INTERNATIONAL
TRADE AND FINANCE

INTERNATIONAL TRADE AND FINANCE

Readings

SECOND EDITION

Robert E. Baldwin
J. David Richardson

University of Wisconsin

Little, Brown and Company
Boston   Toronto

Library of Congress Catalog Card No. 80-84128

ISBN 0-316-07922-7

9 8 7 6 5 4 3

ALP

Published simultaneously in Canada
by Little, Brown & Company (Canada) Limited

Printed in the United States of America

Preface

The world economy faces major international challenges in the 1980's. They range from such monetary problems as controlling the international spill-over from high rates of inflation and improving international financial inter-mediation, to real-side issues that include increasing access to commodity markets as well as to supplies of essential raw materials, and devising politically acceptable means of shifting resources smoothly from declining to expanding industries. Successfully dealing with these international problems will require not only an abundance of goodwill among nations but a widely shared understanding of the economic implications of alternative policies designed to solve them.

This book of readings deals with the above situations and other key monetary, commercial and investment issues that we face in the 1980's, and with important analytical developments that help illuminate these problems. A selected list of topics is examined in detail rather than providing brief coverage of every issue arising in international economics. Although this approach necessitates the omission of some topics and causes some overlapping among the papers, the advantages of permitting readers to examine the views of different authors in some depth was thought to outweigh these costs. Textbooks must necessarily be brief on many topics; the purpose of a book of readings should be to delve more deeply into matters of special importance.

We selected a particular analytical or policy issue by asking ourselves whether there was wide or growing interest in it among trade economists. We then looked for papers, by authors especially knowledgeable on the subject. which were written in a straightforward, interesting style that could be easily understood by students, even those taking their first course in international economics. In the more controversial policy fields, we also tried to include papers that represented divergent views. Although we have had varying success in meeting these standards for each topic, we believe that the readings supplement the material covered in trade textbooks in a way that can enrich and enliven courses in international economics.

We have written introductions to each part in order to place the various selections in better perspective as well as sometimes to supplement, synthesize, or critique different viewpoints. Some of the material covered in these introductions may need to be updated because of the rapid pace of developments in international economics, but we are confident that students will benefit considerably from reading them. We have further tried to help students by providing an index (unlike most books of readings) and by including the bibliographical references listed by the various authors.

As in the first edition, the readings are divided into six parts. However, thirty-two of the thirty-four selections differ from those in the first edition. Part I consists of papers that supplement or modify the simplified factor-proportions theory of international trade and that summarize empirical tests of different trade theories. Part II deals with modern arguments for and against trade liberalization. In addition to the papers presenting these arguments, there are selections that discuss the political and economic policies shaping trade policies, and that present evidence concerning the impact of imports on prices. Part III is comprised of readings exploring several trade-policy topics that will be discussed extensively during the 1980's. These include the so-called New International Economic Order (NIEO) proposals of the developing countries, adjustment assistance for workers displaced by imports, the transfer of technology to developing economies, the international oil cartel, U.S. agricultural exports, and various rules and institutional mechanisms for maintaining order in international trading relationships.

Part IV concerns multinational corporations, outlining their complex interaction with governments, labor movements, and each other, and charting how this interaction has changed in the 1970's. Both traditional and non-traditional economic analyses of multinational corporate influence are presented. Part V summarizes some of the dramatic structural changes in international macroeconomics during the last decade. It includes an assessment of how efficiently the managed-floating exchange-rate system has been working and how much insulation it has provided for each national economy from its global counterpart. It also includes a discussion of how best to analyze modern economic interdependence, where the principal contenders are approaches that rest on equilibrium in good markets and those that rest on equilibrium in financial markets. Part VI of the book analyzes several actual or proposed changes in the international financial systems that will continue to receive attention in the 1980's. Some of these changes involve maintaining adequate international surveillance over exchange rate policies, reducing the dependence of countries on the U.S. dollar as a reserve asset, and adjusting to the balance-of-payments burden imposed by sharp increases in oil prices. In addition, this section includes analyses of the European Monetary System as well as the Eurodollar and other international money markets.

Contents

I

Theories of International Trade

II

Protectionism versus Trade Liberalization

III

Trade Policy Issues for the 1980s

IV

Multinational Enterprises

V

The Performance of Floating Exchange Rates and International Transmission of Macroeconomic Flux

VI

Structural Change in International Financial Relations

I

Theories of International Trade

The standard two-factor (capital and labor) model of international trade is highly useful for understanding the general equilibrium framework in which the structure of trade is determined. It is not a particularly good theory for predicting actual patterns of specialization among countries. During much of the post World War II period, for example, when the United States clearly possessed the highest stock of physical capital to labor of any major trading country, the exports of the United States were—in contrast to the logical implications of the theory—labor-intensive compared to U.S. import-competing production. Another unexpected result is the capital-intensive nature of exports compared to import-competing production in a number of less developed countries that are obviously well endowed with labor relative to capital. As a consequence of such paradoxical relationships, economists in recent years have devoted considerable efforts to modifying the simple factor-proportions theory by relaxing some of its assumptions. The four selections in Part I are examples of these efforts.

The article by Robert E. Baldwin summarizes the major possible explanations for the paradoxical nature of U.S. trade and then reports on various empirical tests of these explanations. One modification of the simple theory that receives strong empirical support in Baldwin's study as well as in other investigations involves taking account of the different levels of training and education—that is, human capital—among workers. Compared to most other countries the United States is abundant in human capital, and the higher average wage and average years of education of workers employed in export industries in contrast to import-competing sectors indicates that this factor supply condition influences the U.S. trade pattern in a manner consistent with a multifactor theory of international trade.

Another alternative theory (one that goes back to David Ricardo) supported by U.S. trade data is that intercountry differences in technology significantly affect the nature of production specialization and consequent trading patterns. The higher proportion of research and development expenditures as well as of scientists and engineers in U.S. export industries than in import-competing activities that Baldwin confirms was discovered earlier by Donald Keesing (1968)[1] and researchers at the Harvard Graduate School of Business, specifically, Gary C. Hufbauer (1968)[2] and William Gruber and Raymond Vernon (1968).[3] A key person in the Harvard group was Vernon who, in 1966, published the classic article on the product cycle that is reprinted in Part I. Vernon not only emphasizes the role of intercountry technological differences in determining trading patterns but indicates how these technological disparities change over time.

Vernon argues that the high average per capita income level in the United States coupled with the high labor costs in this country shape the nature of U.S. inventions and innovations toward labor-saving, luxury-oriented consumer and industrial goods. The need for rapid and easy communications between producers and consumers during the early stages in which such products are being perfected makes it desirable to locate production facilities initially within the United States. Foreign markets are served through exports. As a new product gradually matures, however, United States firms begin to shift production to other advanced countries in order to take advantage of lower labor costs and to be nearer these expanding markets. As the product approaches the standardized stage, production facilities are also located in the less developed countries. Eventually, a flow of net exports is established from both the other advanced countries and the less developed economies, with the United States becoming a net importer of the item.

An obvious implication of Vernon's analysis is that a continual flow of new products is necessary if the United States is to maintain a strong export position in manufacturing. Another point that was not obvious at the time he wrote is that the product cycle theory has applicability beyond the United States. The industrial countries of Europe as well as Japan now possess the technological capability to create new product lines that pass through the same stages described by Vernon with respect to the United States. We are still a long way from understanding why a particular innovation comes about in a particular country, but such examples as the development of small, fuel-efficient cars in a space-scarce, natural resource-poor country like Japan are consistent with the economically induced explanation for the nature of U.S. innovations put forth by Vernon.

Staffan Linder also relates the innovation process to the nature of domestic demand. He argues that in manufacturing, in contrast to the production of natural-resource products, intercountry differences in demand and demand-induced technology shape world trade patterns more than differences in factor endowments. According to Linder, a manufactured product usually will not be exported until after a domestic demand for the product exists, because a clear domestic need for a product must exist before it will be produced, and the market must be close to the production site to obtain the flow of information between buyers and sellers required to perfect a new product. The nature of domestic demand depends to a large extent on the level of per capita income. Since the range of potential imports also depends upon the pattern of domestic demand (and thus per capita income), it follows—according to Linder—that the intensity of trade in differentiated manufactured goods will be higher the closer the per capita income levels of two countries. A rough test by Linder (not included in this book) gave some support to his hypothesis, but it was too crude to warrant any firm conclusions.

The selection by Herbert G. Grubel extends the work of Vernon and Linder by attempting to explain the extensive (and growing) volume of intraindustry trade among industrial countries. As the author notes, a certain proportion of intraindustry trade can be easily explained by reference to such factors as transportation costs and seasonal fluctuations in output and demand. This trade can easily be fit into a factor-proportion theory by introducing transport costs and time. Much of the intraindustry trade, however, occurs in nonhomogeneous product lines where such factors do not seem to play a significant role. One can argue that when two-way trade takes place between similar but not identical products, the issue is simply one of classification; if one places different products into different industries on a sufficiently fine basis, all intra-industry trade will disappear. Although formally correct, this argument glosses over the interesting economic question involved in the literature on intraindustry trade: Why do countries both export and import manufactured goods whose production location does not seem to be related to any discernable differences in factor endowments?

Grubel's explanation of such intraindustry trade emphasizes economies of scale in the sense of long production runs together with intercountry differences in the distribution of income and in tastes. For example, even if technology and per capita incomes are identical in two countries, a higher degree of concentration of incomes in particular income classes can give one country a cost advantage over the other for products consumed by persons in these income classes due to its ability to undertake longer production runs for these products. Clearly, differences in consumer tastes between countries also can give rise to trade advantages based on longer production runs. Still another source of intraindustry trade noted by Grubel is the development of different products based upon a stochastic process of invention.

One should not conclude from the four selections included in Part I that relative factor proportions are not important in influencing trade patterns but rather that such productive factors as human capital and natural resources must also be introduced into the traditional model. Furthermore, it is evident that temporary differences in technology, economies of scale, governmental trade policies, and other factors also play a significant role in determining the commodity structure of world trade. The task now is to ascertain the relative importance of these various elements from country to country and at different times.

Notes

1. Donald Keesing, "The Impact of Research and Development on United States Trade" in Peter Kenen and Robert Lawrence, eds., *The Open Economy: Essays on International Trade and Finance,* Columbia University Press, New York, 1968.
2. Gary C. Hufbauer, "The Impact of National Characteristics and Technology on the Commodity Composition of Trade in Manufactured Goods," in R. Vernon (ed.), *The Technology Factor in International Trade,* New York, 1970.
3. William H. Gruber and Raymond Vernon, "The Technology Factor in a World Trade Matrix," in R. Vernon (ed.), *The Technology Factor in International Trade,* New York, 1970.

1

Determinants of the Commodity Structure of U.S. Trade

Robert E. Baldwin

Nearly twenty years ago Wassily Leontief made the surprising discovery that a lower capital-labor ratio was required to produce a representative bundle of U.S. exports than was involved in producing a representative bundle of import-competing goods. The Leontief results and those from similar investigations of other countries[1] effectively destroyed the comfortable confidence of economists in the simple version of the Heckscher-Ohlin trade theory [developed by two Swedish economists, Bertil Ohlin and Eli Heckscher] that had long been accepted mainly on the basis of casual empiricism.[2] However, the "Leontief paradox" also stimulated extensive theoretical and empirical research directed at providing alternative explanations for the commodity-pattern of a country's trade. The purpose of this paper is to test the main alternative hypotheses that have been ad-

From Robert E. Baldwin, "Determinants of the Commodity Structure of U.S. Trade," *American Economic Review,* May 1971, Vol. LXI. No. 1, pp. 126–46. Reprinted by permission. Appendix, some tables, and some footnotes omitted. Professor of economics, University of Wisconsin, Madison. Research for the paper was financed by a grant from the National Science Foundation.

vanced for this purpose, as well as the simple Heckscher-Ohlin theory itself, by using 1958 U.S. labor, capital, and input-output coefficients rather than the 1947 coefficients employed by Leontief. Information from the *1/1000 Sample of the Population of the United States, 1960* plus certain other data relating to the quality of the labor force and various structural characteristics of U.S. industries are also utilized in testing these hypotheses. In addition, the U.S. trade pattern for 1962 rather than 1947 or 1951 is used in making the various calculations.

The Heckscher-Ohlin theorem states that a country's exports use intensively the country's relatively abundant factors. As is well known (see the survey article by Jagdish Bhagwati, 1965), a set of sufficient conditions for the theorem are: (1) identical production functions throughout the world for each commodity as well as qualitatively identical productive factors; (2) production functions homogeneous of degree one with diminishing marginal productivity for each factor; (3) nonreversibility of factor intensities; (4) identity of consumption patterns (in the sense that all goods are consumed in the same proportions) among countries at any given set of international commodity prices; and (5) perfect markets, free trade, no transport costs, and complete international immobility of productive factors. If one adds the condition that there are at least as many commodities as factors and that all countries produce some of each commodity, it also follows that factor-price equalization is achieved.[3] In addition, as Pranab Bardhan has pointed out, the Heckscher-Ohlin theorem holds as long as one country's production functions all differ from those used in the rest of the world by only a neutral efficiency factor.

Obviously, the various conditions required for the Heckscher-Ohlin proposition to be logically valid do not all hold in the real world. However, this does not necessarily mean that the Heckscher-Ohlin theory is a poor theory. If the failure of any of the assumptions to hold does not systematically and significantly bias the conclusions of the model, the theory will generally still accurately predict the nature of trade patterns from a knowledge of relative factor endowments and thus be a "good" theory. Tests such as the one undertaken by Leontief are designed to determine the adequacy of the theory in this sense.

I. ALTERNATIVE EXPLANATIONS OF THE LEONTIEF PARADOX

Fortunately, trade theory has not suffered from a lack of suggested explanations for the Leontief results. Instead, the problem has been to discriminate among the several hypotheses that have been advanced to account for them. Six major (not necessarily mutually exclusive) groups of explanations can be distinguished.[4] These maintain that the actual structure of U.S. trade can be accounted for mainly by: (1) the relative abundance of skilled labor in the United States; (2) an efficiency advantage in favor of the United States in Research and Development (R and D) oriented industries; (3) the scarcity of natural resources in the United States coupled with a complementary relationship between natural resources and capital; (4) factor-intensity reversals sufficiently extensive to upset the Heckscher-Ohlin proposition; (5) a strong U.S. demand bias in favor of capital-intensive goods so that these are imported even though the United States is capital-abundant; (6) high tariffs and other trade-distorting measures that favor the domestic production of labor-intensive products and consequently bias the import bundle against these products.

Skilled Labor

Current interest in the general topic of investment in human resources has served to focus considerable attention recently (see articles by Peter Kenen [1968], Bharadwaj and Bhagwati, and Roskamp and Gordon McMeekin), on the first explanation mentioned above. This explanation was initially put forth by Leontief and Irving Kravis, both of whom pointed out that U.S. export industries employed more highly skilled labor than did import-competing industries. Donald Keesing (1965, 1966, 1968), Kenen (1965), Helen Waehrer, and Merle Yahr have since elaborated both analytically and empirically upon the significance of differential supplies of labor-skills and also demonstrated the importance of this factor for explaining trade patterns of other countries. Kenen has performed the interesting experiment on U.S. data of capitalizing the excess of wages earned by various types of skilled labor above the wages of unskilled laborers in order to obtain an estimate of the value of human capital involved in export- and import-competing production. When the estimates of human capital obtained by discounting at less than 12.7 percent are added to Leontief's physical capital estimates, the paradox is reversed.[5]

A drawback of computing human capital by capitalizing income differentials at a single discount rate is, as Kenen notes, that the method assumes all income differences to be the result of differences in education and other forms of human investment. It also assumes that long-run equilibrium conditions prevail in capital markets.[6] There is considerable evidence that market imperfections due to various economic and social factors as well as differences in ability are significant explanatory variables for earning differentials. Moreover, returns to low levels of education are considerably greater than to high levels of education.[7]

An even more important point is whether it is proper to combine estimates of human and physical capital to determine the capital-labor ratio in trade-oriented production. Such a procedure rests upon the assumption that in the long run, capital moves freely between physical goods and human agents of production. This assumption may be acceptable for a highly developed country like the United States, but it does not seem appropriate for most developing nations where market imperfections even make it difficult to regard all physical capital as fungible in the long run.

R and D Oriented Industries

Keesing (1968) together with Raymond Vernon, William Gruber, and others, have pointed to the significance of research activities in explaining trade patterns. In particular, they found that there is a strong positive correlation between the relative importance of R&D activities in American industries and the exports of American industries as a proportion of total exports of all the major trading countries. These results confirmed the hypothesis that R&D expenditures are a proxy for temporary, comparative-cost advantages provided by the development of new products and productive methods.[8] A more direct method of introducing nonuniform, efficiency differences between domestic and foreign production functions has been followed by Gary Bickel in a study of U.S.-Japanese trade. Bickel used differences among U.S. and Japanese industries in the productive efficiency of capital and labor (derived from empirically estimated CES production functions) as an explanatory variable for differences between the two countries in relative commodity prices. He found that at least 25 percent of the total variation in these prices was attributable to the efficiency factor alone.[9]

Scarcity of U.S. Natural Resources

The third-factor (natural resources) explanation of Leontief's results has been put forth both by Muhammad Diab and by Jaroslav Vanek (1963). Vanek accepts the notion that the United States is capital abundant but states that natural resources and capital are complementary. Therefore, since natural resources are scarce in the United States, both capital and natural resources are conserved through trade. This hypothesis seemed to receive support from calculations that Leontief made in his second article (1956) on the subject. Specifically, when nineteen natural resource industries were excluded from the matrix, the paradox was eliminated.[10]

As William Travis has pointed out (pp. 94–99), this explanation is logically inconsistent with a Heckscher-Ohlin model in which factor-price equalization is achieved.[11] Even though there are other general or specific factors besides labor and capital, a country that is capital abundant relative to the rest of the world will export capital-intensive products compared to its import-competing production. This can be seen in the following way. In a factor-price equalization model where all goods are traded and tastes are identical, the factor proportions used to produce any particular commodity are the same in all countries, and each country consumes all commodities in the same proportions. This implies that each country indirectly consumes each factor in the same proportions. In other words, one can think of each country as starting with given factor supplies and then trading these at common factor prices until a common set of factor-consumption ratios is reached. In the case where natural resource industries are capital-intensive and natural resources are scarce in a capital-abundant country, factor equilibrium may be achieved in two ways: by the capital-abundant country exporting items that are even more capital-using than natural resource products; or by the rest of the world, which is labor-abundant, exporting highly labor-intensive commodities in addition to the capital-intensive, natural resource products.[12]

Reversals of Factor Intensity

One of the most potentially damaging arguments against the Heckscher-Ohlin theory is that factor-intensity crossovers are extensive within relevant ranges of factor prices. Under these circumstances a country's exports to the rest of the world and the rest of the world's exports to the country may be either both capital-intensive or both labor-intensive. Then the Heckscher-Ohlin relationship cannot possibly hold for both trading units. A study by Minhas seemed to indicate that factor-intensity crossovers were in fact extensive. However, subsequent analysis by Leontief (1964), using additional data provided by Minhas, found extremely little evidence of factor-reversals. Several other recent studies[13] also failed to support the Minhas position, but the matter cannot as yet be regarded as finally settled.[14] For example, see the issues raised by Michael Hodd.

Demand Bias

Demand bias is invariably cited as a possible explanation of the Leontief paradox but no writer has strongly argued that this is the major explanation. Indeed it is now usually accepted (see, for example, the article by Arthur Brown and the analysis by Travis, pp. 105–10) that, if final demand in the United States is factor-biased, the bias is towards labor-intensive rather than capital-intensive goods, because of the operation of Engel's law.

Tariffs and Other Distortions

The argument that various tariff and nontariff trade-distorting measures account for Leontief's results has been expounded most cogently by Travis. He arrives at this conclusion after carefully showing the correctness of Leontief's test of the Heckscher-Ohlin theory and then arguing that it is highly unlikely that the failure of the various assumptions of the Heckscher-Ohlin theory to hold (other than the free trade one) could account for Leontief's results.[15]

Another explanation stressing the importance of market imperfections is Diab's suggestion (pp. 53–56) that commodities produced abroad by American corporations or their subsidiaries and with the aid of American capital, know-how, and highly skilled technicians and managers should be regarded as part of U.S. internal trade rather than imports. Since a large part of this production consists of capital-intensive, natural resource products (especially minerals), the paradox might well be reversed if these were excluded from the trade pattern. However, as Travis points out (pp. 110–11), for this argument to be valid it is necessary to explain why American capital, once overseas, does not move into labor-intensive industries in foreign countries.

Although Travis seems to believe this point cannot be explained satisfactorily, there is considerable evidence in the literature on economic development supporting the view that the immobility of foreign capital and know-how between the export and domestic sectors of less developed countries is a real phenomenon and is based on economic factors. Consider, for example, why foreign funds have in the past flowed mainly into export-oriented, natural resource industries in the less developed countries or in tertiary lines that serve to support these industries. Part of the explanation is that there usually is better knowledge in the developed countries concerning profit opportunities in the developing countries with regard to natural resource industries compared to most other products. Because of the generally lower supply elasticities in developed countries for natural resource products than for commodities produced mainly with capital and labor, there tends to be a greater upward pressure on the prices of those natural resource products that are significant inputs into industrial processes than on the prices of most other products, as growth takes place in the advanced countries. This relative price movement alerts investors to the obvious profit opportunities that can be exploited if costs can be kept from rising and thereby leads to a search at home and abroad for new supply-sources as well as for better ways of using existing supply sources. On the other hand, even if highly profitable opportunities exist overseas in product lines outside of the natural resource group, investors are less likely to become aware of them because of the absence of this signaling mechanism.

Other important factors affecting foreigners' decisions to invest in less developed countries are the nature of factor supplies in these countries, the size of markets, and the degree of input-complexity of production. Natural resource conditions are often sufficiently favorable to make foreign investment profitable in large-scale, primary industries that can supply the large markets of developed countries. However, for products that do not rely heavily on the natural resource factor, production costs usually are too high for exports to be internationally competitive. Labor with very little skill is abundant, but without some training this labor is very inefficient even when used in producing the simplest types of manufactures under modern methods.

A lack of trained labor is less of a barrier to the competitive production of manufactured goods for domestic consumption. However, the costs of establishing and supervising productive units abroad tends to be prohibitive unless the optimum plant size is large. But, in industries where the optimum size of productive units is large, domestic demand usually is too small to support efficient production. Still another factor discouraging foreign investment is the more complex system of input requirements (direct and indirect) for manufactures than for primary products. It is more difficult to finance, coordinate, and fully utilize interdependent investment projects in several as compared to a few industries.

After foreign capital moves into export-oriented, natural resource industries in less developed countries, it does not then flow into domestic industries for the same reasons foreign capital does not move directly into these industries. One difference, however, is that foreign firms located within less developed countries have some advantage over outside investors in ascertaining profit opportunities in other fields. However, there is considerable immobility of capital from such foreign-owned and foreign-directed firms into new product lines involving a very different technology from that used for existing production, especially if the optimum plant size is small. Foreign firms engaged, for example, in oil or copper production will vigorously seek out further profit opportunities in their own product lines, including those that establish additional forward and backward production linkages. But, a lack of interest and knowledge concerning the production and marketing of completely different products tends to offset their proximity advantage.

The flow of direct investment funds into developing countries involves not only an increase in the capital stock of these countries, but also an improvement in technology in the sectors affected. This means that, since foreign capital does not move into very many domestically oriented industries, the state of technology in these industries remains backward. Thus, the explanation of why many less developed countries export capital-intensive products may rest on the immobility of capital between the export and domestic sectors and the technological disparity between these sectors compared to the same sectors in developed economies.

Although the analysis has dealt thus far with developed countries, it also has some applicability to resource-abundant countries like Canada. U.S. investment in natural resource industries in Canada tends to create a greater capital and technological disparity between export and domestically oriented industries than would exist without this investment. However, the experience of recent years has shown that as income and domestic markets grow in such developed countries, direct investment by the United States and other advanced countries takes place in product lines that formerly were mainly imported into these countries and are characterized by significant scale economies. This seems to occur partly to take advantage of being located near the market and partly as a defensive response to import competing investments by domestic investors. To the extent that U.S. investment of this sort is in product lines that are more capital-intensive than other U.S. exports, the Leontief paradox tends to be reinforced.

One other matter that should be considered before presenting the empirical results of testing some of the different trade hypotheses is whether the Heckscher-Ohlin proposition should hold with respect to each pair of countries.[16] Given a pure Heckscher-Ohlin-Samuelson model where all goods are traded, the number of products exceeds the number of factors, and factor-price equalization is achieved, the answer is that the proposition need not hold on a bilateral basis. When the number of commodities is greater than the number of productive factors, the precise distribution of world production and trade is indeterminate with a particular distribution of productive factors among countries and a given set of factor prices.[17] It is not necessary, for example, for the most capital-abundant country to export a larger proportion of the total exports of the most capital-intensive product than a less capital-abundant country or indeed to export it at all. Within the limits set by factor prices, the actual pattern of intercountry production of any traded commodity depends upon a host of complex factors related to different historical rates of development. What is required in the Heckscher-Ohlin theory is simply that the capital-labor ratio of a capital-abundant country's total exports be greater than the capital-labor ratio of its imports. It is quite possible for this relationship to hold with regard to a country's total trade but not with respect to its trade with a particular country. As Hodd (p. 22) has pointed out, preventing complete factor-price equalization by introducing transport costs into the two-factor model causes the Heckscher-Ohlin proposition to hold bilaterally as well as multilaterally, but this bilateral relationship can again break down when the model is complicated by additional factors, e.g., natural resources, that are complementary to one of the other factors, e.g., capital. Since Vanek and more recently Lawrence Weiser found evidence of a complementary relationship between capital and natural resources at least for the United States, the several empirical studies that have revealed inconsistencies in the factor-content of trade between two countries and the relative factor-endowment pattern of the two countries should not be regarded as providing evidence that necessarily runs counter to the Heckscher-Ohlin theory as it is now generally formulated.

II. TESTING THE HECKSCHER-OHLIN THEORY AND OTHER TRADE HYPOTHESES

The major results of retesting the Heckscher-Ohlin hypothesis for the United States, using 1962 trade figures and 1958 capital, labor, and intermediate-input data, are presented in Tables 1 and 2. Table 1 presents factor-content (direct and indirect) ratios[18] that compare representative bundles of import competing with export products[19,20] and Table 2 shows the distribution of the labor force by broad occupational groups. . . .

One important result of the test is that the Leontief paradox still holds.[21] The ratio of capital per man-year in import-competing versus

TABLE 1

Factor Requirements (Direct and Indirect) per Million Dollars of United States Exports and Competitive-Import Replacements, 1962

	Imports	Exports	Import/Export Ratio
Net Capital			
All Industries	$2,132,000	$1,876,000	1.14
Excl. Agriculture	1,806,000	1,403,000	1.29
Excl. Natural-Resource Products[a]	1,259,000	1,223,000	1.03
Gross Capital			
All Industries	$2,393,000	$2,196,000	1.09
Excl. Agriculture	2,083,000	1,777,000	1.17
Excl. N. R.	1,582,000	1,599,000	.99
Labor (man-years)			
All Industries	119	131	.91
Excl. Agriculture	100	109	.92
Excl. N. R.	106	107	.99
Net Capital-Labor			
All Industries	$18,000	$14,200	1.27
Excl. Agriculture	18,100	12,800	1.41
Excl. N. R.	11,900	11,500	1.04
Average Years of Education of Labor			
All Industries	9.9	10.1	.98
Excl. Agriculture	10.2	10.6	.96
Excl. N. R.	10.3	10.7	.97
Average Costs of Education of Labor			
All Industries	$10,300	$10,500	.97
Excl. Agriculture	11,000	11,900	.92
Excl. N. R.	11,200	12,200	.92
Net Capital Plus Total Cost of Education ÷ Labor			
All Industries	$28,300	$24,700	1.14
Excl. Agriculture	29,100	24,700	1.18
Excl. N. R.	23,100	23,700	.97
Average Earnings of Labor			
All Industries	$4,570	$4,660	.98
Excl. Agriculture	5,050	5,460	.92
Excl. N. R.	5,030	5,400	.93
Proportion of Engineers and Scientists			
All Industries	.0189	.0255	.74
Excl. Agriculture	.0230	.0352	.65
Excl. N. R.	.0228	.0369	.62
Scale Index			
All Industries	51	56	.91
Excl. Agriculture	55	66	.83
Excl. N. R.	57	67	.85
Unionization Index			
All Industries	59	62	.95
Excl. Agriculture	65	72	.90
Excl. N. R.	65	71	.92

TABLE 1 (continued)

	Imports	Exports	Import/ Export Ratio
Concentration Index			
All Industries	39	40	.98
Excl. Agriculture	42	46	.91
Excl. N. R.	41	46	.89
Proportion of Labor with			
0–8 years of education	.39	.37	1.05
9–12 years of education	.49	.50	.98
13+ years of education	.12	.13	.92

[a]Natural resource products were arbitrarily defined as all agricultural and mining industries (1–10); tobacco manufactures (15); lumber and wood products (20); petroleum refining (31); and primary nonferrous metals manufacturing (38). The list is roughly similar to the one used by Leontief except that petroleum refining is added and nonlivestock agricultural products are included. One could argue quite persuasively that other industries should also be included.

Sources: The coefficients of total requirements (direct and indirect) per dollar of delivery to final demand were taken from U.S. Department of Commerce. The employment figures used to calculate the 1958 direct labor coefficients for the 79 industries covered in the study were furnished by Jack Alterman of the Bureau of Labor Statistics.

The 1958 capital coefficients for industries 12–64 were obtained by reclassifying data given in *Census of Manufactures, 1958.* Net capital is the sum of net book value, work in progress, materials, and finished product inventories. Finished product inventories were adjusted to purchasers prices and, by utilizing the transaction matrix of the input-output table, were distributed to the industries using them. The gross capital coefficients are based on gross book value rather than net book value. The coefficients for the nonmanufacturing sectors are based on a wide variety of sources. They include the two basic Leontief articles (1953 and 1956); the study by Leontief et al., Dert G. Hickman; John W. Kendrick; and Daniel B. Creamer, Sergei P. Dobrovolsky and Israel Borenstein.

Export and import data for the 60 commodity sectors in which trade occurred in 1962 are from *Exports and Imports as Related to Output.* Values of exports and imports for 1962 were adjusted to 1958 prices by deflators that in the case of the manufacturing sectors (13–64) were provided by the Office of Business Economics, Department of Commerce and that for mining and agriculture were obtained from the *1962 Minerals Yearbook* and *Wholesale Prices and Price Indexes,* 1962. Imports were multiplied by ratios of landed value to foreign port value and exports by ratios of producer value to export value in order to make them comparable to the producer-value figures of the input-output table. These ratios were provided by the Office of Business Economics, Department of Commerce.

The Bureau of the Census, *1/1000 Sample of the Population of the United States, 1960* was available in data tape form from the Social Systems Research Institute computation library at the University of Wisconsin. Using the industrial classification system employed by the Census, it is possible to arrange the labor force covered in the census into the same industry groups adopted for the 1958 input-output table. Characteristics relating to years of education, occupations, and earnings were then determined from the data tape for these individuals.

The direct scale and unionization ratios were adapted from Leonard Weiss. The direct scale index for each industry is based on the percentage of employees in establishments with 250 or more employees, and the direct unionization index represents the percentage of an industry's production workers employed in plants where a majority of the workers are covered by collective bargaining contracts. The direct concentration figures, also from the paper by Weiss, are four-firm concentration ratios, adjusted for the local or regional character of certain industries. The row vector of direct ratios for each of the three variables was postmultiplied by the inverse matrix, and weighted averages of the direct and indirect requirements for these characteristics then obtained for each industry by dividing the resulting row vector by the appropriate column sums of the inverse matrix.

TABLE 2

Distribution of Labor Force by Skill Groups, Per Million Dollars of Exports and Competitive-Import Replacements, 1962 (in percentages)

(A) *Six Skill Groups*	Imports	Exports	Import/Export Ratio
I. Professional, technical and managerial	12.0	12.5	.96
II. Clerical and sales	15.2	15.1	1.01
III. Craftsmen and foremen	14.9	15.4	.97
IV. Operatives	30.4	25.1	1.21
V. Laborers (nonfarm) and service	10.3	7.5	1.37
VI. Farmers and farm laborers	17.2	24.4	.70
	100.0	100.0	
(B) *Eleven Skill Groups*			
I. Professional and technical	5.7	6.7	.85
II. Managerial, except farm	6.3	5.8	1.09
III. Craftsmen and foremen	14.9	15.4	.97
IV. Sales	4.4	4.1	1.07
V. Clerical	10.8	11.0	.98
VI. Operatives	30.4	25.1	1.21
VII. Laborers, except farm	6.9	4.3	1.60
VIII. Service, except private household	3.1	2.9	1.07
IX. Farmers and farm managers	11.2	15.8	.71
X. Private household workers	.3	.3	1.00
XI. Farm laborers and foremen	6.0	8.6	.70
	100.0	100.0	

Sources: See Table 1.

export production is 1.27[22] compared to the ratios of 1.30 and 1.06 that Leontief obtained for the 1947 and 1951 trade patterns, respectively.[23,*] Furthermore, in the various stepwise multiple regressions that were performed, the capital-labor ratio always entered first with a statistically significant negative sign as the single variable that best "explained" the trade pattern. However, if natural resource products are excluded, the capital-labor ratio falls to 1.04 when capital is measured on a net basis and to 1.00 when capital is measured in gross terms.

The hypothesis that export production involves higher skill requirements than import competing production also receives support, as the figures on average earnings, average years of education, and average costs of education indicate. A crude measure of the amount of physical and human capital used in export versus import-competing production was cal-

*[Baldwin (1979) subsequently calculated this ratio to be 1.06 for the United States on the basis of 1969 trade data, the 1963 input-output table, and 1963 capital and labor coefficients. —Eds.]

culated by combining the data on physical capital and the costs of education.[24] As Table 1 indicates, adding this measure of human capital to the physical capital figure is not sufficient to reverse the Leontief results for all industries combined but does reverse it when natural resource industries are excluded.

Classifying the labor force involved in export and import competing production by levels of education and by various occupational groups further brings out the importance of the skill factor in explaining U.S. trade. The educational breakdown indicates that the proportions of individuals with 9–12 years of education and especially with 13 or more years of education are higher in export than in import competing production, whereas the share of those with only 0–8 years of education is higher on the import side. As the occupational figures (Table 2) show, farmers and farm laborers, who are among the least educated occupational groups, are considerably more important in export than import competing production. However, nonfarm laborers and operatives, who are also at the lower end of the educational attainment scale, are sufficiently more important in import competing production compared to export activities to make the proportion of the labor force as a whole with only a primary school education more significant in import competing than export production. The other occupations that stand out as more significant on the export than import competing side are professional, technical and managerial employees and craftsmen and foremen. Clerical and sales employees do not differ in their relative importance in export- versus import-competing activities.

The correlation analysis [not included here—Eds.] shows that there is a significant positive relationship between the percentage of engineers and scientists, craftsmen, and farmers in an industry and the net world export surplus of the industry. The percentage of operatives and nonfarm laborers have the expected negative signs but the coefficients are not significant. . . . There is also a statistically significant positive relationship between the importance in an industry of those with more than a high school education and the industry's world trade balance.

Research and development activities also show up as being much more important in export output than in import-competing production. The ratio of the R&D costs involved in producing a representative bundle of import-competing versus export commodities, as calculated from the R&D sector in the input-output table, is .66.[25] The ratio of the number of engineers and natural scientists engaged in import-competing versus export activities is .74.[26] Moreover, as already noted, in the regression model used, the percentage or the absolute number of engineers and scientists in an industry appears as a significant variable that is positively correlated with the industry's export surplus. This relationship is especially strong when natural resource products are excluded from the trade pattern.

Another exercise confirming the importance of this variable is the correlation between the percentage change of exports in each industry from 1947 to 1962 and various characteristics of the labor force in each industry, such as their earnings, years of education, a simple skill index, the absolute importance of engineers and scientists as well as general industry characteristics such as the degree of concentration, unionization, and large-scale employment.[27] The engineers-scientists variable and the concentration ratio are the only two variables that are significantly related (positively) to the growth of exports. When the same variables are used to explain the percentage change in imports, none comes out to be statistically significant.

Beside, determining the trade requirements for engineers and scientists, an estimate was made of the import versus export requirements of top management, i.e., managers, officials, and proprietors earning more than $10,000. Their numbers are larger in export production than in import-competing production, but the proportions of the total labor force engaged in top management activities are about the same on the import and export sides.[28]

Two other industry characteristics of special interest are the relative importance of scale economies and the degree of unionization in import-competing versus export production. Staffan Linder has stressed the point that profitable production for home markets is a necessary condition for manufactured products to be potential export products. Consequently, in industries where scale economies are important, the size of the American market may give the United States an export advantage, quite aside from any other factors. The unionization calculation is aimed at the hypothesis that unions may raise wages above their competitive levels and thus act to offset underlying "real" factors that contribute to a country's comparative advantage.[29] A variable reflecting the degree of industrial concentration is also introduced into the analysis, but it is highly correlated ($r = .87$) with the scale index. As Table 1 indicates, the scale factor, the degree of unionization, and the degree of concentration are all more important for export production than for import-competing activities. However, none of these variables turn out to be statistically significant in the regression analyses of total trade.

In order to indicate the effect of import duties as well as some of the main nontariff trade barriers on the capital-labor ratio employed in import-competing production, import demand elasticities were assigned to the various trading industries in the input-output table and a new per million dollar bundle of competitive-imports was then determined under the assumption that the average duty (or the ad valorem duty-equivalent of the nontariff barrier) in each industry was reduced to zero.[30] The fact that the capital-labor ratio with the new commodity-composition of imports is about 5 percent lower than the ratio computed with the actual import bundle confirms Travis's contention that tariffs operate in the direction of the Leontief paradox.[31] Furthermore, the commercial policies of other countries probably tend to reduce the average capital-labor ratio in export production below its free trade level. A removal of all trade-distorting measures might confirm the expectation of the Heckscher-Ohlin model for the United States, but, based on my own study of tariff and nontariff barriers to trade, I do not think that this would be the case. However, further empirical study of this subject is very much needed.

The effect of an increase in income levels on the capital-labor ratio of import competing production was also estimated by assigning appropriate income elasticities of import demand to various commodity groups.[32] The capital-labor ratio required to produce the increment in imports associated with an increase in income is $17,750 or slightly less than the $18,000 average for the 1962 bundle of competitive imports. Thus, if the U.S. commodity structure of income elasticities of import demand is typical of the pattern for the rest of the world towards the United States, then demand differences related to income differences among countries are not a factor that tends to account for the Leontief paradox.

In addition to determining the factor content of a representative bundle of U.S. exports to all countries as a whole and a representative bundle of competitive imports from the rest of the world, the Heckscher-Ohlin hypothesis was tested with respect to U.S. trade vis-à-vis Western Europe, Japan, Canada, and less developed countries, and an all other group (mainly Oceania).[33] As previously noted, the assumptions necessary for the Heckscher-Ohlin proposition to be logically true with regard to a country's total trade do not imply that the theory must hold on a bilateral basis. However, a regional analysis is useful in revealing additional information on the factors influencing the commodity pattern of U.S. trade. The results of these tests [not shown] are that the Leontief result does not hold with respect to either U.S.-Western European or U.S.-Japanese trade but does exist with respect to trade between the United States and Canada, the United States and less developed countries, and the United States and all other countries. The latter three groups of countries represent regions that are relatively abundant in natural resources. In view of the strong complementary relationship between capital and certain natural resources and the previously made point concerning the international flow of U.S. capital, technology, and top management into export-oriented, natural resource industries in foreign countries, the results with regard to Canada, the less developed countries, and Oceania are not unexpected.[34] The trade patterns with Western Europe and Japan are not as heavily influenced by imports of natural resource products nor is direct foreign investment as important in these regions relative to domestic capital accumulation. Thus, relative domestic supplies of capital and labor play a more important role in determining the trade structure between the United States and these regions.

Although the United States exports comparatively capital-intensive products to Western Europe and Japan, the capital-labor variable does not show up as statistically significant in the multiple regression analysis with respect to these areas. Other factors appear to be more important as determinants of the trade patterns between the United States and these regions. In particular, there is a significant positive relationship between the percentage of engineers and scientists employed in an industry and the industry's net export balance with respect to each of these two regions (as well as for the all other group). The scale variable also shows up as significant for these two regions. Rather surprisingly, the sign of the scale coefficient is negative (largely because of the large export surplus of agricultural products to Western Europe and Japan).[35]

General measures of skill and human capital such as average costs of education, average years of education, and average earnings were found to be statistically significant only in the case of U.S.-Japanese trade. However, the percentage of employees with 13 or more years of education required to produce a given value of output in each industry is significantly correlated (positively) with an industry's net trade balance between the United States and Western Europe, the United States and Japan, and the United States and the all other group. A similar positive correlation holds for U.S.-Western European trade with regard to the proportion of the labor force educated 8 years or less, whereas a significant negative relationship exists for U.S.-Western European and U.S.-Japanese trade with regard to those receiving 9–12 years of education. Dividing the labor force into broad occupational groups further reveals the importance of various types of labor skills in a manner generally consistent with what one would expect from a factor-proportions approach. The significance of the engineers-scientists variable has already been mentioned. The number[36] and percentage of unskilled (nonfarm) workers employed in an industry are significantly correlated (negatively) with the industry's export surplus in the cases of Japan and Canada, and the number (though not percentages) of semiskilled workers enters significantly with the same negative sign for Japan. Furthermore, the number and percentage of skilled workers in an industry is significantly correlated in a positive manner with the industry's net balance of trade between the United States and the less developed countries.

III. CONCLUSIONS

The preceding analysis strongly supports the view that a straightforward application of a two-factor (capital and labor) factor-proportions model along Heckscher-Ohlin lines is inadequate for understanding the pattern of U.S. trade. Not only is the sign of the capital-labor ratio opposite from what would be expected from the model but it is statistically significant in this unexpected direction. What this negative sign seems to reflect is, as Vanek and others have suggested, that there is a strong complementarity between certain natural resources—many forms of which are relatively scarce in the United States—and physical capital.[37] The regional breakdown indicates, for example, that the source of the paradox is the pattern of U.S. trade with Canada, the less developed countries, and the all other group—all of which export a significant volume of natural resource products to the United States. When various natural resource products are eliminated from the factor-content calculations, the overall ratio of capital per worker in import-competing production to capital per worker in export production drops from 1.27 to 1.04. Omitting natural resource industries from the regression data also eliminates the capital-labor ratio as a statistically significant variable. Moreover, in the remaining group there are still some important industries in which the costs of transporting natural resource products required as inputs are relatively high and whose location, therefore, tends to be near the source of the natural resources that are indirectly required for production.

As previously noted, the complementary relationship between physical capital and natural resources need not be offset by U.S. exports of goods that are even more capital-intensive than natural resource products or by other imports of a highly labor-intensive nature, provided the various assumptions of a simple Heckscher-Ohlin model with respect to capital mobility, homogeneity of the labor supply, commerical policy, and technological parity do not hold. Evidence indicating that the capital mobility assumptions do not hold is available in the economic development literature whereas data consistent with the position that the labor-supply, technology, and commercial-policy assumptions of the traditional model do not hold have been presented in this paper. It seems clear from the preceding analysis that the relatively abundant supply of engineers and scientists is an important source of the United States' comparative-advantage position, especially as far as trade in manufactures is concerned. This abundance of highly trained labor gives the United States an export advantage in products requiring relatively large amounts of such labor.[38] Probably of even more importance is the fact that a significant part of this labor group is engaged in research and development activities. Even those working directly in production facilitate the development of product improvements. Thus, in product lines where the technological opportunities for product improvements are favorable, the use of engineers and scientists for research and development activities fosters temporary U.S. trade advantages based on technological differences rather than on relative factor proportions. Just how to weigh the relative importance of these two aspects of the engineers-scientists variable cannot be determined from this study but what evidence there is suggests that both are significant in influencing the pattern of U.S. trade.[39]

The relative supplies of certain other types of labor skills also appear to be important determinants of the structure of U.S. commodity trade. As would be expected in a Heckscher-Ohlin model with several types of labor, the United States not only indirectly exports professional and technical labor but also skilled craftsmen and foremen. Furthermore, we indirectly import semiskilled and unskilled (nonfarm) labor, both of which are usually considered to be comparatively scarce in the United States.

General measures of human capital such as earnings, years of education, and costs of education, fail to capture much of the explanatory power that is given by a breakdown into levels of educational attainment or into traditional skill groups. Part of this may be due to the omission of on-the-job training from the general education variable used in the study. The positive correlation between net exports and average years of education is also weakened by the large export surplus in the agricultural sector, where formal educational requirements are not only low but where the relatively abundant supply of land in the United States plays a significant export-creating role. The existence of social and economic institutional arrangements that impede equilibrating educational adjustments within the labor force and rapid technological progress that frequently changes educational requirements further tend to diminish the statistical significance of gross measures of the stock of human capital as explanatory variables of the U.S. trade pattern. Simple (and imperfect) measures of the degree of scale economies, unionization, and industrial concentration also do not account for the U.S. trade pattern in a statistically significant manner. Protection levels in each industry, on the other hand, do seem to influence the pattern and factor-content of trade to an appreciable extent.

The clearest conclusion to be drawn from the study is, as other writers (see articles by Kenen [1968] and Hufbauer) have emphasized recently, that it is necessary to discard simple, single-factor (e.g., capital per worker) trade theories in favor of multi-factor trade models. In particular, the labor force must be divided into various skill groups and the notion of relative differences in human capital taken into account. Other variables, such as natural resource conditions, technological differences, transportation costs, and commercial policies, must be explicitly included in these models. Furthermore, trade theory should take greater account of the degree of difficulty with which productive factors move among sectors within an economy and especially barriers to the flow of factors abroad into various sectors of an economy. Under this more general approach the relative abundance among countries of the factors of production will still occupy an important place in trade theory but a more complex notion of productive factors will be utilized and other considerations will also play important explanatory roles. Moreover, as we improve our predictive powers with these broader trade models, we must devote greater efforts to understanding the processes that determine the nature of the underlying variables affecting trade patterns. This, in turn, should enable us to construct a more fundamental, dynamic theory of international trade.

Notes

1. See Masahiro Tatemoto and Shinichi Ichimura, Donald F. Wahl, Ranganath Bharadwaj, and Karl W. Roskamp.
2. The simple Heckscher-Ohlin theory is a model in which only capital, labor, and natural resources are the factors of production, and in which such factors as economies of scale and differences in technology do not play a part in determining comparative-cost differences among nations. It should be recognized, however, that Bertil Ohlin, even when presenting what he regarded as a simplified version of his model, divided labor into three skill groups and capital into long-term and short-term capital. Nevertheless, over time most economists have come to label trade models with a two- or three-factor breakdown as simplified versions of the Heckscher-Ohlin theory. More important, they have believed that the broad pattern of a country's trade could be adequately explained with a simple two- or three-factor model. See, for example, Karl-Erik Hansson.
3. Factor-price equalization can, of course, be achieved without the identical-taste assumption. Moreover, it is not necessary for factor-price equalization that each country produce some of every commodity.
4. See Gary C. Hufbauer for a classification that further refines some of the categories listed.
5. However, similar estimates by Bharadwaj and Bhagwati for India have the effect of operating against what would be predicted by the Heckscher-Ohlin theory.
6. By excluding the human capital in laborers, Kenen's method understates the total human capital involved in export- and import-competing production. Since laborers are more important in import-competing than export production, this exclusion has the effect of tending to reverse the paradox.
7. See Gary Becker (pp. 124–27) and Giora Hanoch.
8. This hypothesis also assumes that current R&D expenditures are representative of the stock of innovations that are the source of comparative-cost advantages and that the rate at which innovations are copied is approximately the same among industries.
9. Leontief's explanation (1953, p. 344) of his findings, namely that U.S. labor is some three times more efficient than foreign labor, implies that the efficiency advantage of the United States is highly biased towards saving labor whereas the usual intercountry studies that estimate the elasticity of substitution explicitly assume only factor-neutral efficiency differences. Bickel, for example, uses the neutral efficiency parameters calculated by Kenneth Arrow, Hollis Chenery, Bagicha Minhas, and Robert Solow. There is evidence suggesting that technical progress in the United States has in fact been labor saving. See Paul David and Th. van de Klundert. However, the very large advantage in favor of U.S. labor suggested by Leontief does not seem to be supported by direct studies of comparative labor efficiency. See the article by Mordechai Kreinin.
10. The industries excluded by Leontief tend to be those in which the direct and indirect factor content of immobile natural resources is relatively high. His exclusion of all agricultural industries except livestock and livestock products seems questionable under this criterion.
11. Vanek (1968) also has now proved this proposition rigorously. Travis (p. 97) further notes that the Leontief results are not consistent with the natural resource explanation even in the absence of factor-price equalization.

12. Suppose that country A possesses a relatively abundant supply of capital, K, compared to country B (the rest of the world) in terms of either labor, L, or natural resources, NR, i.e., $K_a/L_a > K_b/L_b$ and $K_a/NR_a > K_b/NR_b$. Because of the equilibrium conditions that the consumption ratios of these factors must be equal and the value of a country's indirect exports of factors must equal its indirect imports of factors, it follows that country A must in effect export capital to country B.

13. See the book by Hal Lary and the articles by Gordon Philpot and Merle Yahr.

14. The possible lack of global univalence between factor prices and commodity prices when goods are produced with specific natural resources as well as with capital and labor should be further investigated. This corresponds to factor-intensity reversals in the two factor-two commodity case. James Ford (p. 60) raises this point.

15. Tariffs can weaken the pattern of indirect factor-trade in a Heckscher-Ohlin model but cannot alone produce paradoxical results. Export subsidies (or some domestic distortion) in lines that intensively use a country's relatively scarce factors are needed to produce these results.

16. Bhagwati (pp. 175–76) raises this issue in his survey article and terms the lack of analysis on this point a serious deficiency in trade theory.

17. The net factor-trade balance is, of course, the same in these circumstances.

18. In testing the relationship between relative factor supplies and the factor content of trade, some writers (Keesing [1965] and Waehrer) compute only the direct factor content of exports and import replacements on the grounds that most intermediate inputs can be imported instead of produced domestically. This procedure confuses an *ex post* test of an equilibrium trade position to determine if the pattern of trade is consistent with the Heckscher-Ohlin theory with such exercises as predicting or planning for the detailed nature of a country's trade pattern, given its factor endowment and a set of international commodity prices. For the latter purpose the investigator must consider the possibility with respect to any possible export product that national income may be made greater by importing intermediate products rather than producing them domestically. Consequently, the optimum position may well be one where many intermediate inputs involved in trade are not produced locally. Lary's study of the potentialities for exports of manufactures in developing nations in which he analyzes only direct value-added ratios illustrates a problem where the use of direct factor-content ratios is the proper procedure. However, given a particular equilibrium pattern of trade, it is necessary to include both the direct and indirect labor and capital involved in producing exports and imports in order to determine a country's net trade balance in factor services via trade in commodities. If only direct coefficients are used, it is possible to conclude, for example, that a capital abundant country exports labor services and imports capital services when in fact it does the opposite. The direct coefficient test thus would erroneously infer that the Heckscher-Ohlin hypothesis failed to hold.

19. The representative export and import-competing bundles do not include any services but instead are composed entirely of traded commodities.

20. Intermediate products imported and then reexported in the form of other products as well as imports containing intermediate inputs that were exported and then reimported should, of course, be excluded in calculating net factor flows. The Leontief method does in fact accomplish this since, for example, foreign produced intermediates that are imported and reexported are counted by the Leontief method on both the import and export side and thus net out in subtracting the factor services involved in exports from those involved in imports. If capital-labor ratios of exports and imports are compared, an incorrect ratio will be obtained but the error factor will not effect whether the quotient is above or below unity—which is the main purpose of the calculation.

21. Gary Hufbauer also obtains this result in his study of U.S. trade in manufactures.

22. An estimate of this capital-labor ratio was also made in which transportation services, travel (weighted by an average of the capital-labor ratios for hotels

and personal services, amusements, and miscellaneous manufactures) and other private services (weighted by an average of the capital-labor ratios for communications and radio and TV broadcasting) were included in the export and import competing bundles. The capital-labor ratio for imports rose to $18,300 and that for exports to $15,000. The import ratio divided by the export ratio was, therefore, 1.22.

23. As Travis (pp. 98–99) has noted, the exclusion of noncompetitive imports from the U.S. import bundle because of the nonavailability in the United States of certain natural resources required for their production could conceivably result in an incorrect inference concerning the Heckscher-Ohlin hypothesis from a Leontief-type test. This would be the case if the production of noncompetitive imports was so highly labor-intensive (and would be so in the United States had the specific natural resources been available) that the capital-labor ratio of total imports, in contrast to just competitive imports, was less than the capital-labor ratio of exports. However, on the basis of a rough survey of the capital-labor ratios for noncompetitive imports produced abroad and given the fact that these imports constitute only about 8 percent of total U.S. commodity imports, it appears to be extremely unlikely that the labor intensity of noncompetitive imports could be so high as to account for the Leontief paradox. Actually, the capital-labor ratio calculated in the paper for competitive imports is so high that the capital-labor ratio for the 8 percent of imports (or 6 percent if traded services are included) which are noncompetitive would have to be negative in order to make the overall capital-labor ratio for imports even equal to the capital-labor ratio for exports.

24. To obtain direct education costs, the figures on years of education from the 1960 sample census, supplemented with data on school retention rates, were multiplied by the 1956 cost figures determined by Theodore Schultz (p. 34). Estimates of foregone earnings were added to these direct costs to obtain total education costs. However, no measure of accumulated interest costs is included in the estimate nor does it include any on-the-job training costs.

25. The R&D sector in the input-output table includes, however, only research and development performed for sale and thus excludes R&D performed within a company.

26. This group includes both individuals engaged in research and development as well as those engaged in current production activities. Using data for eighteen industries and direct requirements only, Kenen (1968) compared the relative importance of the two groups in "explaining" trade patterns and obtained ambiguous results. As Keesing (1968, pp. 175–89) had previously shown, for exports alone, the ratio of scientists and engineers engaged in research and development to the total labor force in the industry is statistically significant whereas the proportion of scientists and engineers in non-R&D activities is not. On the other hand, when an industry's net trade balance is taken as the dependent variable, the opposite result is obtained. Consequently, in view of these results and also because of the similarity between the results obtained in this study from using R&D expenditures and the number of scientists and engineers, it seems best to regard the engineers-scientists variable used here as both a skill measure and a proxy for R&D activities that result in new and improved products.

27. In this exercise the 1947 trade data were classified on the basis of the industrial breakdown in the 1958 input-output table. The various economic characteristics of the industries pertain to the period around 1960.

28. Two other results that may be of interest are that there is no difference between import-competing and export production in the average age of the workers or the proportion who are white.

29. Even assuming that unions do raise wages above competitive levels, this hypothesis depends on the assumption that the resulting competitive disadvantage is not offset by the same force operating in other countries.

30. Using the study by R. J. Ball and K. Marwah, industries listed in the input-output table were divided into five groups and assigned the following import-demand elasticities: crude foodstuffs—.46; manufactured foodstuffs—

2.39; crude materials—.38; semimanufactured products—1.64 and manufactured goods—4.04. Tariff rates for 1962 were obtained by dividing the calculated import duty for an industry by the value of its imports. The nontariff barriers included were the quotas on agricultural products, cotton textiles, and petroleum as well as the American Selling Price system of valuing certain chemicals. See Baldwin (p. 163). In estimating the price effect of the cuts in the degree of protection, it was assumed that the elasticity of foreign import-supply was infinite for all commodities.

31. The indirect effect that reducing duties on products used as intermediate inputs has in increasing domestic production and thus reducing imports was not taken into account in estimating the new import bundle.

32. The income elasticities as well as the commodity classification employed in making the estimate are from the Ball-Marwah article. The particular income elasticities used were: crude foodstuffs .49; manufactured foodstuffs .96; crude materials .87; semimanufactures 1.22; and manufactured goods 2.47.

33. Western Europe consists of all European members of OECD; the less developed countries are composed of other Asia (Asia except for Japan and China Mainland), Africa, and other America (Americas excluding the United States and Canada); and the all other group is made up of Eastern Europe, other Europe, China Mainland, and Oceania. The data on which these regional trade patterns are based are much less detailed than those from which the world trade pattern is derived. Furthermore, the fact that no products are excluded from the export side on the basis of being noncompetitive is a more serious drawback for bilateral analyses than for the analysis of U.S. trade with the rest of the world.

34. As [the tests] indicate, imports from these regions are more capital-intensive than exports to them even when the list of natural resource industries are excluded from the calculations and when human capital is added to physical capital. However, the nature of much of the remaining trade is still greatly influenced by transportation and technical processing considerations that favor location of production in these areas. Such is the case, for example, in the very important food sector . . . where imports from the LDCs are dominated by cane sugar and imports from the all other group by meat as well as for the paper industry . . . where imports of pulp and newsprint from Canada are large. When these two industries are also excluded from the factor content calculations, the ratio of physical plus human capital to labor is lower in import competing than export production for all regions, and the ratio of physical capital to labor is lower in import competing than export production for all regions except the less developed countries.

35. When natural resource products are eliminated, the scale factor is not statistically significant for Western Europe or Japan.

36. A regression equation . . . was estimated in which the independent variables were the capital-output ratio for each industry and the number of employees in each of the six skill groups.

37. As Seiji Naya (p. 567) has pointed out, this complementary relationship has a more general applicability among countries when agricultural products are excluded from the list of natural resource products.

38. In most industries engineers and scientists make up only a small fraction of the labor force. However, in 1960 the proportion was between 5 and 10 percent for thirteen of the sixty input-output industries in which international trade took place.

39. Kenen (1968) concludes from his analysis of this matter that an eclectic approach is still in order.

References

K. J. Arrow, H. B. Chenery, B. S. Minhas, and R. M. Solow, "Capital-Labor Substitution and Economic Efficiency," *Rev. Econ. Statist.*, Aug. 1961, *43*, 225–50.

R. E. Baldwin, *Nontariff Distortions of International Trade,* Washington, 1970.
———, "Determinants of Trade and Investment," *Rev. Econ. Statist.,* Feb. 1979, *61,* 1, 40–48. Ed. reference.
D. S. Ball, "Factor-Intensity Reversals in International Comparison of Factor Costs and Factor Use," *J. Polit. Econ.,* Feb. 1966, *74,* 77–80.
R. J. Ball and K. Marwah, "The U.S. Demand for Imports, 1948–58," *Rev. Econ. Statist.,* Nov. 1962, *44,* 395–401.
P. Bardhan, "International Differences in Production Functions, Trade and Factor Prices," *Econ. J.,* Mar. 1965, *75,* 81–87.
G. S. Becker, *Human Capital,* New York, 1964.
J. Bhagwati, "The Pure Theory of International Trade: A Survey," in *Surveys of Economic Theory: Growth and Development,* New York, 1965, *2,* 173–75.
R. Bharadwaj, "Factor Proportions and the Structure of Indo-U.S. Trade," *Indian Econ. J.,* Oct. 1962, *10,* 105–16.
——— and J. Bhagwati, "Human Capital and the Pattern of Foreign Trade: The Indian Case," *Indian Econ. Rev.,* Oct. 1967, *2,* 117–42.
G. Bickel, *Factor Proportions and Relative Price Under CES Production Functions: An Empirical Study of Japanese-U.S. Comparative Advantage,* Stanford, 1966.
A. J. Brown, "Professor Leontief and the Pattern of World Trade," *Yorkshire Bull. Econ. Soc. Res.,* Nov. 1957, *9,* 63–75.
D. B. Creamer, S. P. Dobrovolsky, and I. Borenstein, *Capital in Manufacturing and Mining,* Princeton, 1960.
P. David and Th. van de Klundert, "Biased Efficiency Growth and Capital-Labor Substitution in the U.S., 1899–1960," *Amer. Econ. Rev.,* June 1965, *55,* 357–94.
M. A. Diab, *The United States Capital Position and the Structure of Its Foreign Trade,* Amsterdam, 1956.
P. T. Ellsworth, "The Structure of American Foreign Trade: A New View Examined," *Rev. Econ. Statist.,* Aug. 1954, *36,* 274–85.
J. L. Ford, *The Ohlin Heckscher Theory of the Basis and Effects of Commodity Trade,* New York, 1965.
W. H. Gruber and R. Vernon, "The Technology Factor in a World Trade Matrix," in R. Vernon (ed.), *The Technology Factor in International Trade,* New York, 1970.
G. Hanoch, "An Economic Analysis of Earning and Schooling," *J. Hum. Resources,* summer 1967, *2,* 310–29.
K. E. Hansson, "A General Theory of the System of Multilateral Trade," *Amer. Econ. Rev.,* Mar. 1952, *42,* 59–68.
B. G. Hickman, *Investment Demand and U.S. Economic Growth,* Washington, 1965.
M. Hodd, "An Empirical Investigation of the Heckscher-Ohlin Theory," *Economica,* Feb. 1967, *34,* 20–29.
G. C. Hufbauer, "The Impact of National Characteristics and Technology on the Commodity Composition of Trade in Manufactured Goods," in R. Vernon (ed.), *The Technology Factor in International Trade,* New York, 1970.
D. Keesing, "The Impact of Research and Development on United States Trade," in P. Kenen and R. Lawrence, eds., *The Open Economy: Essays on International Trade and Finance,* New York, 1968, 175–89.
———, "Labor Skills and Comparative Advantage," *Amer. Econ. Rev. Proc.,* May 1966, *56,* 249–55.
———, "Labor Skills and International Trade: Evaluating Many Trade Flows with a Single Measuring Device," *Rev. Econ. Statist.,* Aug. 1965, *47,* 287–94.
———, "Labor Skills and the Structure of Trade in Manufactures," in P. Kenen and R. Lawrence, eds., *The Open Economy: Essays on International Trade and Finance,* New York, 1968, 3–18.
J. W. Kendrick, *Productivity Trends in the United States,* Princeton, 1961.
P. Kenen, "Nature, Capital and Trade," *J. Polit. Econ.,* Oct. 1965, *73,* 437–60.
———, "Skills, Human Capital and Comparative Advantage," Univ.-Nat. Bur.

Comm. Econ. Res., Conference on Human Resources, Madison, Wisc., Nov. 16, 1968.

I. Kravis, "Wages and Foreign Trade," *Rev. Econ. Statist.*, Feb. 1956, *38*, 14–30.

M. Kreinin, "Comparative Labor Effectiveness and the Leontief Scarce Factor Paradox," *Amer. Econ. Rev.*, Mar. 1965, *55*, 131–40.

H. B. Lary, *Imports of Labor-Intensive Manufactures from Less Developed Countries,* New York, 1968.

W. Leontief, "Domestic Production and Foreign Trade: The American Capital Position Re-examined," *Proc. of the Amer. Philosophical Soc.*, Sept. 1953, *97*, 332–49.

———, "Factor Proportions and the Structure of American Trade: Further Theoretical and Emprical Analysis," *Rev. Econ. Statist.*, Nov. 1956, *38*, 386–407.

———, "International Factor Costs and Factor Use," *Amer. Econ. Rev.*, June 1964, *54*, 335–45.

——— et al., *Studies in the Structure of the American Economy,* New York, 1963.

S. Linder, *An Essay on Trade and Transformation,* New York, 1961.

B. S. Minhas, *An International Comparison of Factor Costs and Factor Use,* Amsterdam, 1963.

S. Naya, "Natural Resources, Factor Mix, and Factor Reversal in International Trade," *Amer. Econ. Rev. Proc.*, May 1967, *57*, 561–70.

B. Ohlin, *Interregional and International Trade,* Cambridge, 1933.

Organization for Economic Cooperation and Development (OECD), Foreign Trade Statistical Bulletins, Series B, Commodity Trade, Jan.–Dec. 1962, Paris, 1963.

G. Philpot, "Labor Quality, Returns to Scale and the Elasticity of Factor Substitution," *Rev. Econ. Statist.*, May 1970, *52*, 194–99.

K. W. Roskamp, "Factor Proportions and Foreign Trade: The Case of West Germany," *Weltwertschaftliches Archiv*, 1963, *91*, 319–26.

K. Roskamp and G. McMeekin, "Factor Proportions, Human Capital and Foreign Trade: The Case of West Germany Reconsidered," *Quart. J. Econ.*, Feb. 1968, *82*, 152–60.

T. Schultz, *The Economic Value of Education,* New York, 1963.

M. Tatemoto and S. Ichimura, "Factor Proportions and Foreign Trade: The Case of Japan," *Rev. Econ. Statist.*, Nov. 1959, *41*, 442–46.

W. P. Travis, *The Theory of Trade and Protection,* Cambridge, 1964.

U.S. Bureau of the Census, *Census of Manufactures, 1958, 1,* Washington, 1961.

———, *Exports and Imports as Related to Output,* Series ES2, No. 5, Washington, 1964.

U.S. Bureau of Labor Statistics, *Wholesale Prices and Price Indexes, 1962,* Bull. 1411, Washington, 1962.

———, *1/1000 Sample of the Population of the United States, 1960,* Social Systems Research Institute, University of Wisconsin, Madison.

U.S. Department of Commerce, "The Transactions Table of the 1958 Input-Output Study and Revised Direct and Total Requirements Data," *Surv. Curr. Bus.*, Sept. 1965, *44*, 45–49.

U.S. Department of Interior, *1962 Minerals Yearbook, 2,* Washington, 1963.

J. Vanek, "The Factor Proportions Theory: The N-Factor Case," *Kyklos*, Oct. 1968, *21*, 749–56.

———, *The Natural Resource Content of United States Foreign Trade, 1870–1955,* Cambridge, 1963.

R. Vernon, "International Investment and International Trade in the Product Cycle," *Quart. J. Econ.*, May 1966, *80*, 190–207.

H. Waehrer, "Wage Rates, Labor Skills, and United States Foreign Trade," in P. Kenen and R. Lawrence, eds., *The Open Economy: Essays on International Trade and Finance,* New York, 1968.

D. F. Wahl, "Capital and Labour Requirements for Canada's Foreign Trade," *Can. J. Econ.*, Aug. 1961, *27*, 349–58.

L. A. Weiser, "Changing Factor Requirements of United States Foreign Trade," *Rev. Econ. Statist.*, Aug. 1968, *50*, 356–60.

L. Weiss, "Concentration and Labor Earnings," Paper 6405, Social Systems Research Institute, University of Wisconsin, 1964.

M. Yahr, "Human Capital and Factor Substitution in the CES Production Function," in P. Kenen and R. Lawrence, eds., *The Open Economy: Essays on International Trade and Finance*, New York, 1968, 70–99.

2

International Investment and International Trade in the Product Cycle

Raymond Vernon

Anyone who has sought to understand the shifts in international trade and international investment over the past twenty years has chafed from time to time under an acute sense of the inadequacy of the available analytical tools. While the comparative cost concept and other basic concepts have rarely failed to provide some help, they have usually carried the analyst only a very little way toward adequate understanding. For the most part, it has been necessary to formulate new concepts in order to explore issues such as the strengths and limitations of import substitution in the development process, the implications of common market arrangements for trade and investment, the underlying reasons for the Leontief paradox, and other critical issues of the day.

As theorists have groped for some more efficient tools, there has been a flowering in international trade and capital theory. But the very proliferation of theory has increased the urgency of the search for unifying concepts. It is doubtful that we shall find many propositions that can match the simplicity, power, and universality of application of the theory

From Raymond Vernon, "International Investment and International Trade in the Product Cycle," *Quarterly Journal of Economics*, May 2, 1966, LXXX, pp. 190–207. Copyright © 1966 by the President and Fellows of Harvard College. Reprinted by permission of John Wiley & Sons, Inc. The preparation of this article was financed in part by a grant from the Ford Foundation to the Harvard Business School to support a study of the implications of United States foreign direct investment. This paper is a by-product of the hypothesis-building stage of the study.

of comparative advantage and the international equilibrating mechanism; but unless the search for better tools goes on, the usefulness of economic theory for the solution of problems in international trade and capital movements will probably decline.

The present paper deals with one promising line of generalization and synthesis which seems to me to have been somewhat neglected by the main stream of trade theory. It puts less emphasis upon comparative cost doctrine and more upon the timing of innovation, the effects of scale economies, and the roles of ignorance and uncertainty in influencing trade patterns. It is an approach with respectable sponsorship, deriving bits and pieces of its inspiration from the writings of such persons as Williams, Kindleberger, MacDougall, Hoffmeyer, and Burenstam-Linder.[1]

Emphases of this sort seem first to have appeared when economists were searching for an explanation of what looked like a persistent, structural shortage of dollars in the world. When the shortage proved ephemeral in the late 1950's, many of the ideas which the shortage had stimulated were tossed overboard as prima facie wrong.[2] Nevertheless, one cannot be exposed to the main currents of international trade for very long without feeling that any theory which neglected the roles of innovation, scale, ignorance and uncertainty would be incomplete.

LOCATION OF NEW PRODUCTS

We begin with the assumption that the enterprises in any one of the advanced countries of the world are not distinguishably different from those in any other advanced country, in terms of their access to scientific knowledge and their capacity to comprehend scientific principles.[3] All of them, we may safely assume, can secure access to the knowledge that exists in the physical, chemical and biological sciences. These sciences at times may be difficult, but they are rarely occult.

It is a mistake to assume, however, that equal access to scientific principles in all the advanced countries means equal probability of the application of these principles in the generation of new products. There is ordinarily a large gap between the knowledge of a scientific principle and the embodiment of the principle in a marketable product. An entrepreneur usually has to intervene to accept the risks involved in testing whether the gap can be bridged.

If all entrepreneurs, wherever located, could be presumed to be equally conscious of and equally responsive to all entrepreneurial opportunities, wherever they arose, the classical view of the dominant role of price in resource allocation might be highly relevant. There is good reason to believe, however, that the entrepreneur's consciousness of and responsiveness to opportunity are a function of ease of communication; and further, that ease of communication is a function of geographical proximity.[4] Accordingly, we abandon the powerful simplifying notion that knowledge is a universal free good, and introduce it as an independent variable in the decision to trade or to invest.

The fact that the search for knowledge is an inseparable part of the decision-making process and that relative ease of access to knowledge can profoundly affect the outcome are now reasonably well established through empirical research.[5] One implication of that fact is that producers in any market are more likely to be aware of the possibility of introducing new products in that market than producers located elsewhere would be.

The United States market offers certain unique kinds of opportunities to those who are in a position to be aware of them.

First, the United States market consists of consumers with an average income which is higher (except for a few anomalies like Kuwait) than that in any other national market—twice as high as that of Western Europe, for instance. Wherever there was a chance to offer a new product responsive to wants at high levels of income, this chance would presumably first be apparent to someone in a position to observe the United States market.

Second, the United States market is characterized by high unit labor costs and relatively unrationed capital compared with practically all other markets. This is a fact which conditions the demand for both consumer goods and industrial products. In the case of consumer goods, for instance, the high cost of laundresses contributes to the origins of the drip-dry shirt and the home washing machine. In the case of industrial goods, high labor cost leads to the early development and use of the conveyor belt, the fork-lift truck, and the automatic control system. It seems to follow that wherever there was a chance successfully to sell a new product responsive to the need to conserve labor, this chance would be apparent first to those in a position to observe the United States market.

Assume, then, that entrepreneurs in the United States are first aware of opportunities to satisfy new wants associated with high income levels or high unit labor costs. Assume further that the evidence of an unfilled need and the hope of some kind of monopoly windfall for the early starter both are sufficiently strong to justify the initial investment that is usually involved in converting an abstract idea into a marketable product. Here we have a reason for expecting a consistently higher rate of expenditure on product development to be undertaken by United States producers than by producers in other countries, at least in lines which promise to substitute capital for labor or which promise to satisfy high-income wants. Therefore, if United States firms spend more than their foreign counterparts on new product development (often misleadingly labeled "research"), this may be due not to some obscure sociological drive for innovation but to more effective communication between the potential market and the potential supplier of the market. This sort of explanation is consistent with the pioneer appearance in the United States (conflicting claims of the Soviet Union notwithstanding) of the sewing machine, the typewriter, the tractor, etc.

At this point in the exposition, it is important once more to emphasize that the discussion so far relates only to innovation in certain kinds of products, namely to those associated with high income and those which substitute capital for labor. Our hypothesis says nothing about industrial innovation in general; this is a larger subject than we have tackled here. There are very few countries that have failed to introduce at least a few products; and there are some, such as Germany and Japan, which have been responsible for a considerable number of such introductions. Germany's outstanding successes in the development and use of plastics may have been due, for instance, to a traditional concern with her lack of a raw materials base, and a recognition that a market might exist in Germany for synthetic substitutes.[6]

Our hypothesis asserts that United States producers are likely to be the first to spy an opportunity for high-income or labor-saving new products.[7] But it goes on to assert that the first producing facilities for such products will be located in the United States. This is not a self-evident proposition. Under the calculus of least cost, production need not automatically take place at a location close to the market, unless the product can be produced and delivered from that location at lowest cost. Besides, now that most major United States companies control facilities situated in one or more locations outside of the United States, the possibility of considering a non-United States location is even more plausible than it might once have been.

Of course, if prospective producers were to make their locational choices on the basis of least-cost considerations, the United States would not always be ruled out. The costs of international transport and United States import duties, for instance, might be so high as to argue for such a location. My guess is, however, that the early producers of a new product intended for the United States market are attracted to a United States location by forces which are far stronger than relative factor-cost and transport considerations. For the reasoning on this point, one has to take a long detour away from comparative cost analysis into areas which fall under the rubrics of communication and external economies.

By now, a considerable amount of empirical work has been done on the factors affecting the location of industry.[8] Many of these studies try to explain observed locational patterns in conventional cost-minimizing terms, by implicit or explicit reference to labor cost and transportation cost. But some explicitly introduce problems of communication and external economies as powerful locational forces. These factors were given special emphasis in the analyses which were a part of the New York Metropolitan

Region Study of the 1950's. At the risk of oversimplifying, I shall try to summarize what these studies suggested.[9]

In the early stages of introduction of a new product, producers were usually confronted with a number of critical, albeit transitory, conditions. For one thing, the product itself may be quite unstandardized for a time; its inputs, its processing, and its final specifications may cover a wide range. Contrast the great variety of automobiles produced and marketed before 1910 with the thoroughly standardized product of the 1930's, or the variegated radio designs of the 1920's with the uniform models of the 1930's. The unstandardized nature of the design at this early stage carries with it a number of locational implications.

First, producers at this stage are particularly concerned with the degree of freedom they have in changing their inputs. Of course, the cost of the inputs is also relevant. But as long as the nature of these inputs cannot be fixed in advance with assurance, the calculation of cost must take into account the general need for flexibility in any locational choice.[10]

Second, the price elasticity of demand for the output of individual firms is comparatively low. This follows from the high degree of production differentiation, or the existence of monopoly in the early stages.[11] One result is, of course, that small cost differences count less in the calculations of the entrepreneur than they are likely to count later on.

Third, the need for swift and effective communication on the part of the producer with customers, suppliers, and even competitors is especially high at this stage. This is a corollary of the fact that a considerable amount of uncertainty remains regarding the ultimate dimensions of the market, the efforts of rivals to preempt that market, the specifications of the inputs needed for production, and the specifications of the products likely to be most successful in the effort.

All of these considerations tend to argue for a location in which communication between the market and the executives directly concerned with the new product is swift and easy, and in which a wide variety of potential types of input that might be needed by the production unit are easily come by. In brief, the producer who sees a market for some new product in the United States may be led to select a United States location for production on the basis of national locational considerations which extend well beyond simple factor cost analysis plus transport considerations.

THE MATURING PRODUCT[12]

As the demand for a product expands, a certain degree of standardization usually takes place. This is not to say that efforts at product differentiation come to an end. On the contrary; such efforts may even intensify, as competitors try to avoid the full brunt of price competition. Moreover, variety may appear as a result of specialization. Radios, for instance, ultimately acquired such specialized forms as clock radios, automobile radios, portable radios, and so on. Nevertheless, though the subcategories may multiply and the efforts at product differentiation increase, a growing acceptance of certain general standards seems to be typical.

Once again, the change has locational implications. First of all, the need for flexibility declines. A commitment to some set of product standards opens up technical possibilities for achieving economies of scale through mass output, and encourages long-term commitments to some given process and some fixed set of facilities. Second, concern about production cost begins to take the place of concern about product characteristics. Even if increased price competition is not yet present, the reduction of the uncertainties surrounding the operation enhances the usefulness of cost projections and increases the attention devoted to cost.

The empirical studies to which I referred earlier suggest that, at this stage in an industry's development, there is likely to be considerable shift in the location of production facilities at least as far as internal United States locations are concerned. The empirical materials on international locational shifts simply have not yet been analyzed sufficiently to tell us very much. A little speculation, however, indicates some hypotheses worth testing.

Picture an industry engaged in the manufacture of the high-income or labor-saving products that are the focus of our discussion. Assume that the industry has begun to settle down in the United States to some degree of large-scale production. Although the first mass market may be located in the United States, some demand for the product begins almost at once to appear elsewhere. For instance, although heavy fork-lift trucks in general may have a comparatively small market in Spain because of the relative cheapness of unskilled labor in that country, some limited demand for the product will appear there almost as soon as the existence of the product is known.

If the product has a high income elasticity of demand or if it is a satisfactory substitute for high-cost labor, the demand in time will begin to grow quite rapidly in relatively advanced countries such as those of Western Europe. Once the market expands in such an advanced country, entrepreneurs will begin to ask themselves whether the time has come to take the risk of setting up a local producing facility.[13]

How long does it take to reach this stage? An adequate answer must surely be a complex one. Producers located in the United States, weighing the wisdom of setting up a new production facility in the importing country, will feel obliged to balance a number of complex considerations. As long as the marginal production cost plus the transport cost of the goods exported from the United States is lower than the average cost of prospective production in the market of import, United States producers will presumably prefer to avoid an investment. But that calculation depends on the producer's ability to project the cost of production in a market in which factor costs and the appropriate technology differ from those at home.

Now and again, the locational force which determined some particular overseas investment is so simple and so powerful that one has little difficulty in identifying it. Otis Elevator's early proliferation of production facilities abroad was quite patently a function of the high cost of shipping assembled elevator cabins to distant locations and the limited scale advantages involved in manufacturing elevator cabins at a single location.[14] Singer's decision to invest in Scotland as early as 1867 was also based on considerations of a sort sympathetic with our hypothesis.[15] It is not unlikely that the overseas demand for its highly standardized product was already sufficiently large at that time to exhaust the obvious scale advantages of manufacturing in a single location, expecially if that location were one of high labor cost.

In an area as complex and "imperfect" as international trade and investment, however, one ought not anticipate that any hypothesis will have more than a limited explanatory power. United States airplane manufacturers surely respond to many "noneconomic" locational forces, such as the desire to play safe in problems of military security. Producers in the United States who have a protected patent position overseas presumably take that fact into account in deciding whether or when to produce abroad. And other producers often are motivated by considerations too complex to reconstruct readily, such as the fortuitous timing of a threat of new competition in the country of import, the level of tariff protection anticipated for the future, the political situation in the country of prospective investment, and so on.

We arrive, then, at the stage at which United States producers have come around to the establishment of production units in the advanced countries. Now a new group of forces are set in train. In an idealized form, Figure 1 [on page 34] suggests what may be anticipated next.

As far as individual United States producers are concerned, the local markets thenceforth will be filled from local production units set up abroad. Once these facilities are in operation, however, more ambitious possibilities for their use may be suggested. When comparing a United States producing facility and a facility in another advanced country, the obvious production-cost differences between the rival producing areas are usually differences due to scale and differences due to labor costs. If the producer is an international firm with producing locations in several countries, its costs of financing capital at the different locations may not be sufficiently different to matter very much. If economies of scale are being fully exploited, the principal differences between any two locations are likely to be labor costs.[16] Accordingly, it may prove wise for the international firm to begin servicing third-country markets from the new location. And if labor cost differences are large enough to offset transport costs, then exports back to the United States may become a possibility as well.

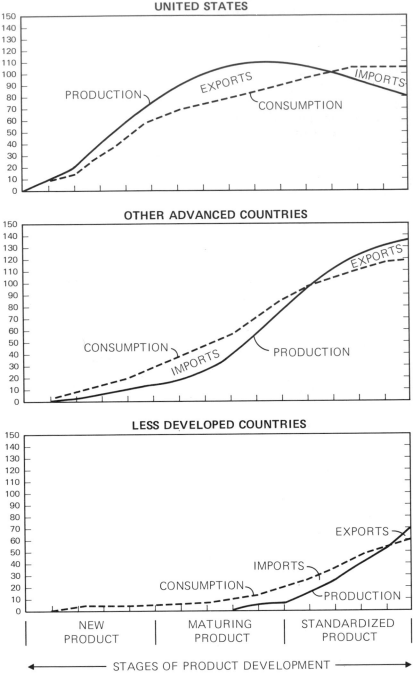

FIGURE 1

Any hypotheses based on the assumption that the United States entrepreneur will react rationally when offered the possibility of a lower-cost location abroad is, of course, somewhat suspect. The decision-making sequence that is used in connection with international investments, according to various empirical studies, is not a model of the rational process.[17] But there is one theme that emerges again and again in such studies. Any threat to the established position of an enterprise is a powerful galvanizing force to action; in fact, if I interpret the empirical work correctly, threat in general is a more reliable stimulus to action than opportunity is likely to be.

In the international investment field, threats appear in various forms once a large-scale export business in manufactured products has developed. Local entrepreneurs located in the countries which are the targets of these exports grow restive at the opportunities they are missing. Local governments concerned with generating employment or promoting growth or balancing their trade accounts begin thinking of ways and means to replace the imports. An international investment by the exporter, therefore, becomes a prudent means of forestalling the loss of a market. In this case, the yield on the investment is seen largely as the avoidance of a loss of income to the system.

The notion that a threat to the status quo is a powerful galvanizing force for international investment also seems to explain what happens after the initial investment. Once such an investment is made by a United States producer, other major producers in the United States sometimes see it as a threat to the status quo. They see themselves as losing position relative to the investing company, with vague intimations of further losses to come. Their "share of the market" is imperiled, viewing "share of the market" in global terms. At the same time, their ability to estimate the production-cost structure of their competitors, operating far away in an unfamiliar foreign area, is impaired; this is a particularly unsettling state because it conjures up the possibility of a return flow of products to the United States and a new source of price competition, based on cost differences of unknown magnitude. The uncertainty can be reduced by emulating the pathfinding investor and by investing in the same area; this may not be an optimizing investment pattern and it may be costly, but it is least disturbing to the status quo.

Pieces of this hypothetical pattern are subject to empirical tests of a sort. So far, at any rate, the empirical tests have been reassuring. The office machinery industry, for instance, has seen repeatedly the phenomenon of the introduction of a new product in the United States, followed by United States exports,[18] followed still later by United States imports. (We have still to test whether the timing of the commencement of overseas production by United States subsidiaries fits into the expected pattern.) In the electrical and electronic products industry, those elements in the pattern which can be measured show up nicely.[19] A broader effort is now under way to test the United States trade patterns of a group of products with high income elasticities; and, here too, the preliminary results are encouraging.[20] On a much more general basis, it is reassuring for our hypotheses to observe that the foreign manufacturing subsidiaries of United States firms have been increasing their exports to third countries.

It will have occurred to the reader by now that the pattern envisaged here also may shed some light on the Leontief paradox.[21] Leontief, it will be recalled, seemed to confound comparative cost theory by establishing the fact that the ratio of capital to labor in United States exports was lower, not higher, than the like ratio in the United States production which had been displaced by competitive imports. The hypothesis suggested in this paper would have the United States exporting high-income and labor-saving products in the early stages of their existence, and importing them later on.[22] In the early stages, the value-added contribution of industries engaged in producing these items probably contains an unusually high proportion of labor cost. This is not so much because the labor is particularly skilled, as is so often suggested. More likely, it is due to a quite different phenomenon. At this stage, the standardization of the manufacturing process has not gotten very far; that is to come later, when the volume of output is high enough and the degree of uncertainty low enough to justify investment in relatively inflexible, capital-intensive facilities. As a result, the production process relies relatively heavily on labor inputs at a time when the United States commands an export position; and the process relies more heavily on capital at a time when imports become important.

This, of course, is an hypothesis which has not yet been subjected to any really rigorous test. But it does open up a line of inquiry into the structure of United States trade which is well worth pursuing.

THE STANDARDIZED PRODUCT

Figure 1, the reader will have observed, carries a panel which suggests that, at an advanced stage in the standardization of some products, the less-developed countries may offer competitive advantages as a production location.

This is a bold projection, which seems on first blush to be wholly at variance with the Heckscher-Ohlin theorem. According to that theorem, one presumably ought to anticipate that the exports of the less-developed countries would tend to be relatively labor-intensive products.

One of the difficulties with the theorem, however, is that it leaves marketing considerations out of account. One reason for the omission is evident. As long as knowledge is regarded as a free good, instantaneously available, and as long as individual producers are regarded as atomistic contributors to the total supply, marketing problems cannot be expected to find much of a place in economic theory. In projecting the patterns of export from less-developed areas, however, we cannot afford to disregard the fact that information comes at a cost; and that entrepreneurs are not readily disposed to pay the price of investigating overseas markets of unknown dimensions and unknown promise. Neither are they eager to venture into situations which they know will demand a constant flow of reliable marketing information from remote sources.

If we can assume that highly standardized products tend to have a well-articulated, easily accessible international market and to sell largely on the basis of price (an assumption inherent in the definition), then it follows that such products will not pose the problem of market information quite so acutely for the less-developed countries. This establishes a necessary if not a sufficient condition for investment in such industries.

Of course, foreign investors seeking an optimum location for a captive facility may not have to concern themselves too much with questions of market information; presumably, they are thoroughly familiar with the marketing end of the business and are looking for a low-cost captive source of supply. In that case, the low cost of labor may be the initial attraction drawing the investor to less-developed areas. But other limitations in such areas, according to our hypothesis, will bias such captive operations toward the production of standardized items. The reasons in this case turn on the part played in the production process by external economics. Manufacturing processes which receive significant inputs from the local economy, such as skilled labor, repairmen, reliable power, spare parts, industrial materials processed according to exacting specification, and so on, are less appropriate to the less-developed areas than those that do not have such requirements. Unhappily, most industrial processes require one or another ingredient of this difficult sort. My guess is, however, that the industries which produce a standardized product are in the best position to avoid the problem, by producing on a vertically-integrated self-sustaining basis.

In speculating about future industrial exports from the less-developed areas, therefore, we are led to think of products with a fairly clear-cut set of economic characteristics.[23] Their production function is such as to require significant inputs of labor; otherwise there is no reason to expect a lower production cost in less-developed countries. At the same time, they are products with a high price elasticity of demand for the output of individual firms; otherwise, there is no strong incentive to take the risks of pioneering with production in a new area. In addition, products whose production process did not rely heavily upon external economies would be more obvious candidates than those which required a more elaborate industrial environment. The implications of remoteness also would be critical; products which could be precisely described by standardized specifications and which could be produced for inventory without fear of obsolescence would be more relevant than those which had less precise specifications and which could not easily be ordered from remote locations. Moreover, high-value items capable of absorbing significant freight costs would be more likely to appear than bulky items low in value by weight. Standardized textile products are, of course, the illustration par excellence of the sort of product that meets the criteria. But other products come to mind such as crude steel, simple fertilizers, newsprint, and so on.

Speculation of this sort draws some support from various interregional experiences in industrial location. In the United States, for example, the "export" industries which moved to the low-wage south in search of lower costs tended to be industries which had no great need for a sophisticated industrial environment and which produced fairly standardized products. In the textile industry, it was the grey goods, cotton sheetings and men's shirt plants that went south; producers of high-style dresses or other unstandardized items were far more reluctant to move. In the electronics industry, it was the mass producers of tubes, resistors and other standardized high-volume components that showed the greatest disposition to move south; custom-built and research-oriented production remained closer to markets and to the main industrial complexes. A similar pattern could be discerned in printing and in chemicals production.[24]

Notes

1. J. H. Williams, "The Theory of International Trade Reconsidered," reprinted as Chap. 2 in his *Postwar Monetary Plans and Other Essays* (Oxford: Basil Blackwell, 1947); C. P. Kindleberger, *The Dollar Shortage* (New York: Wiley, 1950); Erik Hoffmeyer, *Dollar Shortage* (Amsterdam: North-Holland, 1958); Sir Donald MacDougall, *The World Dollar Problem* (London: Macmillan, 1957); Staffan Burenstam-Linder, *An Essay on Trade and Transformation* (Uppsala: Almqvist & Wicksells, 1961).
2. The best summary of the state of trade theory that has come to my attention in recent years is J. Bhagwati, "The Pure Theory of International Trade," *Economic Journal*, LXXIV (Mar. 1964), 1–84. Bhagwati refers obliquely to some of the theories which concern us here; but they receive much less attention than I think they deserve.
3. Some of the account that follows will be found in greatly truncated form in my "The Trade Expansion Act in Perspective," in *Emerging Concepts in Marketing*, Proceedings of the American Marketing Association, December 1962, pp. 384–89. The elaboration here owes a good deal to the perceptive work of Se'ev Hirsch, summarized in his unpublished doctoral thesis, "Location of Industry and International Competitiveness," Harvard Business School, 1965.
4. Note C. P. Kindleberger's reference to the "horizon" of the decision maker, and the view that he can only be rational within that horizon; see his *Foreign Trade and the National Economy* (New Haven: Yale University Press, 1962), p. 15 *passim*.
5. See, for instance, Richard M. Cyert and James G. March, *A Behavioral Theory of the Firm* (Englewood Cliffs, N.J.: Prentice-Hall, 1963), esp. Chap. 6; and Yair Aharoni, *The Foreign Investment Decision Process*, to be published by the Division of Research of the Harvard Business School, 1966.
6. See two excellent studies: C. Freeman, "The Plastics Industry: A Comparative Study of Research and Innovation," in *National Institute Economic Review*, No. 26 (Nov. 1963), p. 22, *et seq.*; G. C. Hufbauer, *Synthetic Materials and the Theory of International Trade* (London: Gerald Duckworth, 1965). A number

of links in the Hufbauer arguments are remarkably similar to some in this paper; but he was not aware of my writings nor I of his until after both had been completed.

7. There is a kind of first-cousin relationship between this simple notion and the "entrained want" concept defined by H. G. Barnett in *Innovation: The Basis of Cultural change* (New York: McGraw-Hill, 1953) p. 148. Albert O. Hirschman, *The Strategy of Economic Development* (New Haven: Yale University Press, 1958), p. 68, also finds the concept helpful in his effort to explain certain aspects of economic development.

8. For a summary of such work, together with a useful bibliography, see John Meyer, "Regional Economics: A Survey," in the *American Economic Review*, LIII (Mar. 1963), 19–54.

9. The points that follow are dealt with at length in the following publications: Raymond Vernon, *Metropolis, 1985* (Cambridge: Harvard University Press, 1960), pp. 38–85; Max Hall (ed.), *Made in New York* (Cambridge: Harvard University Press, 1959), pp. 3–18, 19 *passim*; Robert M. Lichtenberg, *One-Tenth of a Nation* (Cambridge: Harvard University Press, 1960), pp. 31–70.

10. This is, of course, a familiar point elaborated in George F. Stigler, "Production and Distribution in the Short Run," *Journal of Political Economy*, XLVII (June 1939), 305, *et seq.*

11. Hufbauer, *op. cit.*, suggests that the low price elasticity of demand in the first stage may be due simply to the fact that the first market may be a "captive market" unresponsive to price changes; but that later, in order to expand the use of the new product, other markets may be brought in which are more price responsive.

12. Both Hirsch, *op. cit.*, and Freeman, *op. cit.*, make use of a three-stage product classification of the sort used here.

13. M. V. Posner, "International Trade and Technical Change," *Oxford Economic Papers*, Vol. 13 (Oct. 1961), p. 323, *et seq.* presents a stimulating model purporting to explain such familiar trade phenomena as the exchange of machine tools between the United Kingdom and Germany. In the process he offers some particularly helpful notions concerning the size of the "imitation lag" in the responses of competing nations.

14. Dudley M. Phelps, *Migration of Industry to South America* (New York: McGraw-Hill, 1963), p. 4.

15. John H. Dunning, *American Investment in British Manufacturing Industry* (London: George Allen & Unwin, 1958), p. 18. The Dunning book is filled with observations that lend casual support to the main hypotheses of this paper.

16. Note the interesting finding of Mordecai Kreinin in his "The Leontief Scarce-Factor Paradox," *The American Economic Review*, LV (Mar. 1965), 131–39. Kreinin finds that the higher cost of labor in the United States is not explained by a higher rate of labor productivity in this country.

17. Aharoni, *op. cit.*, provides an excellent summary and exhaustive bibliography of the evidence on this point.

18. Reported in U.S. Senate, Interstate and Foreign Commerce Committee, *Hearings on Foreign Commerce*, 1960, pp. 130–39.

19. See Hirsch, *op. cit.*

20. These are to appear in a forthcoming doctoral thesis at the Harvard Business School by Louis T. Wells, tentatively entitled "International Trade and Business Policy."

21. See Wassily Leontief, "Domestic Production and Foreign Trade: The American Capital Position Re-examined," *Proceedings of the American Philosophical Society*, Vol. 97 (Sept. 1953), and "Factor Proportions and the Structure of American Trade: Further Theoretical and Empirical Analysis," *Review of Economics and Statistics*, XXXVIII (Nov. 1956).

22. Of course, if there were some systematic trend in the inputs of new products—for example, if the new products which appeared in the 1960's were more capital-intensive than the new products which appeared in the 1950's—then

the tendencies suggested by our hypotheses might be swamped by such a trend. As long as we do not posit offsetting systematic patterns of this sort, however, the Leontief findings and the hypotheses offered here seem consistent.

23. The concepts sketched out here are presented in more detail in my "Problems and Prospects in the Export of Manufactured Products from the Less-developed Countries," U.N. Conference on Trade and Development, Dec. 16, 1963 (mimeo.).

24. This conclusion derives largely from the industry studies conducted in connection with the New York Metropolitan Region study. There have been some excellent more general analyses of shifts in industrial location among the regions of the United States. See e.g., Victor R. Fuchs, *Changes in the Location of Manufacturing in the United States Since 1929* (New Haven: Yale University Press, 1962). Unfortunately, however, none has been designed, so far as I know, to test hypotheses relating locational shifts to product characteristics such as price elasticity of demand and degree of standardization.

3

Causes of Trade in Primary Products versus Manufactures

Staffan Burenstam Linder

We shall search for a new basic principle to explain the pattern of trade and location. Our contention that the importance of differences in factor proportions has been overestimated does not imply, however, that such differences are unimportant. This will be evident from our subsequent discussion of the principles of trade in, on the one hand, primary products, and, on the other hand, manufactures.

TRADE IN PRIMARY PRODUCTS

We shall retain the factor proportions approach in our analysis of trade in primary products. A country abundantly supplied with a natural resource will be assumed to have a comparative advantage in the exploitation of the resource. . . . The scattered observations on the nature of comparative advantages, which preceded the full-fledged Heckscher-Ohlin factor proportions theory, allotted a strategic role in the formation of the

From Staffan Burenstam Linder, *An Essay on Trade and Transformation* (New York: John Wiley & Sons, 1961), pp. 86–99. Copyright © 1961 by Almqvist & Wiksell. Reprinted by permission. Some footnotes omitted.

trade pattern only to *land endowments*. Capital and labor endowments were not referred to. Thus, it is in harmony with both the Heckscher-Ohlin theory and earlier theory that we use the factor proportions approach in the analysis of trade in primary products.

It is probable that the factor proportions theorem has gained such wide acceptance only because a pattern of trade in primary products, dictated by differences in natural resource endowments, is so plausible. By a suspect analogy, trade in manufactures has been treated as if governed by differences in capital and labor endowments. Explanations of the factor proportions account always begin with a persuasive assertion that the natural-resource-abundant countries export natural-resource-intensive products. We shall now accept this statement but reject its analogous application to the pattern of trade in manufactures.

TRADE IN MANUFACTURES

Among all non-primary products, a country has a range of potential exports. This range of exportable products is determined by *internal demand. It is a necessary, but not a sufficient, condition that a product be consumed (or invested) in the home country for this product to be a potential export product*. This is our basic proposition.

For a product to be consumed (or invested) in a country, there must be a demand for the product at the ruling world market prices. However, in order to make our proposition as meaningful as we can, we want to make the range of potential exports of a country as narrow as possible. Unfortunately, it is not possible, without loss of precision, to adopt a weaker criterion than that there must be a demand at ruling prices. Nonetheless, the reasons—which will be set forth below—why we believe our basic proportion to be correct will enable us to handle intuitively a weaker criterion which will make the range of potential exports of a country narrower. It is really what we may refer to as "representative demand" that is necessary for a good to be a potential export product. It will be evident that, although, for instance, the demand for Cadillacs in Saudi Arabia is not totally absent, this kind of unrepresentative demand is not sufficient to turn luxury cars into potential export products for Saudi Arabia. The meaning of "representative demand" is deplorably loose but may be better understood from our subsequent discussion.

In our proposition we also speak of demand in the "home country." The following inquiry into the reasons why we believe our proposition to be valid will also clarify what we mean more precisely with "home country." It will become evident that an expression such as "market area" might be more exact. But as it would also be more artificial in an international trade theory context, "country" has been preferred. Furthermore, there are forces, both cultural and economic, which tend to make "country" and "market area" interchangeable concepts.

We shall now advance various reasons why we believe our proposition to be valid. These reasons will prove to be variations on the same general theme, namely, unfamiliarity with foreign markets as compared with the domestic market.

Firstly, the decision to take up production of any particular good is likely to be generated by clearly discernible economic needs. In a world of imperfect knowledge, entrepreneurs will react to profit opportunities *of which they are aware*. These would tend to arise from *domestic* needs. Perhaps a need that an entrepreneur has himself experienced has provided the idea on which his entrepreneurship is based.

As a successful firm grows, the local market becomes insufficient for further expansion. The trade horizon of the firm is gradually lifted. But only after what has probably been a considerable period of producing for the domestic market will the entrepreneur become aware of the profit opportunities offered by producing for foreign countries. The export market will not be entered until then. However, once this stage is reached there is nothing to prevent exports from constituting a larger—and even substantially larger—share of total sales than that absorbed by the home market. The smaller the home country is, the larger, *ceteris paribus*, the share of exports of total production is likely to be. Frontiers are arbitrarily drawn lines that we cross when the trade horizon is lifted, and the smaller the country is the sooner these lines will be crossed. Whatever the percentage share of exports, and this is what we want to emphasize, export is the end, not the beginning, of a typical market expansion path. *International trade is really nothing but an extension across national frontiers of a country's own web of economic activity.*

Secondly, to the extent that production of a good is based on invention, we have an additional reason to believe that home market demand is necessary. An invention is, in itself, most likely to have been the outcome of an effort to solve some problem which has been acute in one's own environment. The exploitation of the invention will then, in its first phase, automatically be geared to the home market.

A. P. Usher, in his *A History of Mechanical Inventions*,[1] addresses himself to the question of how inventions are made.[2] This discussion is of great interest for our present purposes. Usher rejects the *transcendentist* approach which describes inventions as the outcome of occasional inspirational insights of great men. Such a theory can possibly serve as a basis for a fascinating essayistic interpretation of isolated phenomena along the road of great inventions. However, it is entirely incapable of analyzing what seems essentially to be a process where insights are accumulated and synthesized.

At the other extreme, we have the *mechanistic* theory of invention. Here, the importance of the individual effort has faded. The inventive process is unfolded under the stresses of necessity. The individual is merely an instrument in a predetermined sequence of events.

Making use of elements from both these theories, but being particularly influenced by the mechanistic approach, Usher presents his own theory of the *cumulative synthesis*. The whole process of technological progress is made up of any number of interrelated sequences of cumulative insights maturing into a synthesis or invention which—in its turn—serves as a basis for the continuance of the process. But the process is not mechanistically determined. The acts of insight and syntheses are not an automatic response with the individual as a mere instrument.

Usher distinguishes between four stages in the sequence leading up to an invention: (1) the perception of a problem; (2) the setting of the stage by bringing together whatever material is essential for a solution; (3) the act of insight; and (4) the critical revision when the new solution is tried out for complete mastery.

This theory of invention lends support to our argument that it is a country's *own* needs which are the mother not only of innovation but also of invention. It must be difficult to become aware of problems and to set the stage for their solution when they do not form part of the inventor's environment. Whether the invention is the product of a one-man effort, as was typical in the old days, or the outcome of institutionalized teamwork in research laboratories, seems to be immaterial in this respect. Research projects as well as one-man efforts, aimed at inventions for commercial exploitation, are likely to be planned for the most obvious needs—the domestic ones. The resulting products will suit the needs of the home market and will only gradually be tried on the export markets.

Whether it is a question of "critical revision" of an invention or product development work in general, it must be carried out in close contact with the market. This gives us a third reason to believe that there must be a home market for an export good, whether it is a consumer good or a capital good. If, for some odd reason, an entrepreneur decided to cater for a demand which did not exist at home, he would probably be unsuccessful as he would not have easy access to crucial information which must be funnelled back and forth between producers and consumers. The trial-and-error period which a new product must also inevitably go through on the market will be the more embarrassing costwise, the less intimate knowledge the producer has of the conditions under which his product will have to be used. And, if there is no home demand, the producer will be completely unfamiliar with such conditions. . . . In a technical sense, it may be possible to solve all problems without such close contact. But, although an entrepreneur lacking testing ground at home may be able to secure necessary information, he would incur additional costs which might be destructive for his effort to achieve the necessary *comparative* advantage. From this standpoint, it may be imperative to begin the expansion path at home. It should be easy to find examples of how producers have sold, or tried to sell, their commodities on markets with which they were not familiar and failed because of the difficulties in adapting to different circumstances. Only if operations are moved to the foreign market can this obstacle be bypassed; but such action comes late on an expansion path and, when it comes, the marketing of the product will no longer be foreign trade.

We have now given three reasons which lend support to the assertion that a particular good will not be produced at a comparative advantage unless there is a domestic market for the good. We have argued: (1) that it is unlikely that an entrepreneur will ever think of satisfying a need that does not exist at home; (2) that, even if this alien need was seen, the basically correct product to fill it might not be conceived of; and (3) that, even if the basically correct product was conceived of, it is still improbable that the product could be finally adapted to unfamiliar conditions without prohibitive costs being incurred. In all, what our arguments amount to is the proposition that production functions are not identical in all countries, but that *the production functions of goods demanded at home are the relatively most advantageous ones*. The necessity of "the support of the home market" is probably stressed by active businessmen as a reflection of the importance of relationships emphasized here.

According to the logic of the reasons we have given in support of our proposition, it is possible to state that exceptions to our proposition are likely to occur in those cases: (1) where it is easy to become aware of the foreign demand in spite of the non-existence of home demand for the product; (2) where the product as such is available without inventive effort; and (3) where no or little product development work is needed.

It might be suspected that Japanese foreign trade contained so many exceptions to the rule that the latter's value was seriously threatened. However, it is easy to become a victim of popular misconceptions about Japanese foreign trade. Passages in W. W. Lockwood's renowned book, *The Economic Development of Japan*,[3] reveal that Japan, in fact, does not constitute an exception but an excellent empirical illustration of our proposition and its meaning. Lockwood is anxious to stress that the (not uncommon) belief that Japan should have built up extensive export industries not producing for the home market is a fallacy. In fact, no category of products seems to have been exported without also having an internal market. The whole of Chapters 6 and 7 are of interest to us in this connection. Three quotations might, however, be sufficient: "Sometimes, indeed, the growth of Japanese industry . . . is attributed mainly to the expansion of overseas demand. This is a misconception, as emphasized earlier, and fails to offer any intelligible explanation of the substance and breadth of Japanese economic development"[4]; "The home demand for Japanese manufactures thus absorbed continuously most of the output of industry. . . . It developed *pari passu* with the expansion of overseas trade"[5]; "In general, as we have seen, Japan tended to export manufactures of the same general type as those used extensively by her own people."[6]

Having determined the range of potential exports of a country, we now wish to determine the *range of potential imports* of a country. The range of these products is more indisputable. It is self-evident that *internal demand determines which products may be imported*. It should be observed that, in this case, demand does not, of course, need to be representative. All products for which there is a demand at going prices are potential import products.

We thus find that *the range of potential exports is identical to, or included in, the range of potential imports*.

SOME FURTHER OBSERVATIONS ON THE PATTERN OF TRADE IN PRIMARY PRODUCTS AND A NOTE ON FOREIGN ENTREPRENEURSHIP

Before we proceed to consider trade in manufactures more carefully, it might be interesting to stop for a while and investigate why a country may export—but not, of course, import—a primary product without there existing any home demand.

An important condition for relative natural-resource endowments to dictate the pattern of trade in primary products is fulfilled in that such products undoubtedly use up relatively much of the natural-resource factor at all relative factor prices. Whether manufactures can be classified according to their factor intensity has been questioned above.

The fact that primary products are natural-resource-intensive makes relative factor proportions of prime importance for the prices of primary products. This carries the additional implication that, because of a strikingly high pre-trade price in natural-resource-scarce countries, foreign demand is easy to become aware of. However, the need for these primary materials is—by virtue of their basic nature in the productive process and because of the large quantities needed—usually self-evident under any circumstances. Furthermore, primary products are often available without particular inventive effort being necessary and their qualitative homogeneity eliminates product development work.

In combination, these facts mean that the forces to which we have attributed great importance in our definition of the potentially possible exports of manufactures obviously cannot exert the same strong influence on trade in primary products. There are likely to be less international differences in production functions as regards primary products than as regards manufactures. And since primary products are characterized by a particular factor intensity, it is clear that the factor proportions theorem is pertinent to trade in primary products. Thus, we must have different explanations for trade in manufactures and for trade in raw materials.

However, it is extremely interesting to note that, even in the case of raw-material exports without the support of a market in the exporting country, *it seldom seems to be entrepreneurs of the exporting country who have taken up production and sought sales outlets on the export market.* Instead, the domination of foreign entrepreneurs recruited from the *importing* country is a typical feature. Even in a country like Sweden, somewhat late in the Industrial Revolution, the initial exploitation of forest resources in the latter half of the nineteenth century was to a considerable extent carried out by foreigners. Singer has called the raw-material sector of underdeveloped countries "foreign sectors."[7] *From the point of view of entrepreneurs, it is domestic demand, i.e., demand in their home country— the importing country—which has stimulated production.* This suggests that, even in the case of raw materials, the various pre-requisites for export production implied in our proposition exert a strong influence. *If entrepreneurship could not move internationally, it is quite possible that our proposition could be applied to trade in primary products as well as manufactures.*

In our model for u-countries [underdeveloped countries], we had occasion to work with the assumption that foreign entrepreneurship will establish raw-material sectors in these countries in cases where domestic entrepreneurs did not engage in such production. We are now in a position to provide an explanation of the mechanism inherent in this assumption. Foreign entrepreneurs will come in to exploit raw-material resources, the utilization of which by domestic entrepreneurs is totally absent, or is proceeding at too slow a rate, because of non-existent domestic demand. They will be attracted by profit opportunities which, owing to the differences in natural-resource endowments, are high enough to overcome the inertia produced by the existence of more familiar alternatives in their home country. This inertia keeps them, however, from entering into other lines of production in u-countries where the profit opportunities are more obscure. Thus, it may well be that differences in natural-resource endowments dictate the pattern of trade in primary products only through their effect on international movements of entrepreneurship, in the absence of which production functions would be too different for the factor proportions explanation to be relevant. One should expect that, *if relative factor proportions were as important in manufacturing industry as in the production of primary goods, the international flow of entrepreneurship into manufacturing industry in u-countries to produce for one's own home market would, with the great differences in the endowment of resources, be as marked as the actual flow into raw-material exploitation.* However, international movements of entrepreneurship in manufacturing industry usually take the form of establishing sales organizations, assembly plants, etc., to increase exports from the home country to foreign markets with a similar demand structure. Perhaps in a study of international flows of entrepreneurship the most significant feature to be explored is to which countries entrepreneurship does *not* flow.

BETWEEN WHICH COUNTRIES IS TRADE IN MANUFACTURES POTENTIALLY MOST INTENSIVE?

It is evident that, with respect to trade in manufactures, the most important step now is to transfer our attention from the determinants of potential trade to the determinants of *actual* trade. However, to acquaint ourselves with all the problems involved in taking this step, we must first solve another, almost equally interesting, problem, i.e., we must ascertain among which trading partners trade could be potentially most intensive.

By "intensive" we do not mean simply the volume of trade. The absolute size of trade is naturally dominated by the size of the trading partners. In order to measure the intensity of trade, we thus have to eliminate the influence exerted by the size of the countries. The method we shall use . . . is to calculate the *propensities* of countries to import from each other.

The more similar the demand structures of two countries, the more intensive, potentially, is the trade between these two countries. If two countries have exactly the same demand structures, *all* the exportables and importables of the one country are also the exportables and importables of the other country.

To determine *which types* of countries may be able to develop intensive trade among themselves, we first have to ascertain which forces determine the demand structures.

A whole array of forces influences the demand structure of a country. We shall, however, argue that the level of average income is the most important single factor and that it has, in fact, a dominating influence on the structure of demand. If this is the case, *similarity of average income levels could be used as an index of similarity of demand structures.* The modal or median incomes are likely to be more representative than the arithmetic mean of the average income, particularly in countries with a pronounced skewness in the distribution of income (such as Kuwait). In a statistical test, modal and median incomes would, however, probably be difficult to find. We shall thus in the following speak of the per capita income, i.e., the arithmetic mean.

We shall try to show that there is a strong relationship between the level of per capita income, on the one hand, and the types of consumer goods and also capital goods demanded, on the other hand.

Let us first consider consumer goods. At higher incomes, products of different kinds, although filling the same basic needs, are likely to replace less sophisticated types of products; furthermore, products filling new needs are added. Such "qualitative changes" in demand are probably very common. Only part of the higher incomes will be expressed in purely quantitative changes in demand. By "quantitative" we mean a change in the volume of demand for the same product. A "qualitative" change is an alteration in the nature of the product.

Qualitative product differences are not well brought out in empirical studies of consumer behavior along the lines first followed by Engel. The qualitative factor is submerged by taking broad groups of goods such as "food" and "clothing." Even if we are specific enough to study changes in demand for a product like toasters, we shall not discern important changes from lower to higher qualities involving extensive alterations in the product as such. The larger the group of commodities we take, the more likely it will be that the income elasticity at all levels of income is in the neighborhood of unity. The income elasticity of demand for aggregate production is necessarily always unity in the long run when Say's law holds, and is very close to unity in the short run. But the more we divide total production into subgroups, the greater will be the variations in income elasticity. If we classify goods in accordance with precise quality specifications, income elasticity with respect to each class of these goods may change within a small income interval from infinitely positive to infinitely negative. In such cases, small differences in income levels may produce substantial differences in the structure of demand. Outside the income interval there is no demand for the product on the home market; outside an even narrower income range there is no "representative demand." In studies of Engel's law, the qualitative aspect is brought to the surface only indirectly when it is explained why, for instance, the proportion of food expenditures has not, as expected, decreased with rising incomes. The reason given is that food *processing* has been carried farther and changed the character of the commodity group.

As far as our study is concerned, when we compare demand structures it is necessary to define goods by specifying quality. Even minor qualitative differences in goods serving the same basic needs may be sufficient to introduce into the demand structure of one country some significant differences compared with that of another country.

The differences in consumer demand caused by per capita income differences should not, however, be exaggerated. Uneven income distribution in a country widens the range of potential exports and imports and results, *ceteris paribus*, in there being a greater overlapping of demands between countries with different per capita incomes than would be the case if incomes were more evenly distributed. High-income-earners in a poor country may demand the same goods as low-income-earners in a rich country.

We shall now take up the question of the composition of demand for capital goods. There is not the same relationship between per capita incomes and the demand for capital goods as there is between per capita incomes and consumer demand. The income elasticity of capital goods is not a meaningful concept. Nevertheless, there is another relationship between per capita incomes and the demand for capital goods which makes it useful to link them together. Per capita income is to a large extent determined by the existing stock of capital goods. The relative amount of capital also determines the qualitative composition of the demand for new capital goods. A capital-abundant country, i.e., a country which, with some likelihood, finds itself on a high level of per capita income, demands more sophisticated capital equipment than a capital-scarce country. Although there is no direct causal relationship, we might thus expect that the differences in the level of per capita incomes would tell us at least something about what differences there will be in the structure of demand for capital goods.

It is probable that the technical possibilities for qualitative variations in capital goods are at least as great as for consumer goods. But why should a capital good of lower quality ever be chosen? It is clear that people on relatively lower per capita income levels select lower qualities of consumer goods in order to be able to diversify their consumption within their given budget. Similarly, the reason for selecting relatively lower quality capital goods in a capital-scarce country is that it is a means of spreading the available capital more evenly.

From the marginalist approach, we know that capital should be spread evenly. In a capital-scarce country this means thinly in comparison with the thick layer of capital in a capital-abundant country. However, "thinly" need not mean "of a lower quality." The marginalist theorem of factor combination is applicable only when we are concerned with capital of a homogeneous quality. It is clear that if a group of 100 workers has 100 hammers, it is rational for each worker to have one hammer and not one worker to have 100 hammers, and the rest no hammers. But it does *not* necessarily follow that we should not give *one* worker an electric hammer (in use perhaps by every worker in a more capital-abundant country and assumed to cost as much as 100 ordinary hammers) and give the other workers no hammers. With different qualities of capital goods, it would, if we prefer to maximize total output rather than employment of labor, be rational to spread capital unevenly if overall productivity thereby increases.

There are also other reasons why capital in capital-scarce countries might not be spread evenly. In the literature on economic development, there has been an extensive discussion as to whether underdeveloped countries should or should not fashion their own less advanced technology in such a way as to enable them to spread their capital more evenly. We shall not go through this literature in any detail as that would entail too great a digression. However, we can find certain arguments there with a bearing on our present problem. It has been said, for instance, that managerial skill might be still more scarce than capital and that, by spreading capital thinly, this resource might be wasted. Furthermore, it has been argued that capital-intensive technology creates profits which provide savings for sustained capital accumulation and growth. The point has also been made that capital-intensive equipment can stimulate management and labor to better performances and help to break the fetters of the past. These two last arguments are in conflict with the allocative approach of marginalism.

To the extent such considerations have influenced, or will influence, the demand for capital goods, and to the extent the use of superior quality capital goods compensates the loss from unemployment of labor, the qualitative differences in capital goods would be less pronounced at different per capita income levels than we might expect. The main differences among countries would be in the quantities of capital goods, because the latest techniques would be adopted in most countries.

Casual empiricism suggests, however, what could probably be confirmed through a more careful investigation, namely, that relative capital scarcity is expressed in the use of relatively low-quality capital goods rather than in the existence of a relatively low number of capital goods of the highest quality. If full employment obtains in a capital-scarce country, this implies that capital goods of lower quality must be in use.

Nonetheless, there will certainly be many overlapping demands in capital goods. To begin with, there are not infinite opportunities for qualitative variations. Furthermore, there is a particular reason why unadvanced techniques should be used in capital-abundant countries, i.e., that implied by differences in capacity use of capital goods. The type of capital goods that it is rational to employ in capital-abundant countries for low-capacity use (such as hobby or reserve equipment) might be economically appropriate for high-capacity use in a capital-scarce country. This will probably create a substantial amount of overlapping demand for capital goods.

Although it is clear that other factors, such as language, culture, religion, and climate, influence the demand structure, we shall work with the hypothesis that the scope for trade is potentially greatest between countries with the same per capita income levels. From this, it follows that *per capita income differences are a potential obstacle* to trade. Goods in the production of which the one country has a comparative advantage are not demanded in the other country, and vice versa. When per capita income differences reach a certain magnitude, trade can only take place in certain qualitatively homogeneous products. Only in such products can there be overlapping demands.

Support for this hypothesis is forthcoming from practical experience. When assessing the market prospects of a foreign area, businessmen devote considerable attention to the per capita income level (and thus not only to total income, which determines the market potential in another sense).

In the literature there is also an interesting, but unfortunately neglected, paper expressing the same thoughts as those we advance:

A country with a large internal market for low-quality goods is more likely to compete successfully in countries with a demand for similar goods than one whose internal markets are mainly in goods of higher quality because less adaptation of production processes to export requirements will be needed in the former case.

Japan's success [in foreign trade] was greatly due to the low purchasing power of the population in the European colonies and semi-colonies.[8]

Notes

1. Revised ed. (Cambridge, Mass., 1954).
2. Usher, Chap. IV, particularly pp. 60–69.
3. Princeton, 1954.
4. Lockwood, p. 364.
5. Lockwood, p. 369.
6. Lockwood, p. 373.
7. Hans W. Singer, "The Distribution of Gains between Investing and Borrowing Countries," *American Economic Review* 40: 473–485 (May 1950).
8. H. Frankel, "Industrialisation of Agricultural Countries and the Possibilities of A New International Division of Labour," *Economic Journal* 53:188–201 (June–September 1943). Quotations from pp. 188 and 189.

4

The Theory of Intra-Industry Trade

Herbert G. Grubel

Goods and services possess nearly infinite numbers of characteristics and no two are ever exactly perfect substitutes for each other. However, for analytical and statistical purposes it is necessary to aggregate production, trade and consumption of goods and services into useful categories. The principle of aggregation used in the compilation of international trade statistics is the proximity of products' substitutability in consumption and/or the similarity of input requirements. At the two-digit SITC [Standard International Trade Classification] level of aggregation the resultant classes of internationally traded goods correspond to "industries" as the concept is used conventionally in economic analysis.

The theory of intra-industry trade analyses the nature, determinants and welfare effects of nations' simultaneous exports and imports of

From Herbert G. Grubel, "The Theory of Intra-Industry Trade," *Studies in International Economics*, I. A. McDougall and R. H. Snape, eds., pp. 35–51. Reprinted by permission of North-Holland Publishing Company.

products belonging to the same industry. The essential difference between traditional and intra-industry trade theory thus is based on the fact that commodities in intra-industry trade are close substitutes in consumption, production, or both. As will be shown below, the most significant results of intra-industry trade theory are found in the analysis of industries where all products have very nearly identical input requirements.

There has been a recent revival of interest in the analysis of international trade in differentiated products, partly because of the inability of the traditional theory to explain much of the expansion of international trade over the last two decades. As has been shown empirically, a very substantial proportion of the growth in intra-EEC [European Economic Community] trade following the customs union formation took the form of intra-industry rather than inter-industry trade.[1] Some interesting empirical and theoretical studies in recent years by Linder [11], Drèze [7], Hufbauer [9], Posner [12], Vernon [13] and others have provided the ingredients for a broad theory of intra-industry trade, which the present paper attempts to formulate.[2]

The first section of the paper contains an explanation of the phenomenon that countries often export and import simultaneously products which are perfect substitutes except for differences in the products' location or timing of manufacture. Section II contains models capable of explaining existing patterns of intra-industry trade in a static world. . . . The [last] section of the paper contains an analysis of the welfare effects flowing from this theory of intra-industry trade.[3]. . .

INTRA-INDUSTRY TRADE IN HOMOGENEOUS PRODUCTS

A certain proportion of intra-industry trade entering quarterly or annual international trade statistics consists of products which from both the ultimate users' and producers' points of view are perfectly homogeneous. Trade in these products is due to a number of causes.

First, there is trade in bulky materials, such as sand, bricks and cement, for which transportation costs are a large fraction of the total cost of the products at the point of consumption and for which the location of manufacturing plants is dictated by the availability of natural resources.

Second, some perfectly homogeneous services enter international trade because of joint production or peculiar technical conditions. Thus banking, shipping and insurance are often exported and imported simultaneously because their production jointly with another traded product is subject to large economies. Electricity often is traded between European countries experiencing peak demand at different hours of the day.

Third, some countries such as Singapore and Hong Kong engage in substantial entrepôt and re-export trade. In the former case commodities are imported and exported in completely unchanged form and the traders' value added consists of providing storage facilities and services of a retailer. Re-export trade involves products subjected to "blending, packaging, bottling, cleaning, sorting, husking and shelling, . . . which leave them essentially unchanged" [2, p. IV]. Many countries distinguish statistically entrepôt and re-export trade from normal trade.

Fourth, government produced distortions of prices are known to have resulted in the simultaneous export and import of identical products by entrepreneurs maximising private profits.[4]

Fifth, seasonal fluctuations in output or demand and natural catastrophies sometimes cause countries to import products and services which at other times they export. Examples of products in this class are fruits and vegetables and tourist services.

Intra-industry trade in perfectly homogeneous products of the types just described can readily be fitted into the analytical framework of the Heckscher-Ohlin model by its proper extension to include consideration of transportation costs (type 1), economies of joint production (second group in type 2), the value added processes[5] rather than commodities (type 3), government activities (type 4), and time (type 5 and first group of type 2). Formal extensions of the Heckscher-Ohlin model in these directions are rather obvious and do not promise to yield very interesting results.

For this reason the remainder of this study will be concerned with international trade in commodities which are considered as the output of the same industry because either they are close but imperfect substitutes from the consumer's point of view or require very similar inputs, or both.

MODELS OF INTRA-INDUSTRY TRADE IN DIFFERENTIATED PRODUCTS

The fundamental problem of the static theory of intra-industry trade is to predict which particular products of a given industry a country exports and imports simultaneously during a given time period, such as a year. The following analysis distinguishes three classes, Heckscher-Ohlin, Economies of Scale, and Technology Gap commodities, for each of which basically different factors determine the pattern of intra-industry trade.

Heckscher-Ohlin Comparative Advantage

There exists intra-industry trade in commodities for which the conventional Heckscher-Ohlin comparative advantage model provides the explanation. These are found mostly in industries where consumer substitutability rather than production similarity serves as the basis of classification. Examples of these are trade in furniture made of wood for furniture made of steel, coarse wool for fine wool, electronic equipment with hand wired circuits for equipment with printed circuits. The relative costs of the primary inputs wood and steel in the case of furniture, labour and capital in the case of electronic equipment provide the basis for the comparative advantage patterns; in the case of wool they are climate and soil.

The similarity of the determinants of trade in this class of intra-industry trade with the inter-industry trade of the textbooks is readily apparent and any rigorous exposition would belabour the obvious.

Economies of Scale

Empirical studies have shown that most manufacturing plants in the industrialised countries of the West are large enough to enjoy nearly all of the reductions in average cost of production that optimum plant size can yield. Recently, however, it has become apparent that substantial lowering of unit production costs results from increasing the length of runs in the production of commodities in a plant of given size.[6] The most important factors in this decrease in unit costs are the reduction in the time during which machines are idle while dies or cutting tools are changed, reduction in inventories of raw materials and finished products, and greater workforce skill due to accumulating experience and greater specialisation. Moreover, the more efficient machines are, the more difficult they are to adapt for different tasks, so that the longer the runs, the more efficient is the available capital equipment.[7]

These scale economies due to length of runs may be considered to be static in the sense that they are independent of any argument about time. Dynamic scale economies have recently been stressed in the work of Arrow [1] and others. These economies accrue to producers as a result of accumulated experience in producing a given product, i.e. "learning by doing," either as a function of time, or of cumulative past output, or both.[8] Static and dynamic scale economies are important in the explanation of some forms of intra-industry trade but in order to facilitate exposition it is assumed . . . that economies of scale are due only to increase in the length of runs. . . . The analysis considers, first, product differentiation based on quality and, secondly, product differentiation based on style, packaging and branding of the product.

In order to bring out the essential nature of intra-industry trade of this type it is assumed that the world consists of only two countries, A and B, with equal and static endowments of capital, labour and raw materials, identical production functions and tastes and, therefore, identical per capita incomes. Only two close substitute consumer products are tradable between the two countries. Assumptions about production techniques, the nature of the difference between the products, public tastes and income distribution are crucial to the following arguments and are introduced at the beginning of each section. The most important point about the theoretical construct just set out is that if the two tradable products are manufactured under the normal diminishing returns, the assumed exact equality of the two countries with respect to production possibilities and consumer preferences means the existence only of border trade of the type discussed above.

Quality Differentiation

Assume that production techniques are static and equal in both countries and that tastes are equal in the sense that a representative group of consumers from each country would choose identical bundles of goods from a given basket with different style and quality characteristics. While per capita incomes are equal, the income distributions are skewed differently, as is shown in Figure 1. The two consumer products are identical in appearance but they differ in price and quality, where quality is defined as an index of measurable performance characteristics such as an automobile's acceleration, smoothness of ride, size of passenger space, etc. All persons with above average incomes purchase the high quality, high priced "model" and persons with below average incomes purchase the low quality, low priced "model." Since country A has the largest number of persons with below average income it is most efficient for country A to specialise in the production of the low price and low quality model, supplying its own population and exporting to meet the demands of B's population with below average income. Country B, in turn produces and exports the high price, high quality model. In terms of Figure 1, all persons in the income distributions of both countries below OP are supplied from

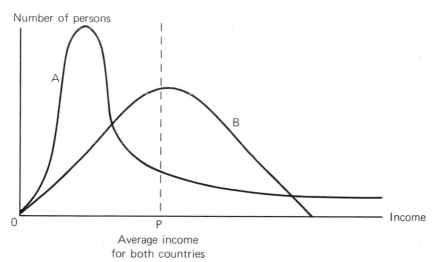

FIGURE 1

production in country A, all those above OP, from production in country B. Because of scale economies there is complete specialisation in production.

The preceding model is the pure case of the more general explanation of trade relationships based on quality of product and income of population developed by Linder [11]. The pure case can be readily extended in several ways. First, differences in the two countries' relative factor proportions and in the two products' input requirements tend to give rise to comparative advantage which may increase, decrease or even wipe out the advantage stemming from scale economies and the supply of the domestic market. Such comparative advantage tends to shift the boundaries of segments on the income frequency distribution supplied by each country. If there are other tradable products it is possible that one country supplies *all* models of one product most cheaply. Second, in a world of more than two countries, overlapping income frequency distributions give rise to opportunities to exploit scale economies through specialisation and export in the same way as in the two-country model.

Third, assume that scale economies are not only a function of the length of runs but also a function of the length of time during which a product has been produced or the total quantity of past output. Such dynamic economies tend to get started during the development of a product and can persist for a long time. Exports would go to countries with all levels of per capita income, but one might expect to find exports to be greater the higher the importing country's average income, holding country size constant.

Fourth, capital goods also come with many combinations of performance characteristics, i.e. in different qualities. The pattern of trade in these producers' goods is determined by the same factors, i.e. static and dynamic scale economies, factor requirements and availabilities and domestic demand. However, capital goods quality is determined by the added element of relative factor proportions required in the *operation* of the machines. Thus, machines with low labour requirements per unit of output tend to be developed and produced in the countries with relative labour scarcity and exported to countries having similar factor endowments.

Generally, extensions of the pure model tend to retain the feature that economies of scale due to length of runs provide opportunity for intra-industry specialisation and trade based on quality differentiation. However, the pure model's implication that the quality of product produced by individual countries is a function of present domestic demand ceases to be valid. For products with low transportation cost relative to price, static and dynamic scale economies can be large enough to enable producers in one country to overcome the comparative cost disadvantages suggested by the traditional factor proportions theory, so that they are the lowest cost suppliers of the specific quality model for the whole world.

Differentiation by Style, Packaging and Branding

Consider a world in which, as before, two countries A and B are identical in every respect, including the shape of their income distribution profile, except that consumers' tastes are different. Thus, confronted with a basket of goods identical in price, quality and performance but different in appearance due to style, packaging or branding, representative consumers from the two countries choose different but overlapping combinations of goods from the basket. The reasons for this difference in taste are found in different historic and cultural developments of the two countries.

From the preceding discussions of differentiation based on quality it is apparent that if the production of a given product style is subject to static and dynamic scale economies, countries specialise in the production of those styles for which domestic demand is greatest and, because of some overlapping of tastes in both countries, certain proportions of this output are exported.

The pure model of trade in products differentiated by style, packaging or branding can be modified in several useful directions. First, cost of production advantages due to a country's favourable factor endowments, on top of scale economies, result in greater exports and smaller imports of the competitive substitutes because consumers in both countries at the margin in their taste preferences are persuaded to opt for the lower priced style of the product. Second, in a world of more than two countries the mutual exchange of style differentiated products is a function of the similarity in countries' cultural background, level of travel among its citizens and exposure to advertising.

Third, if the development of tastes in the sense defined above, *ceteris paribus*, is a function of income levels, then trade in style differentiated products is greater among countries with equal than with different income levels. Fourth, small countries and countries made up of people with persistent and strong cultural differences, such as Belgium and Switzerland, are unable to produce style differentiated products in sufficiently long runs to be competitive with foreign substitutes. These countries can specialise in products where tastes are less important than functional characteristics in the choice of the consumers.[9]

Lastly, it must be noted that in the real world quality and style characteristics of closely competitive substitute products often cannot be separated. Consumers pay attention to both style and quality in matching their taste preferences with available products, given prices and incomes. Producers attempt to design and advertise low quality and low cost products in styles resembling those adopted by successful high quality and high cost substitutes. However, competition, cost and tastes set a finite limit on the substitutability of style and quality, and understanding of the nature of intra-industry trade would not be increased significantly by a more rigorous analysis of substitution and complementarity of style and quality in product design.

Technology Gaps

Consider a world consisting of two countries, A and B, identical in every respect, including their income distribution profiles and consumers' tastes. Both countries engage in research into new product development and improvement in production methods. Success in this research is a stochastic process. Breakthroughs are protected by patents and copyright laws for limited time periods.

As a result of these dynamic changes in production technology and/or product design, over any finite period both countries are likely to export and import simultaneously products which are close substitutes in consumption and require very similar inputs. The fundamental basis for this trade is the existing lag in the effective transfer of production technique for the product. The length for which the so-called "technology gap"[10] persists depends on several factors which are part of a dynamic process discussed below.

Patented breakthroughs in production technology and the discovery of new chemical compounds tend to be more important in products required as inputs into further manufacture, whereas copyrighted designs are more important in consumer goods.

Economically profitable technological innovations do not necessarily lead to technological gap trade. Licensing and foreign investment are substitutes for this trade, especially in products with high transportation costs and in those in which the other country has a comparative cost advantage. On the other hand, patent or copyright protection are not necessary for technological gap trade. If products of new design or produced by new technology are subject to strong initial dynamic economies then a country has a comparative advantage until technology has "settled down" and lack of patent protection leads to imitation abroad. In general, however, static or dynamic economies of scale are not necessary for technological gap intra-industry trade.

If research efforts differ, countries with more research will have a greater ratio of technological gap exports over imports than countries with smaller research efforts. If countries differ in basic factor endowments and consumers' tastes, research is likely to be directed at different objectives in each country and the composition and even the size of the technological gap trade is determined by these factors, especially if there are economies of scale in research in particular areas. . . .

WELFARE EFFECTS OF INTRA-INDUSTRY TRADE

The simple fact that intra-industry trade takes place among free market economies is sufficient evidence that it increases world welfare since all parties to voluntary exchange benefit. In this sense, intra-industry trade and national specialisation in production and export of products having input requirements very similar to imported substitute products is no different from conventional trade in products with very divergent input requirements and poor substitutability in consumption. Therefore, the well known analytical apparatus for the analysis of gains from trade is applicable to intra-industry trade and will not be presented here.

However, the existence of scale economies and monopolistic competition gives rise to problems not normally considered in traditional gains from trade analysis. The welfare implications flowing from the existence of domestic monopolistic competition have been discussed at length in the literature. The conclusion of this discussion most broadly has been that while the divergence of marginal cost and price represents a violation of Pareto-optimality conditions, production and marketing technology in monopolistic industries is such that it is impossible to correct the inequality of marginal cost and price without changing the basic character of the capitalist free enterprise economy. The misallocation of resources due to monopolistic competition therefore is a necessary cost of solving the problem of resource allocation through free markets with consumers' sovereignty.

International specialisation in the production of monopolistically differentiated products increases welfare above the level where monopolistic competition is carried on only by domestic firms, if either, or both, of the two following conditions are met. First, intra-industry trade increases the number of differentiated products on the market. As a result consumers are able to meet more effectively their apparently fundamental desire for variety, individuality and stylishness in their use of consumer goods. Monopoly power is reduced and prices of products are more nearly equal to marginal cost. Second, intra-industry trade lowers the cost of substitute products without necessarily increasing the available number. This cost reduction may be due to the conventional benefits from specialisation under conditions of increasing cost or they may be due additionally to static and dynamic scale economies.

If there are substantial static economies of scale in the production of differentiated products, international trade between countries with very similar resource endowments and tastes is likely to give rise to significant welfare gains which conventional trade theory would have failed to predict. . . .

Notes

1. See Balassa [4] and Grubel [8].
2. See Johnson [10], Caves [5] and Grubel [8] for earlier attempts at providing such a theory and judgments that further extensions of international trade theory in this direction can be expected to be rewarding.
3. This paper is intended to serve as a basis for a thorough empirical analysis of Australia's trade pattern to discover the magnitude and composition of intra-industry trade based on comparative advantage in factor inputs, on quality and style differentiation in combination with economies of scale and on technologi-

cal gaps. Moreover, attempts will be made to discover systematic differences in Australia's intra-industry trade with trading partners at different levels of development.

4. See Bhagwati [3].
5. See the recent literature on effective tariff protection.
6. This phenomenon has been analysed, and empirical information on it has been summarised in Daly et al. [6].
7. [6] p. 39.
8. See Hufbauer [9] for a summary of theoretical and empirical evidence on dynamic scale economies.
9. See Drèze [7] for evidence that Belgium specialises in the production and export of restaurant china and internationally standardised sporting goods.
10. See Posner [12], Hufbauer [9], and Vernon [13].

References

[1] K. J. Arrow, "The Economic Implications of Learning by Doing," *Review of Economic Studies,* July 1962, pp. 155–173.
[2] Australian Commonwealth Bureau of Census and Statistics, *Australian Exports 1967–1968*, Bulletin No. 10, Canberra, 1969.
[3] J. Bhagwati, *The Theory and Practice of Commercial Policy: Departures from Unified Exchange Rates* (Princeton University Press, Princeton, 1968).
[4] B. Balassa, "Tariff Reductions and Trade in Manufactures among Industrial Countries," *American Economic Review*, June 1966, pp. 466–473.
[5] R. E. Caves, Comments on a lecture delivered by H. G. Johnson at the 1968 meetings of the International Economic Association in Montreal, published in: Paul A. Samuelson (ed.), *International Economic Relations* (Macmillan, London, 1969).
[6] D. J. Daley et al., *Scale and Specialisation in Canadian Manufacturing*, Economic Council of Canada, Staff Study No. 21, March 1968.
[7] J. Drèze, "Quelques réflexions sereins sur l'adaptation de l'industrie belge au Marché Commun," *Comptes Rendues des Travaux de la Société Royale d'Economie Politique de Belgique*, no. 275 (December 1960), for the theory and *idem*, "Les exportations intra-CEE en 1958 et la position belge," *Recherches Economiques de Louvain*, XXVII (1961), pp. 717–738, for the empirical evidence supporting the theory.
[8] H. G. Grubel, "Intra-Industry Specialisation and the Pattern of Trade," *Canadian Journal of Economics and Political Science*, August 1967, pp. 374–388.
[9] G. C. Hufbauer, *Synthetic Materials and the Theory of International Trade* (Duckworth, London, 1965).
[10] H. G. Johnson, Lecture at the 1968 meetings of the International Economic Association in Montreal, published in: Paul A. Samuelson (ed.), *International Economic Relations* (Macmillan, London, 1969).
[11] S. B. Linder, *An Essay on Trade and Transformation* (Wiley, New York, 1963).
[12] V. Posner, "International Trade and Technical Change," *Oxford Economic Papers,* October 1961, pp. 323–341.
[13] R. Vernon, "International Investment and International Trade in the Product Cycle," *Quarterly Journal of Economics*, May 1966, pp. 190–207.

II

Protectionism versus Trade Liberalization

No economic policy commands greater agreement among economists than does the desirability of greater trade liberalization for the industrialized countries.[1] Economists have been teaching about the mutual gains of trade for more than two hundred years, yet the world is still far from a position of free trade. In recent years protectionism has actually been increasing. The obvious question arises: Why has liberalization not proceeded further, if it is indeed so desirable an economic policy?

The selection by Robert E. Baldwin confronts the fact that the trade policy of most countries is determined in the political marketplace through a voting process rather than in economic markets. Since most of the important economic policy issues of our times are decided politically, economists are paying increased attention to the manner in which these political markets operate. In their analyses they are utilizing their economic tools and way of thinking to ascertain the extent to which economic policies beneficial to the nation as a whole can be expected to emerge from the political processes of public choice.

Trade policy provides a good example of why public decisions may not promote national welfare. Baldwin points out that unless all citizens are fully aware of the consequences of alternative policies and voting and redistribution costs are absent so that all citizens vote and any losers from trade can be fully compensated, interest groups who in fact are injured by greater liberalization may well succeed in thwarting the achievement of this policy. The failure of these ideal conditions to hold in practice is apparent to the most casual observer. The empirical results Baldwin obtains concerning the interest-group orientation of congressional voting on trade issues are therefore not at all surprising.

One of the most important sources of opposition in the United States to a multilateral lowering of trade barriers is the American union movement. Two selections in Part II attempt to convey the intensity of the opposition from this group. Murray Finley, president of the Amalgamated Clothing and Textile Workers Union, strenuously objects to the import-related losses in jobs in his industry as well as in other industries facing severe import competition. He also argues that the U.S. adjustment assistance program for workers is inadequate. Another of his concerns is the adverse employment and income effects on domestic workers as a result of U.S. direct investment abroad and of technological transfers to foreign firms. Finley, like most labor leaders writing on trade issues, is stronger on rhetoric than on logical analysis backed by careful empirical work. Studies by academic and government economists indicate that labor leaders have greatly exaggerated the adverse effects of increased imports and greater foreign investment on domestic employment.[2]

The article by George Fecteau and John Mara, union officials in the footwear industry, emphasizes the unfairness of foreign competition. The union leaders contend that foreign exporters of shoes have been able to capture a larger share of the U.S. market because of lower costs based on the use of child labor and woefully underpaid workers as well as on the absence of sensible health and safety requirements. Their position is another version of the low-foreign-wage argument for protectionism—a case that makes no economic sense from a national viewpoint. The authors also object to what they consider to be the failure of foreign shoe exporters in both Taiwan and Korea to abide by the import quotas imposed on them under an Orderly Marketing Agreement, and the failure of the U.S. government to play a more vigorous role in limiting footwear imports. This article points up the extreme difficulty of administrating the enforcement of quotas, quite aside from their adverse national economic effects.

The selection from the study by Richard Blackhurst, Nicholas Marian, and Jan Tumlir evaluates various economic arguments for and against further reductions in trade barriers. In addition to the well-known consumption, production, and scale-economy benefits of an expansion in world trade, the authors point to the contributions toward price stability and domestic competitiveness that trade liberalization makes. They recognize, however, that reducing tariff and various nontariff barriers to trade on a multilateral basis entails the loss of jobs and creates lower income levels for some individuals. These individuals may have sufficient political power to prevent liberalizing measures directed at the industries in which they are employed. But, the authors note, not only are the overall net employment effects of multilateral trade liberalization effects very small, but most of the net adverse effects in certain industries are only temporary.[3] They argue that adjustment assistance programs such as the U.S. scheme are the proper way to deal with the transitional costs of liberalization, while any group who is permanently hurt should be compensated through direct grants.

In addition to the income-distribution arguments against moving to a more open trading system, the three authors consider the cases against this policy that stress an excessive reliance on imports and the protection of a national "way of life." Their conclusion, that better ways exist to handle the dependency problem rather than by means of protection, illustrates a key point in the modern analysis of trade policy: Except in a few cases, the objectives that protectionism is designed to achieve can better be attained by direct domestic policies. Unfortunately, we have not succeeded in developing politically feasible policies that in fact offset the economic and social losses to particular income groups due to liberalization (and that are supported or at least accepted by these groups) and still result in a net gain to the rest of society.

The final selection in Part II is from a survey designed to determine whether imported goods are cheaper than comparable goods produced within the United States. The opponents of trade liberalization frequently maintain that importers at the wholesale and retail level do not pass on any lower costs of imports to consumers but instead charge the same price as domestic producers and pocket the difference. Even if competition always keeps the retail prices of imported and domestically produced goods the same, the existence of an import supply tends to keep retail prices below the levels they would reach in the absence of this foreign supply source. Moreover, in this inflation-prone world general tariff reductions should not be expected actually to lower prices but merely to keep them from rising as rapidly as they would otherwise.

Can consumers purchase the same quality product from importers at a lower price than from domestic producers? The survey results indicate that the average retail price of the bundle of imported consumer goods was about 11 percent lower than the average retail price of a comparable bundle of goods produced domestically. Presumably a perception by many domestic consumers that the local product was qualitatively better enabled domestic producers to charge more. Interestingly, the prices of imports from Europe, Japan, and Canada were approximately the same as locally produced goods, whereas imports from the less developed countries were 16 percent lower. Nevertheless, because of the relatively low ratio of dutiable imports to gross national product (about 5 percent) and the low level of tariffs and nontariff barriers in most sectors, the actual price-reducing impact on the U.S. consumer price index of such tariff-reducing negotiations as the Tokyo Round, sponsored by the General Agreement on Tariffs and Trade (GATT), tends to be very small.[4]

Notes

1. Considerable disagreement exists concerning the desirability of lowering trade barriers in the developing countries. Many economists maintain that protection is needed on "infant industry" or even "infant economy" grounds. Many others

favor more open trade policies on the grounds that excessive reliance on im-
port-substitution has hampered development in these countries.
2. See for example, Congressional Budget Office, Congress of the United States,
   U.S. Trade Policy and the Tokyo Round of Multilateral Trade Negotiations
   (Washington: U.S. Government Printing Office, 1979); and Thomas Horst,
   "The Impact of American Investments Abroad on U.S. Exports, Imports, and
   Employment" in *The Impact of International Trade and Investment on Employment,* William G. Dewald (ed.), U.S. Department of Labor, Bureau of International Labor Affairs (Washington: U.S. Government Printing Office, 1978), pp.
   139–151.
3. For evidence on the employment effects of trade liberalization see Robert E.
   Baldwin, John H. Mutti, and J. David Richardson, "Welfare Effects of a Significant Multilateral Tariff Reduction," *Journal of International Economics, 10,*
   3, 1980.
4. See Wayne E. Lewis, *The Effects of Multilateral Trade Liberalization on U.S.
   Domestic Prices,* unpublished doctoral dissertation, The University of Wisconsin, Madison, 1977.

5

The Political Economy of Postwar United States Trade Policy

Robert E. Baldwin

INTRODUCTION

Postwar commercial policy in the United States has been characterized both by major compromises between the political forces favoring
trade liberalization versus protectionism and by significant shifts in the
congressional voting patterns of the two major parties on trade matters.
For example, while the President has been authorized over the years to
reduce most tariffs by as much as 93 percent of their 1945 levels, quantitative restrictions on imports of textiles and apparel, petroleum, steel, and
several agricultural products have also been introduced during the period.
The change in voting behavior is illustrated by the fact that in 1945 an
overwhelming majority of Democrats in the House of Representatives
voted for extending the reciprocal trade program with an additional 50

From Robert E. Baldwin, "The Political Economy of Postwar U.S. Trade Policy,"
The Bulletin, Bulletin 1976–4, New York University, Graduate School of Business
Administration, Center for the Study of Financial Institutions. Reprinted by per-
mission. Some tables and some footnotes omitted.

percent tariff-cutting authority, whereas in 1973 most House Democrats opposed a trade bill that granted the President new significant duty-reducing powers. On the other hand, Republicans in the House opposed further tariff-cutting in 1945 by a very large majority but supported the [1974] trade bill. This paper attempts to explain why U.S. trade policy has emerged in its particular compromised form as well as why realignments in party support have occurred. Particular attention is devoted to the role of pressures from groups with common economic interests as a determinant of trade policies.

Traditional economic theory is not very useful in explaining actual U.S. trade policies. Except when a country can influence its terms of trade by its own actions, this theory concludes that a unilateral shift to free trade is a desirable policy. Even when several countries with monopolistic power participate in multilateral tariff-cutting negotiations, economic analysis suggests that such exercises are likely to be in the best interest of all participants since the trading terms of none of the countries are likely to shift appreciably. Economists have tended to assume that by explaining the advantages of trade liberalization, governments will eventually realize these benefits and introduce policies directed toward this end. In fact, however, actual trade policies in most industrial countries have consisted in recent years of a mixture of protectionism and liberalization. Moreover, it is not clear that the liberalizing actions that have occurred have been influenced to any significant extent by arguments employed by economists.

A MODEL OF TRADE-POLICY BEHAVIOR

Fortunately, within recent years economists have become increasingly concerned with the manner in which public policies are actually determined and have attempted to formulate a theory of public choice.[1] Essentially they have adapted economic theories of private market behavior to political situations in which decisions are determined by majority voting. The following framework for making public decisions represents an effort to apply the theory developed by writers in this new field to the determination of commercial policies in the United States.

A Simple Model

To keep the model as simple as possible initially, suppose the following conditions hold: (1) voters directly determine by majority voting whether a particular public policy is put into effect; (2) there is only one policy issue to be decided within voters' time horizons; (3) the tastes of all voters are identical and homothetic and do not change in the period under consideration; and (4) there is perfect knowledge and there are no costs involved in acquiring or providing information, in voting, and in providing compensation or bribes to any individuals. The objective of each individual is to maximize his welfare, which depends upon the goods and services that he consumes.

The policy under consideration is whether to provide tariff-cutting authority for the purpose of engaging in a multilateral tariff-reducing exercise with other countries.[2] Assume that the terms of trade of the country under consideration do not change as a result of the tariff negotiations. Furthermore, suppose there are no market inefficiencies in the economy other than the existence of tariffs.[3] On the basis of the standard Heckscher-Ohlin-Samuelson model of international trade it follows that those productive factors intensively used in the production of export goods benefit when tariffs are reduced under these circumstances, whereas those utilized relatively intensively in the production of import-competing goods suffer a decline in real income. However, it can also be shown that the gainers under free trade are capable of fully compensating the losers for their income reduction with the gainers still being better off than before the change.[4]

Under the voting framework assumed up to this point the tariff proposal will be acted on favorably whether the gainers are in the majority or not. However, when they are a minority, it is necessary to tie the tariff-cutting exercise to a redistribution scheme that provides net gains to a majority of the electorate.

Modifying the Simple Model

When various assumptions of the model are eased in order to increase the degree of its correspondence with real world conditions, the conclusion that tariff liberalization will always take place under a system of majority voting no longer holds. Suppose that there are costs involved in compensating losers for their injury and that these costs are borne by the gainers. If the gainers are in a minority and the costs of compensating enough losers to achieve a majority voting block are greater than the gains to the majority the liberalization proposal will fail. The existence of voting costs and costs of acquiring information can also serve to thwart tariff liberalization. The gains from duty reductions may be so small to some voters that they are more than offset by the costs of voting. These individuals, consequently, will not vote. Similarly, if the costs of voting exceed the losses incurred by some who are adversely affected by the duty cuts, it will not be worthwhile for these citizens to vote. Consequently, the voting outcome will be determined by the larger gainers and losers, a majority of whom may not support the trade-liberalization proposal.

Probably the best-known reasons for divergences between what is economically desirable and politically feasible are the existence of information costs and the fact that attitudes can be changed by freely supplying certain types of information. Just as it does not pay some voters to incur the costs of voting, it is not rational for many voters to pay the costs of acquiring detailed information about the effects of a particular tariff liberalization.[5] Voters usually are able to acquire some information about most policy proposals at very low cost either as a by-product of their income-earning activities or as consumers of such communication services as newspapers and television. Unless this information indicates that a voter's real income position is likely to be significantly affected by the policy, he generally will not seek out any further information. On the other hand, if his initial information suggests that he may be greatly affected, then it will pay him to invest further to determine more exactly the possible impact of the policy. As Downs points out, this is the reason why producers generally are better informed about tariff policy than consumers.[6] Producers, consequently, arc likely to have more importance in the voting outcome than their numerical importance would suggest, since the poorly informed voters are likely to vote in a somewhat random fashion.

Not only do those who are significantly affected by the tariff liberalization invest time and money to determine in more detail the possible outcome of the policy, but they supply information to other voters in an effort to influence their votes. As William Brock and Stephen Magee have pointed out, producers can be viewed as attempting to maximize their net benefits (or minimize their net losses) from a proposed tariff change by spending an appropriate sum to influence other voters.[7] If those who would lose significantly with duty reductions are unable to bribe the majority gainers into rejecting the liberalization proposal, they still may be able to achieve their objective by spending funds to influence the majority. If would not pay the losers to spend more than the present value of their losses but within this constraint they will spend enough to obtain a majority voting position. When uncertainty is introduced, influencers can be viewed as spending—subject to the above constraint—up to the point where additional outlays equal the resulting increase (decrease) in the expected welfare gain (loss) to them.[8]

Another factor affecting the extent of efforts to influence others is the size of the group sharing a gain or loss of a given magnitude.[9] The smaller the group and thus the greater the gain or loss to any individual member, the more likely will it be rational for an individual to spend enough money to affect the voting outcome. With large groups the minimum outlay needed to have any effect at all is likely to be greater than the gain or loss to the individual. He will hope that others in his group contribute funds to influence other voters but in this case it is not worthwhile for him to do so. Sometimes group pressures (costs) and rewards can be used to force individuals in large groups to provide resources for persuading others to vote in a particular manner. Generally, however, a large group with an aggregate gain or loss that amounts to only a small gain or loss on an individual basis is at a serious disadvantage compared with smaller groups with a smaller total gain or loss yet larger individual gains or losses. This is why consumers and industries consisting of many small firms do not organize to influence tariff policy as extensively as producers in oligopolistic industries and labor unions that dominate particular industries.

So far it has been assumed that there is only one policy matter under consideration, namely, tariff liberalization. However, in practice, voters or their representatives are called upon to decide a series of issues over time. This situation opens up the possibility of logrolling. With vote trading it is possible, for example, for two policies to be defeated even though they would each result in a rise in the community's real income. This could occur if compensation is ruled out on cost grounds and if there is a net loss to a majority of voters when the two policies are combined. But, if compensation is costless, the gainers will be able to offset this unfavorable vote by overcompensating enough losers to obtain a majority. As in the case of a single policy, the lack of the compensation possibility due to high costs is necessary for defeating a series of policies in the public interest. The existence of a number of policy issues also tends to increase the volume of lobbying activity. While it may not pay a group of individuals to establish a lobbying organization on any one issue, it is more likely to pay them to do so if they share common views on a number of the issues.

Another assumption that should be dropped concerns the direct voting procedure of citizens. Most policies are decided by the elected representatives of the voters rather than directly by the voters themselves. In this framework it can be assumed that the elected officials, like other individuals, try to maximize their welfare. To do this as representatives of the voters, they must take actions that will first enable them to be elected and then retain their positions. In a world characterized by the assumptions initially made, competition forces political officials and parties to attempt to maximize the number of votes from the electorate. Unless a politician follows this practice, he will not long retain his office since others can unseat him by doing so. Consequently, the results obtained in the simple, direct voting model will also hold, even though voters express their preferences indirectly. When, however, the various assumptions of the simple model are modified, additional possibilities emerge as to why the tariff-cutting proposal may not be accepted. For example, when there are information costs, it is much easier to set up vote-swapping arrangements when only a small number (rather than the entire electorate) are voting on specific proposals. The existence of political parties, which are associated with representative government, also opens up possibilities for the defeat of such income-raising proposals as a tariff reduction. Party leaders (including elected officials) are primarily concerned with gaining and retaining political power rather than maximizing voter strength. The maximizing behavior is forced upon them when there is a high degree of political competition. But if it is costly to provide information to voters and if there are substantial economies of scale in providing this information, the costs of entering the political market place become high for potential challengers. An incumbent has an advantage in this regard in that he usually can utilize the resources of his party to meet more easily the high costs of campaigning effectively. However, because he wishes to minimize his costs of being elected rather than maximize his vote, he will try to satisfy the preferences of enough voters to prevent others within his own party or in other parties from being able to secure the funds needed to make a successful challenge to his position. One rational means of carrying out this objective is to satisfy the preferences of minority groups who gain or lose significantly when the majority only gains or loses to a moderate degree. Those greatly affected are more likely to provide funds needed to persuade other voters of the candidate's merits and ensure his election.

Still another obvious possibility by which the majority's wishes can be thwarted under representative government is that the representation may not (as in the U.S. Senate) be proportional to the population size. Consequently, the majority of the population favoring trade liberalization may, for example, be in states that do not have a majority in the Senate.

One of the important political advantages of cutting tariffs on a reciprocal basis is that is does not just bring adverse adjustment problems to some industries but, unlike a unilateral tariff reduction, it also opens up improved profit opportunities to selected sectors. Consequently, there will be both business and labor groups who actively oppose tariff cuts and those who favor the reduction. However, if— as seems reasonable—a short-run change in a given amount of income results in a greater change in an individual's utility if it is negative rather than positive, the possibility of serious market losses is likely to provoke more lobbying activities than the chance of large market gains. Therefore, if the large gains and losses from the cut are about equal, politicians are likely to be helped more by opponents to the reductions than proponents of the cuts and, as a result, to oppose tariff liberalization.

Besides introducing into a voting model the fact that citizens express their views on most policy issues only indirectly, it is also important to recognize the existence of an executive branch. The President possesses great power in being able to influence the nature of legislation. Through sympathetic legislators he can introduce specific legislation, and, more importantly, obtain through the press and the information activities of the government, wide dissemination of his views as to why the proposed legislation is meritorious. The various patronage powers of the President also can be used effectively to influence the voting actions of legislators.

One of the main functions of the President is to conduct the country's foreign policy, and in judging his performance many voters put considerable weight on his success in this field. Presidents also find that foreign policy is one of the policy areas over which they can exercise the greatest direct control and thus can most easily pursue their goals. Since it has been the accepted wisdom among most political leaders for many years that closer trading ties among nations improve the chances for harmonious political relations, tariff liberalization provides greater opportunities for a President to gain personal satisfaction by enhancing his international reputation than does a policy of protectionism. However, a President may sometimes find it necessary to offer import protection to particular industries in order to obtain general tariff-reducing authority from the Congress. The general public has also adhered to the view that closer trading ties promote peace, and voters who are affected economically in only a minimal way by tariff liberalization have also tended—though not strongly—to favor a reciprocal duty-reduction policy.

A final set of modifications to the simple model that should be made is to drop the assumptions of identical homothetic tastes and fixed terms of trade. When different taste patterns are permitted (but the fixed trading terms assumption still maintained) it is no longer possible to say that the actual collection of goods rendered under tariff liberalization is sufficient to compensate the losers by appropriate redistribution.[10] However, what can be said is that under tariff liberalization it would be *possible* to obtain a collection of goods under which the losers could be compensated for their loss in the move to the tariff-liberalization policy.[11] As the wide acceptance of the use of changes in consumer and producer surplus as a measure of changes in a community's welfare indicates, many people are willing to accept the *possibility of compensation* as the appropriate welfare criterion.

When the possibility of adverse movements in the country's trading terms in response to tariff liberalization is introduced into the model, tariff-cutting cannot be judged as always desirable even under this welfare criterion. The real income loss associated with the deterioration in the country's trading terms may swamp the consumption and production gains related to the improvement in allocative efficiency. Whether this is so in a particular case could be determined by the measurement of consumer and producer surplus changes, given appropriate parameters such as demand and supply elasticities for exports and imports. If tariff levels among the major trading nations are equal among countries (as they roughly are today for industrial products) and these levels are simultaneously reduced by the same percentage, then a country's terms of trade will improve if the absolute sum of the demand elasticity for the country's exports divided by the sum of its elasticity of export supply and the demand elasticity for its exports is greater than its elasticity of demand for imports divided by the sum of the supply elasticity of imports it faces plus its elasticity of demand for imports. Empirical studies have generally indicated a higher elasticity of demand for U.S. exports than the U.S. demand elasticity for imports but the evidence on supply elasticities is inconclusive.[12] As one investigator notes, reciprocal elimination of tariffs by the United States and her trading partners would involve a net terms-of-trade effect for the United States that could be either positive or negative but in either case very small.[13] Thus, until more evidence is available it seems reasonable to assume that for the United States at least, terms-of-trade shifts are not important enough to negate the welfare benefits of a multilateral tariff-liberalization policy under which the countries involved reduce duties approximately the same degree.

The main conclusions of the preceding analysis can be summarized into several simple hypotheses describing the voting behavior of Congressmen on the issue of granting the President new tariff-cutting authority. First, constituent pressures to vote in a particular manner are not likely to be a decisive factor in determining a representative's voting behavior unless there are politically important economic groups in his district who believe they will be significantly hurt or helped by tariff liberalization. By "important" is meant that either the number of voters in the group or the profits and losses at stake with the tariff change are relatively large. In the United States where imports and exports are a relatively small fraction of GNP, most individual citizens are not likely to exert any pressure on their congressman in this matter. Multi-purposed pressure groups with general consumer or foreign policy concerns, such as the League of Women Voters and the International Chamber of Commerce, will apply some pressure in support of trade liberalization whereas similar organizations like the AFL-CIO will apply general pressures in the opposite direction. But since trade policy is only one of many issues on which these groups have views, under these circumstances, a legislator's response on other issues is likely to be more important in determining whether the members of these organizations actively support or oppose a congressional candidate.

Legislators operating in a situation where there are no strong political pressures either in favor or against trade liberalization are apt to be influenced heavily by the position of their party on the issue. As with individual voters the costs of acquiring reliable information are high for the individual legislator. Consequently, it is sensible for him or her to follow the recommendations either of fellow party members who have become knowledgeable about the subject through membership on the relevant Congressional Committee or of the President, if he is a member of the same party.[14]

In districts where economic interests that represent large numbers of voters or that pay substantial local and national taxes strongly oppose or support trade liberalization, congressmen are more likely to adopt the views of these economic pressure groups rather than those of their party or some other lobbying organization. They can less afford to ignore the loss of votes and campaign contributions that failure to respect these parochial pressures will bring. Industries that are relatively depressed economically and those that have had to contend with rapid increases in imports will tend to be especially energetic in attempting to secure a negative vote by congressmen on trade liberalization.

Given the sometimes conflicting pressures exerted on a Congressman from various lobbying groups, his leadership group in Congress, and the President, an optimal solution for legislators is to seek a compromise among the various interests. For example, faced with a desire on the part of an administration of their own political persuasion for new tariff-cutting authority yet faced also with pressures from certain industries in their districts that claim injury from imports, congressmen are likely to seek legislation combining protective measures for the industries alleging injury and tariff-cutting authority for all other industries. In this way they can minimize vote losses as well as any punitive actions taken by the President or the Congressional leadership. The nature of the compromises actually emerging from Congress thus depends mainly upon four sets of factors: (1) the extent of pressures from economic groups favoring trade liberalization or protectionism; (2) the party positions of Republicans and Democrats on trade issues; (3) the relative strength of the two parties in Congress; and (4) the political affiliation of the President together with the vigor with which the Chief Executive urges that the Congress pass a particular trade policy. Of course, on a more fundamental level the determinants of each of the factors could also be analyzed. However, the viewpoint of this study will be mainly short-run with these various factors being taken as given. . . .

A STATISTICAL ANALYSIS OF VOTING ON THE TRADE ACT OF 1974

. . .To discover whether economic pressures influenced Congressmen's voting on this bill, a list of import-sensitive and export-oriented industries was determined on the basis of testimony before the Ways and Means Committee. If workers or management in any industry opposed the liberalizing features of the bill, the industry was regarded as import sensitive, whereas if members of the industry supported its key provisions, the industry was termed to be export oriented. Table 1 lists the import-sensitive sectors. Only two industries, office and computing equipment (SIC 357) and aircraft (SIC 372), were selected as export-oriented industries.[15]. . .

Having selected a list of import-sensitive and export-oriented industries, the next step was to determine the proportion of workers represented by these industries in each congressional district in each state. The first of these allocations was accomplished by obtaining employment in the industries by county for each state and then aggregating these figures to a Congressional-district basis. For these purposes *County Business Patterns, 1973*, published by the Bureau of the Census, Department of Commerce

TABLE 1

Import-Sensitive Industries, 1973 House and 1974 Senate Hearings

Standard Industrial Classification (SIC) Number	Industry
103	Lead and zinc ores
11	Anthracite coal
12	Bituminous coal and lignite mining
131	Crude petroleum and natural gas
141	Dimension stone
145	Clay, ceramic, and refractory materials
2022	Cheese
2084	Wines, brandy and brandy spirits
2085	Distilled, rectified and blended liquors
2432	Veneer and plywood
26	Paper and allied products
2815	Cyclic intermediates, dyes, organic pigments and cyclic products
282	Plastic materials and synthetic resins
302	Rubber footwear
31	Leather and leather products (includes non-rubber footwear)
321	Flat glass
325	Structural clay products
3262	Vitreous china
3263	Fine earthenware
331	Blast furnaces and basic steel products
3321	Gray iron foundries
3332	Primary smelting and refining of lead
3333	Primary smelting and refining of zinc
342	Hand and edge tools, excluding machine tools
345	Screw machine products
3554	Paper industries machinery
3562	Ball and roller bearings
365	Radio and TV sets
366	Communications equipment
367	Electronic components and accessories
371	Motor vehicles
375	Motorcycles, bicycles and parts
387	Watches, clocks and parts
391	Silverware, plated ware, stainless steel ware
3941	Games and toys
3942	Dolls
3964	Needles, pins, hooks and eyes, etc.

and *Congressional District Data Book, 93rd Congress*, which is also a Bureau of Census document, were utilized.[16] State figures were given directly in *County Business Patterns*.

The dependent variable used in testing the importance of economic factors in the House voting pattern is whether a congressman voted for the 1973 trade bill (a liberal trade vote) or against the bill (a protectionist vote). The independent variables are the political party to which a congressman belongs, the proportions of workers in import-sensitive and export-oriented industries, and finally the campaign contributions from certain unions received during the year 1974 by congressmen who voted for or against the 1973 trade bill and who chose to run for office again in 1974. The unions are the International Brotherhood of Electrical Workers, the Communications Workers of America, and the United Steelworkers of America.[17] All three of these unions actively opposed the trade bill, and presumably their campaign contributions in 1974 were highly correlated with their financial aid to these congressmen in earlier periods.

There are several problems with trying to separate out the effects of economic pressures on a particular vote. Logrolling raises one obvious difficulty. A particular congressman who does not have any significant numbers of import-sensitive or export-oriented industries in his district may vote in a particular way in return for a sympathetic vote on other issues of interest to him from congressmen representing districts where economic interest in the trade bill is considerable. If these votes are distributed in the same proportions as those where economic pressure groups are strong, the results will not be biased. While it seems reasonable to expect this, one cannot be sure of this outcome, and, therefore, logrolling may distort the correlation results. A more serious problem would seem to arise with regard to campaign contributions. Trade is just one of many issues that interests labor unions. A particular congressman may still receive substantial financial help even though he opposes labor's position on trade simply because he supports enough of labor's other positions. However, one again would expect this factor to weaken any relationship between campaign contributions and voting patterns rather than to reverse the expected direction of the relationship. Clearly, there are also many other variables besides the ones included in the analysis that affect voting patterns. If these are systematically correlated with the variables used, the results will be biased. The assumption here is that this is not true.

The directions of the expected relationships between the dependent and independent variables in the analysis are as follows. Since a Republican President proposed the trade legislation, presumably after consultations with Congressional leaders in his party, one would expect Republican congressmen generally to support the bill. On the other hand, a larger proportion of Democrats could be expected to oppose the bill, partly because the AFL-CIO—a major force in the Democratic Party—opposed it and partly because of the absence of White House pressure to vote in a particular manner. The higher the proportion of import-sensitive industries in a congressional district the more likely would one expect a negative vote on the trade bill. Similarly, congressmen from districts with export-oriented industries should tend to vote in favor of the bill. Finally, the higher the political contributions received by a congressman from the three protectionist unions selected, the greater is the likelihood that the congressman will vote against the bill. . . .

[The results of the statistical analysis undertaken showed that party affiliation, union contributions, and the proportion of import-sensitive industries in a Congressional district all were significantly related to voting behavior in the expected direction.[18] However,] the two export-oriented industries did not show up as significant or with the expected sign. . . .

For the Senate the vote selected to test the influence of economic factors was an amendment by Senator McIntyre, a Democrat from New Hampshire, to the Trade Bill of 1974 that prohibited the President from reducing tariffs or duties on manufactured goods for which imports exceed one-third of domestic consumption during three of the last five years. Data on campaign contributions by the three unions were not collected for the Senate so that the independent variables were party status and the proportions of sensitive import-competing and export-oriented industries in each state. [As in the case of the House vote, the likelihood of a negative vote on the bill increased as the proportion of import-sensitive industries in a state rose, and if a Senator was a member of the Democratic Party. Similarly, the proportion of export-oriented industries did not significantly affect voting behavior.] . . .

In summary, the statistical analysis does give support for the hypotheses developed from the model set forth in the early parts of the paper. In particular, workers and management who think they are being adversely affected by imports are apparently able collectively to persuade their congressmen to vote against trade liberalization. However, export-oriented industries are not similarly successful. The problem with a statistical analysis of these industries is that relatively few testify strongly in favor of liberalization. Campaign contributions by protectionist unions are also correlated with voting behavior in the expected direction. In this case, however, the probable correlation of voting on trade issues with voting on other issues not included in the analysis but which are of greater concern to the unions weakens any conclusions about causality that one might draw from this result.

Notes

1. Probably the two best known works in this area are: Anthony Downs, *An Economic Theory of Democracy* (New York: Harper and Brothers, 1957) and James M. Buchanan and Gordon Tullock, *The Calculus of Consent* (Ann Arbor: University of Michigan Press, 1962).
2. Most of the recent investigations of tariffs by economists have not been directed at this issue but rather at explaining the structure of a country's tariffs or changes in this structure. See, for example, . . . J. H. Cheh, "United States Concessions in the Kennedy Round and Short-Run Labor Adjustment Costs,"

Journal of International Economics, Vol. 4, No. 4, November 1974; Richard E. Caves, "Economic Models of Political Choice: Canada's Tariff Structure," *Canadian Journal of Economics,* Vol. 9, No. 2, May 1976, and J. Pincus, "Pressure Groups and the Pattern of Tariffs," *Journal of Political Economy,* Vol. 83, No. 4, August 1975.

3. It is assumed that any purely redistributive changes that would obtain majority support have already been undertaken.

4. Because the assumption of identical, homothetic tastes yields a unique set of non-intersecting community indifference curves, the consumption point for the country after the relative price of imports has fallen due to the tariff liberalization must represent a higher collective income level even if the consumption point does not represent more of all goods.

5. For an extensive analysis of the subject, see Anthony Downs, *op. cit.,* Ch. 13. It is interesting that Downs illustrates his points with the tariff example.

6. Downs, *op. cit.,* pp. 255–6.

7. William A. Brock and Stephen P. Magee, "An Economic Theory of Politics: The Case of Tariffs" (mimeographed).

8. It is assumed that given increments in expenditures eventually result in fewer and fewer favorable votes.

9. For an extensive discussion of this subject, see Mancur Olson, Jr., *The Logic of Collective Action* (New York: Schocken Books, 1968).

10. It does follow, however, that the losers will be unable (without becoming worse off than after the change) to bribe the gainers into not making the change.

11. The standard measurement of net changes in consumer and producer surplus is directed at determining if this type of compensation is possible. As is well known, with fixed international prices, these calculations always yield a net gain as tariffs are lowered.

12. See Stephen P. Magee, "Prices, Incomes, and Foreign Trade," in *International Trade and Finance,* Peter Kenen (ed.), (New York: Cambridge University Press), 1975, for a survey of the empirical results on import and export demand elasticities. In his work on supply elasticities, Magee obtained a higher U.S. supply elasticity for total exports than import supply elasticity for finished manufactures into the United States, *op. cit.,* p. 183. However, a widely used set of estimates by John Floyd ("The Overvaluation of the Dollar: A Note on the International Price Mechanism," *American Economic Review,* March 1965) places both the demand elasticity for U.S. exports higher than the U.S. demand for imports and the U.S. supply elasticity of exports lower than the supply elasticity of imports for the United States.

13. Giorgio Basevi, "The Restrictive Effect of the U.S. Tariff and Its Welfare Effect," *American Economic Review,* Vol. LVIII, No. 4, September 1968, p. 851.

14. These will not always be the same. However, usually the President first checks with his fellow party members in Congress to make sure his recommendations will be supported by these members.

15. The proportion of import-competing and export-oriented industries to the total labor force is .077 and .012, respectively.

16. For some industries in some countries, employment data is not given in *County Business Patterns* because of disclosure problems. However, in most of these cases, it is possible to determine a reasonable figure by taking the mid-point of the employment-size classes which are given in the tables. When employment in a particular industry is in the open-ended size-class, 500 or more, a figure is determined either by subtracting the sum of all other industries from an appropriate sub-total for manufacturing or by utilizing the employment-size classes given by state for reporting units with 500 or more employees. Combining counties into Congressional districts required the use of even more personal judgment, since counties are often not contiguous with Congressional districts. The use of tables in the *Congressional District Data Book* that list the division of cities into the various Congressional districts was helpful in allocating a given county into more than one Congressional district.

17. The information on contributions was obtained from records on file at the National Information Center on Political Finance (Citizen's Research Foundation), Washington, D.C.
18. Since the independent variable [is] not continuous, probit analysis was employed rather than ordinary least-squares regressions. However, for comparison purposes ordinary least-squares regressions . . . were also run. They gave essentially the same results as the probit analysis.

6

Foreign Trade and United States Employment

Murray H. Finley

My invitation to this conference suggested that I give my "unvarnished" view of the relationship between foreign trade and investment and employment. I was delighted to accept the invitation for two reasons. First, I was pleased to know that at least there were some in government who recognized and acknowledged that there *is* a relationship between foreign trade, investment, and employment. Often it seems to us in the labor movement that many people, both in and out of government, do not accept the relationship and if they do, would prefer to simply sweep this fact under the rug. Most seem to consider it a low-priority problem that can be dealt with at some time in the future—if it has to be dealt with at all.

Secondly, I was pleased to come because I believe that the relationship between foreign trade, investment, and employment is extremely important; that the labor movement has something significant to say that no one else is saying, and that should be heard.

The "unvarnished" message that the labor movement is working hard to get across is simply this:

- That jobs are the fundamental base on which our economic and social well-being rest;

From Murray H. Finley, "Foreign Trade and U.S. Employment," *The Impact of International Trade and Employment*, William G. Dewald, ed. (Washington, D.C.: U.S. Department of Labor, 1978), pp. 129–134. Mr. Finley, who is President of the Amalgamated Clothing and Textile Workers Union, delivered this speech at the U.S. Department of Labor Conference on the Impact of International Trade and Investment on Employment, December 2, 1976.

- That no lasting social or economic progress can be made, or political stability maintained, either within the United States or elsewhere in the free world, unless the U.S. economy remains strong. The increasing international interdependence not only means that the United States cannot act in isolation from the rest of the world, but also that our own economic health is essential to the economic and social welfare of the entire international community.
- That there are things happening as a result of our foreign trade policies that are undermining U.S. economic strength—and these things should not go uncorrected. These things include the loss of jobs to imports, the continuing flow of investment capital overseas, and the accelerating transfer of technology without planning or recognition of the impact of such transfers. All of these factors are contributing to the steady shift in this country toward a service-oriented economy rather than a production economy—a shift we believe has serious implications for the future growth of this country.

It sounds glamorous to say we will be engaged in transportation, in communication, in banking, in services. We will be a kind of technological and managerial elite who will send our production offshore, but consume in abundance at home. We supply the computers and the brains; the rest of the world supplies the resources and the brawn. That is, in my judgment, a total misconception about what would happen. If such a service-oriented economy ever did come to its own, there would be a separation between those who don't have the skills to participate in the good life and those who do. A two-class society would develop: an under class and those in the elite who manage the rest of the world.

There are political dangers besides the domestic economic dangers I've mentioned. The high consumption, nonproduction service oriented economy sounds very good at least if you're an elite, but this assumes a peaceful political world. Can we imagine what could happen if we produced no steel, or plastic, or electronics etc., but only managed their production in the rest of the world. We'd be left with an elite with no one to manage around the world.

In our judgment, undermining the industrial base of this country cannot but lead to serious political consequences. We need a strong production oriented economy to maintain our military and political strength. But we also need a strong production oriented economy to provide basic industrial employment.

Now, probably, most of you had already decided what I was going to say today before I started. You probably expect me to say that imports are flooding the country, that American workers are losing their jobs; that something has to be done. I won't disappoint you.

Imports—in many industries, including my own—are flooding the country. Let me cite a few examples.

- In my own industry—textiles and apparel—imports have increased dramatically since 1970. In 1975, the quantity of foreign-made suits entering the domestic market was more than double the 1970 level. Jacket imports were up about 75 percent and trousers imports were higher by 35 percent. The import penetration rate of the domestic market for suits increased from 6.3 percent in 1970 to 9.5 percent in 1975. For coats and jackets, the penetration rate for the same period increased from 16.3 percent to 22.0 percent. For trousers, the rate increased from 7.5 percent to 13.4 percent. The 1976 figures are even more elevated.
- In the specialty steel industry, the story is similar. Imports this year have already increased 12.5 percent over last year. The quotas apparently are already filled. Obviously, imports would go higher without the quotas.
- The shoe industry has been all but destroyed by imports. In the ten-year period 1965–75 imports of shoes and footwear increased 1,000 percent—with a resulting decline in the U.S. domestic industry of more than 30 percent—and it is still going down. Ten years ago, imports accounted for less than 20 percent of domestic consumption—today they make up about half of the total.
- Black and white TVs—the industry has been wiped out by imports—70 percent are imported. This last year, the penetration rate for color TVs has shot up to 35 percent.
- It is not just the labor intensive, consumer goods industries which are affected by imports. Between 1971 and 1975, imports of capital goods increased 132 percent, or almost twice the rate for all manufactured goods.

WORKERS ARE LOSING JOBS

The debate over how many jobs have been lost both to imports and foreign investment is not going to be solved here today. But there is no question that jobs have been lost—and that the number stretches into the hundreds of thousands, even millions—depending on when you want to start counting and on what kind of assumptions you make—especially as to what *might* have happened if there had been no foreign investment, and no increase in imports.

But even if we cannot provide irrefutable macro data, there are plenty of micro data to tell the story. It is not only sufficiently convincing to provide a basis for public policy determination, but also represents such serious disruptions in individuals' lives that attention *must* be paid to it. To the hundreds of thousands of individuals who have lost their jobs because of imports, to talk about the broad picture is most unpersuasive.

The caseload data from the International Trade Commission and the Department of Labor provide one indication of the extent of job displacement resulting from our foreign trade policies. Under the 1974 Trade Act, adjustment assistance petitions have been filed for about 435,000 workers. Labor Department figures show that through the first six months of this year more than 160,000 workers had been certified as eligible for assistance. In my own industry—men's and boys' apparel—we know that at least 45,000 workers have already lost their jobs, and the remaining thousands are distinctly uneasy. We filed TAA [Trade Adjustment Assistance] petitions for close to 50,000 workers and have had eligibility certified for approximately 35,000. And in filing for these 50,000, we used certain arbitrary yardsticks that left out a lot of affected workers. First, a cutoff date of 1974. Second, only cases where unemployment reached 15 percent or more. This is only in our industry alone, and not even the total industry, but basically only tailored clothing, shirts, and some of the outerwear industry.

In the footwear industry, about 80,000 have lost jobs. Just through the first six months of this year, more than 160,000 workers whose jobs were lost to imports have been certified as eligible for TAA. However, none of these figures count those who lost their jobs because of increased foreign investment—when U.S. companies establish new plants overseas rather than here; and serve foreign or even U.S. markets from overseas plants instead of from U.S. plants.

As I mentioned, it is not just the economic problems that concern us—but the very human ones that lie behind all these figures. Let me quote from a letter I received a couple of weeks ago. The letter is from one of our members in New Albany, Indiana. The plant in which she was employed closed a short time ago.

> Mr. President Murray H. Finley, I would like some information on whether and if there is anything that can be done about the imports and the illegal aliens in this country. We at the H. A. Seinsheimers Mens Clothing have been closed down because of imports. Is it fair for us to be out of jobs and isn't there a way to deal with this business through legislation. I hope . . . unemployment pay is nice. But it isn't enough the way prices are and this small town doesn't have many jobs if you are over 40 and besides you can't be paying in on your Social Security. Thank you very much, Mrs. Mary Harris.

I haven't answered this member of ours. I am hoping someone at this conference will provide an answer. But I can't bring myself to answer on the broad, overall picture of trade and a promise that somewhere down the road, adjustments will be made. She is asking, "What can be done?" And she is talking about herself and the 450 other people who have just lost their jobs in New Albany, Indiana.

SOMETHING HAS TO BE DONE

All of us here no doubt agree that something has to be done. But many—maybe most—believe that the "liberalized" Trade Adjustment Assistance program fills that bill. It does not. Of course, we intend to make full use of it—because it is there. We have an obligation to do the best we can for members who lose their jobs because of imports. If as a result of the federal legislation they are able to get $1,200 additional dollars as a kind of employment burial pay, we have an obligation to seek it out for them. But it is a Band-Aid approach when a tourniquet is called for. I am often asked, why isn't TAA enough? Why isn't it a good answer?

There are two reasons why not:

- It doesn't get to the root of the problem, and
- TAA doesn't work—it is not effective in helping the individuals who need help.

Let me talk about the second point—the kind of help actually received by workers displaced by imports. There are at least 435,000 workers on whose behalf petitions for assistance have been filed since enactment of the Trade Act. Of these, only 160,000 workers have been certified as eligible. Of these, only 106,000 have managed to make their way through the maze of regulation and procedure and have actually applied for assistance. Of these, only 58,000 had received any payments by last June, 1975. So only about one in eight has actually been helped. And what help they get is minimal. Through June 1976, they had received an average of about $1,200 apiece. Only 24 workers had received financial job search assistance and only 23 workers received relocation assistance. This is out of at least 435,000 workers on whose behalf petitions have been filed. It is in fact a Band-Aid program, and a small one at that!

We made a study to see what happens once the petitions are approved and eligibility certified. And I will tell you, it is a maze. We had a situation in Illinois where a large plant closed with about 500 workers. They were certified as eligible, but far from automatically. It was impossible simply to go to the various employment service field offices, most of which didn't even know how to handle petitions for trade adjustment assistance. They just were not trained to do it. We ended up almost desperately writing to the governor, the secretary of labor, I think, to President Ford and possibly President-elect Carter. And this was not, by the way, an unusual case. We generally have to fight for the workers' certification.

We know some 35,000 have been certified in our industry. But we can't even tell you how many got trade adjustment assistance nor how much. We know some did. But we don't know how to find out the full story. There is no mechanism to notify workers potentially eligible for TAA to get them to the employment office to get the money. This, by the way, may be a year after they were laid off as a result of the impact of imports. While money, when it comes, is always welcome to an unemployed worker, it obviously does not handle the problem that it was meant to handle, that is to get them into new jobs.

A study of adjustment assistance in the shoe industry as reported in the Monthly Labor Review bears this out [1]. The study found that only one of the sample of 185 workers who were laid off had participated in a government training program, only one had received a relocation allowance, and only five had been placed in jobs through the efforts of the local state employment service agency—in this case the Massachusetts employment service. One-fourth of those laid off never found another job. Half were not employed full time, and real wages for those who were employed had declined almost 18 percent from prelayoff levels.

The report also found that workers waited an average 19.4 months between the date of layoff and the receipt of their first TAA check. That this long delay is typical is substantiated by numerous reports from my own union. Our field people report "horrendous red-tape" involved in getting help to our members from the state employment service agencies. In Illinois, for example, the state employment service simply failed to do the job it was supposed to do—and this despite repeated meetings with state personnel, and repeated reassurances that the problems with local offices had been corrected. In our view, the time lags between application and receipt of benefits are inexcusable.

One "safeguard" supposedly built into the Trade Reform Act was the advisory committees through which the labor movement and other affected groups could participate in all aspects of foreign trade policy development. The idea was that through the advisory committees, constituent problems could either be quickly resolved or avoided in the first place. I and other officers of our union are members of the Advisory Committee for Trade Negotiations, the Labor Policy Advisory Committee, and the labor sector of the Advisory Committee for Textile Apparel and Leather Products. Meetings have certainly been held and we have participated; even presented detailed positions on specific problems facing workers in our industry. But these meetings have been designed more to brief us on the issues that will arise in the multilateral negotiations to take place in Geneva, not to get our advice or to resolve problems. What I sense is happening is that the meetings are being carefully orchestrated so that most of the time is spent on being briefed. What little time is spent on advising is to no avail because the negotiators ignore the advice—and, in fact, had already developed predetermined positions before the advice was given. Thus, instead of a safeguard, to assure that trade policy is consistent with national interests and goals, I and many of my colleagues feel that we are engaged in a charade—designed merely to meet the literal requirements of the Trade Act. But the Labor Policy Advisory Committee is not in any real sense *advisory*.

Now to go back to the first point—that TAA simply does not get to the roots of the problem. Adjustment assistance is based on the premise that so-called free trade provides benefits to all of us, and that the cost of these benefits should not be borne unequally by the few who suffer immediate (but supposedly temporary) injury, but should be spread among all taxpayers. We in the labor movement have learned to our sorrow that this premise, and the presumptions underlying the program, are wrong.

First, we don't have a free trade situation or anything approaching it in the world today—if indeed we ever did. The United States may or may not be operating on a free trade basis, depending on how loosely you want to define it. But we are alone among the trading nations in acting as if the free trade concept were fact and not fancy. Such common phenomena as administered prices, nontariff barriers, local content laws, preferential trading agreements, and subsidized exports make a mockery of "free trade." The labor movement expects U.S. policy to start from a recognition of things as they are—not from an imaginary world, as we might like it to be.

Second, and most important—U.S. policy, particularly foreign trade policy—must become the natural outgrowth of national economic policy. Foreign trade questions, foreign investment issues cannot be resolved or even considered apart from domestic economic concerns. Our foreign trade and investment policy must be an adjunct of national economic policy—they must serve *national* needs—not the other way around. Let me briefly sketch the picture as we see it.

ON THE HOME FRONT

There can be no question that the United States is the strongest nation in the free world. I am speaking here in economic terms. There is nothing chauvinistic in recognition of the fact that we have more resources, and use them better, than any other nation. Our resources—skilled labor, capital, technology, management capability, natural wealth, climate, and social organization—all combine to make us the strongest economic unit. Yet at the present time our economy is in trouble—teetering on the brink of recovery—and I say that advisedly.

- There are almost 8 million American workers unemployed [creating] a festering sore on the economy, a severe drain on the federal budget (about $17 billion this year), and a drag on GNP growth. This is not to mention the individual hardship that the unemployed incur.

- We are told that an insufficient amount of capital investment is being made to create the new jobs that must be created in order to reduce unemployment.
- We read of potential shortages both of essential raw materials and of production capacity to convert these basic materials for our industries. Shortages are forecast in such basic industries as aluminum, copper, lead, and zinc.
- The wholesale price index has been rising steadily over the year and in the past few months, fairly sharply, signaling an increase in the rate of inflation in the very near future.

There has been a long-term decline in the average rate of productivity growth—which not only affects the U.S. ability to compete in world markets but also means a slower rate of improvement in the average worker's standard of living. Between 1948 and 1966, productivity in the United States increased each year at an average rate of 2.4 percent. But between 1966 and 1973, the average rate of productivity increase dropped to only 1.7 percent. This decline in productivity growth occurred at the same time that there has been a gradual shift of the economy from the goods producing sector to the service sector; and this really worries us.

Twenty-five years ago, only 30 percent of the GNP was attributable to the service sector of the economy and almost 60 percent to the goods producing sector. Since that time there has been a steady increase in the service sector and a steady decline in the goods producing sector. Last year, the two sectors were about even—but clearly the service sector has the forward momentum.

In our view there is a connection between these two developments—the decline in productivity growth and the trend toward a service oriented economy. Since technology is more readily applied to manufacturing—to the production of goods—than it is to the provision of services, it is in this area that the greatest improvements in productivity can be made. And without productivity growth, there can be no improvement in the general standard of living. We all here today may be surfeited with material goods, and maybe our college educated, middle-class children are ready to spurn materialistic things, and return to the "simple life." But let me remind you that the 26 million citizens whose income is below the poverty level are not ready to give up on improving their material and physical well being. Nor, I venture to say, are the tens of millions more whose income currently falls somewhere between the $5,500 poverty level and the $14,000 median family income. They are already savoring the simple life. And they don't like it. Improvements in the general standard of living—and therefore in productivity—are not only viable goals, they are still very fundamental goals.

So here we have the U.S. economy—the keystone of the world economy—the rock on which the free world economy *must* depend—and there are ominous signs that the rock is turning to sand.

THE PICTURE OUTSIDE THE U.S.

What is happening in the rest of the world? In the developed countries, the pace of recovery is no better than in the United States, and in many it is even worse. Great Britain's situation is almost desperate. I can only say as an aside, if we looked at the history of what we are doing with direct foreign investment, and what Britain did in the 1800s and 1890s, in terms of portfolio investment, becoming a Rentier economy, we are going on the same road and unless we turn it around, in my judgment, we will end up with the same dire results. Italy is also in a bad way. France, with rising inflation [is] in serious trouble. Even Japan has an inflation rate considerably higher than our own, and its recovery is faltering, if not actually stopped. Only West Germany is doing well. The situation is worse when we look at the developing countries—except the OPEC [Organization of Petroleum Exporting Countries] which, of course, are doing very nicely. Many of the developing countries, dependent as they are on exports of raw materials to buy the goods they need for development, and sometimes simply to maintain a subsistence standard of living for their people, are seeking ways to parlay their control over raw material resources into greater benefits and returns for themselves.

The newly established cartels—of which the bauxite producers' association is probably the most successful—the demands for a new International Economic Order for debt repayment deferments, for special trade preferences, and for U.S. financing of price stabilizing buffer stocks—all of these efforts are indicative of the basic economic insecurity of these nations. The success of these nations in improving their economic and social well-being is completely dependent on a healthy world economy—and the world economy cannot prosper without a strong, growing U.S. economy. If the U.S. economy fails; if our recovery falters and we slide into another recession, which is the way the signs are pointing at the moment, the free world economy may come down like a house of cards. That is why it is so important to pay attention first and foremost to what is happening in the United States. And that is why it is so important to pay attention to what is happening to U.S. employment—to jobs that are the base on which the economy stands.

Let us look for a moment to what is happening in foreign trade and investment.

U.S. FOREIGN TRADE AND INVESTMENT TRENDS

Perhaps the most significant international development in the past ten to fifteen years is the rise of the multinational corporation and the spread of U.S. capital and technology throughout the world. In 1975, the value of U.S. direct investment abroad was two and [a] half times as much as it was ten years before, increasing from $52 billion to more than $133 billion. Annual expenditures for plant and equipment by majority owned affiliates of U.S. companies abroad trebled in 10 years, increasing from $8.6 billion in 1966 to an expected $27.1 billion this year. And there is no end in sight. At the same time that this capital is going out of the country, we are told that we are facing a capital shortage in the United States.

We are also told, don't worry; foreign investment is good for the U.S. economy. Foreign investment, it is said, creates jobs. It brings in more money than flows out. And besides, we are told, even if some workers lose their jobs, other jobs will quickly become available. I don't believe it!

- If that were really so, then how can you account for the fact that the Commerce Department survey of 298 multinational corporations showed that overall employment in their foreign affiliates grew by 26.5 percent between 1966 and 1970, whereas employment in these companies' domestic plants grew by only 5.7 percent—less than a quarter of the rate of increase of employment overseas? Where is the job creation here? Or what accounts for the fact that production worker employment increased 14.5 percent faster for the MNCs overseas than for the U.S. domestic plants?
- If it were true, how can you account for the fact that balance-of-payments income from direct investment declined by 47 percent in 1975? Last year income was only $9.5 billion, considerably less than the $13.4 billion that was added to the book value of direct investment that year.
- If it were true that other jobs are going to become available, how can you account for the stubbornly high unemployment rate—almost 8 percent—which at the moment seems to be going up, not down?

We have been told that one of our international obligations is to recognize the need of developing countries to industrialize and to obtain a larger share of the world trade. We don't disagree. But the point I want to make here is that this will not be done unless the U.S. economy is strong. There will be no problem in improving the terms of trade for developing countries, or increasing their share of the world's economic pie, if the pie itself is bigger. We are also told that we should trust the market mechanism; that left alone everything will come out all right. All I can say on that is, we cannot afford to simply let things happen, on the theory that the market is the best arbiter and most efficient allocator of resources. The fact is that the market doesn't work very well. For example, there was no sense in the Russian grain deal which eliminated the U.S. grain surplus, led to tight supplies and set off a furious round of inflation. There is no sense in closing down plants here, as we are in the case of aluminum, simply to open up new ones overseas, and at the same time paying higher prices for the aluminum we need, when for the same price we could develop substitute sources of aluminum in the United States, and keep the jobs in the United States. It makes no sense to continue to keep millions of American workers on an unproductive income maintenance program, and at the same time, through discriminatory tax incentives, encourage U.S. companies not only to go overseas but to increase their capital expenditures overseas.

What we have to decide is where we want to go, where we want to be, and then do the things that are necessary to get there. The first step obviously is a full employment policy, a domestic program that through a carefully planned, integrated program brings us to full employment within the next four years.

The second step is to stop doing the things that interfere with the goal of full employment. High on the list is the development of a foreign trade policy that is firmly based on and completely consistent with national economic and social policy. Not the kind of backward nod in the direction of national goals that is epitomized by the trade adjustment assistance pro gram. But a forward-looking program where such ineffectual artifices are not necessary and are not even considered.

Reference

1. McCarthy, James E. "Contrasting Experiences with Trade Adjustment Assistance." *Monthly Labor Review*, 6 (June 1975), 25–30.

7

It's a Walkover for Shoe Imports

George Fecteau and John Mara

It is difficult to conceive of a major American industry or group of workers who have suffered more from unfair imports than those engaged in the manufacture of shoes.

In less than a decade the ever-growing avalanche of footwear imports has wiped out at least 70,000 American jobs. Moreover, an estimated

From George Fecteau and John Mara, "It's a Walkover for Shoe Imports." This article originally appeared in *Viewpoint* (Vol. 9, No. 2, Second Quarter, 1979), a quarterly magazine published by the Industrial Union Department, AFL-CIO. Reprinted with permission.

150,000 job opportunities, most of which would have been filled by young people and members of minority groups, were killed off by shoe imports.

With import penetration rates reaching 50% or over for the last three years, hardly a month goes by without the closing of another shoe plant, frequently in a small community where the shoe plant is the only real industry and the largest employer.

More than 350 shoe factories have shut down in the last 10 years, reducing the number of plants from well over 1,000 to less than 700. Companies manufacturing non-rubber footwear in the United States have declined from about 650 to about 325, and many of them have become major importers with an increasing volume of their sales derived from shoes they buy abroad.

By 1977 the situation had become so bad that the U.S. government was reluctantly forced to act. However, instead of imposing import quotas covering all countries, which our unions and the domestic industry had requested in our escape clause petition, the United States applied two Band-Aids to our gaping wounds by entering into Orderly Marketing Agreements [OMAs] with Taiwan and Korea, two of the more than a score of countries exporting footwear to our shores.

Predictably, both Taiwan and Korea have ignored the OMAs and have continued to increase their exports to the U.S. As Senator John A. Durkin of New Hampshire recently wrote in an article for the *Portsmouth Herald* in his state, the only thing orderly about these Orderly Marketing Agreements is "the systematic closing of shoe factories" across the United States.

Shoes are produced in 37 states and nearly half the factories employ less than 100 workers. Many of the companies are small, family-owned enterprises and a high proportion are located in small rural towns. A high proportion of these plants are—or were—the primary source of income for their communities.

Thus, when a shoe plant shuts down, the whole community suffers. Families are often forced to move. Shops and other small businesses go bankrupt. The tax base of the community is undermined and the impact is felt in the schools, in decreased civic services, in a general decline in the standard of living.

Much has been made by the Carter Administration and by others of the "adjustment assistance" offered to shoe workers who lose their jobs to imports. This aid does sometimes temporarily cushion the hard blow of a job loss. But in the long run adjustment assistance becomes burial insurance for the jobs our workers no longer have.

Unfortunately, some of the most influential newspapers still stubbornly adhere to a long outdated editorial policy touting the myth of "free trade." An important part of this myth holds that shoe factories are among the most expendable in the give-and-take of international trade. Because these plants are highly labor-intensive and employ technology that any country can buy or imitate, a segment of the press and its allies in academia argue that America should be willing to sacrifice its shoe plants—and our jobs—in order to aid the uplifting of underdeveloped countries.

The myth embraces a number of misconceptions, including (1) shoe imports keep prices down and thereby fight inflation; (2) American shoe workers will ultimately find better jobs and be better off, and (3) the sacrifice of our jobs and communities somehow improves our relations with other countries.

All of these are based not only on fallacies but on fantasies of the most dangerously deluding kind. The "anti-inflation" part of the myth has a hollow ring to everyone who has bought a pair of shoes in recent years. In fact, as shoe imports have increased, shoe prices have risen inexorably.

When virtually all shoes worn in America were also made here, U.S. shoe prices were the lowest in the world, based upon the number of hours a person had to work to earn a pair of shoes.

What the theoreticians have forgotten, if indeed they were ever taught, is that it was America's productive capacity that gave us the highest standard of living of any nation in history—not imports. And when that productive capacity is finally undermined, as it is being slowly undermined every day by imports of everything from cheese to automobiles, our standard of living will gradually sink back to levels most of us would find unthinkable today.

The second fallacy of the myth—that American workers in labor-intensive industries like footwear will wind up in better jobs—would be ludicrous if it were not for the dimension of the human tragedies that have been experienced by shoe workers and others who fall into the so-called "low-end" category.

All over this country you can find the despairing former shoe workers, the broken homes, the depressed communities that have suffered permanent damage from imports. Some of the once thriving shoe towns in Massachusetts, Pennsylvania, Missouri and a score of other states are veritable ghost towns today. Some of these towns, like Lowell, Massachusetts, are literally being burned to the ground by professional arsonists working for the predatory sharks who buy closed shoe factories for a song and destroy them for the insurance.

The third element of the myth—that unrestricted imports improve U.S. relations with other nations—is, if anything, more demonstrably ridiculous than the other parts of the "free trade" fantasy.

All America has to do is look around at the rest of the world and try to count the reliable friends we have today as compared with, say, the 1950s or, for that matter, with any previous epoch since 1776. Our foreign policy is, quite obviously, losing us friends, and "free trade" is an integral part of that forlorn policy.

Actually, our so-called trading partners have come to regard us with disdain and often with outright arrogance. The prime ministers of

Japan and Germany, two nations from which we accepted unconditional surrender in 1945, now lecture the President of the United States on how we should run our internal fiscal affairs. And even the smaller countries thumb their noses at us, though most of them have received substantial gifts from the bounty of American taxpayers—an increasingly restive group that includes shoe workers, steel workers, textile workers, color television workers and many others whose jobs are being wiped out by imports.

Other "justifications" offered for our open door policy on imports—quality and productivity—do not apply to footwear any more than they do to most other imports. American shoe workers are the most productive in the world and American footwear is the universally imitated standard for every other shoe producing country. Indeed, a recent test conducted by the magazine *Runner's World* in the Pennsylvania State University's Biomechanic Laboratories proved that U.S. made athletic footwear performed better and lasted longer than its foreign competitors in virtually all categories.

What gives foreign-made footwear the edge in our market is purely and simply price: *the wholesale—not the retail—price*. Wages paid workers, including child labor, in Taiwan, Hong Kong, and Korea are often less than 40 cents an hour and the working and environmental conditions are abominable. Our Occupational Health and Safety Laws and environmental statutes would not permit domestic factories to operate under the conditions prevailing in shoe plants in many other countries.

Lane Kirkland, secretary-treasurer of the AFL-CIO, put the fictitious theory of "consumer benefits" from imports in its proper perspective at the IUD [Industrial Union Department] conference on Trade and Jobs in 1977 when he attacked "the proposition that the consumer has an inalienable, top priority right to $4 Korean shoes, regardless of the conditions under which they are made, the human, social and economic cost of lost American jobs, and of who really gets the $4."

"This principle," said Kirkland, "is mostly expounded by those who get their shoes at Gucci." He referred, of course, to the higher profits on shoe imports by retailers who, quite obviously, have not shared them with the American consumer.

The critical question is this: Should American workers, many of whom are the primary source of support for their families, be forced to compete with child labor or woefully underpaid workers in Hong Kong, Korea, Taiwan or anywhere else where workers are exploited in sweat shops that would have made Dickens think the mid-19th century British factories he deplored were, by comparison, heaven on earth?

Unfortunately, the United States government believes American workers should be forced to engage in such one-sided and, in a real sense, inhuman competition that has caused a proliferation of sweat shops abroad. For more than a decade our unions and the domestic industry have been trying in vain to obtain relief from the steadily rising tide of footwear imports. Here is a capsule record of those efforts:

> *In 1968 shoe imports had captured 21.5% of the U.S. market.* President Johnson was persuaded to direct the Tariff Commission (now the International Trade Commission [ITC]) to investigate the economic conditions of the U.S. footwear industry, which had already suffered for some years from the import invasion. Little more came of this investigation than a verification that yes, things were indeed getting serious in the industry.
>
> *In 1971 imports had won 33.5% of our footwear market.* A second investigation again verified the increasing injury to the domestic industry and its workers but President Nixon ignored the mounting evidence of injury and refused to provide relief.
>
> *By 1974 imports had risen to 37.2%* and the Congress—pointedly citing the tragic plight of the shoe industry—passed the new Trade Act to give injured U.S. industries a way to receive faster, more effective relief from imports.
>
> In 1975 our unions joined the American Footwear Industries Association (AFIA) in petitioning the International Trade Commission for relief under Section 201, the "escape clause" provision of the new Act. In a unanimous decision, the ITC recommended relief. But on Good Friday, 1976, President Ford turned us down.
>
> *By mid-1976, after Ford rejected relief, shoe imports soared to record monthly rates of 50%.* At the end of that year imports were approaching 400 million pair—almost two pairs of shoes for every man, woman and child residing in the United States.

At this point, the Senate Finance Committee, which has jurisdiction over trade matters, took the unusual step of formally asking the ITC to reopen the escape clause case and our unions again joined with the industry in a new petition.

With shoe imports shooting past the 50% mark in the spring of 1977, once again the ITC unanimously recommended relief. Unbelievably, President Carter hesitated and in April, just a few days before the IUD Trade and Jobs Conference opened in Washington, he indicated he might reject the ITC recommendation. The member unions of the Industrial Union Department of the AFL-CIO rose up as one at the conference and the resulting protest got the banner headline and lead story on the front page of the *Washington Post* next morning.

President Carter then had some second thoughts. He assigned his Special Trade Representative, Robert Strauss, to negotiate Orderly Marketing Agreements with Taiwan and Korea.

Although George Meany, president of the AFL-CIO; I. W. Abel, then president of the IUD as well as the United Steelworkers of America, and other labor leaders joined our shoe unions in urging the President to impose quotas on imports from all countries—the *only* realistic approach to the problem—Mr. Carter and Ambassador Strauss went right ahead and signed the OMAs with just two countries—Taiwan and Korea.

The results of those two innocuous agreements were, as we have said, entirely predictable. They have failed. We will let Sen. John Durkin give you the measure of their failure in the following excerpt from his article in the *Portsmouth Herald:*

> The impending closure of the Converse shoe factory in Berlin (N.H.), with the loss of over 800 jobs, reminds us of a simple fact—this Administration's policy on shoe imports, like that of its predecessors is a disaster. . . .
>
> In 1976, Taiwan sent 65 million pairs of rubber soled and fabric based shoes to this country. In 1977, the Administration and Taiwan reached an agreement to limit Taiwan exports to the U.S. Yet in 1978, Taiwan sent 97.5 million pairs of similar shoes, a one-third increase. . . .
>
> Korea has also contributed to the problem. In 1976, Korea sent 31.4 million pairs of rubber soled and fabric based shoes. In 1978, once again after the Administration and Korea supposedly reached agreement to limit shoe imports, this total rose to an astounding 59 million pairs—an 88% increase in just two years.

Nit-pickers may argue that some of the shoes the senator cites in his totals were not covered by the OMAs. Non-rubber shoes were the main target of the agreements. (Apparently the Administration felt our canvas-and-rubber shoe factories were expendable all along.) However, to give the reader a handle on what has happened to the non-rubber portion of our domestic shoe industry we will quote from a letter addressed to Ambassador Strauss on January 11 this year by Frederick A. Meister, president of the AFIA:

> The Administration's import relief program for non-rubber footwear is in danger of virtually complete failure.
>
> After 18 months of the OMA's and the attendant "side letters," and the best efforts of our manufacturers to compete, we have received little, if any, import relief. . . .
>
> Total non-rubber imports remain at all-time high levels because increases in imports from the noncontrolled countries in 1978 will be almost exactly equal to the 48 million pair cutback from the base year for Korea and Taiwan. Moreover, the surge in non-rubber from uncontrolled countries is accelerating. . . .

Actually, as the AFIA and our unions had previously reminded Strauss, both Taiwan and Korea had exceeded their agreed levels in the first year of the OMAs. Moreover, while ostensibly cutting back non-rubber shipments to the U.S. in recent months, they have increased their rubber footwear exports astronomically, as Sen. Durkin noted.

In fact, rubber footwear imports from all countries have shot up from 115 million in 1976 to 175 million in 1978—a 52% increase in just two years. Non-rubber imports again approached the 400 million mark (370 million to be precise) in 1978 and at year end domestic production was declining.

There is not space here—nor in this entire magazine—to catalogue the numerous parts of the Orderly Marketing Agreements broken by Taiwan and Korea, nor to cite the galaxy of end-runs around the OMAs by Hong Kong, the Philippines, Italy, Brazil, Uruguay and others. Suffice to say, that the experience of our shoe industry and its workers over the past two years of these ersatz agreements raises some very serious questions, not only for the industry but for all others, and, ultimately for America's whole industrial base.

The most obvious question it raises is this: How can we trust other countries to live up to the complicated codes being formulated at the Multilateral Trade Negotiations in Geneva, if they can't observe relatively simple agreements like the OMAs designed to govern footwear imports into the United States?

The only solution, as the failure of these agreements proves, is for the United States to impose quantitative restrictions—quotas—on all footwear imports. As Lloyd McBride, president of the Steelworkers, points out elsewhere in this issue of *Viewpoint*, quotas have worked for the domestic specialty steel industry. Since they went into effect in June, 1976, they have increased employment dramatically, generated capital investment substantially, enabled the U.S. specialty steel industry to maintain its traditional lead in technology, and have proved to be anti-inflationary as a Labor Department study certifies.

The quotas on specialty steel represent the only major import restraint program now in effect that is working as the Trade Act of 1974 intended. This being the case, it would seem only prudent for President Carter, not only to extend the quotas on specialty steel imports, but to apply import quotas to footwear and to all other imports that are robbing American workers of their jobs.

8

The Issue of Further Reductions in Barriers to International Trade

Richard Blackhurst, Nicolas Marian, and Jan Tumlir

. . . We begin with a consideration of the benefits to be expected from further trade liberalization, and then turn to an analysis of four arguments commonly employed by those who question or oppose efforts to extend the international division of labour.

At the outset, two common misconceptions regarding trade liberalization should be noted. In popular discussions it is often held that the benefit a particular country derives from trade liberalization consists of the resulting increase in exports. With proper qualifications, this may do as a shorthand expression. An unexamined emphasis on export expansion, however, entails the danger of the accompanying increase in imports being considered the "cost" of achieving the benefit. A negotiating team guided by this view could easily fall into the mercantilist trap of seeking to maximize the volume of additional exports and to minimize additional imports. . . .

To arrive at a more meaningful view of the benefits of trade liberalization, it is necessary to consider what the economy must give up in order to produce the additional exports—in technical terms, their "opportunity cost." For example, if the land, labour, and capital used to produce $100 worth of additional exports would have, in the absence of trade liberalization, produced $92 worth of other products, the gain to the economy is measured not by the $100 increase in exports, but by the $8 increase in the value of the (new) output of the relocated factors of production. The additional imports, moreover, are an integral part of the export expansion because they ultimately replace the foregone output in the other sectors of the economy (without which the economy would be poorer rather than richer following liberalization). In summary, the ultimate purpose of trade liberalization is not to maximize a country's exports, or even world trade, but rather to bring about a more productive use of resources.

Nor is it possible to salvage the popular view by arguing that as long as there are idle factors of production, they can be employed to pro-

From Richard Blackhurst, Nicolas Marian, and Jan Tumlir, *Trade Liberalization, Protectionism, and Interdependence,* GATT Study No. 5 (Geneva: General Agreement on Tariffs and Trade, 1977), pp. 21–42. Reprinted by permission. Some tables and some footnotes omitted.

duce the additional exports without the need to forego other output. In a situation in which there are unemployed factors of production, there is no reason—other than considerations of comparative advantage—for favouring employment in the export sector over employment in the import-competing or non-traded "home" good sectors. If there are unemployed factors, the situation will involve some combination of structural problems, deficient aggregate demand, or excessive wages, but not exclusively, or even primarily, deficient production for export. More generally, the argument that trade liberalization should not be thought of primarily in terms of a long-run solution to unemployment problems is the logical counterpart of the argument that increased restrictions on imports represent an inefficient and ultimately ineffective way of solving unemployment problems.[1] The fundamental point in each instance is that changes in trade barriers have a permanent effect on the efficiency with which resources are used, but not on the level of utilization.

Another potential source of confusion in discussions of trade liberalization is of more recent origin. It is the view that the switch from fixed exchange rates to floating rates between the major currencies has reduced the importance of trade liberalization—in particular, of reductions in tariffs—because movements in exchange rates produce changes in the competitiveness of domestic goods vis-à-vis foreign goods that are as large or larger than the wedge caused by trade restrictions.

The policy of trade liberalization is generally based on long-term considerations. It follows that the appropriate comparison is between the impact of exchange rate changes and the impact of tariffs, respectively, on competitiveness in the long run. Following this line, we find first that evidence for the period since the beginning of widespread floating early in 1973 suggests that long-run changes in exchange rates are influenced to an important extent by differences in rates of inflation between countries—an interpretation supported by the International Monetary Fund [IMF], the Organization for Economic Co-operation and Development, and many individual experts. This means that exchange rate movements act in the direction of *maintaining* the competitive relationship between domestic goods and goods produced abroad. Exchange rate changes also do not change relative prices within a country's tradeable goods sector.

Trade restrictions, in contrast, directly alter the relative competitiveness in favour of the domestic version of the goods; they also alter relative prices within a country's tradeable goods sector. A price distortion is created because the imported version is taxed or otherwise restricted, while the domestic version is not. It follows that a reduction in the trade restriction improves the competitiveness of the imported version by reducing the degree of price distortion. As we explain in more detail below, it is through such reductions in price distortions that trade liberalization leads to an increase in productive efficiency and national income.

In summary, when seen in a long-run perspective, changes in tariffs have a definite impact on the relative competitiveness of domestic and foreign goods, whereas changes in exchange rates have little or no permanent impact on relative competitiveness. It is clear that the importance of trade liberalization is independent of whether exchange rates are fixed or floating.

There is one other aspect of exchange rates that should be mentioned. Countries' attitudes toward international trade and trade liberalization are influenced by their perceptions of the extent to which other countries are "playing by the rules." As far as exchange rate policy is concerned, this means that it is important that there is a general belief that each country is—to use the language of the proposed second amendment to the IMF Articles of Agreement—avoiding the manipulation of "exchange rates or the international monetary system in order to prevent effective balance-of-payments adjustment or to gain an unfair competitive advantage over other" countries. . . .

1. THE BENEFITS OF REDUCTIONS IN TRADE BARRIERS

The benefits to be expected from trade liberalization may be classified into consumption gains, production gains, economies of scale gains, gains from a more competitive domestic economy, and a contribution to domestic price stability. The first three constitute the basic motivation for the pursuit of freer trade, while the latter two are "fringe benefits" in the sense that they contribute to the achievement of goals which are being pursued principally through policies other than trade liberalization.

All the benefits presuppose that trade liberalization will reduce the retail prices of both imported commodities and their domestically produced substitutes. This simple conclusion is sometimes denied by the claim that the exporters, importers or retailers simply pocket the savings from the duty reduction. A closely related argument is that imports from low-cost sources are retailed in the importing country at prices comparable to those of high-cost domestic products, yielding a high profit to the importer but little extra benefit to the consumer. It is therefore necessary to begin with a brief look at the argument that the consumer does not benefit from trade liberalization.

Suppose retailers do not change their selling price following the duty reduction. Assuming they were earning normal profits before, they are now earning abnormally high profits. Since the higher profits are made only on the imported version, each retailer will reduce his purchases of the domestic version, putting downward pressure on its price, and try to increase total sales by stocking even more of the imported version. Seeking to expand sales so as to increase total profit, each retailer will be willing to settle for a slightly smaller profit per unit of sales. The price-cutting will continue until the profit from retailing the particular product is back to normal (that is, to a level that gives the retailer a competitive rate of return on investment). At that point the price of the imported version will have fallen by approximately the amount of duty reduction, while the extent of the decline in the price of the domestic version will depend on the degree of substitutability, in the eyes of consumers, between the two versions (the better substitutes they are, the larger will be the decline in the price of the domestic version).

Exactly the same sequence of events would occur in the case of retailers who were selling the low-cost imported version for the same price as the higher-cost domestic version. The only possible difference is that this situation may involve an import quota that limits the low-cost foreign version to a small fraction of total domestic consumption. If so, the high mark-ups can be maintained (with the windfall profit going to whoever gets the import or export licences). However, this is not an argument against but *for* further trade liberalization.

As long as there is free entry into retailing and foreign exporters are free to sell to any domestic buyer, the duty reduction will be passed on to consumers.[2] Only if there is monopoly can the retailer(s) retain some of the duty savings. But they will also pass a part of the savings on to consumers, for in such a setting a monopolist can increase his total profit by reducing the price in order to increase sales. The fact that they will not reduce it by the full amount of the duty reduction is not an argument against trade liberalization. It *is* an argument for eliminating obstacles to freedom of entry and freedom of transactions.[3]

Finally, the allegation that trade liberalization does not reduce prices to the consumer acquires a superficial plausibility in an inflation-prone world in which absolute price declines have become rare. In this situation, trade liberalization is likely to result in smaller-than-otherwise price increases rather than price declines. This is especially likely when the tariff reductions or liberalization of quantitative restrictions are staged over time, as is usually the case. In any case the benefit to consumers is equivalent to that of an absolute price decline in a situation of general price-level stability.

The discussion now turns to the five sources of gain that come with trade liberalization. Because the first three are generally well-known, . . . that part of the discussion has been kept very brief.

Consumption Gains

Everyone is a consumer, and most are also producers. In their role of consumer, people benefit directly from the lower price. Part of this gain represents a transfer from whoever was benefiting from the artificially high price, generally domestic producers of the product, plus the national treasury if a tariff is involved. (If a quantitative restriction is eliminated, the identity of former beneficiaries—other than domestic producers—will depend on how the quota allocations were administered.) The important point, however, is that the total direct benefit to consumers will exceed the transfer from these other groups, and therefore there is a net gain to the country as a whole.

Production Gains

Many people also gain in their role of producers—that is, as suppliers of labour services, capital, and land. Inefficiently produced domestic output is replaced by imports, permitting the reallocation of some domestic land, labour, and capital away from low productivity industries and into more productive employment in those industries in which the country has a comparative advantage. Some specialized producers may lose from trade liberalization, but the gains of the others will more than balance the losses (we return to this point below). The traditional view that the new employment necessarily will be in a different industry is now subject to the important qualification that at least a part of the impact of trade liberalization is likely to take the form of an increase in specialization within industries and firms. This has implications both for the transitional adjustment costs (discussed in the next section), and for the "economies of scale" gains from trade liberalization to which the discussion now turns.

Economies of Scale Gains

There is a second source of gain at the production level. Trade liberalization enlarges the market in which each country's tradeable goods industries compete, bringing with it the opportunity to gain from the cost reductions that under certain circumstances accompany increases in the scale of operations. Three types of scale-related efficiency gains are possible. There are, first, the well-known economies that come with larger scale plants in those industries in which the minimum efficient size plant is "large." Such economies of scale are most likely to occur in one-product plants producing relatively standardized goods.

. . . [Secondly,] multi-product firms producing differentiated versions of the same or similar goods have the possibility of horizontal specialization or, as it is now often referred to, intra-industry specialization (Grubel and Lloyd, 1975). The third source of scale-related gains springs from increased vertical specialization. Once the scale of production reaches a certain level, parts, components, and accessories that were formerly produced by the final users themselves can be supplied by separate factories whose specialization often makes possible significant cost reductions.

Gains from a More Competitive Domestic Economy

Enlargement of the market via trade liberalization brings important benefits through its impact on the degree of competition between foreign and domestic firms in the domestic market. This is particularly true for those industries in which efficient size firms are so large relative to the domestic market that there are only a few firms in each country.

Automobile production is a case in point. . . . The industry is dominated in most countries by two firms—Italy and Germany representing the extremes with one firm, and three firms, respectively.

In the absence of international trade, the industry would be highly concentrated in every producing country. Alternatively, with liberal trade in automobiles . . . seven [industrial] countries approximate one large market. . . .

Important sources of inefficiency in protected oligopolistic industries often include—besides artificially high prices—sluggish responses to changes in consumer preferences and the use of outmoded production methods, the few sheltered firms adopting a "live and let live" or "don't rock the boat" attitude. By providing increased competition, trade liberalization will force such firms to abandon complacent attitudes and adopt efficient production technology. It is also likely to stimulate a search for *new* technologically superior processes. Both considerations point to a positive correlation between the degree of exposure to world market competition and the rate of technological progress in export and import-competing industries.

Central to this discussion is the extent to which it is necessary to make a trade-off between competition and efficient scales of operation. Faced with industries whose minimum efficient size firms are large relative to the domestic economy, a country whose domestic market is largely insulated from the world market must choose between attempting to control concentrated oligopolies operating a small number of efficient scale plants, and the use of anti-trust policies to enforce competition among several firms operating sub-optimal scale production facilities. By supporting and participating in continuing trade liberalization, such a country can progressively reduce the need to choose the "least bad" of the two alternatives as far as the import-competing industries are concerned, eventually reaching a level of openness that permits the simultaneous attainment of all of the advantages of competition and of efficient scales of operation. The usefulness of trade liberalization as an anti-trust device is limited because it directly affects only import-competing industries, but it clearly is a valuable auxiliary policy in the effort to reduce the extent and use of market power.

Contribution to Domestic Price Stability

Although it is now widely accepted that inflation is fundamentally a monetary problem requiring a monetary solution, trade liberalization can be a very useful adjunct to the basic policy package. To begin with, the lower (than otherwise) prices will have a one-time beneficial effect on the wholesale and consumer prices indices. This was the motivation, for example, behind the unilateral reduction of Australian tariffs in 1973, and the unilateral reduction by the Federal Republic of Germany of tariffs in 1956 and 1957, and the liberalization of import quotas for textiles and clothing in 1973. A similar explanation holds for the decision of several countries to implement the Kennedy Round tariff reductions ahead of schedule.

There is a second effect, related to the benefit from more competition, which is lasting and much more important. Efforts to control inflation, particularly in recent years, have frequently been made more difficult by the price and wage behaviour of uncompetitive business and labour groups. It is not unusual, for example, for a government to find itself faced with a painful choice between abandoning its monetary stabilization programme in order to "validate" excessive price and wage settlements, or sticking with the stabilization programme and risking a rise in the unemployment rate. Trade liberalization is an effective way of simultaneously reducing price and wage pressures.[4] In the presence of effective competition from foreign producers, and a credible commitment by the government not to return to the previous (higher) level of protection, there will be a parallel restraint on both prices and wages, the restraint on one being more tolerable because the other is also under restraint. Both the chronic nature of the current inflation and the priority attached to controlling it give this particular benefit of trade liberalization a special significance in the present situation.

2. EVALUATION OF ARGUMENTS AGAINST FURTHER REDUCTIONS IN TRADE BARRIERS

A failure to keep in mind the benefits that accompany increased international specialization explains only a part of the simultaneous decline in support for further trade liberalization and increase in protectionist pressures. The active element in this shift in opinion is provided by arguments which stress various potential disadvantages of moves toward freer trade. The purpose of this section is to examine briefly the more common arguments against further trade liberalization. In slightly altered form the same points are mentioned frequently by those who argue for increased restrictions.

The decline in interest in trade liberalization owes little to the traditional "terms of trade" and "infant industry" arguments for protection. The terms of trade motivation is minor, in part because reciprocal reductions in barriers—to the extent that they have any lasting terms of trade effects—are likely to result in offsetting gains and losses for each participating country, and in part because single-country market power usually is in the hands of sellers rather than buyers, which means that export restrictions are the preferred terms of trade device. The infant industry argument has played a similar minor role in recent developments. Its use during the postwar period has been confined mostly to the developing countries, and if any change has occurred in recent years, it has probably been in the direction of a reduced reliance on this argument as a justification for widespread protection.[5]. . .

Domestic Income Distribution Effects

[One argument that has an important negative impact on attitudes toward greater trade liberalization] centres on the potential income effects of [such] liberalization. Since the overall effect of [trade] liberalization is an unobjectionable increase in aggregate national income, the explanation of this source of opposition must lie in the existence of differential income effects between various groups within the economy.[6] Two such differential effects are possible: (i) the adjustments set in motion by trade liberalization may involve temporarily lower earnings and other transitional adjustments costs for some of the labour and capital employed in the affected import-competing firms; or (ii) a permanent redistribution of income between various domestic groups.

When opponents of trade liberalization discuss transitional income effects, the word "transitional" is seldom used, and the analysis frequently involves the implicit assumption that workers who are displaced by increased imports will remain unemployed forever. Apart from the obvious point that such unemployment need only be temporary—for example, the export industries will be expanding simultaneously—there are various factors which serve to reduce the extent to which people who are currently employed in the affected industries become involuntarily unemployed. They include the standard practice of staging the reductions in barriers over a number of years (five annual reductions of 20 percent for the Kennedy Round tariff cuts), thereby allowing natural attrition of labour and routine depreciation of capital equipment to play a major role in the adjustment; if the domestic demand for a commodity is expanding, an increase in both the absolute and relative importance of imports is compatible with a stable—even growing—level of domestic production; and, to the extent that trade liberalization stimulates specialization within an industry and a subsequent increase in both imports and exports of the industry's products, the need for geographic and occupational mobility is reduced.

While these factors will mitigate the extent of the involuntary unemployment in the import-competing sector, it is unlikely that they will eliminate it entirely. The appropriate policy for dealing with any such remaining transitional unemployment is the provision of adjustment assistance: that is, the distribution of government funds to compensate those who suffer transitional declines in income, and to help cover the costs to workers of searching for new employment opportunities and (if necessary) moving and/or retraining.

Programmes of adjustment assistance already exist in some countries. In the United States, for example, the 1974 Trade Act established a new adjustment assistance programme with a basic benefit of 70 per cent of salary to be paid for a maximum of 52 weeks (78 weeks for workers over 60 years of age, and those enrolled in a training programme), plus counselling, a relocation allowance, and a job search allowance. A recent evaluation of this programme offers some insight into the question of the duration of transitional unemployment associated with increased competition from imports. Statistics for the period April 1975 through September 1976 reveal that the average benefit check was for a 30 week period. That is, the average period of unemployment for workers who became involuntarily unemployed because of increased imports, in the midst of the worst recession in 40 years, was 30 weeks (well within the benefit period). This is not a description of a situation in which trade liberalization leads to chronic unemployment problems.

Granting all of these considerations, there is still the fact that some people, usually older workers, will be permanently hurt by trade liberalization. However, a concern for their interests is not a good argument against liberalization. Such workers represent a very small group, while the gain to society as a whole from reduced trade barriers is large. Sharing that gain is better than foregoing it.

There is an important distinction to be made between the number of people in the import-competing industries who become involuntarily unemployed as a result of trade liberalization, and the impact of liberalization on the overall level of unemployment. As far as the latter is concerned, there is no reason to expect liberalization to have an important effect on the level of aggregate unemployment since the expanding export sector will be withdrawing people from the ranks of the unemployed at the same time as some workers from import-competing industries are joining those ranks.[7] This does not mean that the export industries will hire the people released by the import-competing industries—for example, their skills may not correspond to the needs of the export industries, or they may be living in a different part of the country. At any point in time, however, there is always some unemployment, if only frictional. The expansion of the export industries would draw on workers frictionally unemployed, new entrants to the labour force, and others who are unemployed for reasons unconnected with trade liberalization. In this sense unemployment can be said to be "fungible."

The newly created jobs in the export industry generally are higher-income jobs. When this additional income is spent, it creates still more employment opportunities into which most of the workers released from the import-competing industries will be eventually absorbed. It is in this way that liberalization increases efficiency and raises national income.

One of the most serious problems facing trade liberalization, especially during periods of economic slack, is that the *existing jobs* in the import-competing industries are occupied by people who know their jobs are threatened, whereas the identities ("names and addresses") of the workers who would fill the *new jobs* created by trade liberalization in the export sector and elsewhere are largely unknown. There tends, therefore, to be an asymmetry in the attitude of workers as a group towards liberaliza- tion, even though the net impact on the overall level of unemployment is likely to be negligible. Nor are the problems which this creates for policy makers limited to periods of above-average unemployment.

Another important asymmetry which also works against efforts to promote trade liberalization, arises from the fact that the benefits from trade liberalization are spread over the general population, whereas the transitional adjustment costs are focused on certain groups of workers and owners of capital in the affected import-competing industries. Suppose, for example, that a reduction in a certain trade restriction would benefit each of 10 million consumers by an average of $14 (for a total gain of $140 million), while the same reduction would impose transitional adjustments costs totalling $35 million on six firms employing a total of 5,000 people.[8] Three important conclusions follow. First, the reduction in the trade bar- rier clearly is in the national interest because there is a net increase in national material welfare of $105 million. (If the public feels concern for the threatened workers and owners, the appropriate response is to reduce the import restriction and to introduce an adjustment assistance pro- gramme in order to transfer to the affected workers and owners $35 million—or more—of the $140 million benefit received by consumers.) Second, it is unlikely that many individual consumers will bother to incur the expense (time and money) of becoming informed on this issue, and the expense of "lobbying" for the reduction in the import barrier, because they correctly anticipate that these costs are likely to exceed the potential indi- vidual benefit ($14 in this example). Third, the "per employee" and "per owner" transitional adjustment costs in the import competing industry are large enough that it pays individually for them to be informed and to bring pressure to bear on politicians and policy makers not to reduce the import restriction. In summary, since the information and effort required to influence government policy making have a cost, a simple cost-benefit ap- proach is sufficient to explain why threatened import-competing industries do most of the lobbying in the commercial policy area, and why countries often forego liberalization, or raise trade barriers, even though it is clear that such actions reduce national economic welfare. . . .

These findings are significant and worth reemphasizing, for the ex- istence of two such important asymmetries between the general benefits available from trade liberalization and the extent of public pressure for liberalization—each the product of an incentive system which is biased against trade liberalization as far as the generation of direct political sup- port is concerned—goes a long way towards explaining much of the cur- rent malaise in the area of international commercial policy. It is clearly a situation which calls for considerable statesmanship at both the national and international levels.

Finally, it is useful to note that while there is a good deal of discussion of the "costs of adjustment," very little is heard regarding the "costs of not adjusting." Although in essence this involves nothing more than a reminder of the gains from liberalizing trade, looking at the issue from this angle does serve to emphasize that a decision to forego trade liberalization is not a decision to avoid costs, but rather a decision to substitute one kind of cost for another. . . .

The second category of income effects includes all of the permanent income redistribution effects—that is, the redistribution effects that are expected to persist once the economy has completed the transitional adjustments. To the extent that such issues enter into commercial policy decisions, the main interest is in the redistribution of income between various domestic groups of consumers and producers which was brought about by trade restrictions and which would be reversed or "undone" by trade liberalization. For example, protection of the agricultural sector raises food prices and transfers income from food buyers to owners of agricultural land. Since lower income groups spend a relatively larger share of their income on food, this amounts to a regressive consumption tax, the proceeds of which go to the landowners. In a similar way, protection of domestic producers from the competition of imports of such items as low cost textiles and inexpensive shoes involves taxing the income groups that consume these items in order to maintain wages and profits of domestic producers at artificially high levels.[9]

When the production either of exports or of import-competing goods is geographically concentrated within a country, international commercial policy is sometimes seen as a device for influencing the interregional distribution of income. For owners of capital assets that are specific to the affected industry, income effects associated with changes in domestic and foreign trade restrictions are long-run effects. Obvious examples include owners of agricultural land and mines, as well as capital equipment which has no alternative use and which cannot be fully depreciated ("written off") during the period over which the reductions in barriers are staged. Alternatively, such inter-regional income effects are short-to-intermediate-run effects for labour and for owners of capital assets which are occupationally or geographically mobile.

Although it is difficult to generalize regarding the relative importance in commercial policy making of the two types of income effects—the transitional effects and the permanent redistribution effects—casual observation suggests that with the exception of distributional issues between agricultural and non-agricultural interests, concern with the transitional income effects of trade liberalization dominates. In any case, neither type of income effect offers a convincing basis for opposing trade liberalization. The transitional effects can be covered by adjustment assistance, and there are more efficient methods for achieving permanent redistribution effects, . . . assuming of course that such effects are in the national interest. . . .

Excessive Dependence on Imports

A concern about excessive dependence on foreign supplies of key products is [another] reason put forward by those who question the wisdom of further trade liberalization. While in the past such a concern was considered part of the traditional "national defence" argument for (selective) protection, events of the last few years—including the petroleum embargo of late 1973, and the more general worry over the future adequacy of world supplies of many basic commodities—have given rise to a peace-time version of that traditional argument. In its most specific form, this view stresses that the larger the share of imports in total domestic consumption of a product, the greater is the country's exposure to possible embargoes and the actions of producer cartels.

Space limitations preclude a detailed discussion of the complex decisions involved in situations in which there is a risk of embargoes. . . . However, in addition to a general observation regarding the difficulties of enforcing a selective embargo during peace-time, there is a point regarding stockpiling that is worth mentioning. When an important commodity is simply not available (that is, not "producible") domestically, a country worried about a possible embargo has only the option of stockpiling. This alternative, however, is equally applicable to a situation in which the choice is between protecting a high-cost domestic source, or buying cheaply on the world market. As long as the good is storable,[10] a country can stockpile enough to cover its needs either during the anticipated duration of a disruption, or during the length of time required to establish or resurrect the domestic industry in the event that foreign supplies were threatened. The necessary calculation involves a comparison of stockpiling costs with the cost of permanently protecting a comparison of stockpiling costs with the cost of permanently protecting an inefficient domestic industry, and it is plausible to assume that in many instances stockpiles plus reduced trade barriers would be less costly than continued high levels of protection.

As for the issue of the degree of exposure to the actions of producers' cartels, this is not worrisome unless cartel action is a serious possibility for a range of tradeable goods. Despite considerable rhetoric to the contrary, this does not appear to be the case, and in the great majority of situations a fear of international producer cartels is an inappropriate rationale for protecting high-cost domestic industries. Three comments may be made in this connexion. First, the prospects for effective permanent or even semi-permanent cartelization of the world market for any major commodity other than petroleum appear rather limited. . . . Second, there is the fact that a key requirement for a successful international cartel is that the number of actual *and potential* producers is small. But the fewer producers there are, the smaller will be the number of countries who have the option of producing the good domestically. That is, if there is a good chance of organizing a successful cartel, the situation by definition is one in which few if any non-members will have the option of producing the commodity domestically (cartels also tend to set prices at a level that makes production in non-members uneconomical). A third point concerns the potential for widespread misuse of this argument. Modern economies are complex, and there are a large number of products that could be considered crucial to their smooth functioning, which means that virtually any domestic industry of any consequence that is having trouble with foreign competitors can lobby for self-benefiting protection on the grounds that the smooth functioning of the home economy should not be left to the "whims of foreign cartels."

The "trade dependence" issue occasionally extends beyond a specific worry about monopolistic foreign suppliers of particular commodities, or of being isolated during wartime, to stress that any increase in the share of foreign trade in national income makes a country more "dependent." The use of this adjective, with its obvious negative connotation, to characterize the result of increases in international specialization is unfortunate and misleading. For an individual household to be truly independent would require that it produce all of the goods and services that its members consume. As soon as any specialization in production occurs, we become "dependent" on others. In fact, all of us, city dweller and rural farmer alike, are almost totally dependent on others for virtually everything we consume.

The only concern in these circumstances should be that the supplies of what we consume be as decentralized and competitive as possible so as to minimize the chances of the suppliers artificially reducing or interrupting the flows of goods or services. (There is a parallel here with the general proposition that a diversified portfolio minimizes the risk of investment loss.) But this guiding principle says nothing about the import component of those supplies. It is concerned with the "condition" of supplies, not with their geographic origin. And, as we have seen, trade liberalization is an effective way of insuring that the supplies of many goods and services to households (and firms) are decentralized and competitive.

Protecting a National "Way of Life"

Among the non-economic arguments, one invoked by those who question or oppose further trade liberalization, is that increased openness to foreign trade will threaten a desirable national way of life. This argument has a strong political/philosophical orientation and a very long tradition:

> It was held by Plato and other Greek philosophers that foreign trade was in itself to be regarded as inimical to the atmosphere of the ideal state. The austerity of the alleged self-sufficiency of Sparta was contrasted favourably with the cosmopolitan atmosphere of Athens, whose prosperity depended on foreign trade. (Robbins, 1939, page 111.)

Assuming that a decision to opt for less openness in order to protect a traditional way of life reflected a true national consensus—and not the interests of a small elite who either are wealthy enough to ignore the cost in terms of a lower national income, or who see increased openness to foreign trade as a threat to their own privileges and prerogatives—then restrictions on trade would be justified.[11]

A post-World War II variant of the "way of life" argument is, in many ways, the exact opposite of the traditional version. Whereas the latter generally stresses the virtue of preserving a quiet semi-rural or pastoral lifestyle, the new variant stresses the advantages of having a large industrial sector. In this instance, the concern is that openness to world markets will result in an undesirably small industrial sector. This argument, which differs from the infant industry and import-substitution arguments in that it explicitly recognizes that the larger industrial sector is being purchased at some sacrifice of national income, is open to the same criticism as most of the other arguments for protection—namely, that the first-best policy is a government subsidy to domestic industrial production, not restrictions on trade. This follows from the fact that the goal is not reduced openness *per se,* but a larger industrial sector.

3. SUMMARY

Two main themes emerge from this review of the case for further trade liberalization. First, there are the accompanying benefits, primarily gains to national income and economic growth achieved through a more efficient use of a nation's labour, capital, and land. To these must be added the fringe or auxiliary benefits in the areas of competition policy and inflation control.

The second theme draws on an important development in the modern literature on international commercial policy. Central to this advance is the simple proposition that if a country's economy has a problem, the alternative corrective policies can be ranked according to their efficiency in solving it. . . . For commercial policy the major finding is that, with the exception of situations involving terms of trade or "conserving a way of life" considerations, a restriction on the flow of goods and services between countries is not the best policy.

As Corden stresses in his recent book, *"the link between the case for free trade and the case for laissez-faire has been broken"* (1974, page 4, emphasis in the original). H. G. Johnson (1976, p. 189) adds:

> . . . given the existence of a situation requiring intervention of some kind, there are many policy options available and generally (but not always) the best policy does not involve intervention in the freedom of *international* trade as such. The general implications of this theme are obvious—a shift of attention from commercial policy and a focus on *laisser-faire*-versus-intervention to a focus on optimal policy-making as such, with trade-

policy intervention issues appearing at a secondary, tertiary, or still lower level of policy analysis.

This general theme recurs several times above, for example in the arguments that trade restrictions are an inefficient (and ultimately ineffective) method of reducing unemployment, an inefficient (and often inequitable) way of affecting the distribution of national income, and an inefficient (and probably counter-productive) method of reducing macroeconomic instability.

Later, in the same paper (p. 194), Johnson summarizes the point succinctly:

> The current theory of protection leads to only one, rather aseptic, conclusion: that tariffs and similar devices are very unlikely to constitute first-best policies for anything that is thought to require a policy in the first place.

Combining this with the knowledge of the income gains that come with reductions in trade barriers, we arrive at the modern case for further trade liberalization.

Notes

1. . . . It is true that import restrictions may offer some *short-run* help with unemployment problems, provided there is no retaliation. But the "no retaliation" assumption clearly is unrealistic, especially in circumstances in which many countries are experiencing above-average levels of unemployment.
2. If there is freedom of entry and freedom of transaction, the threat of potential competition will insure that the exporting, importing and retailing activities are competitive, even if there are only a few firms actually in the business. This also holds for the foreign producers, except in the case of "natural monopolies" in industries in which the optimum size firm/plant is very large relative to the market. . . .
3. The "freedom of transaction" question often is a serious problem when imports are restricted by a formal or informal quota rather than by a tariff. There are, briefly, three ways of organizing an import quota system: first-come first-served until the quota is filled; the auctioning off of licences to domestic or foreign residents; and government allocation of licences or *de facto* permits to existing importers or foreign producers/exporters, usually on the basis of historical market shares. The first two methods preserve freedom of entry and freedom of transaction because any individual can participate. This is not true of the third method, which is by far the most frequently used of the three. The practice of formally or informally tying quota licences to particular importers or foreign exporters/producers, especially when a relatively small number of firms is involved, greatly facilitates collusion and monopolistic behaviour because newcomers are excluded by virtue of being unable to obtain a licence. . . .
4. Although this approach works directly only on the import-competing industries, there are likely to be indirect beneficial effects in other sectors. More specifically, price and wage behaviour in the export industries already is moderated by the desire to remain competitive in foreign markets. By adding the import-competing industries to the list of those whose temptation to exploit market power is restrained by foreign competition, the government will gain additional political support for its efforts to control such behaviour in those industries that are involved only in the domestic market (that is, the "home goods" or "non-tradeable goods" industries).

5. A limited exception to this generalization regarding reduced reliance on the infant industry argument, is the current use of the argument in *industrial* countries as a rationale for advocating protection of "advanced technology" industries. . . .

6. In most countries import duties are no longer an important source of government revenue. For those countries that still depend heavily on this method of collecting revenue, an analysis of the implications of trade liberalization would have to allow for the costs and/or benefits of alternative sources of tax revenue and/or reduced government expenditures. . . .

7. A point that is not widely appreciated is that the higher the unemployment rate, the more likely it is that the expanding export industries will be able to locate idle workers with the desired skills, and therefore the smaller will be the net impact of trade liberalization on the overall level of unemployment (that is, the easier it is for the export industries to locate idle people with the necessary skills, the more likely it is that they will be withdrawing people from the ranks of the unemployed at the same rate as people from the import-competing industries are joining those ranks). Another point that goes against the popular wisdom that trade liberalization must be reserved for periods of economic prosperity is the fact that the United States Reciprocal Trade Agreements Act was passed in 1934, virtually at the bottom of the Great Depression.

8. Since the benefits and costs are flows — the former into perpetuity, the latter over the adjustment period — the figures in the example are hypothetical discounted present values.

9. To the extent that labour is more mobile than capital assets, the chief function of protection is to maintain the private value of the capital assets at a level in excess of their true social value — that is, at a value in excess of what their value would be if the output were priced at world market prices.

   To say that wages and profits in protected industries are artificially high does *not* imply that they are higher than the national average; in fact, if the economy is reasonably competitive, wages (adjusted for skill differences) and profits are likely to be in the vicinity of the national average; they are, nonetheless, artificially high relative to what they would be *in that industry* in the absence of protection. Put somewhat differently, by taxing consumers through artificially high prices, protection allows labour and capital in an inefficient industry to earn a wage or rate of return equal to that in the efficient sectors of the economy (the national average wage and rate of return being, of course, lower than they would be if the labour and capital currently in the inefficient industries were in efficient industries instead).

10. "Storable" does not mean storable forever. Many perishable goods can be stockpiled by continuously adding new output to the stockpile and withdrawing older units for current consumption.

11. Of all of the arguments for protection considered in this paper, the "way of life" argument is the only one for which trade restrictions is the first best policy. . . . The reason is that it is the only one which views the level of imports *per se* — and not, for example, the level of output of import-competing industries — as the policy target; all of the others consider import restrictions as a device for avoiding or minimizing some other problem.

9

Imports and Consumer Prices: A Survey Analysis

William R. Cline

INTRODUCTION

It is a critical time for public policy on imports. In recent years there have been several protectionist actions. The United States has negotiated voluntary quotas on imports of shoes from Korea and Taiwan, on color television sets from Japan, and on specialty steel. The administration has implemented a program of trigger prices for steel that, in effect, limits steel imports (though not as severely as alternative measures might have done). The United States has renewed bilateral agreements on import quotas for textile products under the MultiFibers Arrangement, restricting imports from 18 principal supplying countries. Moreover, there are calls for much·more extensive protection against imports. Largely the result of high unemployment stemming from the worst recession since the 1930s (in 1974–1975), these protectionist forces may derive additional support from concerns about the sharp decline of the dollar and the large trade balance deficits experienced in 1977 and 1978.

Yet there is another economic problem that is paramount for the country: inflation. For several months in 1978 the consumer price index accelerated to annual inflation rates on the order of 10 percent. The administration's program of wage and price guidelines, and its package of measures announced on November 1, 1978, to deal with the declining dollar and inflation (including an increase in the discount rate by a full percentage point) are ample evidence that at this juncture inflation is the country's number one problem.

Imports play a vital role in fighting inflation. This study seeks to examine, perhaps more rigorously than ever before, one aspect of that anti-inflation role: the extent to which imports provide a savings to consumers by making available products at prices below those of comparable domestic products. To the extent that imports do restrain inflation, the calls for increased protection directly jeopardize the prospects for dealing with

From William R. Cline, *Imports and Consumer Prices: A Survey Analysis* (Washington, D.C.: American Retail Federation, 1979); published in abbreviated form in *Journal of Retailing* 55 (1), Spring 1979, pp. 3–24. Reprinted by permission. Some tables and some footnotes omitted.

the most serious economic problem, inflation. Protection would aggravate inflation in two ways. First, by reducing the availability of cheaper imported goods (if they are cheaper—the main subject of this study) increased protection would cause a shift to more costly domestic supply. Second, by limiting the availability of total supply, protection would lead to an indirect rise in prices, as domestic firms raised their prices and consumers paid more in order to reach a new equilibrium between smaller supply and, therefore, smaller demand (which could only be reduced by the discouragement to consumption coming from higher prices).

Some advocates of higher protection maintain that imports do not restrain inflation because retailers do not pass on to consumers the savings available from imported products, but pocket large profits instead. As evidence these critics cite a recent study by the Library of Congress that implied that retail stores charge higher markups on imports than on domestic products.[1]

These critics miss a major point about the inflation-retarding role of imports. Even if imports are sold to consumers at prices identical to those of domestic products, the very presence of imports causes the prices for domestic goods to be lower than they otherwise would be. For products with monopolistic tendencies, imports provide a source of competition that restrains prices domestic firms can charge. For products with competitive organization, imports hold down prices simply by virtue of the fact that they raise total supply, causing supply to equate with demand at a lower price (that is, a price where consumers will buy enough more to absorb the added supply).

However, a legitimate empirical question is whether indeed imports are cheaper than domestic products of comparable quality. If they are, then there is a *direct* anti-inflationary contribution of imports in addition to their indirect role of increasing supply.

The purpose of this study is to examine whether imports are cheaper to the consumer than domestic goods of comparable quality. The method applied in the study is that of survey analysis. This study employs a large sample survey of prices for imports and domestic goods. The Survey Research Laboratory of the University of Illinois carried out the survey in retail establishments of all major types and in diverse geographical locations. The survey collected price data on well-specified products, providing the maximum possible assurance that the quality of product was comparable for domestic and imported goods. . . .

. . . To begin with, the sample was large. Approximately 4,300 price observations were collected on 168 specifically identified products. Too often in congressional testimony on import prices one side has produced an assortment of cheap imported sweaters (for example) while the other side has produced its own small collection of import items just as expensive as domestic equivalents. This level of discourse is inadequate to the formulation of public policy. Instead, this study employs a large and scientifically designed sample survey that can provide the basis for a rigorous answer to the question of whether the American consumer receives a direct savings on imported products.

The sample draws from geographically diverse areas, in order to be representative of U.S. consumption. The sample was evenly divided among Los Angeles, Chicago, Philadelphia, and Atlanta.

The products sampled were chosen for their representativeness of consumption and imports. A total of 168 products entered the sample:[2] 41 in footwear, and the remainder in hardgoods. Therefore, the product coverage encompasses the full range of consumer items found in retail stores. The only main consumer products excluded are automobiles, food products, and pharmaceuticals.

Each product was defined in relatively specific terms. . . . The instructions to enumerators were to make the utmost effort at collecting prices only for comparable quality items for the product in question. . . . Because of the detailed specifications assigned to each product, and in view of the instructions to enumerators, it is reasonable to expect that the price observations for imports and domestic products refer to products of comparable quality. Any remaining divergences in quality among observations should be random, and with the large sample taken, that randomness should pose no problem (because there will be enough observations that those erring in one direction will be offset by those erring in the other).

The sample was designed to obtain equal numbers of observations for imports and for domestic products, in order to provide the basis for analysis of the difference between the prices of the two. In particular, for each of the 168 specific products, an attempt was made to obtain, in each of the four cities, 6 observations on domestic goods and 6 observations on imported goods.

The sample design also took into account the type of retail outlet. In each city for each product, an attempt was made to obtain at least one domestic and one import observation from each of the four store types: chain, department, discount, and specialty. In addition, the survey data recorded whether the product was on sale or not. Although the basic analysis below uses the actual transactions price (that is, the sale price if the product was on sale), in the cases of sale items the original price was recorded as well, for the analysis of markdowns.

Finally, the period of the survey, August 1978, was selected after discussion with retail merchandising experts, as a "typical" period for the survey. In particular, the survey was timed to avoid the end of season clearance sales that are common in July. Moreover, summer items were avoided in favor of fall items, in order to avoid leftover stock likely to be on sale. . . .

Weighted Aggregate Results

Table 1 presents the central empirical results of this study. In this table, the relative importance of each product group is taken into account. . . .

The calculations underlying Table 1 follow these steps. First, within Regions A (Europe, Japan, and Canada) and B (Latin America and Asia) separately, the weighted average ratio of import price to domestic price is calculated for the product group in question. For the various hardgoods categories, each individual sample product is weighted in proportion to the value of imports in 1975 . . . for the specific region. Thus, a single figure is obtained for the percentage difference of import price from domestic price for each of the 11 sub-categories of hardgoods, for Region A and Region B separately. For apparel and footwear, the import data are of aggregation that make the use of the entire categories preferable to any attempt to distinguish sub-categories. (In particular, the trade data do not

TABLE 1

Percentage Difference of Import Price from Domestic Price[a]

Product Group	Imports from Europe, Japan, Canada (Region A)	Imports from Latin America, Asia (Region B)	All imports
I. Apparel	+ 4.3%	−11.6%	− 8.7%
II. Footwear	+19.9%	−23.5%	−11.5%
III. Hardgoods			
Watches, clocks	+74.4%	−13.8%	+31.2%
Tools	−30.4%	−25.8%	−29.9%
Recreational goods	+12.5%	−34.1%	− 4.9%
Small appliances	+ 8.7%	− 9.1%	+ 7.8%
Typewriters, calculators	−27.6%	−27.2%	−27.6%
Housewares	−15.6%	−29.9%	−19.4%
Radio, TV, stereo	−30.0%	−30.2%	−30.0%
Photographic equipment	+ 8.9%	−26.4%	+ 6.0%
Furniture	−10.4%	+ 1.8%	− 8.5%
Floor, wall coverings	−14.1%	n.a.	−14.1%
Miscellaneous	+ 1.0%	−19.9%	− 7.8%
Subtotal, hardgoods	− 5.4%	−23.7%	−11.8%
All Products	− 0.4%	−16.3%	−10.8%

[a]Within regions, weighting is proportional to the value of imports by product group. . . . Weights between regions for individual product groups are proportional to quantity of imports, determined from relative import values as adjusted by relative price from each region. For footwear, weights between regions are based directly on 1977 data for number of pairs imported (International Trade Commission data).

divide by the categories "men's, women's, boys', and girls'.") Because of the large number of products in each of these broad categories (52 for apparel, 41 for footwear), and because of the frequent occurrence of products with an extremely small number of observations from the region in question, it was necessary to weight each product by the number of import observations for apparel and footwear.[3]

The first two columns of Table 1 report the results of these calculations for Regions A and B separately. As shown in the table, imports from Region B are systematically cheaper than domestic supply. These imports from developing countries are cheaper by approximately 12 percent for apparel, 24 percent for footwear, and 24 percent for hardgoods. (The weighted average figure for all hardgoods uses the import value for each sub-category as the basis for weighting.) Imports for Region A are slightly more expensive than domestic supply in apparel (4 percent) and in footwear (20 percent). These results suggest the influence of fashion and brand attraction in these softgoods. In hardgoods, by contrast, even the imports from Region A are cheaper than domestic supply. Here, certain subsectors are especially important to the overall result. In the category for radios, televisions, and stereos, in particular, imports from Region A are 30 percent cheaper than domestic supply, and this category accounts for 25 percent of the value of hardgoods imports from Region A. . . . The only hardgoods categories where there appears to be a premium for taste or fashion for imports from Region A are watches and clocks, and photographic equipment.

At the aggregate level, imports from Region A are almost identical in price to domestic products. The savings on imported hardgoods are offset by premiums on imports of apparel and shoes from these industrial countries. From Region B, by contrast, aggregate imports are much cheaper than domestic supply, costing 16 percent less (average based on import value weights).

In order to arrive at a final evaluation of the relative price of imports, it is necessary to aggregate imports from both Regions A and B. The procedure followed in Table 1 does so while retaining the valuable information about the different relative prices for the two regions. The final column of the table is a weighted average difference of import price from domestic price. The weights as between Regions A and B for each product group are quantity weights. For footwear, these quantity weights are available directly from 1977 data on the number of pairs imported from each region.[4] For the other product categories, the content is too heterogeneous to make weighting for observed "units" meaningful. Therefore the quantity weights are derived indirectly. The import values . . . are used as the basis for the weights, but only after "deflating" the import value for Region A by the relative price of Region A goods compared to Region B goods as implied by the first two columns of Table 1. These "deflated" values then provide the basis for quantity weights to obtain the weighted average import price relative to domestic price (final column, Table 1).

The aggregate results shown in the final column of Table 1 show that overall imports are indeed cheaper than domestic supply. Imports are cheaper in each of the three broad categories: apparel, footwear, and hardgoods. Moreover, imports are cheaper than domestic supply by a considerable degree: approximately 9 percent for apparel, 12 percent for footwear, and 12 percent for hardgoods. A final aggregate price comparison is obtained by weighting each of the three broad product categories in proportion to total imports. . . . This final aggregate estimate finds that *overall imports are 10.8 percent cheaper than domestic products.*

The crucial role of supply from developing countries in this aggregate result deserves highlighting. The aggregate result for Region A alone shows imports almost identical in price to domestic products. It is the large saving on import from developing countries (Region B) that derives the final result whereby aggregate imports are approximately 11 percent cheaper than domestic supply.

Table 1 also may shed light on the role of protective quotas as opposed to such influences as taste and brand identification. In the sectors of apparel and footwear, U.S. imports from Region B are subject to severe quota controls. In both of these sectors, Region A supply is considerably more expensive than supply from Region B (by 18 percent and 57 percent, respectively). In the sector of radios, television sets, and stereos, by contrast, the principal U.S. quota restriction is against imports of color television sets from Japan, in Region A. And in this sector, supply from Region A is just as cheap as supply from Region B—both being 30 percent cheaper than domestic supply. These patterns suggest that the presence of quotas facilitates the charging of higher prices by the suppliers not subject to the quotas. In clothing and footwear, the restraint on lower cost supply from developing countries appears to facilitate the charging of high prices by European and Japanese suppliers. In the case of television sets, limits on low-cost imports facilitate the charging of high prices from the main alternative supplier—domestic U.S. production—leading to a wide price difference between domestic and imported supply. These patterns imply that loosening up these quotas would provide savings to the American consumer by permitting a larger shift from more expensive domestic supply to cheaper imports (in the case of television sets) and from expensive domestic, European, and Japanese supply to cheaper supply from developing countries, in the case of apparel and footwear.

Savings to the Consumer

The results presented in Table 1 may be used to estimate the total annual savings to the American consumer made possible by the availability of imports. These savings arise because, unit for unit and holding quality constant insofar as possible, imports are found to be cheaper than domestic production. The present flow of imports therefore provides a direct savings to the consumer; if the consumer had to shift entirely to domestic supply he would lose on each unit shifted because of the higher price for domestic supply. And of course if imports were abolished there would be an enormous additional *indirect* cost to consumers, because domestic prices would not stay fixed (or even continue inflating at their previous rate) but would rise to close the gap caused by the decrease in total supply as imports ceased. The estimate here concentrates solely on the *direct* consumer savings from imports, not the additional indirect savings represented by the fact that domestic prices would be even higher in the absence of imports.

In order to estimate the direct savings to American consumers made possible by imports, it is first necessary to consider the amount they spend currently on imported goods. In the first half of 1978, total retail sales by general merchandise, apparel and furniture firms amounted to $83.3 billion,[5] so that total retail sales for 1978 may be estimated as approximately $167 billion. This figure corresponds approximately to the total sales of stores in the universe of retail firms handling merchandise of the type examined in this study: essentially, manufactured consumer goods excluding automobiles and food. On the basis of information from the retail trade industry, the share of imports in total retail sales is approximately eleven percent. Therefore, total retail sales of imported merchandise amount to an estimated $18.4 billion for 1978. The calculations of Table 1 showed that imports cost the consumer 10.8 percent less than domestic supply. Therefore, if consumers had to rely on domestic supply alone, they would have to pay 12 percent higher prices[6] for each unit previously imported (the *direct* effect, excluding indirect effects of an induced rise in the price of domestic goods). Applying this 12 percent figure to the base $18.3 billion spent on consumer imports in 1978, the resulting estimate is that *American consumers save $2.2 billion annually by obtaining imported goods at prices below those of domestic goods. . . .*

Notes

1. U.S. House of Representatives, Committee on Ways and Means, *Library of Congress Study on Imports and Consumer Prices* (Washington, D.C.: U.S. Government Printing Office, 1977).
2. Because there were too few observations available for some of these products, the surveyors also took observations on "substitute" products. In those cases where the substitutes were very close to the original product, the analysis merges their observations with those for the original product. Otherwise the substitute products are omitted from the analysis. . . .
3. An additional detail of the calculations is that they are not merely the weighted average of the ratio of import to domestic price. That average would be biased upwards; a single ratio could swamp all others, because the upper limit of the ratio is infinity while the lower limit is zero even though the true mean for random variation would be unity. To take this assymetry into account, all cases with the ratio of import price to domestic price greater than unity were first inverted,

then averaged (weighting); then the inverse was taken of this weighted inverse. Then that weighted average was combined with the weighted average of all ratios below unity to obtain the overall price ratio. Thus:

$$R = \sum_i w_i \frac{P_{mi}}{P_{di}} + \frac{1}{\sum_j w_j \frac{P_{dj}}{P_{mj}}}$$

where R is the weighted average ratio of import to domestic price, w is the product weight, P_m and P_d are import and domestic price respectively, and subscript i and j refer to all cases with product price ratio P_m/P_d below and above unity, respectively.

4. According to I.T.C. data, 72.3 percent of the quantity of nonrubber footwear came from Region B in 1977, and 27.7 percent from Region A. International Trade Commission, "Non-Rubber Footwear: U.S. Production, Imports for Consumption, Apparent U.S. Consumption, Employment, Wholesale Price Index, and Consumer Price Index: Fourth Calendar Quarter 1977" (Washington, D.C.: I.T.C., 1978).

5. U.S. Department of Commerce, *Current Business Reports: Monthly Retail Sales and Accounts Receivable,* BR-78-06, June 1978, p. 4.

6. That is, $1.00/(1.00 - 0.108) = 1.12$.

III

Trade Policy Issues for the 1980s

The 1970s were tumultuous times for trade policy. The oil embargo and subsequent very large price increases imposed by the Organization of Petroleum Exporting Countries (OPEC) caused serious economic disruptions from which neither the developed countries nor the non-oil producing developing countries have yet fully recovered. The developing countries launched a drive directed at the advanced industrial nations to achieve a "new international economic order" that entails basic changes in the trade policies followed by the advanced industrial countries. Before finally agreeing upon new codes of good international behavior in the nontariff field as well as a further significant cut in tariffs, negotiators from the 99 countries participating in the GATT-sponsored Tokyo Round of multilateral trade negotiations engaged in much hard bargaining and sometimes bitter debate that threatened harmonious trading relations. Moreover, even while this trade-liberalizing effort was going on, the successful efforts of the newly industrializing countries to penetrate the markets of older industrial economies such as the United States began to generate vigorous demands in the older industrial countries for selective import restrictions. Much of the 1980s will be devoted to dealing with these and the other problems and policies that emerged in the 1970s. But if the past thirty years are any guide to the future, we can also count upon major new and unexpected trade issues to arise.

The selections in Part III focus primarily upon trade policies that we already know will be of concern during the rest of the 1980s. The first selection takes up the call by the developing countries for a New International Economic Order (NIEO)—a set of proposals that involves such actions as establishing international commodity agreements for many primary products, increasing official development assistance on the part of the advanced economies, providing general debt relief to the developing countries, enlarging preferential treatment for imports from developing countries into the markets of the industrial nations, and increasing the flow of technology from developed to developing countries. Views on these proposals range from being highly critical (see the paper by Mordechai Kreinin and J. M. Finger cited in W. M. Corden's bibliographical appendix) to being almost completely supportive (see the Brandt Commission report)[1], but we have selected an essay that comes closer to the mainstream of official reaction in the developed countries.

Corden is sympathetic with the goals of the developing countries, but he is somewhat skeptical about the efficacy of the means they are advocating. For example, he notes that commodity price-stabilization schemes may achieve price stability at the cost of increasing the degree of instability of export earnings. Analyses of previous schemes also seems to indicate, as he points out, that the size of the buffer stocks being proposed are too small to accomplish their price-stabilization objectives. Nevertheless, Corden concludes that it may be worthwhile to try to establish a few additional buffer stock programs. In general, however, he would place more emphasis than the NIEO does upon market-orientated trade and development policies as the best means of stimulating growth.

One NIEO proposal is that the developed countries should further lower their barriers to imports of manufactured goods, especially on those products of particular interest to the developing countries. However, even at current levels of protection, exports of manufactured products from these countries have been increasing at a very rapid rate. Between 1970 and 1977, for example, exports of manufacturers from the developing countries increased at an annual rate of 22 percent, and the developing country share of world exports of manufactures rose from 10.2 percent to 13.1 percent. Moreover, exports were concentrated in labor-intensive product lines such as footwear, textiles, and certain electronics. The resultant pressures for increased protectionism were discussed in the selections of Part II.

An alternative approach to protectionism in dealing with disruptive import competition is to provide adjustment assistance to the affected firms and workers. The selection by George R. Neumann summarizes and evaluates existing policies in the United States and other industrial countries for assisting trade-displaced workers. As Neumann notes, the present U.S. program can be criticized on the grounds that it offers little aid for individuals permanently separated from their jobs. For those who are only temporarily unemployed, the assistance is generally adequate—and in some cases more than adequate in the sense that it encourages workers to remain unemployed. Moreover, the fact that most recipients of adjustment assistance return to their former employers[2] indicates that the program is being used to handle seasonal and cyclical unemployment problems rather than to facilitate the shift of workers to more internationally competitive sectors. Neumann offers various suggestions on how more effectively to carry out the program's purpose. Clearly few tasks on an agenda for the 1980s will be more difficult than devising an adjustment assistance program that meets the legitimate concerns for income distribution yet does not sacrifice the national income benefits of a liberal trade policy.

The paper by Stephen P. Magee is relevant to another important NIEO issue, namely the transfer of technology through multinational corporations to less developed countries. Building upon Vernon's product-cycle theory (see Part I) as well as the works of others (see the list of references at the end of Magee's article), Magee develops a life cycle theory of technology for entire industries that emphasizes the ability of information creators to appropriate the returns from new information as an important determinant of both the structure of industries and the types of knowledge created. One of his interesting conclusions is that multinational corporations and private markets will undersupply simple product technologies and those technologies using unskilled labor because appropriation of the returns from such new technologies is difficult. He then suggests policy measures for stimulating the creation of such much-needed technologies.

No set of readings on trade issues for the 1980s can be complete without a selection covering the real side of the international oil problem. The congressional testimonies by Morris Adelman and Theodore Moran outline the economics of the oil cartel and also touch on the political aspects of relations between OPEC and the oil-importing countries. The message from Adelman—a long-time oil expert who obviously had sharp disagreements with those who directed U.S. oil policy at the time he spoke—is that trying to strike an economic and political deal with the oil-producing governments to assure "adequate" supplies to the consuming nations makes no sense; the oil producers will aim to produce enough oil to maximize their revenues. According to Adelman the only sensible reaction to the cartel by consuming nations is to introduce economic measures such as a tax that is proportional to the price of oil as a means of diverting some of the cartel's revenue to their own treasuries or to institute an import-quota auction system for the purpose of disrupting cartel cohesion.

Moran, whose predictions about the continued rise in oil prices proved quite accurate, also argues that it is increasingly feasible to countervail OPEC's pressures for higher prices because of the need for the cartel members to absorb more and more excess capacity. Besides endorsing Adelman's auction proposal, he recommends a policy that rewards in economic, political, and military terms those members who meet their increased revenue needs by expanding output and penalizes those who try to meet this goal by raising prices. One wonders, however, if the consuming nations possess the degree of unity needed to make these various countervailing actions effective.

One of the bright spots in U.S. export performance is agriculture. Sugar and dairy products are uncompetitive internationally and are heavily protected, but U.S. exports of grains and oilseeds have increased very rapidly in the last ten years. The net export surplus of agricultural trade rose from $7 billion to $15 billion between 1973 and 1979. D. Gale Johnson analyzes the re-emergence of U.S. agriculture as a net export sector in terms of comparative-advantage theory. He concludes that three factors have been important for this change: modifications in our agricultural price-support programs and exchange-rate policies, significant resource adjustments in agriculture, and the introduction of high technology into this field. Moreover, Johnson is optimistic about this sector's future growth, especially if continued progress can be made to reduce the many barriers erected by other countries against our agricultural exports.

The final selection by Robert E. Baldwin summarizes and evaluates the accomplishments of the Tokyo Round of multilateral trade negotiations and suggests areas where further negotiations are needed. The negotiations were successful beyond expectation in achieving agreement on new codes of international conduct with regard to the use by governments of such nontariff measures as export and domestic subsidies, government purchasing policies, product standards, and customs valuation practices. The fact that most developing countries have not signed the codes, however, and the lack of any significant use of the new codes thus far by the industrial signatories raise concerns about whether the codes will become effective arrangements for maintaining a liberal trading order. An encouraging sign, on the other hand, is the negotiating activity that has already begun in the area of services which together with restrictive business practices and state enterprise trade are major areas where further international negotiations are very much needed.

Notes

1. Report of the Independent Commission on International Development Issues (the Brandt Commission Report), North–South: *A Programme for Survival,* (Cambridge, Mass.: The MIT Press, 1980).
2. This relationship has been reconfirmed in a 1978–79 survey of workers receiving aid in 1976 under the United States program. See J. David Richardon, "Trade Adjustment Assistance Under the U.S. Trade Act of 1974: An Analytical Examination and Worker Survey" in Jagdish Bhagwati and T. N. Srinivasan, eds., *Import Competition and Response,* Chicago: University of Chicago Press.

10

The NIEO Proposals: A Cool Look

W. M. Corden

RAISING AND STABILIZING PRICES OF PRIMARY-PRODUCT EXPORTS

Much of the inspiration for the proposals for a "new international economic order" (NIEO) comes from the success of the oil cartel. Surely, it was thought, prices of other commodities exported by developing countries could also be raised by appropriate cartel action. This aim of raising average prices of commodities in real terms is one element in the various NIEO commodity proposals. Sometimes it is associated with the view that there has been a long-term tendency for the terms of trade of developing countries to deteriorate and that it is necessary to reverse this tendency. In fact, there is no clear evidence that there has been any such long-term terms-of-trade trend, even though a belief in it has become widely entrenched.[1] In any case, can prices be raised; and if they could, would it be desirable?

Raising prices cannot just be brought about by a public authority buying up commodities. Eventually there must be production restrictions. Individual countries and groups of them have, of course, practised such policies, notably the European Community in its common agricultural policy. In this case a failure to restrict production sufficiently has led to the need to subsidise exports on a large scale (something that cannot be done for the world as a whole). The only international agreement with export quotas that has lasted for many years is the International Tin Agreement. In the 1960s the International Coffee Agreement succeeded in raising prices. Before World War II there were other agreements, notably the Rubber Agreement. But there are difficulties, and these explain why there are few such agreements and why many have failed in the past.

Criteria for a Successful Cartel

For a cartel to succeed, all potential producers of significant quantities must be members. If existing producers restrict production, new ones that are not members will eventually fill the gap and, finally, the pattern of world production may shift towards the less economic producers. If the

From W. M. Corden, *The NIEO Proposals: A Cool Look*, Thames Essay No. 21 (London: Trade Policy Research Centre, 1979). Reprinted by permission.

cartel is seen as being limited to developing countries, there is the problem that many commodities of export interest to developing countries are produced in developed countries. Cartels have more chance of surviving if they have the support of consuming countries, but the latter can hardly be expected to back schemes over a prolonged period that are intended to have a substantial price-raising effect.

If all producing countries are members of the cartel the pattern of production may become too rigid, the more dynamic producers—those that are more ready to adopt technical improvements—being prevented from expanding and thus losing incentives to make improvements. Even within a given producing country there may be adverse effects. Export restrictions are usually enforced with export quotas or production quotas for individual producers, and the pattern of production is then rigidified, with a bias against potential new producers. But this could be avoided if export taxes were used as the method of restricting exports. The history of the natural rubber industry bears out many of these difficulties. Furthermore, the production of many commodity exports is labour intensive and the labour may be rather immobile. Export restrictions may then create unemployment, at least in the short run.

Finally, the raising of prices will, in time, lead to substitution away from the products concerned, partly through the development of new substitutes. This appears to have happened in the case of tin, and is certainly a danger in the case of rubber and other products where there are synthetic substitutes. The gains to producers are thus likely to be short term and the losses will emerge later. Oil would appear to be somewhat of a special case, although even here a country such as Saudi Arabia, which expects to be an exporter many years hence, needs to take long-term substitution effects into account.

All these issues have been explored at length in the economic literature.[2] The desirability of cartels from the point of view of developing countries cannot be ruled out, but in practice there seems to be limited scope. An attempt to regulate the world market is currently being made in the case of sugar where an agreement was concluded in 1977—but one that the European Community (an important producer) has not joined. It does seem that there are not many products which lend themselves to cartelisation as readily as oil—a very low elasticity of demand in the short and medium run with long lead times required to develop substitutes. Most important, a high proportion of supply needs to come from a few producers—in the case of oil, Saudi Arabia, Iran and the Gulf States, in the case of coffee, Brazil, and for rubber, Malaysia and Indonesia.

Case for Buffer Stocks

When one comes to proposals for *stabilising* commodity prices, as distinct from *raising* them, other issues arise. The basic idea is to establish internationally-managed buffer stocks which will buy and sell particular commodities so as to keep their prices fairly stable around a trend. The trend might still be set by market forces. The main difficulty is for the buffer authority to detect the trend; if it fails to do so it will either accumulate stocks or run out of them. Essentially it must speculate on market forces and, if the buffer stock turns out to be profitable, it will also turn out to be stabilising.

This raises the question of why an internationally or nationally-managed buffer stock authority should be better at detecting trends than private speculators. The view that private speculation is destabilising while public speculation would be stabilising is difficult to support, even though it is widely held and underlies current proposals for commodity price stabilisation. It implies that private speculation is based on foolish views about the future, always tending to exaggerate current trends and subject to sudden changes of expectations. On the other hand, public bodies would be sensible, never tend to move with fashions and would be much better at assessing underlying trends. It is not necessary to show that the "free market" works perfectly to conclude that the people who happen to operate on behalf of governments may be just as wise or foolish as those who work on behalf of private firms. One need not go to the other extreme and suppose that public authorities must always do worse and that private speculation must always be stabilising, with commodity markets necessarily being "efficient."

Adding some public speculators to private speculators may finally make very little difference, or, at least, the nature of the difference may not be easily predictable. Furthermore, to some extent publicly-controlled buffer stocks would replace private speculation. It might also be added that individual governments, just like private firms, are free to build up stocks if they believe that market forces will eventually cause the price to rise. They need not wait on the establishment of an international buffer stock agency.

In the case of an international authority there is the danger that it will be subject to political pressures; and when the initiative has come from the export countries, it is likely to try to keep prices up. It will then accumulate stocks for long periods, eventually having to unload them at a loss as its fund approaches a financial crisis. By trying to hold up prices against a trend it would increase uncertainties and make life harder for private operators in the market. It *ought* to make life easier by making prices more stable, but in practice may make them less certain. Private operators will have to speculate not only about underlying market trends but also about the behaviour of the buffer stock managers and the political forces that will continually press on them.

There are two other difficulties about these buffer stock proposals. First, the stabilising of prices does not necessarily stabilise export earnings. It will do so in the case of those commodities where the sources of price fluctuations come mainly from the demand side. But when instability originates mainly from supply fluctuations, price changes actually help to stabilise earnings. When the harvest falls prices rise and so export income is maintained—how much depending on the elasticity of demand (although it can be shown that when the elasticities of supply and demand are *both* very low, price changes destabilise earnings even when the instability originates from the supply side).

Secondly, analyses of past fluctuations show that very large buffer stocks, involving huge financial investments—considerably larger than envisaged in current proposals—would be required to make a significant impact and avoid price fluctuations of, say, more than 15 percent either side of the trend. The only prolonged post-World War II commodity agreement involving a buffer stock has been the International Tin Agreement, and it has been shown that the tin buffer stock in the past actually made very little difference to the tin price.[3]

When one looks back at the sharp fluctuations in commodity prices of recent years one may feel that surely these could have been avoided, since there were times when private speculators panicked or overshot the mark. It is this very understandable feeling that explains the widespread belief in both developed and developing countries that government-run buffer stocks are desirable. But here it must be remembered that to some extent these fluctuations originated in the public sector. One source of these fluctuations was the instability of aggregate demand in industrial countries, which had a partial origin in instabilities in economic policies and in tendencies for the managers of aggregate demand to go to extremes, to delay adjustments and to fail to recognise trends. Public decision-makers seem as prone to over-shooting policies and to various follies as are private operators. These mistakes are difficult to recognise at the time, but are easy to criticise with hindsight.

In spite of all these doubts and qualifications—which help to explain why so few commodity agreements with buffer stocks have been established in the past—it may be worthwhile trying to establish a few more internationally-controlled or nationally-controlled buffer stocks, and these may do some good. But too much should not be expected from them. They are unlikely to succeed in avoiding major fluctuations in prices. At their best they may succeed in smoothing out short-term fluctuations, rather like a competent central bank can smooth out short-term fluctuations in the exchange rate. At their worst they will try to hold up prices against a trend, borrow to cover losses and eventually have to be bailed out by their sponsoring governments. Undoubtedly the pricing decisions of the managers will be subject to powerful conflicting pressures and it will be impressive if the agreements survive as long as the International Tin Agreement has survived.

Common Fund

The "integrated programme for commodities" proposed by the Secretariat of the United Nations Conference on Trade and Development (UNCTAD) consists essentially of the establishment of a Common Fund of, perhaps, $6,000 million which would finance commodity buffer stocks. The Fund is expected to encourage the negotiation of commodity agreements for the ten to eighteen commodities of export interest to the developing countries.[4] There would still be separate negotiations, arrangements and organisations for each commodity, since each agreement would be autonomous, controlled by the countries directly concerned. But the Fund would play both a catalytic and a financing role. The Fund would obtain equity capital from governments. In addition, it would borrow on the security of the commodity stocks it financed, the borrowing being guaranteed also by the member governments. Existing commodity agreements (the main ones being tin, coffee and cocoa) would be financially assisted, although they would retain their autonomy. The idea of a "Second Window" for the financing of a variety of other measures is also under discussion. The other measures would include storage facilities, diversification programmes, marketing and marketing-related productivity improvements, crop insurance and measures to secure improvements in shipping and transportation facilities.

In fact, the details of what the Common Fund would do and how it would operate have not really been settled yet. The main objective of the Group of 77, as the developing countries in UNCTAD are known, is to get the agreement of the developed countries for its establishment. Negotiations are still in progress. But the establishment of the Fund will, above all, depend on the agreement of the United States, Germany, and Japan, especially the first. These countries did not initially view the idea with enthusiasm, but they seem to be coming round. They, and other industrial countries, agreed "in principle," at the end of the Conference on International Economic Cooperation in Paris in June 1977, to the establishment of a Fund. It, therefore, seems likely that some kind of Common Fund will be established.

For the Group of 77 the Common Fund has become the touchstone of the developed countries' sincerity in wishing to work towards a "new international economic order." An agreement on the Fund is only the first step, however, in what is bound to be a prolonged negotiating process, since for each commodity separate buffer stock negotiations are meant to take place. It must also be added that, even if the United States Administration agrees to the Fund, it will have to run the gauntlet of Congress if there is to be a substantial contribution from the United States.

Congress may be more sympathetic if the Fund's clear objective is to stabilise prices rather than to raise their average levels.

One must welcome the healthy pragmatism that has induced the UNCTAD Secretariat and the Group of 77 to narrow down their initially ambitious ideas about raising commodity prices, stabilising them, indexing them and financing diversification of production to such a specific and limited proposal. Of course, the broader objectives are not dismissed and may be helped by the Common Fund. But at least a practical first-step proposal has come out of all the generalities.

The critics have queried whether a Common Fund is really needed. Why cannot each group of interested countries develop its own commodity agreement and borrow either from the International Monetary Fund (IMF) or on the world's capital markets? In response to this it might be argued that *if* the desirability of buffer stocks is accepted, there does seem to be some case for a central body that will initiate negotiations and help with funding. Furthermore, there may be some economies (though probably small) from the "pooling" aspect of the Fund. To the extent that the various commodity prices do not move in concert—and there have been some very divergent movements in the past because of supply factors and political changes in supplying countries—the Fund may be able to use finance acquired from sales of stocks of one commodity to finance purchases of stocks of another.

The "Second Window" really involves setting up one more aid agency. The sums proposed for it are modest. One question is whether it will have the net result of increasing the total funds for aid provided by the developed countries, or whether it will lead to an equivalent reduction in the money available for the World Bank and for bilateral aid. Clearly, in thinking up these sorts of proposals—as in the case of the link between special drawing rights (SDRs) and aid referred to below—the proponents do rather optimistically believe that it is a way of extracting more aid in total. "Second Window" aid will tend to go to countries for which commodity exports are important. These are not necessarily the most deserving countries. Probably the size of the international bureaucracy will be increased, although a wise policy could avoid this to a great extent by using the World Bank as research advisor and administrative agent for particular aid projects. Much will hinge on how the "Second Window" is run and—more precisely—who is initially appointed to run it.

The idea of the Common Fund has acquired such momentum that something is bound to happen. In the light of the broader issues raised by the NIEO and the deeper problems of economic development it is a small and almost irrelevant proposal. But its defenders would say that something is better than nothing.

OPENING UP MARKETS FOR MANUFACTURED GOODS

The Group of 77 have hoisted their flag to the mast of the Generalised System of Preferences (GSP). This system became effective in the European Community and Japan in 1971 and the United States in 1976. It is shot through with exceptions and limitations so that it has, in fact, made very little difference to the exports of manufactures of developing countries. It has not prevented "voluntary" export restraints and import quotas, and its benefits have been deliberately withheld or restricted in the case of exports from those very countries which are the most successful exporters of manufactures. Extraordinarily, too, it excludes textiles and clothing which account for much of the total exports of manufactures of developing countries. The fault is *not* that of the developing countries but of the various pressure groups in the developed countries.

Towards Freer Trade

Detailed studies have shown that in terms of results the scheme has been a failure because of the exceptions and limitations. The developing countries would apparently benefit much more from a general movement towards freer trade. In fact, they have benefited more from the reduction of tariffs which resulted from the Kennedy Round of multilateral trade negotiations, concluded in 1967, even though they did not participate in those negotiations.[5] Above all, they would benefit from a general attack on non-tariff measures; that is, on import quotas and voluntary export restraints.

The members of the Group of 77 may be wise to put less stress on the GSP and more on general reduction of protection by the developed countries. The developing countries do not need preferences to break into and retain markets for labour-intensive goods in the developed world. They have a natural comparative advantage in this respect. They just need an open and fair go. They need to know that when a market has been broken into, possibly with considerable investment of resources, it will not soon be closed again. One of the limitations of the GSP is that it only applies for ten years. By contrast, reductions in most-favoured-nation (MFN) tariffs resulting from multilateral negotiations, conducted under the auspices of the General Agreement on Tariffs and Trade (GATT), are permanent—apart from the temporary imposition of anti-dumping duties and special "safeguard" arrangements against sudden surges of imports of particular products.

The conclusion follows that the Group of 77 should participate in multilateral trade negotiations, trying to get reductions in tariffs on those goods in which they have a special export interests. This is where they should use all the bargaining power they have. If they are prepared to threaten to restrict supplies of some raw materials, they should use the threats for a good purpose, to open up markets for their goods. It is here that propaganda is needed. They can make common cause not only with consumer interests, and the general tendency towards "consumerism" in the developed countries, but also with those industrial interests which would benefit from those extra exports *to* developing countries that would result if only the latter were able to trade and develop more. Perhaps their most effective allies in the developed countries would be the much maligned multinational enterprises.

A fight on this front seems justified, but it must be admitted that there are tremendous obstacles within the developed countries, especially at a time of recession. The interest groups on the other side are powerful They include the labour unions in the United States. In addition, the interests of different developing countries do not coincide—at least in the short run. The immediate beneficiaries of a general opening-up of markets of the developed countries would be a limited number of developing countries, notably Hong Kong, South Korea, Taiwan, Singapore, India, Brazil, Mexico and Yugoslavia—all countries that have become significant exporters of manufactures, especially of clothing, textiles and footwear. But in time others would benefit.

The idea of working out complicated systems which help the less developed exporters in the developing world as against the more advanced—that is, which handicap Hong Kong, South Korea, Taiwan and India in favour of the beginners in the field—seems, on the surface, appealing. It seems to be a form of infant-industry protection. But such special arrangements reduce the incentives to be successful, since they mean that the open markets may disappear once a country has built up a successful export industry. Furthermore, they provide easy excuses in the industrial countries to give way to pressures from domestic protectionist interests. The more complicated the schemes for freeing trade are, the more they are subject to limitations and "fiddling" of all kinds, and the less they will finally succeed in freeing trade. This is what has happened in the case of the Generalised System of Preferences.

In addition, if tariffs on processed goods in the developed countries were reduced, some countries might export more processed goods and less raw materials, hence creating employment through the extra value added of the processing activity. This benefit could be quite widespread. At present tariffs in developed countries discriminate against such processing.

It may well become recognised in time that the developing countries should hoist their flag to the mast of free or freer trade in manufactures by all developed countries. In the long run they will benefit most if the freeing of trade is non-discriminatory. Once the principle of discrimination and "fiddling" is established it is usually the strong that benefit rather than the weak. It might even pay some of the developing countries to give away something in their own trade restrictions to achieve results.

As for those people in the developed countries who claim to be interested in the welfare of the poor of the developing world, they will have to be taught that "cheap labour" imports ought not to be kept out, and the less they are kept out, the less cheap the labour will get, and the more the poor will benefit. The lesson about cheap labour imports is one that economists have tried to teach for over a hundred years, not with great success. But at least it is a lesson that follows from the pro-market philosophy to which the United States and Germany profess to subscribe.

In view of the increase in restrictions, especially voluntary export restraints, in recent years, pessimism about the prospects for exports of manufactures by developing countries might seem justified. But it must be pointed out that exports of manufactures from developing countries to industrial countries *have* in fact increased a great deal in the last ten years. From 1968 to 1975 they increased more than threefold in value (approximately doubling in real terms). Exports of textiles and clothing increased more than fourfold in value. Severe barriers have been put up against them, especially against exports of textiles and clothing. Nevertheless, the industrial countries have bought an increasing share of their total imports of textiles and clothing from developing countries—from 16 per cent in 1968 to 22 per cent in 1975. But it must be stressed that the share is still quite small. This is true for textiles and clothing, and even more so for exports of manufactures as a whole, where the share was only 7.3 per cent in 1975. There are fifty "dynamic" product lines where the developing countries have been increasing their share of developed-country imports (with another 372 lines where there has been virtually no change), and in this "dynamic" area their share of imports has risen from 11 per cent in 1970 to 17 per cent in 1976.

It is thus quite wrong to think that developing countries have captured the world market for textiles and clothing, let alone for any other major category of manufactures. The share in total consumption of industrial countries, as distinct from imports, is, of course, even smaller. So there is plenty of scope for further expansion. Even with constant shares one would expect the market situation to improve as the industrial countries move out of recession.

The main argument here is that a movement towards free trade by developed countries is in the interests of those developing countries that are, or could become, significant exporters of manufactures. It is not necessary to believe that free trade is the "best" system or that there is "perfect competition" to agree with this view. Furthermore, it does not follow from this particular argument that the developing countries should remove their own restrictions, except insofar as this may be part of a process of bargaining down the restrictions of the developed countries. The focus of this paper is on the interests of the developing countries. Whether particular restrictions are in the interests of the countries that impose them—or of particular interest groups that count politically—is another, and very large, issue. The subject of protection in developing countries will be briefly touched on [in the section discussing the lessons of history].

It might be said that the resistances in the developed countries to opening up their markets are so strong that the cause is hopeless and that, anyway, the developing countries have no bargaining power. But the NIEO is all about power (including the power to withhold commodity supplies), propaganda and political pressure. The issue is whether these weapons are being directed at the right targets.

It is true that many developing countries would not be immediate beneficiaries of more open markets for manufactures. But it is necessary to look ahead. Many of them are potential exporters of labour-intensive manufactures, even if they are not current exporters. This is where their economic future may lie. The less developed among them may in due course become exporters to the more developed, the latter in turn moving gradually into the production of relatively more advanced commodities which are then exported to developed countries as well as being absorbed within the developing world.

REDUCING DEBT AND IMPROVING THE INTERNATIONAL FINANCIAL SYSTEM

The NIEO proposals include various ideas in the financial field. Some have been pushed hard at international discussions while others have only been "floated." Some are concerned with problems that are clearly temporary, while others are not likely to be successful. The lack of prospect of some of these proposals is being gradually realised, as experienced officials in many developing countries always realised.

Special Drawing Rights

A long-standing proposal is that there should be a link between aid to developing countries and the creation of international liquidity through SDRs ("paper gold"). This has been seen as one way of extracting aid finance from developed countries. There is little point in going over the many arguments here, since it has been done so often.[6] Perhaps it is enough to say that the proposal has been firmly rejected by the principal financial nations, notably the United States and Germany. Furthermore, SDRs seem to have little future. They are unimportant in the international financial system, so that, even if there were a link, SDRs would not yield much aid. At present SDRs account for about 3 per cent of total world liquidity.

SDRs were invented at about the same time as there was an explosion of international liquidity in terms of dollars. After the initial small SDR allocation, the world has certainly not chosen to add to the flood of international liquidity which was generated by the American balance-of-payments deficits and by the shift of private holders out of dollars in 1970 and 1971, requiring central banks to take them up, so augmenting their liquidity. The ending of the Bretton Woods "par value" regime may also have reduced the demand for international liquidity, creating even less need for SDRs, although this is a more doubtful proposition.

Changes in the International Monetary System

International liquidity is now mainly generated through the world capital market, notably the Euro-dollar market. It should be realised that, beginning in 1971, there has been an unplanned transformation of the international monetary system. The new system was not the outcome of any negotiations. SDRs have no significant place in it, but the world capital market has a very big place. And the new system appears here to stay.

This raises the issue of the deficits of the developing countries and the possibility of, or need for, "debt remission." Even before the oil crisis and the world recession, developing countries ran current-account deficits, covered partly by official grants, partly by official loans, and partly by loans from the private sector, including suppliers' credits. These deficits were the inevitable counterparts of the transfer of resources from developed to developing countries.

The deficits increased greatly in 1975 and 1976 and, to a considerable extent, were covered by borrowing from private banks. In fact, surpluses of the Organisation for Petroleum Exporting Countries (OPEC) were recycled to end up as loans to other countries, including developing countries. In 1974 more than half of the deficits that corresponded to the OPEC surpluses were run by OECD countries, but in 1975, and to a lesser extent subsequently, have been mainly incurred by developing countries. The surpluses of some OECD countries, notably Germany and Japan, have tended to cancel out the deficits of some other OECD countries, including Italy and Britain and, more recently, the United States. Thus the private capital market did most of the recycling job. It was helped a little by direct lending and aid from OPEC countries and by some official aid and loans from OECD countries. But in the main, the OPEC countries deposited funds in the Euro-dollar market and in New York; the international banks then lent this money to many countries, since 1975 significantly to developing countries. Just a few developing countries were involved. Most of these funds went to about seven countries, and about a third to Brazil and Mexico alone. India and Pakistan, for example, borrowed hardly anything from the private market and their total debt increased very little.

Was this recycling through the private market bad? Does it really present a problem? Should some of the resultant debt be remitted? It is true that for many countries concerned the ratio of debt to gross national product (GNP), or to the value of exports, increased considerably. But the debt was incurred knowingly. If the borrowers try to get the debt remitted, how will they fare the next time they want to borrow? The Government of Brazil has seen this clearly and has not supported such proposals. After all, it was a great help to the developing countries that they were able to borrow so freely, and they may wish to avail themselves of this opportunity again. One can imagine the outcry if they had *not* been able to borrow; if the international banks had been willing to lend to Italy and other developed countries, but had turned developing country borrowers away. The emergence of an international capital market willing to lend to governments on a large scale, with few political questions asked, was a blessing to developing countries at a time of crisis. It may have involved risks for the banks—although not as great as is sometimes said—and some of the borrowing may have been unwise, but the fact is that it helped several developing countries, mainly the more developed among them, over a difficult period.

It is sometimes said that the developing countries had to carry the "burden" of current-account deficits. The suggestion is that the OPEC surpluses must be matched by deficits elsewhere, and these deficits are "burdens." Thus the world should be grateful to Britain, to Italy, to the developing countries, and now to the United States, for bearing this "burden." But this appears to be a false approach. If the developing countries had not been able to borrow, and instead had to cut their imports appropriately, the burden on them would have been greater. A burden was imposed on them by the circumstances that gave rise to the deficits. But the ability to borrow modified the burden. Of course, it did not eliminate it, because there are interest charges (although they are quite low in real terms), and eventually the loans should be repaid. But the burden on the developing countries was lessened by their ability to borrow and incur interest and amortisation commitments rather than having to cut imports immediately so as to avoid a current-account deficit.

The circumstances that gave rise to the large increase in the developing countries' current-account deficits were two. First, there was the oil price rise, which substantially raised the cost of their imports. This burden was not imposed by the developed countries (unless one blames the oil companies for this price rise, which does not seem plausible). Second, there was the world recession, which reduced the demand for the developing countries' exports and so worsened their terms of trade. This was certainly the fault of the developed countries, although the recession may have hurt the developed countries even more than it hurt the developing countries. The question of macro-economic policies in developed countries will be looked at later. It has been estimated that about three-quarters of the deficit of the (non-oil) developing countries during this period can be explained by the recession and about one-quarter by the oil price rise.[7]

It is important to note that both causes of the increase in the developing countries' current-account deficits are essentially temporary. The oil price rise led to deficits because it takes time for countries to adjust their spending to such a shock, and during the adjustment period they naturally borrow, living temporarily above their lower means. The ability to borrow made it possible for many countries, developed and developing, to smooth the adjustment. The situation would have been much worse for them if the OPEC countries had immediately spent all their extra income, rather than lending it on the world capital market and so making a great increase in borrowing possible. The recession can, surely, also be regarded as temporary, although it seems to take longer to come to an end than expected, especially in Western Europe and Japan.

Perhaps some of this discussion is too sanguine. There will be some countries that will get into trouble and need rescheduling of their debts. This is a problem for which the IMF was set up. Such countries may need rescheduling arrangements or additional loans, no doubt with conditions attached. But each case has to be looked at on its own terms. A general remission of debts would seem to be an unrealistic proposal and one that, in any case, would not serve the long-term interests of those developing countries that hope to make future use of the international capital market. The most that one might expect would be the remission of some of the debts incurred to governments—but not to the private sector or to the World Bank—by some of the least developed countries. Such proposals (involving rather small sums) are now under discussion, and some debt remission has recently taken place.

It can certainly be argued that the private capital market did a useful job in recycling some of the OPEC surpluses to developing countries. Some banks made big profits in doing so. On the other hand, they incurred "country risks" which are now attracting attention. With hindsight it appears that some of their loans were banking mistakes. When eventual bad debts are taken into account their profits may turn out not to have been as high as appears when interest rates are looked at. It might also be noted that by no means all developing countries made use of the world capital market. Some did not wish to borrow and some were not considered good enough risks. The market did not meet the needs of all countries and it did not take the place of official aid. The private capital market is concerned with commercial transactions—even when some of the parties to the transactions are governments—and its role should never be confused with that of official aid.

Exchange Rates

Perhaps a word should be said about the attitudes of some developing countries to the exchange-rate regime. They would like exchange rates of developed countries to be fixed relative to each other because a world where exchange rates fluctuate creates problems for them. For example, how should the developing countries hold their reserves? Variable exchange rates create a difficult portfolio-balancing problem. Hence their vision of the NIEO would seem to have elements of the old exchange-rate order in it.

It is true that the less instability and the more certainty there are in the developed world, the better it is for the developing countries that trade with it, borrow from it and deposit their funds in it. The key is the need for general stability, whether in exchange rates, levels of protection, levels of aid, prices of exports and imports or availability of funds to be borrowed. If exchange-rate stability is brought about at the cost of instability in other things, little is achieved. It is unrealistic to suggest that the developed countries should go back to the Bretton Woods system. Even if they did, would there be more stability? There would be the dramatic balance-of-payments crises which many of us remember so well, leading to the sudden imposition of import quotas, to deflationary policies designed to eliminate the deficits and, perhaps, to reductions in aid.

The economy of the developed world is a complex web. To fix one set of prices, namely exchange rates, would not eliminate problems, but might make them worse. If there are underlying forces, or perhaps unwise policies, that give rise to instability in aggregate demand or patterns of demand, it is these forces or policies that have to be dealt with. Perhaps one should interpret the advocacy of fixed—or at least more stable—exchange rates as really a demand for more stability in the developed world. This would seem to be a thoroughly justified demand, made also by many people in developed countries, although it is not easy to satisfy.

Compensatory Financing

Finally, the IMF's compensatory financing facilities should be referred to. Such facilities mean that countries can borrow to cover deficits resulting from fluctuations in export earnings. A compensatory financing scheme is an arrangement where governments can borrow at concessional interest rates to deal with the sort of problem which the developed countries have encountered lately because of the recession. The IMF's facility was created in 1963 but conditions for access were rather severe. They were greatly liberalised in December 1975 and, as a result, in the following sixteen months, over $2,000 million was lent from the facility. This liberalisation was possibly a response to NIEO demands. If countries are concerned about fluctuations in export earnings, compensatory financing seems a far better approach than trying to stabilise export prices through buffer stocks, since the focus is—as it should be—on export earnings rather than export prices.

The revamped IMF scheme involves a substantial sum of money but is still quite modest in relation to the sums that developing countries borrowed in 1975 and 1976 on the private capital market. If it is liberalised further, developing countries will have less need to go to the private capital market on the next occasion when export prices slump. A liberalised scheme would seem to make buffer stock schemes that do not affect price trends—that is, that are purely stabilising—unnecessary. The poorer of the developing countries are likely to be helped more by such a scheme, as they are the countries which have not borrowed much on the private market in recent years. Hence, from this point of view, the IMF facility is highly desirable. Of course, the funds are lent by the IMF to the countries concerned, not given to them, so there is still a debt burden, but presumably it can be liquidated when prices rise again. Since the object is to cover (or part-cover) only those deficits which result from export earnings that are believed to be below trend, only temporary deficits are covered. A natural next step is to transform the scheme from a compensation scheme in nominal terms to one that takes into account fluctuations in *real* earnings. In other words, changes in a country's import prices that are expected to be temporary would become relevant. A country would be compensated for an unexpected rise in import prices as well as for a fall in nominal export earnings.

ARGUMENTS FOR INCREASED DEVELOPMENT AID

It is part of the NIEO proposals that developed countries should give at least 0.7 per cent of their GNPs in official development aid. This has been the target for some time. But actually the share has been falling and has never been near the target. The share for all the countries in the Development Assistance Committee (DAC) of the Organisation for Economic Co-operation and Development (OECD) in 1976 was 0.33 per cent. For the United States it was only 0.25 per cent, for Germany 0.31 per cent, for Japan 0.20 per cent, and for the United Kingdom 0.38 per cent. France's ratio was 0.62 per cent, but there is a special consideration here, to be referred to later. What is the point of such a target? During the targeteering period the ratio for all DAC countries actually declined from 0.42 per cent (1965–67 average) to 0.33 per cent (1976).

At the same time, some of the advocates of the NIEO demand that the aid should be completely untied and uncontrolled. The governments of the developed countries should tax their peoples and hand over the proceeds to the governments of the developing countries, with no questions asked how they are spent. The governments of the developed countries are thought to have an obligation to assist the developing countries. They should provide aid not as an act of grace but as a duty, whether a moral duty or as reparations for evils done in the past. But the governments of the developing countries have complete sovereignty. This is the way the position is sometimes put, although some advocates of the NIEO realise it is extreme and unproductive.

Why Aid?

What is the basis of the aid-giving obligation? Should the rich (including the rich within the developing countries) always help the poor? Or should they only help when they have caused the impoverishment of the poor, possibly through colonial exploitation? There could be some interesting philosophical discussions about the first question, although—in theory at least—many people accept the general obligation. The motivation can be simple humanitarianism. The question of how far the redistribution should go is hardly worth discussing in the present context since any politically and practically conceivable levels of aid would only have marginal effects on incomes in developed countries and on the gap between these and incomes of the bulk of the populations of the developing countries.

A much more difficult question is whether the developed countries should have any guilt feelings on the grounds of having caused the poverty of the developing countries. This is a matter for careful historical analysis, some of which has been done by Richard Cooper in an interesting article dealing with the general question of aid obligation.[8] It might be asked, for example, what responsibility the United States has for the underdevelopment of India and Pakistan. If the colonial experience slowed up India's development, then presumably the reparations should be paid by Britain. It is unlikely that the United States Congress can be persuaded to vote for more aid by being told that the Americans should feel guilty. One would expect aid to be more easily obtainable if Congress feels it is buying goodwill and is given some signs of this goodwill. Furthermore, if the appeal or motivation is basically humanitarian it seems important that Congress and the American people are satisfied that the money is well spent. Unfortunately, this may mean that some of the money has to go on visible, big, projects, and yet this is not necessarily the best way of spending a given sum of money. There has to be some concern about whether the money really encourages economic development, or, even it if does not, whether it benefits the poorer people rather than a small privileged group. These remarks apply not only to the problem of extracting aid from the United States, which still accounts for over 30 per cent of total DAC aid, but to all the donor countries.

There are difficult issues here that have to be faced. All this has been said many times and it is repeated only because of its relevance to the NIEO demands. If the control of the aid flows stays mainly with the donor country the aid may be tied in various ways to benefit export or other domestic interests in the donor country. There are plenty of examples of this. Not only does aid-tying of this kind reduce the real value of any given monetary sum by preventing purchase from the cheapest sources, but it also makes economic management by the developing country's government more difficult. The higher the quality of this government, the less desirable is any form of tying of aid. On the other hand, it could be that if the aid were not tied, there would not be any aid, or much less of it. American food aid, provided by Public Law 480 (PL 480), probably helped to alleviate human suffering in developing countries and so yielded benefits on balance (although, by lowering domestic food prices, it shifted income distribution against food-producing peasants and discouraged domestic production). But if PL 480 had not served the purpose of keeping up the incomes of American farmers—so that a domestic American interest group had become a supporter of aid—there would not have been this aid. Tied aid may be better than no aid.

At present about three-quarters of DAC aid is bilateral and one-quarter multilateral. An objection to bilateral aid is that it is very unevenly distributed between countries. France's high ratio of aid to her GNP is explained by her neo-colonial policy of pouring resources, technical assistance, and Frenchmen generally, into a group of ex-French African countries, as well as into French overseas *Departements*, with a total population of only 30 million or so. Almost half of French bilateral aid goes to *Departements* and territories with a per capita income of over $1000 and a total population of just over two million. The OPEC countries give their aid mainly to Moslem countries; and in the past a high proportion of aid from the United States has gone for political reasons to certain quite small countries, such as South Vietnam, South Korea and Taiwan. Australia also has a fairly high aid ratio (0.51 per cent in 1975–76), but more than half of her aid goes to Papua New Guinea. On average between 1973 and 1975 India received about $2.15 per head per annum while Pakistan received nearly $10, the Philippines $5, Egypt $38, and even Uganda received more, with $2.4.

Another objection to bilateral aid is that it is more prone to be used to help export interests in donor countries. One might then conclude that a higher proportion of DAC aid should go through multilateral agencies, in particular the World Bank and its "soft-loan" associate, the International Development Association (IDA). The trouble is that donors are likely to want to keep control of the money they give away or lend at concessional rates and they are unlikely to forgo the opportunity to benefit some of their domestic interests or to buy political goodwill. With regard to the latter, it must be remembered that the peak of aid in relation of GNP was reached in the 1950s when American aid was, to a great extent, part of the cold war. Furthermore, the donors' aid motivations are likely to be stronger with bilateral aid, because it provides closer and sometimes very human links between donors and recipients. The World Bank is not exactly a generator of enthusiasm and opens few voters' pocketbooks in financing more aid.

A fundamental problem is to make humanitarianism a prime and powerful motive force, as in Sweden and the Netherlands, which give 0.8 per cent of their GNP in aid. This is not a high proportion for prosperous countries, and is much less than is spent by most countries on military purposes, so it does not seem an impossible objective. But one will have to face the fact that in many countries, such as the United States and Germany, public opinion seems to have been less sympathetic to aid than the governments, and it is not sufficient to "work on" governments, or their representatives at international conferences. If as much research were done into aid-giving motivations and into the political processes involved in the determination of total funds for aid as has been done by manufacturers of soap, cigarettes and other products into consumer motivation, perhaps the humanitarian cause might make some progress. Presumably the sponsors of the research, and subsequently the associated advertising and public relations campaigns, would have to be the prospective recipients. But there are obvious difficulties in this line of thought.

Distribution of Aid

A separate issue—although clearly related—is whether aid money is well spent, and how it can be better spent. Should it go primarily to buy political support—the economic and humanitarian benefits being happy by-products—or should the economic aim be dominant? In the latter case, should it be development-oriented—possibly going mainly to those countries which are already fairly well-off, but where aid has a big "pay-off," because local administrations are good and the productivity of aid is high—or should it rather go to help the poor, even if the development effects are less? These are all big issues that are currently much debated. In particular, it has been argued that there is no necessary conflict between development aid (growth) and aid directed mainly to the poor (equity).

In the world of development economics, and especially in the World Bank, there has developed a growing consensus that aid has not helped the poor of the developing countries as much as it should have—that the benefits of high growth rates have not always "trickled down." So the emphasis has shifted to the satisfaction of "basic needs," to use a currently fashionable and somewhat imprecise term. But how to bring about in practice the desired shift in the direction of aid is a more difficult matter. It is not easy for the World Bank to bring about a change when a local government controlled by, or responsive to, a military or urban elite is not cooperating. Even if a shift in aid emphasis could be brought about, the magnitudes of aid that are in prospect could never make a large impact on world poverty if aid just consisted of subsidising the "basic needs" consumption of the poor or physical investment in poor areas. To be significant it has to help generate some kind of domestic "take-off" processes or bring about major technical innovations along "Green Revolution" lines. Even if aid is not the original cause of transformation of attitudes or policies, it could be provided in large doses when a transformation is already in progress. It can help the process along and avoid it becoming aborted because of short-term resource shortages or political difficulties for the "transforming" government.

It has been my impression that *if* one could take the total amount of aid as given and were simply concerned with the welfare of the developing countries, the best vehicle for aid distribution at present would be the World Bank and the IDA. If this is so, this would not be an argument for chanelling all aid through the World Bank—in any case an unrealistic proposal—but for increasing its resources substantially. It is true that the World Bank is moved by intellectual fashions, and not all its staff are wise and well-informed. It can probably be shown that some of the projects it has financed have done more harm than good. It is widely criticised for cumbersome methods (some of which it is trying to improve) and for excessively highly-paid staff, some of whom lack experience of the developing countries on which they have to write reports and who spend too little time in these countries. But the Bank seems to be the best there is. It seems to have a genuine purpose in fostering development and it does represent by far the greatest expertise in the development field. It carefully checks on the way its money is spent. It can do this more thoroughly perhaps than many bilateral donors because it benefits from economies of scale in aid administration. It is also in a stronger position to induce improvements in economic policies in recipient countries, at least as seen by its staff. Sometimes the best procedure may be for a particular donor country to choose the aid recipient and the general field of aid, and to have its name identified with a project, while the World Bank actually administers it. Some of the attractions of bilateral aid are then obtained while at the same time the World Bank's expertise is used. This practice is becoming more common.

Finally, it must be added that there have always been people both on the right and the left who have argued that, in general, aid does more harm than good. This view is recorded for completeness here, as I have not been able to assess it satisfactorily. P. T. Bauer's book, *Dissent on Development,* is the most thorough statement of its right-wing version.

HELPING THE DEVELOPING WORLD— WHAT CAN BE DONE?

Suppose the governments of the developed world really wanted to help the poor of the developing world and that they had the support of their peoples in this desire. In other words, suppose that the developed countries all became like Sweden, or at least like a mythical Sweden. What could be done? The following remarks must clearly be oversimplified, and will seem naive to the experts. But it seems useful, as a basis for discussion, to put forward some possible answers.

First, the governments of the industrial world would see to it that their own economies are prosperous and stable. They would try to get their economies back on an even keel, with high levels of output, employment and growth. This is easier said than done, but it seems important to point out that, in this respect, what is good for OECD countries is likely to be good for the developing countries. High demand and output bring with them better terms of trade for the developing countries. More macro-economic stability brings more stable commodity prices. The various commodity schemes, even if they could overcome their difficulties, would become less necessary. There would be faster technical progress and some of this would spill over to the developing countries. Even if the ratio of aid to GNP did not rise, more aid would be forthcoming. In any case, it seems easier to extract aid out of a prosperous economy. It would be much easier to reduce levels of protection and increases in protection would be avoided. Complicated preferential schemes would be unnecessary if developing countries were allowed to exploit their comparative advantages.

High growth rates in the developed countries would, on past experience, encourage high growth rates of developing countries and the *proportional* gap between them might even lessen. But the *absolute* gap would certainly increase and, since some developing countries would no doubt lag behind, the gap between the fast and slow growers might widen greatly. But it is surely the welfare of the poor—the *absolute* welfare—which should be the first concern. When human misery in terms of material conditions and health is so great, it is surely the first duty of economic policy to try to make some inroads into this problem and leave a concern with a widening gap aside.

Secondly, all trade restrictions, whether tariffs, quotas, voluntary export restraints, and the rest, on imports from developing countries would be removed—not at once, but in a staged and pre-announced process, with appropriate adjustment assistance. The freeing of trade restrictions would be permanent. Once the textile and clothing nettle was grasped, the rest might be easy.

The sense of threat that has been felt in the manufacturing industries of many developed countries since 1975 has been caused much more by a flood of imports from Japan and by the recession than by imports from developing countries. If safeguards are to be allowed to protect industries in developed countries temporarily against sudden, damaging increases in particular imports, the temporariness must be firmly built into the scheme and they must be subject to multilateral surveillance, as has been often suggested.

Thirdly, more aid would be given in explicit grant form, not indirectly through a link with SDRs, concessional loans, debt remission, contribution to a common fund, and so on. More aid (whether in grant or concessional loan form) would be given through the World Bank or, perhaps, in the case of a large donor, through a national institution set up along similar lines and attractive to high quality mobile staff. The aid would not be tied to domestic producer or other interests, nor would it be given to governments of the developing countries unconditionally. It would be given to those governments that followed, in a broad sense, certain efficiency and growth-promoting policies, and policies that helped the poor. While one cannot be sure which are the *best* policies, it is pretty clear that certain existing policies of developing countries are harmful, among them policies of high and uneven protection of import-competing manufacturing industries and systems of widespread controls and licensing which deprive people of initiative.

Fourthly, total aid would be increased, provided the cooperation of developing countries were obtained to ensure its disbursement without too much waste, to ensure that it brings some benefits to more than an elite and to get relevant domestic policies in developing countries improved. It might be appropriate to concentrate the aid on a few countries where it did look like being relatively effective. One might fix on a target, such as the 0.7 per cent figure, if this is useful from a public relations point of view. Most OECD countries, other than Sweden, the Netherlands and Norway, would have to increase their aid—some substantially—to attain this target. Even a 1 per cent figure seems by no means unreasonable provided recipients are available where the aid can be well-spent.

It might be argued that if the donor country or agency is really interested in the economic development of the recipient country it is more important to use aid as a lever to get *policies* right than to give aid for particular projects which appear to be beneficial. With bad policies, the benefits of the best projects can disappear. Furthermore, aid is essentially fungible and a recipient government can leave the financing of certain essential projects to foreigners who happen to approve of these projects, and then use the money saved in directions that may be wasteful.

There are three difficulties about this view. First, it assumes that the aid officials know what is best, something that politicians in developing countries would not necessarily concede. Obviously, one cannot generalise here. Secondly, it assumes that the objective is to help economic development, an assumption that has run through the discussion in this paper. But the overriding objective may really be much less idealistic, namely to buy the goodwill of the recipient country's ruling group. The economic development motive may be no more than a cover, whether conscious or not. In this case the shrewd or cynical policy (not advocated here) is presumably to hand over the money to the rulers and let them do what they like with it. Thirdly, the idea that the use of aid should be closely super-vised, and that its receipt should be associated with the pursuit of better policies, is out of tune with the central NIEO message of non-interference in the internal affairs of the developing countries. The NIEO might be described as the manifesto of a trade union of governments. It has often been said that the NIEO is about "independence" and "self-respect," not primarily about economic development. As it is, there is much resentment about attempts by outsiders to influence economic policies, for example, on the part of the IMF in Latin America.

The desire by many governments of developing countries for noninterference in their internal affairs is quite reasonable, but it is difficult to make it compatible with the receipt of large-scale aid. It is for this reason that these governments have favoured ways of getting aid (resource trans-fers) indirectly or "automatically," whether through an aid-SDR link, through raising prices of commodity exports, or via other possible schemes. But governments and parliaments of developed countries know when they are giving aid, and the larger the amounts, the more they are likely to be interested in the way it is spent. It seems hardly conceivable that the amount of aid from countries such as the United States and Germany could be boosted substantially without their parliaments taking a close interest in what happens to it. On the other hand, a recipient government may justi-fiably resent the pretensions of donors who finance no more than a small proportion of their nation's total investment budget and yet claim the right to regulate its domestic policies.

The delicate balance, between non-interference in internal affairs (avoiding neo-colonialism) and a concern by donors that their aid money is well spent and actually helps to bring about the desired development and improvement of living conditions of the masses, is one that is not easy to strike. In practice, a balance has to be struck with the usual processes of political compromise. The task is easiest when a developing country hap-pens to have a government which, in any case, favours the kinds of policies that donor agencies regard as sound.

THE LESSONS OF HISTORY

Can anything be learned from history about the issues raised and the arguments used in the NIEO debate?

Is there any basis for the rather general argument, sometimes ex-pressed forcefully, that the so-called "old order" which has been imposed by the developed countries, especially by the United States, has operated to the detriment of the developing countries and that the income gap be-tween the developed and the developing countries has been increasing as a result? In fact, the average annual rate of growth of per capita incomes in the developing countries as a group has tended to be about the same as that of the industrial countries over the whole period 1950–75. The rate was 3 per cent in the developing countries (excluding China) and 3.2 per cent in the developed countries.[9]

Thus the proportional gap between the two "worlds" has not changed, although, of course, the absolute gap has increased. These sorts of figures raise many statistical problems, so they should not be taken too seriously in detail. But the broad implications seem to be clear. In the last years, since the 1973 crisis, the rate of growth of developing countries has actually been higher than that of the developed countries. Furthermore, the per capita rates of growth of developing countries during this post-World War II period have been much higher than their growth in earlier periods. The period since World War II has been unprecedented from an economic growth point of view. The developing countries as a whole have grown much faster than the developed countries grew when the latter were in comparable stages of development.

Slow Developers

Within the developing world some countries have grown, relatively, much more slowly—at least compared with other countries, though not in relation to their earlier performance—the most notable case being India, where per capita growth from 1950 to 1975 averaged only 1.5 per cent per annum. On the other hand, some countries have had very high per capita growth rates since about 1960—notably South Korea (7.3 per cent), Singapore (7.6 per cent), Hong Kong (6.3 per cent), Taiwan (6.3 per cent), Thailand (4.5 per cent) and Brazil (4.2 per cent). Mexico is another large country that has done rather well in per capita growth—2.7 per cent since 1950 and 3.7 per cent from 1960 to 1970. This is impressive because of her exceptionally high population growth rate (3.3. per cent over the period 1950–75). Several southern European countries also did very well. Spain (5.1 per cent), Greece (5.4 per cent), and Yugoslavia (4.7 per cent) more or less transformed themselves over the period from less developed to developed countries. Thus the proportional gap between India and the industrial countries has been increasing, but between the countries mentioned above (except Mexico) and the industrial countries the gap has been decreasing.

Within each group, have the poor been lagging behind the rich with the relatively rich spurting ahead? Even this cannot be said in general, although it is true that several of the poorest countries, notably India and Bangladesh, have been low growth countries. On the other hand, one of the richest developing countries, Argentina, has also had a very low growth rate (1.9 per cent for 1950–75 compared with Brazil's 3.7 per cent) and in the group of countries now described as developed, some that were relatively poor at the beginning of the period—Japan and Italy—have had much higher per capita growth rates than those that were relatively rich at the beginning—the United States, Canada, Australia, Britain—and on the figures they appear to have overtaken the last country.

If present growth rates continue in South Asia and in many other developing countries, vast numbers of peoples will remain in poverty for many, many years. So these trends are not satisfactory even though they are remarkable when seen in historical perspective. The central question remains how the poor and relatively slow-growing countries can be trans-formed to be put on a new, higher growth path. What is it that makes a Japan, a South Korea, or a (southern) Brazil? What holds India and Bangladesh back? These are, obviously, vast questions which are, or should be, the central focus of study of development economics. It is not too difficult to identify the sorts of government policies and social attitudes that tend to go with success. What is difficult to explain is why some countries at certain stages of history adopt these policies, or why their peoples acquire certain attitudes, while others do not.

The impression obtained from reading the relevant history is that, other than in very small countries, domestic attitudes and circumstances are crucial, rather than the external "order." After all, the international order (if it can be called that) of the post-war period made it possible for South Korea, Taiwan, Hong Kong, Singapore, Brazil and Mexico to do well, or at least it did not stand sufficiently in their way to hold them back. And this "order" made it possible for Japan to grow at a fantastic rate. Hence, why should it have held back Argentina, India, Bangladesh or Burma? Essentially the same international environment faced them all. Is it seriously suggested that the system discriminated in favour of Brazil and against Argentina?

A great deal of research has been conducted in recent years into the success stories in the developing world. The general theme that emerges is that countries that became export-oriented in their manufactur-ing development because of policies that encouraged exports—or at least because of policies that avoided or reduced a bias towards import substitution—also had high growth rates. Hong Kong, Taiwan, South Korea and Singapore are the most dramatic cases here, although a general shift towards exports was also observable in Brazil and Mexico and some other countries.

The question is whether these policies of trade liberalisation and export encouragement were a major factor in explaining the higher growth rates. In the case of the very small economies it seems possible that they were. In the case of larger economies, it seems more doubtful. There may have been *some* link, although there may also have been more important common causes. A shift towards more rational economic policies and an improvement of economic motivation and incentives may have generally stimulated the economy; some degree of trade liberalisation and export encouragement would have been just one manifestation of more rational policies. A crucial element in some countries may also have been the ability to restrain increases in urban real wages.

It is sometimes argued that these experiences carry no lessons for large economies, notably for India: it is clear that an Indian government could not transform India just by changing her international trading arrangements or by opening her up to foreign capital. But it might transform the more developed part of the Indian economy if it eliminated the great network of incentive-destroying and efficiency-inhibiting controls of which import controls are a part. Furthermore, the experience of Japan shows that it is possible for a large economy to become trade-oriented and to break into the world market.

What has held India, Pakistan and Bangladesh back? An argument could be made that the colonial experience was economically damaging for these countries. This is obviously a complex historical issue where there will never be a clear answer.[10] The British did not try very hard to encourage economic development in the sub-continent; they held back manufacturing industry (for the benefit of British exporters) and, above all, they inhibited local initiative and self-confidence. It does seem relevant that, on the evidence available, the growth rates of India and Pakistan have been higher since independence than in the colonial period. Some British did well out of India, although plenty of capitalists made losses. The financial troubles of the British East India Company are well-known. The British do not seem to have done any worse for India than their predecessors, the Moghuls, and taxed the Indian people less. Perhaps the maintenance of internal order and peace, the introduction of Western technology and contacts, which laid the foundation for subsequent development, and the provision of an infrastructure, notably the railway system, should also be taken into account.

Furthermore, it has to be explained why Ethiopia—which was never colonised—is so backward economically, why Malaysia has done so well and why one of the world's few remaining colonies—Hong Kong—has one of the highest growth rates of all. It could also be argued that Taiwan and South Korea benefited in economic terms from Japanese colonial rule, and that the exceptional economic success of these two countries post-war has something to do with their colonial experiences.

Even the briefest reflections and examples suggest no basis for the opposite conclusion—that it necessarily helped a people's economic growth to have been colonised. Excessively paternalistic regimes, such as that of the Dutch in Indonesia, may have achieved some benefits—for example, in the form of improved health conditions—but must have had adverse effects once independence was achieved through having failed to give experience in responsible self-government.

These brief reflections on the implications of colonialism for *economic* development, or the lack of it, are *not* concerned with the broader issues—the fundamental objection that most people rightly have to being governed by foreigners. Such government is usually in the interests of these foreigners, even though incidentally some economic benefits may ensue to the colonised. It is the offence of colonialism to human dignity, and the memory of this, which appears to lie behind a good deal of the NIEO motivation. In any case, to come back to the main point, even if the colonial experience was at fault in India and Indonesia, as it can be argued that it has been, one cannot blame the international order since independence.

The impression gained from reading studies of Indian economic policy is that there are certain economic policies, most of which still persist, which have led to the failure of India to seize opportunities that some other countries did seize. The complex question is why these unwise and growth-inhibiting policies were pursued and why they persist. It would be presumptuous here to attempt an answer. Two things only seem clear. First, even if ministers and their principal advisers wanted to bring about the necessary radical changes in policies, this would be difficult for domestic social and political reasons. Secondly, the explanations for the attitudes that lie behind these policies have nothing whatever to do with the issues discussed in the NIEO.

The Indian experience thus suggests that the causes of underdevelopment are essentially domestic even though the consequences manifest themselves, among other things, in unwise trade and foreign investment policies, and in low exports. There are social factors, deeply rooted in history, which hold back development, and even the wisest and firmest government would have difficulty overcoming them. But some specific policies—notably an excess of controls and licensing, of cumbersome bureaucratic intervention, too many inefficiently conducted publicly-owned enterprises and a general lack of official sympathy for capitalist initiative (with no socialist motivation along Chinese lines to take its place)—clearly stand in the way of progress.

A somewhat similar situation seems to exist in many of the other slow-growing developing countries. Many of them, like India, have an import-substitution bias in their development policies and the smaller the economy the more harmful this is likely to be. Enterprise is inhibited by excessive controls and bureaucracy. Focusing just on trade aspects, the failure for their exports of manufactures to expand—or at least expand as fast as world trade in general—can be explained much more by supply factors—determined by their own anti-export and growth-inhibiting policies—than by demand factors, that is, by the trade restrictions of developed countries. This generalisation would not, of course, apply to all countries at all times, and must involve an element of judgment.

SUCCESS STORY: JAPAN

From the point of view of deriving some lessons from history it is particularly interesting to look at the experience of Japan.[11] Here is the greatest success story of recent economic history. In 1870 Japan's per capita income was about one-quarter that of Britain and, now, on the figures, it is higher than Britain's. Over the whole period 1870 to 1965 the per capita growth rate averaged about 2.2 per cent, and post-war, 1950–1975, it was 7.5 per cent per annum. Japan broke into world markets and is now the world's third largest trading nation. How was it done? Could currently less-developed countries copy her policies? And was the world "order" facing Japan over the hundred years or so since the Meiji restoration, when her modernisation began, favourable to her?

One thing is clear. Japan encountered great obstacles in her efforts to break into world markets, but, nevertheless, like Hong Kong more recently, she succeeded. She encountered tariff barriers and quotas and had to accept voluntary export restraints, and all this may have held her back a little. But, nevertheless, she became for a time the world's largest exporter of textiles, and more recectly of electronic goods and of motor cars. At the early stage of development it was helpful that the Indian and Chinese markets were virtually free of tariff protection, but in general one cannot say that exporting was made easy for Japan.

As for Japan's own policies, with regard to protection and an import-substitution bias, the message of history is not too clear. At the crucial early stage, from 1866 to 1913, Japan was compelled to follow a free trade policy by treaty. This meant that, from quite an early stage, her industrialisation became export-oriented, and one can to some extent attribute her export success to this policy. But this has to be qualified in two ways. First, the initial development of the textile industry was for the home market, and it helped Japan that she had a large home market. Secondly, governments provided infant-industry protection by starting government enterprises and then selling them to private business. Some private firms were subsidised. Thus the government was active, but at the same time it fostered private enterprise and was market-oriented.

Looking back over the whole period of Japan's modern history there was, on the one hand, a very active, interventionist government and, on the other hand, strong official support for capitalism and the market. The contrast with India is striking: in both cases governments have been active, but in the case of India they have regulated and held back the private sector while in the case of Japan they have worked to foster and encourage it. Since 1911 Japan has certainly not followed a free trade policy. But her protection of manufacturing for the home market has never been such as to discourage a transition from import substitution to exporting. It might be suspected that if, in the last fifty years, there had not been any tariffs or quotas, industry would still have developed in the way it has, although possibly more losses would have been made at early stages of development.

It is well-known that Japan made tremendous efforts to import foreign technology, and still does so. The Japanese went all over the world to learn—and learn they certainly did. They did not permit investment in Japan, so that multinationals were not the media through which technology was transferred. The initiative came, again, from the government. But the world's technology was available to Japan. It was all there, ready to be looked at, read about and, if necessary, bought. This certainly carries a lesson for developing countries today. There is more technology now available, there is foreign aid and technical assistance ready to help developing countries, and most of the developing countries do not have the linguistic difficulties which faced, and still face, the Japanese.

What lessons are to be drawn? Multinationals do not appear to be essential for the transfer and adaptation of foreign technology. If a country has a government of Japanese quality and a people as eager to learn as the Japanese, and with the level of education the Japanese had reached even in the nineteenth century, then such a country can do without the multinationals. But these are big "ifs."

Japan was really a very special case. Japan has always had much lower population growth than developing countries (the long-term average has been about 1.2 per cent compared with 2.4 per cent for all developing countries 1950–75). The administrative machine even at the beginning of the modernisation period was efficient and centralised, and the country had a strong sense of unity and leadership from its elite. The educational level was remarkably high. Financial institutions were well-developed when industrialisation began. The government was willing to bring about radical changes for the sake of economic development. It was willing to tax, and to adapt the country's institutions. For a reason peculiar to the social background of Japan, the government seemed to do almost everything right at the crucial stage in Japan's history and had the people behind it.

It is also true that even in 1868 Japan was relatively advanced. The gap between Japan and Britain was far less than that between India now and the developed world, especially with regard to education. It is not reasonable to take any one aspect of Japanese policy or Japanese experience and suggest that this holds the key. It can be said that an active government, sympathetic to the market and incentives, backed by an educated and disciplined population, and operating in a country with a sense of unity and political stability, can bring about development in all the necessary respects—including a high savings ratio, a development of those industries suited to the country's factor endowment, the import of technology, and raising the level of education. It was not done without strains: there were, after all, three wars. The strains reflected, among other things, a fear that the world "order" was hostile to Japan's economic progress and, especially, a fear of being deprived of vital supplies of raw materials. But the post-war success of Japan certainly shows that the world "order" can accommodate the world's most dynamic nation.

SUMMARY AND CONCLUSIONS

At the risk of oversimplification, the main points of this paper can be summarised as follows.

1. The subject of the NIEO is very sensitive. The issues are political and attitudes have their roots in perceived historical injustices. This essay is only concerned with specific economic proposals. It looks at them from the point of view of the economic interests of the developing countries.

2. Scepticism about proposals for commodity cartels seems justified. Cartels designed to raise prices over a longer period are difficult to set up and maintain, and if set up may do more harm than good. Oil is a special case.

3. Proposals for buffer stocks to stabilise commodity prices hinge on the view that governmental authorities are better speculators than private operators. There are difficulties in the way of buffer stock schemes, which explains why so few have been set up or have lasted. But it may be worth while trying again.

4. The Common Fund proposal is the main concrete proposal to have come out of the NIEO movement. It has become almost symbolic to the Group of 77, and for this reason a Common Fund is likely to be established. Very little has been decided about its precise working. The "Second Window" proposal involves the setting-up of another, rather specialised, international aid agency.

5. The Generalised System of Preferences, on which the Group of 77 have placed so much emphasis in the past, has not made a big impact. Above all, it excludes textiles and clothing.

6. The developing countries need general reduction of protection by developed countries, rather than preferences. There has been discrimination against them, especially through quotas and voluntary export restraints, and the removal and future avoidance of these are more important to them than preferences. They should use their propaganda, power, and pressure to open up markets in a non-discriminatory way. They do not need special privileges to get into developed-country markets, but just open and fair opportunities.

7. The developing countries have had a certain success in breaking into developed-country markets, but there is a long way to go. It is quite wrong to think that they have captured the world market for textiles and clothing, let alone for any other major category of manufactures.

8. Any proposals for remission of the large debts incurred on the private capital markets in recent years are impracticable. The market did well in recycling the oil surpluses. The IMF is the right agency for dealing with debt problems.

9. Proposals to re-establish a fixed exchange-rate are based on misunderstandings, unless they are interpreted more broadly, as a concern with general economic instability generated by macro-economic policies in developed countries.

10. The IMF's compensatory financing scheme has been revamped, possibly in response to NIEO demands. This was a desirable move, and the scheme might be extended to allow not only for export but also for import fluctuations. Compensatory financing is to be preferred to price stabilisation through buffer stocks.

11. There are difficult issues in proposals to increase aid. Arguments in favour of multilateral aid, especially with the World Bank as agency, are given. What is the basis of the aid-giving obligation? How can more aid be extracted from the developed countries? There are two central issues. One is the problem of making humanitarianism a prime and powerful motive force. The other issue is how to ensure that the aid money is well spent, and to reconcile the desire of recipient countries for independence (avoiding "neo-colonialist" interference in aid use and in domestic policies) with the natural interest of donors in wishing to supervise the use of their aid.

12. The developed countries can help the developing world by having high and stable growth rates and by gradually removing all trade restrictions on imports from developing countries. The latter is given particular emphasis in this paper. In addition, aid should be increased, but it may be necessary to concentrate it on those countries where it is likely to be reasonably effective.

13. In looking at the "lessons of history" one finds that the developing world has in fact grown at much the same rate as the developed world since 1950, although there have been important laggards, notably India. Some countries have done very well, and the "old order" has not stood in their way. But the *absolute* gap in real income per head between the bulk of the population in the developing countries and the OECD coun-

tries has, of course, increased. There is still a vast world poverty problem.

14. Slow development can be explained mainly in terms of policies, social attitudes and historical factors that have little or nothing to do with the "international order." More outward-looking trade policies would be helpful for the slower-growing countries. Export orientation seems to have paid off for some of the more successful developing countries. The economic effects of colonialism are discussed.

15. The experience of Japan shows that "it can be done." But, of course, Japan was a very special case. Nevertheless, the post-war success of Japan shows that, in spite of obstacles and even hostility, the world "order" can accommodate the world's most dynamic nation.

Notes

1. See the various references given in [the bibliographical notes at the end of this essay], and also John Spraos, in Stuart Harris (ed.), *Commodity Policy Issues in the North-South Debate* (London: Macmillan, for the Trade Policy Research Centre, forthcoming).

2. They are discussed much more fully, along with stabilisation issues in Harris, Mark Salmon and Ben Smith, *Analysis of Commodity Markets for Policy Purposes*, Thames Essay no. 17 (London: Trade Policy Research Centre, 1978), also to be included in Harris (ed.), *op. cit.*

3. The crucial element was the American strategic stockpile, variations in the size of which were more important than those of the International Tin Agreement's buffer stock. See G. W. Smith and G. R. Schink, "The International Tin Agreement: a Reassessment," *Economic Journal*, Cambridge, No. 86, December 1976, pp. 718–28. The Tin Agreement's resources are to be boosted as the United States has joined it, and for the first time its buffer stock may be adequate to stabilise markets. With the ITA becoming significant and prices continuing to exceed the ceiling, producers are now seeking a rise in floor prices. See Smith, "Commodity Instability: New Order or Old Hat," in *Challenges to a Liberal International Economic Order* (Washington: American Enterprise Institute, 1978).

4. The ten "core" commodities agreed upon at UNCTAD IV in Nairobi in 1976 (when the Common Fund proposal became UNCTAD and Group of 77 policy) are cocoa, coffee, tea, sugar, hard fibres, jute and manufactures, cotton, rubber, copper and tin. Of these ten, there are now buffer stock schemes for tin and cocoa, and one has just been agreed upon for rubber. The coffee scheme provides for a floor price but no buffer stock. Tea is not storable. Cotton is expensive to store. Sugar is a difficult case because much of international trade is subject to bilateral arrangements and because the European Community is a major beet sugar producer. Jute suffers from a long-term problem owing to the development of substitutes. There are large private stocks of copper. In addition, there are seven commodities also under consideration—bananas, wheat, rice, phosphates, meat, wool, iron ore, bauxite—and the whole eighteen cover three-quarters of the developing countries' exports from their agricultural and mineral sectors (excluding petroleum). But some of the last group are substantially exported by developed countries. Rice is a special case with a very small proportion of world production entering trade, and bananas—which are of particular interest to some small developing countries—are not storable.

5. See Mordechai E. Kreinin and J. M. Finger, "A Critical Survey of the New International Economic Order," *Journal of World Trade Law*, London, 1976; Robert E. Baldwin's paper in the present Trade Policy Research Centre series, "MFN Tariff Reductions versus Margins of Preferences" and various detailed studies listed in [the bibliographical notes at the end of this essay].

6. See Y. S. Park, *The Link Between Special Drawing Rights and Development Finance*, Essay in International Finance No. 100 (Princeton: Princeton University Press, for Princeton University International Finance Section, 1973); and J. Williamson, "SDRs: the Link," in Jagdish Bhagwati (ed.), *The New International Economic Order: the North-South Debate* (Cambridge, Mass.: MIT Press, 1977).

7. Harold van B. Cleveland and W. H. Bruce Brittain, "Are the LDCs in Over their Heads," *Foreign Affairs*, New York, July 1977.

8. Richard N. Cooper, "A New International Economic Order for Mutual Gain," *Foreign Policy*, Washington, No. 26, Spring 1977.

9. David Morawetz, *Twenty-Five Years of Economic Development: 1950 to 1975* (Washington: World Bank, 1977). This study is also the source of other figures in this section.

10. The following discussion has been influenced by Angus Maddison, *Class Structure and Economic Growth: India and Pakistan Since the Moghuls* (London: Allen & Unwin, 1971). See also other references in [the bibliographical notes at the end of this essay].

11. See Maddison, *Economic Growth in Japan and the USSR* (London: Allen & Unwin, 1969) especially Chapter 6; and Hugh Patrick and Henry Rosovsky (eds), *Asia's New Giant* (Washington: Brookings Institution, 1976).

Bibliographical Notes

[These notes list] all the references which I have found useful in preparing this essay. Of course, the literature in the field is vast, so this is just a sample, and chance played a part in what I happened to lay my hands on. I do not refer to classic and standard works on development economics by Arthur Lewis, Hla Myint, Albert O. Hirschman and Gunnar Myrdal. . . .

The Broad Issues

A well-written popular introduction to the issues is John Cole, *The Poor of the Earth* (London: Macmillan, 1976). A famous book which analyses the issues rigorously and thoroughly (and shows there is little new since 1966) is Harry G. Johnson, *Economic Policies Toward Less Developed Countries* (Washington: Brookings Institution, 1967). An up-to-date book closely directed to the recent debates, and perhaps now the best book on most of the main NIEO issues, is Alasdair I. MacBean and V. N. Balasubramanyam, *Meeting the Third World Challenge*, 2nd ed. (London: Macmillan, for the Trade Policy Research Centre, 1978). This book contains a comprehensive annotated bibliography. Also on the general issues, see an article written more from a "South" perspective, Carlos F. Diaz-Alejandro, "North–South Relations: the Economic Component," in C. Fred Bergsten and L. B. Krause (eds), *World Politics and International Economics* (Washington: Brookings Institution, 1975).

The NIEO

The "party line"—that is, the UNCTAD position, stated very moderately—can be found in the Secretary-General of UNCTAD's *New Directions and New Structures for Trade and Development*, TD/183 (Geneva: United Nations, 1976). Short of reading United Nations resolutions and speeches one can get a flavour of the NIEO advocates' ways of thinking from Mahbub ul Haq, *The Poverty Curtain: Choices for the Third World* (New York: Columbia University Press, 1976). This Western-trained economist-author is a disillusioned ex-chief planner of Pakistan and is now a senior official at the World Bank, very active in the NIEO world. He holds strong views; this book should be read before reading the critics of the NIEO. A more moderate statement of many of the NIEO views and issues is in the final report of the Commonwealth Experts' Group, *Towards a New International Economic Order* (London: Commonwealth Secretariat, 1977).

A number of papers by Americans sympathetic to the NIEO are in A. Fishlow *et al.*, *Rich and Poor Nations in the World Economy* (New York: McGraw Hill, for the Council on Foreign Relations, 1978). This book also contains an essay by Carlos Diaz-Alejandro, "Delinking North and South: Unshackled or Unhinged," which is "an essay at understanding the mood and substance" behind the influential concept of "delinking the North and the South."

Coming to critical analyses of the NIEO, the most compact and yet comprehensive paper is Mordechai E. Kreinin and J. M. Finger, "A Critical Survey of the New International Economic Order," *Journal of World Trade Law*, London, 1976. Any student of the subject could regard this paper as minimum reading.

Other critical papers are: Herbert G. Grubel, "The Case Against the New International Economic Order," *Weltwirtschaftliches Archiv*, Hamburg, p. 113, 1977; Harry G. Johnson, "The New International Economic Order," *Woodward Court Lecture*, Graduate School of Business, University of Chicago, 1976; Jürgen B. Donges, "The Third World Demand for a New International Economic Order: Government Surveillance versus Market Decision-Taking in Trade and Investment," *Kyklos*, Basle, 30, 1977; Thomas D. Willett, "The Challenges to a Liberal International Order: An Initial Overview," in *Challenges to a Liberal International Economic Order* (Washington: American Enterprise Institute, 1978).

All these approach the subject from the point of view of "Western" professional economists and the first is particularly forceful and thorough. An earlier discussion of these issues, "A Critique of U.N.C.T.A.D.," is in P. T. Bauer, *Dissent on Development* (London: Weidenfeld & Nicholson, 1971). There are also some thought-provoking remarks in the introduction and in the report of the panel discussion in Jagdish N. Bhagwati (ed.), *The New International Economic Order: the North-South Debate* (Cambridge, Mass.: MIT Press, 1977).

Commodity Policy

The UNCTAD proposals are in the Secretary-General of UNCTAD's *An Integrated Programme for Commodities: Specific Proposals for Decision and Action by Governments*, TD/B/C1/193 (Geneva: UNCTAD, 1975). The most detailed review of the Common Fund proposal (though not substantive economic analysis), with practical suggestions at the technical and administrative level, is in a report of a group of experts, *The Common Fund: Report of the Commonwealth Technical Group* (London: Commonwealth Secretariat, 1977).

A valuable and very well-written overview of all the commodity issues is in the report of the House of Lords' *Select Committee on Commodity Prices*, HL 165-I (1976–77) (London: Her Majesty's Stationery Office, 1977). This can be strongly recommended as a general introduction. Another excellent and comprehensive paper is Gordon W. Smith's "Commodity Instability: New Order or Old Hat," in *Challenges to a Liberal International Economic Order* (Washington: American Enterprise Institute, 1978).

Harry Johnson's very critical analysis of the integrated commodity programme is in his "World Inflation, the Developing countries, and an 'Integrated Programme for Commodities'," *Banca Nazionale del Lavoro Quarterly Review*, Rome, December, 1976, and it is also analysed in the various critical papers listed earlier. A detailed study of a fairly technical nature containing much empirical material and simulations of buffer stock operations is in J. R. Behrman, *International Commodity Agreements* (Washington: Overseas Development Council, 1978). Behrman stresses the benefits to consuming countries from commodity price stabilisation. He argues that, because of ratchet effects, commodity price instability has a net inflationary effect, and hence generates vast output losses owing to the anti-inflationary aggregate demand policies which it provokes. His book has a long bibliography, listing in particular many recent empirical studies on commodity issues.

Other useful papers are Robert M. Stern, "World Market Instability in Primary Commodities," *Banca Nazionale del Lavoro Quarterly Review*, Rome, June 1976; G. W. Smith and G. R. Schink, "The International Tin Agreement: a Reassessment," *Economic Journal*, Cambridge, United Kingdom, No. 86, December 1976; Ezriel M. Brook and Enzo R. Grilli, "Commodity Price Stabilisation and the Developing World," *Finance and Development*, World Bank, Washington, 14 March 1977; and the chapters by S. J. Turnovsky and by G. W. Smith in F. G. Adams and S. A. Klein (eds), *Stabilizing World Commodity Markets* (Lexington, Mass.: Lexington Press, 1978).

A standard work which reviews all the commodity policy issues comprehensively, and throws doubt on the need for stabilisation policies (even stabilisation of export earnings) is Alasdair I. MacBean, *Export Instability and Economic Development* (Cambridge, Mass.: Harvard University Press, 1966).

On the alleged tendency of the terms of trade trend to be adverse to developing countries, see Robert E. Lipsey, *Price and Quantity Trends in the Foreign Trade of the United States* (New York: National Bureau of Economic Research, 1963) which is a standard reference; and for figures of recent trends, *Commodity Trade and Price Trends* Report No. EC—166/177 (Washington: World Bank, 1977). A full discussion of the issues—the significance of the terms of trade, problems of measurement, *et cetera*—is in P. T. Bauer, *Dissent on Development* (London: Weidenfeld & Nicholson, 1971). See also Gottfried Haberler, "Modern Challenges to a Liberal International Economic Order: A Historical Perspective," in *Challenges to a Liberal International Economic Order* (Washington: American Enterprise Institute, 1978); and *Select Committee on Commodity Prices, op. cit.,* ch. VII.

Trade in Manufactures

A good summary of the tariff reduction issues is in Kreinin and Finger, *op. cit.* Other key references are Tracy Murray, "How Helpful is the Generalized System of Preferences to Developing Countries," *Economic Journal*, Cambridge, United Kingdom, No. 83, June 1973; J. M. Finger, "Effects of the Kennedy Round Tariff Concessions on the Exports of Developing Countries," *Economic Journal*, No. 86, March 1976; Robert E. Baldwin and Tracy Murray, "MFN Tariff Reductions and LDC Benefits under the GSP," *Economic Journal*, No. 87, March 1977.

Sources of information which I have found useful are *International Trade in Textiles and Developing Countries*, TD/B/C2/174 (Geneva: UNCTAD, 1977); *Recent Trends and Developments in Trade in Manufactures and Semi-Manufactures*, TD/B/C2/175 (Geneva: UNCTAD, 1977); and *Dynamic Products in the Exports of Manufactured Goods from Developing Countries to Developed Market-Economy Countries, 1970 to 1976*, ST/MD/18 (Geneva: UNCTAD, 1978).

General discussions of the problems of market access and of fostering exports of manufactures from developing countries are in I. M. D. Little, Tibor Scitovsky and Maurice Scott, *Industry and Trade in Some Developing Countries* (Oxford: Oxford University Press, 1970); and World Bank Development Policy Staff, *Prospects for Developing Countries 1978–85* (Washington: World Bank, 1977).

International Finance Issues

A good general discussion on international monetary issues affecting developing countries, if a little dated now, is in Johnson, *Economic Policies Toward Less Developed Countries, op. cit.*

On the various financial issues discussed in this paper, see Y. S. Park, *The Link Between Special Drawing Rights and Development Finance*, Essay in International Finance No. 100 (Princeton: Princeton University International Finance Section, September 1973); John Williamson, "SDRs: The Link," in Bhagwati (ed.), *The New International Economic Order: The North-South Debate, op. cit.*; Harold van B. Cleveland and W. H. Bruce Brittain, "Are the LDCs in Over Their Heads?" *Foreign Affairs*, New York, July 1977; Robert Solomon, *A Perspective on the Debt of Developing Countries*, Brookings Papers on Economic Activity, No. 2 (Washington: Brookings Institution, 1977); Louis M. Goreux, "The Use of Compensatory Financing," *Finance and Development*, World Bank, Washington, 14 September, 1977.

Aid

The sources of all information on aid in this paper and in most other papers, are the Annual Reports of the Development Assistance Committee of the OECD, entitled *Development Co-operation*. These reports also contain interesting discussions. Thus, in the 1975 Report there was a chapter on "Aid and Public Support," an issue stressed in this essay. See also for a useful factual survey, Joris J. C. Voorhoeve, "Trends in Official Development Aid," *Finance and Development*, 14 June, 1977.

Two balanced general studies on aid are I. M. D. Little and J. M. Clifford, *International Aid* (London: Allen & Unwin, 1965); and Göran Ohlin, *Foreign Aid Policies Reconsidered* (Paris: Development Centre of the OECD, 1966).

Less balanced, but resting on close study of certain developing countries, is Bauer, *Dissent on Development, op. cit.* In Bauer's view aid generally does more harm than good. The whole of his book might be read as an antidote to the usual optimistic development economics writings. Bauer believes that development must come from within, and that outsiders cannot do much to help. Bauer's negative view of aid is criticised in Alasdair I. MacBean and V. N. Balasubramanyam, *Meeting the Third World Challenge, op. cit.*

A sophisticated discussion of the supposed aid "obligation" of developed countries is in Richard N. Cooper, "A New International Economic Order for Mutual Gain," *Foreign Policy*, Washington, No. 26, Spring 1977. This is a very stimulating paper. As an antidote readers should look at relevant passages in Mahbub ul Haq, *The Poverty Curtain: Choices for the Third World* (New York: Columbia University Press, 1976). These issues, as well as the broader question of the historical roots of the NIEO ideas, are also discussed by Deepak Lal in *Poverty, Power and Prejudice: the North-South Confrontation* (London: Fabian Society, 1978).

Finally, one should perhaps refer to the well-known Pearson Committee, Lester B. Pearson *et al., Partners in Development* (New York: Praeger Publishers, 1969), which deals comprehensively with all the aid issues, although it does not move me to enthusiasm.

Policies of Developing Countries

There is naturally a vast literature on economic policies of developing countries. Here I am only concerned with their trade policies. There are discussions of various issues in Harry G. Johnson, *Economic Policies Toward Less Developed Countries, op. cit.*, but the most important book by far is Little, Scitovsky and Scott, *Industry and Trade in Some Developing Countries, op. cit.*, which stresses the costs of import substitution and controls, and the need for fostering exports of manufactures.

See also Jagdish N. Bhagwati and Padma Desai, *India: Planning for Industrialization* (Oxford: Oxford University Press, 1970); World Bank (Development Policy Staff), *Prospects for Developing Countries, 1978–85, op. cit.*; Bela Balassa, *Policy Reform in Developing Countries* (Oxford: Pergamon Press, 1977); and I.M.D. Little, "Development Challenges to a Liberal International Economic Order," in *Challenges to a Liberal International Economic Order* (Washington: American Enterprise Institute, 1978). The last is a succinct, forceful statement of the case against protection and controls.

An interesting and sceptical review of current fashions in development economics, and especially the new emphasis on redistribution rather than growth (out of which the "basic needs" theme has sprung), is in Deepak Lal, "Distribution and Development: a Review Article," *World Development*, Oxford, 1976.

Historical Experience

The broad view of the post-war development record can be obtained from David Morawetz, *Twenty-five Years of Economic Development:* 1950 *to* 1975 (Washington: World Bank, 1977).

On India, see the fascinating book by Angus Maddison, *Class Structure and Economic Growth: India and Pakistan Since the Moghuls* (London: Allen & Unwin, 1971); and also Bhagwati and Desai, *India: Planning for Industrialization, op. cit.,* 1970. On Japan an excellent source is Angus Maddison, *Economic Growth in Japan and the USSR* (London: Allen & Unwin, 1969), which is directed closely to the questions asked in this paper, and is very clear and concise. See also various chapters in Hugh Patrick and Henry Rosovsky (eds), *Asia's New Giant* (Washington: Brookings Institution, 1976), which is likely to become the standard reference on the modern Japanese economy.

Reflections on the colonial experience are in Bauer, *Dessent on Development, op. cit.,* and in Cooper, "A New International Economic Order for Mutual Gain," *op. cit.* A major work on the subject is David K. Fieldhouse, *Economics and Empire* 1830–1914 (London: Weidenfeld & Nicholson, 1973).

11

Adjustment Assistance for Trade-Displaced Workers

George R. Neumann

A primary obstacle hindering the expansion of trade among nations has been the large dislocation costs borne by individuals. Despite a more than twenty-year period of official concern with this problem in the United States, relatively little has been done to minimize the burden that falls on trade-displaced workers. Thus, even with the development of specific programs such as the Trade Adjustment Assistance (TAA) program in 1962, and the substantially expanded 1974 version, the political pressure against expanded trade continues to exist. In this paper we review the evidence on adjustment-assistance efforts, both domestic and foreign, and suggest an alternative approach to the issue. The plan of the paper is as follows.

From George R. Neumann, "Adjustment Assistance for Trade-Displaced Workers," *The New International Economic Order*, David B. H. Denoon, ed., 1979. Reprinted by permission of New York University Press and Macmillan, London and Basingstoke. Some tables omitted.

In section I the development of adjustment-assistance programs in the United States is reviewed, and their major problems are discussed in section II. The third section of the paper examines the adjustment-assistance programs of other countries and suggests modification in the existing U.S. adjustment-assistance program. In the fourth section the costs of trade adjustment assistance commensurate with the employment changes estimated by Deardorff, Stern, and Greene are presented. The final section summarizes the major results. This paper is concerned with adjustment assistance for displaced workers. Related programs exist to provide aid to firms, but as few firms have made use of these programs, we have focused on programs designed for displaced workers.

I. ADJUSTMENT ASSISTANCE IN THE UNITED STATES

Prior to the Trade Expansion Act of 1962 the only means available for workers affected by increased trade was escape-clause relief. Although present in some earlier trade agreements, the idea of escape-clause relief was formalized in the Trade Agreements Act of 1951. Such actions, effective in principle, are costly, both in economic and political terms. Raising tariffs or establishing quotas reduces, or eliminates entirely, the benefits of trade; consequently, the directness of this approach has prevented its use in most circumstances. Between 1947 and 1962, the president invoked escape clause relief in only fifteen of forty-one cases.[1] Infrequent resort to escape-clause relief is due to two major factors: adverse foreign reaction and the bluntness of the instrument. In areas where only a few marginal firms were affected, relief would have to apply to the entire industry; consequently only major disruptions in trading patterns could be treated in this manner. While a temporary use of escape-clause relief may have been helpful, the tendency for "temporary" quotas and tariffs to become permanent has created obstacles for even limited usage. In the period 1947–62, the costs of labor market adjustments were borne mainly by individuals.

The Randall Commission

The inadequacy of escape-clause relief for reallocating the costs of increased trade were recognized by several observers, and various proposals were offered. The most important of these, from the viewpoint of subsequent adoption, was that offered by David McDonald, president of the United Steelworkers of America, in the Randall Commission Report of 1954.[2] The essence of the proposal was that trade-impacted workers should be compensated in some way to reduce their losses. Three programs were suggested by McDonald. The first provided unemployment benefits for up to one year, and for special training, job counseling, and moving allowances. The second program was an early retirement program—

workers were to be given a certain number of weeks' pay for each year of service with the company, and for workers over fifty-five or sixty, benefits equivalent to the social security benefits that a sixty-five-year-old could draw were to be paid. The third program was a revised unemployment insurance, with benefits paid at a higher rate for a longer time.

Although influential in some regards, the Randall Commission had little success in generating a specific program for trade-displaced workers.

Trade Adjustment-Assistance Programs in the U.S.

Formal efforts in providing adjustment assistance to workers can be separated into three periods: 1962–74, under the Trade Expansion Act of 1962 (TEA); 1966–68, under the Automotive Products Trade Act of 1965 (APTA); and 1975 to date under the Trade Act of 1974 (TA). Despite the appearance of overlap in the dating of the first two programs, they actually are distinct, since adjustment assistance was not available under TEA until November 1969. The essential features of the adjustment-assistance programs, which are outlined in Table 1, are quite similar. Differences that arise among the programs are due mainly to the differences in eligibility requirements.

Examination of the characteristics of these adjustment-assistance programs indicates congressional intent clearly. All three programs have the feature that the adjustment to changed trade conditions would be made primarily by individuals finding new jobs. No attempt was made to create new employment opportunities, and even upgrading of workers' skills was not stressed, as no additional training opportunities were created. To facilitate this adjustment, the cash payments made to individuals were significantly larger and were available for a longer period of time, thus eliminating most of the short-term income loss that workers would incur.

The liberality of the benefits available was offset partially by the strictness of the eligibility requirements. Under TEA a recipient had to have been employed at least half-time for the previous three years at some firm, and also to have worked twenty-six weeks of the previous fifty-two at the trade-impacted firm. The effect of this restriction was to focus benefits at workers with "full-time" labor force commitment. Although these individual requirements restricted eligibility somewhat, the greatest restriction was occasioned by the group eligibility determination. Because the Tariff Commission linked adjustment assistance to escape-clause relief, groups were eligible for benefits only if their unemployment was "in major part [due to] . . . concession[s] granted under trade agreements."[3] Since the Kennedy Round tariff cuts did not begin until 1968, the availability of adjustment-assistance benefits under TEA was delayed until 1969.

Group eligibility requirements were loosened under the APTA by replacing the Tariff Commission with the Automotive Agreement Adjustment Assistance Board composed of the secretaries of commerce, labor,

TABLE 1
Characteristics of Adjustment Assistance Under TEA, APTA, and TA

	TEA (1)	APTA (2)	TA (3)
I. Benefits:			
Cash Payments	65% of previous weekly earnings up to a maximum of 70% of average manufacturing weekly earnings	65% of previous weekly earnings up to a maximum of 70% of average manufacturing weekly earnings	70% of previous weekly earnings up to a maximum of 100% of average manufacturing weekly earnings
Job Training and Counseling	Special services not available, but individuals were eligible for services provided under any federal law	Special services not available, but individuals were eligible for services provided under any federal law	Special services not available, but individuals were eligible for services provided under any federal law
Job Search Allowances	None	None	$500 maximum
Relocation Payments	Reasonable and necessary expenses plus 2.5 times average weekly earnings in manufacturing	Reasonable and necessary expenses plus 2.5 times average weekly earnings in manufacturing	80% of reasonable and necessary expenses plus 3.0 times the workers average weekly wage
Maximum Benefit Period	52 weeks: 65 weeks if over 60	52 weeks: 65 weeks if over 60	52 weeks: 78 weeks if over 60
II. Eligibility Requirements:			
A. Individual	Employment in 78 weeks of the previous 156 at wages of $15 per week, and 26 of the 52 weeks with the impacted firm	Employment in 78 weeks of the previous 156 at wages of $15 per week, and 26 of the 52 weeks with the impacted firm	Employment in 26 of the previous 52 weeks with the impacted firm
B. Group Determination Made By	Tariff Commission	Automotive Agreements Adjustment Board	Secretary of Labor

and the treasury, and by changing the legal wording of "in major part" to "a primary factor."[4] This severed the link between escape-clause relief and adjustment assistance for this act but had no bearing on other adjustment-assistance programs. In essence, this was a legal finesse, because escape-clause relief was never considered as an option by any of the parties.[5]

The greatest change in the group eligibility decision process was made by the TA of 1974. The Tariff Commission, renamed the International Trade Commission, was replaced entirely by the secretary of labor in determining eligibility, and determination of eligibility was made dependent on imports having *contributed importantly* to workers' separation. Essentially, this meant that changes in impacts for any reason—even if imports fell but domestic production declined at a greater rate—would make groups eligible for adjustment assistance.

Because of differences in eligibility requirements, these adjustment-assistance programs differed greatly in size. Evidence on the size differences among the programs is given in Table 2. Limiting eligibility to the automobile industry accounts for the small size of the APTA program, but the pronounced size differences between the TEA and TA programs must be attributed to the more liberal definition of trade impact.

The size difference between the programs may be overstated somewhat due to the sharp recession of 1974–75, but this is unlikely to account for all of the sevenfold increase.

The development of trade adjustment programs in the U.S. has proceeded from an exclusive use of escape-clause relief to adjustment-assistance programs applicable to a single firm or to groups of workers. These latter effects, which rely mainly upon short-term income maintenance to smooth the transition to reemployment, have varied degrees of success. Adjustment assistance under the TEA was delayed until November 1969 because of a strict interpretation of eligibility. Further delays

TABLE 2

Characteristics Of United States Adjustment-Assistance Programs

	TEA	APTA	TA (4175–9176)
	(1)	(2)	
Certifications	106	14	435
Denials	171	7	640
Number of Certified Workers	53,970	2,493	105,000
Benefits Paid	$86 million	$4.1 million	NA

Source: Bureau of International Labor Affairs unpublished documents and P. Henle, "Trade Adjustment Assistance: Should It Be Modified?" *Monthly Labor Review,* 100, no. 3, pp. 40–45.

in benefit delivery also occurred during the program's operational period because of the eligibility requirements. In contrast, the adjustment-assistance program operated under the APTA is generally regarded as more successful, in part because of the absence of such delays. Although the adjustment-assistance programs were otherwise similar, the restriction of eligibility in this case to workers from one industry facilitated eligibility determination and benefit delivery. It is not clear how much of this success was due to the program being restricted to one industry and how much was due to the industry being the automobile industry—an industry that has relatively few firms, most of which are organized by one union.

The adjustment-assistance program contained in the TA of 1974 is only slightly different from its predecessors in terms of the kinds of benefits provided but is significantly more available to workers because of the more liberal eligibility requirements. Because of this expanded eligibility, the current adjustment-assistance program far exceeds previous efforts in attempting to aid trade-displaced workers.

In essence, then, the sixteen-year history of adjustment-assistance effects in the United States can be summarized as a continual expansion of the beneficiary population with little change in the basic structure of the programs. Emphasis has been, and is, on the provision of short-term income maintenance with almost no attention to longer-run problems of reemployability and earnings loss.

II. ADJUSTMENT ASSISTANCE: PROBLEMS OF IMPLEMENTATION

Experience with adjustment-assistance programs, despite the numerous changes that have occurred, has generally been less than favorable in the United States. To be fair, the APTA is often considered to have been successful,[6] but this was a very small program, limited to one industry. It is more comparable to private adjustment programs, such as negotiated by the railway workers on Amtrak, or the arrangements negotiated in the West Coast longshoring industry. Larger programs such as the TAA program in the 1962 act and its successor in the 1974 act have found few strong supporters. Organized labor regards these programs as at best "burial insurance," and the opinion of the business community is no higher.[7] Independent observers offer no great support for the program either and even question the conceptual basis for such programs. That the program survives at all in the face of such opposition is surprising and can be explained more by political expediency than by any economic benefit-cost calculation.

Since the experience of the past is often a guide to the future, a critical examination of the deficiencies of past and present adjustment-assistance programs is in order. Before evaluating the problems that have occurred, a knowledge of the population the programs were designed to serve is essential.

Who Are the Trade-Impacted Workers?

Several studies of trade-impacted workers have appeared in recent years, all of which focus on workers who received benefits under the TAA program of the 1962 Trade Expansion Act.[8]

One consistent picture emerges from these studies: TAA recipients tend to be older, less educated, and less skilled than the average unemployed individual. This lack of general skills is usually counterbalanced by a significant amount of time spent with one employer. Consequently, the prelayoff earnings of these individuals were not noticeably atypical of the industry. However, the attribution of such a substantial part of earnings to firm-specific factors implies that a job separation will have much larger effects on this group. Since women appear to be overrepresented among trade-impacted workers, this problem is emphasized.

An important caveat should be added to this description of the trade-impacted worker. The characteristics reported refer to those workers who actually received benefits under the TAA program. Not all workers who are affected by increased trade receive these benefits, and for several reasons one would expect that workers who do receive benefits would differ significantly from other trade-impacted workers. For example, the impact of increased trade does not usually occur immediately—firms generally experience a reduction in demand, or poor growth, several periods in advance. Therefore, mobile workers, reacting to the adverse situation, may quit to find employment in firms or industries that offer more attractive long-run opportunities.[9] Also, since adversely affected firms tend to react by not replacing normal attrition, the net result is that the workers employed when the full trade impact occurs are likely to be those who have the greatest difficulties in making the transition to alternative employment.

This review of the characteristics of TAA recipients who were permanently displaced from previous employment indicates that trade-displaced workers face unusually severe problems when laid off. In general, they are older, less educated, less likely to be skilled workers, and have a significant portion of their work experience with one firm. Prior studies of the relationship of earnings to personal characteristics would lead one to expect poor prospects for reemployment and, if reemployed, a significant decline in earnings, which are also observed. While evidence from the current adjustment-assistance program is limited, there are several reasons to expect that permanent job losers would be as disadvantaged now as previous individuals were. The normal workings of the labor market would result in those workers with the greatest opportunities either leaving a trade-impacted firm earlier, and thus not being eligible for benefits, or finding employment quickly after impact and thus not applying for benefits. This "screening" effect can be expected to be present whenever there is advance notice or expectations of a plant closing. A further reason to expect these characteristics to apply to future job losers is based on the industries that are most affected by impacts. With a few notable exceptions, such as steel, impacts have had their greatest effect in low-wage, labor-intensive industries such as footwear, textiles, and some parts of the electronics industry. Workers in these industries tend to be less skilled than the average U.S. worker, and thus the effect of increased trade tends to concentrate unemployment in these sectors. This effect is likely to diminish as production in the United States becomes more specialized in capital—both human and physical—intensive sectors, but it will still have effects in the near future.

Benefits Provided by TAA: Some General Criticisms

Although access to adjustment-assistance benefits has been increasing since 1962, and thereby meeting some of the objections to increased trade, the TAA programs continue to be criticized about the structure of the programs. The major areas of complaint are: (1) benefits are received with a sometimes substantial lag; (2) the amount and type of benefits are inadequate; and (3) inequities exist in that individuals facing the same problems are treated differently according to the reason for unemployment. In discussing these criticisms, we will be concerned primarily with their applicability to the current program. However, since experience with the current TAA program is limited, we will have to infer some information from the earlier program.

Benefit Delay. Benefit delivery under the 1962 program was characterized by extremely long lags—on average, benefits were received seven months after layoff. The reason for this long lag was the cumbersome eligibility determination process. Investigations had to be made by the Tariff Commission and, following an affirmative finding, the Department of Labor. The information required for these investigations was often not available to workers, and even when it was, the absence of a standard application form until 1972 made it difficult for workers to determine what was needed. Further delays were encountered after an affirmative finding by the Department of Labor, since individuals had to be personally certified by the state employment agencies. Because the information required was different from that normally required for unemployment compensation eligibility, the process would normally be delayed even further as the agencies searched for information.

To some extent, these delays have been minimized in the 1974 TAA program. Investigation is required only by the Department of Labor, and the personal eligibility requirements now require information that is readily available to the state agencies. Despite these changes, delays still exist and will continue to exist. For example, while the Department of

Labor was initially able to rule on petitions for eligibility within sixty days, in the July–September quarter of 1976 only 6 percent of the petitions were ruled on in this time, and over 50 percent took longer than ninety days. While some of this delay is due to the sudden increase in the number of petitions, delays are inherent in any program that has restricted eligibility. It follows, therefore, that if the TAA program is to be differentiated from regular unemployment insurance (UI), delays in benefits of one to three months will occur.

Benefit Adequacy. The most frequent charge against the TAA program is that the benefits provided are inadequate—they do not foster a rapid movement to alternative employment, and they do not compensate the worker for losses incurred. Judgment on this issue must be mixed. On the rapid movement to alternative employment there is ample evidence that the TAA program either has no effect or encourages individuals to remain unemployed longer.[10] Compensation for losses incurred is a different matter. Workers who are permanently separated from their jobs incur large losses in earnings when reemployed, and many do not return to employment at all. For these workers the TAA program provides only short-term income support. However, under the 1974 TAA program, permanent job losers are only a fraction—perhaps a small fraction—of all TAA recipients.[11] For individuals who are on temporary layoff, the TAA program provides substantial compensation, and in some cases overcompensates, for lost earnings. As an example, consider the case of an individual separated in June 1976. Assuming that the individual was earning the average in manufacturing, $208.06 per week, his trade readjustment allowance would be $145.65. This appears to be a substantial difference, but due to the nontaxable nature of these benefits, the weekly difference is only $16.60.[12] Thus, a year's unemployment would mean a difference of only $863 in net income. In multiple-earner families this loss is less and if the member with the lower earnings receives adjustment-assistance benefits may even become a net gain.

This example points out a central problem with the TAA program. Since the major feature of TAA is the payment of unemployment compensation at a higher rate and for a longer period than regular UI programs, it is most successful in aiding those who need assistance least—those on short-term layoff. Indeed, the program can be criticized only because such payments, by linking benefits to unemployment status, implicitly encourage longer spells of unemployment. But for workers who are permanently displaced and who therefore incur the greatest losses, the program offers only short-term support and has little or no effect on subsequent earnings.[13]

Differential Treatment of Trade–Impacted Workers. An issue that frequently arises in discussions of adjustment assistance is why individuals who have lost jobs due to imports should be treated differently from other unemployed individuals. Jobs are continuously being lost, and new ones created, due to many factors—technological change, shifting patterns of taste, population change, and so on. Workers who lose jobs for reasons other than increased trade face the same problems as trade-impacted workers, so the argument goes, and equity would dictate that they be treated similarly. Arguments in support of differential treatment have usually been based on the idea that the government through its policy decisions on tariffs and quotas was in part responsible for the unemployment of trade-impacted workers and therefore was obliged to respond differently. While this argument is not universally accepted, it is the premise upon which the TAA program is based. Implicit in it is the view that all other sources of unemployment are, in some sense, risks of the marketplace that workers must bear. If one accepts this argument, eligibility for the TAA program under the 1962 act follows naturally: benefits were to be provided to individuals whose unemployment was linked to tariff *concessions*. But the 1974 program has removed this link; variation in imports due to any reason can qualify individuals for adjustment assistance. The elimination of this direct relationship makes it difficult to justify the existence of adjustment assistance in its present form and has important implications for the size of the TAA program and the type of individuals who receive benefits. Whereas under the 1962 program recipients of TAA benefits were almost entirely workers who had been prematurely separated from their jobs, under the present program workers who are on short-term layoff and who expect to return to their jobs with no loss of earnings can now receive TAA benefits.[14] Although experience with the TAA program under the 1974 act is limited, what evidence does exist suggests that a profound change has occurred due to severing the link to trade concessions. From April 1975 to September 1976, a total of 1,075 petitions for adjustment assistance was filed with and investigated by the Department of Labor. Of these 435 were certified and 160 were pending by September 30. More than 105,000 workers were receiving payments under the act in the first eighteen months compared with the 54,000 who received benefits under the previous program in five years.[15]

The "type" of trade-impacted worker has also changed. The automobile industry now accounts for the largest number of TAA recipients, and the primary and fabricated metals industries are not far behind. Also, most TAA recipients return to the previous employer, according to the Department of Labor, which is considerably different from the situation under the old program when 70 percent did not find employment even in the same industry.[16]

The blurring of the distinction between adjustment assistance and unemployment compensation raises, as we noted above, questions of equity. Without a linkage to tariff or quota reductions, decisions about eligibility for TAA have a certain arbitrariness. Thus, if imports of foreign cars increase, employees who manufacture bumpers for an automobile manufacturer may be eligible for TAA benefits, but if the bumpers were purchased from a firm that did not make automobiles, its employees would not be eligible for benefits.[17] Similarly, individuals performing service operations, but not the actual manufacture of a product, are not eligible. Further examples could be given, but the point is clear: without direct connection to tariff reductions, an adjustment-assistance program can be limited only by arbitrary restrictions on eligibility. The consequences of such arbitrariness are inevitable. Workers perceive the TAA program as being unfair, and receipt of benefits is regarded as a political matter. Public opinion for programs that provide benefits in arbitrary fashion is unlikely to develop.

In summary, both previous and present adjustment-assistance programs have had critical flaws that have reduced their usefulness. The administrative structure of the 1962 program resulted in lengthy delays in benefit receipt, which severely limited the value of the benefits. Although the procedures were streamlined in the 1974 act, the increase in the number of cases has resulted in lags that are still substantial. One would have to conclude that the present form of adjustment assistance is not readily adaptable to speedy and effective administration.

A judgment about the adequacy of benefits under the adjustment-assistance program must necessarily be mixed. For individuals who are permanently separated from their jobs, the program offers little aid. Adjustment allowances will provide short-term compensation with relatively small financial loss. However, the real loss that these individuals suffered was in their reemployment earnings, if they found jobs at all, and no part of the adjustment program was adequate to prevent this loss. Partly by design—neither the 1962 nor the 1974 programs were designed to compensate workers for financial loss—and partly due to ineffective programs—for example, training—the adjustment-assistance programs have not been able adequately to minimize the burden of adjustment borne by those who are permanently separated from employment. For those workers who are only temporarily unemployed, mostly those covered under the 1974 act, the TAA program provides adequate and in some cases more than adequate compensation. The losses experienced by such workers are both relatively and absolutely small compared with those experienced by permanent separations.

Finally, although the concept of adjustment assistance has been a basic part of U.S. trade policy since 1962, the changed conditions of eligibility for TAA benefits under the 1974 act significantly weaken the rationale for providing such benefits. As the distinction between the Trade Adjustment Assistance program and regular unemployment compensation diminishes, the purpose of adjustment assistance becomes lost.

III. ALTERNATIVE APPROACHES TO ADJUSTMENT ASSISTANCE

The previous sections reviewed problems that beset the current adjustment-assistance program. Some of these problems can be eliminated by minor changes, but the majority seem resolvable only by significant changes in the structure and orientation of the existing program. In considering alternative forms of assistance, a natural reference is the experiences of other countries with similar problems. In the first part of this section we review the labor-market solutions employed by the major trading partners of the United States. Although this information is illuminating, it must be viewed in perspective. Institutions, particularly labor-market institutions, vary widely across countries, and thus what works in one country may not succeed in another. Nonetheless, cross-country comparison can be useful in suggesting the possible elements of an adjustment-assistance program. In the second part of this section we use the insights gained from this review and the discussion of the previous section to outline an alternative adjustment-assistance program.

Adjustment Assistance in Other Countries. [18]

An examination of the adjustment-assistance effects of other countries reveals a most interesting fact: among the major trading partners of the United States—Canada, the United Kingdom, West Germany, Japan, and Sweden—only the United States has a separate program designed to aid workers displaced by foreign trade. There are Trade Adjustment Assistance programs in other countries—for example, Canada and West Germany—but they are designed to provide technical and financial help to firms. What assistance is provided to workers comes from general programs, or, in a few cases, from ad hoc programs restricted to a specific industry. In essence, trade-displaced workers in other countries receive the local equivalent of unemployment insurance in the United States. These "unemployment insurance" programs are similar to that of the United States in that they emphasize cash payments, but they also contain other benefits aimed at relocating or retraining workers. Canada, under the Manpower Mobility Assistance program, pays jobsearch allowances, relocation expenses up to $1,000, and will provide up to $1,500 if an unemployed worker sells a house and moves to a new locality. Job training is also available through the Technical and Vocational Training Assistance Act.

In Great Britain, unemployment compensation is paid under the Redundancy Payments Act of 1965, based on age and experience with a particular firm. Conditional upon having two years of experience, workers aged eighteen to twenty are entitled to one half of one week's pay for each year of experience; those aged twenty-one to thirty-nine are entitled to one week's pay, and workers over forty are entitled to one and one-half week's pay for each year of experience.[19] Training is provided by the Industrial Training Act of 1964, with the training being provided by the firm that hires the worker. The costs of training are paid for by taxes on the firms.

Sweden offers similar incentives for workers to relocate. Unemployment benefits are available, as are job-training programs; relocation expenses; and, of particular importance given Sweden's chronic housing problem, preferential housing treatment.

Limited assistance is available in West Germany and Japan basically due to the peculair labor-market institutions in these countries. Both economies have experienced strong growth since the 1950s and except for brief periods have encountered more labor shortages than surpluses. This experience has led to the development of the institution of lifetime employment—*shūshin koyō*—in Japan, and, in West Germany, a reliance upon immigrant labor from southern Europe. Fluctuations in employment consequently have not had an impact on most workers in the past. There have been exceptions to be sure—coal mining during the late 1950s and early 1960s experienced significant declines in employment due to government-directed rationalization—but these have been isolated cases, and little political support for adjustment assistance has developed.

The rationalization of the coal and steel industries in the Common Market countries provides an interesting exception to the general pattern of adjustment assistance in other countries. In this case, it was explicitly recognized by the individual countries that rationalization of these industries would dislocate many individuals and thereby generate political problems. In response, the European Community adopted an adjustment-assistance program that was quite similar to the TAA program in the United States. It differed in one respect, in that it explicitly attempted to minimize the earnings losses suffered after new employment had been found. The program authorized compensation of individuals at up to 90 percent of previous earnings for fifteen months after displacement. Thus, if an individual could find employment at only 75 percent of previous earnings, the program would pay an additional 15 percent. No evaluation is available, at least in English, of the effects of this program on unemployment patterns or subsequent earnings, but it seems likely that this novel approach must have had some effect.

This review of the adjustment-assistance policies of other countries provides an interesting comparison with U.S. efforts. Although other countries do not have separate programs for workers, the services provided under general programs are similar to those provided under TAA. This is hardly surprising, since the services provided under TAA in the United States are similar to those available under unemployment insurance; the only difference is the slightly more liberal financial benefits and relocation allowances. Not surprising also is that, with the possible exception of Sweden, there is no strong evidence that such programs have much effect. Indeed, this brief review of alternative adjustment practices suggests that the major factor that minimizes the adjustment costs of worker dislocation is the level of aggregate demand. In countries experiencing strong economic growth, the reabsorption of displaced workers is swift and, although information on earnings losses is minimal, there do not appear to be great costs involved in transferring workers to new jobs. This is consistent with the views expressed in the Trade Expansion Act of 1962—adjustment assistance was to be only a minor aid in offsetting the costs of adjustment; a strong economy would be the major factor in minimizing adjustment costs. The experience of the last decade has taught us that, at least in the mature industrial economies, this precondition is not always fulfilled.

An Alternative Approach to Trade Adjustment Assistance

Having reviewed the major aspects of adjustment-assistance programs in the United States and other countries, we can inquire what features would be desirable in a future adjustment-assistance program. The first issue is: Who should receive TAA benefits? In the original TAA program and in most special programs in other countries, eligibility for adjustment assistance was tied to a specific action by the federal government —usually changing tariffs or quotas. Subsequent developments in the 1974 Trade Act led to a greatly expanded eligibility criterion: variations in impacts for any reason could trigger adjustment assistance. The expanded eligibility results in two classes of beneficiaries—those who are permanently separated from employment due to imports, and those who are on temporary layoff and who, therefore, incur only minor losses.[20] The question is: Should both types of individuals receive TAA benefits? The arguments in favor of a broad-based program of adjustment assistance[21] are implicitly based upon the arguments that it is arbitrary to single out one source of government action (e.g., lowering tariffs or quotas) as being deserving of assistance, and ignore other actions (e.g., tax incentives that lead to an [artificial] advantage for overseas production), and that the cost of not distinguishing among recipients is, apart from the obviously larger beneficiary population, small or nonexistent. Both arguments ignore crucial aspects of labor-market behavior. First, the desirability of linking adjustment assistance to some specific action of the government is not related to any concept of merit or causation; rather it is an attempt to identify, in the most efficient manner, those individuals who suffer losses greater than can reasonably be remedied through existing labor-market institutions, such as unemployment insurance. If linking adjustment assistance to tariff changes does not adequately identify those who are particularly injured, then some other criterion can be chosen. Note that one cannot claim that any method is more discriminatory than another. All programs that provide benefits to a subset of the population are inherently discriminatory. The only question one can ask, given a collective desire to direct benefits to workers adversely affected by trade, is whether the eligibility criteria of the program direct benefits to those most severely affected. From this consideration, and the fact that workers on temporary layoff incur little or no loss of earnings upon reemployment, and are covered by regular unemployment insurance during the interim, there appears to be no reason that would support providing benefits at a higher rate to workers whose layoffs were due to increased imports. Indeed, fundamental questions of equity would arise if workers who were otherwise identical and who incurred five weeks of layoff were compensated at different rates. For workers who have been permanently separated from previous employment, the case for adjustment assistance is much stronger, particularly so given the large losses in earnings they incur.

The argument that the provision of adjustment assistance to a broader class of workers will not occasion any indirect costs—that is, the costs of such a program will be higher only due to the expanded population base—ignores the fundamental role wage differentials play in the labor market. In the absence of such benefits, workers would be led not to enter industries that are losing or have lost part of their comparative advantage or, if already employed, would consider leaving the industry in response to the fluctuations in income occasioned by temporary layoffs. But if these fluctuations are eliminated or substantially lessened, as appears to be the case under the current program, the incentive to adjust is lessened. Consequently, the result may be an eventual large mass layoff that labor markets adjust to only with difficulty and with significant lags rather than a series of smaller adjustments that may involve substantially smaller costs.

Both of these considerations argue for a restriction of adjustment-assistance benefits to those workers who are most seriously injured—those who are permanently separated from their jobs. The thrust of the argument would suggest, however, that *all* workers, without regard to the proximate cause of unemployment, should be so aided. In other words, it is in the spirit of these arguments that the word "trade" be dropped from the TAA program and eligibility opened to all workers involved in, say, plant closings. While this has a strong appeal in terms of consistency, there are valid reasons for continuing a modified form of the present program. It is easier both to monitor and to modify a program that has an easily identifiable recipient base, and there may well exist administrative economies as well. It seems clear, however, that the TAA program could serve as a prototype for other programs.

Assuming an eligible population for adjustment assistance that is restricted to those who are permanently separated from previous employment, the question becomes: What elements should form the basis of the TAA program? The problem these individuals face is clearly one of inadequate job opportunities. Elimination of their previous jobs has resulted in a reduction in specific human capital, the effects of which persist for several periods. In practice, it takes a while for individuals to realize that some fraction of their previous productivity was firm-specific and that their value to another firm is less, often substantially. Existing programs do little to change this situation, since employment is not encouraged by subsidizing unemployment, and job-training programs do not in themselves provide jobs. One solution to this problem, which has been used in Great Britain and Sweden, is to provide public works programs. But this is a very blunt weapon, and one that takes time to organize. Furthermore, since the locus of job displacements is continually changing, the number of workers in any one area may be too small for such a program to adequately use the talents available. Thus, while such a program will provide jobs, it may not compensate individuals adequately. Moreover, timely receipt of benefits is unlikely under such a program unless it is functioning as part of a larger public employment program.

Currently proposals are pending in Congress for an overhaul of the welfare program. These proposals, if enacted, are likely to involve an expanded public sector jobs program. Reports indicate, however, that the public sector jobs program will, if enacted, pay wages at the minimum wage level. For most trade-displaced workers even a 25 percent reduction would not reduce their earnings to the minimum wage level, and thus such programs are not likely to have much of an effect on these individuals.

Since the major loss suffered by trade-displaced workers is the precipitous reduction in earnings upon reemployment (which partially accounts for the long spell of unemployment), the most direct way to deal with the problem is to provide a wage subsidy. This, in essence, was the approach of the European Community in dealing with the rationalization of the coal and steel industries, and is similar in principle to the investment tax credit. While the concept of a wage-subsidy plan is clear, there are a number of details which must be treated carefully if the program is to reduce both the amount of unemployment suffered by trade-impacted workers and the earnings loss attendant to reemployment.

First, the wage subsidy should be directed toward eliminating the average loss suffered by individuals. Available information indicates that a subsidy of 20 percent for about three years would eliminate the average loss. Further refinements could be made, such as a different subsidy rate— say, 25 percent—for workers over sixty, or for a rate that declined over time. Once a particular subsidy rate has been decided upon, the question of how to pay it arises. Direct payment to certified individuals seems the most obvious and direct method, but the method provides no incentive for firms to expand employment. In effect, a wage-subsidy paid directly to the worker becomes a generalized transfer payment that occurs independently of the worker's employment status. Conditioning the amount of the subsidy on either previous earnings or reemployment earnings would provide additional incentives for workers to remain unemployed and search longer for higher-paying jobs, thereby increasing their measured unemployment rates. If, however, the subsidy is paid directly to the employer, then the incentives of the worker are not adversely affected and the number of jobs open to the worker will be expanded. In this case, the effect of a wage subsidy paid to the employer leads to shorter durations of unemployment and greater expected earnings upon reemployment.[22]

Although the administrative details of the process would have to be determined, one obvious method would be to issue eligibility cards to all certified workers, which could then be presented to firms during employment interviews. An employer who hires a trade-impacted worker would then be allowed to deduct the subsidy rate—20 percent of actual earnings—from his business income taxes. Thus, a wage subsidy paid in this manner becomes, in essence, a labor tax credit.

Although a wage-subsidy program appears desirable because of its effects on unemployment and earnings, there are several areas in which a wage-subsidy program will differ significantly from current and previous adjustment-assistance efforts. A wage subsidy paid to employers will not, for example, provide benefits to those individuals who do not become reemployed. For those individuals who voluntarily choose not to work—whether due to an optimal timing of the retirement decision or to a desire to, perhaps temporarily, engage in nonmarket activity such as raising a family—there is no real injury due to trade and thus the appropriate assistance is being provided. The option of working is, of course, always available to these individuals. It may be argued, however, that not all individuals who do not find work are voluntary withdrawals from the labor force. In other words, there may exist some areas in which there exists a shortage of job openings. The empirical magnitude of this fraction of labor force withdrawals is a matter of considerable debate; however, the wage-subsidy program can be made flexible enough to provide greater incentives for employment in unusual cases. For example, the wage subsidy could be increased in areas of particularly high unemployment levels, or it could be made dependent upon the workers' length of unemployment. With sufficient flexibility allowed for in the determination of the wage subsidy, there is no reason to believe that this approach would provide lower benefits to workers than the previous approaches.

One area in which complexities arise is that of determining eligibility. If eligibility is not defined strictly, then it is possible that a wage-subsidy program could create incentives for firms to lay off workers and rehire them at subsidized wage rates. If benefits are available to individuals on temporary layoff, it is obvious that a wage subsidy creates incentives for firms to lay off workers, claim injury due to imports, and then benefit from lower wage costs. Even when there are permanent job losses, not all firms or plants completely cease operations, and so in these cases there is also an incentive for firms to lay off more workers than they otherwise would, and to eventually hire them back. There are two ways to eliminate this problem. One is to have a very careful and intensive examination of the existence of trade impact in each case. Precise delineation of which products are affected and which workers were engaged in producing them would be needed. To pursue this route, however, would inevitably lead to the same problems that occurred under the 1962 act; the investigatory lag would result in benefits being delayed, thus reducing their usefulness.

An alternative approach is to limit the applicability of the subsidy to individuals who change employers. This will remove the incentives for firms to place more workers on temporary layoff and will avoid subsidizing firms that would otherwise be unable to compete in a specific product class. Although this requirement seems discriminatory, there is a strong rationale for it: the substantial loss in earnings which trade-impacted workers suffer. Furthermore, if wage subsidies were available to impacted firms, there would not be any incentive to reallocate production to products in which they have a comparative advantage.

In terms of the workers' well-being, the appearance of discrimination among workers is mostly illusory. Since each eligible worker has the option of gaining employment at a different firm, the fact that some may return to their previous employer and not receive any direct benefits from the wage-subsidy program is merely indicative that their value of the return option exceeded the alternative of alternative employment. Firms that have been adversely affected by trade may, indeed, feel that a wage-subsidy plan limited to new hires from other trade-impacted firms is discriminatory, but again it is not. All firms have the option of hiring new employees who are eligible for the wage subsidy. To allow the wage subsidy to apply to previously employed workers would both overcompensate workers (since firm-specific human capital will not have been lost) and conflict with the basic goal of trade adjustment—reallocating workers to jobs in which the United States possesses a comparative advantage.

Finally, we note that a wage-subsidy program, despite its potential benefits, has one important drawback: it lacks visibility to those who are most immediately concerned. A program that provides higher monetary benefits or public service jobs to affected workers provides very tangible evidence of political action. Dollars paid or public sector jobs filled can be easily counted, and although such actions may create opposition among some parts of a politician's constituency, such opposition is weak relative to the political demand for benefits. A wage-subsidy program, even if it creates more jobs and generates higher reemployment earnings, does so in a manner for which it is not easy for a politician to claim credit. Thus, it is obvious that an essential element for the success of such a program is a careful monitoring of the reemployment experiences of trade-impacted workers in order to document the efficiency of such a program.

To summarize, then, a wage-subsidy program, coupled with regular unemployment insurance benefits, is proposed as an alternative to the existing TAA program. The major advantage of this approach is that a wage subsidy program, in contrast to income-maintenance programs that have characterized previous adjustment-assistance programs, provides direct incentives for job creation and thereby for minimizing unemployment among trade-impacted workers. Moreover, as we have outlined it, a wage-subsidy program will have a direct effect upon earnings subsequent to reemployment. Finally, the administrative complexity and cost of operating such a program appear no larger than current efforts. Whether the direct budgetary costs of operating such a program are comparable is a question to which we now turn.

IV. THE BUDGET COSTS OF TRADE ADJUSTMENT ASSISTANCE

A major consideration in the choice of an adjustment-assistance program is the direct budget cost of such programs. All else the same, the program that has the least cost will be the socially most desirable one. In the preceding section we argued that a wage-subsidy program could provide superior benefits to trade-impacted workers; it remains to be shown whether this can be achieved at a reasonable cost. In this section we compute the cost of providing adjustment assistance under three possible programs. To provide an appreciation of the scale of adjustment-assistance programs, we use these estimates to calculate the budget costs that would occur under several of the tariff policies considered by Deardorff, Stern, and Greene.[23]

The average cost of adjustment assistance per recipient can be broken into three components:

a) *unemployment compensation*—which depends upon the benefit rate, previous earnings, and the length of time unemployed.
b) *training and counseling services*—which depend on the fraction who enroll in these programs; and
c) *wage subsidy*—which depends upon the subsidy rate and reemployment earnings.

We consider three programs: program 1—identical to the current TAA program; program 2—all features of the current program are retained and a wage subsidy of 20 percent for three years is added; and program 3—the current TAA program is supplanted by a three-year wage-subsidy program with the subsidy rate declining from 20 to 15 percent, and finally to 10 percent in the last year. Individuals are still eligible for unemployment compensation.[24] . .

The results in Table 3 indicate that a wage-subsidy program such as we have suggested costs the same per worker as the current program;

TABLE 3

Average Cost of Three TAA Programs, Per Individual

	Unemployment compensation	+	Training and job search	+	Wage subsidy	=	Total
Program 1	6,383	+	294	+	0	=	$6,677
Program 2	6,099	+	294	+	4,955	=	$11,348
Program 3	2,481	+	294	+	3,769	=	$6,544

wage-subsidy payments under program 3 turn out to be roughly the same as the extra unemployment benefits available under the current program. The distribution of benefits will be different, however, since wage subsidies will accrue only to those who become reemployed. Under this program there will be more individuals who find employment, so that the net distributive effect will be unclear. Finally, note that the combination of the current TAA program with a wage subsidy results in almost a doubling of the average cost. In essence, the higher unemployment benefits induce individuals to remain unemployed longer, which therefore increases the cost of the program.

Adjustment-Assistance Costs of Alternative Trade Policies

To provide an indication of the magnitude of an adjustment-assistance program, we compute the costs of six tariff-policy options, considered by Deardorff, Stern, and Greene. The six policies considered are those in which U.S. tariffs are reduced from current levels. . . .

. . . Estimates . . . of the costs of providing adjustments assistance [under the three different programs] range in the aggregate from $43 million to $287 million. Compared with TAA expenditures of $170.5 million in 1976, these amounts do not look particularly large. However, these estimates may understate the number of workers eligible for adjustment assistance, since they are based on net displacements from an industry. It is difficult to assess the magnitude of this bias. . . .

V. SUMMARY

In this study of trade adjustment-assistance policies in the United States, we have examined three questions: What types of assistance have been provided? How successful have these programs been? And what alternative could be considered in the future? The assistance provided to trade-impacted workers has been varied, but the trend has clearly been to rely upon specific programs of assistance.

In practice, these programs have met with little success in the United States, and related programs in other countries appear to have had similar results. The failures of these programs to minimize the burden of trade-related job losses can be attributed in part to diverse problems—benefit delay, inappropriate training opportunities, and so on—but the major defect was conceptual. As operated, the programs amounted to expanded unemployment insurance payments. In a labor market characterized by high demand, such programs may have been quite adequate, but in a situation where the closing of one firm has a significant impact on local demand, the result is a lack of jobs. More importantly, since workers' firm-specific knowledge is reduced in value, those who do find jobs suffer substantial earnings declines. The TAA program as operated under the 1962 act and the 1974 act is ill-equipped to deal with these problems. Although short-term income maintenance is provided by the TAA program at a fairly high rate, its effect on the reemployment situation facing most workers is minimal.

In order to minimize the costs borne by trade-displaced workers, an adjustment-assistance program must focus on increasing the employability of the displaced workers. Several options exist, but the nature of trade dislocations and the type of individuals affected render some possibilities infeasible. Retraining efforts have not been successful, basically because they have not been focused on the special problems of the trade-impacted worker, and it may be very difficult to provide the appropriate training. A public employment program could have some effect, but it is a very blunt instrument. A program of wage subsidies, paid to employers of trade-displaced workers, represents a possibility that can minimize the impact of job loss to individuals both by increasing employment opportunities and by eliminating part or all of the earnings loss at relatively low cost. Indeed, a wage subsidy coupled with regular employment insurance in lieu of the present TAA benefits is likely to be less expensive than the current program.

Notes

1. S. Metzger, "Adjustment Assistance," in the U.S. Commission of International Trade and Investment Policy, *United States International Economic Policy in an Interdependent World* (Washington, D.C.: U.S. Government Printing Office, 1971), p. 320.
2. U.S. Commission on Foreign Economic Policy, *Report to the President and the Congress* (Washington, D.C.: U.S. Government Printing Office, 1954). Earlier versions of some of the ideas are credited to John Coleman of the Committee for a National Trade Policy, Meyer Kestenbaum of the Committee for Economic Development, and Stanley Ruttenberg of the (then) Congress of Industrial Organizations in R. Bauer, I. De Sola Pool, and Z. Dexter, *American Business and Public Policy* (New York: Atherton, 1963), pp. 34–35.
3. Public Law 87–794, sec. 301 (c), (2).
4. See J. Manley, "Adjustment Assistance: Experience under the Automotive Products Trade Act of 1965," *Harvard International Law Journal* (Spring 1969): 294–315.
5. The companies involved operated plants in both the United States and Canada, and the union, the UAW, also represented workers on both sides of the border.

Neither party had an incentive, therefore, to press for strong actions such as escape-clause relief.

6. See C. Frank, *Foreign Trade and Domestic Aid* (The Brookings Institution, Washington, D.C., 1977) p. 57.

7. See Committee on Ways and Means, *Trade Reform*, 93rd Cong., 1st sess., for the list of problems that business and organized labor found in the 1962 program.

8. See M. Bale, "Adjustment to Freer Trade: An Analysis of the Adjustment Assistance Provision of the Trade Expansion Act of 1962," Ph.D. dissertation, University of Wisconsin, 1973; J. McCarthy, *Trade Adjustment Assistance: A Case Study of the Shoe Industry in Massachusetts*, Federal Reserve Bank of Boston, Research Report No. 58, 1975; and G. Neumann, *An Evaluation of the Trade Adjustment Assistance Program,* report submitted to the Bureau of International Affairs, U.S. Department of Labor, under contract number ILAB74–23.

9. Brechling provides strong evidence that quits within an industry respond sharply to declining employment opportunities. See F. P. Brechling, "A Time Series Analysis of Labor Turnover," in W. G. Dewald, ed., *The Impact of International Trade and Investment on Employment*, mimeographed (Washington, D.C.: U.S. Department of Labor, 1977).

10. See Neumann, *An Evaluation*, p. 34.

11. Henle, "Trade Adjustment Assistance," p. 44, quotes a Labor Department estimate that 90 percent of all TAA recipients are only temporarily laid off.

12. Assuming an average tax rate of 22 percent—13.2 federal, 5.85 FICA, and 3 percent state.

13. Because of the sharp earnings losses incurred by permanently separated workers, roughly 20 percent, the TAA program is likely to have a significant effect on duration. An individual who was earning x per week receives $0.7x$ as TAA payments. If his best employment offer is $0.8x$, then he is indifferent between working and receiving benefits of $0.7x = (1 - t) \, 0.8x$, where t is the average tax rate. This implies, with no value given to leisure, that workers facing a tax rate greater than 12.5 percent would always exhaust their benefits. More generally, if z denotes the expected percentage loss in earnings at reemployment, an individual will prefer working only if

$$t \leq \frac{0.3 + z}{1 + z}$$

14. It is difficult to understand why all workers on layoff do not petition for TAA eligibility. The process has been streamlined to such a degree that the costs to an individual are small, and the potential gain, in terms of higher benefits, is large. The major costs are of course borne by the government.

15. See Henle, "Trade Adjustment Assistance."

16. Neumann, *An Evaluation*, p. 29.

17. The component parts issue was present under the 1962 act, but the issue arises frequently under the new act also.

18. This section draws extensively on material in chapter 9 of C. Frank, op. cit. 1977, pp. 124–147.

19. See C. Smith, *Redundancy Policies,* BIM Report No. 20, 1974.

20. We say only "minor" losses, since such individuals are eligible for various other income maintenance plans such as regular UI, and negotiated private agreements such as supplementary unemployment benefits.

21. See. e.g., Frank, pp. 124–147.

22. Evidence supporting this assertion is given in N. Kiefer and G. Neumann, "Estimation of Wage Offer Distributions and Reservation Wages," in S. A. Lippman and J. McCall, eds., *Studies in the Theory of Search* (Amsterdam: North-Holland, 1979.) The essential idea is that a wage subsidy to the employer creates, via the conventional demand for labor argument, an incentive for employers to hire trade-impacted workers relative to other factors of production.

23. Alan V. Deardorff, Robert M. Stern, and Mark N. Greene, "The Implication of Alternative Trade Strategies for the United States," in David B. H. Denoon (ed.), The New International Economic Order: a U.S. Response (New York: New York University Press, 1979).

24. For consistency we attribute all unemployment payments as costs of the TAA program. This convention underscores the fact that we are calculating the budgetary and not the social costs of adjustment assistance.

12

Information and the Multinational Corporation: An Appropriability Theory of Direct Foreign Investment

Stephen P. Magee

Here, we analyze private market creation of "information" (technology), relate it to the observed behavior of multinational corporations, and draw policy implications for the purchase of information by the less developed countries (LDCs). The theory proposed is a natural evolution of the views of Hymer (1960), Vernon (1966), and Caves (1971) on foreign direct investment and of Arrow (1962), Demsetz (1969), and Johnson (1970) on the creation and appropriability[1] of the private returns from investments in information. Such a consolidation of views is necessary for systematic consideration of policy proposals aimed at inducing greater "transfers of technology" through multinational corporations. The formulation adopted is based on six ideas.

1. Industries in which the demand for new products is high have a high derived demand for new information.
2. For these industries, investments must be made to create five distinct types of information; specifically, information is required for product
   a. creation;
   b. development;

    c. production functions;

    d. markets; and

    e. appropriability.

    Thus, the term "technology transfer" by private firms is ambiguous until the type of information being transferred is specified.

3. There are decreasing marginal returns on the stock of information applied to a given product and information-saving growth in production in the long run (that is, information flows as a factor of production become relatively less important after some point). Thus, investments in new information will be high early in a product's life and will decrease as it ages. Vernon (1966) developed a technology cycle for individual *products* that is consistent with these statements; we shall build here upon a technology cycle developed elsewhere for entire *industries*.[2]

4. The public-goods aspect of information and the attendant calculations by firms of the appropriability of the private returns from creation of information is one of the most important considerations determining both the type of technology created and the sectoral allocation of private research effort. Private markets bias their information investments toward sophisticated information because appropriability is higher for complicated ideas than for simple ideas.

5. The cost of trading each type of information dictates whether it is transmitted most efficiently intrafirm or extrafirm. Optimum firm size for 2a is small (many products are discovered by lone inventors). Optimum firm size is increased by 2b through 2c because of lower costs of intrafirm movements of new information, economies of scale in the use of new information across many products, greater intrafirm appropriability of the private returns to investments in new information, and greater managerial skill in industries creating new information (the sophistication required to successfully coordinate 2b, 2c, 2d, and 2e dictates that managers in "new product industries" be more highly skilled than the norm; hence, the managerial constraint on firm size will be less in these industries). These considerations explain the correlation (though not necessarily the causation) between the tendency of multinational corporations to be large and their tendency to produce sophisticated, information-intensive products.

6. The legal, political, and economic systems of the LDCs differ significantly from those in the DCs. These and other considerations indicate that their welfare would be increased by modify-

ing their adherence to the Paris Convention (the code of international patent behavior).

We consider only finished manufactured products, as examined in Vernon's (1966) product cycle and in Caves' (1971) "horizontal" type of direct investment; raw materials are excluded in this analysis. There is a long and rich literature on the multinational corporations as conveyors of new products and technologies to the world. The pioneering study by Hymer (1960) on the monopoly advantage held by multinationals in technology and Vernon's (1966) product cycle developed this theme. However, no paper to date has dealt simultaneously with the five different types of information created by firms and their "transfer" to developing countries, with the appropriability question, with optimum firm size, and with the international policy issues that these points raise vis-à-vis the LDCs for information created by multinational corporations.

We apply these six ideas to the multinational corporations and generate the following hypotheses. Multinational corporations are specialists in the production of information that is less efficient to transmit through markets than within firms. Multinational corporations produce sophisticated technologies because appropriability is higher for these than for simple technologies. The appropriability of the returns from these public goods (information) and complementarities among the five types of information dictate large optimum firm size. The large proportion of skilled labor employed by multinationals is an outgrowth of the skilled-labor intensity of the production process for both the *creation* of information and *appropriability* of the returns from information. The relative abundance of skilled labor in the developed countries dictates that they have a comparative advantage in creating and exporting new information. There are diminishing returns to information in the short run. Output growth of new products ultimately has an information-saving bias in production. And all of these considerations generate a technology cycle at the *industry* level.

In Section 1 we develop the hypothesis and discuss the effects of the different types of information on the firm. In Section 2, we discuss some of the conventional wisdoms with respect to the behavior of the multinational corporation and how the theory proposed here provides a convenient framework for organizing and explaining some of the stylized facts of foreign direct investment. In Section 3, we evaluate policy proposals for the transfer of information between developed countries and developing countries and suggest a modified adherence by the LDCs to the Paris Convention.

1. THE HYPOTHESIS

Let us consider the generation of economically useful information. Information is a durable good, in that present resources must be devoted to its creation and its existence results in a stream of future benefits. Information is also a public good, in that once it is created, its use by second parties does not preclude its continued use by the party who discovers it. However, use by second parties does reduce the private return on information created by the first party. This is the "appropriability problem" (see Arrow, 1962).

We should expect that for information of all types, economic actors will invest resources in the generation of information until the expected private returns will be equated to the returns on other investments of equal risk. Four traditional types of information are created by private markets in the generation of new products: information required for (1) discovery of new products, (2) development of the products, (3) development of their production functions, and (4) creation of their markets.

An important fifth type of information affects each of the previous four, namely, (5) knowledge of the degree to which creators of information can appropriate to themselves the returns on the new information. It is a near tautology that the greater the public-goods aspect of new information, the lower its private market appropriability and the more reason for private markets to underinvest in it. Johnson (1970) noted the two ways historically in which society has dealt with this problem of the public-goods nature of information: either the *government* creates the information and provides it freely to private markets or the legal system permits *private* firms to internalize the returns by either creating temporary monopolies through the patent system or allowing restrictions on free trade in information through trade secrets.[3] Is welfare higher with government or private market creation of information?

1.1 Government versus Private Market Creation of Information

Consider a technological breakthrough resulting in the creation of a new product or service whose demand, marginal revenue, and marginal cost curves are represented by D, MR and MC in Figure 1. If private markets develop the ideas and if the rights to the breakthrough are fully protected legally by patents or trade secrets, output of the product will be Q_m, the price will be P_m, monopoly profits will be B, and the gain to society will equal the sum of B and the consumer's surplus triangle A. If the government develops the same product and distributes the information freely, absence of the legally sanctioned monopoly and the presence of many competitive firms will drive market output to the competitive level Q_c, the price to P_c, and the gain to society will equal the consumer's surplus areas $A + B + C$. With a government's free dissemination of the information, welfare is higher than under patent protected creation of the information by area C. These points are developed in some detail in Johnson (1970).

However, the issue of public versus private creation of information is more complicated than this. If welfare is always higher with government

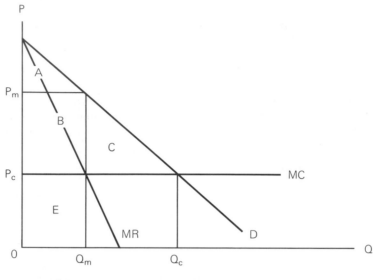

FIGURE 1

distribution of information, why are patents and trade secrets permitted as incentives for creative activity? The previous analysis indicates that there are two alternative ways in which society could be made better off by government intervention. The first would be for the government to let private firms create information through the patent system. Once an important discovery had been made, the government could purchase the discovery from the inventor, pay him the present value of the monopoly profit stream (the current flow equals area B in Figure 1), and provide the information freely to private producers. In this way, welfare would increase by area C. Three difficulties with this solution are that markets in information are not "efficient" (in the way in which some securities are "efficient") so that establishing the present value of new information might be more costly than the social gains from its free provision; sellers of information would attempt to extract the entire social value of the patent, equal to the monopoly profits plus $A + C$, and this would create redistribution problems that would be costly politically; and sellers of patents would waste real resources attempting to influence politicians and bureaucrats equal to, at most, $A + B + C$. Sales of new military technologies to the U.S. Department of Defense are good examples of these problems.

The second solution is for the government to do the research and development itself and make the results freely available. The problem with this solution is that the selection of the research and development projects would be determined as much by political investments and bureaucratic idiosyncracies as by social rates of return. Since organizational costs for political groups in society are far from identical, there is no reason to believe that political investments in pork-barrel lobbying would be proportional to expected social returns on new information. (See Brock and Magee, 1975, for an analysis of investments in politicians.) Thus, the *allocation* of government research and development may be less correlated with social returns in many product areas than the monopoly profits conferred by the patent system. In cases in which the welfare losses from *underprovision* of new products by patent holders is more than offset by the superior private *allocation* of research and development, then private rather than public creation of knowledge is justified. Casual empiricism suggests that private research and development is probably superior for toasters, hand-held hair driers, and radial ply tires, while government research and development is better for some types of agricultural research. An important argument against privately patentable research hinges on varying private appropriability of the returns from such research, given even the protection of the law. The more uncorrelated are private appropriabilities of new information and their social returns, the less efficient is private market allocation of research and development. We examine next the types of information required during the product and industry technology cycle.

1.2 Five Types of Information

New product discovery. The technology cycle developed here differs from Vernon's (1966) product cycle in that we deal here with a cycle for both the product and the entire industry.[4] In spite of some notable exceptions, five papers in the NBER [National Bureau of Economic Research] Study (1962) of inventions indicated that a simple maximization model is a good first approximation in explaining inventive effort (see Nelson, 1962, p. 11). Nevertheless, the discovery of major new products (locomotives, autos, aircraft) is difficult to explain if it is not random. The same is true in explaining why some industries have a high demand for new products. We shall sidestep these problems by assuming that inventions of major new products occur randomly.

The investments in innovation can be described more systematically. This approach is taken because *innovation* rather than *invention* is the focus of multinational corporation activity. Once a major invention has occurred, the expected return on new technology for the components of the new product is high. The development of the automobile increased the returns on improved technologies for carburetors, electrical assemblies, clutches, gears, and even tires (the demand for rubber and rubber substitutes was greatly increased, although synthetic rubber was not commercially successful until the 1940s). Thus many minor inventions follow a major discovery rapidly, until the returns on new information start to decline.

Nelson (1962) has observed that patents for a given *industry* follow an S-curve over a long period of time, reflecting an eventual retardation in new investments in information for creation, development, production, and appropriation of the industry's products. . . . The steeply rising part of the curve reflects the derived demand for components, economies of scale inherent in the production of information, and the complementary applicability of new information to other products in the same industry. At some point in time, the marginal returns decline on the flow of additional information, as the transferability to other products declines and as the market demand for standardization is reached. As industries mature, all of these considerations lead to decreases in the share of industry value added going to investments in information. In effect, growth becomes "information saving in production." Throughout the industry technology cycle, "technological change," "factor productivity," and the effects of "learning by doing" are all endogenous and determined by the existing stock of information and rational investments in new information. As a result, research and development investments and changes in factor productivity should be high early in an industry's life cycle and low late in the cycle. This prediction is supported by the data: the simple correlation between research and development investments as a percent of sales and the average industry age for twenty-nine U.S. three-digit SIC [Standard Industrial Classification] industries in 1967 is $-.34$. Vernon's cycle dealt only with individual products so that he had no theory of the eventual decline in research and development by entire industries. Here, we have provided a rationale and evidence for industry-wide declines in research and development with maturity of the industry.

Another important empirical regularity is that investments by each industry in the *creation* of new products is not necessarily done by the firm that develops the products commercially. For example, Mansfield (1974, p. 151) points out that many industrial innovations are based on relatively "old science." Many inventors and small firms make breakthroughs that result in the creation of new products. Although an increasing proportion of patents has been granted to corporations, private inventors still play an important role (Nelson, 1962, p. 5). Thus, we expect that optimum firm size may be smaller in young industries than in older industries.[5] One reason is that the low appropriability of the private returns on information generated in industries with small optimum firm size is well protected in this stage by the patent system. The patent system is more effective in protecting new products than in protecting the next three types of information.

Product development. Research and development expenditures by large firms are primarily for the development rather than the creation of new products. Mansfield (1974, p. 150) has outlined the stages for which information is important in the development process: "applied research, preparation of product specification, prototype or pilot plant construction, tooling and construction of manufacturing facilities, and manufacturing and marketing start up," with the entire process frequently taking five to ten years. Large amounts of information are required to estimate the costs of each step and high managerial capabilities are needed to coordinate their undertaking. Certain firms, such as multinational corporations, develop comparative advantages in creating information for controlling product development. The information generated by creating one product becomes applicable, through learning by doing, to other new products. Since this information is usually transmitted more efficiently intrafirm than through the market, optimum firm sizes increase in the development stage. Another characteristic of the industry cycle, which parallels Vernon's product cycle, is that product differentiation is high for new industries and low for older industries. The correlation in 1967 between product differentiation and the average industry age for 101 U.S. three-digit SIC industries is $-.29$, indicating that older industries have less product differentiation and more standardized products. Finally, the appropriability problem for this type of information is particularly serious.[6] The patent system does not provide full protection for the early prototypes of many new products. Rivals can free ride on the development process of innovating firms if they can make apparently major though inexpensive changes in the characteristics of the product.

Three important steps remain that are information-intensive: the firm must develop the production function, generate market demand, and appropriate the returns.

Creation of the production function. The most important source of derived demand for information on the supply side is for the development of the production function for the new product. Although economists frequently assume that engineers or technicians provide such functions, actually large and costly investments in information must be made to create the most efficient methods of production. Vernon stresses how the production function shifts from being skilled-labor-intensive early in a *product's* life cycle to unskilled-labor-intensive and captial-intensive late in the cycle. This is consistent with a framework that includes the stock of information along with the other physical inputs in the production function. As that stock increases, diminishing returns and "information saving" growth help explain what Vernon calls "standardized production" processes in stage 3 of his product cycle. With standardized production processes, new investments in information are low, including in information implicit in the human capital employed by the industry (in both production and non production labor). This implies that production wages will be lower for old industries than for new ones. The data are ambiguous on this point: for ninety-three U.S. three-digit SIC industries in 1967 there was no relationship between production wages and the average age of the industry. However, when the same data are aggregated to seventeen two-digit SIC categories, the correlation between the two variables equals − .30, as expected.

An important structural factor also explains the eventual standardization of the production process for an entire industry. As patents begin to lapse, monopoly and oligopoly structures characteristic of the early life of some new industries begin to crumble. Increased competition erodes the private market appropriability of the returns from new production technologies so that the production function is "frozen" or becomes standardized at the most efficient process extant. Although processes are protected by patents, patents provide less appropriability to processes (especially simple ones) than to products. As a result, industry structure is relatively more important in protecting production technologies. If industry structure does not change, then the existing structure plus the normal economic process already discussed (diminishing returns on information and so forth) will eventually standardize the production process.

Market creation. The firm introducing new products must invest in information to discover the market *and* to determine the most efficient method of communicating information to consumers on the existence of a new product or technique. In this section, we discuss only the second type: communication investments or advertising. Since the amount of information conveyed must be higher for new industries, we expect a negative correlation between the age of the industry and the amount of advertising done. At the three-digit SIC level in the United States for 1967, we had only thirteen observations on these two variables and they were uncorrelated. The only supporting empirical evidence is indirect: the correlation between advertising as a percent of sales and research and development as a percentage of sales for sixteen four-digit SIC industries in the United States in 1967 is .37. Of course, the causation in this relationship may be determined by the joint dependence of both variables on another variable, such as market structure.

Nelson (1970) has drawn a distinction in the advertising literature between "search" goods and "experience" goods. With experience goods, it is impossible to determine from physical examination whether the goods actually live up to the advertisements for them. With a search good, on the other hand, the qualities advertised can be tested by visual inspection before purchase. Advertising by search-good firms must communicate information (because it can be easily disproved) while that conveyed by experience-good firms creates only brand loyalty. But there is an economic logic to firms specializing in the marketing of many experience goods (see Telser, 1976), establishing brand recognition, and becoming large in the process. The reputations of these firms convey market information and are established by firms' consistency in selling goods of a predictable quality. This reduces the costs of search and uncertainty about product quality for purchasers. For example, in retailing, consumers frequently use firm names rather than product names in selecting the quality and prices of products that they are going to sample before purchase. There is a natural hierarchy of retail stores whose ranking from low to high quality products goes from a discount store to a Zayre to a J. C. Penney to a Sears and finally to a Saks Fifth Avenue.

A similar process is at work with the multinational corporations. They specialize in the development, production, and marketing of an experience good, namely, new information. The quality of the technology they produce and the price at which it is sold is determined partly by the accumulated experience of the market as to the reliability of past information sold by each firm. Multinational corporations provide an important screening device for the retailing of new information. However, in the development of markets, they differ somewhat from the Nelson (1970) dichotomy since they are selling experience goods and yet their advertising must convey verifiable search information, namely, on *existence* of a new product.

The appropriability problem for returns to advertising will be more severe for search goods and homogeneous goods than for experience goods and differentiated products since returns on advertising for the latter are more firm specific. The positive correlation noted earlier between industry research and development and advertising is consistent with this observation. For all industries, including older search-goods type industries whose products contain little new technology, appropriability of the returns on firm advertising should increase with industry concentration.

Appropriability. We have discussed the appropriability problem for each of four types of information created by multinationals. We consider here a final investment in information, namely, the determination of how much must be invested to stop interlopers from copying these types of information. As noted earlier, society attempts to remedy free riding caused by the public-goods nature of information—through patents, trade secrets, and legal means—but the protection is never complete. If a firm develops a new product with a one-shot next period stream of $1 million in monopoly profits, than an interloper wishing to copy the idea (who feels that the probability equals p that he could win an infringement suit brought by the innovating firm) would be willing to invest up to $p/(1 + r)$ times $1 million in legal fees in this period to protect his infringement (r is the return on a risk-equivalent investment). The knowledge of this possibility will certainly affect the amounts invested in information by the innovating firm.

Lack of appropriability is analogous to depreciation of the information investments. In the development stage, the multinational corporation must estimate the anticipated depreciation rates on each of the expected information investments in product creation, product development, production function development, and market development. Higher expected depreciation rates result in smaller investments in information. Thus, the firm must invest in information to determine the probability of leakage of new ideas, the reduction in revenues if information is lost, the cost of legal and extralegal remedies to prevent leakage, and the cost of punishing interlopers. The firm will invest in private appropriation schemes until the marginal dollar spent equals the marginal dollar of the expected present value of revenue saved.

It should be pointed out that generation and implementation of this information, as well as of the previous four types, is skilled-labor-intensive. For example, computer firms invest to camouflage the technology in new models of their computers to prevent copying by rival firms. The rational firm will create artificial and sophisticated masking devices, artificial product differentiation, and expend resources to appropriate the returns on earlier investments. These are more efficiently done intrafirm than through the market. Although these appear to be wasteful from a social point of view, they are an inherent by-product, and in some cases a sine qua non for the creation of information by private markets. The current success of a firm in its appropriability investments affects its expectations about the future appropriability of returns on present investments and, hence, the supply of future information.

The two most important variables affecting appropriability are the efficiency of the legal system in preserving appropriability and the industry structure. For a given legal system, the more "potentially" competitive the industry, the more likely that investments by one firm in information will be copied by rival firms. A monopolist has no appropriability problem unless there are "potential" entrants who can enter to emulate innovations made by the monopolist (for expositional ease, the term "potential entrant" is ignored in succeeding discussions of market structure).

One irony is that private expenditures by individuals and firms to prevent loss of appropriability are also public goods. The first firm in an industry may expend large sums to establish proprietary rights and precedents for technologies appropriate to the industry. Since subsequent innovators do not share in these investments, but benefit from the appropriability protection they provide, such innovators take a free ride and private investments in appropriability will be too low. Monopolistic or cartelized industries are less plagued by this problem than competitive industries since their collusion on other matters provides a useful framework in which to share the costs of private enforcement of appropriability. The less developed countries are at a disadvantage on this score since they specialize in products with competitive market structures. This is *one* explanation of the low level of research and development by the LDCs.

A more important question is why so little research and development is devoted to the creation of simple, unskilled-labor technologies, which are in high demand in LDCs. There are good economic reasons why production technologies developed by the multinationals are "inappropriate" for developing countries. One reason multinationals do not develop simple technologies is that their appropriability is so low that they are not profitable. It is impossible, even with patents, to prevent the rapid depreciation of returns on ideas that have high social returns but low private returns. Multinationals, for example, generally cannot capture the return on discovery of a superior rearrangement of unskilled laborers. As a result, they cannot be expected to create unskilled-labor technologies. The gap between the private and social rate of return on this information for LDC firms is also high. Developing countries do not possess skilled labor forces, they specialize in industries that are highly competitive and they produce old and standardized products with no experience-goods characteristics. On the other hand, it is possible that for some industries, the social return is also low so that the existing technology is the optimum.

Vernon (1966) gave some convincing reasons why production will occur early in the product cycle in developed countries and late in the cycle in developing countries. These arguments carry over to the industry technology cycle. In order for the production functions to match different factor markets, production functions should be skilled-labor-intensive early in the cycle and unskilled-labor-intensive late in the cycle. But variation in technology is costly so that the firm creates initially a technology that lies between the two extremes. During the cycle, modification costs prohibit the technology from having as much variance as factor markets. The average factor-intensity of the production function created early in the cycle is thus biased away from techniques using unskilled labor for two reasons: unskilled-labor-intensive production occurs much later in the technology cycle so that it gets a lower weight because of *discounting* and returns on the development of unskilled-labor-intensive and simple technologies are *less appropriable*.

Finally, the appropriability theory provides a compelling argument for the fact that multinational corporations have biased their research away from simple, unskilled-labor-intensive technologies. The appropriability of these types of information is lower than for sophisticated technologies. We have already established that concentrated industry structures are more favorable than competitive ones to the private creation of information. A rational monopolist or collusive oligopoly will prevent or delay the introduction of a randomly discovered new unskilled-labor-intensive technology with *low* appropriability if it is highly substitutable for an existing technology that has a higher *private* present value because of its *higher* appropriability.

1.3 Optimum Firm Size

There is a problem of determining the direction of causation in relating the creation of information to the structure of industry. We know one reason why monopolists will be more likely than perfect competitors to invest in information: they will be more successful in appropriating the returns (the naive counterargument is that because of sloth, they will underinvest in information). But causation can run the other way. Firms creating information may expand to internalize the externality that new information creates. Let us summarize the arguments as to why firms that create information will be larger.

First, though the relationship is far from perfect, there is a tendency for new products to be "experience" goods and for standardized products to be "search" goods. Optimum firm size will be larger, *ceteris paribus*, for retailers of experience goods. For multinationals subsidiaries are more likely than licensing for experience goods.

A second point is that sales of many high technology products must be accompanied by sales of service information. The firm's optimum size is expanded because of service subsidiaries in the information creating industry. IBM's servicing is a case in point.

Third, the average number of products produced by information creating firms should be greater than the number produced by other firms because of complementarities in the use of new information across products. Fourth, complementarities among the last four types of information (development, production, marketing, and appropriability) and their more effective intrafirm rather than extrafirm transmission increase firm size.

Fifth, there is risk associated with the creation of new products. Negative covariation in the returns to creating different products suggests that multiproduct developments will reduce both risk and costs to the firm. For example, mistakes made in developing one product can be avoided in subsequent ones. In many cases, this information (regarding minor failures) cannot be transmitted through markets as efficiently as intrafirm. For this reason larger firms will be more efficient in minimizing the costs of duplication of errors.

Sixth, as products become older and the technology diffuses, the spread narrows between the buyer's and the seller's evaluations of the information created by the firm. This reduces the cost of market transactions, since less search is required, so that licensing is likely late in the cycle and subsidiaries are important early in the cycle.

In summary, what do we expect to happen to optimum firm and plant size through the technology cycle? We know that small firms and inventors create many new products. Optimum firm size should then be smaller for new product industries. However, optimum firm size grows rapidly as the product ages, that is, as the firm exploits the patent in the information-intensive stage of development, production, marketing, and appropriation. The market shares of the largest firms will then decline slowly as the appropriability of the returns on information falls because of entry and increased competition from other firms. Vernon's (1966) product cycle did not deal with this question of optimum *firm* size. He did

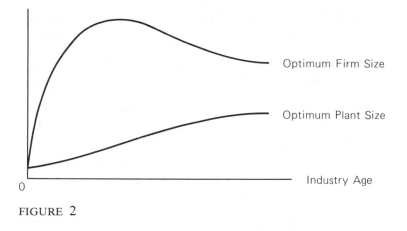

FIGURE 2

suggest that optimum *plant* size might rise through his cycle as mechanization and assembly-line production accompanied the standardization of production. All of these considerations suggest the relationship between optimum firm size and optimum plant size through the technology cycle shown in Figure 2.

The evidence on the hypothesized relationship between optimum firm size (or industry structure) and industry age is mixed. . . . The correlation between [the four-firm concentration ratio and the average product age for 137 four-digit SIC industries in the United States in 1967] . . . is low. However, it is clear that the older industries are less concentrated than the rest. The youngest industry was 11.7 years old and the oldest was 39.3 years old: 25.5 years is the midpoint of this range.

We divide the industries into two groups: there are 119 industries with ages below, and eighteen with ages above, 25.5 years. The average four-firm concentration ratio was 34 percent for the younger group (with a standard deviation of 15 percent), and 26 percent for the older group (with a standard deviation of 9 percent). A Behrens–Fisher t test of the difference in the means indicates that they are significantly different at the .01 level. An F-test of the difference in the variances shows them to be significantly different at the .025 level. Although we find no evidence for increasing concentration with age for the very youngest industries, the very oldest industries are less concentrated than the rest, as hypothesized. . . .

2. APPROPRIABILITY, THE TECHNOLOGY CYCLE, AND THE STYLIZED FACTS

The previous discussion provides a framework within which to interpret recent discussions of the multinational corporation, direct investment, and technology transfers. The framework here emphasizes that multinational corporations generate new products requiring large investments in five complementary types of information. It is fruitful to treat information like any other tangible good and to think of the international operations of the multinational corporations as international trade in this commodity (see Helleiner, 1975). The revenue from trade in information is the present value of the monopoly profit streams permitted by international patent agreements and trade secrets. The price of the information is the present value of the monopoly profit streams permitted by international patent agreements and trade secrets. The price of the information is the monopoly element in the price of the new product. What implications follow from this approach?

Since *international trade* in information is analogous to international trade generally, both exporters and importers will play optimum tariff games (see Rodriguez, 1975). Importers will tax it and exporters will restrict its flow (for example the opposition of the U.S. government to General Electric's sale of jet engines to France in 1972). Importing regions mistakenly equate the monopoly profits on new products with export taxes by exporting countries. Monopoly profits are consistent with competitive rates of return on investments in information ex ante.

Information importers should realize that levying optimum tariffs on information can increase their welfare but will *reduce* the quantity of information imported below free trade levels and hence reduce the "transfer of technology." In the same context, some discussions of "technology gaps" get very sloppy. If we think of technology transfer as international trade in information, then the phrase "technology gap" is a misunderstood catchword equivalent to other equally misdirected phrases such as "fuel gaps," "wine gaps," and "cloth gaps"—any situation in which a country is a net importer of a product. Some regions have comparative advantages in creating information and others comparative disadvantages. The theory of comparative advantages applies to trade in information just as it applies to steel, autos, and textiles: countries that do not have a comparative advantage in creating it should import it.[7]

It is clear why horizontal direct investment and product *differentiation* are correlated. Caves (1974, p. 136) has said: ". . . the multinational making horizontal investments tends to flourish in just those industries afflicted with strong product differentiation, and perhaps other sources of high entry barriers as well." This association is more than affliction: in fact, a cornerstone of the appropriability theory is the important behavioral link between the creation of information and concentrated market structures. Brand loyalty in the marketing of experience goods, information, and product differentiation are important instruments used by private firms in appropriating the returns on new information. If product differentiation and barriers to entry were eliminated, investments in privately created information would fall, and Caves' own industrial organization theory of direct investment would be weakened.

New products are exported to *foreign markets* long before the originating firm sets up production facilities abroad. Vernon (1966) cited several important reasons for this; however, another is suggested by appropriability. Appropriability suggests that depreciation of new information increases with the number and the geographical dispersion of plants, since both the probability of leakage and the costs of preventing leakage increase.

The U.S. data are consistent with this hypothesis. The correlation in 1967 between industry age and the U.S. geographical concentration of industry employment for thirty-two three-digit SIC industries is −.35, indicating that production for young industries is concentrated in a few locations while production for older industries is widely dispersed. If developing countries wished to speed up production relocation for new products within their national borders, guarantees of greater appropriability of returns would increase transfers of technology by private firms.

The term *defensive investment* may be a misnomer for the normal process of increased competition as entrants erode the rents to innovating firms (as appropriability is being lost). Rather than "following each other around," multinationals may be simply increasing industry competition (for industries well into the cycle). Another explanation is that multinationals are free riding on the information investments of their rivals. If one firm succeeds in marketing a new product in a given country, its multinational competitors will follow.

Takeovers of host country production facilities and *mergers* of multinationals with host country firms are normal consequences of the expansion in optimum firm size early in an industry's technology cycle. They may be aimed at slowing the depreciation of the stock of information by absorbing the most likely interlopers. This is another example of expansion to internalize an externality. Limits to take-overs by host country governments, through forced joint ventures or forced licensing, redistribute current income to the host country but reduce optimum firm size, appropriability, and future information flows. Since these policies are equivalent to taxation, they should be evaluated by host governments in an optimum tariff framework.

The phrase *transfer of technology* must be refined. First, the connotation of a costless gift should be discarded: all information transfers entail some cost. There are many ways in which information is transmitted: intrafirm transmission through the multinational corporations, market transfer through licensing, and government transfer through aid. Second, for the multinationals, we have already emphasized that several types of information are created and transferable, and the type of information transferred should be specified. Third, the fact that existing information is a public good does not mean that speeding up its transmission is a welfare improvement. For example, a policy imposed speedup in the transfer of sophisticated production technology may cause its premature introduction into unskilled-labor-abundant countries.

As indicated in Figure 2, optimum firm size should fall after the innovation stage in the technology cycle. This suggests that *licensing* should increase relative to direct investment after some point. These market, rather than intrafirm, transactions will increase since increased market information about the technology possessed by the multinational corporation reduces the variance in the valuation of the technology and thereby reduces market search costs.

Finally, since multinationals can practice price discrimination across markets, there is the question of whether LDCs pay more or less than DCs for identical technology imports. Johnson (1970, p. 41) speculates that the price elasticities of import demand for high-technology goods are higher in LDCs than DCs. If the marginal delivered costs of the products are similar worldwide, then the elasticities indicate that discriminating monopolists would charge the LDCs less than the DCs for new technology. However, the Vaitsos (1974) study shows that Johnson's (1970) speculation does not apply to Colombia: priced paid by Colombia for its imports are much higher than the world average. If this is true generally, then the view that international *price discrimination* permits LDCs to pay less than their pro rata share of the worldwide costs of generating new information may be false.[8] (Such assertions must be tempered by the realization that the LDCs will not import the new technology until later in the technology cycle. This consideration will lower their pro rata share.)

How much more than the world price do the LDCs pay for their information-intensive goods? The only evidence presented here comes from the Vaitsos (1974) study. Matching a sample of $5 million in pharmaceutical imports into Colombia with Vaitsos' price estimates indicates that $3 million of the $5 million in imports (60 percent) are payments in excess of the world price.

If international price discrimination in these high technology products could be costlessly eliminated, Colombia's welfare would increase by $4.5 million at current world prices, or by almost the value of existing imports. These calculations can be illustrated in Figure 1. Let P_c be the world price and P_m the price now paid for the sample of pharmaceutical imports. Area E, $2 million, corresponds to the cost of the imports at world prices, and area B, $3 million, is the excess Colombia pays because of international price discrimination. If Colombia purchased the pharmaceuticals at world prices, Colombia's consumer's surplus and welfare would increase by the current discriminatory monopoly profit paid to foreign exporters, area B ($3 million), and the eliminated deadweight loss from discrimination, area C ($1.5 million). (With linear demand curves, area C is always one half of area B.)

3. CONCLUSIONS AND POLICY IMPLICATIONS

We examine here the role of the multinational corporations as international traders in information. We stress the ambiguity and possible meaninglessness of the traditional use of the term "technology gap," suggest a redefinition, and enumerate five types of information generated by the multinational corporations: information for product creation, for product development, for development of production functions, for market creation, and for appropriability. We review for entire industries a technology life cycle that parallels Vernon's (1966) cycle for individual products. We note that private market generation of new information and new techniques may require concentrated industry structures and large optimum firm size. Thus, any policy proposal aimed at "increasing private market technology transfer" through reducing the market power of the multinationals via increased intraindustry competition is close to a contradiction in terms. Multinational corporations are successful in transferring technology either because they have expanded to internalize the externality created by the public-goods aspect of new information or because they have been in industries with high concentration initially. These and other implications follow directly from the "appropriability theory" of foreign direct investment.

Two types of information may be seriously underprovided by existing private means: simple product technologies; and unskilled-labor-using production technologies. Multinational corporations and private markets undersupply this information because they cannot appropriate the returns. They will delay introduction of simple technologies (with *low* appropriability) if their introduction lowers sufficiently the returns on existing sophisticated technologies (with *high* appropriability). LDC firms also will not undertake these projects because small optimum firm size, free entry, and standardized products and processes reduce the private appropriability of returns. This leaves an excess of the social return over the private return. Solutions to these problems could come from government financed research or from government tax-subsidy incentives. The evidence suggests that the creation of information is responsive to such economic incentives. Governments could increase the supply of both types of technologies if they were willing to purchase these new technologies at their social rather than private value. The multinationals are probably not suited to create these types of information, given existing incentive structures. Even if incentives were provided, I suspect that they would largely continue to specialize in the more sophisticated technologies demanded in the DCs.

An economic criterion was suggested here for whether governments or private firms were more efficient at creating new information. Both institutions suffer from inefficient social *allocations* of investments in the types of information created: governments because of differential organization costs of lobbies advocating alternative research projects and firms because of differential appropriability of the private returns across information investments. If the government is more efficient on this allocation question, it should create the information. If private firms are more efficient on the allocation question, then the decision hinges on the trade-off between superior private allocation but suboptimal private supply due to patent-induced monopoly practices versus inferior government allocation but superior supply of the information if the government distributes it freely.

We emphasize that information is not a free good and that even though existing information has nearly a zero marginal cost, the LDCs would not want to "steal" it if this would cut their future information imports below the optimum levels. This issue of price hinges on the empirical question of the importance of LDC markets in calculations by technology creators of the profit maximizing levels of future technology to be supplied to the world: if LDC markets are unimportant, then LDCs should push the effective prices they pay for existing technologies as low as possible since this will not affect the supply of future information to themselves or to the world.

To the extent the multinationals are important sources of current information flows to the LDCs, neither the impression of strict codes of conduct nor revisions of the Paris Convention in favor of technology importers will encourage them to increase their real flows of information to the LDCs. Applying greater political pressure to the multinationals (equivalent to increased taxation of their information creation in the LDCs) pushes back their target date for movement of production facilities to the LDCs in the technology cycle. This reduces the weight of the LDC relative factor-price structure in the present value calculations for the type of production function to create for new products and thereby accentuates the "inappropriate technology" problem. LDCs should evaluate all technology policies in an optimum tariff framework since the price as well as the amount of "technology transferred" is critical for welfare calculations. LDC "codes of conduct for technology" should be carefully formulated so as not to restrict future information flows below optimum levels. I suspect that a number of the current policy proposals will be beneficial to the LDCs (the welfare gain from cutting the price on existing technologies will more than offset the welfare loss from reduced flows of future information). These proposals include limitations on all of the following: restricting package licensing, tied purchases, contract durations, quality control, and territorial constraints.[9]

Two of these proposals deserve special attention. The first is aimed at the current practice of sellers of technology restricting exports of new products from the purchaser's country. Creators of information gain from this ability to engage in price discrimination across countries. But the higher variance that this causes in the world price of information is an important welfare cost to technology purchasers. There is no social rationale for the cost of computers to differ between Colombia and Peru because of political boundaries.

The second proposal is for the LDCs to modify their adherence to the International Convention for the Protection of Industrial Property (the Paris Convention). This treaty was first signed in Paris in 1883, has been revised half a dozen times, and has grown from including eleven countries in 1884 to seventy-eight in 1970. The terms of the convention are largely devised by technology exporting countries and so they cannot be expected to be optimal for technology importers. Since the legal systems and the types of technology demanded in LDCs differ from those in the DCs, we should expect the socially optimal legal instruments protecting rights to privately created information to differ. Differences have evolved naturally. For example, the average duration for patents in forty-five LDCs is only eleven years while it is seventeen years in fourteen DCs.[10] Because of the simplicity of the types of information demanded in the LDCs, it is appropriate for them to have patents that are easier to obtain and of shorter duration. Such a legal instrument is the "utility model."[11] It is much easier to obtain than a patent and of shorter duration, generally of three to six years. It has been used with great success in Japan and Germany, two countries with rapid technical change in the last two decades. Utility model patents were 52 percent of new patent applications (and patents granted) published in Japan in 1972.[12] (Japan and Germany accounted for 440,000 of the 770,000 new patents published by ten major developed countries in 1972; the United States was a poor third with only 75,000 published new patents.)[13] The LDCs would gain by shifting their laws away from the longer duration patents (favored by technology *exporters* in the Paris Convention) toward the simpler and shorter utility models.

Multinational corporations have received strong criticisms in recent years; some were justified and some not. Critics should remember that the patent system and trademark laws stimulate the private creation of new ideas by explicitly guaranteeing that successful innovators can behave outrageously for, say, seventeen years. The appropriability theory indicates that limitations on particularly onerous types of outrageous behavior should be dictated by the optimal supply of information, and not by mindless cuts in firm size.

Notes

1. By "appropriability" we mean the ability of private originators of ideas to obtain for themselves the pecuniary value of the ideas to society.
2. See Magee (1977).
3. Alternatively, the government could auction the right to produce each unit of

the new information and its utilization would be the same as under free provision. For expositional ease, use of the term "free provision by the government" hereafter includes the possibility of auction.

4. See Magee (1977) for greater detail on the industry technology cycle. The three stages are similar to Vernon's (1966): invention, innovation, and standardization.

5. Enos (1962, p. 304) reports that almost all of the nine major inventions for thermal cracking and catalytic cracking in the petroleum industry were made by men who were close to the oil industry but who were not attached to the major firms. Mueller (1962) found that fifteen out of twenty-five of DuPont's major new products and processes were not discovered by DuPont scientists. There were "on-the-shelf" or existing technologies that DuPont purchased from individuals or smaller firms.

6. For this reason, process patents, utility models, and patents for the "mechanical arts" are frequently shorter than other patents (see United Nations Conference on Trade and Development, 1975a).

7. About 6 percent of world patents granted in 1970 were made by LDCs and only 1 percent were held by nationals of LDCs (United Nations Conference on Trade and Development, 1975b).

8. Table 14 in the United Nations Conference on Trade and Development (1975a, p. 53) also provides evidence in this area. It indicates that, for all four of the major product areas considered, the proportion of DCs who excluded patentability *exceeded* the proportion of LDCs excluding patentability. The hypothesis that the DCs are "stealing" more technology than the LDCs should be investigated, since both the Vaitsos (1974) and UNCTAD (1975a) results are consistent with it.

9. See the United Nations Conference on Trade and Development (UNCTAD), 1975c, pp. 20–28, for descriptions of these proposals, and UNCTAD, 1975a, pp. 20–29 for abuses.

10. These averages were calculated from UNCTAD (1975a, Table 15, p. 54).

11. Utility models are discussed in UNCTAD (1975a, p. 4) and UNCTAD (1975b, p. 37).

12. See UNCTAD (1975a, p. 19).

13. Ibid.

References

Aliber, R. 1970, "A Theory of Direct Foreign Investment" in C. P. Kindleberger, ed., *The International Corporation* (The MIT Press, Cambridge, Mass.).

Arrow, K. J., 1962, "Economic Welfare and the Allocation of Resources for Invention" in *The Rate and Direction of Inventive Activity: Economic and Social Factors*, a report of the National Bureau of Economic Research (Princeton University Press, Princeton).

Bhagwati, J., 1972, "R. Vernon's *Sovereignty at Bay: The Multinational Spread of U.S. Enterprises*," *Journal of International Economics*, 2, 455–459.

Brock, W. A., and S. P. Magee, 1975, *The Economics of Pork-Barrel Politics*, Center for Mathematical Studies in Business and Economics, University of Chicago, Report 7511, February.

Caves, R., 1971, "International Corporations: The Industrial Economics of Foreign Investment," *Economica*, 38, 1–27.

———,1974, "Industrial Organization" in J. H. Dunning, ed., *Economic Analysis and the Multinational Enterprise* (Praeger, New York).

Demsetz, H., 1969, "Information and Efficiency: Another Viewpoint," *Journal of Law and Economics*, 12, 1–22.

Enos, J. L., 1962, "Invention and Innovation in the Petroleum Refining Industry" in *The Rate and Direction of Inventive Activity: Economic and Social Factors* (Princeton University Press, Princeton), 299–321.

Helleiner, G. K., 1975, "The Role of Multinational Corporations in the Less Developed Countries' Trade in Technology," *World Development*, 3, 161–189.

Hufbauer, G., 1970, "The Impact of National Characteristics and Technology on the Commodity Composition of Trade in Manufactured Goods" in R. Vernon, ed. *The Technology Factor in International Trade*, Universities-National Bureau Conference Series (Columbia University Press, New York).

Hymer, S. H., 1966, *The International Operation of National Firms: A Study of Direct Foreign Investment* (MIT Press, Cambridge, Mass.).

Johnson, H. G., 1970, "Multinational Corporations and International Oligopoly: The Non-American Challenge" in C. P. Kindleberger, ed., *The International Corporation* (MIT Press, Cambridge, Mass.).

Kindleberger, C. P., 1974, "Size of Firm and Size of Nation" in J. H. Dunning, ed. *Economic Analysis and the Multinational Enterprise* (Praeger, New York).

Magee, S. P., 1977, "Multinational Corporations, the Industry Cycle and Development," *Journal of World Trade Law*.

Mansfield, E. 1974, "Technology and Technological Change" in J. H. Dunning, ed., *Economic Analysis and the Multinational Enterprise* (Praeger, New York).

Mueller, W. F., 1962, "The Origins of the Basic Inventions Underlying DuPont's Major Product and Process Innovations, 1920 to 1950" in National Bureau of Economic Research, *The Rate and Direction of Inventive Activity: Economic and Social Factors* (Princeton University Press, Princeton)

National Bureau of Economic Research, 1962, *The Rate and Direction of Inventive Activity: Economic and Social Factors* (Princeton University Press, Princeton).

Nelson, P., 1970, "Information and Consumer Behavior," *Journal of Political Economy*, 78, 311–329.

Nelson, R., 1962, "Introduction" to National Bureau of Economic Research, *The Rate and Direction of Inventive Activity: Economic and Social Factors* (Princeton University Press, Princeton).

Rodriguez, C., 1975, "Trade in Technological Knowledge and the National Advantage," *Journal of Political Economy*, 83, 121–135.

Telser, L., 1976, "Comments on Political Information," *Journal of Law and Economics*, 19, August.

United Nations Conference on Trade and Development, 1975a, *The Role of the Patent System in the Transfer of Technology to Developing Countries* (United Nations, New York), TD/B/AC, 11/19/Rev. 1.

——, 1975b, *Major Issues Arising from the Transfer of Technology to Developing Countries* (United Nations, New York), TD/B/AC, 11/10/Rev. 2.

——, 1975c, *An International Code of Conduct on Transfer of Technology* (United Nations, New York), TD/B/C, 6/AC, 1/2/Supp., 1/Rev. 1.

Vaitsos, C., 1974, *Intercountry Income Distribution and Transnational Enterprises* (Clarendon, Oxford).

Vernon, R., 1966, "International Investment and International Trade in the Product Cycle," *Quarterly Journal of Economics*, 80, 190–207.

13

Statements on Oil and OPEC

Murray A. Adelman and Theodore H. Moran

PREPARED STATEMENT OF M. A. ADELMAN

I thank the Committee for the invitation to testify. . . .

Cartel A Burden and Danger

We can set aside doomsday rhetoric and cartel apologetics. Direct tribute to the cartel is over $125 million per year worldwide, about a fourth paid by us. Building new energy sources at home diverts capital and labor and thereby lowers our real income. The industrialized countries have so far largely avoided beggar-my-neighbor policies to adjust balances of payments, but their resolution seems to be wearing thin, and there could be heavy effects on world trade. The less developed countries are in much worse straits.

OPEC [Organization of Petroleum Exporting Countries] success in monopolizing a natural resource has inspired strife all over the world. Patches of barren ground or ocean seem worth fighting for; the Law of the Sea conferences have failed; there are confrontations from the Aegean to the East China Sea. Investment in minerals in the less developed countries decreases as they try to follow the OPEC examples both in taking over properties and trying to form cartels. There has also been political damage. . . . And cartel revenues are fueling an arms race which could go nuclear.

It is a long overdue question, why the procartel policy has persisted so long, and what good it is supposed to be doing. I suggest that there are three reasons, all honestly believed, all of them delusive and harmful.

First, since 1945 and particularly since 1950, it has been our policy to subsidize the oil producers in order to have friends at the Persian Gulf and oppose Russian advances in that area. We could do it directly for a tiny percent of the cartel tribute. It would be not only cheaper but much more effective. Governments would be much more amenable to American wishes and interests if they were directly dependent on us, and if they did not have billions of dollars with which to pursue their own adventures.

From *Energy Independence or Interdependence: The Agenda with OPEC*. Hearings before the Subcommittee on Energy of the Joint Economic Committee, Congress of the United States, January 12 and 13, 1977, pp. 7–15 and 39–44.

Saudi Arabia as a supposed force for moderation in Middle East politics is based on just one thing: its money. If we were to subsidize Egypt directly, not only would we save billions, the money would go farther. The Egyptians would also like it much better: "It has long been ruefully said in Cairo that the [Saudi] Arabs are determined to fight to the last Egyptian."[1]

The second reason, which has only gained currency in the last few years, is that high prices are good because they discourage energy consumption. But that is no reason for pouring out billions in tribute. If we collect an excise tax on oil products, we can use it to subsidize low income consumers, energy research, or for any other useful purpose.

The third delusion is the belief that we face a long-run energy shortage. Now, regardless of what we think about demand growth, fossil fuels reserves, etc., the belief in shortage is nonsense. Except when a government deliberately holds a price below the market-clearing level, any shortage, any excess of demand over supply, forces up the price and closes the "gap." In any but the short run, the amount supplied will equal the amount demanded. When a monopolist swears, his hand on his heart, that he will never let us run short, we had better believe him. For if supply is less than demand, he will raise his price and increase his profits. Under competition, prices will be less and profits approach the normal level for marginal production—but again, no shortage.

If Saudi Arabia enforces a "production ceiling" on its output, and if the amount demanded worldwide really exceeds world capacity, the price will rise. It is merely a problem of tactics: whether the Saudis prefer to raise the price directly or indirectly. But a price rise there will be in either case.

Price is the only issue; energy "needs" and "gaps" and "shortages" are time-wasting confusion.

Our foreign-policy makers, in and out of the government, continue to labor under a mythical problem: "Will the oil producing governments produce enough for our needs? We must somehow induce them to do this. We are interdependent—they need the money, we need the oil. Let us make some kind of agreement, with both economic and political elements, to make it worth their while."

This is all illusion. The cartel governments will aim to produce enough oil to maximize their revenues—no more or less. Maximum revenue means also maximum political clout, for the royal road to power is money.

Therefore despite any political diversity these nations agree on the cartel objective: maximum revenues. They may disagree on what price would maximize revenues, in short or long run. Moreove, a price which maximizes for one may not do it for another. Moreover, they do not agree on how to divide up those gains; the discord has been contained, so far. But thoughts of splitting the socalled OPEC moderates from OPEC extremists, linkage with nonoil issues, political settlements, etc. disregard the nature of the cartel and are addressed to phantoms. . . .

*"Dependence" Nothing But Monopoly: No Monopoly, No
Dependence. "Interdependence" Is Myth*

Dependence on any nations or persons requires, first, an essential
product or service; second, its control by a single hand or united group. We
need food, but farmers cannot deny us food so long as they are many and
not united, hence we are not dependent on farmers. We are dependent on
those persons who in concert control the supply of oil, and may restrict its
production. Control of supply is the essence of monopoly, and dependence
only an aspect of monopoly.

The cartel of the oil-producing nations has two special features
which increase dependence.

(a) Oil is a nondurable good, needed in a continuing stream. It is
quite unlike the metals. The service we get out of steel or
aluminum is embodied in an enormous stock of durable instruments. The stock is consumed only very slowly. So a year's
cutoff by a steel or aluminum monopoly would deny us only
the small annual increase in the stock, and we would have
enough time to retrieve the situation. Oil stocks are normally a
small percent of current consumption, and a cutoff does quick
damage.

(b) The oil cartel is composed of sovereign states. Some of them
have accumulated very large foreign-exchange holdings, and
can the more easily do without current income.

The cartel nations are not dependent on us, because
we have no monopolies comparable to their oil monopoly.
However much they need our food or industrial products, they
are sure of getting them by normal purchase, if not from one
country then from another. The industrial nations are not
united to control prices, and are not going to cut off their supply. (Nor, in my opinion, should they try.)

Trade may be called "interdependence," if we prefer
five syllables to one. Aside from this, to speak of "interdependence" between oil producing and consuming nations simply
ignores the market structures on both sides of the fence. Of
course a few people are getting rich out of that trade, and will
use all their influence to help increase cartel revenues and prevent any resistance.

(c) We are dependent on cartel oil, but not on Arab oil. If we
imported not a drop of Arab oil, it would be replaced by
non-Arab oil at little additional expense or trouble. But
neither would this exclusion do us much good, because as will
now be explained the problem is not an "embargo" but a production cutback.

"Embargo" Never Was. "Energy Independence" Impossible

During the production cutback of 1973–74 (the so-called "embargo") the industrialized democracies fell apart. Member nations of the European Economic Community broke their own law, the Treaty of Rome, which prohibits restrictions on movements of goods, in order to help cut off the Netherlands. As in the 1930s, Europeans hastened to make friends with the tiger, in the hope he would go eat someone else.

Yet the fraction of oil imports lost was not greatly different among the "friendly" French (as the Arabs saw them) or British, or the "odiously neutral" Japanese, or the "enemy"—meaning us:[2] And we were the only one who produced most of the oil it consumed.

A selective embargo against the United States was and is impossible. If oil becomes more scarce in some consuming countries, prices are higher there. Those producer nations who do not cut back increase profits by diverting expots to those countries, until prices are roughly equalized. (The oil companies did well to anticipate the inevitable and do the complex logistics.) The non-Arab governments have no difficulty in doing well by doing good. American imports are now around 7 million barrels daily (mbd) and by 1980 may be 9 mbd. Non-Arab OPEC capacity is today 14.5 million, and growing.

This is both good and bad news. The Arabs cannot hurt us without hurting everybody even worse, since we import much less of our oil consumption. But in hurting everybody else they also exert pressure on us. Therefore even zero U.S. oil imports would not remove energy dependence, hardly mitigate it. *Energy independence is literally impossible.* So long as the cartel keeps prices very high, and the oil producing nations get richer, they can more easily afford production cut-backs, and we are more subject to blackmail.

Moreover, if the cartel runs into trouble, a temporary production cutback is an obvious way to clean out inventories, jack up prices, and scare consuming nations. It will be used when and as the cartel needs to use it. No political settlement has the slightest relevance to this clear and present danger. The Administration has been "unwilling to depict publicly and vividly the danger of another deliberate, unfriendly embargo by nations, notably Saudi Arabia and Iran, which Mr. Kissinger regards as essential to stability and American interests in the Middle East.[3] It is the last of the cover-ups. . . .

Cartel Remains Strong But Fragile

All cartels including this one are fragile because they fix the price at a level where it would pay any individual member to expand output by means of secret price cuts, which when matched by enough rivals would break up the whole scheme. This cartel is strong because it has prevented the chiselling from getting started.

High cartel prices are self-reinforcing. They promote lower supply instead of higher. With large enough revenues, the cartel nations can fulfill their spending plans and commitments. The higher the price, the easier to pay debts and stay solvent. Then the less the pressure on them to gain some extra revenues by shading the price.

High prices cause lower production in noncartel countries as well. Windfall profits to domestic producers are so repugnant to public opinion that special taxes or price controls hold back expansion or (as in Canada) actually decrease investment in oil and gas production. Another variant of the perverse effect: Norway and Mexico would speed up the rate of development and exploration if prices were not expected to go higher. (In economists' jargon, these are "backward bending supply curves" in cartel and non-cartel countries.)

But strength one way is fragility the other way. Lower prices would make cartel countries strapped for cash, and more likely to reduce prices still more to get badly needed incremental sales. The self-reinforcing and cumulative tendency either way is what makes a cartel unstable.

Another source of strength: the cartel members are sovereign nations, and can suppress competition by force or the threat of force. Iran can limit outshipments from the Persian Gulf. Saudi Arabia can invade and occupy its neighbors. Distances are short, local populations scanty, the terrain ideal for a quick grab. Today they account for 6 million barrels daily of capacity, and they can be taken out quickly. The knowledge of such a backstop is an important cartel strength.

The chances seem small of reduced world demand breaking the cartel. In 1974, there was a large reduction in volume, accomplished in only a few months, hence with greater shock value than conservation and new supplies could ever do. Yet there was a 50 percent increase in the price. . . . This is not a market where prices are set by competitive supply and demand. We are dealing with a cartel which is in process of learning how high the world price can be pushed.

The cartel can live with selling fewer barrels than in 1973. The ultimate question is: can Saudi Arabia take the whole burden of excess capacity, letting the others produce as much as they wish? How far down will Saudi Arabia be willing to go?

We can dismiss the nonsense, however seriously urged by some Americans, that Saudi Arabia would rather produce less oil, but makes a sacrifice for the good of the world. But undoubtedly they could if need be meet their commitments with considerably less than current output.

Professor Moran calculates about $32 billion annually a minimum acceptable Saudi income.[4] At prices of $15 (or $20) per barrel, this could be met with 6 (or with 4.5) million barrels daily. Assume the Saudis would be content with that production, if they were certain of getting it. But certainty is impossible. That is the basic cartel problem. Suppose total OPEC production is lower than expected by one or two mbd, a fluctuation or error of only 3 to 6 percent. Then if Saudi Arabia is the residual supplier of 6 mbd, and absorbs the 1–2 mbd decrease, it is a 20 to 40 percent loss. (If they are producing 8 mbd, it is 15 to 30 percent.) Simple prudence will not let the Saudis permit output to go that low, while others produce as they like. They will need and demand compensation, in the form of either a higher share or of an agreement for others to cut back proportionately.

Similarly, suppose it is profitable to raise the cartel price by a third because the sales loss would be only about 10 percent (elasticity of demand assumed as −0.37). If even half the loss fell on Saudi Arabia, it would be no gain for them even if eveything happened exactly as planned. They could not agree to it. This is the basic reason for Saudi caution since the great days of 1974. They want to postpone as long as possible their role as residual supplier, and keep their market share as high as possible for as long as possible.

The real danger to cartel cohesion, therefore, is not slack demand for their oil, but rather the difficulty of assigning the inevitable excess capacity. To speak of Saudi Arabia (and the rest of the Southern Gulf) as residual suppliers is correct, but too simple. There are difficulties and dangers in their acting this role. Their danger is our opportunity.

Obsession with "Assuring Adequate Supplies" A Powerful Aid to the Cartel

The "backward bending supply curves" noted earlier are a special case of a powerful delusion in both consuming and producing countries. Products which emerge from the earth—including food and timber but especially minerals—are not viewed as subject to the economic axiom; all products are scarce. It takes scarce resources to produce (or extract or grow) them. Scarcity is a matter of degree, and is measured by price, which registers the pressure of demand upon supply, and also regulates each of them. If a product becomes more scarce, the higher price will ration it, encourage new supplies, and promote substitution. And this may be painful—nobody enjoys paying higher prices and skimping on the use of a necessary good.

But minerals, above all oil, are not viewed in that common sense way. Either one has "enough" or "not enough." A producing nation which is also a consumer finds it hard to regard the oil as a national asset, whose value should be maximized for the sake of the nation. It is rather considered a duty to insure that "there will always be enough for us," and better to err on the side of conservatism, and assume more will be "needed." Since this usually means a subsidized low price, it is at least partly a self-fulfilling prophecy. Keep it at home in the ground, where it is safe. (It is really too good for wretched foreigners anyway.) If we're to be all right, we must resist all blandishments to produce for the sake of humanity, or the world community, or whatever. Investment and production decisions are difficult, but when in doubt, don't.

Non-producing nations share the same delusions, from the unhappy side. If we can't find our own, then let's line up supplies for the future, and assure "access" by offering the producing nations any political or economic premium. If the producers are not content with last year's prize, we must give them more . . . and more. Nothing is too much to give for oil, since without it the wheels would all be standing still.

This is nonsense, and "access" is a non-problem. Whatever the amount available, it will be rationed mostly by price. But we must live with the consequences of these delusions. So long as governmental thinking is paralyzed by "gaps" and "shortages," not only will much oil stay in the ground, but consuming nations will outsmart each other, and normal market forces will act with great difficulty and very slowly. I turn now to two feasible means of active resistance.

If All Consuming Nations Levy A Percentage Tax They Can Divert Most Cartel Revenues into Their Own Treasuries

Over time, the cartel will raise prices until the higher take per barrel no longer compensates for the lower volume. This is the price which maximizes profits. We cannot prevent this and should not fool ourselves that any agreement will keep the cartel nations from charging their optimal price, as far as they can discern it. But consuming countries acting together could divert the bulk of cartel revenues right into their own treasuries, through a tax proportional to the price of oil.

For example, assume we levy a tax per barrel equal to twice the Persian Gulf price. The tax would then automatically rise and fall with the Persian Gulf price. The same Persian Gulf price which maximized cartel revenues in the absence of the tax would maximize cartel revenues with the tax. If the producer countries raised the price higher, it would lose so much volume as to cost them money. Two-thirds of the cartel revenues would be diverted into consuming-country treasuries. They could use the monies to reimburse low-income consumers, or for any other purpose. . . .

The proportional tax will only work if most consuming countries levy it together. At present they are too bemused with fear of shortage and empty slogans like "cooperation and dialogue." They have yet to face the fact of a monopoly, which is going to keep raising the price despite all the pretty words addressed to them.

Yet oddly enough, the chances are fair that consuming countries will drift into this policy without meaning to. It depends more on how quickly the cartel governments raise the price, than on how high. If the cartel nations are content to keep raising the price by small increments, as they have done since the end of 1974, then balances of payments can adjust. Higher priced oil imports mean a gradual adjustment in many directions: some oil importing nations will devalue in small steps; they will import less of all goods, including oil; some will have higher exports, not necessarily to the oil producers. Producer country surpluses will be gradually invested through world capital markets, and less developed-countries will be covered by "loans." But large sudden changes in oil prices force consuming country governments to take strong action to check imports, including taxes or tariffs on crude oil or products. Therefore consuming countries may find themselves taking one step after another, inadvertently doing what they would never dream of doing deliberately—levying a proportional or more-than-proportional tax.

This is another reason why the larger cartelists, chiefly Saudi Arabia, will continue to practice moderation as long as the consuming countries are in recession or at least not peak prosperity. Another reason is that they fear that the burden of restriction may in the future fall chiefly upon them   as it has not fallen in the recent past

Import Quota Auctions

Every cartel with excess capacity is vulnerable to disruption. Hence what the oil cartel nations really fear, as Iraq said so well in the autumn of 1975, when threatening Kuwait for a trifling price cut, is "competitive bidding among producers," i.e., among producing nations.

The United States could take the hint. As a large buyer, it could inject some competition, exploit the cartel's one weakness, lower its own import costs and disrupt cartel cohesion. . . .

Briefly, it provides that imports be fixed monthly to equate demand with supply at prevailing prices. (Mistakes are easily correctible the following month.) Import entitlements or tickets would be sold monthly at public auction to anyone paying in advance. This would create a primary market of some 200 million tickets monthly. Resale of tickets would be permitted. In order to allow forward planning and term contracts, a part of the tickets could be issued valid for future periods.

The cartel nations would not buy tickets, at first, and tickets would be very cheap. So much the better for getting the system off to a smooth start. But a ticket would be worth up to $12 to a cartel nation. Nearly $2.5 billions' worth of them would be up for grabs, month after month. Cheating by a cartel government would be easy. They could bid for tickets, through third parties, or buy them. A cartel country would sell at the cartel price and not even the customers would know that it was chiselling, by buying tickets, thereby rebating to the United States Treasury.

Today, governments chisel only on peripheral short-term supplies, and word gets around quickly. The great bulk of the oil moves at publicly known contract prices, and buying companies are not free to shop around for small bargains. The costs and risks of losing continuity of supply are too great when handling large amounts of liquids. The quota auction would separate the movement of oil from the bargaining over cartel surpluses. The total amount of cartel surplus would be on the block every month.

Any country wanting extra revenues would buy more tickets to sell more barrels. Any country which lost business would recoup itself by buying tickets, jostling other cartelists. The tickets would not stay cheap for long. Without any interference in industry logistics or disturbance of the flow of oil, and with a handful of employees administering the auctions, the United States would pocket substantial revenues.

No serious argument has ever been offered against the quota auction system.[5] The burden of proof ought to be on those who assume that every cartel nation would resist temptation indefinitely, month after month. We need only one defector to get the process started. As it develops, the big cartelists would be the holdouts. Then imports from Saudi Arabia would drop, to be replaced by imports from producing nations who were more eager or needy for money—i.e., whose interests were closer to ours.

The import quota auction system has often been misunderstood or misrepresented as a government purchasing monopoly. That would be a logistical horror. It would also lose the secrecy in chiseling.[6] The United States as buyer would need to make long term purchases, thereby legitimizing a cartel price—just the contrary of what is desirable.

Cartel Cannot Soon Be Quickly Destroyed, But Should Not Be Helped

The cartel could have been prevented from ever getting started, and as recently as two years ago it might have been quickly destroyed. That is not feasible now. The profits of their raid on the world economy have been so huge that if the cartel collapsed tomorrow, the most strenuous violent efforts would be made to put it together again. Strength may give rise to extreme tactics, but so also may weakness. There could, as pointed out earlier, be a production cutback to put the price back up again. Hence the need for a stockpile, to prevent both Arabs and non-Arabs from scaring us out of any rational counter-action. . . .

Some would claim that as things stand today, there is nothing at all which the United States or other nations can do. If so, we should at least not collaborate with our oppressors. Let us make no deal which would tie our hands, and prevent us from using any future opportunities for resistence. There is nothing to be gained by freezing a dismal present into the indefinite future. . . .

PREPARED STATEMENT OF THEODORE H. MORAN

Oil Prices and the Future of OPEC[7]

Mr. Chairman, in your letter of invitation to appear today you suggested that I might be able to use research I have been conducting under the sponsorship of Resources for the Future to address two questions of interest to your Committee, namely: (1) what will life with OPEC be like for the United States (and for the world) over the medium term in the future? And (2) will the glue that binds OPEC together continue to stick?

My calculations suggest that the answer to the first question is fairly straightforward. Life with OPEC will be difficult and painful. Adjusting to the emergence of OPEC does not mean having to accommodate to a one-time increase in the price of oil, which is now over. Rather it means having to face a regular and steady push toward higher real prices for petroleum this year, next year, and each year in the future. This appraisal is not contradicted by the apparent "moderation" of OPEC in this year: a 5 percent to 10 percent increase in oil prices in the first half of 1977, followed by another increase later in the year.[8] Had the economic recovery been stronger in the OECD [Organization for Economic Cooperation and Development] countries, as Sheik Yamani admitted, Saudi Arabia would have gone along with an even greater price increase. The most optimistic prediction one can make about OPEC behavior between now and 1980 (and beyond) is that the price of oil will rise in real terms as fast as the macroeconomic policies of the major industrial countries can adjust. That could mean an average annual price jump of 10 to 15 percent above the OECD rate of inflation.

The answer to the second question is more ambiguous. To keep prices high (or raise them higher) will require OPEC to absorb larger and larger amounts of spare capacity in the late 1970's. In the past most of this spare capacity has been able to be shunted off, with only a small amount of tension, onto OPEC members for whom the marginal utility of the revenues foregone was near zero. Before the end of the decade, this will no longer be possible. Instead, approximately 6 mbd of idle facilities will have to be held by governments who feel they "need" the revenues those facilities would generate. This has implications that are not now widely appreciated.

A large amount of spare capacity in the hands of governments who would like to use it is a tremendously unstable situation for a producers' group that is trying to restrict production. It renders the group vulnerable to the efforts of consumers to play one producer against another and thus weaken the group's ability to collude. But it does not ensure, by itself, that OPEC will break up. Indeed the rational way for OPEC to respond to this vulnerability will be to establish a system of explicit pro-rationing, with a faithful commitment to higher prices being the reward for the members accepting the decision on who must accept how much spare capacity.

Thus, life with OPEC over the middle term will be costly and difficult. But, between now and the early 1980s, the oil-importing countries (led by the United States) will face an unprecedented opportunity to moderate the impact of the energy crises that otherwise will surely come by applying a little solvent to the glue that holds OPEC together. This will require establishing procedures to reward differentially those members who choose to alleviate their financial "squeezes" by expanding volume rather than by restricting it. If the oil-importing countries do not seize this opportunity, however—specifically if the United States continues to drift along with no identifiable energy policy in the vague hope that the energy crisis will somehow disappear—they will find themselves having to shift ever larger annual amounts of real resources to the OPEC nations with traumatic implications for the Third World, for the Fourth World, for the weaker industrial countries and for the international financial system as a whole.

Let me turn to the analysis of these points.

What will life with OPEC be like over the medium term? Since 1973 the conventional prediction in the U.S. government and in private business circles has been that energy prices would remain level, or decline slightly, in real terms between the date of the prediction and 1980. This seemed a reasonable expectation as long as the OPEC countries were awash in petrodollar revenues, supposedly unable to "absorb" them and searching anxiously for ways to recycle them. But the conventional prediction will prove false precisely because constant real oil prices will not generate enough revenues to finance programs that civilian or military elites in the OPEC countries consider too important to give up if they have any choice in the matter.

The perception about the extent to which the oil exporting states will "need" petroleum revenues for their government budgets has taken a quantum leap since 1973 for three reasons: (1) there has been a worldwide explosion in the cost of heavy equipment and construction; (2) the diseconomies of scale of rapid growth have proven very great in the OPEC countries; (3) the goals that the OPEC nations have set for themselves ("development," "welfare," "defense," international "influence") have proved to be enormously expensive. As a result the "Development Plans" of the major OPEC governments would be, if carried out, prohibitively costly. But that is an unrealistic standard—such Plans were typically too grandiose to begin with. What is striking is that even small fractions of the economic, social, and military plans of the major OPEC governments will be too costly to finance if oil prices "only" remain constant.

Iran, for example, planned to spend $112 billion between 1973 and 1978 to lay the foundation for a modern state before the country's petroleum capacity begins to dwindle in the mid-1980's. The Iranian Plan and Budget Organization projected a net revenue surplus, after the completion of all projects, of more than $11 billion. But before the end of 1975 the Iranian government already faced both balance of payments and fiscal deficits. A recalculation of the cost of the programs more realistically suggests that the total Plan will cost at least 50 percent more than the initial estimate of $112 billion dollars. Of this jump, approximately 15 percent will be due to the higher price of imported goods if current trends continue; 35 percent will be generated internally. Even if Iran is able to export oil at full capacity from 1976 through the end of the Five Year Plan with oil prices rising no more than the 15 percent decreed by the majority of the OPEC members for 1977, it will still be able to finance only about half of the civilian projects contemplated by the Plan and perhaps even a smaller fraction of the military and internal security programs desired by the Shah. At the same time, the authorities in Tehran are facing pressures for additional programs—food subsidies, public housing, rural development—that are needed to retain the present level of domestic political stability. Iran has, not surprisingly, been the forefront of those oil exporting countries pushing for dramatically higher oil prices.

Saudi Arabia is discovering that its oil earnings are buying even less than the Iranians when measured against the original expectations of the Central Planning Office in Rüyadh. The Five Year Plan announced for 1975–1980 was supposed to cost $142 billion. In fact it will cost much more than double that figure. (Of the rise in program costs in the Saudi plan, 5 to 10 percent have thus far been "imported inflation." The remainder can be attributed to domestic causes). Few outside analysts thought that the timetable contemplated in the plan was even faintly realistic. Now subsequent calculations indicate that even if the Saudis were to stretch out the plan over a twenty-year period, and drop many projects altogether, they will still have to earn more than $30 billion per year to finance their budget on a current basis. Even if Saudi authorities drop their expectations about economic development dramatically (especially industrial development that requires the use of foreign workers), place no more than moderate priority on national defense and popular welfare, and maintain their interest in domestic stability and the ability to influence intra-Arab affairs (via aid) at current levels, they will have to finance programs at a rate of $30 to $35 billion (1976 prices) in the late 1970s–early 1980s. Should oil prices rise no more than 5 percent to 10 percent in 1977 and remain constant (in real terms) thereafter, the Saudi government will have to export 8–9 mbd per year to cover its expenditures or else draw down its financial reserves at a very fast rate. (With massive cutbacks and stretch-outs of programs, Saudi financial reserves will probably peak in 1978 at not much more than $50 billion and decline steadily after that.)

But what about those in the royal family or in the Council of Ministers who dislike the high level of economic activity and the pace of public spending in Saudi Arabia, and who would like to go back to the relative quiet of the pre-1973 period? Or what about the assertion, made by Sheik Yamani and others, that Saudi Arabia could cut production to 3 mbd, or even 1 mbd, without feeling the effects. Due to the high current level of official reserves, the Saudi government could easily do this for a short period of time. Thus the threat should be given serious consideration in the event of another Middle East war (although the behavior of other oil exporters with excess capacity at the time would be crucial to the effectiveness of a Saudi production cut). As a longer term strategy, however, one has to weigh the credibility of the Yamani assertion against the kind of domestic upheaval that might result against a future government that tried it. A Saudi government that had already stretched the country's Five Year Plan out over 20 years (and placed stringent limits on the spending of ministers concerned with national defense, economic development, or social stability) would, by 1979, have an annual budget of $26 billion remaining even if it suddenly reduced expenditures on new infrastructure, gas gathering, and industrial projects to zero. That would require exports of 6.4 mbd to finance on a current basis. It could cut its budget to $24 billion by also stopping new municipal water projects completely and eliminating the entire food subsidy program. That would require exports of 5.9 mbd. It could cut its budget to $20 billion by also firing half of the bureaucrats in the Saudi administration. That would still require exports of 4.9 mbd. It could cut its budget to $17 billion by also stopping all foreign aid (predominantly to other Arab states). That would require exports of 4.2 mbd. It could cut its budget to $14 billion by also eliminating all expenditures on military construction and equipment. That would get to the 3.5 mbd mark. And so on.

The record of survival for regimes that try to stop, or reverse, the process of social mobilization and rising expectations once it is started should not recommend this as a promising strategy for a monarchy.

These projections do not mean, of course, that Saudi Arabia will have any inclination to break away from OPEC if its export level does not earn the country $30 billion each year. It simply means that below that level the Saudis will either have to expand their market share at the expense of their OPEC colleagues or to become more sympathetic to the urgings of their fellow members for an escalation in the real price of oil.

Prominent among those members will be the high-population, high-mobilization societies—such as Algeria, Indonesia, Nigeria, Iraq, and Venezuela. Before 1980 ten or eleven of the thirteen members of OPEC will likely be facing current fiscal deficits. Indeed, depending upon how the market for OPEC oil is divided, all thirteen countries could be experiencing deficits.[9]

What will this financial squeeze do to the "glue" that holds OPEC together?

OPEC's approaching financial squeeze could be, paradoxically, either the catalyst for the producers' association to perfect its structure as a cartel, or the opportunity for the major oil-importing countries to weaken the ability of the association to collude and thus moderate the impact of the continuing energy crisis. The most plausible calculations of demand for OPEC exports in 1980, for example, indicate a figure of 29–30 mbd (million barrels per day oil equivalent) at current prices, including oil, natural gas, and petroleum products.[10]

With the expanding appetite for revenues, this will mean that by 1980, with a 5 percent to 10 percent price rise in 1977 and constant real prices thereafter, OPEC will have to absorb not merely 17 mbd in aggregate spare capacity but more than 6 mbd of spare capacity in the hands of governments for whom the marginal utility of the revenues foregone is high. While the near-term matching of OPEC revenues with perceived OPEC needs will be close, the medium-term prospects—after Alaskan, North Sea, and other sources come on-line—portray a far different picture. In the late 1970's and early 1980's, the market will be a mirror-image of the post-1973 market, with more sellers than there are buyers at the given OPEC price.

Does this mean that OPEC will fall apart spontaneously and the energy crisis thereby disappear? Such a hope surfaces perennially in Washington as government officials try to persuade themselves that if they do nothing the problem will vanish.[11] But there is little justification for it.

It is based on the assumption that, instead of gaining experience and sophistication in the years since 1973 (or, indeed, since 1971), the OPEC members will be less skillful in balancing supply and demand in the future than they have been until now. More plausible is the expectation that, if left to themselves, the OPEC countries will do what is most rational from the point of view of their own self-interest: namely, assign explicit market shares and reward compliance (as well as ease internal tensions) with generous and dependable price hikes.

Will the United States be able to rely upon the "special relationship" with Saudi Arabia that has been the centerpiece of Secretary Kissinger's approach to OPEC? This will be a policy approach of increasing fragility over the next three or four years, especially if the United States continues to ignore the sources of strength that reinforce its own position in that relationship. As the real or perceived revenue needs of the OPEC governments mount, the Saudis will become caught, unavoidably, in having to make a zero-sum choice: either to side with the other members of OPEC that are cutting back on development projects and are angry about the cost of industrial equipment and weapons imported from the West, or to provoke their wrath by following a unilateral policy designed as a favor to the United States, Europe, and Japan. Thus, reliance upon the gratuitous goodwill of a "moderate" Saudi Arabia assumes that the Saudis will regularly and dependably put the interests of consumers above the interests of their fellow producers, Arab and non-Arab alike, and stand ready, at the same time, to withstand the mounting wrath of their neighbors and fellow exporters (a wrath the depths of whose intensity is being demonstrated only mildly in the first quarter of 1977). More plausibly, Saudi Arabia will probably limit its role as a "moderate" in the future as it has in 1976–7 to ensuring that the shift of resources demanded by the other members of OPEC is kept within bounds that does not "strangle" or "destroy" the strong, developed economies of the West.

How high might an explicit OPEC cartel be likely to raise oil prices? Since even the scaled-down versions of the OPEC development plans would require more than a doubling of the oil price in real terms by 1980 (under the most favorable assumptions about supply and demand elasticities), and since a doubling of the oil price would be counterproductive if it produced another severe recession in the West, the primary constraint on the cartel's price strategy would probably be the fear of an adverse impact on industrial activity in the OECD countries. Thus, depending on how well the macroeconomic policies of the U.S., Europe, and Japan will be able to cope with the strain, OPEC price raises might range from "only" 5 percent when the large Western economies are shaky (or when OPEC members want some political favor like pressure for a favorable Middle East settlement) to 10 percent to 15 percent above the rate of OECD inflation when the large Western economies are relatively robust.

While this push will ultimately be constrained by the price of substitutes (for example, shale oil or gasified coal), it could in the meantime have a severely adverse impact on the weaker OECD economies, such as Italy and the United Kingdom, and a devastating impact on the Third and Fourth Worlds.[12]

What are the policy implications of this analysis for the United States? There are three principal implications for U.S. policy:

(1) The energy crisis is not dead. It is only resting, and will soon reappear with potentially more devastating consequences. (For example, the apparent "ease" with which Third World countries have expanded their debt to more than $130 billion since the 1973 oil price jump does not mean that future increases in their import bills will be handled with equal ease. Instead, "ease" in financing the last round means that future rounds will be much tougher to finance).

(2) Relations between the major oil-importing countries and OPEC will, necessarily, become more tense and strained in the next years as both sides realize that (while neither wants to kill the goose) they are engaged in a largely zero-sum struggle for real resources that each side feels is necessary for its economic health, social welfare, and national power. There will be no easy, amicable resolution to the problems in the relations between the oil-exporting and the oil-importing countries.

(There is one heartening corollary to the above point. The "financial squeeze" projected for OPEC means that the petrodollar surplus "problem" is vanishing as abruptly as it appeared, and the justification for pushing every possible policy designed to sop up those petrodollars [especially selling massive amounts of military arms] has disappeared.)

(3) The balance of power is not inevitably tilting, however, in favor of the OPEC countries. The need for oil exporters who desire higher revenues to absorb large amounts of spare capacity will render OPEC vulnerable to the possibility of the oil-importing countries playing one producer off against another. (As a corollary to this point, conservation measures in the United States plus efforts to stimulate non-OPEC sources of supply will in the future greatly complicate OPEC's future ability to operate as a cartel. A few years ago Secretary Kissinger's call for conservation measures to reduce U.S. consumption by 1 mbd died a quiet death within the Ford administration as other advisers warned that the sacrifice of American consumers could easily be matched by an offsetting reduction in Saudi output that would, if anything, be welcomed by Saudi financial authorities. By the late 1970's this will no longer be possible for Saudi Arabia.)

How might the oil-importing countries, led by the United States, strengthen the power they have to countervail OPEC's pressure for higher prices?

The tactical options range from open confrontation (which would probably be both inefficient and undesirable) to quiet subtlety. But the strategic principle would remain the same: to weaken the ability of the OPEC members to collude by rewarding differentially (in economic, political, and military terms) those members who choose to augment their revenues by expanding output rather than by restricting it.

Economically, it could include the plan suggested by M. A. Adelman, for example, to auction import tickets for the U.S. market by secret bidding.[13] This system would favor any hard-pressed government anxious to expand its market share by discounting its price, while giving OPEC as a whole minimal opportunity to monitor either who the cheaters were or how large the discounts became. Since Professor Adelman is here today I shall not elaborate on the pros and cons of this system, except to point out that the intensification of the spare-capacity-cum-financial-squeeze problem within OPEC will create a favorable environment for its success. With 6 mbd of idle facilities in the hands of governments that need the revenues those facilities produce, there will be a continuous buyers' market, with more sellers anxious to dispose of their product than there are customers.

Politically and militarily this approach could make the continuation of crucial services provided to OPEC countries by American suppliers contingent upon certain production or price targets being met over specified periods of time. The operative wisdom in the U.S. government at the present time is that any good or service supplied by Americans would be instantly and painlessly provided by others if the U.S. government threatened to stop or slow its provision. For some goods and services that is certainly true. But for others it is patently false. Clearly there is a spectrum from housing construction carried out by private American companies (which could be easily replaced) to sophisticated military equipment and intelligence information provided by American government agencies (which could not be replaced at all). The United States currently has extensive commercial, financial, labor, communications, cryptographic, engineering, cultural, educational, managerial, military, and intelligence-sharing programs with the governments of Iran and Saudi Arabia, for example. Yet it has never taken an inventory of how many of these could be replaced, at what cost, with how long a disruption, and with what reaction among pro-U.S. elements in the civilian and military elites if the United States were forced, because of OPEC policy, to make an "agonizing reappraisal" of the structure of relations between ourselves and either of the two countries.

In the case of Saudi Arabia, these are both price-hawks and price-doves influential in the governmental hierarchy. The price-doves argue that from the point of view of the country's national interest the only way to retard Iran's military expenditures and curb its imperial ambitions is through preventing oil prices from rising. These voices could be strengthened with carefully orchestrated American encouragement.

The main point to be considered as the U.S. government (both Congress and the Executive) begins at last to give energy policy the priority it deserves is that OPEC will be pressing for ever higher real prices for oil. The United States can remain passive only at great economic and political cost. It must begin to develop the tools to counteract that pressure.

Notes

1. Cairo correspondent, in *London Economist*, November 13, 1976, p. 83.
2. Imports, Four Large Nations, 1973–74:

Nation	Amounts (Million barrels per day)						Percent		
	Sept.	Oct.	Nov.	Dec.	Jan.	Feb.	Nov.–Jan. Sept.–Oct.	Nov.–Feb. Sept.–Oct.	Dec.–Feb. Sept.–Nov.
United States	6.4	6.5	6.9	5.9	5.4	5.2	0.94	0.91	0.83
United Kingdom	1.8	3.0	2.4	2.0	2.7	2.2	.98	.97	.95
France	2.7	2.8	3.0	2.2	2.7	2.7	.95	.95	.89
Japan	5.2	6.0	5.4	5.3	5.0	5.5	.93	.95	.95

Note: U.S. inventories bottomed in January, thereafter increased.

Source: *Petroleum Industry Trends* (Parra, Ramos & Parra, London).

Spot crude prices peaked in January, thereafter decreased.

There is no satisfactory way to measure the shortfall, i.e. the difference between what a country wished to buy, at current prices, and what was available. The above table would look different, but not substantially so, if we used a different base period. But there is a strong reason not to go beyond January or at most February 1974, since the accumulation of inventories means that more was being supplied than consumed. Hence the two extreme right-hand columns exaggerate the real shortfall in the United States.

3. Edward Cowan, in *New York Times*, January 2, 1977, Section 4, page 2.

4. Theodore H. Moran, "Why Oil Prices Go Up: OPEC Wants Them," *Foreign Policy*, No. 25, Winter 1976, p. 65. It would be better to subtract the amount of foreign investment income, which will be substantial by 1980.

5. It was endorsed by President-elect Carter's energy task force. See *Oil & Gas Journal*, January 10, 1977.

6. Some proponents of such a monopoly recognize (inadequately, I think) the loss of secrecy as well as the supply difficulties, but urge that it would not be serious because a given landed price would leave the Persian Gulf f.o.b. price unclear because of the possible variations through freight and quality. Unfortunately these are quite small relative to the price, so a serious reduction would be impossible to hide. See Christopher D. Stone and Jack MacNamara, "How to Take on OPEC," *New York Times Magazine*, December 12, 1976, pp. 38-44.

7. This testimony is drawn from a larger study, entitled *Oil Prices and the Future of OPEC: The Political Economy of Tension and Stability in the Organization of Petroleum Exporting Countries* (Washington, D.C.: Resources for the Future, work in progress.)

8. For an appraisal of the impact of the two-tier price system on OPEC, see infra., footnote 4.

9. The measure here is fiscal deficits, not balance of payments deficits which will lag somewhat behind fiscal deficits, depending on the country. For the assumptions about the rate of growth of non-petroleum revenues during the simulation period, see Moran, *Oil Prices and the Future of OPEC: the Political Economy of Tension and Stability in the Organization of Petroleum Exporting Countries* (Washington: Resources for the Future, in progress 1977).

10. On the demand side, the "base case" in my study assumes an aggregate growth in (non-Communist) world energy demand of 4% per year. The projection is consistent with an average GNP growth of 5.0% per year, with an income elasticity of energy consumption of 1.0, a price elasticity of -0.15, and an appropriate lag effect as an energy-intensive capital stock is replaced by less energy-intensive capital goods. On the supply side the "base case" includes cautious assumptions about output, such as a steady decline in U.S. "lower 48" oil and gas production even with price decontrol, a continuing slowdown in nuclear construction, a one year delay in the Alaskan pipeline, Mexican oil production of only 1.1 mbd in 1980, Egyptian oil production of only 0.5 mbd in 1980, Chinese oil exports of only 0.5 mbd in 1980. From this "base case" comes the figure of 6.1 mbd of spare capacity in the hands of governments for whom the marginal utility of the revenues foregone is high. Under three plausible alternative scenarios unwanted spare capacity rises as high as 8.9 mbd. Under four plausible alternative scenarios unwanted spare capacity drops as low as 5.3 mbd. Only if demand is substantially higher than 4% per year *and* supply is substantially lower than the cautious projections made in the base case does spare capacity drop below 3.0 mbd.

11. Indeed, there is occasional wishful thinking that the present two-tier price system constitutes the beginning of OPEC's break-up. While the next six months could highlight the potential for extreme tension that exists among the OPEC members, and indicate how disruptive a Saudi Arabia that refuses to act as a residual balancer to accommodate the price level decreed by the other members could be, the probable outcome will be merely a price rise very close to Saudi Arabia's 5% rather than the beginning of a "breakup."

If the two-tier price system continues through the first quarter of 1977, the eleven members of OPEC who try to hold their price rise at 10% will suffer an *aggregate net revenue loss of 16%* in comparison to a rapid capitulation to the 5% level. In terms of the strain on their budgets, their tax receipts will be running *a full 25%* behind what they were in the second half of 1976. For some countries, such as Iran, Kuwait, and Venezuela, whose heavy crudes compete directly with Saudi Arabia's the net revenue loss could be much greater. For this reason, if Saudi Arabia holds firm to its rumored production intentions and if the oil companies are aggressive price shoppers, I would expect the eleven to discover rapidly that adopting the 5% formula (openly or covertly) will be in their own best interest.

Analysis: *For the aggregate net revenue loss*

1. Demand for OPEC exports in the last quarter of 1976 was about 32 mbd with an inventory build-up of 3–4 mbd, for a "real" demand level of approximately 29.5 mbd.

2. Demand in the first quarter of 1977 will equal about 29.5 mbd minus the inventory drawdown of about 3.5 mbd and minus almost 0.5 mbd in fewer bunkers, or 25.5 mbd.

3. I assume that if all the OPEC countries had adopted an equal 5% price rise the Saudi share of the market would be about 7.0 mbd and the Abu Dhabi share about 1.2 mbd, for a market of 17.3 mbd for the other eleven (25.5–8.2).

4. If, instead, Saudi Arabia increases its production to 9.8 mbd and Abu Dhabi to 2.0 mbd, the market for the other eleven will be 13.7 mbd (25.5–11.8).

5. Thus the eleven lose 3.6 mbd in volume or 21% (3.6/17.3), but gain 5% in price (a rise of 10% instead of 5%) for a net loss of 16% in revenues.

For the quarter to quarter comparison

1. Demand for OPEC oil in the first quarter of 1977 will equal (from above) 25.5 mbd.

2. If Saudi Arabia exports at 9.8 mbd and Abu Dhabi at 2.0, the other eleven members of OPEC will share a market of 13.7 mbd.

3. During the last quarter of 1976 Saudi Arabia exported at a rate of 9.2 mbd and Abu Dhabi at 1.6 mbd, leaving the other eleven a market of 21.2 mbd (32.0–10.8).

4. Thus, the eleven will have a market 7.5 mbd smaller (21.2–13.7) or 35% less (7.5/21.2) than the last quarter of 1976.

12. The non-OPEC LDCs "lose" about $13 billion per year on account of the past increases in oil prices, and "gain back" about $5 billion per year in aid from OPEC (with over half of that going to Arab states). The analysis presented here suggests that the opportunity cost of giving aid will rise for most members of OPEC over the next 5 years—that is, foreign aid will constitute an increasingly sharp "sacrifice" in terms of other programs foregone. Thus one would predict a *declining* rather than a rising level of foreign aid from OPEC between now and the early 1980s. Indeed the decline has already begun. Iranian aid dropped 41% if one compares the budget for 1975–76 (1354) with the budget for 1976–77 (1355).

13. M. A. Adelman, "Import Quota Ticket Auctions," *Challenge,* January–February 1976.

14

Comparative Advantage of United States Agriculture

D. Gale Johnson

DEVELOPMENT OF AGRICULTURE'S TRADE SURPLUS

The large net export surplus in U.S. agricultural trade is a recent phenomenon. Starting with fiscal year 1974 the net trade surplus has exceeded $10 billion annually. In fiscal 1973, the net positive trade balance was $7.2 billion, more than treble that of the previous year. Since 1973 the net export surplus has continued to increase and reached $15 billion in fiscal 1979.[1]

During the last half of the nineteenth century the United States followed the pattern associated with developing countries. As late as 1880 agricultural exports accounted for 80 percent of total exports, and there was a significant excess of agricultural exports over agricultural imports. In the years immediately prior to World War I agricultural exports still accounted for approximately half of total exports. Even as late as the mid-1920s, when the United States had emerged as a major industrial nation, agricultural exports were 40 percent of total exports.

However, 1922 was the beginning of two decades (save but one year) during which the value of U.S. agricultural imports exceeded the value of agricultural exports. It was not until the early years of World War II that the United States once again became a net exporter of agricultural products. This development was almost certainly caused by the disruptions of production and transport during the war rather than any fundamental improvement in the comparative advantage of U.S. agriculture.

The net export of agricultural products lasted only a few years. In 1950 imports once again exceeded exports and continued to do so through 1956, even though during most of this period the United States supplied substantial quantities of agricultural products to other nations at low cost or free through its aid programs. It was not until the early 1960s that agricultural exports would have exceeded agricultural imports if there had been no P.L. 480, the food aid program. It is not possible to pinpoint the exact year when the transition would have occurred since some of the food aid shipments displaced commercial exports.

From D. Gale Johnson, "World Agricultural and Trade Policies: Impact on U.S. Agriculture," *Contemporary Economic Problems 1979*, William Fellner, Project Director. Reprinted by permission of the American Enterprise Institute.

What was responsible for the large increase in the net agricultural surplus during the 1970s? . . . [The major objective] of this essay is to explain why American agriculture has emerged with such a large export surplus. For the moment, however, we shall consider only the role of prices and quantities and any changes that may have occurred in our trade barriers that might have influenced the quantity of imports. The next section will consider factors that may explain the significant change in the comparative advantage of agriculture during the 1970s.

In 1971 the value of agricultural exports was $8.0 billion; imports $6.1 billion. By 1977 the value of agricultural exports had trebled, and the value of imports had somewhat more than doubled. The growth in the value of exports was due to a 54 percent increase in quantity and a 94 percent increase in prices. Import volume increased by 19 percent while import unit values increased by 104 percent.[2] Thus, the growth of export volume was almost three times as great as the growth of import volume while export prices increased somewhat less than import prices.

The significant increase in the U.S. net agricultural trade balance has been the result of maintaining a constant or slightly increasing share of world exports and a declining share of world imports. One possible explanation for our declining share of world imports of agricultural products might be that our barriers to imports increased during the 1970s. This explanation has little or no validity. The farm products that were heavily protected during the 1960s, such as dairy products and sugar, are the same products heavily protected during the 1970s. Most of our agricultural imports enter either duty free (rubber, coffee, cocoa, tea, palm oil) or at rates of 5 percent or less. In 1976 the average import duty on dutiable farm products (one half of imports) was 7 percent; a decade earlier the duty averaged 10.8 percent.[3]

The only apparent significant increase in the protection of agricultural products in the 1970s compared with the 1960s has been for beef. But this increase has been more apparent than real. We do have import restrictions on beef and veal in the guise of voluntary export restraints by the major exporters. The restraints have had some effect on beef and veal imports during the 1970s, but the effects have been small. During part of the 1970s the restraints were removed, and in 1974 imports were below those that would have been permitted under the program. The maximum restraint in any year was probably 10 to 20 percent, with the lower figure the more probable. In 1978, in the face of rising domestic beef prices, the restraints on beef imports were increased by 200 million pounds, or more than 15 percent.[4] In announcing the 1979 restraint level, the U.S. Department of Agriculture estimated that in the absence of restraints the imports of beef and veal subject to the restraints might have been 6 percent greater.[5] There are significant imports outside the restraint system, primarily cooked and processed beef from countries subject to hoof and mouth disease. Imports of cooked and canned beef are not controlled at all, and duties are very low, generally less than 5 percent. . . .

As noted above, the quantity of agricultural exports increased by more than 50 percent from 1971 through 1977, which accounted for a significant part of the increase in the value of exports. This growth was due to production increases for major export products and a decline in domestic utilization of some of the same products. While total agricultural output increased by 12 percent between the first two years of this decade and 1977 and 1978, livestock output remained unchanged. Thus crops accounted for all the increase in output, and essentially all the increased crop output was available for export. Significant production increases were realized for four major exports—feed grains, food grains, oilseeds, and cotton, with the largest increase for oilseeds.

During 1977 and 1978 the United States used lower absolute amounts of all grains than during the first two years of the decade.[6] While the domestic use of soybeans has increased gradually during the decade, the export of soybeans increased from 52 percent of production for the first two years to 58 percent in 1977 and 56 percent in 1978.[7] Thus restraint in the domestic demand for the major export products also contributed to the expansion of agricultural exports, though the major factor was output growth.

COMPARATIVE ADVANTAGE OF U.S. AGRICULTURE

The United States stands in a singularly unique trade relationship with the rest of the world. It is a major net exporter of agricultural products and a large net importer of other raw materials. It is a major net exporter of high technology products such as airplanes, computers, sophisticated military hardware, and complex machinery but a large net importer of a wide variety of standardized manufactured producer and consumer goods. Our major comparative advantages seem to be in two quite disparate areas— high technology products and a primary industry, namely agriculture.

There may well be less of an anomaly in our trade pattern than the previous sentence implies. It can be argued, and I will so argue, that American agriculture is today a high technology sector of our economy. While there is no clear definition of high technology, most would agree that certain characteristics are associated with such an industry or sector: a relatively high ratio of capital to labor; rapid changes in the methods or techniques of production; a high rate of adoption of new and improved inputs; and a relatively large annual flow of resources into research. Where these characteristics prevail, the transfer of technology to other countries is difficult compared with, say, the production of such products as radios, television sets, textiles, or steel. Admittedly the description of a high technology sector is imprecise and impressionistic, but yet the characteristics indicated may be helpful in putting the comparative advantage of U.S. agriculture in proper perspective.

Three inappropriate explanations of the comparative advantage of U.S. agriculture are frequently offered. It is quite common for foreigners, especially those from Western Europe and Japan, to attribute the high productivity of American agriculture to the enormous amount of excellent land and the generally favorable characteristics of our climate. It is true that we are blessed with much land of excellent quality; there exists nowhere else in the world an equivalent area of high-quality land such as exists in the American corn belt. Another explanation for the high productivity is the large size of American farms compared with those in Western Europe or in most other parts of the world outside the centrally planned economies. This statement is empirically valid. A third explanation is that American agriculture employs relatively few workers, and the ratio of land area per worker is very much greater than almost anywhere else in the world. Comparable ratios exist only in Canada and Australia.

Although the facts on which these explanations are based can be verified, they were equally valid, at least in a relative sense, when the United States was a net importer of agricultural products. The explanations probably rest on the mistaken impression that the United States has been a net exporter of agricultural products throughout the past century or more. But, as has been noted, agriculture's substantial comparative advantage has emerged only recently.

The reemergence of U.S. agriculture as a net exporter in the early 1960s was due, in my opinion, to three important factors: (1) modification of our agricultural price, incomes, and exchange rate policies; (2) significant resource adjustments in agriculture after World War II; and (3) the emergence of U.S. agriculture as a high technology sector. Each was important, and there have been significant interrelationships among the three.

Policy Modifications

During the 1950s, price supports for the major grains and cotton were established at levels significantly above market clearing prices. Large stocks were accumulated by the government even though efforts were made to reduce production. Exports declined during the early 1950s, and efforts to reduce the accumulation of stocks included the expansion of food aid and the payment of export subsidies on commercial sales. Starting in the late 1950s price support levels were lowered, and by 1966 price supports for most commodities were at or below international prices. When the price supports were above market clearing levels, export subsidies were used to maintain an acceptable level of exports or the quantity of exports was adversely affected. When price supports significantly influenced the domestic price, exports were largely determined by the kind and extent of governmental intervention. When price supports were lowered, the markct was permitted to function in allocating the available supply between domestic and export uses, and there can be little doubt that exports increased significantly as a consequence.

Schuh has argued that the overvaluation of the U.S. dollar prior to the 1971 devaluation had imposed substantial costs upon agriculture, restraining the growth of exports and adding to the resource adjustments required to obtain a satisfactory level of labor returns in agriculture.[8] The overvaluation of the dollar resulted in a lower level of prices of farm products in the domestic market and in greater difficulty in competing for resources with all sectors of the economy except the other export-oriented industries. There can be little doubt that the devaluation of the dollar in 1971 and the floating of the dollar in 1973 encouraged agricultural exports and improved the relative profitability of agricultural production in the United States. Consequently, the change in exchange rate policy clearly contributed to the size of the net agricultural trade surplus in recent years, even though other factors may have been primarily responsible for the transition from a net import to a net export position.

Resource Adjustments

The significant resource adjustments that occurred in agriculture after World War II were described in my article in *Contemporary Economic Problems 1977*. These changes included a rapid reduction in the labor input per unit of farm output and an increase in the amount of capital per worker. Very importantly, argriculture became more fully integrated into the economy, and the off-farm income of farm people increased significantly so that by the mid-1960s approximately half the net income of farm operator families was derived from off-farm sources. Although real farm prices declined by more than 20 percent from the early 1950s to 1970, the per capita disposable income of the farm population increased from about 60 percent of the nonfarm population's in the early 1950s to about 75 percent by 1970.

A High Technology Sector

What is today described as modern agriculture is a recent development. The first of the new high-yielding varieties—hybrid corn—became available only during the mid-1930s. It was not planted on half the corn area until 1942. The second important new high-yielding variety—grain sorghums—did not become available until the mid-1950s. Grain yields in the United States in 1930 were very little greater than they had been six decades earlier. The benefits of agricultural research until the 1930s were relatively small and were confined primarily to labor-saving inventions. Output-increasing innovations did not occur until there were significant breakthroughs in plant breeding. Once the yield potentials of several major economic crops were increased significantly, numerous other innovations and adjustments occurred that resulted in substantial increases in yield and output.

Between 1910–1914 and 1937–1941 crop production per acre increased by 8 percent; from 1937–1941 to 1950–1954 by 15 percent; from 1937–1941 to 1960–1964 by 51 percent and to 1975–1978 by 100 percent.[9] Almost all the increase in output per acre of cropland occurred after 1955 and much of it since 1964.

Farm output per hour of farm work increased even more dramatically over the same period—by 660 percent between 1937–1941 and 1976. Again most of the improvement occurred after 1955, though less so than for the increase in crop production per acre. Output per farm worker nearly doubled between 1937–1941 and 1950–1954 and then doubled again by 1960–1964 and again by 1976.[10]

Modern agriculture is highly dependent upon the services of many other sectors of the economy. It depends upon major continuing research efforts in both the public and private sectors. It depends upon competitive and innovative input sectors that continuously introduce new and improved products and supplies them on a timely and assured basis. It depends upon an efficient marketing and transport sector that minimizes costs of delivering inputs to farms and of delivering the output of farms to processors and consumers. American agriculture is favored on all of these scores. This is not to say that similar circumstances do not exist in any other part of the world, but only a limited number of countries provide as effective a setting for agriculture as is available for U.S. agriculture. Certainly the agricultures of the centrally planned economies are not supported with the same degree of effectiveness. Nor are the agricultures of the developing countries similarly favored.

American agriculture is supported by a large and varied set of research institutions. In 1974 approximately a quarter of the world's agricultural research expenditures was made in the United States. The share of this research undertaken in the industrial sector is much larger in the United States than in any other economy. The firms that do the relevant research are primarily in the agricultural input industries. Such firms obviously draw upon both the basic and applied research of the federal and state agricultural research institutions. A substantial amount of research being undertaken in the input-producing firms means a relatively rapid productive utilization of recent research results. It can also be argued that there is more competition among agricultural research institutions in the United States than in the rest of the world, even within the publicly supported sector. Each state has one or more agricultural experiment stations, and the federal government has a number of different research enterprises. While some of the support for state research comes from the federal government, funds supplied by state governments dominate.

The amount of capital per farm worker has dramatically increased since 1950. In constant 1978 dollars the value of production assets per farm worker has increased from $40,000 in 1950 to $150,000 in 1978. If one excludes all land and buildings, the increase has been from approximately $9,000 in 1950 to $28,000 in 1978. A large part of the increase in capital per worker occurred after 1960. Production assets per worker in 1978 dollars as of 1960 was $55,000 and other than land and buildings, $14,000.[11] In 1976 the 500 largest industrial corporations had $39,000 of assets per employee; production assets per farm worker were almost $125,000 by the end of 1976.[12]

A further indication of the capital intensity of U.S. agriculture is the relative importance of annual capital consumption to net product. In 1977 capital consumption, including capital consumption allowance, was 40 percent of agriculture's net national product.[13] For all nonfinancial corporations capital consumption, including the capital consumption allowance, was approximately 12 percent of net domestic product. The high relative capital consumption of agriculture occurs even though its major production asset, namely land, is not considered in the estimates of capital consumption. Perhaps the most important implication of high ratio of capital consumption allowances to net product in agriculture is that it indicates a rapid turnover in the stock of capital equipment and the degree to which the capital stock represents the newest and most modern equipment available.

Important as material capital may be in a high technology sector, human capital is at least as important. One form of human capital is utilized in the development of new knowledge, primarily in the public and private research institutions. But the material capital and the new knowledge must be combined with other resources by the farm operator or entrepreneur.

Modern agriculture is highly complex. Change is rapid; adjustment to new conditions is continuous. There is a continuing flow of new knowledge and new inputs. Agriculture is subject to wider price variations than most other sectors of the economy and, in addition, is subject to numerous natural conditions over which it has no control. Efficient allocation of resources is both complicated and difficult, requiring a high level of skill. By comparison with other sectors of the economy, farm firms are relatively small. This means that the increasing productivity of agriculture depends upon the capacities of hundreds of thousands of entrepreneurs.

The effects of education on productivity may be divided into two parts—the worker effect and the allocative effect. According to Finis Welch, the worker effect refers to improvement in production as education is increased, with other factors of production held constant. Education may also improve allocative efficiency or ability to acquire and utilize information about costs and the productive characteristics of other inputs, including the characteristics of unfamiliar inputs such as new seed varieties or new machines or new methods of cultivation. Welch concluded that agriculture "is probably atypical inasmuch as a larger share of the productive value of education may refer to allocative ability than in most industries."[14]

Welch's analysis of data for U.S. agriculture shows that the return to the operators with the most education, namely college graduates, is substantially higher than for all other educational levels. A significant part of the increased return to the college graduate is attributed to expenditures on research, which contribute to the changing and dynamic characteristics of agriculture. In effect, as Schultz has argued, "the value of schooling in farming depends on the opportunities that farmers have to modernize their production." As Schultz has noted, modern agriculture is in a continuous state of disequilibrium because it undergoes rapid changes as new knowledge and new inputs become available. Before complete adjustment can be made to any set of conditions, new potentialities have been made available. He concludes: "There is enough evidence to give validity to the hypothesis that the ability to deal successfully with economic disequilibria is enhanced by education and that this ability is one of the major benefits of education accruing to people privately in a modernizing economy."[15]

In a recent article, Welch summarizes a number of studies of the returns to education in agriculture related to allocative efficiency. His conclusion was:

> Based on what by now is a large body of accrued evidence, it seems clear that in U.S. agriculture—a particularly dynamic technical setting—education enhances allocative efficiency. Furthermore, increased scale increases incentives for "correct" decisions and results not only in the "purchase" of more education for operators of larger farms but in related investments that enhance response.[16]

Since the end of World War II there has been a significant absolute and relative increase in the educational levels of farm operators in the United States. Simultaneously there has been a substantial increase in the scale or size of farms. Since 1960 gross sales per farm, measured in constant dollars, have more than doubled. Another measure of farm scale—farm output per farm—increased 86 percent between 1960 and 1977.[17]

There has been a significant increase in the years of school completed by farmers and farm managers during the past two decades. For male farmers and farm managers twenty-five years old or more, the median years of schooling completed in 1960 was 8.7 years; in 1970, 10.6. For all males in the labor force the increase was from 11.0 to 12.3 years. By 1970 the years of school had exceeded twelve years for three age groups—twenty-five to twenty-nine, thirty to thirty-four, and thirty-five to forty-four. In 1960 the median years of schooling for the thirty-five to forty-four age group was 9.9. Available data indicate a continued increase in years of school completed through 1975, especially for the forty-five to sixty-four age group—from 9.0 years in 1970 to 10.9 years in 1975.[18]

The increase in educational attainment for farm operators represents two factors. The first is that the gap between years of school completed by urban and rural residents has been largely eliminated over the past three decades. The second is the influence of mobility. If one follows the age cohorts from 1960 to 1970, the data indicate that farm operators in the forty-five to fifty-four age group in 1970 completed 0.9 more years of school than did the same cohort a decade earlier. Quite obviously, the farm operators who remained in agriculture had more years of schooling than those who left for other economic activities.

Transferring Agricultural Technology

A characteristic of modern agriculture is that many significant improvements are location specific. In other words, crop varieties and some production practices are specifically adapted to the soil and climatic conditions of limited geographical areas. In order to take advantage of the matching of local conditions with the most appropriate varieties, production methods, and equipment, agriculture must be supplied with the continuing output of sophisticated research and with the required inputs. American agriculture is greatly favored on both counts.

An important implication of the location specificity of much of modern agriculture is that it is difficult effectively to transfer varieties and production methods from one part of the world to another. Although modern research has produced crop varieties that are less sensitive to certain climatic conditions, such as length of day, than were crop varieties developed as recently as two decades ago, the advantages of technological leadership remain very great.

Maintaining Agriculture's Comparative Advantage

If appropriate governmental policies are followed, U.S. agriculture should retain its comparative advantage into the indefinite future. Continued support of agricultural research is essential, as are price and incomes policies that permit the market to allocate available supplies between domestic and foreign consumers and permit farmers a high degree of freedom in utilizing their resources in an efficient manner. Agriculture's comparative advantage would be more striking if its major products faced trade barriers in its export markets similar to those enjoyed by most industrial products. We should, of course, reduce those of our own barriers that interfere with efficient use of the world's agricultural resources. We have much to gain from a substantial reduction in trade barriers, including our own. . . .

Notes

1. *Outlook for U.S. Agricultural Exports* (February 16, 1979), p. 2.
2. *FATUS* (March 1978), pp. 45–46, and (September 1978), pp. 112–14. The quantity indexes are for fiscal years; the unit values for calendar years. Publication of these series has been discontinued, at least temporarily.

3. *FATUS* (August 1977), pp. 80–84.
4. U.S. Department of Agriculture, Economic, Statistics, and Cooperatives Services, *Livestock and Meat Situation,* no. 221 (June 1978), p. 4.
5. U.S. Department of Agriculture, *News,* December 29, 1978.
6. *World Agricultural Situation,* no. 18 (December 1978), p. 38.
7. *FATUS* (November 1973), p. 34.
8. G. Edward Schuh, "The Exchange Rate and U.S. Agriculture," *American Journal of Agricultural Economics,* vol. 56, no. 1 (February 1974), pp. 1–13.
9. U.S. Department of Agriculture, Economic Research Service, *Changes in Farm Production and Efficiency 1977,* Statistical Bulletin no. 581 (November 1977), p. 19; and *Agricultural Outlook,* no. 40 (January–February 1979), p. 18.
10. *Changes in Farm Production and Efficiency 1977,* p. 45.
11. Calculated from Board of Governors of the Federal Reserve System, Division of Research and Statistics, *Agricultural Finance Databook: Annual Series* (September 1976), table 512.1; and U.S. Department of Agriculture, Economics, Statistics, and Cooperatives Services, *Balance Sheet of the Farming Sector, 1978,* Supplement no. 1, Agricultural Information Bulletin no. 416 (October 1978).
12. U.S. Department of Commerce, Bureau of the Census, *Statistical Abstract of the United States 1977,* p. 563; and *Balance Sheet of the Farming Sector, 1978,* p. 27.
13. *Survey of Current Business* (December 1978), pp. 1–3.
14. Finis Welch, "Education in Production," *Journal of Political Economy,* vol. 78, no. 1 (January/February 1970), p. 47.
15. Theodore W. Schultz, "The Value of the Ability to Deal with Disequilibria," *Journal of Economic Literature,* vol. 13, no. 3 (September 1975), pp. 841 and 843.
16. Finis Welch, "The Role of Human Investments in Agriculture," in *Distortions of Agricultural Incentives,* Theodore W. Schultz, ed. (Bloomington: Indiana University Press, 1978), p. 274.
17. Based on *Changes in Farm Production and Efficiency 1977,* pp. 6–7; *Agricultural Outlook* (December 1978), p. 21; and U.S. Department of Agriculture, *Agricultural Statistics 1977,* p. 422.
18. U.S. Department of Commerce, Bureau of the Census, *Census of Population 1960,* vol. 5B, *Educational Attainment,* table 8; and ibid., *1970,* table 11. For each age group under forty-five, the percentage of farm operators and managers who had completed at least four years of college doubled between 1960 and 1970. For the cohorts aged thirty-five to forty-four and forty-five to fifty-four in 1960, the decline in the number of farm operators was 33 percent and 42 percent, respectively. The decline in the number with four or more years of college was 17 percent and 20 percent.

15

The Tokyo Round of Multilateral Trade Negotiations

Robert E. Baldwin

INTRODUCTION

As the Multilateral Trade Negotiations (also known as the Tokyo Round) draw to a conclusion, the U.S. Congress faces a significant choice; it can either accept or reject without amendment a proposed set of rules of "good" behavior in international commerce that will shape the conduct of international trade for at least the rest of this century.* The rules were drawn up in more than five years of negotiations aimed both at further cutting tariffs and at reducing or eliminating nontariff impediments to and distortions of international trade. Ministers of the ninety-nine nations involved agreed in the inaugural Tokyo Declaration that where the reduction or elimination of such nontariff impediments was not appropriate they should at least be brought "under more effective international discipline."

The emphasis on nontariff distortions of trade makes the current negotiating round different from the six previous trade-liberalizing exercises held since World War II within the framework of the General Agreement on Tariffs and Trade (GATT). Earlier negotiations focused primarily on reducing tariffs. The last multilateral effort, the so-called Kennedy Round lasting from 1962 to 1967, cut import duties in the major industrial nations by an average of 35 percent for dutiable manufactures and 20 percent for agricultural products. As a result, the average duty for dutiable manufactured goods declined to only about 10 percent in the United States, the European Community, and Japan by the conclusion of the Kennedy Round cuts. This is in contrast to a U.S. tariff level for dutiable imports of nearly 60 percent in 1931. Further tariff reductions of about 33 percent for all participants are scheduled as part of the agreements reached in the Tokyo Round negotiations.

The most significant part of these agreements, however, is the series of detailed codes spelling out permissible and nonpermissible

Reprinted from Robert E. Baldwin, *The Multilateral Trade Negotiations: Toward Greater Liberalization?*, Special Analysis, 1979, pp. 1–2 and 8–30, by permission of the American Enterprise Institute; and from Robert E. Baldwin, *Beyond the Tokyo Round Negotiations*, Thames Essay No. 22 (London: Trade Policy Research Centre, 1979), pp. 23–33, by permission.

*[The proposed codes were approved by Congress in the Trade Agreements Act of 1979. Most other industrial countries also promptly approved the codes, but, as of July 1980, only a few developing countries had signed them.—Eds.]

"good" behavior by governments in almost all areas where nontariff measures have threatened the basic trade-liberalizing objective of the GATT. Consideration of these codes is especially timely not merely because the negotiations have just ended but also because, unlike tariff reductions, the codes must be approved by both houses of Congress before they can be implemented. The implementing bill will not only approve the agreements and any administrative actions needed to implement them but will repeal and amend any existing laws that must be changed for them to take effect. In accordance with the 1974 Trade Act, no amendments to the implementing bill will be permitted in either the House or Senate, and the bill must be voted on no more than ninety legislation days from its introduction in Congress. According to present plans, the President will submit the implementing bill to Congress in May.

The purpose of this analysis is to assist in evaluating the results of the Tokyo Round, especially the package agreement on nontariff measures. This package covers subsidies and countervailing duties, antidumping practices, government procurement policies, valuation and licensing practices, technical barriers to trade (standards), differential and more favorable treatment for developing countries, safeguard actions for balance of payments and developmental purposes, and dispute settlement and surveillance procedures under the GATT. The negotiators failed to reach agreement on codes covering safeguards against injurious imports and commercial counterfeiting, but the hope is that final agreement on these subjects will be reached within a few months.* Moreover, the participants agreed to reassess in the near future the GATT provisions relating to export restraints. In addition, specific agreements have been reached with regard to steel, aircraft, certain agricultural products, and several nontariff measures of only bilateral interest. The following analysis will describe the measures or practices that have led to the desire for improved codes, the nature of the agreed upon or proposed codes and how they differ from existing GATT rules, and finally a brief evaluation of each. After appraising the mechanisms established to secure compliance with the different nontariff codes, the various other agreements concluded will be examined more closely, including the tariff-cutting formula that has been adopted. . . .

THE NONTARIFF AGREEMENTS

. . .

Subsidies and Countervailing Duties

Two trends of recent years have been especially important in focusing attention on the potential trade-distorting effects of subsidies.

---

*[As of July 1980, no agreement on a safeguards code had been reached, and the short-run prospects for such an agreement were not favorable.—Eds.]

One is the increasing economic intervention by governments in order to redistribute income toward various groups that the electorate regards as "socially deserving," while the other is the growing degree of openness and interdependence among the major trading nations. As a result, there are many more types of government subsidies than when the GATT was first adopted, and any given subsidy is now likely to have a more direct effect on trade than in the late 1940s.

Selective subsidies that affect production activities, that is, those that are not merely lump-sum income transfers, tend to misallocate economic resources and thereby reduce the potential output of the international community unless the subsidies serve to offset other economic distortions that cannot be eliminated or handled by better means. There are, in fact, a number of circumstances where subsidies can be justified on this ground. For example, some types of socially desirable research may not take place if a firm fears that the results will become freely available to its competitors and make it impossible to recoup the costs of undertaking the research. Similarly, the stickiness of wages along with imperfections of capital markets may justify temporary subsidies to particular regions or specific industries. But if the reason for the subsidy is to promote economic efficiency and growth, the subsidy should be only temporary. However, one may wish to assist a particular group simply on equity grounds or for some other noneconomic reason. Moreover, various political or social factors may prevent the government from providing direct income grants that do not distort production. In these circumstances international political and economic problems often arise because distorting production may produce not just temporary but permanent income losses to citizens of other countries.

Article III of the GATT explicitly permits "the payment of subsidies exclusively to domestic producers." However, Article XVI requires that members who maintain a subsidy "which operates directly or indirectly to increase exports . . . or reduce imports . . . shall notify the Contracting Parties . . . of the estimated effects of the subsidization."[1] If "it is determined that serious prejudice to the interests of any contracting party is caused or threatened by such subsidization," the country granting the subsidy "shall, upon request, discuss . . . the possibility of limiting the subsidization." In 1955 a section added to the article stated that any subsidy on the export of a nonprimary product resulting "in the sale of such product for export at a price lower than the comparable price charged . . . in the domestic market" should cease after January 1958 or "the earliest, practicable date thereafter." At the insistence of the United States export subsidies on primary products; that is, agricultural products and minerals, were not prohibited, although they were not to give a member "more than an equitable share of world export trade" in the affected product.

While open and direct export subsidy of manufactured goods by the advanced industrial countries has been kept to a minimum since the late 1950s, various indirect subsidies have developed that the new code tries to control more effectively. First it strengthens the GATT condemnation of government export subsidies on nonprimary products by stating flatly that they should not be granted. This ban is also extended to minerals. More important, by eliminating the requirement that export subsidies result in a lower sales price abroad than at home, it recognizes that under conditions of imperfect competition export subsidies need not always result in dual pricing. An updated list of export subsidies is also provided that includes such measures as currency retention schemes, internal freight rates more favorable for export goods than for domestic products, and special tax, credit, and insurance-rate breaks for exporters. However, export tax benefits such as those provided when U.S. firms form a Domestic International Sales Corporation (DISC) may still be permitted under these latter rules, and the financing of exports at only slightly more than the government's borrowing rate will definitely still be allowed.

In carrying out their wide-ranging efforts for income redistribution and full employment, governments provide extensive domestic subsidies for specific industries, for example, coal, steel, shipping and shipbuilding, textiles, aircraft, and electronics; for specific regions, such as depressed areas; and even for broad product sectors and activities, for example, manufacturing, agriculture, education, health services, and research. The subsidizing means include favorable tax treatment (tax holidays and deferrals, accelerated depreciation, investment credits), below-market borrowing privileges, the payment of fringe benefits, production subsidies, wage subsidies, lump-sum payments, and the sale of government-owned services at favorable rates. It does not take an economist to appreciate that domestic firms receiving this kind of assistance are able to compete more effectively against foreign imports and also in export markets.

As already noted, Article XVI of the GATT provides for consultation only if a member believes another's subsidies are seriously prejudicing its interests. An alternative route for settling such disputes is the use of Article XXIII, which relates to "nullification or impairment" of benefits accruing under the General Agreement. If a contracting party considers that any of these benefits is being nullified or impaired, it can, after the failure of bilateral consultations, have the matter referred to the contracting parties as a whole. Over time the procedure has evolved of appointing a working party or panel of experts to investigate the dispute and report on the merits of the alleged nullification or impairment in terms of the Articles of Agreement. After receiving the report the contracting parties can, if they deem the circumstances warrant it, authorize one of the parties to suspend concessions it has granted to the offending party. The use of the panel or working party to settle disputes has been infrequent, however. Between 1948 and 1977 only thirty-five disputes of all types reached this state, and their frequency has diminished sharply in recent years.[2]

The greater use of domestic subsidies in most industrial countries other than the United States coupled with the vagueness of existing GATT provisions covering subsidies and the inadequate mechanism for dispute settlement prompted the United States to press in the Tokyo Round negotiations for substantial changes in the rules on domestic subsidies. The code that has evolved explicitly recognizes the right of signatories to use domestic subsidies "for the promotion of social and economic policy objectives," including the elimination of industrial, economic, and social disadvantages of specific regions, and restructuring of certain sectors adversely affected by trade and other economic policies, the maintenance of employment, and the encouragement of research and development programs. It also lists means of subsidization (with the implication that they are legitimate and need not be temporary) to meet these objectives, such as government financing of commercial enterprises, government provision of operational services to these enterprises, government financing of research, and various fiscal incentives to private firms. The code also explicitly recognizes, however, that domestic subsidies may cause or threaten to cause serious prejudice, especially when they adversely affect "the conditions of normal competition," and the signatories agree to seek to avoid causing such injury. Moreover, the dispute settlement mechanism is improved for both export and domestic subsidies. If consultations with other members fail to satisfy a signatory who believes another nations's domestic subsidy causes injury to its own domestic industry, nullification or impairment of its GATT benefits, or serious prejudice to its interests, the dispute can be referred to a committee of signatories of the code for conciliation. If the matter remains unresolved, any signatory involved can request that the committee appoint a panel of experts to present its findings concerning the rights and obligations of the parties involved. The committee may then authorize appropriate countermeasures based on the panel's report.

For countries that subsidize more extensively than the United States, the incentive to agree to tighter controls over both export and domestic subsidies is to obtain an "injury clause" in the U.S. countervailing duty law. Countervailing duties are discriminatory levies on imported goods permitted under the GATT (Article VI) to offset any government subsidy on the "manufacture, production or export of any merchandise" if the effect of the subsidy is "to cause or threaten material injury" to a domestic industry. Imposing countervailing duties to handle the problem of foreign subsidies is quite different from utilizing the provisions of Articles XVI and XXIII. The countervailing-duty route can be used only against subsidized imports, since imposing import duties obviously does not offset a country's loss of an export market because of foreign subsidies. More important, the decision whether to countervail is made entirely by the importing country according to its established procedures. Other countries have been concerned for many years because U.S. procedures do not require proof of material injury before countervailing duties can be imposed on subsidized imports. However, U.S. negotiators agreed to accept the normal GATT requirement that material injury must be caused or threatened before countervailing can take place. Nevertheless, provisional countervailing measures can be taken after a preliminary finding that a subsidy exists and there is sufficient evidence of injury. The criteria listed in the code for determining injury also specify that the effects of the subsidy on the volume of imports as well as their price must be taken into consideration.

One might conclude from the language of the subsidies/countervailing duty code that the United States will not receive any benefits that do not already exist in the various GATT articles dealing with subsidies, even though the country is giving up its right to countervail without proof of material injury and may be implicitly accepting the legitimacy of many domestic subsidies of other countries. A more appropriate view, in my opinion, is that the code represents a potentially significant accomplishment that may enable the international community to control in a realistic manner the trade-distorting effects of domestic subsidies, particularly those that reduce the exports of another country. The United States has never literally enforced its own subsidy and countervailing duty law; to do so would create an administrative nightmare and lead to such extensive retaliation that our international economic and political position would be jeopardized. On the other hand, the various provisions of the GATT that apply to subsidies, especially to domestic subsidies, are vague and scattered throughout the document. Moreover, the dispute settlement mechanism under Article XXIII is more a means of resolving unusual situations not covered by the specific articles of the agreement than a regular procedure for settling ordinary disputes that arise in the operation of trade policies. Consequently, it has been difficult to find a sensible intermediate position between countervailing against every trivial foreign subsidy and ignoring all but the most flagrant trade-distorting subsidies. The introduction of an injury clause into U.S. law coupled with the creation of a dispute settlement committee for subsidies alone may enable us to attain such a position. The word "may" is used because the key to the code's success is how effective the dispute settlement and enforcement mechanism will be. Since this issue applies to all the codes, it will be considered later in this chapter.

Anit-Dumping Practices

One of the few areas of progress on nontariff measures in the Kennedy Round was agreement on a code dealing with anti-dumping practices. The United States signed the document as an Executive Agreement, but the Congress strongly objected to the fact that it was never submitted to that body for approval. A law was passed directing the International Trade Commission to ignore the new code in making its decisions on whether injury occurred as a result of dumping. The new anti-dumping agreement reached in the Tokyo Round affords an opportunity to eliminate this highly unsatisfactory state of affairs, since it will be part of the package submitted to Congress for approval and the implementing bill will contain any necessary changes in U.S. law.

The new agreement on the implementation of anti-dumping practices under Article VI of GATT differs from the previous one mainly in two respects: the determination of injury and the establishment of a dispute settlement mechanism. The impetus for revision of the anti-dumping code was the desire to make its injury provisions consistent with those negotiated in the code on subsidies and countervailing duties. Like those in the latter code, the provisions of the new agreement specify that both the volume of dumped imports and their effect on prices in domestic markets be considered in determining injury. The illustrative list of factors to consider in examining the impact of dumping on the industry concerned is made consistent with the subsidies code, as is the provision cautioning that demonstrated injury under the code must be caused by dumped imports rather than other economic factors. Both the subsidies/countervailing duties and anti-dumping codes state in footnotes that "injury" is to mean material injury to a domestic industry. However, the revised U.S. anti-dumping law to be submitted as part of the implementing bill apparently will simply specify that injury not be "immaterial" rather than use the phrase "material injury."

Although a committee on anti-dumping practices had been established under the old code, its purpose had been merely to facilitate periodic consultations among members on matters relating to the administration of anti-dumping systems. The new agreement makes the powers of the committee similar to those of committees established under the other nontariff codes. It can perform a conciliation role in disputes, appoint panels to examine the matters under dispute, and authorize retaliatory actions.

Safeguards

Article XIX of the General Agreement permits member countries to withdraw or modify a concession (such as a tariff reduction) previously granted "if, as a result of unforeseen developments," a product is being imported in such increased quantities "as to cause or threaten serious injury to domestic producers." But consultations with exporting countries must take place prior to or immediately after the withdrawal or modification and, if equivalent concessions on other products are not agreed upon, these exporting countries can withdraw some of their own concessions.

These "escape clauses" or safeguards have not worked well in recent years. Most of the major industrial trading nations have entered into various bilateral agreements with other countries outside the GATT framework, whereby these other countries "voluntarily" agree to limit their exports of particular products. This procedure permits the importing country to discriminate against the exports of one or more countries and does not involve the granting of offsetting concessions by the importing nation. The exporting nations have not complained of "nullification and impairment" under Article XXIII because of the threat of even more severe restriction if the matter gets into the hands of national legislators.

A draft code under consideration attempts to bring the various types of safeguards back within the GATT framework and to spell out in more detail the procedures each country must follow in carrying out such actions. On the latter point the code sets forth (as the relevant U.S. law does) a list of indicators to be considered in determining serious injury and also specifies that safeguard measures should be only temporary and progressively liberalized. A committee on safeguard measures, composed of the signatories to this code, is also established for surveillance and dispute settlement. Whether a country will have the right to restrict imports from only a few sources—that is, to discriminate against certain countries—and whether "voluntary" export restraints and "orderly" marketing agreements will be allowed under Article XIX is still under discussion. Reportedly, the European Community [EC] is strongly urging that selective discrimination be permitted. The developing countries, on the other hand, are vigorously opposing the proposal, since they believe it will be used mainly against them for both economic and political purposes.

The most-favored-nation principle (MFN), that is, nondiscrimination among countries with respect to trade policies, has already been so widely breached that it is somewhat hard to become concerned about a limited policy of selectivity. For example, the European Community discriminates against nonmembers such as the United States. The EC also gives special preferential treatment to the former colonies of its members as well as to several other states. Both of these actions are permitted under current GATT rules. There are other customs unions and free trade areas in the world, including, for example, the arrangement between the United States and Canada on automobiles and automobile parts. The granting of tariff preferences to the developing countries and the fact that the new codes will discriminate against nonsignatories are further indications that the most-favored-nation principle is widely violated in actual practice.

More important than the MFN principle is whether economic adjustments occur in the injured industry so that the import restrictions are in fact only temporary. Unless solid evidence of adjustment efforts is required, the same conditions justifying the initial relief are likely to persist for years. Under these circumstances it is difficult, as experience with textiles indicates, not to find some way of continuing the import relief. If pressures were exerted on industries that resulted in the gradual movement of resources out of these sectors into more productive lines, the matter of temporary discrimination would not seem so significant. Unfortunately neither U.S. law nor GATT rules deal effectively with the adjustment problem.

Government Procurement

Purchasing policies by governments are excluded from the GATT principle of nondiscrimination under Article III. But favoritism toward domestic producers in government nonmilitary purchasing has increasingly irritated exporters as government purchases have escalated in recent years. The United States discriminates against foreign exporters on the basis of the so-called Buy American Act of 1933.[3] It has been implemented by generally giving U.S. producers a 6 percent price preference over foreigners. However, small firms and those in depressed areas receive a 12 percent price preference, and the Defense Department gives U.S. producers a 50 percent preference on all nonmilitary purchases. Many states and municipalities in the United States also have purchasing rules that openly discriminate against foreigners. Other countries do not have such explicitly discriminating legislation, but this does not mean that they do not favor their domestic producers over foreign bidders. A study of the share of domestic purchases in total nonmilitary spending by governments suggests that by using various administrative means other nations are every bit as discriminatory as the United States.[4]

Stating in a code that governments should not discriminate against foreign products or suppliers in the their purchasing policies is obviously merely a first step. Discrimination is the result not only of deliberate efforts to favor local producers but also of ignorance on the part of purchasing agents who are reluctant to spend the time and take the risks involved in purchasing from foreign suppliers. Consequently, it is necessary for nations to establish administrative procedures that enable foreigners to learn about and participate in bidding opportunities, meet the required specifications, find out why any bid was rejected, and have access to a dispute settlement mechanism. In short, the entire procurement process must be made more open or transparent so that discrimination is made more difficult. The new government procurement code in the Tokyo Round attempts to do this. It contains detailed rules relating to such matters as describing the technical specifications for a product, publishing notices of bidding opportunities, qualifying as a possible supplier, determining the time allocated for submitting bids, awarding contracts, furnishing knowledge about bids, and reviewing complaints.

The code is clearly in the interest of the United States. The governments of most other industrial countries own or control a much larger part of secondary and tertiary economic activities than does the U.S. government. Moreover, the purchases of these industries often involve the type of high technology capital goods for which the United States has a competitive production advantage. While opportunities for trade worth as much as $20 billion a year could open up in foreign government purchasing markets now closed to U.S. exporters, there are still several important government agencies and classes of products excluded from the general provisions of the code. For example, most countries exclude telecommunications equipment, and the U.S. Defense Department omits such items as textiles, shoes, and specialty steel from its list of eligible products.

Customs Valuation and Licensing

Two other areas where administrative practices sometimes restrict trade needlessly are valuing imports for the assessment of customs duties and issuing import licenses. The United States has nine different methods of determining customs value and has been severely criticized by foreign countries who charge that these methods are not applied in a uniform manner.

In addition, foreign governments argue that one of the nine methods, the so-called American selling price (ASP) is blatantly unfair. In the Tariff Act of 1922 some congressmen succeeded in raising the level of protection on a particular group of products of special interest to them not by raising the *rates* at which imports were taxed (since this would have made these rates embarrassingly high) but by raising the *base* on which the rates were levied.[5] Specifically, the duty was levied on the value of similar products produced in the United States rather than, as usual, on the export value of the items themselves. Suppose, for example, the selling price of a unit of some benzenoid chemical produced in the United States is $150, while the export value of the same commodity produced in Germany is $90. If a 40 percent tariff is levied on the American selling price, the duty is $60, whereas if levied on the export value, it is only $36. Under the ASP system the landed price of the foreign-produced chemical will, when transport costs are included, exceed the price of its American substitute. However, under the usual method of valuing imports, the foreign product will be cheaper if the various costs of shipping the product to the United States do not exceed $24, that is, $150 minus $90 minus $36. One of the few nontariff items negotiated in the Kennedy Round was the elimination of the ASP system, but Congress failed to accept this part of the package. If the new code on customs valuation is accepted by Congress, however, the ASP system will be abolished.

The new code sets out five methods of determining customs value. The first is the primary method, while the others are secondary methods to be followed in sequence if the primary method fails. The primary method values imports at their transaction value, that is "the price actually paid or payable for the goods when sold for export to the country of importation" plus certain costs and expenses incurred with respect to the imported goods that are not included in the price paid. Examples of these are selling commissions, brokerage fees, packing costs, royalties and license fees, and "assists," such as the plans or various tools that help the importer use or sell the product.

If the customs value cannot be ascertained under the primary method, the next method is to ascertain the transaction value of identical goods exported to the same country at or about the same time as the goods under consideration. The third method is to use the transaction value of similar (rather than identical) goods exported to the same country at the same time. Failing the existence of adequate information for this procedure, the importer can request that either the value be deduced from the unit price at which identical or similar goods imported at the same time are resold in the country of importation less appropriate transportation costs, profit margins, and the like, or be computed from material, manufacturing, and other costs and margins in the country of exportation. Both a committee on customs valuation consisting of the parties to the agreement and a technical committee on customs valuation under the auspices of the Customs Cooperation Council are established to facilitate dispute settlement. The customs valuation committee can request the technical committee to examine a disputed matter or create a panel for this purpose.

The transactions-value method is similar to the actual-value method that is cited in Article VII of the GATT as the preferred way of valuing imports for customs purposes. However, the growing practices of providing various services and assets free of charge or at reduced cost along with the product makes it necessary to elaborate how to calculate this value. Article VII merely states that, when the actual value cannot be determined, the value should be "based on the nearest ascertainable equivalent of such value." Spelling out in detail just what these other valuation methods are and the order in which they should be followed should go far in reducing the irritations of traders over customs valuation procedures.

Since U.S. exporters often complain that foreign customs officials arbitrarily increase the value of American products as well as that foreign customs procedures are uncertain, the new code deserves the support of Congress. Elimination of ASP is a concession in the technical sense of the word, but presumably this will be taken into account in determining the overall balance of concessions with other countries. As a customs valuation method, however, it deserves to be abolished, since it is deceitful in its purpose and grants a particular set of producers protective privilege that may no longer be warranted. Alternative, more transparent means for assistance exist, if these producers are being seriously injured or threatened with injury by imports.

Many countries, mainly developing nations, have import licensing systems for such purposes as facilitating the allocation of scarce foreign exchange. However, the red tape involved in obtaining these licenses sometimes makes them significant barriers to trade. An import licensing code, similar to those proposed for government procurement and customs valuation, tries to minimize any trade-distorting effects by specifying that the rules for submitting import-licensing applications be published, that the forms and procedures be as simple as possible, and that licenses not be refused for minor documentation errors or variations in value, quantity, or weight of the licensed product.

A section on automatic import licensing, that is, a system under which licenses are granted freely, states that import licensing should continue only "as long as the circumstances which gave rise to its introduction prevail" and that properly completed applications should be approved immediately on receipt or at least within a maximum of ten working days. In order to prevent discrimination among countries when licenses are not automatically issued, signatories agree to furnish information upon request concerning the past allocation by country and to publish the rules for applying for licenses as far in advance as possible of the opening date of submission. The period of license validity is not to be so short as to preclude imports, and governments are not to discourage the full utilization of quotas. In addition to dealing with other licensing technicalities that sometime distort trade, the code establishes a committee on import licensing to facilitate consultation and the settling of disputes.

Since 38 percent of U.S. industrial exports now go to developing countries, the reduction in delays and frustrations on the part of American exporters that this code promises should also be very much appreciated by the Congress.

Technical Barriers to Trade (Standards) and Commercial Counterfeiting

The customs valuation and import licensing problems faced by exporters and importers are often child's play when compared with those arising from the many product standards with which these traders must contend. In customs valuation and import licensing, clearly identifiable governmental authorities issue regulations and make decisions. But product requirements relating to health, safety, environmental protection, national security, technology, packaging, marking and labeling, and the like are set out in many different places within the government and the private sector and are often difficult to discover by potential exporters or importers.

The standards code agreed upon by the negotiators states that technical regulations and certification procedures shall not be formulated or applied in a manner that creates obstacles to international trade or discriminates against the products of particular countries. To carry out these goals a series of procedures is agreed upon. When framing new standards and cetification rules governments are to publish notices of this intent, provide copies of the proposed rules upon request, and allow enough time before their adoption for interested parties to comment upon them. Each adherent to the code shall ensure that "an enquiry point exists which is able to answer all reasonable enquiries from interested parties" regarding any technical regulation or certification system. Moreover, the signatories agree upon request to advise other members, especially the developing countries, on how best to meet their technical regulations.

There are two levels of obligations in carrying out these and other provisions in the code. For technical regulations and cetification procedures set by central governments, the signatories "shall ensure that" these agencies comply with the code. For the various rules formulated by regional, state, local, and private organizations, the code requires its adherents to "take such reasonable means as may be available to them" to ensure compliance.

While encouraging the harmonization of standards among nations, the code is not intended to interfere with the right of countries to adopt rules that meet their particular goals in areas such as health, safety, and environmental protection. The dispute settlement mechanism is similar to that in the other codes. First, a member must enter into bilateral discussions if requested by another signatory. If the dispute is not resolved in these consultations, the matter can be referred to the committee on technical barriers to trade that is established under the code, which can then appoint technical expert groups or panels to consider the issues, consult with the disputants, and make recommendations or rulings on the matter. The committee reviews the finding of these groups and can authorize retaliatory actions.

Like the other technical codes, the one on standards represents a valuable attempt to reduce needless distortions of international trade. Furthermore, since the process of making rules and regulations is already more open in the United States than in many other countries, the efforts to publicize this process and to disseminate more widely knowledge about such rules is very much in U.S. interests.

With regard to trademarks and trade names U.S. negotiators have argued, not that rules and regulations are sometimes needlessly trade-distorting, but that more rules and regulations are needed to prevent "unfair" trade. Foreign producers sometimes affix the trademark or trade name of another firm on their products without permission. The United States has proposed discouraging this commercial counterfeiting by requiring that such merchandise be detained or seized at the time of importation, if the appropriate authorities are requested to do so by the person having the right to the protection of the trademark and trade name. Steps also would be taken to settle disputes and to prevent the misuse of this procedure to block imports. The reaction of other countries to the U.S. proposal has led to optimism that an agreement in this area can be reached within a few months.

Special and Differential Treatment for Developing Countries

Not only have the developing countries been accorded more favorable treatment in the tariff field by means of tariff preferences and exclusion from the full reciprocity requirement, but they have also been given special privileges in the various codes dealing with nontariff trade barriers. In the subsidies code, for example, developing countries are excluded from the ban on export subsidies, provided they agree "to reduce or eliminate export subsidies" when these are inconsistent with their "competitive needs." If they agree to this provision, other countries cannot take countervailing actions against their export subsidies in accordance with Article VI of GATT. However, developing country signatories also agree that their export subsidies shall not be used in a manner that causes adverse effects to the trade or production of another signatory, and action against these subsidies can be taken by resorting to the panel procedure under Articles XVI and XXIII. Similarly, the government procurement code permits developing countries to negotiate the exclusion of certain entities or products from the rules, while the safeguards code being considered contains a provision whereby the developed countries agree to make an effort to avoid safeguard actions on products of special interest to the developing nations. In addition to these special provisions, a general "enabling clause" has been agreed upon that provides a firmer legal basis for continuing tariff preferences and more favorable treatment with regard to nontariff trade barriers. Since this modifies the basic most-favored-nation principle set forth in Article I of the GATT, it was negotiated in the so-called Framework or GATT Reform Group. The clause merely states: "Notwithstanding the provisions of Article I in the General Agreement, contracting parties may accord differential and more favorable treatment to developing countries, without according such treatment to other contracting parties." This applies to tariffs, nontariff measures, regional or global arrangements among developing countries for reducing or eliminating tariffs, and special treatment for the least developed of the developing nations. The developed countries further agree not to expect reciprocal reductions in tariffs and nontariff barriers by the developing countries in trade negotiations if these are inconsistent with the developmental, financial, and trade needs of the latter countries. The text also contains the following clause dealing with the "graduation" of the developing countries to fuller GATT responsibilities:

> Less developed contracting parties expect that their capacity to make contributions or negotiated concessions or take mutually agreed upon action under the provisions and procedures of the General Agreement would improve with the progressive development of their economies and improvement in their trade situation and they would accordingly expect to participate more fully in the framework of rights and obligations under the General Agreement.

There is, however, no mechanism to determine when a developing country has reached the stage when it should assume these greater responsibilities. It has not been determined whether the text covering these points should appear as a new GATT article or be adopted by the members as a declaration or decision.

Safeguards for Balance of Payments and Development Purposes

Another issue considered by the Framework Group was measures taken for balance of payments and development purposes. The phrasing of Article XII dealing with restrictions to safeguard the balance of payments implies that, while quantitative controls over imports are permissible for this purpose, an import surchange is not. However, countries have in fact quite often used this method, which most economists think is less distorting than quantitative restrictions. The declaration on the subject recognizes this fact and states that countries should use measures that are the least disruptive of trade. The signatories also declare their conviction that restrictive trade measures are in general an inefficient means of maintaining or restoring balance of payments equilibrium. The developing countries are also permitted in Article XVIII of the GATT to restrict imports for another purpose, namely, to implement their development programs. However, the provisions of the article are complex and quite stringent. The declaration broadens the reasons for taking such actions and makes them less difficult to meet.

Dispute Settlement and Surveillance Procedures for the Various Codes

Each of the major codes provides for a committee composed of the code's signatories to facilitate the settlement of disputes that have failed to be resolved through consultations between the disputants. Although the mechanisms differ somewhat from code to code, each committee elects its own chairman and can establish a panel of experts of from three to five members to review the facts of the case and make such findings as will assist the committee in making recommendations or giving rulings. The committee or a panel can also play a conciliating role in the dispute. Preference is given to government officials in selecting panel members from lists of qualified persons supplied by the signatories. After receiving the panel report the committee itself makes recommendations to the parties involved or rules on the matter. If the recommendations are not followed, the committee can take further appropriate action including, for example, the authorization of appropriate countermeasures. Some of the codes also specify that the committee keep under surveillance any matter on which it has made a recommendation or ruling.

In addition to the provisions in each code on dispute settlement, an Understanding Regarding Notification, Consultation, Dispute Settlement and Surveillance was agreed upon in the GATT Reform Group "with a view of improving and refining" the mechanism under Articles XXII (on consultation) and XXIII (on nullification or impairment). Under these articles the contracting parties (the entire GATT membership) rather than any committee appoint panels or working groups, receive the panel reports, make recommendations and rulings, and keep relevant matters under surveillance. The director-general proposes the composition of any panel to the contracting parties for approval. According to the understanding, members of a panel should "preferably be governmental." Moreover, while a panel "should make an objective assessment of the matter before it, including an objective assessment of the facts of the case and the applicability of and conformity with the General Agreement," it should make only such other findings as will assist the contracting parties in making recommendations or rulings "if so requested." Besides stating that the contracting parties shall keep under surveillance any matter on which they have made a recommendation or rule, the understanding includes a provision committing them "to conduct a regular and systematic review of developments in the trading system."

In evaluating the prospects for enforcing the various codes, it is necessary to consider why the panel procedure has not worked as well in recent years as in GATT's first decade. Hudec points out that the fundamental reason is the breakdown in substantive consensus about GATT rules: some members feel that certain rules are no longer valid and that certain important trade problems are not covered in the document.[6] The main purpose of negotiating new codes has been to amplify and modify the older GATT rules in order to meet these objections. Even if the new codes do handle these problems, however, it is still necessary to establish procedures that facilitate their enforcement. Although the basic intentions of the participants are good, they cannot be carried out unless the rules and procedures are framed so as to discourage partiality. In recent years governments have tended to regard complaints as hostile diplomatic acts and have exerted strong pressures on other governments not to activate the dispute settlement mechanism. Morover, once panels have been established, pressures have been brought on their members—usually representatives of the different governments in GATT—for favorable findings or for settlement of the dispute prior to making such findings. In all of this the "big" trading powers have a considerable advantage over the developing nations and the smaller industrial countries. Consequently, as Hudec points out, "the pressures for compliance tend to vary according to the relative power of the governments involved, creating an inequitable situation in which the rules bind the weak but not the strong.[7]

Two steps to help prevent this outcome would be to enable the GATT secretariat itself to request the establishment of panels and to ensure that nongovernmental individuals are well represented on such panels.

Unfortunately, the secretariat will not be allowed to activate the panel mechanism under the new codes or Article XXIII, and government officials will still be given preference as panel members. One cannot, therefore, help but wonder whether the same unsatisfactory procedures will continue by which many potential disputes never surface because of heavy-handed political and economic pressures or are smoothed over once they do surface rather than being settled on the basis of consistently applied rules. On the other hand, the creation of so many separate committees that can establish panels would seem to indicate that the GATT members at least expect many more disputes and panel decisions than in the recent past.

One part of the enforcement mechanism that is not likely to be very effective is that enabling the various committees to authorize retaliation or other appropriate action when their recommendations are not followed. Only once in its history has the GATT membership authorized retaliation.[8] Rather than trying to enforce panel decisions, the GATT membership has tended to accept a panel's decision and then to rely upon the resulting international pressures to secure compliance. Usually, the parties to the dispute have accepted the panel findings, although in a famous 1976 decision on tax practices relating to export subsidies neither the United States nor the other party to the dispute, the European Community, implemented the panel's decision. The fact of the matter is that governments are far from willing to yield the kind of authority that would make retaliation sanctioned by other GATT members an effective compliance measure. If retaliation is used too frequently, it is likely to push members into using pressures to block the formation of panels or into withdrawing from the various codes. Nonetheless, the dispute settlement procedure can be effective without this last step, provided the procedure is regularly utilized and the decisions are realistic yet impartial and well reasoned.

OECD Steel Committee

An agreement reached outside the GATT framework but with important implications for the trade negotiations is the creation of a new International Steel Committee within the Organization of Economic Cooperation and Development (OECD). The committee's mandate states that governments need to work together not only to "ensure that trade in steel will remain as unrestricted and free of distortion as possible" and to "encourage reduction of barriers to trade" but "enable governments to act promptly to cope with crisis situations in close consultations with interested trading partners," to "facilitate needed structural adaptations . . . and promote rational allocation of productive resources," to "avoid encouraging economically unjustified investments," and to "facilitate multilateral cooperation consistent with the need to maintain competition, to anticipate and, to the extent possible, prevent problems." Among the committee's functions are following world supply and demand conditions in steel and developing "common perspectives" as well as establishing "where appropriate, multilateral objectives or guidelines for government policies."

The U.S. steel industry is reportedly pleased with the creation of this international committee. However, one must be somewhat concerned that the committee might turn into a cartel-like arrangement blocking needed adjustment in the industry and reducing its long-run efficiency.

Aircraft Agreement

Early in the Tokyo Round there was considerable hope for a series of sector negotiations in which the various tariffs and nontariff measures affecting a particular product line would be discussed within one group rather than among different groups organized on the basis of types of non-tariff trade barriers. The only manufacturing area where such negotiations have been successful is the aircraft industry. Led by the United States, the participants have reached an agreement that frees trade on all civil aircraft and engines and on most parts and that commits the signatories to limit trade-restricting actions with regard to standards, government purchasing policies, quantitative restrictions, financing, and inducements. A committee on trade in civil aircraft is established for surveillance, consultation, and dispute settlement purposes. In view of the fact that U.S. dominance of the aircraft market is threatened by the announced intentions of the European Community, Canada, and Japan to build national aerospace industries of their own, this agreement should be widely appreciated in this country.

Agriculture

Agricultural trade barriers have long been among the most difficult to remove, for fairly obvious political reasons. The current negotiations have proved to be no exception to this general experience. Reportedly, tariff and nontariff concessions affecting almost $4 billion worth of U.S. agricultural exports (out of total agricultural exports of about $27 billion) were made by other countries. These cover meat, grain products, tobacco, fruit, vegetables, wine, nuts, and oilseed.

Agreements have also been reached on dairy products and bovine meat. These agreements establish councils for exchanging information about production and marketing conditions and for consultations among member representatives concerning world conditions and policies in these product areas. In addition, the dairy arrangement establishes minimum prices for milk powders, butter, milk fat, and cheese below which commercial trade is prohibited. An effort has also been made under the auspices of the United Nations Conference on Trade and Development (UNCTAD) to formulate a new wheat trade convention to replace the one expiring in June 1979. So far this has not succeeded. There are still disagreements over the size of the wheat reserves to be held as well as the prices at which to add and subtract from these reserves.

THE TARIFF-CUTTING FORMULA

In the Kennedy Round negotiations the tariff-reducing rule finally agreed upon was a cut of 50 percent across the board, subject to a "bare minimum" of exceptions. (Of course, the fact that the average cut in manufactures came to 35 percent meant there was considerable slippage in the "bare minimum" notion.) The European Community pressed vigorously for a so-called harmonization formula whereby the higher the duty on an item, the greater the percentage cut in the duty. The United States opposed this approach for several reasons. The major one was the belief that, since all the harmonization formulas proposed by the EC resulted in a very modest average duty reduction, the EC was using this argument as a means of opposing a significant tariff reduction. Moreover, while there are good consumer-welfare reasons for reducing high duties a greater percentage, it seemed unfair to subject producers in high-duty industries to considerably greater pressures from import competition than producers in low-duty industries. The high-duty industries are often precisely the ones where the difficulties of adjustment for labor and capital are the greatest. Congress recognized this fact by allowing cuts of up to 100 percent for tariffs of 5 percent or below but of only 50 percent for duty rates above 5 percent. Furthermore, a constant percentage cut already puts high-duty industries under somewhat greater import pressure than low-duty industries. Suppose, for example, that the international prices of two products are fixed at $100 each, and the import duty on one is 50 percent while on the other 10 percent. When the first good is imported, it will sell for $150 in the domestic market (ignoring transport and other costs), whereas the other good will sell domestically for $110 when imported. Cutting the duty 50 percent on each will reduce the selling price on the first product to $125, or by 16.7 percent, and on the second to $105, or by only 4.5 percent.

In the Tokyo Round negotiations the United States proposed a tariff-cutting formula of 60 percent across the board. (This was the maximum cutting authority permitted under the 1974 Trade Act, although again duties of 5 percent or less could be completely eliminated.) The European Community countered with a harmonization formula. Specifically, the percentage cut in each duty would be the level of the duty itself. Moreover, the process would be repeated four successive times to reach the final rate. For example, a 40 percent duty would be cut by 40 percent to 24 percent. This would then be cut 24 percent to 18.2 percent; the 18.2 percent figure would be reduced by 18.2 percent to 14.9 percent. This would finally be cut by 14.9 percent to 12.7 percent. While for high duties the cut under this formula would be greater than the 60 percent proposal of the United States, the average cut on all dutiable items would amount to only about 30 percent.

In various simulations the United States discovered that with likely exceptions the employment and trade effects from a given average percentage cut achieved through harmonization formulas were actually somewhat more favorable for this country than those resulting from a uniform cut. In view of the strong position taken by the EC on the issue and the absence of real enthusiasm in this country for a significant cut such as 60 percent, the United States tentatively agreed to the harmonization approach provided the average cut was considerably greater than the EC's formula yielded. The final formula agreed upon was proposed by the Swiss. The rate at which a duty is cut is the rate of duty itself divided by the duty rate plus 0.14. Thus, the rate at which a 30 percent duty would be cut is $0.30/(0.30 + 0.14) = 0.68$ or 68 percent. There is no economic rationale for the particular formula. It was selected from among others because it gave an average cut of about 40 percent (before exceptions) and most governments found the degree of harmonization acceptable. The United States is constrained somewhat in following the formula in that it cannot reduce any tariff above 5 percent by more than 60 percent. However, it can—and did—reduce duties 5 percent or below by more than this percentage in order to raise its average cut after exceptions to a level comparable to that of the other major participants. The average percentage cut on dutiable manufactures that will be made by the United States is 31 percent.

As one who was involved in the harmonization hassle in the Kennedy Round, I can only express admiration at the ability of the Tokyo Round technicians to sell to their more practical-minded superiors and to private business and labor groups an esoteric formula like $t/(t + 0.14)$ (where t is the tariff rate) as the tariff-reducing rule for the Multilateral Trade Negotiations. Moreover, one wonders why industries that must, for example, accept a 59 percent cut in their protective tariff because the level of this duty is 20 percent do not object to the undue burden when they observe a duty cut of only 42 percent in industries protected by a 10 percent tariff. Perhaps such factors as the fairly low levels of most duties, the eight-to-ten-year stretchout period for the duty reductions, and recent fluctuations in exchange rates that dwarf these tariff cuts have greatly diminished the concerns of various economic groups over the exact nature of the tariff reductions affecting them.

There is understandable concern by legislators over the possible adverse employment effects of the tariff reductions. However, detailed studies of these effects indicate not only that the overall employment impact is likely to be extremely small but that instances of adverse regional or industry effects can generally be easily absorbed through normal labor turnover and market growth in the region or industry as well as by staging the cuts over eight to ten years. My own simulation of a 50 percent reduction (with certain product exceptions) yields a net impact on total employment of only −15,000 jobs or about 2/100 of 1 percent of the labor force.[9] Studies by Deardorff and Stern and by Cline and others estimate the aggregate employment impact of a 50 percent cut at −24,000 and +24,000 jobs, respectively.[10]

Regional and occupational effects are also quite small. For example, the labor impact in New England— the region which incurs the largest net loss, according to my calculations—is only −3,000 jobs. When one considers that this number is based on a 50 percent rather than a 30 percent reduction, that a major import-sensitive New England industry (footwear) included in the 50 percent calculations is in fact being excluded from any duty reductions, and finally that the cuts will be staged over at least eight years, the conclusion can only be that this (or any other) region should not be concerned about adverse employment effects from the Tokyo Round tariff reductions.

Since there is much evidence that the U.S. comparative advantage position in international trade is based on a relatively abundant supply of human capital and an ability to create new technology, it is not surprising that the demand for highly skilled workers tends to increase whereas that for comparatively unskilled workers tends to decline as a result of a multilateral tariff reduction. These effects are, however, again very small. My estimates are that a 50 percent cut would tend to increase employment of those involved in research and development by 14/100 of 1 percent and of other professional and technical workers by 8/100 of 1 percent. On the other hand, the initial impact on semiskilled and unskilled production workers is an employment decline of 14/100 of 1 percent and 8/100 of 1 percent, respectively, in the number employed in these skill groups. However, the estimates do show that certain industries in which recent market growth has been low or negative could be faced with a considerable adjustment problem when faced with a 50 percent duty reduction. These include certain textile products not subject to quotas, nonrubber footwear, electronic tubes, glass products, ceramic tiles, pottery products, and primary lead and zinc.

The response to these occupation and industry figures should not be to demand that no duty cuts producing these results be made but rather to try to ensure that adjustment takes place in a noninjurious manner. Reciprocal duty reductions afford the country one of its few opportunities of moving to a higher living standard in a predictable and controllable manner. (Just the static net welfare gain to the nation of a 50 percent reciprocal cut is estimated at over $1 billion.)[11] By combining active adjustment assistance policies with less-than-formula cuts and longer staging periods, affected workers can be shifted either to higher earning positions, or, if necessary, be protected until they voluntarily leave or retire. The preferred approach is to use adjustment assistance policies, but unfortunately our programs in this field are still quite primitive and lack political support from labor. Consequently, the administration has used the technique of either excluding from duty cuts most of the above industries or reducing tariffs in these sectors only modestly. While this is a second-best approach, it should at least eliminate any credible charges that the actual duty reductions will cause appreciable injury to any industry or occupational group. . . .

NEW AREAS FOR NEGOTIATION

The prospects for preventing either the intensification of protectionism or the rapid growth of government-managed international trade depend . . . upon the development of new or better rules in areas of recent protectionist activity that were not covered in any significant detail in the Tokyo Round negotiations. New international rules are most needed in the trade with respect to: state-owned or state-controlled enterprises that compete with trading firms subject to the constraints of the private-enterprise system; restrictive trading practices by business; and trade in services. While they will not be discussed further here, efforts are also needed within the GATT framework to contain the use of multiple legal approaches to harass importers;[12] and to ensure that trading blocs do not act as permanent obstacles to trade liberalisation on a multilateral basis. Moreover, in addition to these traditional areas of trading relationships, there are an increasing number of "grey" areas in which trade matters and policies traditionally excluded from consideration within the framework of commercial policy are becoming more interdependent and which, therefore, require greater efforts at policy coordination. These include the interrelationships between trade and policies affecting the balance-of-payments, aid and debt servicing, international investment, technology transfers and commodity agreements. Most of these subjects are best dealt with in forums other than the GATT, but this organisation should become more deeply involved in coordinating policies in these various fields.

State Enterprise Trade

. . . Governments in market-oriented economies are to an increasing extent taking over trading and producing activities traditionally undertaken by private enterprise. Private firms competing internationally with such state-owned enterprises frequently claim they must contend with dumping and subsidisation practices by these state firms that are impossible to detect and thus broach through the standard GATT articles relating to these matters. Nor has Article XVII on state-trading enterprises proved to be effective in dealing with this type of trade. If, as some think, East-West trade will grow significantly in the near future, the issue of minimising trade distortions in a trading world where state-owned and private firms compete and resolving the international conflicts resulting from this competition will become even more important within a few years.

Attempting to determine whether state-owned enterprises are engaged in dumping or export subsidisation is likely to be an exercise in futility. There is, however, a simple and feasible alternative for dealing with this type of trade. First, it should be recognised that from the overall welfare viewpoint of the importing country, dumping and export subsidisation are not in themselves economic "bads." These activities tend to increase real income in the importing country at the expense of the exporting country. What is really objectionable about them is if they result in such large-scale and sudden import-competing pressures that domestic workers and capital-owners suffer serious injury. The GATT "serious injury" test for imposing temporary import controls can be interpreted as determining when equity considerations for the affected factors dominate the total welfare-increasing effects of a great import supply. Extending this thought to state-trading leads to the conclusion that on the import side the "safeguard" rules of the GATT can be used to deal with this type of trade. Import restraints would be imposed only if it were determined that the increased imports from state-trading firms caused or threatened to cause serious injury to a domestic industry. What would differ, however, from the usual use of this article is that, if import restraints were deemed to be appropriate, there would not have to be a link between these actions and domestic measures of adjustment.

The export side is more difficult to deal with. Under some circumstances, state enterprises are established to carry out some fundamental goals relating to growth or equity considerations, for which the government is willing to sacrifice short-run efficiency considerations. Provided governments compensate for the withdrawal of the import "concessions," or accept an equivalent withdrawal of "concessions" by exporters, there is little that can be done about such actions. Others may not approve of them but sovereignty over internal affairs must be a recognised fact of international life. In other cases, though, government enterprises come into being and are operated at a loss because of political pressures to bail out economically weak firms. The loss of export markets to foreigners is the same as if quotas or subsidies had been employed to prop up the industry. And, just as the use of quantitative import restrictions as a safeguard measure should be tied to plans for adjusting to the realities of world resource conditions, so too should such plans be part of government take-overs of weak firms. Unless governments extend this principle to public ownership under these circumstances, this procedure will become more and more important as a loophole in the GATT rules. Of course, it is not always easy to distinguish these two sets of cases, but that is a function for GATT panels.

Restrictive Business Practices

Unlike the charter of the International Trade Organisation, which was proposed (but not accepted) shortly after World War II, the articles of the GATT do not include any rules concerning restrictive business practice. The omission of such rules seems hard to justify, especially in view of the rapid growth of multinational enterprises. The tariff-reducing provisions of the GATT are aimed in part at eliminating windfall profits that accrue to domestic producers because of government restrictions. Yet it is evident that many firms sending goods abroad also possess the market power to extract monopoly profits. Moreover, they often can engage in discriminatory pricing policies among countries—a practice condemned in the GATT if it causes "material injury."

The reasons for the omission of a code on business practices stem from the pro-government and pro-business (as opposed to pro-consumer) bias of the GATT. Consumer interests were of some concern to the founders of GATT, but import duties, for example, were regarded primarily as highly visible instruments of governments that restrict access to both output markets and supplies and thereby jeopardise international political stability. Tariff reduction, therefore, was an important matter of concern to governments. The various provisions dealing with internal taxes, health and safety standards, national security, *et cetera*, indicate other areas where the interests of governments were either protected or promoted in the GATT. The producer bias of the agreement manifests itself in such areas as dumping and subsidisation. Consumers in countries receiving dumped or subsidised goods gain from the lower prices resulting from such actions. The interests, however, of domestic producers who might suffer economic losses are given priority over consumers; and they have the right to request their governments to impose anti-dumping or countervailing duties if foreign producers sell below their domestic price. Similarly, some governments do not regard the pricing policies of exporting firms as proper concerns of governments, even though such policies may raise prices to domestic consumers.

Pressure for the establishment of a code on restrictive business practices has not come from consumers, who are poorly organised, but from the governments of developing countries and, interestingly, from some governments of developed countries as well. The developing countries complain that the absence of effective competition from domestic producers makes them prime targets for monopolistic exploitation by producers in the industrialised economies. Producers in certain developed countries, the United States for instance, where foreign monopolistic practices are generally unlawful, have become concerned about the diversionary impact of restrictionist agreements among private producers in other countries.

If the GATT is to become an effective central organisation for dealing with international trading problems that reduce world income and increase political tensions among nations, the gap in its articles of agreement on private business practices must be filled. What would be involved is simply the extension to all international trade of the kind of anti-monopoly rules that currently apply to domestic trade in most industrialised countries. Agreements such as that concluded between European Community and Japanese steel producers would not be permitted. Similarly, the developing countries as well as the smaller industrial countries would be able to prevent the kind of discriminatory pricing practices among countries recently illustrated within the European Community by exports of bananas to its various members. The settlement of disputes arising under the new code would represent a major new responsibility for the GATT; and it would severely test the "panel" approach to resolving controversies, but the challenge to the organisation must be accepted.

Trade in Services

The seven rounds of multilateral trade negotiations that have been held under the GATT since World War II, including the Tokyo Round negotiations, have dealt primarily with government measures affecting international trade in physical goods. Even if the subject matter of the GATT is restricted to trade issues, not only should its scope be enlarged to include private business practices affecting trade but the scope of trade should also be broadened to include services.

The services sector has come to provide a major source of employment and income in the more industrialised countries. In the United States and Canada about 60 per cent of the labour force is employed in this sector and 60 per cent of the GNP originates there. For West Germany, France, Japan, and the United Kingdom, the labour force figure is between 40 and 50 per cent, while the GNP percentage ranges from 40 to 60 per cent.[13] While many service sectors do not engage in international transactions, the fact that trade in "invisibles" now accounts for about 25 to 30 per cent of all international transactions indicates, in a crude way, the importance of service activities in international trade. Moreover, the services sector, like the industrial sector. is undergoing an increasing degree of internationalisation and inter-country penetration.[14]

Rather than attempting to delineate the proper scope for any negotiations on restrictions on international transactions in the services sector by framing a definition distinguishing "goods" from "services"—a task that is by no means a simple one—it seems most useful to deal with the services issue by concentrating on various private and public measures affecting the international activities of those industries traditionally listed as engaged in supplying services. It has been through the efforts of these industries that the subject has received greater attention in the 1970s and future negotiations will probably be framed in specific industry terms. A recent report by an inter-agency task force of the United States Administration, set up to investigate the subject, examined eighteen service industries, namely: accounting, advertising, auto-truck leasing, banking, communications, computer services, construction engineering, education services, employment services, equipment leasing, franchising, health services, hotels, motels, insurance, legal services, motion pictures, civil aviation and shipping.[15] Of these industries, insurance, motion pictures, civil aviation, shipping and construction engineering were considered to be faced with serious international problems from an American viewpoint.

These include extensive government subsidisation, government ownership, restrictive licensing arrangements, duties and quotas, standards that sometimes discriminate needlessly against foreign firms and government purchasing policies that favour domestic suppliers. Such measures also impede the trading activities of the other industries included in the above list. Though the problems are not as serious for these industries as the other five, they are likely to become more burdensome unless international action to reduce trade distortions in services is taken soon.

Not surprisingly, the task force in the United States concluded that government policies with regard to the foreign investment activities of service industries were even more constraining than those affecting trading activities in services. The services sector is a good case of where it is difficult to separate trade and investment matters, since to provide the service, foreign investment is often necessary.

American trade negotiators actually possessed the authority under the Trade Act of 1974 to negotiate on services in the Tokyo Round negotiations and most other delegates presumably could easily have obtained such authority under their parliamentary forms of government. There was general agreement though not to press for such negotiations in view of the absence of detailed knowledge about the problems involved and the complexity of the other issues to be discussed. This situation is likely to be corrected in the near future as more private and government studies of barriers to international trade in services are undertaken.

Setting aside investment and repatriation questions, there is no difference, in principle, between the distortions affecting trade in services and those affecting trade in goods. For example, a subsidy to a domestic shipping or film industry is no different from a subsidy to a domestic coal or computer industry. What distinguishes the services sector from the goods sector (and probably accounts for its exclusion thus far from GATT negotiations) is the greater extent to which services are subject to national policies that are inconsistent with a market solution to resource allocation. Nations believe they need a certain size shipping industry for national defence purposes; they want a national airline system for reasons of pride and prestige; or they wish to encourage a local film industry in order to preserve and enhance the country's cultural heritage. As stated earlier, while others may not always agree with a particular country's mix of such goals, the right of a country to make such judgments must be respected. These objectives, however, usually do not imply fixed trade positions in each area. A country may be quite willing to reduce its domestic shipping activities in return for trade concessions in other service areas or in commodity fields. In other worlds, negotiations of the traditional GATT variety can still be mutually productive to the participants, even in areas where "non-economic" national goals apply. This applies with even greater force to the several service fields where self-interest on the part of the industry rather than any lofty national goal is the basis of the protectionism. The various GATT codes developed for dealing with subsidies, government procurement *et cetera* also can be readily applied to the services area. A Code of Liberalisation of Current Invisible Operations has been negotiated in the Organisation for Economic Cooperation and Development but it is only partially effective and has not served to control the protectionist trend in the services sector of the world economy.

A beginning has been made on the subject with the setting up of a working party by the Trade Committee of the OECD to develop an inventory of restrictions on international transactions in the services sector.

INTEGRATING TRADE ISSUES AND RELATED POLICIES

Balance of Payments Policy

The increasing interdependence of national economies as well as the growing degree of state intervention in economic life is making the need for international coordination of economic policies in different fields ever more urgent. One international non-trade subject that is touched on explicitly in the GATT is balance-of-payments policy. Countries are permitted to introduce quotas on a temporary basis when faced with significant balance-of-payments problems. Oddly, the use of a uniform import levy, or surcharge, in these circumstances was considered inconsistent with the GATT. One of the changes achieved in the Tokyo Round negotiations that most observers agreed was much needed was to give preference to a uniform import levy over quotas as a trade measure for meeting balance-of-payments crises.

Trade, Aid and Financial Policies

Another relationship between trade policy and balance-of-payments conditions that is becoming more important concerns the trade, aid and financial policies of the developed countries towards the developing nations. Private banks, national governments, and international institutions are providing financial assistance and advice to foster capital formation and industrialisation in developing countries. At the same time, the established industrial countries are becoming increasingly reluctant to accept exports of certain manufactures from these countries. The only way the developing countries, though, can earn the foreign exchange needed to amortise their external debt is to increase their exports. Financial groups within the advanced industrialised countries are anxious to avoid defaults on the part of the developing countries, while other domestic economic interests exert pressures that increase the likelihood of such defaults. Obviously there is a need for better coordination of trade and financial aid policies, not just within individual countries but between the GATT, the

World Bank and the aid and export credit agencies of the major industrial countries. The World Bank would seem to be the best organisation for the leadership role in this effort.

International Investment

A frequent proposal over the last several years has been to establish a GATT-like organisation that would deal with international investment issues. The rapid rise of direct investment by multinational enterprises in both smaller developed and developing countries has been especially important in leading to this proposal. These enterprises have often been accused of a long list of "unfair" practices ranging from engaging in discriminatory pricing and investment practices to using their power to promote the political influence of a foreign state. But another source of pressure for such an organisation stems from private firms which engage in international investment and object to the many government controls over investment and the repatriation of earnings that hamper their operations. The impact of these policies on trade patterns can be illustrated with reference to the services industries discussed earlier.

The previously cited OECD code on invisibles as well as another OECD code, on the Liberalisation of Capital Movements, covers some of these matters, but as noted earlier, they are not very effective. An OECD code covering the behaviour of multinational enterprises in foreign countries also exists. None of these codes provides though for any dispute-settlement procedures as does the GATT; nor do the codes have the binding force, such as it is, of agreements signed within the GATT framework.

Pressures for an agreement and organisation to control direct investment activities of multinational enterprises have weakened in recent years. In part this seems due to the greater investment activities of multinationals based in other countries besides the United States; for example, a surprising amount of investment by multinationals domiciled in the developing countries is taking place. Most developing countries and small industrial nations have also passed legislation controlling the activities of multinational enterprises and have found these to be quite effective in satisfying their national goals with respect to these private organisations. Consequently, while conceptually a GATT-type institution is needed in the investment field, the lack of a strong demand for it at this time makes it an issue of lower priority.

Technology Transfers

As industrialisation spreads among the developing countries, the concerns about the transfer of technology increase in both developing and developed countries. Countries in which industrialisation is beginning to take hold fear that firms in the advanced industrialised countries make available only obsolete and non-competitive technology and extract monopolistic profits when making available this technology. On the other hand, labour groups in the advanced industrialised economies often claim that the full social cost in the country, in particular those associated with labour displacement, are not taken into account in the transfer process. Both of these sets of concerns lead to requests for some type of control over the international transfer of technology.

If as has been suggested, the GATT is broadened to include both private business practices and trade in services, issues relating to technology transfer can be handled within this new framework. Charges concerning the unreasonable pricing of technological services, for example, could be handled in the same manner as similar charges concerning trade in physical goods. Issues relating to the national benefits and costs of technology transfers are best handled at the national level and through other GATT channels. Rapid transfers causing significant unemployment in a domestic industry, for example, can be dealt with most effectively through a country's own industrial adaptation policies and the safeguard rules of the GATT.

Commodity Agreements

The key request of the developing countries in their proposals for a New International Economic Order, namely an Integrated Commodities Program, also raises trade issues outside of the traditional GATT framework. While the ITO charter included a chapter on commodity agreements, the GATT does not bring these agreements under its jurisdiction. This has caused few problems to date because of the failure of most such agreements, but the likelihood that commodity agreements will grow in importance increases the prospects of conflicts between GATT rules and the operation of these agreements. It is quite unlikely, however, that the primary product agreements in which the developing countries are interested will ever be brought within the GATT, since many affected countries are not GATT members. Thus it is very important that the representatives from the GATT participate in the establishment of commodity agreements so as to minimise needless conflicts on rules and procedures. A permanent consultative arrangement is also essential between the GATT and the various commodity organisations.

Multiple Exchange Rates

Multiple exchange rates are still another non-trade policy measure with important implications for the structure of trade. Obviously different exchange rates for different goods have similar effects to tariffs and export subsidies on the goods. Fortunately the fact that most developed countries have adopted uniform exchange rates for commodity transactions since the late 1950s has prevented any serious conflicts between exchange-rate and trade policy from arising among the major trading nations. However, a different exchange rate for capital transactions has sometimes been used in these countries and, as concern about liberalisation in services increases, a need for greater coordination on this matter will arise. The exchange-rate practices of the developing countries pose a more serious problem. These countries often use multiple exchange rates in commodity transactions; and their gradual liberalisation *vis-à-vis* international trade as they assume greater GATT responsibilities could be negated by offsetting changes in multiple exchange rates. Such matters are theoretically covered by Article XXIII of the GATT, which deals with actions by members that impair the value of concessions granted by other members, but there should be a more detailed statement of possible objectionable measures, including multiple exchange rates, in the Article. A formal consultative arrangement between the International Monetary Fund (IMF) and the GATT is also needed to ensure that measures taken to deal with balance-of-payments crises are consistent with GATT rules.

Notes

1. The contracting parties are the members of the GATT acting in a collective manner.
2. Robert E. Hudec, *The GATT Legal System and World Trade Diplomacy* (New York: Praeger Publishers, 1975), appendix A; and Robert E. Hudec, *Adjudication of International Trade Disputes*, Thames Essay no. 16 (London: Trade Policy Research Centre, 1978), pp. 5–6, n. 2.
3. 41 U.S.C. 10a–10d.
4. Robert E. Baldwin, *Nontariff Distortions of International Trade* (Washington, D.C.: Brookings Institution, 1970), pp. 70–78.
5. The products now covered are benzenoid chemicals, rubber-soled footwear, canned clams, and certain knit gloves.
6. Hudec, *Adjudication of International Trade Disputes*, p. 11.
7. Ibid., p. 3.
8. Ibid., p. 82.
9. Robert E. Baldwin and Wayne E. Lewis, "U.S. Tariff Effects on Trade and Employment in Detailed SIC Industries" in William G. Dewald, ed., *The Impact of International Trade and Investment on Employment* (Washington, D.C.: U.S. Department of Labor, 1978).
10. Alan V. Deardorff and Robert M. Stern, "A Disaggregated Model of World Production and Trade," presented to a conference on Micro Modeling for International Trade Policy, University of Western Ontario, London, Ontario, February 23–24, 1979, processed; and W. Cline, N. Kawanabe, T. Kronsjo, and T. Williams, *Trade Negotiations in the Tokyo Round* (Washington, D.C.: Brookings Institution, 1978).
11. Robert E. Baldwin, John H. Mutti, and J. David Richardson, "Welfare Effects in the United States of a Significant Multilateral Tariff Reduction," Journal of International Economies, 10, (August 1980).
12. The development of this form of non-tariff protection is discussed, in the American context, in Malmgren, "Significance of Trade Policies in the World Economic Outlook," *The World Economy*, October 1977.
13. High Level Group on Trade and Related Problems, *Policy Perspectives for International Trade and Economic Relations*, Rey Report (Paris: OECD Secretariat, 1972).
14. An early review of restrictions on international transactions in the services sector of the world economy, on which subsequent studies have been based, is

contained in Brian Griffiths, *Invisible Barriers to Invisible Trade* (London: Macmillan, for the Trade Policy Research Centre, 1975).

15. Task Force on Services and Multilateral Trade Negotiations, *US Service Industries in World Markets: Current Problems and Future Policy Development* (Washington: Department of Commerce, 1976).

IV

Multinational Enterprises

The three readings in Part IV on direct foreign investment are divergent in substance, approach, and perspective, as seems typical of any sample of work on this controversial subject. The one theme common to all is concern over control or power. That fact is not surprising, since control and market power are the distinguishing characteristics of most multinational enterprises—enterprises for which the domain of operations and control span a wider set of nations than the domain of ownership.

C. Fred Bergsten, Thomas Horst, and Theodore H. Moran delve into the power struggle between multinational corporate affiliates and labor unions. Both these authors and Stephen Hymer discuss the way in which multinationals can be a channel for "extraterritorial" application of home-country policies on host countries. All three papers illustrate the confrontation between the market power of the multinational and the political power of the host country.

Most of these power conflicts take place over the distribution of rents (spoils) among multinationals, immobile factors of production, and governments. Rents exist because, as Hymer and Paul Streeten both stress, multinational corporations are never perfect competitors. They are not forced by the market to accept the minimal (normal-profits) price that would assure their survival—not in product or technology markets where they are large sellers, and not in factor markets where they are large buyers. Nor, for that matter, should governments or labor unions be seen as perfect competitors. Rather they too have market power in the wages and taxes they charge and in the quantity of services they offer to multinationals. The appropriate model of multinational corporate behavior may thus be something between trilateral monopoly (corporations, unions, governments) and pentagonal monopoly (given that home-country and host-country labor may be in conflict, and home-country and host-country governments as well). It's no wonder Hymer feels that the behavior of "the multinational corporation raises more questions than economic theory can answer."

Economics has not yet developed any well-accepted theory of multilateral monopoly or oligopoly, whether international or not.

One recent change in this complicated structure is a slight and tentative decline in intergovernment and interunion conflict over multinationals. Bergsten, Horst, and Moran cite the evidence for both: the first, halting steps toward an intergovernmental code of conduct that would control and harmonize policy toward multinationals, similar perhaps to the General Agreement on Tariffs and Trade (GATT); and the beginnings of transnational cooperation among labor unions (information exchanges, simultaneous bargaining, sympathy strikes). Bergsten, Horst, and Moran also provide numerous counterexamples of residual conflict, so that ample room still remains for Hymer's concern that "at present large corporations are consciously moving towards an international perspective much faster than other institutions and especially much faster than governments. . . ."

Hymer's concern over the globalization of corporate enterprise is, however, somewhat less palpable today than when he wrote. The other contributions, written in the late 1970s, discuss the deceleration of global reach, especially by U.S. corporations. Both describe the increasing willingness of multinationals to engage in joint ventures with host-country partners, to train skilled workers and managers in the host-country, and to conduct some research and development there.

Some of this trend reflects the growing shares of firms from Japan and less developed countries (see Streeten) in global direct investment. Yet even U.S. multinationals have become more accommodating to host-country pressures, for example, by reducing their insistence on wholly owned affiliates. Streeten's vision is of increasing prominence for smaller, flexible multinationals, whose "special advantage would consist not in the monopolistic package of capital, technology, and marketing, but in special skills." These smaller multinationals would "use more capital-saving techniques . . . and design products more adapted to the consumption and production needs of the poor—hoes, simple power tillers, and bicycles, rather than air conditioners, expensive cars, and equipment for luxury apartments. . . ." This vision will be slow in materializing, at best, however, and is just wishful thinking at worst. Small may be beautiful, but it's not very likely: Almost all the dramatic crosspenetration of U.S. markets by European and Japanese multinationals in the 1970s (see Bergsten, Horst, and Moran) has been by familiar oligopolistic giants.

This crosspenetration of multinationals within the developed world poses some interesting puzzles. One is why it happened in the sequence it did, with burgeoning growth of U.S. investment in Europe during the 1960s, and burgeoning growth of European and Japanese investment in the U.S. during the 1970s. Bergsten, Horst, and Moran point to the change in relative currency values as the most important reason, but they provide little explanation. The dollar was overvalued in the 1960s; its depreciation corrected that overvaluation in the 1970s. It is tempting to jump to the conclusion that the overvalued dollar made foreign corporations relatively cheap for Americans in the 1960s, and the depreciated dollar made U.S. corporations relatively cheap for the rest of the world in the 1970s. Yet such simple reasoning is false. It fails to recognize that when Japanese direct investment in the U.S. yields dollar returns, the Japanese are then not only paying fewer yen for dollar assets but are earning fewer yen on their dollar profits. Neither their *rate* of return nor the relative attractiveness of real investment at home and abroad need be affected by exchange rates.

A more accurate explanation for the striking correlation between exchange rates and direct foreign investment may begin with Raymond Vernon's paper in Part I of this reader: Most foreign direct investment takes place in the tradables industry, as the natural extension of exporting. The overvalued dollar of the 1960s was accompanied by a low relative price of tradables to nontradables in the U.S.—low compared to both a general-equilibrium norm and relative prices abroad. Production of tradable products in the U.S. was consequently discouraged, and production abroad encouraged, with a concomitant inducement for U.S. tradables producers to invest abroad. The inducement was eliminated or reversed by dollar depreciation in the 1970s.

A second puzzle raised by crosspenetration is what direct investment does to the industrial market structure. The potential loss associated with worldwide oligopoly as multinational corporations displace or acquire smaller national firms and collude among themselves affects the whole world. But the problem is more complex than it appears on the surface, for certain direct investments may reduce monopolistic market power. Direct investment in a host country where one manufacturer previously had a monopoly position will reduce market concentration in that country; direct investment by smaller multinational oligopolists may reduce the world market power wielded by the largest multinational oligopolists.

Moreover, Hymer points out that economic opinion is divided on whether market concentration and oligopoly is uniformly "bad." More market concentration may imply more research and development, with consequent innovation and faster growth. If so, the static losses from oligopoly and market power are the price paid for dynamic gains, which may outweigh those losses in terms of social welfare. Similarly, the corporation may consider market power and concentration a part of the return which makes innovation profitable. Streeten's argument that developing countries, because they are small, could be painlessly exempted from paying for such supernormal returns seems flawed. It fails to explain what would induce any sensible firm to accept a lower return on one part of its investments, even a very small part (investments in developing countries), than on another (investments in developed countries). Even small developing countries can kill the goose that lays the golden eggs, or more accurately, cause her to move her nest to more hospitable habitats.

Besides the substantive differences among the readings discussed above, the articles differ in approach and perspective. Bergsten, Horst, and Moran believe that many conclusions from "traditional models," employing competitive and general-equilibrium assumptions, carry over qualitatively into the more complicated world of multinationals. Some of these conclusions are initially arresting—for example, that the optimal home-country policy toward capital outflows may be taxation, not laissez-faire, or that commodity trade may be so close a substitute for direct investment that the latter has *no* effect on equilibrium wages, employment, or distributive shares of labor and capital. Hymer and Streeten do not demonstrate that abstractly-reasoned conclusions like these *fail* to carry over in the real world, but they certainly doubt it. Their approaches would, by contrast, stress gaming, bargaining, organizational behavior, and conflict resolution.

With respect to perspective, Bergsten, Horst, and Moran are candid about the several options. Most frequently, their discussion proceeds from the perspective of what is economically best for the home country, taken as an aggregate. For example, from the perspective of U.S. welfare, they approve of Domestic International Sales Corporations (DISC's) and restricting the U.S. investment tax credit to U.S. plant and equipment spending only— as offsets to U.S. tax incentives for foreign direct investment that became outdated in the 1970s. But they also evaluate multinationals from the perspective of subgroups within a national economy, most extensively with respect to the welfare of labor. In closing, they carefully remind the reader of the fallacies of composition and decomposition: What is good for labor is not necessarily good for the nation as a whole, and vice versa.

Hymer and Streeten, by contrast, proceed from either the perspective of global welfare or that of the host country. Hymer discusses how multinationals may stifle "infant entrepreneurship" within a host country, or promote a political/economic alliance of foreign interests and host country elites that find it in their interest to perpetuate unbalanced, enclave-based growth.

Within the various perspectives found in the readings in Part IV lie the explanations for many apparently contradictory conclusions and irreconcilible differences regarding this theme.

16

Home-Country Policy
Toward Multinationals

*C. Fred Bergsten, Thomas Horst, and
Theodore H. Moran*

AN OVERVIEW

THE UNITED STATES has no consistent, coherent policy toward
foreign direct investment and multinational enterprises. Nor has it ever had
one. But many specific policies have a major impact on foreign direct investment, and most of them have a proinvestment orientation. The tilt
began to change in the past few years, as both the administration and Congress began to respond to mounting internal criticism of multinationals.

Most of the individual measures directed explicitly at foreign direct
investment were developed within the context of a particular functional
issue: tax policy, foreign policy, trade policy, balance-of-payments policy.
There has been little effort to relate one policy to another or to any overall
approach to foreign direct investment. Indeed, there has been no agency in
the U.S. government to coordinate the different policies affecting foreign
direct investment: the Treasury Department largely determines tax and
balance-of-payments policy, the Department of State usually determines
expropriation policy and aid-related measures, the Overseas Private Investment Corporation has the major role in shaping investment insurance
and guarantees, and the Department of Justice, Federal Trade Commission, and Securities and Exchange Commission have their respective functional responsibilities. Domestic macroeconomic policy and trade policy,
which have major effects on foreign direct investment, are separate responsibilities and are made with little attention to their implications for foreign
direct investment.

Such an evolution in policymaking is understandable. Many
policies, particularly in the tax area, were formulated before multinational
enterprises became important to U.S. economic and foreign policy. Later,
when multinationals grew to be a potent force, government policy usually
focused on dealing with short-term crises—political relations with an ex-
propriating country, a balance-of-payments deficit, domestic economic

decline—rather than the long-term, structural issues regarding foreign direct investment. Even today, many policymakers (including those engaged in international economic policy, let alone the majority, whose orientation is primarily domestic) have little awareness of the foreign investment impact of their policies.

The new importance of the activities of these firms . . . , however, brings into question the appropriateness of existing policies. It also suggests the need to develop an overall policy toward multinational enterprises and the need to coordinate that policy with other U.S. economic and foreign policies. The sharp increase in the flow of direct investment into the United States by foreign-based multinational enterprises (toward which U.S. policies are also largely ad hoc) adds to the importance of assessing U.S. policy.

The Policy Prescriptions of Traditional Analysis

Classical international investment theory suggests that the United States, as a home country, could pursue one of two basically different goals. One is to *maximize global economic welfare.* This is the focus of most economic analysis, which avoids explicit treatment of distributional issues, either among or within countries.

Adoption of a global welfare goal, however, does not determine the specific nature of policy. If all markets were perfectly competitive and no externalities existed, the government's role would be abstention from interference with foreign direct investment. But because much investment is carried on by firms in oligopolistic industries, the market is not perfectly competitive. Further distortions are caused by market interventions by other home and host governments. In addition, important externalities— such as pollution and international politics—are often related to such investments. Therefore, maximizing the contribution of foreign direct investment to global economic welfare may require active national policies on a wide range of specific issues.

Second, the United States could seek to *maximize its national economic welfare.*[1] This could require the application of optimum capital controls, either taxes or quantitative limits on foreign direct investment. (Limits could apply to not only capital but technology and other factor flows, as well.) Such controls would be primarily for limiting the level of investment to increase the returns from each unit. Controls might also be used to alter the industry composition of investment. In practice, there are two constraints on the use of optimum capital controls: the user must be large enough to significantly affect the rate of return on its overseas investments, and offsetting retaliation must be avoided or at least limited.[2]

The United States might be able to overcome both constraints. Though its previous near-monopoly position as a home country for multinational enterprises is eroding, the United States still has a far greater share of foreign investment than any other country. In addition, foreign retaliation is less likely than retaliation against efforts to install an optimum tariff on imports of goods. Indeed, some countries seek to reduce incoming direct investment and might welcome U.S. limitations. At a minimum, the schizophrenic attitude with which most host countries view U.S. investment limits the likelihood of their reacting sharply, as was indeed the case when the United States limited capital exports by American-based firms from 1965 to 1974 for balance-of-payments purposes. Finally, no international rules or institutions authorize retaliation to new barriers to foreign direct investment similar to those authorized by the General Agreement on Tariffs and Trade regarding new barriers to international trade.

There are several ways that unrestricted foreign direct investment could lower the national welfare of the United States and thus call for optimum capital controls. Traditional economic analysis focuses on comparative rates of return on alternative investment opportunities; it thus regards the higher pretax rates on foreign (than on domestic) investment as evidence that foreign investment promotes world welfare. From the national standpoint of the home country, however, the comparison should be made between domestic earnings and foreign earnings *after the payment of foreign taxes,* which represents the return on the investment to the home country.[3] . . .

In addition, an individual firm contemplating an investment abroad may ignore the impact of its activity on the return on other U.S. foreign direct investment. When the outstanding stock is already quite large, as is the case for the United States, the reduction in income of other investors could offset the return on the new investments.[4] This consideration is most relevant for perfectly competitive industries; it is less applicable to the oligopolistic industries that characterize much of foreign direct investment.

A third consideration of national interest is that foreign investments (direct or portfolio) are subject to default, confiscation, repudiation, or other forms of host-country manipulation which, unlike domestic defaults or bankruptcies, can negate the whole worth of the investment from the standpoint of the home country. This risk alone does not appear insignificant; slightly more than $2 billion of U.S. foreign direct investment has been so lost during the entire postwar period.

Finally, an important element in traditional analysis is the impact of foreign direct investment on the terms of trade of the home country. For example, in this view, the major benefit that Great Britain derived from its heavy foreign investment in the years before 1914 is the development of cheap sources of raw materials and the railroads to transport them efficiently. The development of other foreign factors of production, including labor, can have similar effects. But foreign investment can lead to reduced export prices for the home country if it generates new competition for home-country production.[5] Hence the net impact of foreign direct investment on the home country's terms of trade is positive in some cases and negative in others.

Traditional economics does point to certain clear benefits to the home country from foreign direct investment. Exports of capital increase the returns on capital invested at home. By increasing foreign incomes, they improve the demand for home-country exports. In addition, they may raise the level of total world savings and investment and, hence, the future level of sustainable consumption.

There are many shortcomings in the traditional approach. Most analyses assume, explicitly or implicitly: perfect competition, complete knowledge of foreign and domestic investment opportunities, no externalities, no foreign retaliation, perfect substitutability between domestic and foreign investments, full employment (or at least no concern about transitional adjustment problems), and balance-of-payments equilibrium. Yet many of these conditions are not met in the real world. Once they are abandoned, "it is impossible to say with certainty whether . . . investing abroad is preferable to investing at home. . . . Much depends on the industries and the conditions in which the investment takes place."

The most important shortcoming is the static nature of traditional analysis. Yet multinational enterprises argue that merely maintaining static foreign direct investment would reduce the rate of return over time and, thus, weaken their global competitive position. On the other hand, the dynamic effects of foreign direct investment, many argue, have been unfavorable to the home country. This is because the "developmental benefits of capital accumulation," including technological progress and increases in productivity, accrue to the host country.[6] The argument takes contemporary form in the charge by the AFL-CIO that foreign direct investment is eroding the industrial bases of the American economy.

Given the conflicting effects, traditional, general equilibrium economics cannot provide guidance in finding policies which would maximize the gain from foreign direct investment. As Jasay concluded in 1960:

> A conflict between private and social investment optima is entirely possible; what appears impossible is to *establish the presumption of a general bias* for private overseas investment to be either too large or too small. Nor can therefore a general recommendation be made for public policy in this regard.[7]

Present United States Policy

The deficiencies in traditional analysis of international investment help explain why home countries such as the United States have been reluctant to accept its policy prescriptions without qualification. The alternative is not, however, another logically coherent theory, but rather an eclectic, ad hoc approach. Sometimes the goal may be global or national welfare, as measured by a traditional analyst; but often the goal lies outside the classical realm, for example promoting domestic employment, maintaining the balance of payments, or improving access to raw materials. In some instances, the conclusion is that foreign investment should be encouraged; in others, the opposite prescription is reached. Because ad hoc analyses are often the rationalizations for current policies, a review of their effect on international investment follows.

Present U.S. policy deals directly with foreign direct investment in three areas: taxation of foreign income, insurance against noncommercial risks faced by foreign direct investment in particular countries, and expropriation. In addition, capital outflows to finance foreign direct investment were limited from 1965 until early 1974 by quantitative controls aimed at strengthening the U.S. international financial position.

Beyond these specific measures, a number of general U.S. policies affect foreign direct investment by U.S.-based firms. Antitrust policy extends to at least some of their foreign operations. The National Labor Relations Act, which provides much of the framework for labor-management negotiations, covers foreign direct investment as well as domestic investment. Several aspects of trade policy directly affect foreign direct investment. The international monetary policy of the United States has had several important effects on multinational enterprises. In a broad sense, all national policies—growth policy, industrial policy, manpower policy, the level and structure of taxation, indeed all efforts to maintain political and social stability—have an impact on investment decisions.

In addition, the United States is a participant in several international agreements that affect foreign direct investment: the articles of agreement of the International Monetary Fund (IMF), the code of liberalization of capital movements of the Organisation for Economic Cooperation and Development (OECD), and the International Center for the Settlement of Investment Disputes (ICSID) managed by the World Bank. Furthermore, the United States has in recent years participated in a series of international discussions aimed at forging new arrangements regarding multinational enterprises. The most important of these is the Committee on International Investment and Multinational Enterprises (CIME) established in the OECD, which in mid-1976 promulgated guidelines for multinational enterprises, a decision on national treatment, and a decision on international investment incentives and disincentives. None of these international efforts, however, has significantly affected U.S. policy toward foreign direct investment.

American *taxation* of foreign direct investment has two main features: (1) the foreign tax credit through which income, withholding, and certain other taxes paid to foreign central governments are credited against U.S. tax liabilities; and (2) tax deferral, through which no U.S. tax is levied on the income of subsidiaries incorporated in other countries until that income is repatriated. Other features of the U.S. tax code that have an important impact on foreign direct investment are the investment tax credit and the provision for domestic international sales corporations, both of which reduce effective tax rates on domestic investment. (President Carter has proposed the elimination of both tax deferral and the domestic international sales corporations.)

The basic tax laws covering foreign income were adopted without any systematic reference to home-country policy toward foreign direct investment. These provisions clearly did not aim at maximizing U.S. national welfare. This would have called for full taxation of foreign income without any credit against taxes paid abroad. Indeed, giving credit for foreign taxes suggests that the economic rationale was promotion of world welfare by avoiding tax distortions on the global allocation of capital.

Tax deferral, however, is counter to both national and global welfare. Its apparent aim was to preclude disadvantage for American-based companies competing with local firms (or multinationals based elsewhere, since all other home countries practice deferral or exemption). . . . However, . . . the overall U.S. tax system no longer provides any net incentive to invest abroad rather than at home. Current policy in this key area is roughly neutral toward foreign direct investment, the proinvestment tilt of the past having declined sharply since the early 1960s.

The postwar U.S. programs of *investment insurance and guarantees* for foreign direct investment sought to promote development in certain foreign countries. Several minor provisions of the tax code also had such a purpose, but the insurance program was the major policy instrument for implementing a cardinal tenet of postwar U.S. foreign policy: that American foreign direct investment could spur economic development around the world and was, thus, a major component of U.S. foreign assistance. The purpose of the program was to insure foreign direct investment against some of the noncommercial risks of investing in the countries covered: the threat of war, expropriation, and currency nonconvertibility. It began as a component of the Marshall Plan, to induce U.S. investment in Western Europe. Since 1959, however, it has been limited to the developing countries. Until 1971, the insurance and guarantees were administered by the successive U.S. foreign aid agencies, as part of overall assistance policy.

Since 1971, the program has been managed by the Overseas Private Investment Corporation (OPIC), an independent government corporation. Congress has increasingly required OPIC to focus on financial rather than developmental principles. In practice, OPIC's emphasis has shifted from the development of poorer countries and support for multinationals toward protecting other short-run U.S. economic interests, particularly jobs and the balance of payments. Indeed, each corporate application for OPIC coverage must estimate the "U.S. effects" of the proposed investment, and OPIC has turned down requests because an adverse impact on U.S. employment or the trade balance seemed likely.

In addition, as the incidence of foreign expropriations rose, OPIC insurance fees increased and its terms hardened. It has financed few extractive investments in recent years, both because fewer projects have been undertaken by American-based multinationals and because OPIC has reduced the share of such ventures in its portfolio because of the risk. And the proportion of its insurance directed to the poorest countries has declined in recent years (see Table 1).

The ostensible goal of OPIC insurance is global welfare, attained by offsetting some of the peculiar noneconomic risks that discourage foreign direct investment. Its record of financial self-sufficiency suggests that it does not represent a net subsidy to U.S.-based firms. In recent years, however, its goals have become increasingly nontraditional (notably, U.S. employment), and it may no longer equate the conditions of domestic and foreign investment. It has certainly become less attractive, in general, to the multinational enterprises. Its primary goal has never been to maximize the national economic welfare of the United States.

The third major policy explicitly directed at foreign direct investment relates to *expropriation* without fair, prompt, and adequate compensation. The United States traditionally has taken a dim view of such actions, on two grounds: that defense of U.S. nationals in their activities abroad (as tourists, missionaries, or investors) was a responsibility of U.S. foreign policy; and that "arbitrary" foreign seizure of private U.S. property retards the free flow of international investment. American multinationals

TABLE 1

Share of Overseas Private Investment Corporation (OPIC) Insurance Coverage in Third and Fourth Worlds, November 1973 and February 1976

Insurance program[a]	THIRD WORLD[b]		FOURTH WORLD[c]	
	November 1973	February 1976	November 1973	February 1976
Inconvertibility	56.9	73.0	43.1	27.0
Expropriation	51.5	55.4	48.5	44.6
War risk	49.4	55.1	50.6	44.9
Total	51.6	58.4	48.4	41.6

[a]Current (as opposed to contingent or maximum) coverage.

[b]All of South America except Bolivia and Paraguay; all of East Asia; Yugoslavia, Portugal, Greece, Turkey, Iran, and Israel.

[c]All of Africa, South Asia, Central America, and the Caribbean.

Source: Author calculations, based on OPIC data obtained through private communication.

occasionally sought such retaliation in earlier periods but have seldom done so in recent years; their earlier fear that any single expropriation would trigger additional expropriations was replaced by the fear that U.S. retaliation would trigger more expropriations.

In 1962, Congress added the Hickenlooper amendment to the Foreign Assistance Act. The amendment required the United States to automatically cease all bilateral aid to any country that expropriated private U.S. property without fair compensation or without taking the appropriate steps. In 1972, through the Gonzalez amendment, Congress applied the same principle to U.S. support for soft loans from the Inter-American Development Bank, the allocation of import quotas for sugar, and all U.S. contributions to the international lending institutions (World Bank, International Development Association, Inter-American Development Bank, Asian Development Bank).

In practice, however, the principle of automatic, retaliation has been administered quite flexibly. The Hickenlooper amendment was applied only once, and the Gonzalez amendment has never been formally applied, though both have been used as levers to achieve U.S. objectives in a few investment disputes. In 1973, the Hickenlooper amendment lost much of its force when automaticity was eliminated by providing for a presidential waiver of its aid cut-off. A similar change was implicitly added to the Gonzalez amendment. And in 1974, when Congress extended the possible scope of sanctions against expropriation, the President was free to designate countries for preferences, even if they violated sanctions against appropriation, if he should determine "that such designation will be in the national economic interest" (88 Stat. 2067–68).

The fourth area in which the United States directly addresses foreign direct investment is *balance-of-payments* policy. From February 1965 through January 1974, first (through 1967) on a voluntary basis and then on a mandatory basis, the amount of capital that U.S.-based multinational enterprises could export from the United States was limited to reduce the deficit in the U.S. balance of payments. The program did not limit foreign plant and equipment expenditures by American-based firms but only the ways in which such investment could be financed. The program was administered by the Office of Foreign Direct Investment (OFDI) within the Department of Commerce.

The controls were instituted in an effort to offset the effects on the U.S. balance of payments of the growing overvaluation of the dollar.[8] The overvaluation itself provided an increasing incentive for U.S.-based firms to invest abroad rather than in the United States, because of the improving competitive position of other countries. Thus the controls were in reality a second-best (or third-best) policy, adopted to restore the status quo ante rather than to achieve any positive goal. Indeed, the controls were removed soon after the second devaluation of the dollar and the widespread adoption of flexible exchange rates.

Even so, the controls sparked conflict between the United States and several host countries (notably Canada, Australia, and France), which recognized that the U.S. action threatened to deprive them of some of the benefits (capital inflows and reinvested earnings) of foreign direct investment. Hence they became concerned about the effects of the U.S. action on their balance-of-payments positions and capital markets. And they worried politically about the extraterritorial reach of U.S. policy implied by its effort to dictate to subsidiaries (including those in which U.S. parents were minority owners) how they should divide their earnings between reinvestment and repatriation to the United States.

In addition to these policies aimed directly at foreign direct investment, there have been a series of attempts by the U.S. government throughout the postwar period to control specific activities of the foreign subsidiaries of U.S.-based firms to promote U.S. foreign policy or internal economic objectives. In implementing its policy of controlling exports to the communist countries, the United States restricted sales of foreign subsidiaries through its leverage over their U.S. parents. Some of these restrictions were coordinated through the coordinating committee of NATO (COCOM), but several of the U.S. efforts triggered clashes with host countries. In recent years, this policy has been attempted infrequently (and carried through even more infrequently)[9] because of the general easing of U.S. trade policy toward the communist countries and the growing ability of host countries to reject U.S. efforts to control firms incorporated in their territories.

The United States has also on occasion tried to apply its antitrust policies and securities disclosure policies in other countries. Several U.S. efforts to apply its antitrust law have triggered conflicts with other countries, particularly in Canada and Western Europe. In one recent case, the Federal Trade Commission argued that competition in the domestic U.S. photocopier market could be increased if Xerox Corporation spun off its European and Japanese subsidiaries, since Xerox's own subsidiaries were potential competitors in the U.S. market. No spin-offs were required in the consent decree ending the case, however. At the same time, domestic antitrust policy has probably increased the level of foreign direct investment by U.S.-based firms and brought on the emergence of conglomerates in the 1960s, by precluding both further market expansion by U.S. firms and takeovers of competitors in their own industries.

The National Labor Relations Act, along with several other pieces of legislation, governs labor-management relations in the United States by requiring management to negotiate with legally constituted labor unions and to provide them with adequate data as a basis for such negotiations.

The act applies in principle to international as well as domestic operations. However, the several efforts by labor to use it to defend its interests vis-à-vis the multinational enterprises (to restrain foreign direct investment) have failed totally. . . . Labor law has had no impact thus far on foreign direct investment.

The international monetary policy of the United States can have an important effect on foreign direct investment. In the late 1960s, the United States permitted the dollar to become overvalued because it viewed devaluation as disruptive both to the functioning of the international monetary system and its leadership of the noncommunist world. The over-valuation heightened the incentive for U.S.-based multinational enter-prises to invest abroad rather than in the United States (and for foreign-based multinational enterprises to invest at home, or in third countries, rather than in the United States). Subsequent devaluations of the dollar and adoption of flexible exchange rates restored equilibrium in national competitive positions.

Facets of U.S. trade policy also affect foreign direct investment. Its generally liberal treatment of imports permits the foreign affiliates of U.S.-based firms to sell to the U.S. market, though its high effective tariffs and nontariff barriers discourage such activities in a few industries (includ-ing some processed raw materials, textiles, and benzenoid chemicals). Its exemption from duties of U.S.-made components of imports, in sections 806.30 and 807 of the Tariff Schedule, facilitates the assembly of finished products abroad. On the other hand, the steady U.S. effort to negotiate reductions in the trade barriers of other countries has reduced the incentive for investing behind tariff and nontariff walls.

Several provisions of the Trade Act of 1974 addressed problems raised by multinational enterprise. The program of trade adjustment assis-tance, inaugurated in the Trade Expansion Act of 1962 to assist workers displaced by imports to adjust into new endeavors, was extended to pro-vide for assistance to communities where "the transfer of firms or subdivi-sions of firms located in such area to foreign countries have contributed importantly" to job layoffs. A new section of the law requests that "firms relocating in foreign countries" provide at least sixty days' advance notice to their workers and to the Secretary of Labor and Secretary of Commerce, make maximum use of adjustment assistance, offer new jobs to employees "who are totally or partially separated as a result of the move," and "assist in relocating employees to other locations in the United States where em-ployment opportunities exist."

In addition to its national policy measures, there are international measures that the United States has agreed to. The Articles of Agreement of the International Monetary Fund, developed in Bretton Woods in 1944–45, permit individual countries to control capital movements (in con-tradistinction to current account transactions, which could be checked only when the international community agreed that such checks were needed for balance-of-payments reasons). The architects of the Bretton Woods Agreements were thinking primarily of portfolio investment, not multinational enterprises. By the middle 1950s, the United States sought international support for freeing the flow of foreign direct investment. The Organisation for European Economic Co-operation adopted a code of liberalization of capital movements, which was incorporated in the OECD with its creation in 1960. The United States launched a further effort in the OECD in 1973 to assure "national treatment" for direct investors in all member countries and to limit the use of disincentives to such investment maintained by member countries. The OECD countries agreed in 1976 to notify each other of deviations from the newly agreed norms and new consultative procedures. Simultaneously, the United States has taken a largely skeptical view of the efforts by the United Nations, beginning in 1973 with the appointment of its Group of Eminent Persons, to implement mandatory international checks on the activities of multinational enterprises without parallel agreements on the policies of governments toward foreign direct investment.

In the OECD negotiations of 1973–76, the United States also sought checks on certain host-country incentives, particularly tax concessions, to foreign direct investment. The agreement is quite weak, however; for example, incentives in the guise of regional policies, not aimed explicitly at foreign direct investment, are exempt. So U.S. policy in international forums still largely supports foreign direct investment and freedom of action for multinational enterprises, unlike its retrenchment in taxation, OPIC insurance, and trade policy. Indeed, the U.S. opposition to the proposals of the Group of Eminent Persons, for example, is couched in terms of "assuring the rights of multinational corporations."

This review of U.S. policy points to several conclusions. First, there is no coordinated overall program. Each individual measure affecting foreign direct investment, either directly or indirectly, has developed largely in a separate functional area, in response to problems in that area at a particular point in time. The government is not organized to coordinate the separate policies, and each agency is largely autonomous in managing the impact on foreign direct investment of policies within its area of responsibility.

Second, these individual policies display a common theme: support of foreign direct investment by U.S.-based multinational enterprises, both by encouraging the investment itself and by defending the firms against adverse treatment in host countries. The traditional government attitude is that there is a high coincidence between the interests of the multinational enterprises and the country as a whole.

In practice, the specific policy measures adopted toward foreign direct investment point toward different underlying objectives. Some seek to promote world welfare. Some seek to promote nontraditional objectives of the United States. Views vary as to the motives underlying the proinvestment U.S. approach. Interestingly, there has been no effort to apply optimum capital controls to promote the national economic welfare.

Third, in a number of areas the proinvestment tilt is being reduced. Doubts about the identity of interests between the firms and the country are increasingly translated into law. The changes implemented so far limit support to the firms, rather than actually restrict their activities.

The Policies of Other Home Countries

Other home countries have the same policy options as does the United States. They can seek to promote global welfare, their national welfare, or more immediate goals through either supporting or restricting foreign direct investment. With the exception of Japan, other home countries have been no more coherent than the United States in formulating such policies. As in the case of the United States, some of their macroeconomic policies, particularly regarding exchange rates, have had a major impact on the level of their foreign direct investment.

Eleven home countries accounted for over 95 percent of the stock of all foreign direct investment by market economies in 1971; the United States alone accounted for 52 percent. . . . The United Kingdom, the original leader in this area, still is the second largest home country by a wide margin (14.5 percent, compared to 5.8 percent for France). The most rapid growth is exhibited by Germany and Japan. Germany increased its share of the world stock of foreign direct investment from 2.8 percent in 1967 to 4.4 percent in 1971, and Japan more than doubled its share from 1.3 percent to 2.7 percent during the same period. Indeed, from 1967 to 1971, Japanese and German foreign direct investment grew at average annual rates of 28.3 percent and 22.8 percent, respectively, compared to U.S. and U.K. rates of 9.2 percent and 6.5 percent, respectively. Among firms based in various countries, there are important differences in the structure as well as the magnitude of foreign direct investment. For example, about 60 percent of the foreign affiliates of U.S.-based multinationals are wholly owned by the parent, compared to under 30 percent of the affiliates of Japanese-based parents.

The importance of foreign direct investment to a home (or host) country should be judged in comparison to the size of the country, not in absolute terms. Switzerland had over $1,000 foreign direct investment per capita, more by far than any other country in 1971 . . . Sweden was second ($425), slightly ahead of the United States and the United Kingdom ($415 and $422, respectively). Canada, the Netherlands, and Belgium had around $300; France, $186; Germany, $119; and Italy and Japan, around $50.

There is some similarity between this measure of openness and openness in terms of international trade. Switzerland, Sweden, the United Kingdom, Canada, and the Low Countries are relatively open on both counts, while France and Japan are relatively closed. However, there are several notable exceptions: the United States is far more open in terms of international investment than international trade, while Germany and Italy are much more trade-oriented. In 1971, the international production of U.S.-based firms was almost four times larger than U.S. exports, whereas international production by firms based in Germany, Italy, and Japan were only about 40 percent of the exports of those countries (see Table 2).

The three countries (the United States, the United Kingdom, and Switzerland) which loom largest by far, both in absolute terms and relative to their national exports, are also the three whose exchange rates were demonstrably overvalued, in terms of the international competitive

TABLE 2

Exports of Major Home Countries Compared to Estimated Foreign Production of the Multinationals Based in Each, 1971

Home country	Exports in millions of dollars	ESTIMATED FOREIGN PRODUCTION	
		In millions of dollars[a]	As percentage of exports
United States	43,492	172,000	395.5
Switzerland	5,728	13,500	235.7
United Kingdom	22,367	48,000	214.6
France	20,420	19,100	93.5
Sweden	7,465	6,900	92.4
Canada	17,582	11,900	67.7
Belgium	12,392	6,500	52.4
Netherlands	13,927	7,200	51.7
Italy	15,111	6,700	44.3
Japan	24,019	9,000	37.5
Germany	39,040	14,600	37.4

[a]Estimated foreign production equals the book value of foreign direct investment multiplied by the factor 2. The factor was derived as follows: the ratio of foreign sales to book value of foreign direct investment was estimated from 1970 U.S. data on gross sales of majority-owned foreign affiliates and book value of U.S. foreign direct investment. Gross sales of majority-owned foreign affiliates (approximately $157 billion) includes transactions between foreign affiliates and parent corporations (approximately $20.3 billion) and interforeign affiliate sales (approximately $28.1 billion), which together account for about 30 percent of gross foreign affiliate sales. The book value of U.S. foreign direct investment in 1970 amounted to $78.1 billion. The resulting ratio of gross sales to book value is 2:1.

Source: UN, *Multinational Corporations in World Development,* ST/ECA/190 (1973), p. 159.

positions of their economies, throughout much of the era of fixed exchange rates.[10] The two countries whose foreign production ranged farthest beneath their exports in 1971, Germany and Japan, had the most demonstrably undervalued exchange rates during the 1960s, the boom period for foreign direct investment.[11] Hence there is a priori evidence that exchange rates affect trade and investment patterns. The acceleration of foreign direct investment by multinational enterprises based in Germany and Japan since the realignment of exchange rates beginning in 1971, and the sharp increase in the role of the United States as a host country, adds credence to this observation.

The international monetary policies of home countries thus appear to have an important bearing on their patterns of foreign direct investment. In addition, all home countries must decide how to tax the income on foreign direct investment; most have provisions similar to those of the United States for crediting taxes paid abroad against tax liabilities at home. Germany exempts income from countries with whom it has tax treaties and has a tax-sparing credit for income from developing countries. France exempts 95 percent of all foreign income from any taxation in France. A couple of small home countries exempt all foreign income from domestic taxes, while others deduct foreign income taxes from taxable income rather than credit them against domestic taxes.

Fifteen home countries also insure and guarantee some foreign direct investment by their firms in developing countries. . . . Most programs focus on the developmental effects of proposed investments in the host countries. A few, including Australia's, seek to promote the type of investment that meets host-country preferences by offering premium rates for joint ventures. However, several of the programs (including the Japanese and Australian) are not limited to covering investments in developing countries.

In addition, a number of the programs (including France's) explicitly link the extension of insurance to an expansion of home-country exports. The Japanese program originally was limited to investments that would help the balance of payments. Several (including the Canadian, Japanese, and British) are managed by the export promotion agencies of their governments. The Japanese scheme, in addition, applies to portfolio investment in non-Japanese companies if the investment is used to develop mineral resources for import by Japan under long-term supply contracts. All of the national insurance and guarantee programs are, of course, selective, and support specific projects that meet their criteria.

Virtually all home countries, for balance-of-payments reasons, have controlled exports of capital to finance foreign direct investment. Several (the United Kingdom, Japan, France, Sweden) used such controls regularly, applying them in response to the immediate balance-of-payments situation. None has tried to use its controls to maximize its national welfare (indeed none, with the exception of Britain in earlier periods, has had enough market power to contemplate doing so). The objective was simply to limit the immediate balance-of-payments deficit.

Though the United States is historically hostile to such controls, it applied them when it was concerned with its balance of payments. The United Kingdom, which generally permitted outflows despite its exchange controls, also tightened its rules considerably during the 1960s. Germany and Japan, on the contrary, tried to increase their foreign direct investment outflows in the late 1960s and early 1970s, to reduce their balance-of-payments surpluses and avoid adjusting their current account positions. Their efforts failed to prevent sizable revaluations of both currencies.

There have also been efforts by home countries to use their multi-national enterprises in the extractive industries to assure access to imported raw materials. . . . They have been almost wholly unsuccessful. Indeed, none of the home countries of the multinational oil companies appeared to do any better than other oil-importing countries during the OPEC production cutback (and embargo) in 1973–74, whether or not they actively sought preferential treatment from their firms (as did the United Kingdom and, probably, France).[12]

Two home countries, Japan and Sweden, instituted fairly comprehensive policies regarding foreign direct investment by firms based within their jurisdictions. Throughout most of the postwar period, Japan exercised tight control over outgoing (and incoming) foreign direct investment. In 1968, it officially sought to promote various national goals through foreign direct investment. . . . Some of these goals were traditional: improving the terms of trade by improving access to foreign raw materials, meeting an increasing share of home demand in some industries from cheaper sources abroad, and avoiding further pollution and intensity of land use in the home islands.

The basically laissez-faire attitudes of other home countries developed during an earlier era when host countries had similarly laissez-faire policies. Now, host countries increasingly are able to tilt the benefits of foreign direct investment in their direction. Whether home countries will maintain their traditional policies when host countries seek to maximize their national gain—and whether domestic political forces within home countries will enable them to do so—remains to be seen. The decline in support for foreign direct investment in U.S. and Swedish policy may be a partial response to this changed environment.

Answers to these questions turn on the [impacts] of both foreign direct investment and new host-country policies on home countries. [Among the most controversial of these impacts is the impact on home-country labor.]

U.S. MULTINATIONAL CORPORATIONS
AND U.S. LABOR

AMERICAN LABOR has several concerns about foreign direct investment: first, that it exports jobs. If production that could have remained competitive at home is transferred abroad, there is an immediate loss of jobs. And if, over time, the investment erodes the home country's competitive strength, including its technological or capital bases, there will be long-term job losses.

Labor believes, also, that foreign direct investment erodes labor's share of national income. Traditional economics suggests that export of capital reduces the stock of capital in the home country and enhances its returns at the expense of labor; some argue that the income shift in recent years has been sizable. Both of these issues pit workers in home countries against workers in host countries. Host-country labor benefits not only from the jobs and technology exported from the home country but also from the larger national income that results from a flow of capital to their country from the home country. So important differences between the attitudes of home-country and host-country labor toward multinational enterprises are to be expected.[13]

There are other concerns, however, that are common to labor in both home and host countries. One is the threat that multinationals pose to labor's ideological and institutional position. Labor in all countries is affected when multinationals do not recognize host-country unions, invest in anti-union countries, exploit host-country workers by evading local work standards, invest in countries without such standards, pay substandard wages, or support regimes that have policies opposed by labor (such as apartheid in South Africa and suppression of human rights in post-Allende Chile). Home-country labor may oppose the low wages and weak unions of host countries for pragmatic reasons, too, thinking that they attract investment and add to the export of jobs.

Finally, labor is intensely concerned over the effect on its bargaining position of the internationalization of business. Blue-collar labor is essentially immobile, internationally. There are exceptions within Europe and between Canada and the United States, but the importance of family and community ties to most workers limits their mobility even in those areas. And labor is almost wholly immobile across oceans and between northern and southern hemispheres, for reasons of both geographical distance and cultural (including linguistic) differences. Capital and management, on the other hand, are highly mobile across national boundaries. Runaway plants can now run halfway around the globe, but strikes by national unions affect only portions of the earnings of a multinational, in contrast to the total earnings of a firm that operates completely within a single country.

The importance of this concern to labor in the United States is confirmed by the apparent antipathy of the AFL-CIO to foreign direct investment in the United States by foreign-based multinationals. Logically, the AFL-CIO should see such investment as a means of importing jobs, consistent with its view that outgoing foreign direct investment exports jobs. However, the increase in jobs is not, in American organized labor's view, a welcome trade-off for a decrease in bargaining position. The leadership of the AFL-CIO—where concern for bargaining power is most manifest within the U.S. labor movement—is apparently no more eager to deal with a multinational Mitsubishi than with a multinational Dow Chemical.

Unions in countries that traditionally play host to subsidiaries share the view of the AFL-CIO. The international mobility of plants means the prospect of loss of jobs. Negotiating with the management of a subsidiary seems pointless, because the firm's decisions are made in the home country. And, though the multinational may pay higher wages than local employers, it may ignore local labor practices and traditional working conditions.

The mobility of multinational enterprises, in fact, may not be as great as labor believes. As the International Labour Office, itself, points out, most production runs in most industries are based on long-term investments which cannot be easily shifted, excess capacity is frequently unavailable in alternative sites, the large investment losses and large severance payments would be incurred by precipitate shifts. Indeed, a multinational may be *more* susceptible to labor action than a nonmultinational, because its national components often depend heavily on each other. The Labour Office also points out that subsidiaries are subject to local laws, that personnel officials are almost always drawn from the local population, and that the corporate interests within a multinational are so similar that the actual locus of decisionmaking—whether the parent or the subsidiary—may not matter to the negotiations.

Nevertheless, international shifts of production within an existing family of plants is, by definition, unique to multinationals. And the power of this unique position can manifest itself in practices that are threatening to labor: substituting overtime for excess capacity, for example, or effecting changes in local laws that have hitherto deterred a multinational's flexibility. Hence, relative mobility and its effect on relative bargaining positions is the root of labor's antagonism toward multinational enterprises. Before we turn to the alternatives available to labor in dealing with multinationals, the issues of job displacement and income distribution must be placed in perspective.

Job Displacement

The AFL-CIO cites numerous instances of job losses because of foreign investment, but it does not ask whether these jobs could have been maintained without the foreign investment. The multinationals cite their growing domestic employment, but they do not ask whether it would rise even faster without foreign investment. Neither labor's nor the multinationals' argument takes into account all the information necessary to trace the effect of foreign direct investment on U.S. employment.

But the job effect of foreign direct investment cannot be ignored. It is impossible to fulfill desired employment levels through macroeconomic policy. As the recent past illustrates, macroeconomic policy is not flexible, the forecasts it relies on often go awry, and the inflationary costs of a policy devoted fully to reducing unemployment may be simply too high for society to pay. Even if macroeconomic policy could ensure full employment, foreign direct investment can still cause transitional costs by triggering a shift in the structure of the work force. . . .

[One of] the most recent and detailed [studies] is by Robert F. Frank and Richard T. Freeman.[14] On the assumption that exports could substitute for all foreign affiliate production, they seek to measure the probable extent of that substitution given the inferior cost competitiveness of domestic production. They measure the annual effect of foreign direct investment, not the effect of several years. And they include in their calculation (through the use of input-output tables) the indirect effects on suppliers in addition to the direct effect on the investing industries. Finally, they include changes in the labor market to assess the real impact on workers, including both employed workers and potential workers.

Frank and Freeman find that the annual effect ranges between the creation of a small number of jobs (about 11,000) and the displacement of a sizable number (about one million) and conclude that the annual loss is 120,000–260,000 jobs, 70 percent in the investing industry and the remainder in supplying industries. There are large differences among the twenty-one industries disaggregated by their data, but in none is creation of jobs more likely than displacement. They go on to minimize the net effect, however, by citing an increase of one week in the average period of unemployment and an average of seven weeks before the majority of workers who lost their jobs because of foreign direct investment were reemployed. Thus, even Frank and Freeman's pessimistic assumption that foreign investment substitutes for U.S. exports suggests that one should look at factors like macroeconomic policy rather than foreign investment to explain the high rates of domestic unemployment experienced in the 1970s.

Distribution of Income

Even if exchange rate adjustments or some combination of monetary and fiscal policy offset loss of jobs, the question of who benefits from foreign direct investment would remain. Because the distribution of national income between labor and capital has received so much attention from economic theorists, let us review the principles of the traditional analysis. . . .

Although international trade theory usually assumes that only commodities move in international exchange, several writers consider the economic consequences of the international movement of capital and labor. As early as 1904, Arthur C. Pigou argued that a tariff protecting domestic labor from cheap imports could be undermined by domestic capitalists investing abroad.[15] If the tariff succeeded in raising the wages of labor and depressing the return on capital, foreign investment opportunities would become more attractive and domestic labor would suffer as domestic capital was transferred overseas. The relation between international trade and investment was further explored in 1919 by Eli Heckscher, who reasoned that international trade (disregarding tariffs and transport costs) could actually equalize both wage rates and the returns on capital between two trading countries.[16] Even though one country might start with more capital and, consequently, higher wages than the other country, trade between the two would lower wages in one country and raise them in the other until they were equal. The first country's wages fall because it imports goods that take advantage of cheap labor and exports goods that take advantage of abundant capital. Thus if international trade were completely free of tariffs and transport costs, the original differences in national wage rates and returns on capital would disappear and, with them, the economic incentive to international investment or emigration.

Fourteen years after the Heckscher study, Bertil Ohlin backpedaled a bit by denying the possibility of *complete* equality in wage rates and returns on capital. However, he reaffirmed the general principle:

> The exchange of goods cannot bring about a complete equalization of factor prices. Interregional differences remain, and call forth factor movements, whenever the difference is great enough to overcome the obstacles. Factor prices are in this way brought into completer harmony as between regions; the need for interregional trade, and consequently its volume, are reduced. Thus factor movements act as a substitute for the movements of commodities.[17]

But in 1948, Paul A. Samuelson showed that under the conventional (if strict) assumptions, complete equalization is a distinct possibility.[18] It remained, however, for Robert A. Mundell in 1957 to show the exact theoretic relation between international trade and investment: either free trade or free investment equalizes wages and capital returns, and barriers to one will only stimulate the other.[19]

If one were to apply the traditional theory to U.S. investment and labor, the effect of foreign investment on income distribution would be very small because international trade would adjust to offset the effect. To compensate for the loss of capital, the United States would cut both exports of capital intensive goods and imports of labor intensive goods, and the terms of trade, labor's wage, and labor's share of national income would remain unchanged. While labor must adjust by transferring from one industry to another, the burden is transitional, not permanent.

If international trade cannot or will not adjust, however, fewer laborers would have to switch from one industry to another, but labor's real wages and its share of national income would suffer permanent harm from the foreign investment. An extreme example is considered by Lester C. Thurow.[20] With only one commodity produced at home or abroad, no international trade would flow except as return on international investment. Foreign investment cannot, by assumption, be offset by switching production from the exported to the imported commodity. Thus the real wage of labor must fall until the substitution of labor for capital within the industry can compensate for the loss of domestic capital.

According to Thurow's estimates, the free international flow of capital would raise the real income of all Americans by less than 1 percent if the rest of the world had as much labor but only half as much capital as the United States. The redistribution of income within the United States would be substantial, however: the real income of labor would fall by over 8 percent while the real return on capital would jump by more than 22 percent.[21] With the opportunities for substitution between commodities ruled out, the estimated swings in the distribution of income from labor to capital are substantial.

Similar calculations have been made by Peggy B. Musgrave. Using a one-sector model like Thurow's, and including the tax consequences of foreign investment, Musgrave estimates that domestic utilization of the entire $80 billion of American capital invested abroad through 1968 would have raised labor's share from 77.2 percent to 79.4 percent of national income and diminished capital's from 22.8 percent to 20.6 percent, a shift of about $25 billion, or $125 per American, in 1974.[22] While this estimate is not as large as Thurow's, it also implies that foreign investment significantly reduces labor's share of U.S. national income.

There are three severe limitations on the usefulness of the Thurow–Musgrave analysis. The first is the omission of international trade adjustments which, as just noted, can wholly compensate for any shift in income distribution triggered by the foreign investment. Second is the failure to recognize that foreign direct investment by American multinationals does not equate to net capital outflow from the United States, both because those firms finance a majority of their investments with foreign capital and because whatever export of funds takes place tightens the U.S. capital market and attracts incoming capital. Third, they give short shift to the transfer of technology.[23] Thurow considers the possibility that American foreign investment increases foreign productivity but assumes that the benefits are shared by all factors generally, including foreign capital, rather than by American capital in particular.

Alternative Labor Strategies

Though it is doubtful that multinational enterprises export significant numbers of jobs from the United States or adversely affect labor's share of American income distribution, some jobs are exported . . . and the position of labor in collective bargaining is weakened by the multinationalization of business. In addition, labor's belief, whether well-founded or not, that jobs are exported has led it to search for effective means to countervail the perceived power of multinational enterprises.

These efforts follow two broad strategies: reducing the mobility of the multinational enterprises and increasing labor's own ability to counter that mobility. Tactically, labor can pursue these strategies either through purely national efforts, usually in league with their own governments, or internationally, by coordinating the activities of labor across borders or by promoting intergovernmental agreements. Table 3 displays specific approaches and examples of each. In any approach, home-country and host-country labor may seek to promote their own interests, the interests of each other, or both. And a labor union can pursue different approaches simultaneously, for no single approach could achieve all of labor's objectives.

Reducing Multinationals' Power through National Effort. The most serious efforts by national labor to check the power of multinational enterprises have been made in the United States and Sweden. In 1969 and 1970, two major U.S. unions challenged foreign investment by the firms under the authority of the National Labor Relations Act (NLRA), which compels business to bargain with labor over its investment decisions that affect employees in the bargaining unit.[24] They were unable to demonstrate that the investments caused an actual reduction in U.S. employment, however, or even that foreign investment data were germane to collective bargaining. Since these failures, U.S. labor has made no effort to use the NLRA to strengthen its position vis-à-vis multinational enterprises.

TABLE 3

Examples of Four Labor Strategies for Countervailing Power of Multinationals

	STRATEGY	
Tactic	Reducing multinationals' power	Increasing labor's power
National effort	U.S. Burke-Hartke bill; Swedish insurance program	Germany's Mitbestimmung (codetermination); Swedish requirement for union approval of investment
International effort	Attempts toward U.N. guidelines and GATT clause on fair labor standards	Genk strike, Saint-Gobain strike, Michelin strike (solidarity action); U.S.-Canada Automotive Pact (international collective bargaining)

The AFL-CIO in 1971 developed and sponsored an alternative approach, the Burke-Hartke bill, which sought to legislate four major new constraints on multinational enterprises. First, it would increase the taxation of their foreign income by eliminating the deferral of taxation of such income until it is repatriated to the United States and by permitting them to treat payment of foreign taxes only as deductions, rather than credits, against their U.S. tax liabilities. Second, it would require presidential licensing of all foreign direct investments and exports of technology, with decisions based on a number of criteria including the effect on U.S. jobs. Third, more complete corporate disclosure of international activities would be required. Fourth, U.S. imports, especially those produced abroad with American-made components, would be curtailed, partly to prevent American firms from meeting domestic demand through foreign production. . . . Changes in the U.S. tax code in 1975 accomplished a small part of the first of these union objectives. However, the other components of the Burke-Hartke approach were rejected by both the administration and Congress.

Sweden is the only other home country in which labor has made a major effort to check locally based multinationals through national legislation, and it has succeeded in structuring two Swedish laws relating to multinational enterprises. First, Swedish legislation authorizing government insurance for foreign direct investment in developing countries requires that the insured firm meet specific standards in such matters as collective bargaining rights; compensation, for wage losses during illnesses, injuries, and layoff; pensions; and several other health and welfare matters. This law sought to help labor in host countries, rather than in Sweden, and pursues interests common to home-country and host-country labor. Swedish-based firms ignore the insurance program, however, rather than meet its conditions.

Swedish unions have also increased the power of home-country labor to cope directly with multinationals. . . . Sweden in 1974 adopted legislation requiring all capital outflows for foreign direct investment by Swedish-based firms to be approved by the Swedish government. All corporate applications for such permission must be accompanied by statements on the proposed investment from both blue-collar and white-collar unions. But no applications have been denied, and it is too early to know how much advantage Swedish labor will derive from their opportunity.

Increasing Labor's Power through National Effort. Workers in Germany, and to some extent other continental European countries and Great Britain, are going a different route to improve their power to countervail the power of multinationals. Rather than allying with the home-country government to overturn corporate decisions that are already made, these unions have for many years sought national and European Community legislation giving them equal representation with management on all supervisory boards—Mitbestimmung, or codetermination. This effort, motivated by a wide range of concerns, preceded the present attention to multinationals and, indeed, since the 1950s has gone forward in a few industries. The most concrete success to date of codetermination vis-à-vis foreign investments came in Germany in early 1975, when the opposition of Volkswagen workers to the firm's proposed investment in the United States helped delay the project and forced the retirement of the management that proposed it.

American unions show little interest in codetermination. (For different reasons, neither do the communist-dominated unions of Italy and France.) Indeed, this is the only one of the four possible strategies U.S. unions have not pursued. Their history of arm's-length confrontation with industry and the hostility to labor of many U.S. firms make the unions wary of any cooperative steps. The clout of the AFL-CIO is largely based on its representation of a distinctive part of the body politic and on the collective power of member unions, which would become diluted through codetermination. Indeed, AFL-CIO leadership views labor representatives on the boards of German firms as being co-opted by management.

Increasing Labor's Power through International Effort. The Volkswagen case also provides a fascinating instance of informal transnational union cooperation, because the opposition of the Volkswagen workers to the investment was at least partly stimulated by Leonard Woodcock, president of the United Auto Workers (UAW) of the United States, during a week-long visit to Wolfsburg. To Woodcock, Volkswagen investment in the United States would have meant simply a shift of jobs from the three large American automakers to Volkswagen, rather than a creation of additional jobs, because demand in the industry at that time was depressed. And in reaching this conclusion he was no doubt in agreement with the appraisal of VW management—that U.S. investment was necessary to retain its share of the U.S. market.[25]

Secretary-General Charles Levinson of the International Federation of Chemical and General Workers' Unions (ICF), suggests that multinational collective bargaining will evolve through three stages: "company-wide support of a single union in one country" in a dispute with a foreign subsidiary or parent firm, "multiple negotiations with a company in several countries at the same time," and finally "integrated negotiations around common demands."[26] The ultimate objective would presumably be multinational collective bargaining, with a single multinational union composed of members from all relevant countries confronting each multinational enterprise (or industry), and operating under the requirements of international law.

National unions have already taken action within each stage. British and American unions supported their Belgian counterparts in a strike against a Ford Motor plant in Genk in 1968, in pursuit of efforts by the International Metalworkers Federation to achieve "upward harmonization of wages." French, German, Italian, and American glass workers simultaneously struck the Saint-Gobain group of companies in early 1969. French and Italian workers, supported at least morally by other European rubber-worker's unions, struck Michelin in 1971 to protest new investments in Canada. The International Federation of Air Line Pilots Associations staged the world's first multinational, multicompany, shutdown in 1972 when it blocked much of the world's air transportation for a day in an effort to persuade the United Nations to adopt sanctions against countries that harbored skyjackers. American and Canadian auto workers bargained jointly with Chrysler (and simultaneously with General Motors and Ford) within the context of U.S.-Canada automotive pact, achieving wage parity across national borders. In all of the other cases, however, it is unclear whether labor's efforts significantly affected the eventual outcome.

Coordinating and implementing international efforts require certain effort on the part of labor, such as collecting data on the profits and practices of all the subsidiaries of individual firms. The most advanced effort is that of the International Metalworkers' Federation, which has a computer bank on wages and working conditions at forty-seven representative plants of fifteen world auto companies. The secretariats transmit data and technical advice to member unions to help them in specific negotiations, and work generally to strengthen individual unions. Company councils are formed by unions in different countries, and meetings are sought with management to discuss both specific issues and overall corporate investment policy.[27] Common termination dates are sought for labor contracts in different countries, making simultaneous strikes possible. When "solidarity action" is actually needed, unions in nonstriking countries may refuse to work overtime or to otherwise help to offset declining output, and may give financial assistance to the strikers. Almost 25 percent of a group of American multinationals and 40 percent of a group of foreignbased multinationals, responding to a poll in early 1975, reported that they had already experienced at least some of these types of union solidarity.

There are a number of fundamental structural differences among labor organizations in different countries, however, which make the multinationalization of labor extremely difficult. One difference is bargaining method: some are highly decentralized and operate mainly at the firm or even plant level, as in the United States; some operate at the industry level, as in Western Europe; and some are highly centralized, engaging in national bargaining across all industries, as in Sweden. (Only the U.S. model appears widely applicable on the international level.) Another difference is the degree of unionization within a country: less than 25 percent of American workers are unionized, whereas almost all Scandinavian workers are union members. In countries where union membership is nonuniversal, any skewness in union composition will affect strategy. Too, ideological differences among unions in different countries remain: some are still dedicated to gaining control of their governments or of achieving broad objectives such as codetermination. And most of them harbor the bureaucratic fear that internationalization would weaken them.

In addition, workers compare their position to other workers within their own countries, rather than to workers in their industry in other countries. This is particularly true of multinational workers in developing countries, whose pay is usually high by national standards though low in comparison to workers in the same industries in the industrialized countries.

There have been recent disagreements between national unions in different countries, triggered by the differences outlined here. Canadian members of the AFL-CIO, for example, denounced the federation's pursuit of tight quotas on U.S. imports and foreign direct investments and threatened to leave the federation unless Canada were exempt from any such steps. In 1974, Japanese auto workers rejected United Auto Worker requests for their help in persuading Japanese auto firms to accept voluntary export restraints on their sales to the United States. The United Rubber Workers supported countervailing duties on U.S. sales of Michelin tires. The International Federation of Petroleum and Chemical Unions opposed the ICF stress on company councils on the grounds that low-paid workers in developing countries could not be asked to help high-paid workers in industrial countries.

Despite the difficulties, a number of U.S. unions participate in efforts to multinationalize labor, both to help unions in other countries and to seek help for their own activities; on the other hand, virtually all of these unions also supported the Burke-Hartke efforts to slash foreign direct investment by American firms, which would hurt labor in other countries. Solidarity actions obviously will be combined with other strategies in union confrontation with the power of multinationals.

Reducing Multinational Power through International Effort. For many years, labor groups have sought to add to international trade agreements (General Agreement on Tariffs and Trade) requirements covering working conditions and pay. (Such requirements were included in the charter of the stillborn International Trade Organization.) More recently, some labor groups have been in the forefront of the efforts to use the United Nations to set new international rules, or at least guidelines, on the operations of multinational enterprises.

Summary & Conclusions

Though none of the four strategies available to labor has achieved dramatic success, all are building toward it. And though many multinationals are skeptical that international collective bargaining will ever occur, others see it as inevitable. But internationalization of labor has progressed very slowly compared with internationalization of business, and it is viewed even by its most ardent devotees—the dedicated people who manage the international trade secretariats in Geneva—as requiring a decade or more to become a significant force in world industrial relations. In any event, eventual multinationalization appears to be a component of labor's strategy, both to gain psychic redress against the superior mobility of capital and management and to defend its more tangible economic interests.

This analysis suggests that labor's primary recourse, particularly in the short run, is to governments of both host and home countries; indeed much of labor's success in countervailing the power of corporations within national borders has come through influencing government policy. National legislation is required to regulate working standards, minimum wages, bargaining with representative unions, and allowing actions by labor such as strikes. Though collective bargaining in the United States first occurred before the 1930s, it was the legislation of that and subsequent periods that enabled U.S. labor to begin to exercise effective countervailing power.

Just as labor within individual countries once had to both organize itself and get government help to cope with the national spread of industry, so must world labor organize itself internationally and get help from both home and host governments, through both national and international policies, to cope with the multinationalization of the corporate sector. We should thus expect it to pursue a two-track strategy, with a heavy emphasis in the immediate future on seeking government help.

Two specific U.S. policy changes could be sought. Though sympathy strikes across national borders may be effective in keeping a firm from increasing production in one country to offset the production cutback of a struck plant in another country, such strikes are illegal in the United States and many other countries. Legalizing sympathy strikes in the United States would permit workers of the parent company to support strikes by workers in its foreign subsidiaries and would enable American labor to play a larger role in international union cooperation.

Second, the jurisdiction of the National Labor Relations Board could be extended to cover foreign direct investment. This could raise problems of extraterritoriality, because data might be required from subsidiaries incorporated in other countries. On the other hand, the board could get information from the parent regarding its transactions with the subsidiary, and penalties could be applied simply to the parent.

In closing, it must be added that labor's interests and priorities may in some cases run counter to national interests. Multinational labor may benefit only the relatively elite workers, while national labor may simply protect positions already acquired; in either case, the conditions for the majority of workers could well be worsened. Hence labor can no more be permitted to dictate national policy than can business.

Widespread controls over foreign direct investment, as advocated by the AFL-CIO and as effected in Sweden, could adversely affect the national economic welfare of the home country (as well as welfare in host countries). Codetermination, in practice, could bring either co-option of labor by business, reducing labor's countervailing power, or collusion of labor and business against broad public interests.

Notes

1. Some analysts argue that the national welfare of the world's dominant economic power is maximized by a free international economic system, because the dominant power is best able to exploit its opportunities. They reject the distinction between national and global welfare, at least for the United States at the present time and Britain in the nineteenth century. An important empirical question is whether the United States does exercise dominant world economic power in any meaningful sense.

2. Host countries, recognizing that the United States or a small group of home countries possess such power, recommended (through the United Nations Group of Eminent Persons, whose conclusions they dominate) "that home countries do not hamper the process of transfer by multinational corporations of the production of labor-intensive and low-skill products to developing countries, and that they protect the domestic work force displaced by this transfer, through adjustment assistance measures." United Nations, *The Impact of Multinational Corporations on the Development Process and on International Relations*, ST/ESA/6 (May 1974), p. 75.

3. Considerable amounts of foreign direct investment by U.S.-based firms might, on this criterion, still be viewed as promoting the national interest of the United States. Glenn P. Jenkins and Brian D. Wright, "Taxation of Income of Multinational Corporations: The Case of the United States Petroleum Industry," *The Review of Economics and Statistics*, vol. 57 (February 1975), p. 10, conclude that "although the U.S. petroleum corporations paid no U.S. tax on their foreign income over the years 1969 to 1972 the rate of return net of foreign taxes from their foreign investments compares favorably with the gross rate of return on domestic corporate investment." Transfer pricing and tax considerations would have to be taken into account, however, before one could conclude that these rates of return were fully comparable.

4. In 1973, the book value of foreign direct investment by U.S.-based firms rose by about $12.9 billion. Given a 10 percent return on those investments in their first year—a generous assumption—they produced earnings of about $1.3 billion. The book value outstanding at the end of 1972 was $94.3 billion, on which earnings in 1972 were $11.5 billion. Thus, if the new investments reduced the rate of return on the outstanding stock by 12 percent, they would adversely affect overall earnings. *Survey of Current Business*, vol. 54 (August 1974), p. 16.

5. A home country can, in theory, cope with unfavorable effects of foreign direct investment on its terms of trade by placing an optimum tariff on the trade flows, themselves. Sophisticated analyses of foreign direct investment by traditional economists integrate the concepts of optimum tariffs and optimum capital controls in arriving at an overall optimizing foreign economic policy for an individual country.

6. Marvin Frankel, "Home Versus Foreign Investment: A Case Against Capital Export," *Kyklos*, vol. 18, fasc. 3 (1965), pp. 411–33. He estimates that this factor alone assures a negative impact of foreign direct investment on the home

country unless its yield is at least 250 percent of the available return on domestic investment.

7. A. E. Jasay, "The Social Choice Between Home and Overseas Investment," *Economic Journal,* vol. 70 (March 1960), p. 113.

8. The *net* reduction in the U.S. balance-of-payments deficit probably fell far short of the *gross* shift of corporate financing to foreign capital markets, because of offsetting capital flows induced by the higher interest rates abroad triggered by the increase in foreign borrowing by U.S. firms. See Martin F. J. Prachowny, *A Structural Model of the U.S. Balance of Payments* (Amsterdam: North Holland, 1969), and David Morawetz, "The Effect of Financial Capital Flows and Transfers on the U.S. Balance of Payments Current Account," *Journal of International Economics,* vol. 1 (November 1971), pp. 426–27. For a contrary view, see Peter H. Lindert, "The Payments Impact of Foreign Investment Controls," *Journal of Finance,* vol. 26 (December 1971), pp. 1083–99.

9. During 1974, the United States sought to block sales to Cuba of locomotives from Argentina and trucks from Canada manufactured by subsidiaries of U.S.-based multinational enterprises. In both instances, the United States backed down when it became clear the countries intended to proceed.

10. The British pound may have been overvalued before World War I; it was clearly overvalued during 1925–31, as well as in most of the postwar period. Some observers argue that the dollar was overvalued as early as 1960; the overvaluation grew rapidly from 1965 to 1971. For both countries, the international roles of their currencies provided financing for the resulting balance-of-payments deficits and enabled them—indeed, induced them—to maintain overvalued exchange rates. Even when their balance-of-payments deficits could be reconciled with international financial equilibrium, the international competitive position of their domestic production eroded and foreign direct investment grew. Switzerland, the only other country whose foreign production exceeded its exports, also experienced steady capital inflows over time and hence developed an exchange rate overvalued in terms of the international competitive position of its economy. For a complete analysis of these international monetary phenomena see C. Fred Bergsten, *The Dilemmas of the Dollar: The Economics and Politics of United States International Monetary Policy* (New York University Press, 1975).

11. Italy, whose foreign production was also less than 50 percent of its exports, also maintained what some observers maintain was an undervalued exchange rate.

12. Robert B. Stobaugh, "The Oil Companies in Crisis," *Daedalus* (Fall 1975), pp. 179–202, finds that Royal Dutch/Shell cut U.K. oil supplies by 10–15 percent despite government demands. Petrofina and ten other companies boycotted Belgium to force the government to permit them to charge higher prices; France got better treatment from American-based firms than from French companies, despite its efforts to gain preferential treatment from the latter; the United States, home base to most of the companies, got the poorest treatment of all.

13. B. C. Roberts and Jonathan May, "The Response of Multinational Enterprises to International Trade Union Pressures," *British Journal of Industrial Relations,* vol. 12, no. 3 (November 1974), conclude that "conflicts of interest between unions in home and host countries of multinational enterprises . . . at bottom are probably the main obstacle to effective international union collaboration," p. 416.

14. "The Impact of United States Direct Foreign Investment on Domestic Unemployment" (May 1975; processed).

15. *Protective and Preferential Import Duties* (London: McMillan, 1904), pp. 59–60.

16. "The Effect of Foreign Trade on the Distribution of Income," in *Readings in the Theory of International Trade,* vol. 4, Blakiston Series of Republished Articles on Economics (Blakiston, 1950), pp. 272–300.

17. *Interregional and International Trade* (Harvard University Press, 1935), p. 169.
18. "International Trade and the Equalisation of Factor Prices," *Economic Journal,* vol. 58 (June 1948), pp. 163–84.
19. "International Trade and Factor Mobility," *American Economic Review,* vol. 47 (June 1957), pp. 321–35.
20. "Multinational Companies and the American Distribution of Income" (1973; processed).
21. Ibid., table 4, p. 13.
22. *Direct Investment Abroad and the Multinationals: Effects on the United States Economy,* report prepared for the Subcommittee on Multinational Corporations of the Senate Foreign Relations Committee (GPO, 1975), p. 97. Estimates are based on an elasticity of substitution between capital and labor of 0.75 and on a definition of capital which includes structures, equipment, and inventory, but not land or cash.
23. Musgrave, *Direct Investment Abroad and the Multinationals,* p. 97, notes the existence of technology transfer but assumes that its significance is limited to the multinationals' repatriation of royalties and fees. This seems an understatement, since the higher-than-average returns earned by foreign investors may include an imputed return on know-how.
24. The International Union of Electrical, Radio, and Machine Workers (IUE) raised the subject of foreign investments with General Electric during negotiations for their 1969–72 labor agreement, and in 1970 the United Auto Workers attacked Ford Motor's decision to produce Pinto engines and gear boxes at its English and German subsidiaries. The cases are traced and the applicability of the National Labor Relations Act is analyzed in Duane Kujawa, "Foreign Sourcing and the Duty to Bargain Under the NLRA," in Duane Kujawa, ed., *American Labor and the Multinational Corporation* (Praeger, 1973), pp. 253–58.
25. Subsequently, when demand for automobiles revived with the recovery of the world economy in late 1975 and 1976, both the German auto workers and the UAW withdrew their objections to the investment.
26. Charles Levinson, *International Trade Unionism* (London: Allen and Unwin, 1972), pp. 110–11. See, esp., chap. 4.
27. Philips Lamp agreed in 1969 to give its unions advance notice of all production transfers within the European Community—and did so six times in the next four years. Hirschfield, *The Multinational Union Challenges the Multinational Company,* p. 25.

17

The Efficiency (Contradictions) of Multinational Corporations

Stephen Hymer

Multinational corporations are a substitute for the market as a method of organizing international exchange. They are "islands of conscious power in an ocean of unconscious cooperation," to use D. H. Robertson's phrase.[1] This essay examines some of the contradictions of this latest stage in the development of private business enterprise.

At the outset, we should note that the multinational corporation raises more questions than economic theory can answer. Multinational corporations are typically large firms operating in imperfect markets and the question of their efficiency is a question of the efficiency of oligopolistic decision making, an area where much of welfare economics breaks down, especially the proposition that competition allocates resources efficiently and that there is a harmony between private profit maximization and the general interest. Moreover, multinational corporations bring into high definition such social and political problems as want creation, alienation, domination, and the relationship or interface between corporations and national states (including the question of imperialism), which cannot be analyzed in purely "economic" terms.

DIVISION OF LABOR AND THE EXTENT OF THE FIRM

Our starting point is the fact that there are two kinds of division of labor: the division of labor between firms coordinated by the markets; and the division of labor within firms, coordinated by entrepreneurs. International trade theory has been mainly concerned with the first of these and has long stressed the desirability of widening international markets to increase the division of labor and exchange. Far less attention has been paid to the parallel proposition that the division of labor within a firm is limited by the extent of the firm and the economic and social questions this raises. . . .

The qualitative evidence on the structure of business enterprise and its evolution through time suggests that both size and internationality

From Stephen Hymer, "The Efficiency (Contradictions) of Multinational Corporations," *American Economic Review,* May 1970, Vol. LX, No. 2, pp. 441–453. Reprinted by permission. Some footnotes omitted.

have important positive effects on a firm's strength and ability. Since the beginning of the industrial revolution there has been a steady increase in the size of manufacturing firms, so persistent that it might almost be formulated as a general law of capital accumulation. These increases in size were accompanied by important changes in organizational structure involving both increased subdivision or differentiation of tasks and increased integration through the creation of new organs of control. Business administration became a highly specialized activity with its own elaborate division of labor; and the corporation developed a brain to consciously coordinate the various specialties and to plan for the survival of the organism as a whole.

Chandler[2] distinguishes three major stages in the development of corporate capital. First, the Marshallian firm, organized at the factory level, confined to a single function and a single industry, and tightly controlled by one or a few men who, as it were, see everything, and decide everything. The second stage emerged in the United States at the end of the nineteenth century when rapid growth and the merger movement led to large national corporations, and a new structure of administration was developed to deal with the new strategy of continent-wide, vertically integrated production and marketing. The family firm gave way to the modern corporation with a highly elaborate administrative structure to organize the many disparate units of a giant enterprise. The next stage, the multidivisional corporation, began in the 1920's and gathered great momentum after the second World War. It too was a response to a new marketing strategy. To meet the conditions of continuous innovation, corporations were decentralized into several divisions, each specializing in one product line and organized as an almost autonomous unit similar in structure to the national corporation. At the same time, an enlarged corporate brain was created in the form of the general office to coordinate the various divisions and to plan overall growth and survival. This form is highly flexible and can operate in several industries and adjust quickly to rapidly changing demands and technology.

With each step in the development of business administration, capital obtained new power and new horizons. As Chandler and Redlich[3] point out, there are three levels of business administration. Level three, the lowest level, is concerned with managing the day-to-day operations of the enterprise; i.e., keeping it going within the established framework. Level two is responsible for coordinating the managers at level three. Level one's function is goal determination and planning; i.e., setting the framework for the lower levels. In the Marshallian firm all three levels are embodied in one entrepreneur. In the national corporation, the top two levels are separated from the bottom level. In the multidivisional corporation, differentiation is far more complete; level three is completely split off from level two and is concentrated in the general office whose specific function is strategy, not tactics.

In other words, the process of capital accumulation has become more and more specialized through time. As the corporation evolved, it developed an elaborate system of internal division of labor, able to absorb and apply both physical sciences and the social sciences to business activity on a scale which could not be imagined in earlier years. At the same time, it developed a higher brain to command its very large concentration of wealth. This gave it the power to invest on a much larger scale and with a much wider time-horizon than the smaller, less developed firms that preceded it. The modern multidivisional corporation is thus a far cry from the Marshallian firm in both its vision and its strength. The Marshallian capitalist ruled his factory from an office on the second floor. At the turn of the century, the president of a large national corporation was lodged in a higher building, say on the seventh floor, with wider perspectives and greater power. In the giant corporation of today, managers rule from the top of skyscrapers; on a clear day, they can almost see the world.

Each step in the evolution of business enterprise had important implications for the structure of the international economy, just as each excursion into the international economy provided new challenges to the corporation and speeded its evolutionary development. In a world of Marshallian firms, commodity trade and portfolio capital were the main engines of international exchange. Movement of enterprise between countries was sharply limited because firms were small and lacked the appropriate administrative structure. The diffusion of Marshall's vital fourth factor, organization, from advanced to less advanced countries was therefore exceedingly slow. Movements of portfolio capital were substantial, at times, because the small Marshallian firms were associated with a highly developed banking and financial system. But the ability of less advanced countries to absorb capital (and technology) was limited to the rate at which they could build up their own organizations, a slow and difficult process given the negative policies of most governments in Africa, Asia, and Latin America, especially those in colonial dependencies. The range of goods which could be produced was thus restricted and the possibility for international trade to equalize factor prices was severely limited.[4]

The national corporation opened new possibilities of transferring organizational abilities internationally. The new administrative structure and financial power enabled firms to undertake direct foreign investments and organize large-scale production in mining and manufacturing in foreign countries. However, this migration of business enterprise occurred only on a limited scale and was usually restricted to a narrow activity; i.e., to acquiring raw materials used by the parent company or to exploiting some technological advance or differentiated product developed by the parent company. Moreover, to the extent that investment strengthened the firm's market control, its effect was considerably less beneficial and perhaps even negative.

The modern multidivision or conglomerate enterprise is a much more powerful organizational form than the national corporation and appears capable of integrating world production and exchange to a much larger extent. Larger size and a more advanced administrative structure give it a much wider horizon leading in many cases to a global outlook and a transformation to the stage of multinational enterprise. It seems that after a certain point, a corporation comes to think in terms of its world market position rather than merely its United States or European market position and to plan in terms of worldwide factor availabilities and demand patterns. Since the process is just beginning, it is difficult to evaluate how strong this tendency will be. However, it is clear that at present large corporations are consciously moving towards an international perspective much faster than other institutions and especially much faster than governments, and are in the vanguard of planners of the new international economy created by the aeronautical and electronic revolutions. Since multinational corporations also have great financial and technical resources, they will certainly have many successes and will be able to speed up the spread of technology and to organize activities until now impossible. They are a large step forward but this is not, however, the same thing as saying that they serve the general interest as well as their own, that they are the best way to exploit the possibilities of modern science, or that they do not create certain highly intractable problems which greatly impede their efficiency. We turn to these considerations.

BIGNESS AND FEWNESS

Multinational corporations enlarge the domain of centrally planned world production and decrease the domain of decentralized market-directed specialization and exchange. Bigness is thus paid for, in part, by fewness, and a decline in competition since the size of the market is limited by the size of the firm. The precise effect of the present wave of direct investment on seller concentration in world markets is not well established. On the one hand, improved communications are breaking down barriers to trade and widening the market facing most buyers. On the other hand, direct foreign investment tends to reduce the number of alternatives facing sellers and to stay the forces of international competition. A great deal of statistical work needs to be done to evaluate the net effect of these two tendencies and establish the exact trend in the level of seller concentration, taking into account the growing international nature of the market. All that can be said at present is that the world level of concentration is much higher than it would be if foreign investment and domestic mergers were restricted. Since most countries are encouraging mergers at home and foreign investment abroad, for better or worse, the opportunity to increase competition by maintaining numbers is not being taken up.

Direct foreign investment thus has a dual nature. It is an instrument which allows business firms to transfer capital, technology, and organizational skill from one country to another. It is also an instrument for restraining competition between firms of different nations. Analyzing any particular case is an exceedingly complex matter, as the antitrust literature shows. For present purposes, the important point is to note that the general presumption of international trade economists in favor of free trade and free factor movements, on the grounds of allocative efficiency, does not apply to direct foreign investment because of the anticompetitive effect inherently associated with it. Just as in antitrust theory there are recognized reasons, within the framework of neoclassical economics, for preventing a firm from merging with another firm or from increasing its share of the market by growth, there are also international antitrust reasons for preventing a firm of one country from taking over a firm in another country or from acquiring or increasing its share of foreign production. Since this point can be easily misunderstood, it is important to stress that this is not a second-best argument but a genuine argument on antimonopoly grounds for interfering in international markets. A restriction on direct investment or a policy to break up a multinational corporation may be in some cases the only way of establishing a higher degree of competition in that industry. National antitrust measures cannot substitute for international antitrust when, for example, one of the major potential competitors to a domestic firm is its sister or parent affiliate within the same multinational group. In short, when we leave the conditions of perfect competition we lose the assumption of the invisible hand.

This argument, it should be noted, provides an important rationale for the infant entrepreneur argument supporting protection. Temporary protection of a weak firm from a stronger firm can improve the competitive structure of the industry in future periods by maintaining numbers. In the present context, the cost of this protection would have to be borne by the country that offers it while the benefits would accrue to the world as a whole. Thus, in reverse of the usual arguments, myopic behavior will lead to too little protection rather than too much. This presents a particularly acute problem in the case of underdeveloped countries. These countries typically do not sell commodities or buy capital or technology in competitive markets where there is an established price at which they can trade whatever quantity they want. Instead, they frequently face only a few potential buyers of their raw materials or their manufactured goods and a few potential sellers of a particular technology. The price they receive or pay therefore depends on their skill and strength in bargaining and not on market conditions alone. The less developed the country, the greater its disadvantage in the bargaining process because it has fewer organizations that are in any way a match for the giant companies with which it is dealing. Given the oligopolistic front maintained by the firms from developed countries, the underdeveloped countries need to devote an important share of their scarce resources to building up national enterprises which they can control and use in bargaining with foreign oligopolists. Ironically, their stronger bargaining position, by increasing competitiveness, may improve general welfare in the rich countries as well—although it will harm those in the monopoly position.

THE INTERNATIONAL "TRICKLE DOWN"

Many economists, in dealing with oligopoly, prefer to stress . . . that the competition that counts lies in creative destruction through the introduction of new technology and new products. In that case, an oligopolistic market structure, even though it interferes with static optimum allocation, may be a necessary or at least a contributing factor to dynamic optimum allocation in a private enterprise system, because it allows innovators to capture some of the benefits of their discoveries and thus provides the incentive for research and development. The record of the United States shows that one certainly cannot fault oligopoly on the grounds that it does not produce a very rapid rate of technological change and product innovation. (Indeed it is easier to argue that the rate of change is too high.) One can expect international oligopoly via multinational corporations to provide the same kind of dynamic environment for the world economy as a whole.

The question of efficiency therefore hinges on the direction of change rather than the rate of change. An analysis of this problem involves an excursion into unexplored terrain since we do not now have an adequate theory on how corporations choose between the available paths of innovation. We certainly cannot assume that market forces compel firms to choose the optimum path. It is true that an innovation must, to some extent, meet the market test for a corporation to survive. However, what is at stake here is not whether the consumer has some choice but rather whether an oligopolistically competitive market structure provides him with the full range of choices possible. Oligopolists tend to copy each other, and their predictions as to what the consumer wants are often self-fulfilling, since in fact this is all that the consumer is offered. If we had only large numbers of independent decision centers could we assume that all avenues had been explored.

Since we cannot possibly treat this complex topic in any detail in the present paper, let us simply examine one theory of innovation closely associated with the multinational corporation and the international demonstration effect. The marketing literature suggests new products typically follow a cycle known as trickle-down or two-stage marketing. An innovation is first adopted by a small group of individuals who act as opinion leaders and is then copied by others via the demonstration effect. In this process, the rich get more votes than everyone else, first of all because they have more money, second of all because they have discretionary income and can afford to be experimental, and, third, because they have high status and are more likely to be copied. The principle of consumer sovereignty cannot easily be applied to this process since, at most, only the special group in the first stage of the marketing process has something approaching a free choice. The rest have only the choice between conforming or being isolated.

In the international economy, trickle-down marketing takes the form of the international demonstration effect. Products are first introduced in the United States or Europe and then spread to other countries. Multinational corporations speed up this process by making it easier to transfer new products and marketing methods to less advanced countries. One of the key motives for direct investment, cited by corporations, is to gain control over marketing facilities in order to facilitate the spread of their products. If firms were denied control over communication and marketing facilities in the foreign countries and we had a regime of national firms (private or socialized) rather than multinational firms, the pattern of output would almost certainly be quite different than the one that is now observed. There would be more centers of innovation, and probably more variety of choices offered to the consumers, as each country developed products suited to its particular characteristics. Products from one country would spread to other countries either through trade or imitation but the movement would be coordinated by market competition rather than the planning decisions of top management in a few corporations whose interest it is to foreclose competition, to restrict the choices offered, and to insure the survival of their own organizations. It is difficult to speak with professional certainty in this badly neglected field, but it does not appear to be socially efficient to allow corporations to monopolize information on new possibilities created by science.

THE INTERNATIONAL HIERARCHY OF
DECISION MAKING

Marshall, like Marx, thought that the "chief fact in the form of modern civilization, the kernel of the modern economic problem . . ."[5] was the division of labor within the factory between those who plan and organize economic activity and those who work for them. In the modern corporation the hierarchical structure of command and authority has been greatly elaborated from the simple division between owners and workers in the Marshallian firm, but the tensions and conflicts of autocracy remain. They take on particular importance in the multinational corporation where problems of nationalism and problems of authoritarianism intertwine.

Multinational corporations are torn in two directions. On the one hand, they must adapt to local circumstances in each country. This calls for decentralized decision making. On the other hand, they must coordinate their activities in various parts of the world and stimulate the flow of ideas from one part of their empire to another. This calls for centralized controls. They must therefore develop an organizational structure to balance the need to coordinate and integrate operations with the need to adapt to a patchwork quilt of languages, laws, and customs. One solution is division of labor based on nationality. Day-to-day management in each country is left to nationals of that country who are intimately familiar with local conditions and practices and best suited to deal with local problems and local government. These nationals remain rooted in one spot, but above them is a layer of people who move around from country to country, as bees among flowers, transmitting information from one subsidiary to another and from the lower levels to the general office at the apex of the corporate structure. In the nature of things, these people, for the most part, will be citizens of the country of the parent corporation, just as we now find that the top executives of most of the major corporations in the United States are drawn from a relatively small homogeneous cultural group quite distinct from the population of the United States as a whole.

This creates two types of problems. In the first place, there is the internal problem of creating incentives for foreigners whose access to the top corporate positions will be necessarily limited. The second problem is far more important and is in the nature of an external diseconomy. The subsidiaries of multinational corporations are frequently amongst the largest corporations in their country of operations and their top executives play an influential role in the political, social, and cultural life of the country. Yet these people, whatever their title, occupy at best a medium position in the corporate structure and are restricted in authority and horizons to a lower level of decision making. The country whose economy is dominated by the foreign investment can easily develop a branch plant outlook, not only with reference to economic matters, but throughout the range of governmental and educational decision making.

Thus there are important social and political costs to international specialization in entrepreneurship based on multinational corporations. The multinational corporation tends to create a world in its own image by creating a division of labor between countries that corresponds to the division of labor between various levels of the corporate hierarchy. It will tend to centralize high-level decision-making occupations in a few key cities in the advanced countries (surrounded by regional subcapitals) and confine the rest of the world to lower levels of activity and income; i.e., to the status of provincial capitals, towns, and villages in a New Imperial System. Income, status, authority, and consumption patterns will radiate out from the centers in a declining fashion and the hinterland will be denied independence and equality.[6]

This pattern contrasts quite sharply with the free trade system which offered both income equality and national independence. According to the factor price equalization theorem, trade allows a country to choose its own style and still share fully in the riches of the world. Whether large or small and even if its resource endowment is highly skewed, it can achieve factor price equalization with the rest of the world by varying the composition of output without surrendering its control over its capital stock and without the need for its members to leave the country to find employment elsewhere. Now the stakes seem to have gone up. In order to reap the gains from international exchange, a country has to become integrated into a corporate international structure of centralized planning and control in which it plays a very dependent role.

Countries may not be willing to play this game nor to completely break with it and the possibility arises, in part suggested by the Canadian experience, of getting the worst of both worlds. Canada has allowed an almost unrestricted inflow of capital and as a result has surrendered a great deal of national independence. At the same time, she has adopted a number of policies, including high tariffs, which prevent international corporations from fully rationalizing production on a continent-wide basis. The record shows that foreign subsidiaries in Canada tend to perform at levels equal to their Canadian counterparts rather than at the higher levels of efficiency of their parent corporations. This suggests that many of the benefits of foreign investment have been emasculated while many of the costs remain.

BIG CORPORATIONS: SMALL COUNTRIES

The efficiency with which multinational corporations can allocate resources internationally depends in large part on government policy decisions. If government decision making were independent of the structure of the private sector, we could view it as an exogenous factor and safely ignore it in an essay devoted to the multinational corporation. However, an increase in the importance of multinational corporations relative to national corporations will clearly have an important impact on both the ability and willingness of governments to carry out certain types of economic policies. An analysis of the efficiency of multinational corporations must take this into account and analyze, for example, its effect on government capital formation in the crucial sectors of infrastructures and human capital. This aspect is particularly important with regard to the problem of underdevelopment—clearly the greatest instance of inefficiency in today's international economy.

Analyses of the role of foreign investment in underdeveloped countries often focus on the great disparity between the bargaining power of the corporation and the bargaining power of the government. The corporations are large and modern and have international horizons. The governments are typically administratively weak and have very limited information outside their narrow confines. In any particular negotiation between one country and one company, power in the form of flexibility, knowledge, and liquidity is usually greater on the private side than on the public side of the table.

The problem of unequal bargaining power can be illustrated with a simple model (developed in collaboration with Stephen Resnick).[7] This model focuses on the feedback relationship between the government and the foreign corporation. The government provides certain support services to the corporation: protection, infrastructure, help in the creation of a labor force, land laws, etc. The corporation in return pays the government taxes and royalties. This is a trading relationship in which two main variables are involved: (1) the tax rate (t); and (2) the fraction of government expenditure devoted to support services (g). The outcome is determined by a process of bargaining which, for simplicity, can be viewed in a purely duopolistic form—one government and one country—though it, in fact, usually arises in a more complicated structure where there are several corporations and several power groups involved. The government, we assume, is interested in maximizing its surplus (total revenue from foreign firms less the cost of support services). The corporation is interested in maximizing profits after taxes. At one extreme the government may be very strong and choose (g) and (t) such as to make profit zero (we assume normal profits are included in cost) and to make the government surplus as large as possible. This seldom, if ever, occurs in underdeveloped countries where the bargaining tends to go in the opposite direction. The corporation sets (t) as low as possible, subject to the constraint that the government has enough money to: (a) provide necessary infrastructures; (b) remain in power and maintain law and order for the corporation. Since the government has little surplus it does not have the money to provide capital or services for other industries. This is in keeping with the foreign investor's interest, since the growth of other industries would compete away factors of production and would create interest groups who might challenge the corporation's hegemony. Provided that the political forces are kept under control in this system, the country can remain in its state of underdevelopment for a long period.

Such extreme cases are no longer possible because of the increased political strength of the local middle class in most underdeveloped countries and because of the changed nature of foreign investment. Modern multinational corporations are interested in manufacturing in underdeveloped countries and not just in raw materials and therefore want a growing market for advanced products and an educated, urbanized labor force. They are no longer tied to traditional backward governments, but have a stake in an active government sector which promotes growth and provides education and infrastructure. The "new foreign investment" is, then, a far cry from the "Banana Republic" kind, but important dangers remain.

Statistics on income distribution show that the top one-third of the population typically gets about 60 percent of the total income. It is this top group which provides the direct and indirect labor force for large-scale manufacturing as well as the market. An alliance between this group and foreign investors represents a formidable bargaining force vis-à-vis the remaining two-thirds of the population. A government expenditure policy based on such an alliance would concentrate on the modern high-income sector, leaving the rest of the population as a source of unlimited supply of cheap labor for services and for menial work. Growth in these circumstances would retain its uneven quality and all the inefficiency that implies, albeit in a more advanced and progressive form than characterized the enclave economies of the previous round of foreign investment.

MULTINATIONAL CORPORATIONS AND SUPRANATIONALITY

Multinational corporations create serious problems in the developed world as well. The most important of these, from the limited perspective of this essay, is that they reduce the ability of the government to control the economy. Multinational corporations, because of their size and international connections, have a certain flexibility for escaping regulations imposed in one country. The nature and effectiveness of traditional policy instruments—monetary policy, fiscal policy, antitrust policy, taxation policy, wage and income policy—change when important segments of the economy are foreign-owned. This has long been recognized in countries such as Canada, but it is now becoming obvious that even the United States has reached the point where the international commitments of its corporations reduce the room for flexibility in national economic policy formation. If foreign investment continues to grow at anything like the rate of the last ten or fifteen years, this problem will become an extremely serious one for all North Atlantic countries.

This contradiction between multinational corporations and nation states has important bearing on the efficiency of the multinational corporation. The main problem, stated most simply, is as follows: if national power is eroded, who is to perform the government's functions? For example, if nation states, because of the openness of their economy, cannot control the level of aggregate economic activity through traditional monetary and fiscal policy instruments, multinational agencies will need to be developed to maintain full employment and price stability. Yet such organizations do not exist at present, nor can they be quickly built. Either one must argue that the Keynesian problem has somehow been solved by the creation of the multinational corporation (along with a host of other problems) or else one must agree that it is not feasible to have international business integration via direct foreign investment proceeding at a much faster rate than political integration. Yet, this seems to be precisely what is happening. Most of the large American firms have already staked out their claims in the European market and many of the leading European firms are now rapidly entering foreign markets, including those of the United States. A predominance of multinational corporations in the North Atlantic economy seems therefore to be a *fait accompli*. Government cooperation is not growing at anywhere as rapid a rate. If serious problems arise, governments are likely to reassert their power and attempt greater regulation and control over the business enterprises within their jurisdictions. Economists will rightly point out that these restrictions create inefficiencies in the allocation of the economic resources. It is important, however, to realize the role played by a too liberal policy towards private capital, movements and mergers that created the multinational industrial structure.

CONCLUSION: SOME SUBJECTIVE EVALUATIONS

This essay has presented a list of advantages and disadvantages of multinational corporations. Assuming there are no important omissions and that each point taken by itself is valid, the question arises as to what weights should be attached to the various arguments. One simple summation, offered here without proof, is as follows: The large corporation illustrates how real and important are the advantages of large-scale planning, but it does not tell us how best to achieve wider domains of conscious coordination. Broadly speaking, there are two main directions in which one can proceed. Multinational corporations integrate one industry over many countries. The alternative is to integrate many industries over one country and to develop noncorporate linkages between countries for the free flow of goods and, more important, the free flow of information. The advantage of the second direction is that it keeps the economy within the boundary of the polity and the society. It thus causes less tension and creates the possibility of bringing economic power under control by removing the wastes of oligopolistic anarchy. This would allow more scope for solving the two major economic problems of today, affluence and poverty, than the first alternative. The trend, however, is clearly in the direction of the first alternative. The coming age of multinational corporations should represent a great step forward in the efficiency with which the world uses its economic resources, but it will create grave social and political problems and will be very uneven in exploiting and distributing the benefits of modern science and technology. In a word, the multinational corporation reveals the power of size and the danger of leaving it uncontrolled.

Notes

1. D. H. Robertson quoted in R. H. Coase, "The Nature of the Firm," *Economica,* New Series, 1937, pp. 386–405. Reprinted in G. S. Stigler and K. E. Boulding, *Readings in Price Theory* (Richard D. Irwin, Inc., 1932).

2. Alfred D. Chandler, *Strategy and Structure* (Doubleday & Co., 1961).
3. Alfred D. Chandler and Fritz Redlich, "Recent Developments in American Business Administration and Their Conceptualization," *Bus. Hist. Rev.,* Spring 1961.
4. Stephen Hymer and Stephen Resnick, "International Trade and Uneven Development," in J. N. Bhagwati, R. W. Jones, R. A. Mundell, Jaroslav Vanek, eds., *Kindleberger Festschrift* (M.I.T. Press, forthcoming).
5. Alfred Marshall, *Principles of Economics* (Macmillan, 1961), pp. 74–75.
6. This point is developed more fully in S. Hymer, "The Multinational Corporation and Uneven Development," in J. Bhagwati, ed., *Economics and World Order* (World Law Fund, 1970).
7. S. Hymer and S. Resnick, "Interactions between the Government and the Private Sector in Underdeveloped Countries: Government Expenditure Policy and the Reflection Ratio," Ian Stewart, ed., *Economic-Development and Structural Change* (Edinburgh: Edinburgh Univ. Press, 1969). Published in French as "Les Interactions entre le Gouvernement et leur Secteur Privé," *L'Actualité Economique,* Oct.–Dec., 1968.

18

Multinationals Revisited

Paul Streeten

The multinational is no longer so multifashionable. It is true that much is still being written about it, and this reviewer of some recent books and articles on the subject [see references at the end of the article] succumbs to the Swiftian thought that he who can make one word grow where there were two before is a true benefactor of mankind. Yet, in spite of the continuing controversy, some of the steam has gone out of the debate. There is no longer the sharp separation between those who think that what is good for General Motors is good for humanity and those who see in the multinational corporations the devil incorporated.

The reasons for this lowering of the temperature are to be found in five recent trends that suggest that the role of multinational corporations in development has to be reassessed.

First, there has been a shift in bargaining power between multinationals and their host countries, greater restrictions on the inflow of packaged technology, a change in emphasis from production to research and development and marketing, among other factors, that have increased

From Paul Streeten, "Multinationals Revisited," *Finance and Development*, June 1979, Vol. 16, pp. 39–42.

the uncertainties of direct foreign investment. As a result, there is some evidence that it has become the policy of multinational companies to shift from equity investment, ownership of capital, and managerial control of overseas facilities to the sale of technology, management services, and marketing as a means to earn returns on corporate assets, at least in those countries that have policies against inflows of packaged technology (Baranson, 1978).

Second, many more nations are now competing with U.S. multinationals in setting up foreign activities, which means that the controversy is no longer dominated by nationalistic considerations. Japanese and European firms figure prominently among the new multinationals. The number of U.S. companies among the world's top 12 multinationals declined in all of the 13 major industry groups except aerospace between 1959 and 1976, whereas continental European companies increased their representatives among the top 12 multinationals in 9 of the 13 industries, and the Japanese scored gains in 8 (Franko, 1978). The reasons for this are to be found in the decline of U.S. predominance in technology transfer; in the fact that foreign production follows exports, and exports from these countries steadily rose; in the steady growth of European and Japanese capacity to innovate; and in the greater adaptability—both politically and economically— of these companies to the needs of host countries. For example, Michelin's radial tires, Bosch's fuel injection equipment, and French, German, and Japanese locomotives, aircraft, and automobiles are more energy saving than their American counterparts.

Third, developing countries themselves are now establishing multinationals. In addition to companies from the Organization of Petroleum Exporting Countries (OPEC), and firms established in tax-haven countries, the leading countries where multinationals are being established are Argentina, Brazil, Colombia, Hong Kong, India, the Republic of Korea, Peru, the Philippines, Singapore, and Taiwan. According to ... Wells (1977), in Indonesia "Asian LDC investors together account for more investment than either Japanese, North American, or European investors, omitting mining and petroleum." It may well be that these firms use more appropriate technology and are better adapted and more adaptable to local conditions. Wells notes that there is a strong preference in the developing countries for multinational corporations from similar countries. Korean companies put up buildings in Kuwait, pave roads in Ecuador, and have applied to Portugal for permission to set up an electronics plant; Taiwanese companies build steel mills in Nigeria; and Filipino companies restore shrines in Indonesia. Hindustan Machine Tools (India) is helping Algeria to develop a machine tool industry; Tata (India) is beating Mercedes trucks in Malaysia; and Stelux, a Hong Kong-based company with interests in manufacturing, banking and real estate, bought into the Bulova Watch Company in the United States. C. P. Wong of Stelux improved the performance of the U.S. company. There are other instances of Third World multinationals that have aimed at acquiring shares in firms in developing countries (Heenan and Keegan, 1979).

The data on the extent of developing countries' foreign investment are inadequate and the evidence is anecdotal. A partial listing of major Third World multinationals in *Fortune* (August 14, 1978) contains 33 corporations with estimated sales in 1977 ranging from $500 million to over $22,000 million, totaling $80,000 million.

If there is a challenge, it is no longer uniquely American; and if multinationals are instruments of neocolonialism, the instrument has been adopted by some ex-colonies, and at least one colony (Hong Kong), and is used against others. (Excluding mining and petroleum, Hong Kong is, for example, the second largest investor in Indonesia.) Neither developed nor developing countries are any longer predominantly recipients of multinationals from a single home country.

Fourth, not only do host countries deal with a greater variety of foreign companies, comparing their political and economic attractions, weighing them against their costs, and playing them off against one another, but also the large multinationals are being replaced by smaller and more flexible firms. And increasingly alternative organizations to the traditional form of multinational enterprise are becoming available: banks, retailers, consulting firms, and trading companies are acting as instruments of technology transfer.

Fifth, some multinationals from developed countries have accommodated themselves more to the needs of the developing countries, although IBM and Coca-Cola left India rather than permit joint ownership. Centrally planned economies increasingly welcome the multinationals, which in turn like investing there, partly because "you cannot be nationalized."

Several distinguished authors, former U.S. Under Secretary of State George Ball, Professor Raymond Vernon, and Harry Johnson among them, had predicted that sovereignty would be at bay and some of these authors even suggested that the nation state, confronted with large and ever more powerful multinationals, would wither away.

> Competition among nation-states for the economic favours of the corporation and the xenophobic character of the nation state itself will prevent the formation of a conspiracy or cartel of nation-states to exploit the economic potentialities of the international business in the service of national power. Therefore, the long-run trend will be toward the dwindling of the power of the national state relative to the corporation.

Such was Harry Johnson's (1975) vision of the future. The nation state has shown considerable resilience in the face of multinationals; its demise, as with reports of Mark Twain's death, have been somewhat exaggerated. The Colombians succeeded in extracting substantial sums from their multinationals. The Indians dealt successfully with firms that introduced inappropriate technologies and products. The Andean Group and OPEC showed that solidarity among groups of developing countries in dealing with multinationals is possible and can pay.

STILL IMPORTANT FORCE

This is not to say that multinationals are no longer an important force. It has been estimated that the foreign production of multinationals accounts for as much as 20 per cent of world output, and that intrafirm trade of these companies (defined narrowly as trade between firms linked through majority ownership) constitutes 25 per cent of international trade in manufacturing. There has been an increase in the proportion of U.S. technology receipts, which are intrafirm. The share of total U.S. imports accounted for by intrafirm transactions of multinationals based in the United States rose from 25 per cent in 1966 to 32 per cent in 1975. The share of these transactions from developing countries showed a rise from 30 per cent in 1966 to 35 per cent in 1975; however, this rise can be accounted for by the rise in the price of petroleum imports, which constitute the largest category of imports from developing countries. The share of U.S. intrafirm trade in manufactures from developing countries declined from 16 per cent in 1966 to 10 per cent in 1976. But control can take many forms other than majority ownership in subsidiaries. And multinationals are adept in assuming these other forms (UNCTAD, 1978).

An essential feature of the multinational enterprise is a special advantage over the local rival, who knows the local conditions and the local language better than the foreigner. This advantage must be sufficiently large to permit rents to be collected that exceed the extra costs of geographical and cultural distance. It may consist in a natural monopoly, in size, in risk-spreading, in good will, or in proprietary knowledge acquired through research and development expenditure. It may be bestowed upon a firm by what Veblen called "business methods," like advertising, or by "production methods," like superior knowledge or larger scale.

It was recognized quite early that it is wrong for multinationals to benefit from a natural monopoly in which know-how is widespread, such as that enjoyed by public utilities. As a result, these enterprises were nationalized early. Host countries also learned to appropriate for themselves a larger share of the monopoly rents in minerals. In manufacturing, monopoly profits for multinationals were generated partly as a result of high levels of protection, on which the companies often insisted, and excessive subsidies and tax concessions, and partly as a result of trade names, market-sharing agreements, and other monopolistic practices.

Expenditure on the creation of this advantage does not vary with the unit operating costs in a particular country, which may be quite low compared with the prices charged. The large fixed costs that arise from research and development, exploration, scale, or advertising make the allocation of these costs between operations in different countries arbitrary within wide limits. But while one school of thought has used this to justify companies charging prices substantially in excess of the incremental costs of operating in a particular country, as a way of recouping what are regarded as necessary overhead expenditures, another school has emphasized the element of monopoly profit in these pricing policies. The existence of such profits or rents (which may be concealed, for example, through transfer pricing of imported inputs, management or license fees, interest rates on intrafirm loans, and royalties) implies that the "marginal productivity of investment curve," which relates returns to amounts invested, has vertical branches, within the limits of which the division of gains between the host country and firm is a matter for bargaining. Higher shares going to host countries would not be accompanied by reduced investment or lower operating efficiency, as the conventional theory has maintained.

This theory states that any policy that raises costs to the multinational is bound to lead to reduced capital or technology inflow. Policymakers have to "trade off" their desire for raising taxes, imposing conditions about local participation or training, or limiting remittances abroad against the advantages of more foreign capital and know-how. Though their relationship to the foreign enterprise may be a love-hate relationship, at the margin they have to make up their minds whether they love or hate the investment of the foreign company.

But the correct analysis must start from the monopolistic advantage of the firm and the monopoly rent that it yields. There will, therefore, be a range between a high "rate of return" to the company that will make the operation just acceptable to the host country and a low rate that will make it just worthwhile for the company. The maximum point of this range is determined by the host country's ability to acquire the advantage in an alternative way, or to do without it; the minimum point being set by the operating costs to the company of conducting the activity in the country.

It might be objected that if governments were to beat down returns to such low levels that they barely covered their local operating costs and did not permit firms to recoup a contribution to their overhead expenditures (such as those on research and development), they would kill the goose that lays the golden eggs. Pharmaceutical companies, for example, would have to go out of business if they were allowed to charge only the direct costs of producing drugs, for the sources of their research funds would dry up.

But this is not a valid objection as far as developing countries are concerned. The argument may hold for advanced, industrial countries. In deciding upon its research expenditure the company usually has the large markets of the advanced countries in mind. Anything it gets from the small, relatively poor markets of the developing countries over and above operating expenses is frequently a bonus. To forgo that bonus would not reduce its research expenditure. The potential bargaining strength of the developing countries (where they have the ability, solidarity, and knowledge) lies precisely in their small size: an instance of the importance of being unimportant.

TOWARD A POLICY

Any developing country has to ask itself four questions in evolving a policy toward multinationals—a positive answer to each giving rise to the next question. (1) Are foreign enterprises wanted at all? Some countries, though their number is declining, may reject outright the idea of foreigners making profits in their country. (2) Is the particular product or product range wanted? Many products of multinationals are overspecified, over-processed, overpackaged, oversophisticated, developed for high income, high-saving markets, produced by capital-intensive techniques and, while catering for the masses in richer countries, can cater for only a small upper crust in poorer countries. (3) Should the product be imported or produced at home? Home production could be for the domestic market or for export. (4) Is direct foreign investment the best way to assemble the package of management, capital, and know-how? The host country has a variety of choices. It can borrow the capital, hire managers, and acquire a license; use domestic inputs for some components of the "package"; or use consultancy services, management contracts, importing houses, or banks. If it is decided that direct foreign investment in the form of a multinational subsidiary is the best way of assembling the package, the terms of the negotiation will have to be settled, so that the host country strikes the best bargain, consistent with efficient operation of the multinational. This is an area in which international organizations, like the World Bank, could give technical assistance to host countries. (Bilateral technical assistance would be suspected of taking the side of the companies.)

The correct approach is therefore a combination of cost-benefit analysis and a bargaining framework. In one sense, though not a very significant one, the two approaches amount to the same thing. It is always possible, formally, to regard forgoing the second-best bargain to any given bargain as an element in the "opportunity cost" (the cost of forgoing the alternative) of the bargain in question. If, then, all bargains are ranked in order of preference, only the best bargain will show an excess of benefit over cost. But this is a purely formal way of getting round the difficulty of distinguishing between cost-benefit and bargaining issues. It would be more illuminating to say that cost-benefit analysis is useful in ranking the bargains, so that the host country knows what it should go for and what it will sacrifice with any concession, whereas the bargaining framework is necessary to strike the best bargain within the numerous items for negotiation. Here a number of issues may arise; do elements in the bargain in one country affect bargains in other countries? Can concession on one front be traded for counterconcessions on another? Are there clear areas of common interests that can be delineated from areas of conflicting interests? More fundamentally: can the government negotiators take a truly independent position that reflects the interests of their country, or do they not represent partial group interests within their own countries, that are aligned with the interests of the foreign company?

Bergsten, Horst, and Moran in their book *American Multinationals and American Interests* distinguish between four conventional schools of thought. The imperialist and mercantilist school argues that there is a joint effort by U.S. multinationals and the U.S. Government to dominate the world both politically and economically. The sovereignty-at-bay thesis (Raymond Vernon, 1971) holds that multinational firms have become dominant over all nation states, both host and home, with largely beneficial effects on all concerned. The global reach school (Barnet and Müller, 1974), while agreeing that the firms have become dominant, concludes that the effects can be detrimental for both home and host countries. There is also the view espoused by labor unions in the United States that multinationals hurt the United States and benefit foreign countries. Bergsten, Horst, and Moran find that none of these (somewhat oversimplified) models really fits and propose a policy to get the best out of these firms. They find that the main distortions to be corrected arise from competitive government policies, by both host and home governments (with respect to tax policies, for example), and from the structure and behavior of the companies. The type of rules and procedures that we have evolved in the area of trade and money need also to be negotiated in the area of foreign investment and multinational behavior.

Can multinationals make a contribution to meeting basic human needs? Since it follows from the above argument, about the special advantage, that the multinationals from the developed countries are likely to produce and market rather sophisticated products on which oligopoly rents can be earned for some time, they are not likely to make a contribution to the simple producer and consumer goods that a basic needs approach calls for. (They may, however, contribute to intermediate goods, capital goods, and exports.) Such products would be readily imitated by local competitors and the rents soon eroded. There can be a conflict between the basic goods the poor need and the advertised consumer goods of the multinationals.

The chairman of a multinational food company writes in the *Columbia Business Journal* on the subject of marketing in developing countries:

> How often we see in developing countries that the poorer the economic outlook the more important the small luxury of a flavored soft drink or

smoke . . . to the dismay of many would-be benefactors the poorer the malnourished are, the more likely they are to spend a disproportionate amount of whatever they have on some luxury rather than on what they need. . . . Observe, study, learn. We try to do it at [our company]. It seems to pay off for us. Perhaps it will for you too.

It is probable that the new multinationals from the developing countries will be more adapted to local needs. The costs to the host country are likely to be lower and the technology and product design more appropriate to local conditions. They often are of smaller scale, use more capital saving techniques, create more jobs, are better adapted to the supply and social conditions in the host country, are more responsive to requests for exporting, local participation, joint ventures, or local training, and design products more adapted to the consumption and production needs of the poor—hoes, simple power tillers, and bicycles, rather than air conditioners, expensive cars, and equipment for luxury apartments. Their special advantage would consist not in the monopolistic package of capital, technology, and marketing, but in special skills. Their costs of overcoming geographical and cultural distance are often less than those of multinationals from industrial countries. Their relative bargaining power is weaker. The visible hand of these multinationals is less visible than that of U.S. companies. Because of these characteristics, their ability to survive in a world in which developing countries become increasingly interdependent among themselves is increased.

References

Jack Daranson, *Technology and the Multinationals* (Lexington, Lexington Books, 1978).

R. J. Barnet and R. Müller, *Global Reach: The Power of the Multinational Corporations* (New York, Simon and Schuster, 1974).

C. Fred Bergsten, Thomas Horst, and Theodore M. Moran, *American Multinationals and American Interests* (Washington, Brookings Institution, 1978).

Lawrence G. Franko, "Multinationals: the End of U.S. Dominance," *Harvard Business Review* (Nov.–Dec. 1978).

David A. Heenan and Warren J. Keegan, "The Rise of Third World Multinationals," *Harvard Business Review* (Jan.–Feb. 1979).

Harry G. Johnson, *Technology and Economic Interdependence* (London, MacMillan Press, 1975).

UNCTAD Seminar Programme, *Intra-firm Transactions and Their Impact on Trade and Development,* May 1978. Report Series No. 2, UNCTAD/OSG/174.

Raymond Vernon, *Sovereignty at Bay: The Multinational Spread of U.S. Enterprises* (New York, Basic Books, 1971).

Louis T. Wells, Jr., "The Internationalization of Firms from Developing Countries" in *Multinationals from Small Countries*, Tamir Agmon and Charles P. Kindleberger, editors (Cambridge, MIT Press, 1977).

V

The Performance of Floating Exchange Rates and International Transmission of Macroeconomic Flux

A decade ago, most of the entries in Part V would have concerned policy under pegged exchange rates, with a few references (almost as afterthoughts) to what life would be like in the unlikely world of floating exchange rates. Times have changed quickly, and today the emphasis is reversed. The most important currencies float against each other (albeit periodically with substantial central bank management). Pegged rates are restricted mostly to developing countries[1] and to the European Monetary System, discussed in Part VI.

In Part V, all of the contributions except those of Michael Mussa and Jude Wanniski reflect the pervasive importance of variable exchange rates. Jacques R. Artus and John H. Young set the stage by even-handedly discussing how floating rates have failed to live up to the expectations of their proponents but have also failed to live down to the fears of their detractors. Many of the issues that receive brief mention in their synthetic and temperate paper are covered in greater detail in subsequent papers.

Volatility has probably been the most surprising aspect of exchange-rate variability since 1973. The observation that "recently large exchange-rate changes cannot be justified by 'fundamental' trends" has been heard so often as to become a platitude. Commentators usually have in mind two initially bewildering features of exchange-rate variation. First, exchange-rate variation has been larger and sharper than variation in any of the underlying variables we usually look at to explain exchange rates—money stocks, prices, interest rates, trade balances, and other such factors. Second, it has not always corresponded even to the *timing* of changes in the underlying determinants. Exchange rates have varied, for example, up to 10 percent in the course of a few days with no significant changes in any of their "fundamental" determinants.

Some experts (for example, Scott Pardee and Dennis Weatherstone) explain such volatility and unpredictability as being caused by capricious and destabilizing speculative movements of "hot money." To others (for example, John Rutledge), this explanation only begs the question. What fundamental changes cause the hot money to move? Economists such as Rutledge only grudgingly and occasionally accept the answers "animal spirits," "herd instincts," and "stampedes." They have too much faith in the ongoing presence of "fundamentals-watchers"—those who try to make quick, huge profits from any irrational "animals" in a "herd" by transacting oppositely to them. The fundamentals-watchers thereby stop any irrational "stampede" before it starts and cause the "herd" to bunch up close to the trail of the fundamentals. Nor will fundamentals-watchers be dismayed by large, irrational "herds." Far from feeling swamped and losing their cool sensibility, they may actually welcome the opportunity to earn larger profits than ever.

The hypothesis that actual exchange rates (or any other prices) will closely track their equilibrium values, as determined by fundamental determinants, is known as the "efficient-markets hypothesis." This hypothesis is occasionally hard to reconcile with experience (Artus and Young observe that the forward market for Italian lira disappeared in early 1976). But, in general, statistical studies have shown its implications to be remarkably consistent with the data. Such studies are described in the somewhat technical paper by Richard M. Levich. Among other things, these studies examine data on exchange rates over time to see if forecasts of those exchange rates, based for example on the economist's models of interest arbitrage or of forward speculation (Levich's equations 1 and 2, respectively), show any systematic pattern of forecast error. If they do, and if such information could be exploited for profit, then foreign exchange markets would be said to be inefficient. To illustrate, if forecasts tended to generate "serial correlation"—day-by-day runs of rising or falling forecast errors—then exchange rates would appear to be following not fundamentals but the "bandwagon" discussed by both Rutledge and Weatherstone. Profits could be made by selling or buying at the beginning of a run and reversing the position before its end.

The importance of such studies is that if the foreign exchange market can be shown to be efficient, then it is tantamount to showing that destabilizing speculators (the irrational "herd") are always dominated by rational speculators (the "fundamentals-watchers"). In that event, one of the most important arguments for central-bank concern over market-determined exchange rates—destabilizing speculation—would have no practical significance. The case for cleanly floating exchange rates would be strengthened considerably.

One problem with this inference, however, is that it tempts people to conclude that finding inefficiency would *justify* central-bank intervention in the foreign exchange market. Yet market failure does not necessarily suggest government success. In fact, protracted and unanticipated central-bank intervention itself might cause exchange-rate movements that appear inefficient, even though the underlying private market really was efficient. And central banks *do* continue to intervene extensively under floating rates (Rutledge), sometimes doing "their best in what may be a losing cause. . . ," conducting "damage control" or "rearguard actions" (Pardee).

Even if destabilizing speculation is granted as a possibly important phenomenon, more economically satisfying explanations can be made for the volatility and apparent unpredictability of exchange rates. These explanations rest on a careful consideration of fundamental determinants. Observers are slowly accepting the fact that good economic reasons exist for the observed short-run volatility of flexible economic magnitudes, such as exchange rates, to be greater than their observed long-run volatility. For good reasons, their observed short-run volatility can also be greater than any predicted volatility based on a narrow view of fundamentals.[2] Most explanations spring from the interplay between flexible economic variables and "sluggish" economic variables—those which respond only slowly to unanticipated economic shocks.

Illustrations of sluggish economic variables abound. Producers are reluctant to change commodity prices frequently or dramatically. Costs of materials, labor services, and rentals are often contractually rigid in the short run. It is sometimes much less costly to allow flexible inventories and order backlogs to adjust than to alter output. Saving and dis-saving to compensate for unexpected capital losses and gains takes time, as does the conversion of saving and dis-saving into real capital. Government policies are adapted to economic flux with well known lags in recognition, implementation, and response.

The contrast between flexible and sluggish variables has an important consequence. Flexible economic variables must do the work of sluggish economic variables, as well as their own work, in the short run after an unanticipated shock. Flexible daily supplies of foreign exchange and flexible demands for it, for example will be affected in the short run not only by what we normally believe to be their fundamental determinants but also by pressures which spill over into the foreign exchange market from other places. These pressures include transitory frustration of savings-investment preferences, temporary failure of commodity and input markets to clear, and short-run divergence between anticipations and realizations.[3] Flexible exchange rates are affected by the same familiar fundamentals and the same less familiar spillovers from sluggish economic behavior.

Not all sluggish economic behavior causes the exchange rate to be more volatile than otherwise, but some does. Artus and Young discuss the sluggish responsiveness of export and import demands to relative price changes, which can cause not only perverse trade balance results from exogenous price shocks (the "J-curve") but also perverse exchange-rate changes from exogenous capital-account shocks (depreciation from a capital inflow and appreciation from an outflow).[4] They also discuss the case, better summarized in the abstract and analytically challenging paper by Rudiger Dornbusch, in which the sluggish response of commodity prices to excess supply or demand causes exchange rates to "overshoot" their new long-run equilibrium value consistent with a monetary shock. That is, monetary expansion can bring about depreciation that is greater in the short run than in the long run, and greater than will appear warranted by "long-run fundamentals." (Monetary contraction will have symmetric effects.) The important lesson of overshooting is that the instability of exchange rates can often exceed the instability of policy. Even relatively stable policy will not assure relatively stable exchange rates.

Much modern work in international economics starts from the hypothesis that financial asset markets clear quite rapidly by price variation in contrast to sluggish commodity and factor markets. The exchange rate is, after all, a relative asset price of one money in terms of another. It should therefore respond rapidly and primarily to economic shocks as they affect demands for and supplies of money and assets that substitute for money (time deposits in banks, including Euro-banks [see Part VI], commercial paper, bonds, and so on). Dornbusch calls this hypothesis the "portfolio-balance" approach to exchange-rate determination, but it is more conventionally referred to as the "asset approach." Its implications are striking. For example, current account surpluses have no tendency to lead to instantaneous appreciation. Exchange rates don't immediately adjust to the current account, but rather to asset stocks, and current account imbalance may persist for some time even under flexible exchange rates (as Artus and Young ruefully reflect). Only sluggishly over time will current account surpluses cause appreciation, and then because the increase in domestically-owned foreign assets that they implicitly represent (see note 2, Artus and Young) causes appreciation sufficient to make wealth-holders content to hold their gradually changing asset portfolios (see Dornbusch).

The "monetary approach" to the exchange rate that Dornbusch also summarizes is a special case of the asset approach.[5] Assets that are portfolio substitutes for money are ignored, except insofar as they affect "the" interest rate—the alternative cost of holding money. Exchange rates respond in a qualitatively familiar way to monetary growth in such a model, but its quantitative implications are somewhat surprising: The exchange rate is unit elastic with respect to the money stock. Surprising also by comparison to Keynesian approaches (summarized by both Dornbusch and Marina v. N. Whitman) is the fact that greater real gross national product (GNP) growth and lower interest rates cause domestic currency to *appreciate* in the foreign exchange market, not to depreciate—because both increase the demand for money in the face of an unchanging supply.

Economic reasons that explain why the *timing* of changes in exchange rates does not match the timing of changes in allegedly fundamental determinants are also becoming well known. Income is to be earned in correctly anticipating movements of flexible economic variables such as exchange rates. Exchange rates will therefore respond immediately to any change in *expectations* regarding their fundamental determinants, as Artus and Young stress—even before the determinants themselves change, and sometimes even when they never change. Expectations in turn are altered in response to any new relevant information. Among such data are announcements of policy intentions by governments and corrections of former anticipations when fundamental changes are actually revealed.

This reasoning suggests that exchange rates respond to errors in forecasting a fundamental change, not to the fundamental change itself. Since a forecast error can be either positive or negative, the movement of the exchange rate at the exact moment of some fundamental change can itself be either positive or negative—to the consternation of commentators who rely on simple, immediate, and unambiguous relationships between exchange rates and money stocks, prices, trade balances, and the like.

The lesson in this for all decision makers on the international monetary scene is that to understand and to predict exchange rates, we must understand and predict how expectations are generated (Dornbusch provides an explicit model), how forecasts are formulated and updated, and how information about impending fundamental changes is disseminated. If, by contrast, we understand only how exchange rates are related in the long run to the fundamental changes themselves, we will be wrong as often as we are right.

Policy authorities are not excluded. In fact, if private decision makers understand what makes policy authorities react better than the authorities understand the private sector, then private agents will often be able to anticipate policy and take steps that alter its influence in a surprising way, or that undermine its effectiveness. The same will often be true if the private sector has more information than the government or better understands expectations formation and other economic behavior. For this reason Pardee, a senior official in the Federal Reserve System, is at pains to defend the government's informational advantage over the private sector and its ability to forecast and interpret more accurately. Note that government policy, in this way of looking at the economy, is systematic and can be predicted by private agents. It is thus not wholly exogenous. This fact complicates greatly discussions of whether government policy—most pertinently, exchange-market intervention aimed at damping the volatility of rates—really works and, if so, whether it really advances economic goals.

But of what concern are the volatility and predictability of variables as exotic as exchange rates? The answer is that exchange rates aren't exotic. They are frequently neglected fundamental determinants of *domestic* economic prosperity—most importantly of jobs, profits, wages, and prices, and not only the jobs, profits, wages, and prices tied up with exports and imports. Point-for-point, changes in exchange rates probably have broader effects on an economy than do bond prices, stock prices, or any other price, as Artus and Young discuss.

This effect holds true even in the U.S., as Whitman eloquently shows. As the 1970s progressed, it became less and less useful to approximate the U.S. as a "closed" economy. It too was affected by the integration of markets across national borders. Market integration brings with it, for example, sympathetic price variation to the extent that exchange rates are fixed, and exchange-rate induced price changes to the extent that they vary. Whitman describes these occurrences not only for commodity prices but also for profits. She does not go as far in this regard as Wanniski, who challenges the reader with the vision, formulated by Robert A. Mundell and Arthur B. Laffer, of a fully integrated world. In their world, the "law of one price" holds for all commodity prices (purchasing power parity), for all asset prices (perfect capital mobility), and would hold for all factor prices except for productivity differences. Wanniski represents (persuasively) an extreme point of view in the opinion of most economists. Most hold views closer to Whitman's evaluation of the empirical evidence on inexact global price/exchange-rate synchronization, and closer to her (and Dornbusch's) discussion of finite "elasticities of substitution" between domestic and foreign goods to their "real" (relative) price. Both suggest that while the world may be interdependent, it is less than perfectly integrated. Nations still seem to be producing differentiated products such as autos, not homogeneous products such as apples (Wanniski's example). Commodity trade still seems motivated by the taste for variety more than by arbitrage aimed at establishing purchasing-power-parity relations between prices and exchange rates.

Variable exchange rates can also have significant effects on employment and capacity utilization—again, even in the U.S. Consider a 10 percent decline in the average value of the dollar that is induced by international reshuffling of assets. In the presence of any price sluggishness,[6] a 10 percent depreciation of this sort improves U.S. international price competitiveness about as much (or as little) as an extra 10 percent tax on all imports (dutiable and nondutiable) coupled *with* an extra 10 percent subsidy to all exports. Groups in this country that clamor for protection from a "flood of imports" or for a "fair shake for American exporters" are sometimes reluctant to appreciate this symmetry, feeling better protected or encouraged by import barriers and export promotion than by exchange rates. No evidence, either empirical or anecdotal, supports their feelings.

The quantitative impact of exchange-rate changes on real economic activity depends most importantly on how close the economy already is to full employment and capacity. If it has already been achieved, the impact may be zero. At the other extreme, if the economy is so far away from that achievement that exchange rate changes have insignificant effects on the trend in prices of domestically-produced goods, then the impact is maximal.

Exchange rates can also affect the domestic cost of living. Many people understand the most straightforward channel. If foreign desires to hold dollar-denominated assets weaken, the resulting dollar depreciation feeds directly into higher U.S. prices of imported merchandise (including raw materials such as natural gas and manufactured inputs such as steel, whose higher prices become higher costs for other U.S. producers). But most people give insufficient weight to three other influences of such exchange-rate changes on domestic prices. All three are summarized by Whitman, and all are important when monetary authorities are "accommodative"—that is, when they have or sense a responsibility to "bend with the wind" as they are "leaning against it" (see Artus and Young).

1. Wage-price spirals are aggravated by the familiar exchange-rate/price link described above. The aggravation is greater the closer the economy is to full employment and capacity.
2. U.S. producers of the large quantity of goods competing with imports are also prompted to raise their prices when the dollar depreciates. To raise prices as dramatically as import prices rise is not usually in their interests, but the induced increase in strictly domestic prices will be greater the more homogeneous the commodity (apples rather than autos), the more difficult it is to expand import-competitive domestic capacity, and the less slack there is in the overall economy.
3. U.S. producers of exportable goods are also prompted to raise prices when the dollar depreciates—even if they don't themselves engage in exports! Increased foreign demand for U.S. products encourages active exporters to raise prices somewhat, except at very low levels of capacity utilization. That encourages nonexporting U.S. producers of exportable products to raise their prices, too, partly from imitation, partly from finding local U.S. demand shifting toward them

and away from the active exporters. Once again, the induced increase in strictly domestic prices will be greater the more homogeneous the commodity, the more difficult it is to increase U.S. production of exportable products (again, whether exported or not), and the less slack there is in the overall economy.

The domestic price effects of exchange-rate changes can also prompt wage/profit effects. Dollar depreciation causes U.S. real wages to fall unless nominal wages are adjusted upward (see Artus and Young). If they are adjusted upward enough to restore the standard of living, costs will rise throughout the economy. Other prices will rise in turn, and depreciation may simply breed inflation, with few or no real effects. If the initial depreciation was policy-motivated, aiming at, perhaps, increased price competitiveness for domestic producers relative to foreigners, or at a reduced trade deficit, it will fail. But the authorities may be tempted to try again, and the recurring sequence of depreciation, inflation, wage escalation, and more inflation is a vicious circle. Its analog in appreciating countries is referred to as a "virtuous circle." In the extreme, vicious and virtuous circles break the link between exchange rates and any real magnitude, so that exchange rates end up influencing and being influenced only by prices and other nominal variables. Dornbusch and Artus and Young discuss these tendencies, which also provide grounds for Wanniski's denial that exchange rates have real effects. Plausibly, such circles are one of the underappreciated consequences (and causes) of exchange-rate variation in the 1970s. Exchange-rate variability seems universally to have increased attentiveness to real income, and encouraged the spread of automatic indexing of wages, salaries, and transfers to prices through cost-of-living adjustments.

That variable exchange rates themselves can sometimes cause flux in jobs, prices, and incomes—especially when that variability is caused by asset shifts and portfolio rebalancing, as stressed by the asset and monetary approaches—is the key to understanding why exchange rates do not insulate an economy in the way that was once supposed (see Artus and Young). Whitman summarizes the surprising lack of evidence for insulation under flexible exchange rates. Empirical work that might have been expected to show declining international synchronization of cycles in real output, money stocks, and prices usually turns out to be inconclusive.

These same domestic impacts of exchange rates undermine simpleminded approaches to international policy coordination. One such simple approach that was popular in the late 1970s is the "locomotive approach" to global expansion. On the basis of Keynesian logic, it was argued that the "locomotive economies" with relatively strong payments positions (Japan, Germany, and the U.S.) should pursue an expansionary policy to draw themselves and the rest of the world out of a global slump. Advocates of the "convoy approach" added the imperative that other countries coordinate and apply their own policies expansively as their payments positions allowed. The chief problem with both approaches was their neglect of the fact that if expansion took place to any great extent through monetary growth, then capital outflows from the expanding economies would cause significant enough depreciation to improve their trade balances,[7] with deterioration of trade balances elsewhere in the world, and corresponding *contractionary* effects on those economies. The chance for such perverse transmission of policy under floating exchange rates with high capital mobility is implicit in Dornbusch's discussion of the Mundell-Fleming model, and is explicit in Whitman's paper. The policy coordination she proposes is better informed than that sketched above.[8]

In light of these macroeconomic complications from variable exchange rates, might fixed exchange rates be better after all? Wanniski says yes, and likens their resource savings to those of currency union among the fifty states (replacing fifty "mom and pop" moneys with the "money supermarket"). What he neglects, however, is that all practical mechanisms for officially stabilizing exchange rates also employ resources. These resources are devoted to exchange-market monitoring and intervention, to administration of official-reserve mechanisms, and to supporting policies. His regional Federal Reserve banks, after all, hire employees, use space, and purchase materials, and whether or not a supermarket uses fewer resources than do fifty corner grocers is uncertain.

Fixed exchange rates have their own problems, some of which are described by Mussa. For example, monetary authorities are forced sooner or later to allow their intervention in the foreign exchange market to affect the monetary base (currency, coins, and commercial-bank deposits at the central bank). When the central bank buys official reserves, commercial banks receive new deposits at the central bank, and the base (and money supply) expands. When the central bank sells official reserves, the base (and the money supply) contracts. Attempts to "sterilize" these effects (perhaps by offsetting open-market sales and purchases, respectively) cannot generally go on forever and are technically very difficult for the great majority of countries without open market operations. The result, even for managed floating, is familiar from the gold standard: Balance-of-payments surpluses or currency-dampening exchange-market intervention tend to expand the money stock; deficits and currency-propping intervention contract the money stock. Payments needs or exchange-rate concerns eventually come to dominate monetary policy, which is therefore weakened in its ability to meet other macroeconomic goals.

Reserve-currency monetary policy can come to dominate monetary events elsewhere in the world, as Whitman mentions and Wanniski emphasizes.

So which is better—clean floating, managed floating, adjustably pegged rates, rigidly fixed rates? Wanniski opts for the last; Artus and Young are more agnostic. The answer depends on time and place. The question will arise again in Part VI in considering the European Monetary System.

Notes

1. Since they usually peg to one or more of the most important currencies, their exchange rates are stable only against those, and vary against others in lockstep with the currencies pegged to. *All* countries in today's world are hence subject to at least some continuous exchange-rate variation.
2. A readable survey of these reasons is Susan Schadler, "Sources of Exchange-Rate Variability: Theory and Empirical Evidence," International Monetary Fund *Staff Papers*, 24 (July 1977), pp. 253–296.
3. A graphic, extreme, and long-lived example is that American energy-related price controls in the late 1970s almost certainly generated additional spillover demands for imported petroleum products by interfering with market clearing within the U.S. economy. Some of the additional flow of dollars received by foreign oil producers was converted steadily to foreign-currency assets to insure diversified financial portfolios, and the dollar was therefore weaker in the foreign exchange market than it would otherwise have been. (This example is so familiar that many commentators now treat it as "fundamental" in its own right.)
4. A. J. Britton, "The Dynamic Stability of the Foreign Exchange Market," *Economic Journal*, 80 (March 1970), pp. 91–96; Jürg Niehans, "Some Doubts About the Efficacy of Monetary Policy Under Flexible Exchange Rates," *Journal of International Economics*, 5 (August 1975), pp. 275–281.
5. One might question Mussa's characterization of the monetary approach as primarily applicable to the long run. The money supply process and money demand behavior are arguably just as predictable (stable) in the short run as any other economic behavior. If equilibrium is realized more quickly and regularly in cash-balance holding behavior than in other markets, the monetary approach may be appropriate in both the short run and the long run. However, other typical assumptions underlying the monetary approach are not likely to hold in the short run after most exogenous shocks—for example, invariant real GNP and a continuous purchasing-power-parity relationship among national price levels. See Dornbusch on the latter.
6. Wanniski, Mundell, and Laffer deny that exchange rate changes have *any* real effects, short run or long run, because they doubt the possibility of persistent price sluggishness when commodity markets are global and purchasing power parity holds.
7. The positive price effects of the depreciation on the expanding country's trade balance would have to dominate the negative effect of higher domestic incomes and prices.
8. Information exchange among governments can be valuable in its own right in shaping intelligent policy, as is implicit in the discussion above of the informational advantage of government over the private sector.

19

Fixed and Flexible Exchange Rates: A Renewal of the Debate

Jacques R. Artus and John H. Young

For some time the view has been developing that the flexible exchange rate system has not accomplished as much as many of its supporters had hoped. More recently, in the discussions associated with the adoption of the European Monetary System, there has been a renewal of interest in the advantages and disadvantages of adopting some form of pegging. It may be time, therefore, to review the extent to which a decade of analysis and experience has altered the thinking on the choice of an exchange rate system. As in the earlier debate, the discussion of fixed and flexible rates in recent years has been almost exclusively directed to the choice of exchange rate systems for developed countries, and the scope of this paper is similarly limited.

The case for a flexible exchange rate system was generally based on hopes of what would result, and the case against on fears of what might happen. Section I of this paper provides a critical analysis of some of the views widely held by adherents of flexible rates. It is pointed out that few today would defend flexible rates on the grounds that they permit governments to take advantage of a long-term trade-off between employment and wage increases, and thus make it possible for countries to have permanently higher rates of economic activity at the expense of higher inflation. Also, it is argued that many adherents of flexible rates gave inadequate weight to the slow speed of adjustment to relative price changes in the goods markets. They thus exaggerated the contribution that exchange rate changes would make in the short run to external adjustment, and similarly overestimated the extent to which flexible rates would insulate countries from external influences and leave them free to pursue domestic objectives through the use of domestic economic policies.

From Jacques R. Artus and John H. Young, "Fixed and Flexible Exchange Rates: A Renewal of the Debate," *Staff Papers,* Vol. 26, No. 4, December 1979. Reprinted by permission of the International Monetary Fund. Some tables, figures, and footnotes omitted. Mr. Artus, Chief of the External Adjustment Division of the Research Department, holds degrees from the Faculty of Law and Economics in Paris and from the University of California at Berkeley. Mr. Young, Deputy Director of the Research Department when this paper was prepared, is now Deputy Director of the African Department. He holds degrees from Queen's University, Kingston, Ontario, and Cambridge University.

Section II takes a similarly critical approach to some of the fears raised by opponents of flexible rates. Some of the concerns are found to have had some basis, particularly the fear that flexible rates would tend to be fluctuating rates, and it is suggested that exchange rates might continue to show considerable instability even under relatively stable underlying economic and financial conditions. There is less empirical evidence to justify other concerns, namely, that flexible rates would have adverse effects on trade and capital flows, but some of the most marked exchange rate instability has been too recent to show much effect as yet. Finally, a brief analysis is given of the complex and mixed relationship between flexible rates and inflation. . . .

I. THE CASE FOR FLEXIBLE EXCHANGE RATES

Much of the earlier support for flexible rates was based on the weakness of the pegged rate system, and Milton Friedman's classic article published in 1953 promised only modest benefits from the adoption of flexible rates. In the main, flexible rates were expected to isolate a country from monetary disturbances originating abroad and to help reconcile countries' divergent rates of monetary growth. It was also expected that flexible rates would lead to a smooth working of the external adjustment process without exchange crises or the need for controls on trade and capital flows. Many of those who supported flexible rates in the 1960s, however, expected much more from them. They believed, in particular, that there was a long-term trade-off between employment and inflation, and saw exchange rate flexibility as an opportunity for individual countries to adopt price-employment objectives of their own choosing. It was also widely held that flexible rates would help to achieve stable growth, in particular by providing a significant measure of insulation from external shocks, real as well as monetary. In the event, the flexible exchange rate system has not accomplished all that its supporters had hoped, and we consider each of the areas in which developments have turned out somewhat differently than expected.

Flexible Rates and the Trade-off

The case for exchange rate flexibility was initially built on a belief that various countries cannot for long maintain the same inflation rate because of the undesirable but unavoidable tendency for governments to mismanage their currencies to various degrees. This was clearly the view advanced by Friedman (1953, pp. 179–80):

> Governments of "advanced" nations are no longer willing to submit themselves to the harsh discipline of the gold standard or any other standard involving rigid exchange rates. They will evade its discipline by direct controls over trade if that will suffice and will change exchange rates before

they will surrender control over domestic monetary policy. Perhaps a few modern inflations will establish a climate in which such behavior does not qualify as "advanced"; in the meantime we had best recognize the necessity of allowing exchange rates to adjust to internal policies rather than the reverse.

Differential rates of inflation must inevitably lead to exchange rate adjustments, and flexible exchange rates were seen to provide the least inconvenient form of adjustment. Flexible rates were not viewed as the first-best system, but only as a second-best system that had to be used because political realities made the fixed rate system unworkable.

This argument based on political realism was soon, however, to be accompanied by the view that it would be desirable for countries to be left free to choose their own inflation rates because there is a long-term trade-off between inflation and unemployment. The choice of the inflation rate came to be seen as an important prerogative of a government, and flexible exchange rates were going to make it possible for each country to maintain its optimal inflation rate. This view was apparent, for example, in Johnson (1969, p. 18):

> On the one hand, there exists a great rift between nations like the United Kingdom and the United States, which are anxious to maintain high levels of employment and are prepared to pay a price for it in terms of domestic inflation, and other nations, notably Western Germany, which are strongly adverse to inflation. Under the present fixed exchange rate system, these nations are pitched against each other in a battle over the rate of inflation that is to prevail in the world economy.... Flexible rates would allow each country to pursue the mixture of unemployment and price trend objectives it prefers, consistent with international equilibrium, equilibrium being secured by appreciation of the currencies of "price stability" countries relative to the currencies of "full employment" countries.

The notion that countries were faced with a trade-off between inflation and unemployment enjoyed considerable vogue during the 1960s, following Phillips's article in 1958. A case can be made that the notion that there was any significant long-run trade-off between inflation and unemployment was never consistent with well-established generalizations about economic behavior. This is indicated by the low-key way in which the original basic criticism of the trade-off was made. Milton Friedman's initial critique of the long-term trade-off was made as part of a comment on a paper by Robert Solow. As Friedman (1966, pp. 58–60) put it in a very matter-of-fact fashion:

> The basic fallacy is to suppose that there is a trade-off between inflation and employment; that is, to suppose that by inflating more over any long period of time, you can have on the average a lower level of unemployment. ... By speeding up the rate of monetary expansion and aggregate demand, you can unquestionably increase output and employment temporarily ... only until people adjust their anticipations ... from a logical

point of view, the true trade-off is between unemployment today and unemployment at a later date. It is not between unemployment and inflation.
There is no long-run, stable trade-off between inflation and unemployment.

Similarly, when Phelps (1972) looked back at his critical analysis of the
long-run trade-off argument, he drew attention in a footnote to the fact
that Professors Fellner and Wallich had put forward similar views at Yale
University prior to the discovery of the Phillips curve, and such reasoning
could be found in the writings of Von Mises in the 1920s and between the
lines of the work of the classical economists.

It is, nevertheless, easy to see how the trade-off concept caught on
among economists and policymakers. In the first place, it was really a cod-
ification of experience rather than a new idea. In the past, it had generally
been true that periods of recession or depression had been characterized by
reduced wage and price increases, and in the extreme case by absolute
declines. Similarly, periods of prosperity had usually been associated with
higher than average wage and price increases. It was not surprising, therefore, that plotting wage increases on the vertical axis and unemployment on
the horizontal axis led to a cluster of points that suggested a curve that was
downward sloping to the right. Second, there appeared to be ample evidence that economies react in this way in the short run, with the rate of
wage increase declining when unemployment was relatively high and tending to rise during periods of relatively low unemployment. From this, it was
only one step to the view that a stable Phillips curve could be combined
with a preference function for a particular society to derive an optimum
choice of unemployment and inflation for an economy. Since it was assumed that each economy had its unique Phillips curve and its unique set of
preferences for inflation and unemployment, it was not to be expected that
countries would choose the same level of wage and price increases.

As indicated above, the final step in which the Phillips curve was
used to choose a particular combination of unemployment and inflation
over the long run was the one which might have given pause; and it was
certainly true that few were prepared to take this step without qualifications. Some, for example, recognized that after a time wage earners would
start building expected future price increases into their wage bargains and
that any particular trade-off would not be stable. It was argued, however,
that it would take time for wage earners to adjust to rising prices, and that
employment gains could be made today at the expense of higher inflation
and unemployment at some later stage. This kind of *apres nous le déluge*
thinking served temporarily to maintain a rear-guard action, but with the
surge of inflation in the late 1960s it became impossible to ignore the not-
so-long-run inflationary effects of trying to raise employment permanently
by using expansionary monetary or fiscal policies. There would thus be few
today who would argue for flexible exchange rates on the grounds that they

give countries a significant amount of freedom over the long run to choose a higher level of employment at the expense of more rapid price increases. The case for flexible rates as a first-best system on these grounds can be dismissed. As will be argued later in this paper, the more prosaic case based on political realities cannot be dismissed as easily.

Flexible Rates and External Adjustment

Flexible rates were also expected to facilitate greatly the working of the international adjustment process, particularly among industrial countries. In the longer run, flexible rates would ensure that, at any given level of economic activity, the supply of and demand for foreign exchange orginating from current account transactions would be consistent with the foreign investment flows that reflect longer-run differences in propensities to save and in investment opportunities among countries. In the short run, they would ensure that financing flows would be available to offset any short-run excess demand for, or supply of, foreign exchange originating from current account transactions and longer-run foreign investment flows without unduly large variations in the exchange rate. Demand-management policies would thus be free from external constraints.

Many of the advocates of flexible rates were, of course, careful to point out that flexible rates were not an instant cure for all external adjustment problems. They recognized that, in particular, protracted imbalances inherited from the fixed rate period could not be eliminated overnight. More generally, they realized that trade flows would adjust to exchange rate changes only after a certain lag. It was also appreciated that, where underlying economic conditions were unstable, private capital flows might be insufficient to prevent some exchange rate overshooting while adjustments in the goods market were taking place. On the whole, however, flexible rates were expected to prevent the recurrence of the protracted external maladjustments experienced in the 1960s and early 1970s, and to eliminate gradually the imbalances inherited from the past at little cost in terms of exchange rate stability.

To a large extent, these expectations have not been realized. To begin with, the adjustment process in the goods market has not worked well. The Federal Republic of Germany, Japan, and Switzerland have maintained very strong current account positions despite the appreciation of their currencies both before and after the establishment of flexible rates. The total current account surplus of these three countries increased from about $8 billion in 1972 to $31 billion in 1978. On the other side, the United States has continued to experience recurring current account deficits despite the marked effective depreciation of the U.S. dollar that took place during that period. There is, of course, no reason to expect all industrial countries to have the same balance of payments structure, since there may be long-run differences among countries in propensities to save and in opportunities for investment. What is required for payments equilibrium, however, is that capital flows should also adjust to differing savings and investment propensities. It has been noted that existing financial conditions in the major surplus countries, the Federal Republic of Germany and Japan, are not well suited for channeling savings abroad on a regular basis. (See Kindleberger (1976) for the Federal Republic of Germany and McKinnon (1978) for Japan.) In the present case, the fact that this pattern of current account balances is not an equilibrium one is apparent from the pressures on exchange markets that it generates.[1]

The difficulties with the adjustment process in the goods markets are also apparent from the resurgence of trade restrictions (see International Monetary Fund (1978)). The argument that flexible rates would remove the balance of payments motive for restrictions on international trade has clearly not been validated. Countries do not seem to be prepared to accept Friedman's (1969, p. 118) view that "if you have a flexible rate and you reduce tariffs, movements in the exchange rate will automatically protect you against having any adverse balance of payments effects, and therefore you are not exporting or importing unemployment." Instead, there has been a tendency toward protectionism on current transactions.

The persistence of the same pattern of current account imbalances eight years after the currency realignment of 1971 and six years after the widespread adoption of flexible rates cannot be blamed on any failure of exchange rates to move. Over a number of years, rates have changed in the right direction and by large amounts. It is, of course, easy to point out that either the current balances or the private capital flows would have had to adjust if the authorities had not intervened in the foreign exchange markets. This, however, is begging the question. The authorities intervened because current account imbalances were putting excessive strains on exchange markets. It is these strains that must be explained.

Economic developments in the 1970s had the unfortunate effect of increasing existing current account imbalances (see Artus (1979)). A marked reduction of the long-run rates of growth in the three surplus countries, the Federal Republic of Germany, Japan, and Switzerland, was accompanied by a fall in domestic investment relative to saving.[2] At the same time, the main deficit country, the United States, was faced with a gradual fall in its production of natural gas and crude petroleum, which led to a sharp increase in its dependence on imports of energy. The position of U.S. manufacturers in their domestic markets was also eroded by the continuous growth of Japanese exports and the emergence of such countries as the Republic of China, the Republic of Korea, and Singapore and Hong Kong as major exporters.

These developments, however, do not explain fully the failure of the adjustment process to work more effectively over the past few years. Another reason seems to be that not enough consideration was given to the requirements for a successful adjustment through exchange rate changes. It has been known since the development of the absorption approach in the late 1940s, and the rediscovery of the monetary approach by Polak (1957), Johnson (1958), and others, that current balances can be changed only if domestic absorption is changed relative to output, and that changes in exchange rates are not likely to have much lasting effect on this ratio via the effects of relative prices or otherwise if the monetary authorities are willing to validate any incipient price changes brought about by exchange rate changes. In particular, if a country is running a large deficit on its current account and wishes to alter this situation, it will have to cut its absorption through the use of a more restrictive monetary and fiscal policy unless it has spare capacity available.

A restrictive policy alone, however, may contribute only to an extended period of unemployment and an extremely slow adjustment in the relative prices between domestic goods and foreign goods[3] because of the downward inflexibility of goods and factor prices that may prevail in the short and medium run. The advantage of an accompanying exchange rate devaluation is that it changes relative prices directly. If the changes in relative prices are sustained and the foreign trade price elasticities are significant, the decrease in the real domestic demand for goods in general may be offset by a switch in foreign and domestic demands toward domestic goods, so that there is no fall in the level of output.

In brief, flexible rates can play a useful role only if three interdependent conditions are met: (1) there is a supporting demand-management policy, (2) changes in the relative prices between domestic goods and foreign goods are sustained, and (3) a shift in relative prices leads to a switch in domestic and foreign demand between foreign goods and domestic goods.

The first condition for effective adjustment through flexible exchange rates was not often present during the past five years. Flexible rates did not work better because, in part, demand-management policies were not usually directed toward adjustment of current account imbalances.[4] Cutting the inflation rate, even at the cost of sluggish domestic aggregate demand, was the major policy target in the surplus countries, while the United States placed a higher priority on reducing unemployment in the short run. . . .

The lack of supporting demand-management policies was not the only problem. A persistent change in the price ratio between domestic goods and foreign goods implies a sustained change in the real wage rate. In the period of high inflation that has prevailed since the early 1970s, money illusion and wage adjustment lags have been reduced and, with explicit and implicit wage indexation clauses widespread in labor contracts, an adjustment of real wages is difficult to bring about. Johnson (1969) and others argued that, under a flexible exchange rate system, exchange rate adjustments would occur gradually, and their impact on the cost of living might remain unnoticed.[5] The integration of the world economy has now proceeded so far, however, that the residents of few, if any, countries have the illusion that the local currency price of imported goods is not a major determinant of the cost of living. In fact, they may be particularly sensitive to exchange rate induced domestic price changes. Exchange rate changes may thus fail to have a lasting effect on the real wage rate, even if the initial impact is to move it back to its equilibrium level. Labor resistance, at least in the case of a depreciation, may gradually move it back to its initial disequilibrium position.

This vicious circle mechanism has been heavily focused on by the critics of flexible rates; see, for example, Economistes Belges de Langue Française (1977). This effect should not, however, be exaggerated. First, the lags involved in the adjustment of the money wage rate to the consumer price index have not been eliminated. Second, and more important, the adjustment of the money wage rates to the consumer price index is not beyond the power of the authorities to alter. This will be discussed in Section II. What is striking, in fact, is the size and persistence of the effective changes in relative labor costs and goods prices brought about by the exchange rate changes, at least for the major industrial countries. . . .

A further disappointment as far as flexible rates and the adjustment process are concerned has been the slow speed of adjustment to changes in relative costs and prices in the goods markets. The extreme case is provided by Switzerland, where exports were still rising in 1978 *in volume terms* despite the 30 to 50 per cent loss in cost and price competitiveness experienced during the previous five years. Swiss exporters are highly specialized and do not have in many cases the possibility of shifting their production to the domestic market. Instead, they have shifted the composition of their export sales toward highly technical products and luxury goods with low price elasticities. The adjustment is certainly easier in larger and more diversified economies, but even in such cases it remains a lengthy process. It is very common to point out that, in order to become established or to expand in a new market, it is important to develop a distribution network, parts and service suppliers, and a reputation for reliability and quality. During the 1960s, German, Japanese, and Swiss manufacturers supplied high-quality goods at very competitive prices, and developed entrenched market positions in a number of products. In the process, these countries became strongly export oriented. Such a process cannot be reversed rapidly.

This is not to say that foreign trade flows do not respond in time to variations in relative prices. General economic reasoning and the historical evidence is convincing on this point, and the bulk of the econometric results point in the same direction.[6] Stern, Francis, and Schumacher (1976), after reviewing more than 130 studies on price elasticities in international trade, conclude that "typical" long-run demand elasticities vary between −0.50 and −1.50 for total imports and between −0.50 and −2.00 for total exports. The studies reviewed are based on data for the 1950s and 1960s. The estimates may be somewhat too high for the 1970s if, as McKinnon (1978) argues, a floating rate regime increases exchange rate uncertainties and weakens the incentives of traders to respond to cost and price differentials among countries. Estimates based on more recent studies tend to show, however, that while the long-run price elasticities may be smaller now they remain substantial. Estimates from the International Monetary Fund's world trade model (see Deppler and Ripley (1978) for a description of the model) that are derived from data that cover the period through 1977, for example, suggest a range of −0.50 to −1.00 for total imports and of −0.50 to −1.50 for total exports.

Econometric estimates of the time lags involved in price effects range widely in the literature from no lag to a mean lag of three or four years. The most persuasive studies tend to find a mean lag of about two years; see, for example, Beenstock and Minford (1976). Over the first few quarters, the volume effects of an unanticipated change in the exchange rate is bound to be small, if only because of the long lags between orders and deliveries. In the Fund's world trade model, for example, the sum of the elasticities of demand for imports and exports is smaller than unity for 9 of the 14 industrial countries over the first year and a half. . . . With the perverse effects of an exchange rate change on the terms of trade that prevail over that period (Spitäller (1979)), the result is the well-known J-curve effect. Initially, the trade balance worsens with an exchange rate depreciation and improves with an appreciation. This kind of lag no doubt explains why countries are often tempted to use more direct tools, such as trade controls, despite their welfare costs.

Flexible Rates and Stable Growth

Another major argument for flexible rates was that they would make it possible for national authorities to achieve more stable rates of economic growth. The argument was based on three propositions: (1) flexible rates insulate a country's level of economic activity from foreign expansion and contraction; (2) flexible rates increase the degree of control of the authorities over the money supply and allow them to use both monetary and fiscal policy to influence the level of economic activity without constraint from the external balance; (3) the efficacy of monetary policy is greatly enhanced by flexible rates, that is, the effect of a given change in the money supply on the level of economic activity is larger under flexible rates.

The events of recent years suggest that all three of these propositions are questionable. The degree of economic interdependence seems to have been, if anything, greater since 1973 than before, particularly among

European countries, whether in the "snake" arrangement or not. Similarly, there has been no sign either of greater economic stability brought about by an increase in the control of the authorities over the money supply or of much evidence of an increase in the efficacy of such policies.

The conclusion of greater insulation from variations in economic activity abroad under flexible rates is based on two assumptions: (1) a real external disturbance leads to an exchange rate change and (2) the exchange rate change prevents the external disturbance from having an effect on the domestic economy. The effect of a fall in foreign demand, for example, is seen to lead to a depreciation of the exchange rate rather than to a deterioration of the trade balance, which would have a deflationary effect on the domestic economy. These two assumptions, however, seem to be valid only to a limited extent.

Whether an external disturbance leads to an exchange rate change will depend in part on whether the disturbance is viewed as being temporary. In the case of a temporary disturbance, capital flows may have a stabilizing influence on the exchange rate as market participants maintain their views on the longer-term equilibrium value of the exchange rate. When the background is stable and there is a belief in a "normal" exchange rate, as during much of the period in which the Canadian dollar floated in the 1950s, offsetting effects of this kind have been found. Indeed, it is possible to envisage capital flows playing an even more active role. If the fall in foreign demand results from a recession abroad, accompanied by a decrease in the rate of return on investment, capital may tend to move to the home country, where the level of economic activity is sustained and the interest rates are higher. Modigliani and Askari (1973) argue that this factor may more than offset the effect of the worsening of the trade balance, so that the exchange rate appreciates rather than depreciates. In this case, flexible rates would increase the impact of foreign disturbances on domestic economic activity.

In the above discussion of the external adjustment process, however, it was noted that capital flows had not offset completely the effects of demand induced disturbances on the current account in recent years. As pointed out in that discussion, the key factor in the failure of the exchange rate to provide insulation is the lag in the response of trade flows to changes in relative prices.

All the major econometric models of world trade—including the LINK model presented in Ball (1973) and the Fund's world trade model described in Deppler and Ripley (1978)—show conclusively that year-to-year changes in the volume of imports and exports are dominated by variations in real aggregate demand. During the first one or two years, offsetting effects that may result from exchange rate induced variations in relative prices are generally only a small fraction of the effects of demand changes. Even over a longer period (for example three years) the effect of demand changes remains large relative to the offsetting effects of exchange rate changes. Some calculations of the magnitudes of the fall in exchange rates necessary to offset increases in demand for 14 industrial countries based on the Fund's world trade model were included in the Fund's *Annual Report, 1978.* The results indicate that an increase of 1 per cent in manufacturing output maintained for three years has a strong negative effect on the trade balance in all 14 countries, ranging from 1½ to 3⅓ per cent of 1977 imports. It was estimated, by comparison, that in most cases exchange rate declines of 5 to 15 per cent would be necessary to produce the same trade balance effects.

There are, thus, strong grounds for concluding that a flexible rate does not provide an automatic mechanism that will insulate a country's level of economic activity from foreign expansion and contraction.[7] If a flexible rate contributes to a more stable rate of growth, it would be because it frees the authorities from any balance of payments constraint and allows them to direct demand-management policies toward the achievement of domestic stability, or because it increases the degree of control of the authorities over the money supply and enhances the efficacy of demand-management policies.

Until recently, it was thought that flexible rates would allow the authorities to control the money supply (or, more precisely, the monetary base); and, indeed, that is true if the flexible rate regime is one where the monetary authorities never worry about exchange rate developments in forming their monetary policy. It has become obvious in recent years, however, that such a policy of benign neglect may lead in many cases to exchange rate instability. Artus (1976) and Dornbusch (1977), among others, have focused attention on the high elasticity of the exchange rate with respect to (unanticipated) changes in the money supply. While there is some difficulty in explaining this high elasticity (a further discussion of this issue is given later), the evidence is clear that uncoordinated monetary policy changes among countries often tend to lead to large changes in exchange rates. Even if the money supply is kept stable in the various countries, exchange rate instability may be a problem because of the short-run instability of the demand for money.

These considerations do not, of course, detract from the fact that flexible rates allow the authorities to maintain, in the longer run, a monetary growth that is consistent with their ability to keep a low inflation rate. They do, however, indicate the consequences that can follow from attempts to use monetary policy to affect the level of economic activity over the short run without regard to the effects on the exchange rate.

The argument that flexible rates enhance the efficacy of demand-management policies, particularly monetary policies, has also turned out to be somewhat deceptive. The argument is similar to the one presented for insulation. It was derived from the observation that the change in money supply is likely to be accompanied by a variation in the exchange rate that would reinforce the effect of the money supply change. As discussed above, however, the response of the volume of the foreign trade flows to a change in the exchange rate is likely to be so small in the short run that the additional expansionary effect would not be noticeable. A further weakness in the efficacy argument is that price increases caused by the exchange rate depreciation may sharply reduce the expansionary effect of the increase in the money supply. Monetary policies affect the level of economic activity only if prices in the goods markets adjust slowly to a monetary change. By speeding up the price adjustment, flexible rates reduce the efficacy of monetary policies.[8]

The efficacy argument is also to some extent misleading. The magnitude of the effect of a given policy change is important, but it is even more important that the effect of that policy change be foreseeable. There is not, unhappily, much reason to believe that flexible rates increase the extent to which the authorities can reliably estimate the quantitative effect of a certain discretionary change in monetary policies. This effect will depend to a large extent on the behavior of the exchange rate and the magnitude and timing of the effects of exchange rate changes on prices and on the level of economic activity in the short run. In this area, it is particularly difficult to make reasonably accurate forecasts.

II. THE CASE AGAINST FLEXIBLE EXCHANGE RATES

If the advantages of flexible rates have fallen short of the expectations of their advocates, it must also be recognized that their drawbacks have been less damaging than was anticipated by their detractors. The word drawback may not even be appropriate to characterize the disasters that some suggested would occur if flexible rates were adopted. It was argued—for example, by Roosa (1967, p. 52)—that, as a practical matter, a system of flexible rates was not workable. As he put it:

> . . . I have never met anyone who has attained the competence of a seasoned trader who would be prepared to continue in the business if, by some sleight of hand, all parities were to be abandoned and the central banks were barred from entering the markets in their own currencies. Many, and I include myself, would probably want to withdraw from trading activities even under the sort of flexible-rate system in which the central banks were allowed a role, so long as there were no parity guidelines to get us into the right ball park.

These fears were rapidly discarded as experience was gained with the new system. Three other traditional arguments against flexible rates have, however, shown more staying power, but only in a milder form than initially advanced. The first is that flexible rates are inherently unstable; the second, that exchange rate uncertainties disrupt domestic and international economic relations; and the third, that flexible rates promote faster inflation.

Exchange Rate Instability

Advocates of flexible rates had suggested that exchange rates would reflect "underlying economic conditions"; as long as these conditions were stable, exchange rates would also be stable. The underlying economic conditions in question were not precisely defined, but the impression was left that exchange rates would move only to the extent necessary to offset differential rates of inflation and to compensate for changes in real factors, such as tastes and production techniques, that usually take place only gradually. These views, however, never seemed to prevail completely over the argument that flexible rates would be unstable and would disrupt domestic and international economic relations.

After six years of flexible rates, a good deal of evidence has been accumulated that indicates that flexible rates tend to be unstable in the commonsense meaning of moving up and down a lot from day to day, month to month, and year to year. . . .

Much of the exchange rate instability . . . reflects the marked domestic and international instability of recent years, including the breakup of the par value system, the oil price increase of 1973, high and divergent inflation rates, and the worldwide recession followed by recoveries at varying rates among industrial countries. However, there are also a number of developments that suggest that exchange markets with flexible rates may be characterized by the kind of instability generally found in other markets that are strongly influenced by expectations. . . . In all these cases, there seems to be the same lack of parallelism in the short run between the exchange rate change and the broad movements in the major monetary aggregates and price indicators.[9] Exchange rates were sticky for a certain period, then changed suddenly, overshot, and finally moved back to some extent, a pattern that is alien to the gradual adjustment expected by advocates of flexible rates.

In part, the stickiness of exchange rates reflected governmental intervention. . . . In addition, however, reasons for the instability must be found in the nature of the exchange rate determination process. Nordhaus (1978, p. 250) has argued that volatility is to be expected in an "auction market" such as the exchange market under floating rates simply because there are incessant surprises. As he puts it:

> In those pure auction markets where prices are the main shock-absorber, considerable price volatility is the result. These conditions generally prevail in raw foods and commodities markets, in markets for many financial instruments such as common stocks, or when a regime of pure floating exchange rates exists. Such volatility is an intrinsic feature of real-world auction markets—markets in which there are incessant surprises due to

weather, changes in taste, inventions, political upheaval, inflation, recession, and boom, etc.[10]

This auction market characteristic is important, but it certainly does not account fully for the magnitude of the observed short-run exchange rate movements. To understand why a large measure of instability may be an inherent characteristic of flexible rates, it is useful to review recent developments in the analysis of exchange rate determination. The basis of this analysis is that exchange rates among currencies are the relative prices of these currencies and [are] therefore sensitive to any change in the supply of, or demand for, financial assets denominated in these currencies. Indeed, at every point in time the exchange rate must be at such a level that the amount of financial assets denominated in a particular currency matches the amount that market participants desire to hold. This is not to say that relative prices in the goods markets do not influence exchange rates, but the adjustment process in the goods markets works so much more slowly than in the financial asset markets that they play a somewhat secondary role in the short run.[11] The important contribution of this approach is that, by treating exchange rates as financial asset prices, it focuses attention on the strong influence of expectations. Thus, it is not only the amount of assets available today that influences asset prices but also the amount expected to be available tomorrow. It is the instability of these expectations that appears to be a major factor in short-run exchange rate instability.[12]

It is easy to explain why the expectations of market participants tend to be unstable. Forecasting the future course of monetary and other management policies in different countries relative to each other is normally, at best, a matter of guesswork. Mussa (1976), among others, has pointed out how tenuous the information that forms the base for such forecasts usually is, and how any new piece of information, even if somewhat unreliable, may lead to a substantial revision of exchange rate expectations and a sharp movement in the spot rate.[13] The instability of expectations is increased further if market participants have reason to believe that domestic price changes related to exchange rate variations may lead to accommodating changes in the money supply. Furthermore, the money supply is not the only element that affects the exchange rate, so that, even if the authorities gradually stabilize expectations with respect to monetary policies by respecting preannounced monetary policy targets, exchange rate expectations would not necessarily be stable.

All these elements are, of course, not new to the debate. The new element, however, is the realization that, once the authorities refuse to be limited to policies that will keep the exchange rate along a predetermined time path or at a certain parity, market participants will normally be quite uncertain as to the future path of the exchange rate even when underlying economic conditions are not markedly unstable. Thus, there seems every likelihood that flexible rates will continue to show some short-term instability in response to the inherent instability of market participants' expectations. Of course, the more unstable the underlying economic conditions are, the more unstable expectations will be.

The instability of expectations is not the only factor leading to exchange rate instability. Various institutional rigidities have also been focused on in the context of the asset market approach to explain exchange rate instability. McKinnon (1976) has pointed out that there might be an inadequate supply of private capital available for taking net positions in either the forward or spot markets on the basis of long-term exchange rate expectations.[14] Thus cyclical variations in the demand for foreign exchange originating from trade or financial activities that may be sustained for a number of years may lead to large exchange rate movements because of a lack of investors with both the funds and the willingness to take a longer-run open position. Branson (1977), Dornbusch (1976), and Kouri (1976) have, rather, focused on the slow speed of adjustment in the goods markets in cases of unexpected monetary policy changes to explain exchange rate instability. Although their models differ, they all embody the hypothesis that asset markets are continuously in equilibrium, while the goods markets adjust only gradually. They show that under such conditions the immediate response of the exchange rate to a monetary policy change overshoots the new longer-run equilibrium rate.

This "monetarist" explanation of exchange rate movements should not obscure the fact that the inadequate current balance adjustment discussed in Section I is also one of the causes of exchange rate instability. The first reason is that a current account surplus leads to an accumulation of net foreign assets. This in turn may lead to an appreciating exchange rate to the extent that a fall in the relative price of foreign assets is needed as an incentive for domestic agents to increase the share of these assets in their portfolios. Probably more important, however, is the impact of current balance developments on exchange rate expectations. The emergence of a current account surplus that is not related to temporary disturbances may, at times, be rightly interpreted as an indication that a rise in the real exchange rate is required if a lasting adjustment is to take place.[15] How much of a change in the nominal rate will be necessary to bring about the needed adjustment is, however, the type of question that cannot be answered with any degree of certainty. Market participants will, therefore, continually reassess their views of the needed exchange rate change on the basis of actual current balance developments without always being able to discount properly the effects of temporary divergences in economic cycles, J-curve effects of exchange rate changes, and so forth.

A further possible source of instability in the present system is related to the fact that several currencies are held by central banks as part of their international reserves. Any major action to change the composition of these reserves could lead to sharp exchange rate movements and disorderly market conditions. Because holders of large reserves are conscious of the possible harmful effects of their actions on the value of their portfolios and on the system as a whole, they tend to avoid major portfolio shifts. As a result, they may maintain larger stocks of certain reserve currencies than they would choose to have, and the possibility that some of these balances might come on the market creates uncertainty in the minds of both private and official holders. The overhang of official sterling balances seems to have played a destabilizing role through 1976.[16] More recently, there have been signs that actual or potential diversification out of U.S. dollar reserve balances was a factor in the weak behavior of the U.S. dollar in 1978.

The inherent instability of expectations, limitations on the role of stabilizing capital movements, the slow speed of adjustment in the goods markets, the persistence of current account imbalances, and the existence of a multiple reserve currency system account for much of the volatility in exchange market behavior in recent years. There are, moreover, cases in which extrapolative expectations or bandwagon behavior on the part of market participants appears to have played a role. Dooley and Shafer (1976) have found some tentative evidence indicating that such effects may occur, and it is hard to explain exchange market developments in October 1978 without reference to extrapolative expectations or bandwagon effects. Out of 22 market days in October, the U.S. dollar depreciated against the deutsche mark on 19 days, with the other 3 days characterized by relatively flat movements.

The Costs of Instability

While the evidence is building up to suggest that a floating rate system is characterized by a good deal of what is commonly regarded as exchange rate instability, it is not clear how important any detrimental effects of this instability have been or will prove to be. With forward rates of exchange seeming to contain little information on actual movements of spot rates in the future (see Cornell (1977)), this instability is probably accompanied by an increase in uncertainty. It is difficult, however, to assess the detrimental effects that may follow from the increase in uncertainty. These detrimental effects could include (1) a reduction in foreign trade, (2) a decline in foreign investment, and (3) the adverse effects resulting from changes in the value of reserve currencies.

The risks of a dislocation of international economic relations was a major theme of the critics of a flexible rate system in the 1950s and 1960s. It was argued that exchange rate flexibility, by increasing the uncertainty associated with international transactions, would discourage both foreign trade and international investment.[17] The additional uncertainty associated with foreign trade could be related to the risk of exchange rate changes during the period between contract and settlement, or to the risk of changes in the relative cost and price competitiveness of countries because of exchange rate changes. Supporters of flexible rates argued that forward markets could be used to take care of the first type of risk, and that over the longer run exchange rate changes would reflect changes in price and cost competitiveness.

The experience of the past few years has indicated that some of the difficulties likely to be encountered by those engaging in international transactions were treated rather casually in the earlier debate. It might appear that a businessman has eliminated exchange risk if he covers his position with a forward transaction, but, if his competitor does not and is thereby able to offer goods at a lower price, the forward transaction does not eliminate all the consequences of a change in the spot rate. Further, little was said about the difficulties firms would encounter in avoiding major fluctuations in their profit figures, and the problems that would be posed by their own internal accounting arrangements or externally applied accounting standards.

While life may have become more complicated for those engaged in international transactions, this does not necessarily mean that there has been a significant effect on foreign trade or investment. Indeed, to date, the statistical evidence tends to be negative. Hooper and Kohlhagen (1978) introduced various proxies for exchange rate uncertainty (variability) in import and export volume equations for the United States and the Federal Republic of Germany for 1965–75, and found they did not play any significant role. Various tests making use of the Fund's world trade model have also failed to detect any systematic effects of exchange rate uncertainty on disaggregated trade flows for individual industrial countries through 1977.

The evolution of the trade pattern of the snake countries is also interesting in this context. While the proportion of intra-snake manufacturing trade to non-snake trade expanded in the late 1960s and early 1970s, it contracted slightly between 1972 and 1977 despite the increased stability of intra-snake exchange rates relative to exchange rates with non-snake countries during that period.[18] Such tests are not precise enough to reject the hypothesis that exchange rate instability has had harmful effects on foreign trade flows. But even taking into account the limitations of the data and the fact that there are likely to be long lags in the response of trade to exchange rate instability, these tests do raise doubts that *major* effects have been present.

Exchange rate instability did not have more of an effect on international trade in part because facilities for hedging have normally remained adequate. It is only in a few instances, such as the case of the Italian lira in early 1976, that forward markets have dried up because of excessive uncertainty.[19] The costs of hedging in such markets as measured by the bid-ask spreads have increased with the move to flexible rates, but they still represent only a minute fraction (usually about $1/10$ of 1 per cent or less) of the value of a currency. Forward contracts for as long as a year are not unusual, and, at a price, a trader can always cover by borrowing in one market and lending in the other. In many cases, multinational corporations can hedge internally by matching the timing of their future receipts and disbursements in particular currencies. It remains difficult, however, to hedge against the risk that exchange rate movements that are sustained for, say, two to three years may temporarily change relative costs and prices in the goods markets.

It is even more difficult to assess the effects of exchange rate instability on long-term investment flows, which cannot be easily covered in forward markets or through other hedging mechanisms. So far, little evidence has accumulated that financial and nonfinancial enterprises have significantly curtailed international capital movements in response to exchange rate fluctuations. To the extent that it is expected that changes in relative price levels and shifts in exchange rates will tend to be offsetting, some built-in safeguards are present, and the other major determinants of investment flows then tend to dominate decisions. These include, in foreign direct investment, positive advantages in terms of direct access to material inputs, skilled labor, markets, and so forth. It is worth emphasizing, however, that even if exchange rates adjust to relative price and cost levels over the long run, instability in exchange rates and relative prices in the short run can have detrimental effects, because in planning their investment strategy firms must put a high weight on expected rates of return in the early years of a project. These rates of return are uncertain in situations of exchange rate instability.

Exchange rate instability involving a major reserve currency raises particular problems. For example, developments with respect to the U.S. dollar in 1978 had major repercussions throughout the system, as virtually every country found some of its important bilateral rates changing significantly. Moreover, with the bulk of official reserves held in U.S. dollars, this meant major changes in the value of international reserves, and put pressure on reserve holders to consider diversifying their portfolios. The precipitous decline in the U.S. dollar relative to the deutsche mark and the Japanese yen generated a pronounced reaction against the floating system. It may turn out, retrospectively, that this was a structural change that needed to take place and would have been difficult in the extreme to bring about without the contribution made by the free play of market forces. The immediate effect, however, was to add to the disillusionment with the floating rate system.

These brief comments on the costs of exchange rate instability have touched upon the conventional quantifiable costs. While there are clearly some grounds for the kind of irritation that seems to have developed about the operation of the flexible rate system, the extent of the reaction is somewhat surprising.[20] Why is it that it is rare these days to hear vigorous criticism of fluctuations in other financial markets, such as the equity or bond markets, and such strong feelings about exchange rate fluctuations? Complacency about stock market fluctuations was not always the general rule. Keynes's comments in his *General Theory* (p. 159) are well known:

> Speculators may do no harm as bubbles on a steady stream of enterprise. But the position is serious when enterprise becomes the bubble on a whirlpool of speculation. When the capital development of a country becomes a by-product of the activities of a casino, the job is likely to be ill-done. The measure of success attained by Wall Street, regarded as an institution of which the proper social purpose is to direct new investment into the most profitable channels in terms of future yield, cannot be claimed as one of the outstanding triumphs of *laissez-faire* capitalism—which is not surprising, if I am right in thinking that the best brains of Wall Street have been in fact directed towards a different object.[21]

There is little echo of this view in current discussions of equity markets, but clearly there is a good deal of this kind of sentiment in discussions of exchange markets. There are, no doubt, many reasons for this, the most obvious being that any "cure" for equity market instability may be either impossible to find or worse than the disease. Decades of experience under the gold standard and under par values do not, however, suggest that stability in exchange rates is either impossible or necessarily hazardous to the effective operation of economies. Moreover, the ordinary public can escape direct involvement in equity markets, even if some of their resources are committed to these markets by their pension funds or insurance companies. The exchange rate, however, has very broad effects on all who produce or consume goods and services that are traded internationally. Thus, the statement that no government can be indifferent to the exchange rate is as much a political as an economic observation.

Flexible Rates and Inflation

Few characteristics of modern society have failed to be identified as a cause of inflation, and flexible rates are no exception. The fact that the present inflation originated and developed under pegged rates at least limits the extent to which flexible rates can be identified as a possible culprit. Even among those who have no doubt that persistent increases in prices in terms of any particular currency cannot occur unless the authorities responsible for that currency follow accommodating policies, there are some who argue that there are inflationary risks associated with flexible rates. These arguments are all variants of the notion that it is harder to maintain the discipline of prudent monetary and fiscal policies under flexible rates than under fixed rates.

It has often been suggested, for example, that changes in exchange rates can exercise asymmetrical effects. It is argued that nominal prices in goods markets are inflexible downward, so that initially the increase in the domestic prices of goods tends to be larger in depreciating countries than the decrease in these prices in appreciating countries. Whether this is so is arguable, but in any case a permanent effect on the overall price levels in the two countries is not to be expected as long as no change is made in their demand-management policies. Thus, the argument has to be pushed one step further.

The second level of the argument is that the money wage rate is inflexible downward.[22] Thus, a fall in the domestic prices of traded goods leads to a fall in profit margins and in the level of economic activity in the appreciating country, while in the depreciating country a rise in wages in response to the depreciation reduces any increase in profit margins or in the level of economic activity. There is, thus, a fall in the aggregate level of economic activity for the two countries taken together. Under such conditions, the monetary and fiscal authorities may take expansionary action, and exchange rate variations could thus lead to more expansionary policies and thus to a higher rate of inflation for the world as a whole.

A criticism of this line of argument has been raised by Crockett and Goldstein (1976). This criticism is that the exchange rate instability under discussion is to a large extent short run. Given the slowness of the effects of exchange rate changes on activity levels and resource allocation in the goods markets, it is unlikely that short-run exchange rate movements have any noticeable effects on these variables and unemployment. There is, therefore, no reason to suppose that the authorities will adopt more expansionary policies in response to week-to-week or month-to-month fluctuations. This general point is valid, but there are also cases of longer-run exchange rate instability.

It has also been argued that undue reliance on the exchange rate to correct certain external and domestic imbalances can push a country into a vicious circle of depreciation and inflation. Typical cases are those where labor unions succeed in obtaining an increase in the money wage rate that exceeds the increase in the marginal value product of labor, or where an exogenous shock, such as the oil price increase of 1973, leads to a deterioration in the terms of trade. If real wage rates are inflexible downward and demand-management policies are accommodating, then currency depreciation can lead to price increases, owing to the presence of imported goods in the price index, and this in turn leads to higher increases in wages that lead to higher prices, more depreciation, and a further feedback to prices, wages, and the exchange rate.

Asymmetrical price and wage effects and vicious circles would have very limited effects on inflation if the authorities did not accommodate incipient domestic costs and price increases by following expansionary monetary policies. Thus, it is demand-management policies rather than flexible rates that are the fundamental factor, and the case for a positive association of flexible rates and inflation rests on the view that there may be occasions in which the authorities feel constrained to accommodate incipient domestic cost and price increases rather than accept temporary unemployment. Against this must be counterbalanced the greater freedom stable countries have had to pursue prudent policies, and thereby to enjoy a virtuous circle of currency appreciation and falling rates of price increase. It should also be noted that depreciating rates have not freed governments from pressures to take strong action to check adverse developments. Indeed, rapid depreciation is widely regarded as clear evidence of imprudent policies, and the fact that an underlying disequilibrium is not masked by a fixed rate and restrictions on the flow of goods and capital has in a number of cases played a positive role in bringing about adjustment.

Notes

1. Artus (1979) contains a detailed discussion of this issue.
2. The current account surplus is by definition equal to domestic output minus domestic absorption, or to domestic saving minus domestic investment.
3. The argument presented here in terms of domestic goods and foreign goods needs to be modified when the elasticity of substitution between internationally tradable goods produced by the various countries is extremely high. In such a case, the argument must be developed to some extent in terms of internationally tradable goods versus nontradable goods.
4. For a detailed analysis of the policy choices made by the Federal Republic of Germany, France, the United Kingdom, the United States, and Sweden during 1972–75, see Black (1977).
5. As Kindleberger (1969, p. 95) humorously put it, it is only "banana republics" that get excepted by Johnson from flexible rates on the ground that "they do not have the illusion that the price of bananas in local money is a major determinant of the cost of living, as contrasted with the price of imported goods."
6. It should not be necessary for the economics profession to repeat the unfortunate experience of the early postwar period, when the notion of a dollar shortage was developed despite the difficulty of reconciling such a result with economic theory and economic history. "Prices don't matter" is a proposition on about the same plane as "money doesn't matter."
7. It similarly follows that real disturbances originating at home will tend to be transmitted abroad in large measure under flexible rates, and thus their effects on the domestic economy will be diffused.

   This conclusion is also verified by empirical studies (e.g., Ripley (1978)), which seem to suggest that the international transmission of fluctuations in economic activity is no less powerful under flexible rates than under fixed rates.
8. It is mainly on the basis of this argument that many authors, such as Argy (1975), have concluded that monetary policy will tend to have stronger price and weaker employment effects in the short run under flexible rates.
9. The 26 per cent and 34 per cent depreciations of the U.S. dollar against the deutsche mark and Japanese yen, respectively, from end-June 1977 to end-October 1978 in particular, were out of proportion with underlying developments, at least in terms of either rates of monetary growth or inflation rate differentials. Rates of change in MI and the gross national product (GNP) deflators are indicated below. A comparison based on other monetary and price indicators can be found in the Fund's *Annual Report, 1979* (Table 11, p. 38).

	MONEY (MI) (PERCENTAGE CHANGES BASED ON PERIOD AVERAGES)				GNP DEFLATOR (PERCENTAGE CHANGE)			
	1975	1976	1977	1978	1975	1976	1977	1978
Germany, Fed. Rep.	14.1	10.2	8.3	13.8	6.7	3.3	3.6	3.5
Japan	10.3	14.2	7.0	10.8	12.8	5.5	5.4	3.7
United States	4.5	5.1	7.2	8.3	9.6	5.2	5.9	7.2

10. Nordhaus also points out that the day-to-day variability of the Dow-Jones industrial average in the recent period had been almost 0.5 per cent a day, compared with 0.1 and 0.2 per cent for the nominal value of the U.S. dollar as measured by a trade-weighted index.

11. Several variants of this "asset market" approach are presented in the papers included in *Scandinavian Journal of Economics*, Vol. 78 (No. 2, 1976), and discussed in Bilson (1979), Dornbusch and Krugman (1976), Schadler (1977), and Isard (1978).

12. Here also the word *unstable* is used in its commonsense meaning of moving up and down frequently, rather than in the sense of moving continuously away from equilibrium once disturbed.

13. Countries may have monetary targets, but in practice such targets are not often respected for long and thus do not necessarily stabilize the expectations of market participants with respect to the future time paths of money supplies.

14. As Isard (1978) notes, the unwillingness of banks and multinational corporations to take open positions on the basis of longer-run exchange rate expectations is to some extent related to the imprecision of these expectations.

15. At other times, the surplus on current account may be the result of factors that provide their own offset to the current account surplus in the form of capital flows.

16. In February 1977, a medium-term stand-by credit facility of the equivalent of $3 billion was extended to the Bank of England by a group of European central banks and the central banks of Canada, Japan, and the United States. This facility could only be drawn on if U. K. official reserves were less than the equivalent of $6,750 million, and it has not been used in the succeeding two years.

17. In his *Treatise on Money*, Keynes (p. 333 and pp. 333–34) differentiated between the effects of exchange rate fluctuations on foreign trade and foreign investment. On the first, he commented: "So far as foreign trade is concerned, I think that the advantage of fixing the maximum fluctuations of the foreign exchanges within the quite narrow limits is usually much over-estimated. It is, indeed, little more than a convenience." On international investment his view was different: "When we come to Foreign Lending, however, the advantages of a fixed exchange rate must . . . be estimated much higher. In this case the contracts between borrower and lender may cover a far longer period than would be contemplated by any practicable dealings in forward exchange."

18. The snake countries considered here are Belgium-Luxembourg, Denmark, the Federal Republic of Germany, the Netherlands, and Norway.

19. Forward markets do not exist for the currencies of a number of developing countries. Normally, however, these currencies are pegged to a major currency, and the forward market for that currency can be used for hedging purposes. Those currencies that are pegged to a basket can achieve partial hedging by operating in the forward market of a major currency.

20. Surveys of U. S. entrepreneurs are reviewed in Burtle and Mooney (1976). For a survey of U. K. entrepreneurs, see Oppenheimer (1978). U. K. businessmen seem to react more negatively than their U. S. counterparts to exchange rate instability.

21. It is interesting that one of Keynes's proposals for dealing with this problem, namely, a "substantial Government transfer tax on all transactions" to discourage the "predominance of speculation over enterprise" in the stock market, has recently been repeated by Tobin (1978) for exchange market transactions.

22. It has been pointed out that, given prevailing inflationary conditions, the inflexibility problem is not relevant since there is sufficient room for rates of change of prices and money wages to be reduced because of exchange rate movements without ever becoming negative (see, for example, Claasen (1976)). This point is not crucial, however, since the downward inflexibility may apply to some extent to the rate of change of the money wage rate as well as to its level.

References

Argy, Victor, "The Dynamics of Monetary Policy under Flexible Exchange Rates: An Exploratory Analysis," in *Papers in Monetary Economics* (Reserve Bank of Australia, 1975), pp. 1–42.

Artus, Jacques R. (1976), "Exchange Rate Stability and Managed Floating: The Experience of the Federal Republic of Germany," *Staff Papers*, Vol. 23 (July 1976), pp. 312–33.

———(1979), "Persistent Surpluses and Deficits on Current Accounts Among Major Industrial Countries" (unpublished, International Monetary Fund, May 24, 1979).

Ball, Robert J., ed., *The International Linkage of National Economic Models* (Amsterdam, 1973).

Beenstock, M. C., and A. P. L. Minford, "A Quarterly Econometric Model of Trade and Prices 1955–1972," in *Inflation in Open Economies*, ed. by J. M. Parkin and G. Zis (University of Manchester, 1976).

Bilson, John F. O., "Recent Developments in Monetary Models of Exchange Rate Determination," *Staff Papers*, Vol. 26 (June 1979), pp. 201–23.

Black, Stanley W., *Floating Exchange Rates and National Economic Policy* (Yale University Press, 1977).

Branson, William H., "Asset Markets and Relative Prices in Exchange Rate Determination," *Sozialwissenschaftlich Annalen*, Vol. 1 (1977).

Burtle, James, and Sean Mooney, "International Trade and Investment under Floating Rates: The Reaction of Business to the Floating Rate System," in *Exchange Rate Flexibility*, Proceedings of a Conference on Exchange Rate Flexibility and the International Monetary System, Sponsored by the American Enterprise Institute for Public Policy Research and the U.S. Department of the Treasury, ed. by Jacob S. Dreyer, Gottfried Haberler, and Thomas D. Willett (Washington, 1976).

Claasen, Emil-Maria, "World Inflation Under Flexibile Exchange Rates," *Scandinavian Journal of Economics,* Vol. 78 (No. 2, 1976), pp. 346–65.

Cornell, Bradford, "Spot Rates, Forward Rates and Exchange Market Efficiency," *Journal of Financial Economics*, Vol. 5 (August 1977), pp. 55–65.

Crockett, Andrew D., and Morris Goldstein, "Inflation Under Fixed and Flexible Exchange Rates," *Staff Papers*, Vol. 23 (November 1976), pp. 509–44.

Deppler, Michael C., and Duncan Ripley, "The World Trade Model: Merchandise Flows," *Staff Papers*, Vol. 25 (March 1978), pp. 147–206.

Dooley, Michael P., and Jeffrey R. Shafer, "Analysis of Short-Run Exchange Rate Behavior, March 1973 to September 1975," International Finance Discussion Paper, No. 76, Board of Governors of the Federal Reserve System (Washington, February 1976).

Dornbusch, Rudiger (1976), "Expectations and Exchange Rate Dynamics," *Journal of Political Economy*, Vol. 84 (December 1976), pp. 1161–76.

———(1977), "What Have We Learned from the Float?" (unpublished, Massachusetts Institute of Technology, February 24, 1977).

————, and Paul Krugman, "Flexible Exchange Rates in the Short Run," *Brookings Papers on Economic Activity: 3* (1976), pp. 537–75.

Economistes Belges de Langue Française, 2 congrès, 5/6 Novembre 1976: *Economies ouvertes face aux mutations internationales: rapport préparatoire* (Centre Interuniversitaire de Formation Permanente).

Friedman, Milton (1953), "The Case for Flexible Exchange Rates," in his *Essays in Positive Economics* (University of Chicago Press, 1953), pp. 157–203.

————(1966), "Comments," in *Guidelines, Informal Controls, and the Market Place: Policy Choices in a Full Employment Economy*, ed. by George P. Shultz and Robert Z. Aliber (University of Chicago Press, 1966), pp. 55–61.

————(1969), "Discussion," in *The International Adjustment Mechanism*, Federal Reserve Bank of Boston, Conference Series, No. 2 (October 1969), pp. 109–19.

Hooper, Peter, and S. W. Kohlhagen, "The Effect of Exchange Rate Uncertainty on the Prices and Volume of International Trade," *Journal of International Economics*, Vol. 8 (November 1978), pp. 483–511.

International Monetary Fund (1978), *The Rise in Protectionism*, IMF Pamphlet Series, No. 24 (Washington, 1978).

————, *Annual Report of the Executive Board for the Financial Year Ended April 30, 1978* and *1979* (Washington, 1978 and 1979).

Isard, Peter, *Exchange-Rate Determination: A Survey of Popular Views and Recent Models*, Princeton Studies in International Finance, No. 42, International Finance Section, Princeton University (May 1978).

Johnson, Harry G. (1958), "Towards a General Theory of the Balance of Payments: Studies in Pure Theory," in his *International Trade and Economic Growth* (London, 1958).

————(1969), "The Case for Flexible Exchange Rates, 1969," Federal Reserve Bank of St. Louis, *Review*, Vol. 51 (No. 6, June 1969), pp. 12–24.

Keynes, John Maynard (1930), *The Treatise on Money,* Vol. 2 (London, 1930).

————(1936), *The General Theory of Employment, Interest, and Money* (New York, 1936).

Kindleberger, Charles P. (1969), "The Case for Fixed Exchange Rates, 1969," in *The International Adjustment Mechanism*, Federal Reserve Bank of Boston, Conference Series, No. 2 (October 1969), pp. 93–108.

————(1976), "Germany's Persistent Balance-of-Payments Disequilibrium Revisited," Banca Nazionale del Lavoro, *Quarterly Review,* Vol. 29 (June 1976), pp. 135–64.

Kouri, Pentti J. K., "The Exchange Rate and the Balance of Payments in the Short Run and the Long Run: A Monetary Approach," *Scandinavian Journal of Economics*, Vol. 78 (No. 2, 1976), pp. 280–304.

McKinnon, Ronald I. (1976), "Floating Foreign Exchange Rates 1973–74: The Emperor's New Clothes," in *Institutional Arrangements and the Inflation Problem*, ed. by Karl Brunner and Allan H. Meltzer, Carnegie-Rochester Conference on Public Policy, Vol. 3 (Amsterdam, 1976), pp. 79–114.

————, (1978) "Exchange-Rate Instability, Trade Balances, and Monetary Policies in Japan and the United States" (mimeographed, Stanford University).

Modigliani, Franco, and Hossein Askari, "The International Transfer of Capital and the Propagation of Domestic Disturbances Under Alternative Payments Systems," Banca Nazionale del Lavoro, *Quarterly Review*, Vol. 26 (December 1973), pp. 295–310.

Mussa, Michael, "The Exchange Rate, the Balance of Payments and Monetary and Fiscal Policy Under a Regime of Controlled Floating," *Scandinavian Journal of Economics*, Vol. 78 (No. 2, 1976), pp. 229–48.

Nordhaus, William D., "Statement," in *The Decline of the Dollar*, Hearings Before the Subcommittee on Foreign Economic Policy (95th Congress, 2nd Session, Washington, June 22, 1978), pp. 249–53.

Oppenheimer, Peter, *et al, Business Views on Exchange Rate Policy: An Independent Study by a Group of Leading Economists*, commissioned by Confederation of British Industry (London, July 1978).

Phelps, Edmund S., *Inflation Policy and Unemployment Theory: The Cost-Benefit Approach to Monetary Planning* (New York, 1972).

Polak, J. J., "Monetary Analysis of Income Formation and Payments Problems," *Staff Papers*, Vol. 6 (November 1957), pp. 1–50; reprinted in *The Monetary Approach to the Balance of Payments* (International Monetary Fund, Washington, 1977), pp. 15–64.

Ripley, Duncan M., "The Transmission of Fluctuations in Economic Activity: Some Recent Evidence," in *Managed Exchange-Rate Flexibility: The Recent Experience*, Federal Reserve Bank of Boston, Conference Series, No. 20 (October 1978), pp. 1–21.

Roosa, Robert V., "Second Lecture," in Milton Friedman and Robert V. Roosa, *The Balance of Payments: Free Versus Fixed Exchange Rates*, American Enterprise Institute for Public Policy Research, Rational Debate Seminars, No. 4 (Washington, 1967), pp. 25–67.

Schadler, Susan, "Sources of Exchange Rate Variability: Theory and Empirical Evidence," *Staff Papers*, Vol. 24 (July 1977), pp. 253–96.

Stern, Robert M., Jonathan Francis, and Bruce Schumacher, *Price Elasticities in International Trade: An Annotated Bibliography* (London, 1976).

Tobin, James, "A Proposal for International Monetary Reform," Cowles Foundation for Research in Economics, Discussion Paper No. 506 (Yale University, October 1978). This is scheduled for publication in the *Eastern Economic Journal*.

20

An Economist's View of the Foreign Exchange Market: Report on Interviews with West Coast Foreign Exchange Dealers

John Rutledge

INTRODUCTION

The large variations in bilateral exchange rates observed since the adoption of floating exchange rates in 1973 have caused concern over the operation of foreign exchange markets under flexible rates. Recent international agreements to counter "erratic fluctuations and disorderly market

From John Rutledge, "An Economist's View of the Foreign Exchange Market: Report on Interviews with West Coast Foreign Exchange Dealers," in *Exchange Rate Flexibility*, Jacob S. Dreyer, Gottfried Haberler, and Thomas D. Willett, eds. (Washington, D.C.: American Enterprise Institute, 1978), pp. 83–88. Reprinted by permission.

conditions" have amplified this concern and generated considerable discussion of the appropriate official intervention policy for ensuring orderly markets.

There is now substantial agreement that "disorderly markets" are not to be identified by reference to some target rate or by simply looking at the magnitude of exchange rate variations. Instead, they should be identified by certain characteristics of technical market performance. Moreover, it would appear desirable to use the accumulated experience of market traders in selecting and evaluating these characteristics. This paper reports information on exchange market performance based on several recent interviews with West Coast foreign exchange dealers.

THE ROLE OF PRIVATE SPECULATORS IN A REGIME OF FLEXIBLE EXCHANGE RATES

If asset prices are to serve their function as signals for efficient resource allocation, they must successfully transmit all relevant information about present and future market developments to the ultimate suppliers and demanders of the asset. In the foreign exchange markets (when they are not dominated by official intervention), the information-transmitting function of exchange rates depends largely on the actions of private speculators.

By private speculators we mean those market participants who gather and process information about the likely behavior of the many factors which determine exchange market equilibrium, and then use that information to buy and sell currencies in anticipation of price movements. Speculators can act on their own behalf, or as agents for ultimate wealth holders engaging in no other business activity, or they can use their anticipations about likely exchange market developments to make decisions about the size, timing, and placement of ordinary business transactions. By definition, then, there are a great many who play the role of private speculator in the foreign exchange markets.

Asset markets in which prices accurately reflect all available information are called efficient markets. There exists massive evidence that equity markets in the United States are efficient markets. New information about firms' underlying return distributions is quickly reflected in price changes; there is no evidence of cyclical, or otherwise easily predictable, variations of stock prices about their equilibrium values; and stock prices do not systematically overreact or underreact to new releases of information.

We are now in a period of furious research activity in international finance, asking the same questions about exchange rates that we once asked about stock prices. Do the markets always overreact? Are there "bandwagon effects"? Do exchange rates move cyclically? Do exchange rates reflect the underlying determinants of exchange market equilibrium? Is speculative activity stabilizing or destabilizing? One must reflect for a moment on why we are having such a difficult time nailing down answers to these questions for the exchange markets when they have been so convincingly demonstrated for equity markets.

The answer, of course, is that stock prices are determined entirely by private traders—there are literally thousands of observations of stock price behavior from which to draw conclusions. There is no direct official intervention in the equity markets. In contrast, *there has never been a significant length of time during which exchange rates have been determined entirely by private market forces, free of all official intervention.* As a consequence, the researcher's job becomes much more difficult. Weak-form tests* for efficient markets—which simply examine observed price behavior for evidence of inefficient cyclical and nonrandom price movements—cannot discriminate between price movements caused by private speculators and those caused by the intervention authorities. Strong-form tests,† which account for official intervention by building detailed structural models of exchange market equilibrium, are the appropriate alternatives. Effective application of strong-form tests, however, is still beyond our reach since there are nearly as many competing hypotheses about the formation of speculators' expectations as there are independent market observations, since official intervention data are both confidential and unreliable.

Having pointed out some of the major difficulties with traditional approaches to examining the performance of private speculators, I shall report the preliminary results of a second—or perhaps third best approach: interviewing participants in the foreign exchange markets. The objective is to obtain some information about the technical efficiency of the foreign exchange markets in facilitating transactions between ultimate buyers and sellers, and about private traders' views of the role of official intervention in international exchange markets.

DO PRIVATE SPECULATORS CREATE BANDWAGON EFFECTS?

The hypothesis that private speculators exert a stabilizing influence on the foreign exchange market is based on the presumption that private speculators evaluate the fundamental determinants of exchange market equilibrium, then take open positions based on the difference between the market rate and their forecast of the equilibrium rate, or their forecast of some range of rates compatible with exchange market equilibrium. Speculative purchases of currencies which traders feel are temporarily undervalued and speculative sales of currencies which traders feel are temporar-

---

*[Weak-form tests test whether the market has made use of all profit-creating information in lagged prices only.—Eds.]

†[Strong-form tests test whether the market has made use of *all* profit-creating information.—Eds.]

ily overvalued tend to eliminate foreseeable (that is, ex ante) deviations of the market exchange rate from the rate implied by the fundamentals. If speculators fail to perform this stabilizing role then, in principle, exchange rates could diverge from "equilibrium" rates for substantial periods of time, causing transactions to be based on a set of inefficient prices.

The econometric problems outlined above make it difficult to make empirical judgments on the behavior of speculators since the float. My view, however, is that, in principle, there is little difference between the equity markets and the foreign exchange markets. The presumption is thus that foreign exchange markets, like equity markets, are "efficient markets," and that speculators play a largely stabilizing role. We shall, therefore, take stabilizing speculation and efficient markets as the null hypothesis: it remains for critics of floating rates to present evidence that private speculators have exhibited unstable behavior. One such allegation that has received much recent attention is that speculators generate "bandwagon effects."

In all the discussions of bandwagon effects and destabilizing speculation, I have yet to see a careful description of the precise roles played by various market traders. The basic story, however, goes something like this. A group of speculators in a smoke-filled room decides to take a currency (the Bolumbian Mambo, for example) for a ride. They begin massive purchases of mambos. Other speculators, seeing the mambo rate rise, will not want to miss out on a good thing, and they will also place buy orders for mambos. Thus for a time the increases in rates will—in bootstraps fashion—beget further rises in rates, until the mambo rate is far out of line with the underlying equilibrium rate.

Then—and this is where the art comes in—the smart speculators dump their mambos at the premium price and reap handsome profits. Other speculators, of course, catch the scent and place their mambos on offer. As a result there is a prolonged decline in the mambo rate.

Viewed as a time series, then, bandwagon effects imply a speculative bubble in the exchange rate. Clearly, from a welfare point of view such exchange rate movements serve little useful economic purpose.[1] Worse still, the false signals given off during the transitory exchange rate movement may distort real resource flows and result in a decrease in net welfare.

Markets which are dominated by bandwagon effects provide the strongest case for official intervention. Central bank intervention that succeeds in smoothing out bandwagon cycles—or, in the spirit of Kondratieff and Jevons, what we may call "Bernstein Cycles"—will not only avoid costly resource misallocations associated with disequilibrium exchange rates; it will also make a profit for the public treasury (a wealth transfer that would have been applauded neither by Marshall nor by Fisher, although certainly by Galbraith).

Not surprisingly, this rationale for official intervention has not been overlooked by the authorities. The foreign exchange reports of the

Federal Reserve Bank of New York tell of speculative attacks on the dollar and other currencies, and of central banks defending their currencies from speculative onslaughts. Furthermore, speculative activity is often characterized as unreliable, as capricious, and as overreacting to each snatch of news as it hits the foreign exchange market. Thus, the existence of bandwagon cycles is an important issue for policy as well as for theory.

As my earlier arguments imply, however, it is not very easy to test for the existence of bandwagon effects over relatively short time periods.

To augment the statistical studies, I have asked several foreign exchange traders for their views on the existence of bandwagon effects. Invariably traders responded yes, that private speculators can and do have powerful effects on exchange rate movements, and that speculators gang up on an exchange rate to force adjustments.

Before we pick up our intervention shovels and head for the trenches, however, note that exchange market intimates overwhelmingly felt that such speculative swings in exchange rates were mainly an intraday phenomenon, lasting for a few hours. I did not see any agreement with the story that bandwagons can persist for several months at a time, or that they can be used to explain the mysterious behavior of the dollar-mark rate over the past three years.

Nor did traders feel that there was any reliable way of distinguishing short-run speculative pressure on a currency from fundamental adjustments due to changing evaluations of market forces. Speculative cycles in exchange rates, it seems, can only be identified through the rear-view mirror. One trader, when asked about speculative "cycles" remarked, "I have been in this business for more than twenty years, and have yet to see one."

Official intervention, on the other hand, presumes that the authorities are endowed with the ability to discriminate between exchange rate adjustments which are bandwagon-induced and those which are more fundamental. U.S. intervention, moreover, has been based on the existence of recognizable bandwagon cycles lasting for several months—witness the practice of repaying swaps within several months, and the sizable U.S. one-way intervention pursued during early 1975. It would seem that the burden of proof on both counts ought to be with the intervention authorities. They have supplied no evidence, to my knowledge, either that speculators cause bandwagon effects, or that they—the intervention authorities—are especially good at picking out these effects from all the other factors which impinge on exchange markets.

IS THERE ENOUGH SPECULATION?

Paradoxically, many of the same people who urge that speculators are responsible for large and prolonged bandwagon cycles argue at other times that there is not enough private speculation to give depth and stability to the foreign exchange markets. The problem, they say, is that the inter-bank market is too thin—traders are either unable or unwilling to take "large enough" open positions in foreign exchange. This is the legacy of the Herstatt and Franklin National failures.

Traders with whom I talked agree that they are more cautious in foreign exchange operations today than they were in the quasi-fixed-rate era; open positions are smaller, and bid-asked spreads are wider for both spot and forward exchange. This is not because speculators are faint-hearted, however, but rather because the variability of the underlying determinants of exchange market equilibrium has increased. It is also because "the drinks are no longer on the house," that is, traders cannot always count on a benevolent central bank to guarantee that they can complete a transaction for a customer with little exchange risk. As with any other industry, when a subsidy is reduced or removed, the volume of business done by the industry shrinks.

It has also been suggested by some analysts that today's foreign exchange markets are so thin that a fairly large purchase order—say DM 30 million—would disrupt the market, and would unduly interfere with a trader's sleep while he tried to sneak his order into Australia, Hong Kong, and London at various points during the night. Traders indicate that this is not so! To be sure, a West Coast trader would send for an aspirin if he received such an order late Friday afternoon, when both New York and the European markets are closed. But there are two reasons why this is not likely to be a major problem. First, customers are usually able to forsee such large purchases, and would likely time their order to coincide with the most favorable market conditions. Second, the risk to the trader can be partly shifted to the customer if the trader contracts on a "best I can do" basis, rather than at a quoted rate. Naturally, traders say, if a customer demands a quotation one will be given, and it will include a premium for the estimated impact of the contract on the exchange rate, plus an allowance for risk.

The final point we shall consider is that institutional constraints on traders' speculative positions inhibit the stabilizing speculation that would otherwise be forthcoming. Such constraints could conceivably interfere with market efficiency. Traders claim that this is incorrect. First, huge intraday open positions can be carried while meeting *any* constraint on overnight open positions. Second, constraints on forward open positions typically do not differentiate according to maturity. A trader can carry a forward open position in a currency by simultaneously buying a contract for one maturity and selling a contract for a different maturity, while showing zero open position in total forward contracts for that currency.

A corollary of this argument is that auditing schedules of banks and other firms prevent them from holding positions long enough to speculate on medium-term movements in the fundamentals. I propose, to the contrary, that the horizon of the speculators is irrelevant to questions about market efficiency. Even if speculators only act on two-week horizons, every future date at which we observe the exchange markets will have been preceded by days during which that date was within the speculators' horizon.

In summary, traders with whom I spoke agreed that the system of market-determined exchange rates, while not perfect, has performed admirably in spite of the generally high level of uncertainty about the underlying economic and financial conditions over the past three years. Exchange market participants react quickly to new market information, but do not generate the variety of cyclical or "bandwagon" exchange rate behavior which have been used to justify prolonged periods of market intervention.

Notes

1. Except the transfer of wealth from dumb speculators to smart ones which after all, both Marshall and Fisher agree is only right.

21

Commentary on the Rutledge Paper

Scott Pardee and Dennis Weatherstone

SCOTT PARDEE

... For many years, academic people have been talking to academic people about foreign exchange, and market people have been talking to market people about foreign exchange, but neither group has talked very much to the other. This meeting is an opportunity to clear the air. We may disagree, but at least we will know more precisely the points on which we disagree. Now, my responsibilities are to conduct the foreign exchange operations of the Federal Reserve System. At this meeting so far, I have received a lot of free—and conflicting—advice on our operations. I would like to outline my view of the Federal Reserve's role in the exchange market. . . .

We have several advantages over other market participants. We have the great advantage of being an insider in an insider's market. The exchange market, after all, is a money market. The Federal Reserve Bank of New York carries out foreign currency operations under the authoriza-

Commentaries on the Rutledge paper by Scott Pardee and Dennis Weatherstone from *Exchange Rate Flexibility*, Jacob S. Dreyer, Gottfried Haberler, and Thomas D. Willett, eds. (Washington, D.C.: American Enterprise Institute, 1978), pp. 111–119. Reprinted by permission.

tion and directive of the Federal Open Market Committee, which also sets domestic money market policy. Knowing what U.S. monetary policy is, and is likely to be, is a great advantage in evaluating conditions in the exchange market.

In view of the Treasury's responsibilities in international financial policy, we also consult closely with Treasury officials. The Federal Reserve System would not operate in the exchange market over Treasury objection. Indeed, the New York Federal Reserve has a more direct responsibility to the Treasury even than this, since we also serve as fiscal agent for the Treasury's Exchange Stabilization Fund in its foreign currency operations. Thus, we operate in the context of a broader range of U.S. international financial policies, beyond monetary policy as such.

Moreover, the Federal Reserve has close working relationships with foreign central banks, which have substantial information both about conditions in their money and exchange markets and about their own policies. This link with foreign central banks is especially important, since the major exchange market for every currency is not in New York but elsewhere. The more we know about conditions in those markets the better we can operate in the New York exchange market itself.

In addition, the Foreign Department of the New York Federal Reserve has close contacts with other participants in the exchange markets both in the United States and abroad. All those contacts and relationships allow us to gain a more complete picture of the situation at hand.

I might add that we also have at our disposal the immense data-collecting services of the U.S. Government, again the Federal Reserve and the Treasury in particular. This gives us access to data which are not yet available—in their raw form not available at all—to other participants in the market. We also have the benefit of the economic research being carried out in these institutions. In some cases, to be sure, research economists give us numbers we do not need, such as weighted average exchange rates. (After all, the market deals in real money, not in weighted averages.) Moreover, research economists have a poor track record in forecasting certain developments in the international area, particularly on projecting the U.S. trade balance. Nonetheless, since market people tend to concentrate on short-run transitory factors, the longer-term perspective of the research economist contributes in an important way to our understanding of more fundamental developments.

Finally, the Federal Reserve has a valuable legacy from the era of Charles Coombs, who has recently retired to private life after serving as head of the Foreign Department of the Federal Reserve Bank of New York for some fifteen years. From the wide range of operations he undertook during those years, he has left us with ample resources, in the form of the swap arrangements, and a full arsenal of tested intervention techniques. As a master of personal diplomacy, he earned for us an immense measure of good will with our counterparts in other central banks. Because of this, when we do intervene we can be extremely effective.

I have stressed our advantages in the marketplace, but we also have serious constraints. Some of them are obvious. Central banks are occasionally obliged to intervene in a situation in which the economic fundamentals may be very unfavorable and government may be weak or indecisive in resolving the problem. In such cases, central bankers do their best in what may be a losing cause. We are careful, however, to characterize such operations as "damage-control" or "rear-guard" actions.

Other constraints are what I will call simply "overriding considerations." One is the trade-off between domestic and international objectives of policy. In the Federal Reserve, domestic monetary policy objectives often hold sway over international objectives. Or the overriding considerations may arise from broader economic policy choices. At such times it is often forgotten that exchange market intervention by itself is not a policy solution. It is a signal that something is wrong; the bigger the intervention, the bigger the problem. To backstop or eliminate the need for intervention other policy actions are necessary.

For example, a great deal has been said here of the recent declines of the Italian lira, the pound sterling, and the French franc. In each case there was heavy exchange market intervention by the central bank concerned, but the intervention was not immediately supplemented by other policy measures. At least one participant in this meeting has drawn on these examples to suggest that central bank intervention in the exchange market is futile, if not perverse. But no one has mentioned the recent Belgian experience. The Belgian franc also fell under heavy speculation in early 1976, but the Belgian government responded forcefully and in an orthodox manner. The government issued strong denials of any intention to change the exchange rate. The central bank not only intervened massively in the market, it allowed this intervention to tighten domestic liquidity and even raised some domestic interest rates. Exchange controls were tightened and the budget was trimmed. This approach worked, and Belguim is now enjoying a significant reflow of funds. My point is that each situation should be analyzed on its own merits.

More broadly, there are times of clear government crisis when a central bank should make its presence known in the exchange market. The Federal Reserve's operations on November 22, 1963, the day that President Kennedy was assassinated, offer an example of effective intervention. On other occasions, however, political considerations may render exchange market intervention ineffective. Time and again in recent years the markets have been disrupted by loose talk about exchange rates by government officials and politicians.

For this reason, my first rule for floating would be in the form of a commandment to government officials: "Thou shalt not talk about the exchange rate in public." Anything said, even with the best of intentions, can backfire. Some of the wide volatility of exchange rates in recent years has reflected the market's response to statements and mis-impressions left by government officials. . . .

To comment generally on the papers, . . . the role of the speculator is vastly overemphasized. The exchange market has many functions, only one of which is to serve as a vehicle for speculation. Even among the forces motivating exchange traders, speculation may not be particularly important. Fear of loss can be a more impelling force than desire for profit. Moreover, by focussing on the isolated question of the effects of central bank intervention, the papers tend to neglect the importance of broader economic policies for exchange rate determination. Also, the assumption of traders' rationality bothers me. Modern decision theory has shown that the assumption of rationality may yield misleading results in ambiguous situations—and the exchange markets are rife with such situations. Perhaps we should look into the recently developed "catastrophe theory" now being applied to "fight or flight" situations in behavioral sciences. This entails some highly sophisticated mathematics, but to me some of the results seem to fit more closely with actual behavior in the marketplace than do the models presented here.

DENNIS WEATHERSTONE

. . . Turning to Rutledge's paper, the "speculator theme" has been almost worn out today. Bernstein is, of course, right in saying that it is not necessarily a dirty word. Economists, though, regard it differently, I believe, from the market and Congress. In New York, everybody is concerned about the use, or misuse, of that word, while in Washington people often talk about speculators as though they are helpful individuals, contributing to a good market. In New York clients frequently walk into the room and before relating their exchange problems feel it necessary to say for the record that they never speculate. Only once have I ever met a person who admitted to being a foreign currency speculator.

A word now on the bandwagon effect. We ask if there is or is not a bandwagon. I do not think one gets a true perspective from the West Coast. There is no doubt at all in my mind that, in 1973 and 1974, there was a bandwagon. We saw it operating, as big positions were being set up, and the market knew which banks were involved. If a bank or group of banks fairly clearly was moving $500 million, $1 billion, or $2 billion, how could a trader sit back and call that movement wrong? In the short run, he would trade the same way. Thereby he may make the currency movement exaggerated, but he is not there to lose money. Fighting the market majority can be an expensive luxury.

There was, then, a bandwagon market. How long it carried on is a little difficult to say. I believe, however, that the bandwagon was just one of the problems of 1973 and 1974. We had an exceptionally difficult time for determining proper exchange rates, with the imbalances created by the huge oil price increase, the oil embargo, the development of sharply different inflation rates, the International Equalization Tax, and the abolition of the Office of Foreign Direct Investment. All were unusual and major factors, making it impossible to guess which way rates should go, and how far.

The problem was magnified by the big speculative positions. I believe that the market is now in much better shape, and that this improvement is due only in part to the actions of central banks. The way to learn one has been wrong is to lose money, and painful lessons were learned. Look at the list of banks that lost money in 1974 in foreign exchange. The market learned its lesson and subsequently improved. . . .

Today, we could say that we have worked out a fine set of rules for intervention. We have considered inflation differentials, interest rates, balance of trade, capital flows, and so on, and it would seem reasonable. But as soon as we walk out of the room, the rules may turn out to be wrong. Or perhaps in a week they may turn out to be wrong. A precise workable solution through rules is not possible. Let us therefore have a minimum of intervention. Let the market decide as best it can. Let us exercise judgment, have the central banks correct disorderly markets, and, when they do it, give them a good deal of scope and opportunity to do it properly.

. . . Several of us have said that we do not consider the forward market to be deficient although it is not always what it appears to be when we are looking for quotations for the long term. There is a good market up to one year, and the market beyond one year is not bad either. My bank is willing to give quotations up to five years, in the Canadian dollar, the pound sterling, the deutsche mark, and the Swiss franc, and, three, sometimes five, years in the Japanese yen. These are currencies that are actively used in trade and investment, and there tends to be quite a good two-way interest in them.

We, however, prefer to make the market directly with our own commercial customers. We are a commercial bank, and we do not see much to be gained by putting our rates into the open market for those long periods if that only enables another bank to trade those currencies long date for their commercial customers. We would rather encourage as many commercial customers as we can to come directly to us. We think that our role as a major market maker well equips us to quote in the long-date market. Therefore, though it may be said there is no market, business can be done even if there is none in the accepted sense of the term. The other point is that those who say there is no possibility to do long-date transactions often mean they do not like the price, which is a different matter.

. . . I referred a little earlier to the particular problems of 1973 and 1974. . . . I can remember a commercial customer saying to me that he really did not know what to do. In 1973 and 1974 he started by hedging all his positions, and he lost money. Then he decided not to hedge any positions, because he decided he did not understand it sufficiently, and he lost money. He decided then to hedge half, and he still lost money. I said to him that in 1975 he must have made money, and he said that was exactly right. The explanation was that in 1975, there was a logical market, and his was a logical company. He did not make money in the illogical markets because he thought logically.

The New York market has become a better foreign exchange market. There has not been a rush, as there was on the continent after the Herstatt collapse and other incidents, to slap controls on the banks, inhibiting them from taking reasonable positions during the day and inhibiting them from making good forward markets. The system that has been adopted here so far has been to collect information on banks' positions. The banks in New York have been responsive to this. The authorities can now monitor the banks' positions, with the possibility of talking about them intelligently. The absence of rigid rules reflects recognition that there should be different rules for different banks with different abilities. . . .

22

Tests of Forecasting Models and Market Efficiency in the International Money Market

Richard M. Levich

I. INTRODUCTION

Over the last twenty years, a substantial research effort has been directed toward developing and testing the efficient-market hypothesis. Stated simply, an efficient market is one "in which prices always 'fully reflect' available information" (Fama, 1970). Investors collect and process information in order to assess the value of an asset. Trading occurs so that

From Richard M. Levich, "Tests of Forecasting Models and Market Efficiency in the International Money Market," in *The Economics of Exchange Rates*, Jacob A. Frenkel and Harry G. Johnson, eds., © 1978, Addison-Wesley Publishing Company, Inc., pp. 129–158. Reprinted with permission. Some tables, footnotes, and references omitted.

market prices continuously reflect the information set; as a consequence, unusual profit opportunities are quickly eliminated.

The main laboratory for testing the efficient-market hypothesis has been the market for financial claims (primarily equities) in the United States.[1] The [aim of this paper is to examine the hypothesis that prices reflect available information in] the international money market. Stated in this manner, the hypothesis is too general for empirical testing. Therefore, two more specific hypotheses are formulated:[2]

1. Prices of particular financial claims imply accurate and consistent forecasts of future spot exchange rates.
2. Unusual speculative profits should not be earned by investors who use exchange-rate forecasts based on publicly available information.

The first hypothesis draws on the assumption that prices reflect information. Since investors' expectations of the future spot exchange rate are part of the information set, observed prices of spot rates, forward rates, and interest rates, for example, should reflect the market's consensus estimate of the future spot rate. A test of this hypothesis can be based on the statistical properties of exchange-rate forecasts implied by market prices. Under the null hypothesis that the international money market is efficient, these statistical properties should agree with our theoretical expectations.

The second hypothesis considers the usefulness of exchange-rate forecasts based on publicly available information. One risky investment opportunity is speculation in forward contracts. Market efficiency suggests that publicly available forecasts of the future spot rate should not lead to unusual profits in forward speculation.

These ideas are definitely not new. Statements describing the speed of foreign-exchange traders and the efficiency of foreign-exchange markets can be found in Ricardo (1811), Goschen (1862), and Walras (1874). . . .

Overall this research suggests that we cannot reject either hypothesis. First, although exchange-rate forecasts based on market prices are not perfect, they do display many statistical properties consistent with efficient use of available information. Second, publicly available forecasts do not lead to unusual profits in forward speculation. This research, therefore, cannot reject the hypothesis that the international money market is efficient.

II. STATISTICAL METHODS AND EXCHANGE-RATE FORECASTING

One approach to the exchange-rate forecasting problem is to specify a structural model of the economy. If the spot rate can be expressed as a function of lagged endogenous variables and exogenous variables, and if forecasts of the future values of the exogenous variables are available, then a conditional forecast of the future spot rate can be generated. This is not the approach adopted here.

Alternatively, forecasting can rely on principles associated with spot and forward currency speculation. An early statement that the interest-rate differential between assets denominated in two currencies should reflect anticipated exchange-rate changes is associated with Irving Fisher (1896).[3] The basic thrust of Fisher's analysis is that for the asset market to clear, investors demand a higher nominal return on assets denominated in a (relatively) depreciating unit of account; investors accept a lower nominal return on assets denominated in a (relatively) appreciating unit of account. In a world of certainty, the market's implied one-period ahead forecast of the spot rate is given by:

$$\hat{S}_{t+1} = S_t \; \frac{1 + r_d}{1 + r_f} \tag{1}$$

where

S_t = Spot exchange rate (in domestic currency per unit foreign currency) at time t,

r_d = One-period interest rate on domestic currency asset, and

r_f = One-period interest rate on foreign currency asset.

Equation (1) represents a great simplification; to forecast the future spot rate we need only two inputs—the interest rates. The cost is that we no longer see how underlying economic variables affect the exchange rate. Implicitly, we are acting as though Eq. (1) is the reduced form equation for the spot rate in a correctly specified structural model. In effect, we are relying on asset markets to be efficient processors of information on exchange-rate expectations.

In the case where interest rate parity holds, spot speculation and forward speculation are equivalent investments.[4] Equation (1) can then be re-written as

$$\hat{S}_{t+1} = F_t \tag{2}$$

where F = one-period forward rate at time t. The formulation assumes that the forward market efficiently reflects information on exchange-rate expectations.[5]

Both Eqs. (1) and (2) assume a world of certainty and no transaction costs. When transaction costs exist it is easily shown that the forecast point estimate becomes a neutral band with upper bound (U) and lower bound (L) given by

$$U = \hat{S}_{t+1}/\Omega$$
$$L = \Omega\hat{S}_{t+1}$$

where

$$\Omega = \prod_{i=1}^{n} (1 - t_i),$$

t_i = cost of transaction i,

and n is the number of transactions required to take the speculative position. The presence of transaction costs may therefore lead to forecast errors even under perfect foresight and rational behavior.

If market forces are efficient in assessing information about the future spot exchange rate, then a large fraction of sample observations should be bounded by the neutral band. In this case, we will not reject hypothesis one. However, if the fraction of observations bounded is low, there are two alternative conclusions. First, it may be that market participants are inefficient in processing exchange rate expectations. Second, it may be that Eqs. (1) and (2) are not the correct reduced-form models of exchange rates which market participants use to set prices. This conundrum is common to any data which reject market efficiency and empirically, there is no technique for distinguishing the correct conclusion.

When uncertainty exists, forecast errors may arise because unanticipated events occur after the forecast is formulated. In this case, Eqs. (1) and (2) should be modified to include an error term, u_{t+1}. If the mean of the error term is zero, the forecast is unbiased. Furthermore, if the market is efficient, the error terms will be serially uncorrelated.

It is, however, possible for the forecasts to be biased with a nonzero mean error term.[6] It should be underscored that the existence of bias does not necessarily imply market inefficiency. It is conceivable that equilibrium expected returns are set so that the compensation for bearing exchange risk is nonzero.

Another explanation for bias is currency preference (Aliber, 1973). The currency preference argument is that there may be a convenience or other nonpecuniary yield associated with a currency. For example, a London importer (who is risk averse) may hold dollar balances to lessen exposure to exchange risk and to reduce transaction costs from trading in and out of sterling. A U.S. investor may hold Swiss franc assets to benefit from anonymity in the Swiss banking system. In both examples, the nominal interest rate does not adequately measure the desirability of these assets for investors.

The empirical evidence on forecasting bias in Eqs. (1) and (2) is mixed.[7]

Another approach to forecasting which uses market data is based on time-series analysis.[8] In an efficient market, the price of spot exchange itself will reflect the information set. If the underlying factors determining exchange rates are generated by a stationary process, the time-series description of the spot rate may be useful for forecasting. One possible description of the spot series is a random-walk model with zero drift which leads to the forecast

$$\hat{S}_{t+1} = S_t. \tag{3}$$

It should be emphasized that the random-walk description of the exchange rate is not the only model consistent with market efficiency. Equation (3) was selected because it is a naïve model that may have been postulated by market participants during this period.[9]

Notes

1. For a survey of the efficient markets literature see Fama (1970, 1976). Surveys with special reference to international financial markets are in Kohlhagen (1976) and Levich (1978).
2. A more fundamental hypothesis is that unusual profit opportunities in covered interest arbitrage are quickly eliminated. This hypothesis is more fundamental in the sense that efficiency here rests on the relatively simple process of policing a boundary condition; all inputs for this single period model are known with certainty. Earlier research reported by Frenkel and Levich (1975, 1977) indicates that when transaction costs are included and the financial assets are comparable in terms of risk, unusual arbitrage profits are quickly eliminated. It is therefore appropriate to test hypotheses which consider uncertainty.
3. Fisher presents data for the period 1865–1895 on Indian debt, partly denominated in silver and partly denominated in gold. Interest on the silver bonds is paid by draft on India (in rupees) and interest on the gold bonds is paid in gold. Both securities are traded in London. Fisher also presents a matching time series on rupee exchange rates. He concludes:
   > From 1884 exchange fell much more rapidly than before, and the difference in the two rates of interest rose accordingly, amounting in one year to 1.1%. Since the two bonds were issued by the same government, possess the same degree of security, are quoted side by side in the same market and are in fact similar in all important respects *except in the standard in which they are expressed*, the results afford substantial proof that the fall of exchange (after it once began) was discounted in advance. Of course investors did not form perfectly definite estimates of the future fall, but the fear of a fall predominated in varying degrees over the hope of a rise. (p. 390, emphasis added.)
4. A proof of the statement assuming uncertainty is in Tsiang (1959). pp. 86–92.
5. There is substantial literature to support this assumption. For example, Working (1961) argues that "Futures prices tend to be highly reliable estimates of what should be expected on the basis of contemporarily available information. . . ."
6. For a theoretical description of the sources of bias, see Stockman (1978). An alternative explanation based on international portfolio theory is in Solnik (1973).
7. Fisher (1896) observed that a 0.2 to 0.3 percent interest rate differential between gold and silver assets existed, even when the exchange rate was unchanged. A reexamination of this data (Levich, 1977) indicates that, under the 25-year sample period, the null hypothesis that the error terms have mean zero and are serially uncorrelated cannot be rejected. For evidence on other periods see Kohlhagen (1975), Bilson (1976) and Frenkel (1977).

8. For an explanation of time-series estimation methods, see Box and Jenkins (1970) and Nelson (1973). For a comprehensive analysis of the determination of exchange rates implementing a time-series analysis approach, see Hodrick (1978).
9. A time-series analysis of weekly spot exchange rates over the period 1973–1975 indicates that the strict random-walk model is valid only for the Italian lira and the Swiss franc. However, the precise time-series specification could only be learned using in-sample observations. See Levich (1977).

References

Aliber, Robert Z. "The Interest Rate Parity Theorem: A Reinterpretation. *Journal of Political Economy*, *81*, No. 6 (November/December 1973): 1451–1459.

Box, G. E. P., and G. M. Jenkins. *Time Series Analysis*. San Francisco: Holden-Day, 1970.

Fama, Eugene F. "Efficient Capital Markets: A Review of Theory and Empirical Work," *Journal of Finance*, *25*, No. 2 (May, 1970): 383–417.

———. *Foundations of Finance*. New York: Basic Books, 1976.

Fama, Eugene F., Lawrence Fisher, Michael C. Jensen, and Richard Roll. "The Adjustment of Stock Prices to New Information." *International Economic Review*, *10*, No. 1 (February, 1969): 1–21.

Fisher, Irving. "Appreciation and Interest." *Publications of the American Economic Association*, *11*, No. 4 (August, 1896): 331–442.

Frenkel, Jacob A. "The Forward Exchange Rate, Expectations and the Demand for Money: The German Hyperinflation." *American Economic Review*, *67*, No. 4 (September, 1977): 653–670.

Frenkel, Jacob A., and Richard M. Levich. "Covered Interest Arbitrage: Unexploited Profits?" *Journal of Political Economy*, *83*, No. 2 (April, 1975): 325–338.

———. "Transaction Costs and Interest Arbitrage: Tranquil Versus Turbulent Periods." *Journal of Political Economy*, *85*, No. 6 (December, 1977): 1209–1226.

Goschen, George J. *The Theory of the Foreign Exchange*. 3d ed. London, 1862. Reprinted 4th ed. London: Pitman House, 1932.

Hodrick, Robert J. "An Empirical Analysis of the Monetary Approach to the Determination of the Exchange Rate." in *The Economics of Exchange Rates*, Jacob A. Frenkel and Harry G. Johnson, eds., Boston: Addison-Wesley, 1978.

Kohlhagen, Steven W. "The Forward Rate as an Unbiased Estimator of the Future Spot Rate." Mimeographed. University of California, Berkeley, 1975.

———. "The Foreign Exchange Markets—Models, Tests and Empirical Evidence." Presented at the U.S. Treasury Workshop on Technical Studies on Economic Interdependence and Exchange Rate Flexibility, Washington, D.C., February 26–27, 1976.

Levich, Richard M. "The International Money Market: Tests of Forecasting Models and Market Efficiency." Unpublished Ph.D. dissertation, University of Chicago, 1977.

———. "The Efficiency of Markets for Foreign Exchange: A Survey." in R. Dornbusch and J. A. Frenkel (eds.), *International Economic Policy: An Assessment of Theory and Evidence*. 1978 (forthcoming).

Nelson, Charles R. "The Prediction Performance of the FRB-MIT-Penn Model of the U.S. Economy." *American Economic Review*, *62*, No. 5 (December, 1972): 902–917.

———. *Applied Time Series Analysis*. San Francisco: Holden-Day, 1973.

Ricardo, David. *Reply to Mr. Bosanquet's Practical Observations on the Report of the Bullion Committee*. London, 1811.

Solnik, Bruno H. *European Capital Markets*. Boston: D.C. Health-Lexington, 1973.

Stockman, Alan C. "Risk, Information and Forward Exchange Rates." in *The Economics of Exchange Rates,* Jacob A. Frenkel and Harry G. Johnson, eds., Boston: Addison-Wesley, 1978.

Tsiang, S. C. "The Theory of Forward Exchange and the Effects of Government Intervention on the Forward Market." *Staff Papers, 7,* No. 1 (April, 1959): 75–106.

Walras, Leon. *Elements of Pure Economics.* 1st ed. 1874. Translated by W. Jaffe. New York: Kelly, 1969.

Working, Holbrook. "New Concepts Concerning Futures Markets and Prices." *American Economic Review, 51* (May, 1961): 160–163.

23

The Monetary Approach to the Balance of Payments

Michael Mussa

The purpose of this [paper is] to expound the basic features of the "monetary approach" to the balance of payments; . . . it will be argued that a monetary approach is essential for sensible discussion of the behaviour of the balance of payments.

The monetary approach to the balance of payments consists of a set of broad principles which are shared by a wide class of specific theoretical models. . . . These broad principles will be summarised into three basic features of the monetary approach.[1]

A. AN ESSENTIALLY MONETARY PHENOMENON

The first feature is summarised in the fundamental proposition: *the balance of payments is an essentially (but not exclusively) monetary phenomenon*. In this proposition, the term "the balance of payments" refers specifically to the Official Settlements Balance, that is, to the "money account." The official settlements balance is in surplus (deficit) when the monetary authorities of a country are purchasing (selling) foreign exchange assets in order to prevent their own money from appreciating (depreciating) relative to other monies. Thus, analysis of the balance of payments only

From Michael Mussa, "Tariffs and the Balance of Payments: A Monetary Approach," in *The Monetary Approach to the Balance of Payments,* Jacob A. Frenkel and Harry G. Johnson, eds., 1976. Reprinted by permission of the University of Toronto Press and George Allen & Unwin (Publishers) Ltd. Some figures, footnotes, and references omitted.

makes sense in an explicitly monetary model, and, in this sense, the balance of payments is an essentially monetary phenomenon.[2] Or, to give the point a more provocative tone, analysis of the balance of payments in a theoretical framework where money is not explicitly present, is prima facie, nonsense.

The monetary approach has a limited perspective. It does not attempt to provide a theory of the balance-of-payments accounts. These accounts include the trade account, the service account, the short-term and long-term capital accounts, and the private and government transfer accounts, as well as the official settlements account. The monetary approach concentrates on the official settlements account and lumps everything else into a single category: "items above the line." The rules of double entry book-keeping require that the net sum of all items which appear above the line equal the official settlements balance. The monetary approach attempts to provide only a theory of this net sum, not to explain its decomposition.

The narrowness of the monetary approach in its concentration on the official settlements account is complemented by the breadth of the monetary approach in its conception of "an essentially monetary phenomenon." To say that something is "an essentially monetary phenomenon" says that money plays a vital role, but does not imply that *only* money plays a role. The monetary approach takes explicit account of the influence of "real" variables such as levels of income and interest rates on the behaviour of the balance of payments. Indeed, a primary purpose of the present article is . . . to dispel the confusion which has associated the monetary approach with the view that "only money matters."

B. THE DEMAND FOR MONEY AND THE SUPPLY OF MONEY

To some extent, this confusion has been generated because of a second basic feature of the monetary approach: *the use of the money supply process and, particularly, the demand for money function as the central theoretical relationships around which to organise thought concerning the balance of payments*. The basic rationale for this principle of organisation is that we are interested in the behaviour of the money account for which the demand for money and the supply of money should be of prime importance. The same principle would apply if we were interested in the steel account; we would organise the analysis around the demand for and supply of steel.

The importance of the principle of organisation is dramatised by contrasting it with the frequently employed procedure of treating the balance of payments as the excess of exports over imports. Given the rules of double entry book-keeping, this procedure is formally correct, provided

that the import demand and the export supply functions are correctly specified. But, it does not focus on the prime determinants of the behaviour of
the money account; and, in practice, it is rarely the case that the demand
and supply functions are correctly specified. Usually, the import demand
function and the export supply function abstract from monetary variables
with the result that the demand for money and the supply of money are
either ignored or treated as passive in the analysis of the money account.

Of course, if the organisation of the analysis of the balance of
payments around the demand for money function and the money supply
process is to make much sense, the demand for money and the money
supply process must be stable functions of a limited set of variables. Fortunately, extensive empirical analysis has established the existence of both a
stable money demand function and a stable money supply process. Given
these stable relationships, it follows that if any policy or parametric change
is to have an effect on the balance of payments, it must cause a divergence
between what the demand for money would have been in the absence of
the policy or parametric change and what the supply of money would have
been in the absence of any change in the level of official holdings of foreign
exchange. If there is no such divergence, then there can be no long-run,
cumulative effect on the balance of payments. Any initial surplus must be
wiped out by a later deficit and any initial deficit must be wiped out by a
later surplus because people will not be willing to hold either more or less
money than they were previously holding.

If money demand were passive, i.e. if the economy [were] in a
liquidity trap, the monetary approach would have no predictive power. The
cumulative balance-of-payments surplus would be whatever was dictated
by exclusively non-monetary considerations, and the demand for money
would simply adjust to that fact and a non-monetary approach would not
only be justified, it would be required.

A stable money supply process is, in some ways, less essential to
the monetary approach to the balance of payments than a stable money
demand function. That part of the money supply process which deals with
the behaviour of the monetary authorities need not be stable since the
focus of the analysis is usually on the policy choices which are open to the
monetary authority. For this purpose, the behaviour of the monetary authorities is taken as exogenous, and the question that is asked is: what
would be the effect on the balance of payments if the monetary authorities
pursued policy X rather than policy Y? A sensible and useful answer to this
type of question depends only on the assumption of reasonable stable behaviour on the part of other actors in the money supply process.

The monetary approach does not always assume a constant domestic source component of the monetary base, nor does it always assume that
the monetary authorities follow the gold standard rules of the game by
maintaining a constant ratio of foreign exchange reserves to the monetary

base. If the monetary authorities expand the domestic source component of the base in excess of the growth in the implied demand for the base, then the monetary approach predicts that there will be a balance-of-payments deficit equal in magnitude to the excessive expansion of the domestic source component of the base. If the monetary authorities sterilise the balance-of-payments surplus created by, say, the imposition of a tariff, then the monetary approach predicts that there will be a further surplus, equal to the reduction in the domestic source component of the base which is implied by sterilisation, and so on, until the sterilisation operations cease.[3]

The monetary approach forces into the open the question of what the monetary authorities are doing and, hence, isolates effects which arise from a particular policy of parametric change, *per se*, and effects which arise from the induced (and frequently implicit) responses of the monetary authorities. Thus, the monetary approach avoids the unsound and objectionable procedure of concealing the basic determinants of the behaviour of the balance of payments behind such assumptions as "a neutral monetary policy" or "a monetary and fiscal policy which maintains internal balance" or "an accommodating monetary policy."

C. THE LONG RUN AND THE SHORT RUN

The empirical evidence which justifies the assumption of a stable money supply process and a stable money demand function applies to periods of a year or more, rather than to periods of a month or a quarter. These empirical facts account for the third basic feature of the monetary approach: *a concentration on the longer-run consequences of policy and parametric changes for the behaviour of the balance of payments, coupled with an eclectic view of the processes through which these longer-run consequences come about.*

This concentration on "longer-run consequences" does not imply that the nature of the process of adjustment is unimportant or that specific models which lie within the monetary approach can and should ignore the process of adjustment. Rather, the monetary approach takes an eclectic view of the process of adjustment because it seems unlikely that any single model of the process of adjustment will be relevant to all countries, at all time periods, and under all institutional arrangements. The monetary approach seeks to combine a relatively general theory of long-run behaviour with a number of different models of the process of adjustment.

Concerning the concentration of the monetary approach on "longer-run consequences," four comments should be made. Firstly, if these "longer-run consequences" take years or decades to materialise, the monetary approach will not be very useful. It will not be useful for discussing current policy problems because the horizon of the policy maker is typically much shorter than a decade. It will not be useful for empirical analysis because there is great difficulty in sorting out empirical relationships which involve very long lags. Therefore, the advocacy of a monetary approach to the balance of payments necessarily involves the assertion that these "longer-run consequences" materialise within a time horizon of two or three years.

Secondly, while the monetary approach explicitly denies the possibility that the demand for money is passive in the long run, it admits the possibility that the demand for money may be more or less passive in the short run. In the short run, money might operate as a buffer stock which serves to absorb the changes in other variables. In such an event, essentially non-monetary factors would determine the behaviour of the balance of payments in the very short run. The monetary approach, however, denies that this very short run could last very long before monetary factors began to assert themselves and explicitly raises the question of how long the very short run is. Thus, the monetary approach focuses attention on the critical role which monetary factors must play in the process of adjustment.

Thirdly, the monetary approach emphasises that as a fact of accounting, the balance-of-payments surplus is identically equal to the excess of income over expenditure. Hence, any analysis of the process of adjustment must explain how the policy or parametric change which is under investigation generates a divergence between income and expenditure.[4] The monetary approach does not insist that such a divergence may be created only by a real balance effect working directly on expenditure. Expenditure may be affected by changes in interest rates or changes in the values of non-monetary assets. In a world of capital mobility, the requirements of portfolio balance may lead to purchases or sales of assets to the rest of the world.[5] In a variable employment model, the divergence between income and expenditure may come as a result of changes in income rather than changes in expenditure. All of these mechanisms, and conceivably others, can play a role in the process of adjustment. The point is that there must be at least one such mechanism. This mechanism should be explicit, rather than implicit, in the formal model of the process of adjustment.

Fourthly, since the monetary approach establishes the long-run balance-of-payments effects of a policy change, it places limits on what is a reasonable analysis of the process of adjustment. If a tariff causes a finite change in foreign exchange reserves in the long run, then an analysis which suggests that a tariff creates a permanent (flow) balance-of-payments surplus is clearly incorrect. The analysis of the process of adjustment must show that as foreign exchange reserves accumulate, the flow balance-of-payments effect of the tariff is gradually reduced and ultimately eliminated. The cumulative balance-of-payments surplus which is implied by the process of adjustment must be equal to the required long-run change in foreign exchange reserves.

Notes

1. The monetary approach to the balance of payments is not a new approach: the basic ideas date back at least to David Hume and his discussion of the price specie flow mechanism. Indeed, up to the 1930s, the monetary approach was *the* recognised approach to the analysis of the balance of payments. For a particularly penetrating discussion of the basic features of the "monetary approach," see Marshall (1926). Also see Keynes (1971).
2. Under a system of freely floating rates, attention is shifted from the balance of payments, which is always zero, to the exchange rate, which moves up and down to absorb the consequences of policy and parametric changes which, under a system of fixed rates, would affect the balance of payments.
3. Some care must be taken in analysing the effects of a policy of sterilisation. If the monetary authorities are selling domestic interest-bearing assets out of their portfolio in order to sterilise a foreign exchange inflow, then the stock of such assets in private hands must be rising and the interest which the government will be required to pay on the privately held government debt will be rising. The effects of a change in the stock of privately held debt and the effects of the change in government interest payments and of the means which are used to finance these interest payments must be dealt with in order to have a complete analysis of the effects of sterilisation. The issue here is akin to the issue of what happens to the budget surplus in a closed economy macro model. For further discussion, see Mussa (1976).
4. The fact that a balance-of-payments surplus requires an excess of income over expenditure is the fundamental principle of the "absorption approach" to balance-of-payments analysis. The monetary approach incorporates this basic principle of the absorption approach in so far as the analysis of the process of adjustment is concerned. For further discussion of the absorption approach, see Alexander (1952) and Johnson (1958).
5. Note that purchases of assets are included with expenditures, and sales of assets are included with income in the calculation of the balance-of-payments surplus as the difference between income and expenditure.

References

Alexander, S. S. (1952) "Effects of a Devaluation on the Trade Balance," *IMF Staff Papers*, vol. II (April 1952), 263–78.

Johnson, H. G. (1958), "Towards a General Theory of the Balance of Payments," in H. G. Johnson, *International Trade and Economic Growth* (London, George Allen & Unwin, 1958), 153–68.

Keynes, John M. (1971), *Tract on Monetary Reform* (London, Macmillan, 1971).

Marshall, Alfred (1926), *Official Papers* (London, Macmillan, 1926), 170–95.

Mussa, Michael (1976), *A Study in Macroeconomics* (Amsterdam, North Holland, 1976).

24

The Mundell-Laffer Hypothesis—A New View of the World Economy

Jude Wanniski

The United States has been passing through an economic night-mare. It seems like just the other day—and it was—that American economists of the first rank spoke confidently of "fine-tuning" the economy to assure a predetermined rate of economic growth within ac-ceptable bounds of inflation and unemployment. And even those in the profession who scoffed at the notion of such fine-tuning, those who argued it could not be done in the fashion prescribed by the New Economics, were prepared to assert that other strategies—usually pertaining to the supply of money—could be called into play to keep the United States on the magic path of non-inflationary growth.

Obviously, the profession has been experiencing an intellectual crisis. Over a six-year period, the pragmatic Republicanism of Richard Nixon shot into the twitching patient every antibody the economic doctors of Cambridge and Chicago prepared. And always the vital signs declined. Money was tightened and money was eased. Mr. Nixon became a Keynes-ian and a "full-employment budget" was installed. Deficits were run on purpose and deficits were run by accident. The Phillips curve, a wondrous device by which politicians supposedly could balance unemployment and inflation along a finely calibrated line, was enshrined in the textbooks. The dollar was devalued and the gold window closed. The Japanese and Ger-mans were reviled as being stubborn, and worse, efficient. The dollar was devalued again, then floated. Wages and prices were controlled through varied stages of stringency, and a jawbone was brandished. At the end of all these exertions, many are beginning to wonder whether the patient was sicker than had been thought or whether the medicine has been making him sicker than he was.

To be sure, the academic theoreticians who pushed these various prescriptions will now all argue that their own brand of medicine was not given time to work—and besides, the patient was poisoned by all those other medicines. They all have a point in that there is rarely enough time in the real world to see a diagnosis and a prescription through; politicians and

From Jude Wanniski, "The Mundell-Laffer Hypothesis." Reprinted with the au-thor's permission from *The Public Interest* No. 39 (Spring 1975), pp. 31–52. © 1975 by National Affairs, Inc.

the public will always want a remedy that doesn't require the patient to get much worse, for very long, before he gets better. That is one of the inevitable political constraints on economic policy, as distinct from economic theory.

But before one laments the constraints that the body politic places on our economic physicians, it is worthwhile seeking out another opinion. It is always possible there is an expert around with a superior diagnosis of our economic illness—one that does not require politically impossible prescriptions. And, in fact, there are *two* such experts around today: Robert A. Mundell, . . . a Canadian who is professor of economics at Columbia University, and Arthur B. Laffer, . . . of the University of [Southern California]. For the past several years, they have attempted to effect what some would call a "Copernican revolution" in economic policy. And, with every passing year, they are getting a somewhat more respectful hearing from their fellow economists—though, of course, theirs is still very much a minority point of view.[1]

It is the purpose of this article to show how the Mundell-Laffer "model" of the world economy works, and why its implications are not politically unattractive—i.e., would not involve a period of suffering by the world's population in order to achieve improvement. The model is really quite simple and, except for its applications, is not even particularly novel. It is just, as Laffer says, "that nobody's thought much about it this way for about 50 years or so."

One of the reasons the Mundell-Laffer hypothesis is getting a respectful hearing these days is that it easily explains phenomena that other theories can explain only with immense difficulty and complication. Though they are not in the business of forecasting, Mundell and Laffer's predictions of what would happen as a result of particular policy changes have held up astonishingly well these past years. Laffer in 1971 said the U.S. dollar devaluation would not mean a turn from deficit to surplus in the U.S. trade balance. There wasn't one. In February 1973, when the dollar was devalued again, he said it would mean "runaway inflation" in the United States. In January 1972—almost two years before the Yom Kippur war—Mundell said the price of oil, and then of other commodities, would rise dramatically if the U.S. economic policy makers proceeded to do what in fact they did. Later in the year, he said that if the Western economies did what they in fact subsequently decided to do, there would be increased world inflation, a general rise in interest rates, and an accelerated use of the Eurodollar. In 1973, he bet an eminent U.S. economist $1 that U.S. inflation would be far worse in 1974 than 1973, and another $1 that sometime in 1974 the price of gold would hit $200.

Maybe Mundell and Laffer were lucky—right for the wrong reasons, as some may say. But it certainly would seem to be worth the effort to understand their reasoning—and, above all, to understand their general view of the economic universe and what it is in this view that fundamentally separates them from the great majority of their peers. Their policy prescriptions—which derive from a kind of synthesis of Keynesian and classical economic thought—make no sense unless one shares their perspective on the economic universe. After all, Columbus would have found it difficult to persuade Queen Isabella that sailing west to the Indies was good policy if he had failed to convince her that the world was round, not flat.

THE WORLD IS A CLOSED ECONOMY

This is where they start: The world economy is truly integrated and has been for a long time. The proposition sounds reasonable enough, perhaps even trite. Yet while most other economists accept the idea to a degree, the prevailing analytical approach to economic problems and policy is based on a quite different notion: that the U.S. economy is in large part independent of the economies of the rest of the world, especially now that monetary policies are not linked through fixed currency exchange rates. From this prevailing notion there follows the idea that, insofar as the U.S. economy experiences fluctuations in rates of inflation as the result of the economic policies of other governments, such disturbances are limited in scope by the U.S. volume of trade with the rest of the world. These disturbances must be small, the conventional wisdom argues, because U.S. trade is so small in relation to the whole of the U.S. economy. In 1971, when the dollar was devalued by 13 per cent, virtually the entire economics profession in the United States calculated that, because U.S. trade was only five per cent of GNP, the effect of the devaluation on the level of U.S. prices would merely be 13 per cent of five, or a little more than a half-point on the Consumer Price Index. This kind of calculation can be made only by viewing the United States as a closed economy, "with international relationships grafted on," says Laffer. But, they argue, the U.S. economy is not a closed economy; nor is that of any other nation. *The only closed economy it makes sense to talk about is the world economy.* One cannot understand the American economy within an American perspective; it must be viewed from the perspective of the world economy.

In simplest terms, what they are saying is that prices are tied together around the world, not only by the volume of goods shipped back and forth, but by rapid communication of price changes. To verify this, one of Laffer's students, Moon Hoe Lee, went to the trouble of studying nine countries from 1900 to 1972. He found that (1) their general price indexes indeed moved in step during the period, as long as their exchange rates were unchanged; and (2) that when a country devalued or revalued its currency, it experienced roughly equivalent amounts of inflation or deflation. (The only brief exceptions were observed when a country became isolated during wartime, Japan and Italy during World War II being the clearest examples.) What this means is that if a country devalues by 13 per cent against the rest of the world's currencies, you could expect that it would experience higher inflation than the rest of the world *until its prices had risen by 13 per cent more than those of the rest of the world.* So far from such a revision of exchange rates having only a minor effect—via foreign trade—on the Consumer Price Index, it has an exactly proportioned effect relative to the price level in the rest of the world.

This isn't exactly a revolutionary idea but, as Laffer says, it hasn't been thought about for quite a while. Here's J. Lawrence Laughlin writing in 1903:

> The action of the international markets, with telegraphic quotations from every part of the world, precludes the supposition that gold prices could in general remain on a higher level in one country than another (cost of carriage apart), even for a brief time, because, in order to gain the profits merchants would seize the opportunity to send goods to the markets where prices are high.

Laughlin talks about gold, but implicit in his statement is that apples are affected similarly. Say there are a million apples in a country selling at 10¢ each, but that there exists an unqualified demand for 1,000,001 apples. If the extra apple can't be gotten from the rest of the world at less than 11¢, cost of carriage apart, *the price of all apples will rise to 11¢.* In this illustration, the volume of trade involved is only one part in a million—but price still changes by 10 per cent.

Going a step further, Mundell has revived the proposition, and Laffer has documented empirically, that money, like apples and gold, is also subject to these international forces of supply and demand. When, for example, there is an excess demand for money in the United States relative to the rest of the world, we will import money and run a balance of payments surplus—i.e., more money will be coming into this country than is going out. When there is an excess supply of money in the United States, we will export money and run a balance of payments deficit. This idea also has its roots in earlier centuries, but is still a minority view among economists everywhere. Balance of payments deficits are thought to represent not a market phenomenon but a structural problem—i.e., "capital flight" or "undercompetitiveness." . . .

This way of looking at deficits and surpluses in one's balance of payments and balance of trade is strikingly different from the prevailing way, and has large implications for economic policy. But more about that later.

MYTHS OF DEVALUATION

While the above approximates the Mundell-Laffer long-distance view of the economic universe, it is necessary to move in closer and examine the terrain piece by piece before the direction of policy becomes apparent. A most important thesis, again one that cuts against the predominant thinking, is this: *When money supplies and currency exchange rates change, the terms of trade remain unchanged.* Somewhere at the root of our economic policies of the past several years lies exactly the opposite assumption.

Put simply, what Mundell and Laffer say is this: If a bushel of U.S. wheat can be traded for a bottle of Italian wine when $1 equals 100 lire, then, even though the United States devalues the dollar so that it is only equal to 80 lire, the bushel will still trade for the bottle. There may be a temporary confusion, which economists call "money illusion," but it is only temporary. That is, the U.S. farmer may temporarily accept 80 lire in payment for his wheat, because it still equals $1—and his first interest is in dollars. But when he discovers that $1 is now worth only four-fifths of the bottle, he will insist on getting $1.20 worth of lire so he still gets the whole bottle. As a result, *the dollar price of U.S. wheat goes up by the full amount of the devaluation.* Or the lire price of Italian wine goes down.

It is thus the contention of Mundell and Laffer, borne out by considerable empirical evidence, that devaluation has no "real" effects, but results only in price inflation in the devaluing country relative to the country or countries against which the devaluation occurs. By reducing the amount of goods its money can buy, the devaluing country creates an excess demand for its money. If it simply prints more money, there is no balance of payments improvement—which was what devaluation was supposed to achieve. If it doesn't, its citizens will simply import money (by exporting bonds) to satisfy the excess demand, and this will show up as a brief "improvement" in the balance of payments.

But isn't it true, as the textbooks and newspapers have been saying for a generation, that when a country devalues, the goods it imports become more expensive, so it buys fewer of them, while the goods that foreigners buy from it are cheaper, so the foreigners buy more of them? And the net result is a nice improvement in the devaluing country's balance of trade? The answer is: No. . . .

EXCHANGE RATES NEED NEVER CHANGE

According to Mundell-Laffer, the world be much better off with a system designed to keep exchange rates permanently fixed. If 2.5 Deutschemarks will always be equal to $1, or 300 yen always equal $1, all currencies would be identical except in name. *The world would in effect have a common currency.* Interest rates, prices, and the rate of inflation would then be the same everywhere, broadly speaking, just as they are within a large country like the United States with its common currency.

In the Mundell-Laffer scheme of things, a common currency is not a utopian fantasy; it has been around before. For decades prior to World

War I, the world had a simulated common currency as national currencies were tried to the pound sterling and the pound was fixed to gold. In the years after Bretton Woods (1944) until about 1967, or even 1971, the world had a simulated common currency bound to the dollar. The system was flawed, but still enormously successful.

There are substantial benefits to be had, by the world and all its component parts, through use of a common currency, simulated by a properly constructed fixed-exchange-rate system. Conversely, the world and its component economies are now paying an enormous penalty for the absence of a common currency—the penalty of rampant inflation. But before the benefits of a common currency are examined, consider the supposed penalties of not having an independent national currency. Even if, as Mundell and Laffer claim, devaluation does not improve the U.S. competitive position in the world and only causes price inflation, isn't monetary policy useful in stimulating production and employment in the United States, making it worthwhile to retain national control over it? Again, say Mundell and Laffer, the answer is no.

Just as trade between a U.S. wheat farmer and an Italian winemaker is only stimulated momentarily by the confusion of an exchange rate change, so there is no lasting stimulation to commerce internally from pumping money into the system faster than the system is demanding it— i.e., beyond the real growth demands of the economy. There may be a brief confusion in the terms of trade between Kansas farmers, California vintners, and Detroit automakers, or the workers who are paid to produce these goods. But there will be less and less confusion as they learn to read the signals and extract their meaning. As soon as this has been accomplished, the overwhelming effect is price inflation. And, because monetary stimulation increases the rate of inflation, thereby "taxing" cash balances and other financial assets, there is an immediate lowering of real income and offsetting subtraction from output. If the horse will not drink if there is a gallon in the trough, you can't make him drink by adding liquidity.[2]

If monetary stimulation can increase production only by increasing someone's credit at the expense of someone else (a creditor who is paid off in inflated currency, a contractor who has agreed to supply goods and services at a fixed price, or a worker tied to a wage contract), the increased production gained by such deceptive means can be of value to a politician only insofar as the cost of price inflation can be pushed far enough into the future so that some other politician will have to deal with it. If the market becomes conditioned to see immediately through the deception, and discounts the future accordingly, the politician gets no gain whatever.

On the other hand, there are distinct advantages to the politician, and to the economic interests of his constituency, in a common currency or a properly constructed fixed-exchange-rate system.

THE "BONUS" OF A WORLD CURRENCY

The world economy gets a bonus, something extra, by having the economies of scale of a common currency. On narrow grounds, even the opponents of fixed rates agree with this. But Mundell and Laffer go beyond the narrow grounds.

Here is the *usual* financial argument on behalf of fixed rates: Suppose each of the 50 states of the U.S. had its own monetary authority and its own currency. Interest rates and the rate of inflation would vary widely. Business would still be transacted between states, but in each interstate transaction requiring a contract both buyer and seller would have to insure themselves against a change in the exchange rate, say between Kansas and Nebraska. This effort would require a sizable layer of personnel, expertise, and capital, which would otherwise be doing something more useful. As always, consumers would pay higher prices for everything, the cost of "hedging" being added in at the retail level. The dollar cost of providing "hedges" between 50 currencies would run into billions per year.

It may be argued that such an overhead expense is not really a colossal amount of money to pay in order to retain the advantages of independence. In the same way, if it were really deemed important by national governments to have independent monies, the extra tens of billions of dollars worth of resources required to maintain commerce in a world of floating exchange rates could be defended. But Mundell and Laffer identify the costs of floating in a different dimension as well. It is not only that the floating system has financial costs because of added coverage requirements, but also that *there are dramatic and inescapable increases in the amount of error in a system of many, rather than few, monetary authorities.* This point is crucial to an understanding of why the world economy is now in such a mess. It becomes obvious why Mundell can write so casually that, throughout history, "the gains from using a common international medium are so great that some means of creating one have always been found."

Again, consider Kansas and Nebraska. If each had an independent monetary authority, each authority would have to be considerably wiser and more efficient than if they arranged a compact to pool their mistakes. Imagine that on a given day in July, there are a thousand economic transactions in Kansas that have to be made with the available supply of money. If the Kansas monetary authority erred on that day by not anticipating the precise number of transactions and the quantity of money required to make them, one of two things would happen. If the amount of money were insufficient, some of those thousand transactions could not be completed at prevailing prices. Prices would have to fall until the amount of money were sufficient. If prices did not fall (which is likely in that prices seem to go up easier than they come down), some of the transactions would not be completed unless money substitutes were available. Which means the supply of goods would have to fall, resulting in lower output and higher unemployment in Kansas.

Alternatively, if the Kansas authority overshot the mark and produced too much money, all the transactions would be completed, but because buyers had more money than sellers had goods, the prices of goods would be bid up until supply equaled demand. So, on that day in July, if too much money is supplied, there is inflation; if too little is supplied, there is some deflation and some reduced output.

On that same day, the Nebraska authority is having a similar problem. With so many transactions to be completed, only by miraculous good luck is it going to produce the precise amount of money required.

But consider what happens if the Kansas and Nebraska monetary authorities agree to buy and sell each other's currencies at a fixed rate, say one Kansas dollar for one Nebraska dollar. If this is so, and Kansas produces $100 too little money to effect its 1,000 transactions, and Nebraska produces $100 too much, a party in Kansas will observe there are 100 too many Nebraska dollars and 100 too few in his own state. He then borrows 100 Nebraska dollars and presents them at the Kansas monetary authority. In accord with the Kansas-Nebraska agreement, he gets the 100 Kansas dollars he wants for the 100 Nebraska dollars. With this transaction, each state has precisely the amount of money it needs and there is no unemployment in Kansas and no inflation in Nebraska. On the following day, Kansas can overshoot a little and Nebraska undershoot a little, and over the course of months—and certainly years—they can make sure that the use of each other's money nets out to roughly zero. That is, neither state will have a balance of payments deficit or surplus.

But what if, you will wonder, both Kansas and Nebraska undershoot at the same time? Say Kansas is short $100 and Nebraska short $50. In sharing the error, both come up short $75, which means Nebraska is worse off than if it didn't have the agreement, but Kansas is better off. But even if one is going to assume that Nebraska will be consistently right and Kansas consistently wrong, it is still to their mutual advantage to compromise their errors—if only because each gains from the other's prosperity and loses from the other's depression.

This is not simply a theoretical example. *It is, in fact, exactly the way the 12 Federal Reserve Districts operate,* with each responsible for issuing currency in its region. The districts have daily, monthly, and yearly balance of payments deficits and surpluses with one another, but they are so attuned to correcting the money supply to fit demand that the deficits and surpluses are not even apparent to the public, which believes there is only one U.S. currency instead of 12. (Check the left center of any bill for the issuing bank.)

THE BRETTON WOODS SYSTEM

This is almost, but not quite, the way the Bretton Woods system operated. Instead of setting up a system that would approximate the fashion in which the 12 Federal Reserve Districts correct balance of payments differences with each other, by expanding or contracting the money supply, the Bretton Woods agreement tried something else.

Imagine, in the above example, that instead of all 50 states balancing payments with one another by expanding or contracting the money supply, one state had a different role. New York, say, would not have to stay in balance with the other states. Theoretically one state could be excused, because if 49 states have zero balances, the 50th automatically has a balance of zero. New York could then use this extra measure of freedom by making sure that the system *as a whole* had "proper" monetary policy, so that with economic growth in the system *as a whole,* commerce would not be hindered by a paucity or excess of money growth.

What, though, is the *proper* quantity of money? That is the question New York would have constantly to decide. The answer goes something like this: The chief cost of excessive expansion of money is the strain put on the availability of natural resources. If New York raised the quantity of money at too rapid a rate, it would increase the nominal amount of transactions. But, as previously mentioned, this would come about through the destruction of the real value of someone's financial assets.[3] The increase in nominal transactions generated by this artificial means—inflation—results in a more inefficient use of the nation's resources than would otherwise occur. One way New York could solve its hypothetical problem of determining the proper rate of money growth would be to adopt a metal as money, such as gold, thereby tying money creation directly to a natural resource. This, too, is not a theoretical example. It is the way the world economy worked for decades, even centuries, up to 1914. During this period, Great Britain fixed the price of gold by regulating the quantity of money in the world and by buying and selling gold, doing so with such precision that all the while it maintained only a very small inventory of gold. Nor was there a general international monetary agreement in this period. The rest of the world simply found it so advantageous to fix their currencies to the pound sterling, while sterling was fixed to gold, that it occurred *ad hoc.*

This was also the Bretton Woods system, arrived at formally. The United States played the role for the world economy that, in the hypothetical example, New York played for the 50 states, and that Britain played in earlier centuries. Although the Bretton Woods system was flawed, it did provide the framework that made possible a quarter-century of uninterrupted prosperity and growth in the Western economies. The flaw, however, led to its abandonment.

The flaw in Bretton Woods lay in the fact that the people who were responsible for running the system didn't know how it was supposed to work. Go back to our hypothetical New York example. If 49 states are maintaining external balance by expanding or contracting their money supply, and New York is expanding the quantity of money to accommodate economic growth in the system as a whole, then if New York expands too fast everyone in the system has too much money and there is a general inflation. If the other 49 states do not desire to have inflation, they have to print less of their own currencies. If New York keeps pumping out money, and the other 49 states are contracting their monies accordingly, the result is inevitable. At the extreme, everyone in the United States is transacting business with New York dollars. All the states are running huge surpluses in the balance of payments with New York, and New York is running a stupendous balance of payments deficit. But New York doesn't care. It has become the sole supplier of money, and as banker of the game receives in return for its banking service the real goods of all other states.

So it was with Bretton Woods. For a while, everything worked well. After World War II, the United States had most of the gold in the world, far more than it needed. It didn't worry about providing precisely the correct growth of money supplies, but acted in a way that made sure there was more than enough money rather than too little. When the war-torn countries got on their feet, it still did not matter that the United States was overexpanding its money creation, because the others wanted some of the U.S. gold to hold for a rainy day, and they were now prosperous enough to acquire some. By restraining its money growth, West Germany, for example, would import dollars. If the number of dollars were more than needed by West Germans, after being turned in for Deutschemarks, the West German monetary authority, the Bundesbank, would have some left over to buy U.S. gold. After several years of this, the U.S. gold hoard was down from $24 billion to $12 billion, valued at $35 an ounce.

In this arrangement, all the economic incentives drove the United States to create more money than was really needed, and forced the other countries to produce less of their own currencies if they wanted to avoid inflation. People and enterprises all over the world did more and more of their business in dollars, finding the United States always there to supply money when needed, while their own monetary authorities seemed to be cutting back. In exchange for its real good, the banking service, the United States was receiving other real goods—autos, radios, etc.

But it's one thing for New York to drive everyone else's money out of the other 49 states, and quite another for the United States to push out foreign currencies by running constant balance of payments deficits. For the most part, the U.S. deficits were not the fault of the United States, but the natural result of its having been the most efficient supplier of money in the world. The dollar became, says Mundell, "the major intervention currency, a reserve asset for central banks, the standard of contract, the standard of quotation, the invoice currency, the major settlement currency, the major reserve asset for commercial banks, the major traveller's currency, the major external currency for indexing bonds, and the major clearing currency." In so many ways, foreigners were demanding dollars rather than their own national currencies.

GOLD AND DOLLARS

Such was, and still is, the power of the dollar, deriving from the power of the American economy. Just as Kansas is the most efficient supplier of wheat, and Brazil the most efficient supplier of coffee, so the United States is the most efficient supplier of money. It would be ridiculous to expect Kansas to run a zero balance of trade in wheat, importing as much as it exported, or Brazil a zero balance of trade in coffee. So too, it was imperative that the United States run ever increasing deficits in its export of money. Bretton Woods broke down because U.S. politicians and economists did not understand this, and thus did not do the simple things required to perpetuate international economic stability.

What was overlooked was the efficient use of gold in providing a control mechanism and an error signal, as to when the United States was supplying too much money or too little. If the world economic system's real growth, year after year, would average three per cent, and the increase in the world money supply would adverage five per cent, there would be a world inflation rate of two per cent. As a purely private commodity, gold in 1944 at $35 was overpriced. But as world prices moved up year after year, and gold remained at $35 an ounce, eventually it became underpriced. By 1960, external demands for U.S. gold became so great at this bargain price that the U.S. government would sell gold only to other central banks. What emerged then was a collective agreement among central banks not to reduce further U.S. gold stocks. But the gold pool thus formed broke down in 1968 when gold losses to the private market became serious.

According to Mundell and Laffer, what the United States could have done to avoid the last decade of grief was to have concentrated on keeping the dollar more attractive than $35-per-ounce gold. Neither individuals nor central banks would come to the U.S. Treasury with dollars and demand their conversion into gold as long as the level of real growth in the world called for X number of dollars and only X number were supplied. If the United States was afraid of "losing" any more of its $12 billion gold hoard in 1967, it need only have acted in the following fashion: Whenever a foreigner holding, say, $100 showed up and demanded an equivalent amount of gold out of the Treasury hoard, the Federal Reserve would know it had mistakenly issued 100 too many dollars. By contracting the money supply in that amount, the Fed would only have to sit back and wait:

Somebody else in the world, needing 100 dollars in order to make a transaction and finding the world was short by that amount, would come to the Treasury with the equivalent amount of gold and demand dollars.

Instead, by partially closing the gold window in 1968, the United States only succeeded in making the dollar less attractive relative to gold and began the process that culminated in the current economic nightmare. Immediately, the private market developed an unofficial price of gold higher than $35 an ounce. This effectively *immobilized* the gold held by central banks as reserve assets. Why? Central banks hold reserves as a cushion against unexpected international demands, arising from an internal crop failure, for example. But if such demands arose while gold was selling unofficially at higher than $35, the central bank would have to give up its gold at the official price and lose the difference. Every central bank thus locked up its gold and began scraping together new reserves—i.e., dollars. The U.S. central bank, of course, didn't have this concern—acquiring dollar reserves—because it is the central bank that creates dollars.

THE DEMISE OF BRETTON WOODS

At the time, the popular belief in the United States was that the Western European and Japanese economies were amassing these dollar reserves by running trade surpluses with the United States. There was a common vision here of a Japanese manufacturer, using cheap labor, peddling a television set here for dollars, then simply banking the dollars. An American would lose a job, and a substitute job would not be created because the dollars earned by Japan would not be spent. The U.S. economy had become "uncompetitive," or so the story went, and as the balance of payments deficits mounted, the idea took hold that the reason for all this was that the U.S. dollar had become "overvalued."

What Mundell and Laffer say actually occurred was that, as foreign central banks immobilized their gold reserves, "money" became scarcer in these countries. In order to transact business, foreigners borrowed dollars and turned them in at their central banks for their own currency, and month after month the foreign central banks would show larger holdings of dollars. To most Americans, this looked pretty frightening, since these dollars were perceived as claims against U.S. goods and services. *What was not apparent in the balance of payments deficits was the original transaction, the foreign "borrowing" of dollars, which meant that the United States had an equal and offsetting claim against foreign assets.*

In a world economy whose growth depended on a proper growth of the common currency (i.e., the dollar), the United States under the Bretton Woods arrangement would have to run ever larger balance of payments deficits for everyone's good. But Mundell perceived that, by forcing the immobilization of gold, the United States intensified this process and increased its deficits beyond the "normal" level. Then, instead of regaining control of the deficit by tightening up on dollar creation, which would have made possible once again the conversion of dollars into gold (or creating a world money into which the dollar was convertible), a grievous policy error was made. President Johnson sought to slow the outflow of dollars to reduce the U.S. payments deficit, first by voluntary restrictions on U.S. overseas investment (1965), then by making it mandatory (1968). A series of regulations was put in place to keep dollars from going abroad. The result was that the private market found a way around the U.S. regulations, and through financial innovation created a much worse headache for Washington. As Mundell stated in April 1972:

> Failing an international money, a market solution will always develop, but it is one field in which market solutions are not optimal. The commercial banks, using the dollar, have now created an international money. It is the Eurodollar system or the international dollar system.

The financial innovation, which has taken on a life of its own, was the private substitute for the imperfectly working official system. The foreign branches of U.S. commercial banks accommodated the thirst for dollar liquidity abroad that the U.S. government was trying to choke off. Because foreign deposits of U.S. dollars are not subject to the reserve requirements imposed against domestic deposits, the banks could and did become efficient *private creators of money.* When the Fed slowed its creation of dollars, the Eurodollar market speeded up its creation, and vice versa. In an important 1974 empirical study, Laffer found this relationship to hold in each of the last 14 years. *The Federal Reserve could now only kid itself into thinking it could slow down the economy by contracting money growth, or stimulate the economy by expanding money supply.* The marketplace had found a substitute for the Fed.

In their imperfect understanding of what was happening in the world economy from 1967 on, U.S. policy makers dealt a quick *coup de grâce* to the Bretton Woods system. In Mundell's words:

> No event in history can be said to have a single cause. But if one were seeking the most important policy origins of the 1971 [monetary] crisis one would have to blame it on excessive monetary looseness in the U.S. in the first six months of 1971, when monetary expansion was more rapid than in any comparable period in a quarter century! . . . The monetary acceleration exaggerated the overflow of dollars and engulfed Europe in dollar liquidity in the spring of 1971. In August, European central banks demanded gold. Rather than pay it out, the U.S. suspended convertibility. The 1934–71 era of $35 an ounce became a closed book in history.

There followed, between August 1971 and February 1973 (when currency exchange rates were set on a common float), a further comedy of errors. U.S. policy makers, hypnotized by the idea that the U.S. economy was suffering from an overvalued dollar, "won" a 13 per cent devaluation of the dollar in the agreement Treasury Secretary John Connally got from foreign ministers at a meeting in the Smithsonian Institution. The U.S. officials grumbled that the devaluation should have been three or four per cent higher to get all the benefits. As events demonstrated, there were not going to be any benefits at all.

RECREATING THE "MONEY SUPERMARKET"

In the Mundell-Laffer perspective, the world after 1944 had enjoyed all the efficiencies and economies of scale of a "money supermarket." But the flexible—then floating—exchange rates, the supermarket would close and be replaced by "mom and pop" money stores. It is the global equivalent of what would suddenly happen if each of our 50 states were forced off the common U.S. currency into independent monetary systems.

Nor will Mundell and Laffer be surprised if the world comes back to a money supermarket, a fixed-exchange-rate system that again tries to approximate a world currency. In June 1969, at a conference celebrating the 25th anniversary of Bretton Woods, Mundell took note of the powerful forces driving toward exchange-rate flexibility and predicted that by 1980 the world would have tried it, abandoned it, and turned away from any further advocacy of it. It will probably not take that long. Already, many U.S. officials no longer look upon dollar depreciation as signaling an improvement in the U.S. "competitive" position. And West German bankers, economists, and politicians no longer worry that an appreciation of the Deutschemark will harm the German economy. Once this reality is accepted, the "political impracticalities" of putting together a world currency vanish. If politicians can see that their internal economies do not benefit from depreciation of the currency, and if they further see that their internal economies cannot be stimulated to increased output and decreased unemployment by money creation, they will willingly give up this device in order to gain the enormous benefits of the money supermarket, the common currency.

Once this political problem is put aside, all that Laffer and Mundell see is a difficult, but straightforward, engineering problem. In a dozen different ways, the mechanism can be reconstructed so that the benefits of Bretton Woods are back without the flaw of the system. . . .

The economic and social costs of not having such a system operating since 1967, and especially since 1971, have been colossal. Monetary discipline ended when the world moved away from convertibility and onto flexible rates. Much of the world inflation has resulted from the breakdown of Bretton Woods, bringing in its train the crisis in confidence in Western institutions and doubts about the appropriateness of free economies in the modern environment. In return for this mess, the United States now has an independent monetary policy, which amounts to a "right" to have more unemployment when policy errs on the side of tightness and the "right" to have more inflation when policy errs on the side of looseness.

It is still much too early, of course, to estimate the status of the Mundell-Laffer hypothesis. Though many distinguished economists are beginning rather grudgingly to allow that "there may be something in it," resistance and disapproval are still strong. The suggestion that gold (or an equivalent to gold, say a basket of commodities) could have a useful role in international finance certainly raises the hackles of a generation of economists who were raised to think that the "gold standard" was one of yesteryear's most awful superstitions. And the Mundell-Laffer hypothesis does irritate the ideological sensibilities of those—whether economists or politicians—who believe that, world economy or no, a national economic policy can still be "made" by national authorities. And it is always possible that further research and analysis will reveal that Mundell and Laffer have only a part of the truth.

Still, it is unlikely that the hypothesis will simply fade away. . . .

Notes

1. There is no joint Mundell-Laffer paper. Mundell, the prime mover, writes the theory. Laffer, more the empiricist, provides the data support, contributing slices of theoretical inspiration along the way.
2. At one time Mundell believed with the rest of the profession that the government could retard the economy by contracting its money supply, but after so much government manipulation over so many years private commerce has become exceedingly adroit in switching to money imports and substitutes, chiefly trade credit and credit cards, both of which are sources of liquidity.
3. Those who lent money at a fixed rate of interest, or contracted to supply goods or services at a fixed price, or who agreed to work for a year or longer at a fixed wage, discover that the addition of these marginal transactions, through excessive monetary expansion, has put prices up, and their wages have lost purchasing power. While those who borrowed or bought enjoy an offsetting benefit, the net effect is a weakening of the relationship between reward and effort. Henceforth, if excessive policies continue, they will demand compensation in the form of higher interest rates, higher fixed-price contracts, and higher wages and/or cost of living adjustments.

25

International Interdependence and the U.S. Economy

Marina v. N. Whitman

THE AMERICAN ECONOMY: FROM INDEPENDENCE TO INTERDEPENDENCE

Whereas the idea of economic interdependence among nations has always lain at the heart of the pure theory of international trade, it was virtually ignored in the development of macroeconomic analysis and the theory of economic policy in the United States during the two decades immediately after World War II. The Keynesian income-expenditure analysis developed and refined on this side of the Atlantic is fundamentally the analysis of a closed economy, into which "foreign repercussions" are introduced as second-order effects that can alter the magnitude but not the direction of impact of policy measures or other exogenous disturbances on the national economy. The quantity-theory "counterrevolution" that challenged this neo-Keynesian orthodoxy was equally strongly rooted in closed-economy assumptions, substituting domestic monetary policy for domestic fiscal policy as the key macroeconomic variable. And the major survey of inflation theory published by two American economists in the mid-1960s relegated discussion of the influences of foreign prices on domestic inflation to a single footnote.[1]

Today, in contrast, the term "interdependence" is on almost every tongue, and it is scarcely possible to hold—or to read—a serious discussion of any aspect of contemporary major economic problems in the United States, or of the policy responses to those problems, without incorporating the international dimensions of the problems themselves and of the policies proposed to deal with them. This shift in perception and attitude is undoubtedly due in part to the dramatic events of the past few years: the upheavals in the international monetary system, the emergence of the OPEC cartel with its dramatic economic and political effects, the simultaneous development first of explosive inflation and then of severe recession in a large number of countries. But the shift is also rooted in some important changes in the international economic position of the United States—changes that

From Marina v. N. Whitman, "International Interdependence and the U.S. Economy," in *Contemporary Economic Problems 1976*, William Fellner, ed. (Washington, D.C.: American Enterprise Institute, 1977). Reprinted by permission. Some footnotes omitted.

have been taking place gradually over a much longer period of time—as well as in the emergence of new developments in economic theory that have significantly affected the analytical perspective from which economists view the problems confronting economic policy making. These theoretical developments are of course related to and in part stimulated by changes in economic realities—in the data, so to speak. But in their impact on policy analysis, these expansions and shifts in analytical framework tend to take on a life of their own, becoming an independent influence on the way problems and issues are perceived, in addition to the influence that is exerted by changes in the underlying quantitative data.

The Changing Nature of Interdependence

Among the important developments in the underlying data is the change in the real (as opposed to the financial) position of the United States in the world economy over the past quarter century. The United States remains the world's largest national economy, with a gross national product accounting for nearly half that of all the OECD countries combined, and more than three times as large as that of Japan, the second largest non-Communist country. But the U.S. share of world GNP has fallen by more than one-third since 1950: from 39 percent in that year to 25 percent in 1975. In certain important industrial sectors, the U.S. share of world production dropped even more sharply between 1950 and 1970: from 76 percent to 31 percent in the case of motor vehicles and from 46 percent to 20 percent in the case of steel—while, concomitantly, our share of world consumption of industrial materials fell from 42 percent to 27 percent. In international trade, our share of world exports fell more gradually, from 16 percent in 1950 to 12 percent in 1975.

There are exceptions to this pattern of a declining world share in at least two important areas: the United States is today a more important agricultural exporter than ever before, and in the early 1970s continued to hold nearly 70 percent of the total direct investment claims of the world's major capital-exporting nations, about the same proportion as a decade earlier, despite the introduction during the intervening years of several programs designed to limit outflows of capital from the United States. But the drop in the U.S. share of international reserves, at first deliberately encouraged by U.S. policies to help other nations rebuild their war-depleted stocks and then the increasingly troublesome result of an overvalued dollar, was the most precipitous of all: from 50 percent in 1950 to 7 percent in 1974.[2]

Actually, to emphasize the declining share of the United States in the world economy may be to put an unwarranted negative emphasis on a phenomenon that is in large part a result of the rapid recovery and subsequent healthy growth of the economies of other industrialized nations since World War II. Perhaps it would be better to talk, instead, about the growing share of the rest of the world in the global economy. But, however one describes it, there is no question that this shift in relative importance in the "real" side of the global economy has affected the nature of the interactions between the United States economy and the rest of the world. It has been significant particularly because the shift in relative importance has been accompanied by an increase in the openness of the United States economy, and therefore in its sensitivity to influences from abroad. The ratio of imports to GNP in the United States has grown from 4.4 percent in 1950 to 8.3 percent in 1975, and that of exports to GNP from 4.6 percent to 9.8 percent over the same period. Of course, the openness of other industrialized nations has also increased substantially over the same period, and the United States still remains the least open economy in the non-Communist world. The point is simply that the United States is today more deeply involved in two-way interdependence than ten or twenty years ago. It used to be said that "when the United States sneezes, Europe catches pneumonia." Today, it is increasingly clear that we can all catch the flu from each other and that we are mutually dependent on each other for economic health.

The continuing importance of the United States in the world economy, along with the increased sensitivity of the domestic economy to external influences, creates a channel through which developments and policies in the United States have an additional indirect impact on our own economy through their effects on the economies of the rest-of-the-world. In recent years, the most dramatic example of such feedback was the substantial and greater-than-anticipated impact that the depreciation of the U.S. dollar had on the acceleration of domestic inflation, a phenomenon analyzed in greater detail in a later section of this paper. A less dramatic example of such feedback, in an entirely different area, can be observed for domestic corporate profits. The share of foreign earnings in the profits of U.S. corporations has roughly tripled since 1950. At the same time, the share of sales of local affiliates of U.S. firms in the GNP of such important partner countries as Canada, the United Kingdom, West Germany, and France has been increasing steadily. The circular flow from economic developments in this country through the activities of U.S. affiliates to other economies and then back again to domestic corporate profits through the earnings of those affiliates clearly has had a growing impact on real economic activity in the United States.

In contrast to the declining relative importance of the United States on the real side of the world economy in the years since World War II, the international financial position of the United States and the U.S. dollar (which are not always identical) has generally grown stronger throughout most of this period. Under the Bretton Woods system, the dollar came to serve a number of unique international functions, both private and official, and even the major upheavals in international financial markets associated with the termination of that system and the somewhat ambiguous transitional situation that has prevailed since have at most impinged marginally on the international financial status of the dollar.

Oddly enough, while the declining share of the United States in the world economy has been associated with increasing openness of the domestic economy on the real side, the continued or even increasing international importance of the U.S. dollar in the financial sphere has also been associated with an increase in two-way interdependence between the United States and the rest of the world. One result of the very rapid growth of the Eurodollar market, for example, has been that the assets of foreign branches of U.S. banks grew at an average annual rate of nearly 30 percent between 1960 and 1974, much more rapidly than those banks' domestic assets. The most important exposure of U.S. financial markets to influences from abroad, however, has probably come through the dramatic increase in foreign ownership of the U.S. public debt. The proportion of the privately held portion of the U.S. gross public debt held by foreign and international investors—a proportion which ranged between 5 and 9 percent over the period 1958–1970—leaped to the range of 20 to 21 percent in 1971–1973. In flow terms, the massive accumulations of dollars by foreign central banks during 'the monetary turmoil of 1971–1973 meant that some 70 percent of the estimated total federal unified-budget deficit of $66 billion during that period was financed by foreigners, and more than 75 percent of the estimated $30 billion increase in marketable debt outstanding was acquired by foreign holders. Even though econometric evidence suggests that, before 1972, changes in foreign central bank holdings of U.S. Treasury bills had only small, short-term effects on Treasury bill rates, foreign ownership of such a substantial portion of the public debt cannot but expose this important segment of U.S. financial markets to significant influences from abroad.

Even more significant, in the minds of most Americans, than the broad general trends described so far is the rapidly increasing dependence of the United States on other countries for imports of certain specific critical materials—especially on third-world countries for petroleum and a number of important raw materials. Of the thirteen basic industrial raw materials required by a modern economy, for example, the United States was dependent on imports for more than half of its supplies of four of these in 1950, six in 1970, and the number is projected to rise to nine by 1985 and to twelve by the end of the century. The influence of the producing countries on the U.S. economy that these projections imply will be enhanced substantially if the countries that produce these materials are successful in their efforts to create imitations of the OPEC cartel in order to exploit their potential oligopoly power.

Integration, Vulnerability and National Autonomy

Partly as the result of some of the developments just described, both policy makers and the public in the United States appear currently to be having some second thoughts about interdependence. For the first two decades after World War II, the rapid growth of international trade and investment was perceived essentially in classical terms: as a development that enhanced specialization, efficiency, and competition, thus raising output, income, and standards of living in the participating countries. More recently, however, another aspect of this growth of interdependence has been increasingly emphasized: the growing sensitivity of national economies to events and policies originating outside their borders and therefore beyond their control.

This fundamental tension between the rapid increase of international market integration in the sphere of private transactions and the continuing desire for national autonomy in the sphere of public policy is not new. It was stated succinctly in 1968 by Richard Cooper in his now-classic book, *The Economics of Interdependence:* "The central problem of international economic cooperation—and of this book—is *how to keep the manifold benefits of extensive international economic intercourse free of crippling restrictions while at the same time preserving a maximum degree of freedom for each nation to pursue its legitimate economic objectives.*"[3] Most nations have been seriously concerned with this tension for some time. If it has come to prominence in the United States rather later than elsewhere, it is partly because our perceptions of the "dark side" of interdependence have been heightened by a number of dramatic events in the past few years, and partly also because it is only recently that Americans have come to recognize that interdependence has increasingly become a two-way phenomenon.

The reduction in national economic autonomy, or self-determination, that is the concomitant of increasing openness has several aspects. The most obvious of these is the increased vulnerability or sensitivity of the domestic economy to influences originating abroad. The larger the export sector relative to GNP, the more important will shifts in foreign demand be as a source of domestic economic fluctuations. The more dependent a country is on imported oil, the more will domestic prosperity be affected by foreign decisions regarding its supply or price. Such vulnerability is not absolute, of course; it "is a matter of degree and varies with the costs and time involved in developing alternatives. This implies hard policy choices about acceptable degrees of dependence and how willing we are to sacrifice the economic benefits of cheaper foreign supplies"[4]—or, more generally, of international specialization and exchange for the sake of reduced vulnerability. Such problems may ring hollow in the ears of those countries whose vulnerability is far greater and whose available alternatives are far more restricted than ours, but they are real problems nonetheless.

Probably no government has ever regarded a loss of autonomy with equanimity, but the problem is today exacerbated by the fact that, in the years since World War II, the governments of industrialized nations have taken upon themselves (or had thrust upon them by their electorates) responsibility for an increasingly ambitious list of domestic macroeconomic goals. With our own Employment Act of 1946 as a prototype, governments have become responsible for the achievement and maintenance of high levels of employment, for a reasonable degree of price stability, and for an acceptably rapid rate of economic growth. These increased responsibilities are critical to an assessment of the benefits and costs of increased economic interdependence. For, as Cooper has noted, the efficiency implications of pure trade theory argue that, for private transactions, the boundaries of the nation-state should have no significance—that is to say, for private markets in both goods and factors of production, the optimum size of the integrated area is the world. The economic justification for nation-states, then, lies in the existence of public or collective goods—including stabilization targets, the distribution of income, and the regulatory climate—and of differences in the consumption preferences for such goods among the citizens of different nations. The greater the divergences among countries with respect to the transformation curve or the indifference map for public goods, and the greater the weight of such goods in the nation's welfare function, the greater will be the welfare costs of international economic integration that must be set off against the efficiency gains from the integration of private markets.[5]

The increased responsibility for the achievement of collective macroeconomic goals brings into sharp relief another aspect of the reduced autonomy resulting from increased economic openness (under pegged exchange rates): the attenuated effectiveness of domestic policy instruments in achieving these goals. For example, an increase in the marginal propensity to import that generally accompanies international integration of commodity markets reduces the domestic multiplier impact of fiscal policy by increasing the proportion of the impact that leaks into imports, affecting the level of aggregate demand abroad rather than at home. Capital-market integration similarly attenuates the impact of monetary policy on the level of domestic economic activity, as flows of interest-sensitive capital across national boundaries offset the desired change in domestic interest rates or credit-market conditions.

Another characteristic of the governments of industrialized nations in the postwar era is their increasing concern with questions of equity (perceived in terms of the actual distribution of income) rather than simply with questions of efficiency (or the maximization of total potential income). Because the costs and benefits of economic integration tend to fall unevenly on different regions, different factors of production, different industries, and different industries, and different individuals, and because it often proves difficult in practice to tax the gainers to compensate the losers, interdependence becomes a political issue, to be approached with caution by a democratically elected government.

Finally, by increasing the importance to the domestic economy of what happens in the world outside its borders, interdependence creates an enhanced need for the coordination of national economic policies in order to increase the probability of each nation's achieving its own economic goals. For example, the failure of governments to coordinate their macroeconomic policies at least to the extent of knowing what course of action is proposed in one's partner countries and taking this information into account in one's own policy formulation (an iterative process, obviously) is likely to result in macroeconomic overkill—a collective excess of stimulative measures leading to inflationary pressure or of contractionary measures leading to recession and unemployment. Thus, paradoxically, in an interdependent world, "autonomy may at times be increased by yielding some 'sovereignty' in the freedom to formulate economic policy with apparent (but often illusory) independence of other nations' actions."[6] At present, the institutions and instrumentalities for the coordination of national economic policies are relatively undeveloped and inadequate to the expanding tasks being thrust upon them, and neither the United States nor any other industrialized nation is experienced in making the international coordination of economic policies politically acceptable.

ANALYTICAL DEVELOPMENTS AND RECENT EXPERIENCE

Transmission of Economic Disturbances

Concern about the transmission of economic disturbances between the United States and other industrialized nations, and the magnification of these disturbances in the transmission process, has been growing over the past decade, with a tremendous acceleration in the most recent few years. From the post-Korean War period to the mid-1960s, in contrast, the general view in this country, and to a considerable extent in other countries as well, was that the United States was an "island of stability" whose presence helped damp the waves of economic fluctuation in partner countries. Our rate of inflation was well below those generally experienced in other industrialized countries, and our cyclical fluctuations in real economic activity had been growing steadily milder in amplitude and duration. Our balance on goods and services was positive throughout the period, representing a net transfer of U.S. output to the rest of the world, and rose irregularly from $0.5 billion in 1953 to $8.5 billion in 1964.

If the situation is looked at from the other direction, the foreign sector also appeared as a stabilizing influence on the domestic price picture in the United States. Over the period from 1954 to 1970, the rate of price increase for the import component of the GNP deflator was far below the aggregate rate of increase. The same was true, although to a lesser extent, of the export component.

Between the mid-1960s and the end of the Bretton Woods system in mid-1971, the general view of the role of the United States changed substantially: the former "island of stability" came to be regarded as a major exporter of inflation to other countries. One reason for this shift was the change in our domestic rate of inflation. Domestic inflation began to accelerate substantially in 1966, and in 1968–1970 actually rose above the average rate for nine other major industrialized countries. Over the period from 1964 to 1972, furthermore, our balance on goods and services underwent a negative shift of more than $14 billion (from a surplus of $8.5 billion to a deficit of $5.9 billion). This means that a significant share of the excess demand pressure that would otherwise have exerted still greater upward pressure on the domestic price level spilled over instead into foreign markets.

In addition to the changes just described in certain key economic parameters for the U.S. economy, several important analytical developments contributed to the changing perception of our role in the transmission process. A growing body of empirical evidence tended to verify Balassa's 1964 reappraisal of the purchasing-power-parity doctrine, which suggested that the relationships among different price indices vary systematically among countries with different economic characteristics.[7] Specifically, the proposition is that countries with a relatively high real-growth rate based on a rapid rate of productivity increase tend to experience a more rapid rise in the consumer price index relative to the rise in the prices of traded or tradeable goods than do slower-growing countries. According to this theory, rates of increase in the consumer price indices can be considerably greater in fast-growing countries—such as Germany and Japan—than in slower-growing countries—such as the United States and Great Britain—and still be consistent with equal or even slower rates of increase in the indices of tradeable goods prices (such as the wholesale price index or, even more, an index of export prices)—an implication strikingly borne out by the data for the countries just mentioned. This view implies that "inflation in the United States, whether zero or positive, is transmitted in magnified form to some other countries . . ." and "that the United States is capable of 'exporting inflation' to some countries, even if it has no inflation (in terms of the CPI) at home."[8]

Second, recent work on the monetary approach to balance-of-payments theory has stressed a basic asymmetry of the Bretton Woods gold exchange standard: that the United States, by virtue of its reserve-currency status, was alone free to determine its rate of inflation domestically, free of any direct balance-of-payments constraint, while the money supplies and thus the inflation rates in other countries were determined primarily by their balance-of-payments positions and the resulting changes in the international reserve component of the domestic monetary base.[9] Harry Johnson has gone so far as to argue that, if foreign central banks recognize the inevitability of importing inflation from the reserve-currency country, they may go ahead and expand the domestic component of the monetary base in advance, and thus prevent any actual reserve inflow. He thus implies that the price-specie flow mechanism may operate to transmit inflation internationally even in the absence of significant observable flows of international reserves.[10] Obviously, the end of the dollar-based gold-exchange standard in mid-1971 and the shift to generalized floating shortly thereafter significantly reduced (if they did not entirely eliminate) this particular mechanism of transmission.

The erosion of the stabilizing position of the United States in the world economy was well under way by the second half of the 1960s; the parallel shift in the role of the foreign sector in the U.S. economy came somewhat later, though more suddenly. No longer did the prices of exports and imports rise less rapidly than the aggregate domestic price level. On the contrary, between 1970 and 1975, the export component of the GNP deflator rose nearly twice as fast, and the import component nearly three times as fast, as the aggregate index. By 1975, several years after the shift to an exchange-rate regime that presumably increased the ability of countries to insulate themselves from external disturbances, both the United States and the other industrialized nations appeared paradoxically to be importing inflation from each other to a much greater extent than ever before in the postwar period.

There can be little doubt that during 1971–1974 the intensity of the inflationary pressure on the U.S. economy from the foreign trade sector did much to stimulate the shift in the view of this country from an essentially "closed economy" to a "large open economy." For one thing, the apparent impact of the dollar depreciation on the domestic price level took many Americans by surprise. Initial predictions of the magnitude of this inflationary impact were in general far too low. They were underestimates because most of them were based implicitly on the assumptions of the conventional Keynesian model, that elasticities of substitution between domestic and foreign goods are low and that domestic wages and prices are stable (in terms of the home currency) up to the point of full employment. Under these assumptions, depreciation of the dollar in the presence of unemployment would affect the domestic price level only through raising the prices of imported inputs or finished goods. Since imports constituted

about 7.5 percent of GNP during 1971–1973, an effective dollar depreciation of 10 percent, for example, could have been expected to raise the
domestic price level (in terms of the GNP deflator) by about three-quarters
of 1 percent. Furthermore, this represented an upper-bound estimate, inasmuch as the relatively large size of the United States in world markets
made it unlikely that the full amount of the depreciation would be passed
through in the form of increased dollar prices of imports.

During the past five or six years, however, analyses of devaluation
have increasingly incorporated the fundamental assumption of a highly integrated world economy, in contrast to the Keynesian view of the world as
consisting of relatively closed national economies. And the assumptions
underlying this so-called "monetary approach" have very different implications from those of the Keynesian model regarding the impact of an
exchange-rate change on the domestic price level. Specifically, this approach holds that high elasticities of substitution prevail among countries
for most tradeable goods and that, because world markets today are highly
integrated, a single price must prevail in all markets for goods that are close
substitutes for one another. The implication of this view is that competitive
forces will produce offsetting changes in domestic prices, thereby quickly
eliminating the initial shift in relative prices arising from an exchange-rate
change. Under the assumptions of such a perfectly competitive model, the
upper bound on the increase in the domestic price level (as elasticities of
substitution between foreign and domestic goods approach infinity) would
be the amount of the effective depreciation itself.

Several recent empirical investigations have incorporated at least
some of the additional effects of depreciation on the domestic price level
that are implied by the analytical approach described here. In general, they
have yielded estimates of the price level impact of exchange-rate changes
much higher than crude ex ante calculations based on the conventional
Keynesian view, but still well below the long-run upper bound implied by
the monetary approach. Making use of regression results for the period
1950–1971, on the basis of Phillips curve equations that incorporate an
import-price term, Kwack, for example, estimated that the U.S. price level
(as measured by the consumer price index) would rise by about 20 percent
of an effective devaluation of the U.S. dollar, or by two percentage points
in the case of an effective devaluation of 10 percent.[11] Nordhaus and Shoven reached roughly consistent results: using an input-output approach to
estimate the transmission of the price effects of depreciation, they concluded that the 10 percent effective depreciation of the dollar between
November 1972 and August 1973 accounted for between 1.9 and 2.3 percentage points of inflation over that period.[12]

Such studies as these may still not capture the total indirect effects
of depreciation on prices in industries producing exportable and import-
competing goods and, through effects on wages, even in sectors producing

nontradeable output. In particular, the sharp improvement in our net balance on goods and services over the year 1973 (from a deficit of $0.8 billion in the fourth quarter of 1972 to a surplus of $11.6 billion in the fourth quarter of 1973, both in 1958 dollars) represented 38 percent of the total increase in our real GNP that year. At a time when important segments of the economy were straining against capacity limitations, this diversion of nearly 40 percent of the real increase in domestic output from domestic to foreign absorption must have had pervasive effects on the domestic price level.

Still another recent study attempts to take just such a broad view of the external effects on inflation in the United States over the period from mid-1971 to mid-1974, not only encompassing the general aggregate-demand effects but also attempting to decompose the external impact into two parts: the portion of domestic inflation resulting from the effective depreciation of the dollar and the portion due to other "extraordinary" increases in the prices of U.S. exports and imports over the period.[13] . . . It attributed the bulk of these increases to other exogenous disturbances affecting world commodity markets, of which the OPEC-induced increase in prices of petroleum products was the most dramatic example. Here, in contrast to what is the case with depreciation, the higher exogenous prices are associated with a decline in *real* GNP, so that there is no additional inflationary pressure arising from aggregate demand. . . . Some 24 percent, or nearly one-quarter of the three-year rise in the personal consumption deflator is attributable to these "extraordinary" increases in the prices of U.S. exports and imports.[14]

As the authors are careful to point out, their assumption that increases in U.S. export and import prices between 1971 and 1974 were exogenously determined cannot be entirely valid. In reality, "developments within the United States clearly have influenced both the course of the dollar's exchange rate vis-à-vis other currencies, as well as movements in the prices of the commodities that the U.S. imports and exports."[15] Thus their results are best regarded as estimates of an upper limit for the contribution of foreign developments to domestic price increases. Nevertheless, despite the fact that they undoubtedly fail to catch some of the external influences on domestic inflation in the United States and overestimate others, studies such as the ones described here serve to drive home two points. The first is that the foreign sector is an important transmission belt for inflationary impulses, even in such a relatively closed economy as the United States, and that the actual channels of transmission are more varied and complex than those encompassed by the conventional Keynesian analysis. The second is that, in an economy like ours, shifts in *relative* prices, which in recent years appear to have been caused at least as much by fluctuations and disturbances on the supply side as by the vagaries of demand usually stressed in modern economic analysis, are likely to have a substantial and prolonged (although ultimately transient) inflationary effect on the general price level, even in instances where their *real* effects are deflationary.

Interdependence, Transmission and Convergence

The discussion so far has focused on trends in interdependence, on the mechanisms for international transmission of inflation, and on their implications for the economy of the United States. More generally, however, one would expect that an increase in economic openness or interdependence, by widening the channels of transmission on both trade and capital account, would have brought about some convergence or synchronization of economic fluctuations among the participating countries. A priori considerations suggest such convergence not only for price movements under pegged exchange rates, but also for fluctuations in real economic activity as sensitivity to external disturbances increases. The fact that such convergence can occur for a number of reasons other than an increased tendency toward international transmission—such as a common response to some common exogenous disturbance, for example[16]—confuses the statistical evidence but does not alter the basic relationship. Furthermore, the shift from pegged to flexible exchange rates in the period from 1971 to 1973 would be expected to have increased the dispersion among national rates of inflation and among cycles in real economic activity as well. That is, theory suggests that such a shift should reduce the channels of transmission and thus enable countries both to insulate themselves at least partially from disturbances originating abroad and to increase the domestic impact of their own macroeconomic policies.

In recent years quite a number of empirical investigations into various aspects of this convergence-divergence question have been conducted, primarily by inquiring whether the dispersion across industrialized countries of various quantitative measures of both prices and real economic activity has increased or decreased over time. The largest number of such studies has been conducted on the dispersion among national rates of inflation. Unfortunately, because of differences among the various studies in the selection of price indices, of time periods for comparison, of the number and mix of industrialized countries, and of the particular measure of dispersion (in particular, whether the standard deviation, the coefficient of variation,* or both were used), the various results are not directly comparable, and the picture that has emerged is somewhat ambiguous. Some of these studies have shown no clear trend in the dispersion of national inflation rates over the postwar period spanned by the Bretton Woods system. Others, utilizing different price indices, time periods, or country samples, have found some degree of convergence—that is, reduction in

---

*[The coefficient of variation is defined as the standard deviation divided by the mean, a unitless measure of deviation.—Eds.]

dispersion—for the period from the mid-1960s through the early 1970s as compared with the earlier postwar years before about 1963 or 1965. Most of them, however, have found some increase in the standard deviation among national inflation rates beginning in 1971 or 1972 or (at the latest) in 1973—that is, after the end of the Bretton Woods system in mid-1971 or after the move to generalized floating early in 1973. Because the average rate of inflation for all countries in the sample increased markedly during this most recent period, the use of the coefficient of variation as the measure of dispersion reintroduces some ambiguity into the pattern and makes any general conclusion regarding the expected increase in dispersion less certain than it appeared when the standard deviation was used. One study also found an increase in dispersion in 1971–1975 (and even more markedly for 1973–1975) over the average for the 1960s not only for three different price indices but also for an index of stock prices and for representative interest rates.

In a few cases, investigators have gone behind the rates of national price inflation to look at what happened to money supply growth rates in major industrialized countries. Here the results have been somewhat surprising: there is no evidence of increased dispersion among the rates of money supply growth in the flexible-rate period as compared with earlier years. In one of the most detailed of the statistical studies, the author reported that, although he observed an increase in quarter-to-quarter divergences among the money supply growth rates in ten major industrialized countries beginning in 1972, no such change was observable for longer periods. In fact, the monetary policies of the nine other industrialized nations appeared to be closer to those of the United States in the flexible-rate period than they were before the move away from pegged rates. Such evidence led the investigator to conclude that the nature of monetary interdependence has remained fundamentally unchanged in the face of a substantial change in the international monetary system because countries have apparently chosen to continue behaving as if exchange rates were fixed— that is, except for very short-period divergences, to maintain as close coordination of monetary policies as they did before.

In looking at changes in the degree of dispersion of cycles in real economic activity, there is a wide variety of potential proxy variables to choose from. The fact that such cyclical fluctuations take place around underlying growth trends, which themselves differ among countries, complicates the interpretation of the results. And, in fact, two of the three empirical investigations of this question found no particular trend in the dispersion of real GNP growth rates or of "potential output gaps" among major industrial countries over the postwar period, even when the pegged and flexible-rate periods were compared. The most detailed and exhaustive of the empirical studies, however, did discern the sort of changes in dispersion among the potential output gaps of twelve major industrial countries that had been anticipated on a priori grounds.[17] That is, there appears to have been some decline in the dispersion—or increase in the synchronization—of real cycles between 1952–1957 and 1964–1970, presumably as the result of increasing economic integration, and then a decrease in synchronization from the latter period to 1971–1974. The author noted that the decrease in synchronization as a result of greater flexibility in exchange rates was presumably moderated considerably by the impact of a major exogenous shock common to all the countries in the sample: the oil price increases of 1973–1974. She noted, too, that

> the United States' pattern of cyclical movement relative to that of its trading partners . . . is quite different from that of most other industrial countries. It shows reasonably high levels of covariation during periods when external shocks were hypothesized to have harmonized cyclical movements across countries, and practically no covariation when it was thought that fluctuations should have been transmitted through the current account.[18]

This last observation is consistent with the relatively small size of the external sector relative to total GNP in the United States, but it is not fully consistent with some recent National Bureau of Economic Research (NBER) findings on the relationship between the U.S. trade account and business cycles here and abroad. The authors of the NBER study found that there has indeed been a common international growth cycle for nine major industrial countries over the period 1953–1973 and that, perhaps surprisingly, in terms of the degree of association, the United States occupies an intermediate rather than a dominant position. In addition, monthly trade data for the period 1958–1973 show a close connection between movements in the U.S. trade balance and differences in the timing and severity of cycles here and abroad. U.S. exports to four of its major partner countries grew about six times as fast when those countries were in the expansion phase of their own cycles as they did when those countries were in the contraction phase, whereas U.S. imports from these same four countries grew more than three times as fast during cyclical upswings in this country as they did during downswings. Once again, the United States has not always appeared as the cyclical leader: rather, the pattern has been "for other countries to lead the United States into growth recession and for the United States to lead other countries into recovery"—that is, the postwar evidence "provides no support for the popular misconception that the contagion runs in a dominant way from the United States to the other major industrialized nations."[19]

Finally, the various studies described in the previous paragraphs shed little or no light on the question why, despite some tendency toward increased dispersion under flexible rates, a considerable common element remains—in other words, why certain channels of international transmission appear to persist, even under flexible rates. Why do flexible rates appear to provide only limited insulation of national economies one from another, rather than the high degree of insulation implied by simple models focused on the trade balance? One immediate answer is, of course, that the present system is far from the freely floating rates of the textbooks; it is rather a system of managed floating wherein governments still undertake substantial intervention in foreign-exchange markets. But this does not seem to be the whole story.

Most textbook models of the adjustment process under either pegged or floating rates are based on the assumption of instantaneous adjustment in all markets. Most also assume, implicitly if not explicitly, the prevalence of totally inelastic price expectations (that is, actual prices are expected to continue unchanged forever). In fact, however, the existence of adjustment lags in both goods and asset markets and different assumptions about the formulation of price expectations may create channels for the international transmission of inflation under flexible rates in the short run, so that a rise in foreign prices may cause upward pressure on domestic prices before the domestic currency appreciates to its new equilibrium level in the foreign-exchange markets. Furthermore, certain institutional features common to most industrialized economies tend to serve as transmission channels for world inflation: among these are (1) the tendency of monetary authorities to "accommodate" imported inflation by preventing a fall in nominal incomes in the face of a real-income decline caused by worsening terms of trade, and (2) the demand-shift inflation caused by the uneven sectoral impact of a rise in foreign prices and the resulting change in the exchange rate.

More fundamental, however, is the fact that flexible exchange rates cannot be expected to abolish interdependence in an integrated world economy. According to conventional Keynesian closed-economy models, in which the balance of payments is generally equated with the balance on goods and services, exchange-rate flexibility can be expected to strengthen national economic autonomy in three ways. First, by making possible permanent improvement in the balance of payments, such rate flexibility would eliminate the need to use macroeconomic policies for the elimination of balance-of-payments disequilibria as well as for the achievement of domestic targets. Second, by eliminating the "leakage" of domestic multiplier effects through the balance of payments, flexible rates would directly enhance the domestic impact of stabilization policies. And, finally, rate flexibility would insulate the domestic economy against imported inflation by eliminating, through an appreciation of the domestic money, both the direct-cost and the aggregate-demand inflationary pressures caused by a rate of price increase higher abroad than at home.

In a different analytical framework, however, each of these characteristics is seen to have important limitations. The monetary approach to the balance of payments implies that exchange-rate changes can cause only a temporary change in the balance of payments; in the long run, according to this view, the conditions for equilibrium in all markets require that the balance of payments revert to its original level. The applicability of the assumptions underlying the monetary approach and the relevance of stationary-state equilibrium conditions to policy analysis are important issues, but there is no doubt that the insights this approach offers have posed significant questions about the conditions under which an exchange-rate change can be counted on to effect a durable improvement in the balance of payments.

Similarly, the use of a model that focuses on the conditions for money-market equilibrium implies that, if capital is highly mobile internationally in response to interest-rate differentials, a shift from pegged to flexible rates will weaken rather than strengthen the domestic effectiveness of fiscal policy (while the effectiveness of monetary policy will be enhanced). The reasoning is essentially an extension to the open economy of the idea of "crowding out," according to which the interest-rate rise caused by an increased government deficit with an unchanged money supply (or an unchanged rate of money growth) will discourage private investment and thus offset the stimulative effect of the deficit. In the open economy case, the rise in domestic interest rates resulting from stimulative fiscal policy will attract capital inflows, cause the currency to appreciate, and thus lead to a deterioration in the goods and services account which again offsets the desired stimulative effect. Again, the extent to which the assumptions of the model are met and the extent to which such offsetting actually occurs are unsettled issues. But the very possibility that such effects may operate introduces a cautionary note into our expectations about what happens to the domestic efficiency of fiscal policy as the result of a move from pegged to flexible rates.

Finally, there is the fact that flexible exchange rates provide only limited insulation against foreign disturbances in a world of capital mobility. If there are internationally mobile securities and investors sensitive to interest-rate differentials among countries, a change in monetary policy abroad will affect domestic as well as foreign interest rates and will thus impinge on the domestic level of economic activity even under flexible rates. In fact, the impact of certain kinds of disturbance abroad may actually be aggravated rather than lessened by rate flexibility. As an example, Cooper has cited an exogenous shift in asset preferences that increases the foreign demand for domestic securities at constant rates of interest. The result of such a shift would be an appreciation of the domestic currency leading to a current-account deficit and a reduction of domestic aggregate demand and income.[20] Furthermore, even if the foreign disturbance were monetary in origin (the case in which the insulation provided by flexible rates is supposed to be most effective), the existence of capital mobility might still, under certain circumstances, magnify the international transmission process more under flexible than under fixed rates. This could happen if an increase in the foreign price level (together with an accompanying equiproportional appreciation of the domestic currency that would leave the current account exactly unchanged) were to lead to an increase in the net capital outflow from the appreciating country—an increase such as might occur, for example, if the increasing foreign price level were to create expanded profit opportunities abroad. In this case the maintenance of overall equilibrium in the foreign exchange market would cause the domestic currency to appreciate less than in proportion to the rise in the world price level, leading to an improvement on current account and thus an inflationary increase in aggregate demand at home. Thus, the degree (and even the direction) of insulation provided by flexible exchange rates depends both on the type of disturbance that is assumed to dominate in the international arena and on the particular nature of the domestic response. . . .

The Question of Coordination: What and How?

. . . Coordination among governments can relieve the vulnerability resulting from interdependence. It is first important to sort out what is meant by "policy coordination." In fact, it is possible to talk about several different levels of policy coordination. At the lowest level, the phrase can simply mean the avoidance of explicit beggar-my-neighbor policies, such as trade barriers or exchange-rate manipulation, in the solution of domestic economic problems. Although our own record has not been spotless, the United States has tended to take the lead in promoting negative coordination of this sort during the postwar period. This country took the initiative in promoting trade liberalization through successive rounds of multilateral trade negotiations. . . . Since the successful avoidance of beggar-my-neighbor policies requires that countries eschew inconsistent targets for such variables as the current account or the exchange rate, the United States has throughout the discussions and negotiations on international monetary reform stressed the importance of insuring such consistency. To that end, we initially urged a larger role for "objective indicators," or guidelines on balance-of-payments and reserve targets, than most other industrialized countries were willing to accept. The general concept has carried over into the floating-rate context in the suggested guidelines for floating in the Committee of Twenty's "Outline of Reform."[21]

The theoretical insights provided by the monetary approach to balance-of-payments analysis imply that, in a world of managed floating, rules for exchange-market intervention are inadequate to insure that inconsistent targets and exchange-rate manipulation will be avoided, since there is more than one means of pursuing such targets. And, in fact, the recent history of managed floating is replete with instances of countries' supporting their currencies indirectly through foreign borrowing rather than directly in the exchange markets. Fundamentally, in this view, the avoidance of inconsistent external targets requires not merely rules governing exchange-market intervention but rules guaranteeing the compatibility of national monetary policies with each other, and the compatibility of fiscal policies to the extent that they are financed by money creation or affect the demand for money.

The degree of coordination just described is, of course, much more demanding than would be the mere avoidance of restrictive commercial policies and of explicit beggar-my-neighbor behavior. It means positive coordination, not merely in the sense that each country take account of the probable macroeconomic policies of others in setting its own and thus avoid global stimulative or deflationary "overkill," but in the sense that countries actually set macroeconomic targets and plan the policies to achieve them cooperatively, including the coordination of timetables for implementing the policies. And the history of past efforts along these lines is not encouraging. In the early 1960s, for example, efforts to establish guidelines for international cooperation on stabilization policies among OECD countries foundered on disagreement between the United States and the European countries as to how formal and restrictive the agreed principles should be. . . .

The somewhat discouraging experience of the European Economic Community in trying to establish an economic and monetary union shows how difficult it is for nations to make the transition from negative coordination (in the sense of abolishing explicit barriers to international transactions) to positive coordination of national economic policies. But both the logic of analysis and the evidence from recent experience suggest that there is no alternative; the dynamics of tension between the vulnerability created by increasing integration at the market level and the persistence of fragmentation at the policy level suggest that if we do not find ways to make progress on the latter we will inevitably slip backward away from the former. The shift to managed flexibility of exchange rates has alleviated the burden by providing a partial buffer against external disturbances, but the buffer is only partial and the need to take a global approach to macroeconomic policy problems remains.

Notes

1. Martin Bronfenbrenner and F. D. Holzman, "Survey of Inflation Theory," *American Economic Review,* vol. 53, no. 4 (September 1963), pp. 593–661.
2. These proportions refer to gross reserves. The net reserves of the United States (international reserves minus liabilities to foreign official agencies) have been negative in nine of the past ten years.
3. Richard N. Cooper, *The Economics of Interdependence* (New York: McGraw Hill, 1968), p. 5. Emphasis in original.
4. Joseph S. Nye, Jr., "Independence and Interdependence," *Foreign Policy,* no. 22 (Spring 1976), p. 133.

5. For an example in terms of the trade-off between inflation and unemployment, see Marina v. N. Whitman, "Place Prosperity and People Prosperity: The Delineation of Optimum Policy Areas," in Mark Perlman et al., eds., *Spatial, Regional and Population Economics* (New York: Gordon & Breach, 1972), pp. 359–93.

6. Cooper, *The Economics of Interdependence,* pp. 4–5.

7. Bela Balassa, "The Purchasing Power Parity Doctrine: A Reappraisal," *Journal of Political Economy,* vol. 72, no. 6 (December 1964), pp. 584–96; Gottfried Haberler, "International Aspects of U.S. Inflation," in *A New Look at Inflation: Economic Policy in the Early 1970s* (Washington, D.C.: American Enterprise Institute, 1973); Ronald McKinnon, *Monetary Theory and Controlled Flexibility in the Foreign Exchanges,* Essays in International Finance No. 84 (Princeton, N.J.: Princeton University Press, 1971).

8. Gottfried Haberler, "Inflation as a Worldwide Phenomenon—An Overview," in David I. Meiselman and Arthur B. Laffer, *The Phenomenon of Worldwide Inflation* (Washington: American Enterprise Institute, 1975) p. 16. Haberler notes (p. 17) that European complaints about the United States exporting inflation antedated the inflation which started in this country in 1965.

9. For a survey of this literature (which is to be distinguished from the "domestic monetarism" associated above all with the name of Milton Friedman), see Marina v. N. Whitman, "Global Monetarism and the Monetary Approach to the Balance of Payments," *Brookings Papers on Economic Activity,* 1975(3), pp. 491–536. The point is a controversial one, and the evidence on the extent to which countries are actually able to sterilize the impact of reserve flows on their money supplies is not conclusive (Whitman, pp. 522–26).

10. Harry G. Johnson, "Secular Inflation and the International Monetary System," *Journal of Money, Credit, and Banking,* vol. 5, no. 1, pt. 2 (February 1973), p. 516.

11. S. Y. Kwack, "The Effects of Foreign Inflation on Domestic Prices and the Relative Price Advantage of Exchange Rate Changes," in Peter B. Clark, Dennis Logue, and Richard J. Sweeney, eds., *The Effects of Exchange Rate Adjustment* (U.S. Department of the Treasury, forthcoming 1976).

12. William Nordhaus and John Shoven, "Inflation 1973: The Year of Infamy," *Challenge,* May–June 1974, pp. 14–22.

13. Richard Berner et al., "International Sources of Domestic Inflation," Joint Economic Committee, *Studies in Price Stability and Economic Growth,* no. 3 (94th Cong., 1st sess.), August 5, 1975.

14. The authors caution that, because the model is non-linear, "the 15 and 24 percent figures cannot be added to obtain a combined effect for both the depreciation and the exogenous price increases." Ibid., p. 20.

15. Ibid., p. 2.

16. For a detailed analysis of the interrelations between dispersion of national inflation rates and international transmission, see Walter S. Salant, "The International Transmission of Inflation," paper prepared for the Brookings Conference on World Inflation, Washington, D.C., November 21–23, 1974, pp. 5–21.

17. Duncan Ripley, "Cyclical Fluctuations in Industrial Countries" (International Monetary Fund, 1976; processed).

18. Ibid., pp. 8–9.

19. Geoffrey H. Moore and Philip A. Klein, "New International Business Cycle Indicators System: Applying the NBER Indicator Approach to International Growth Cycles" (National Bureau of Economic Research, 1975; processed), pp. 26 and 29. For a more detailed discussion of the "sneeze hypothesis," see Philip A. Klein, *Business Cycles in the Postwar World* (Washington, D.C.: American Enterprise Institute, 1976), pp. 27–43.

20. Richard N. Cooper, "Monetary Theory and Policy in an Open Economy," *Scandinavian Journal of Economics* (forthcoming, 1976).

21. See *Economic Report of the President,* January 1973, Appendix A, Supplement to ch. 5; "Quantitative Indicators from the Point of View of the Overall

Operation of the System" (memorandum submitted by the U.S. deputies of the Committee of Twenty to the secretary, International Monetary Fund, May 17, 1973; processed). Also, International Monetary Fund, "Outline of Reform," "Annexes" 1 and 4, "Reports of Technical Groups: On Indicators," all in *International Monetary Reform: Documents of the Committee of Twenty* (Washington, D.C.: International Monetary Fund, 1974).

26

Monetary Policy under Exchange-Rate Flexibility

Rudiger Dornbusch

This paper . . . attempts to lay out the basic analytical framework that has been developed for the analysis of exchange-rate questions and to relate it to the question of monetary policy. [It] concentrates on the development of the relevant theoretical framework. The main points to be made here are: (i) exchange rates are primarily determined in asset markets with expectations playing a dominant role; (ii) the sharpest formulation of exchange-rate theory is the "monetary approach," Chicago's quantity theory of the open economy; (iii) purchasing power parity is a precarious reed on which to hang short-term exchange-rate theory; (iv) the current account has just made it back as a determinant of exchange rates. . . .

The topic covered in this paper has received an extraordinary amount of professional attention in the last few years and much fruitful research has been accomplished. The fine surveys by Isard (1978), Kohlhagen (1978) and Schadler (1977) will place our sketchy review in the perspective of the literature and the books by Black (1977) and Willett (1977) help relate our topic to the ongoing policy discussions.

. . . We start off with two rock-bottom models that, in an oversimplified manner perhaps, represent exchange-rate theory as viewed by the person in "the Street." These models, purchasing-power parity and a

From Rudiger Dornbusch, "Monetary Policy under Exchange-Rate Flexibility," in *Managed Exchange-Rate Flexibility* by Jacques R. Artus et al. (Boston: Federal Reserve Bank of Boston, 1978). Reprinted by permission. Some footnotes and some references omitted. Rudiger Dornbusch is Professor of Economics at the Massachusetts Institute of Technology. The author gratefully acknowledges helpful discussions with Jeffrey Frankel, Jacob Frenkel, Stanley Fischer and Michael Rothschild as well as financial support from the NSF.

balance-of-payments theory of the exchange rate, each contain, of course, more than a germ of truth and thus serve as a useful introduction to our review.

We proceed from there to more structured models that emphasize macroeconomic interaction or the details of asset markets. These theories can be described as asset-market theories of the exchange rate. Extensions of these models are then considered in an effort to add realism. These extensions deal with expectations, questions of dynamics and of indexing and policy reaction.

A. PURCHASING-POWER PARITY AND THE QUANTITY THEORY

The purchasing-power parity theory of the exchange rate is one of those empirical regularities that are sufficiently true over long periods of time to deserve our attention but deviations from which are pronounced enough to make all the difference in the short run. Clearly, purchasing-power parity (PPP for short) is much like the quantity theory of money and indeed can be viewed as the open economy extension of quantity theory thinking.[1]

1. PPP Theory:

PPP theory argues that exchange rates move over time so as to offset divergent movements in national price levels. A country that experiences a hyperinflation, for example, will experience at the same time a corresponding external depreciation of its currency.

The theory leaves open two important operational questions. The first deals with the channels through which this relation between inflation differentials and depreciation will come about. The second question concerns the extent to which PPP is complete,—does it hold in the short run and is there no responsibility for trend deviations over time?

The extent to which PPP holds exactly, at every point in time, and without trend deviation has been an important issue in trade theory. There is no question that theory has shown the possibility of systematic deviation that arises from the existence of nontraded goods. Specifically, Balassa and Samuelson have argued that because services tend to be nontraded, labor-intensive and show low technical progress as opposed to traded manufactures, we would expect fast-growing and innovating countries to experience an increase in their real price level over time. With prices of tradables equalized, the productivity growth in the traded sector would raise wages and the relative price of nontraded goods and thus the real price level in the fast-growing countries.

A second source of systematic deviation has been pointed out by earlier literature, including Viner, that dealt with the effect of capital flows or current account imbalance. Here it was argued that a borrowing country has a relatively high (real) price level. The argument here relies on the fact that an increase in aggregate demand, financed by borrowing and a current account deficit, would raise the relative price of nontraded goods and thus the real price level. There are thus two reasons for trend deviations or systematic deviations from PPP that serve as important reservations to the generality of the theory.

Setting these reservations aside we are still left with the issue of how rapidly and completely we expect PPP to hold and through what channels it comes about. Here the literature is considerably more diffuse. A hard-core theory, associated with what Marina Whitman (1975) has aptly called "global monetarism" asserts the "law of one price." Goods produced by us and by our competitors behave as if they were perfect substitutes. Simple arbitrage by market participants will establish uniformity of price in closely integrated markets.

This hard-core view is no longer very fashionable except, of course, for raw materials, commodities and food. A more differentiated view would argue that in the short run and perhaps even in the long run there is substantial scope for product differentiation. Under these conditions price adjustment is no longer a matter of arbitrage but rather becomes a question of substitution. When our prices get out of line with those of our competitors so that we become more competitive, then we would expect demand to shift toward our goods, and in a fully employed economy, start putting upward pressure on cost and ultimately prices. The price adjustment here is certainly time-consuming; it depends not only on substitutability between supply sources—Okun's distinction between customer and auction markets is important here—but also on the state of slack in the economy and on the expected persistence of real price changes. The description of this mechanism suggests that deviations from PPP are not only possible, but may persist for some time. . . .

2. Money, Prices and the Exchange Rate

We turn now to a development of the "monetary approach" of exchange-rate theory. This model or approach combines the quantity theory of money—fully flexible prices determined by real money demand and nominal money supply—with strict PPP to arrive at a theory of the exchange rate.

The approach can be simply formulated in terms of a combined theory of monetary equilibrium and exchange-rate determination. Let M, P, V and Y be nominal quantity of money, the price level, velocity and real income. Then the condition of monetary equilibrium can be written as:

$$(2) \qquad \frac{M}{P} V(r,Y) = Y$$

where our notation indicates that velocity may be a function of other variables, such as interest rates, r, or income.

We can rewrite equation (2), solving for the price level, as:

(2)'
$$P = V \frac{M}{Y}$$

which states that for a given velocity an increase in money leads to an equiproportionate rise in the price level. A rise in velocity likewise raises the price level while an increase in real income, by raising real money demand, would lower the equilibrium level of prices.

To go from here to a theory of the exchange rate we draw on a strict version of PPP which states that our price level is equal to foreign prices, P*, converted at the exchange rate, E:

(3)
$$P = P^*E$$

where E is the domestic currency price of foreign exchange. Substituting (3) in (2)' yields an expression for the equilibrium exchange rate:

(4)
$$E = (1/P^*) V \frac{M}{Y}$$

The equilibrium exchange rate depends on nominal money, real output and velocity. An increase in nominal money or in velocity will depreciate the exchange rate in the same proportion. A rise in real income will lead to appreciation. What is the mechanism?

The theory argues that domestic prices are fully flexible, but are linked to world prices by PPP. Given the nominal quantity of money any variations in the demand for money must be offset by compensating changes in the level of prices and thus in the exchange rate. An increase in real money demand, because say of an increase in real income, will be accommodated by a decline in the level of prices so as to raise the real value of the existing nominal money stock. With a decline in our prices, though, we are out of line with world prices and thus require appreciation of the exchange rate.

To complete the theory we note two extensions. First there is symmetry in that the foreign price level, P*, is determined by foreign money demand and supply so that we can write (3) as

(4)'
$$E = \left(\frac{M}{M^*} \right) \left(\frac{V}{V^*} \right) \left(\frac{Y^*}{Y} \right)$$

Clearly then, what matters for exchange-rate determination in this view is *relative* money supplies, velocities and real incomes in the two countries. Our exchange rate will depreciate if, other things equal, our nominal money stock rises relative to that abroad.

The second extension is a specification of a velocity function. Here the tradition has been to assume that velocity depends on real income and the alternative cost of holding money:

$$(5) \qquad\qquad V = Y^{\lambda-1} \exp(\theta r)$$

where r is the nominal rate of interest. The functional form is a matter of expositional convenience and monetary tradition.

Substituting (5) in (4)′ and taking logs we obtain the standard equation of the "monetary approach":

$$(6) \qquad\qquad e = m - m^* + \lambda (y - y^*) + \theta (r - r^*)$$

where e, m, m*, y, y* are logarithms of the corresponding capital letter variables.

In the final form, equation (6) shows that an increase in our relative money stock or a decline in our relative income will lead to depreciation as would a rise in our relative interest rate. The last conclusion is particularly interesting since it certainly is the opposite of the conventional wisdom that a rise in interest rates will lead to appreciation. We return to the question below when we compare the relation between interest rates and the exchange rate in alternative theories. We note here the explanation: an increase in interest rates reduces the demand for real money balances. Given the nominal quantity of money the price level has to rise to reduce the real money stock to its lower equilibrium level. With our prices thus getting out of line internationally a depreciation is required to restore PPP.

B. BALANCE-OF-PAYMENTS THEORY OF EXCHANGE RATES

A textbook view of exchange rates will argue that the exchange rate adjusts to balance receipts and payments arising from international trade in goods, services and assets. The current account is affected by the exchange rate because it changes relative prices and thus competitiveness, the capital account is affected to the extent that expectational considerations are important. The theory can be formulated with the help of equation (7):

$$(7) \qquad\qquad BoP = 0 = C(EP^*/P, Y, Y^*) + K(r, r^*, s)$$

where BoP denotes the balance of payments, EP*/P measures the relative price of foreign goods and thus serves as a measure of our competitiveness, C denotes the current account, K the rate of capital inflow and s is a speculative variable which we disregard for the present.

Figure 1 shows the schedule BB along which our balance of payments is in equilibrium, given prices, foreign income and interest rates. A rise in E or a depreciation of the exchange makes us more competitive and thus improves the current account. To restore overall balance-of-payments equilibrium, lower interest rates are required so as to generate an offsetting rate of capital outflow. We can readily show that in this framework the exchange rate depends on interest rates, activity levels, relative price levels and the exogenous determinants of the composition of world demand:

(8) $E = E(Y, Y^*, r, r^*, P^*/P)$

Specifically, an increase in our income, because of say an autonomous increase in spending, will worsen the current account and thus requires an offsetting depreciation. An increase in foreign prices leads to a precisely offsetting appreciation and an increase in our interest rate leads to an appreciation. The mechanism through which higher interest rates at home lead to an appreciation can be illustrated with the help of Figure 1. In the first place the increase in interest rates will lead to a net capital inflow or a reduced rate of outflow and thus causes the overall balance of payments to move into surplus. The exchange rate will accordingly appreciate—

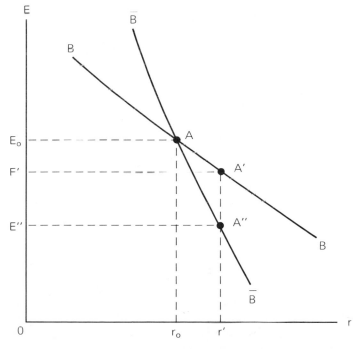

Figure 1

assuming the right elasticities—until we have an offsetting worsening of the current account. This is shown by the move from A to A' on BB.

We may not want to stop at this point but rather recognize that the higher interest rates and the exchange appreciation will exert subsidiary domestic effects. With higher interest rates aggregate demand declines and thus output will fall. The same effect arises from the appreciation and the resulting deterioration of the current account. Thus we have a second round of adjustments to the decline in income which shifts the BB schedule inward over time. The long-run balance-of-payments schedule that incorporates the equilibrium level of income implied by the real exchange rate and interest rate is the steeper schedule $\overline{\text{BB}}$. In the long run we have further appreciation until point A" is reached.

Two points deserve emphasis here. First, the approach views changes in exchange rates as changing (almost one for one) relative prices and competitiveness. It in this respect represents a view opposite to that embodied in the monetary model. Second, it contradicts the monetary model in predicting that an increase in interest rates will lead to an appreciation. I will not pursue this model further, but rather take a specialized version and embody it in a macroeconomic setting.

C. THE MUNDELL-FLEMING MODEL

The balance-of-payments model has drawn attention to the role of capital flows in the determination of exchange rates. This is also the perspective adopted by the modern macroeconomic approach to exchange-rate determination that originated with the pathbreaking work of Mundell (1968) and Fleming (1962). Their theory argues that the exchange rate enters the macroeconomic framework of interest and output determination because changes in exchange rates affect competitiveness. Depreciation acts much in the same way as fiscal policy by affecting the level of demand for domestic goods associated with each level of output and interest rate. A depreciation shifts world demand toward our goods and thus acts in an expansionary manner.

The Mundell-Fleming model is illustrated in Figure 2 for the case of perfect capital mobility. Perfect capital mobility means that there is only one rate of interest at which the balance of payments can be in equilibrium. If the rate were lower, there would be outflows that would swamp any current account surplus and conversely if it was higher. This is illustrated by the horizontal BB schedule. The LM schedule is the conventional representation of monetary equilibrium. Higher income levels raise the demand for money. Given the money stock, interest rates will have to rise to contain money demand to the existing level of supply. Finally, the IS schedule resembles that of a closed economy except that it includes as a component of demand net exports as determined by income and competitiveness. That is why a depreciation will shift the IS schedule out and to the right.

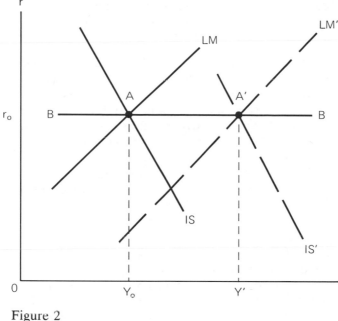

Figure 2

Consider now a monetary expansion indicated by a rightward shift of the LM schedule. The impact effect is of course to lower interest rates and thus to exert an expansionary effect on demand. The decline in interest rates, however, leads to exchange depreciation because of incipient capital outflows. The depreciation in turn enhances our competitiveness raising demand and shifting the IS curve to the right until we reach point A'. Here output and income have risen sufficiently for the increased money stock to be held at the initial rate of interest.

The framework has an important lesson for exchange-rate theory and monetary policy. First, under conditions of perfect capital mobility and given the world rate of interest, monetary policy works not by raising the interest-sensitive components of spending, but rather by generating a depreciation and thereby a current account surplus. Monetary policy works not through the construction sector but rather through the net export component of demand. This is of course a striking result, due in part to the small country assumption. It draws attention to the central role of net exports in aggregate demand and to the link between interest rates and exchange rates. It is the latter link that has become central to recent exchange-rate models.

The theory implies an equilibrium exchange rate which we can obtain either from the condition of goods market equilibrium:[2]

(9) $E = E (r, Y, Y^*, P^*/P, \ldots)$

or as a reduced-form equation of the full system:

$$(10) \qquad\qquad E = E(M, Y^*, \ldots)$$

where the dots denote fiscal policy variables and other exogenous determinants of goods and money demand. It is interesting to note that in (9) an increase in the (world) interest rate, because it reduces aggregate demand and thus creates an excess supply of goods, requires an offsetting depreciation that increases competitiveness and gives rise to a trade surplus.

In its present form the model has three limitations: First, there is no role whatsoever for exchange-rate expectations. This point is important because it implies that strict interest equality must obtain internationally. Second, the model allows for no effect from the depreciation on domestic prices. The depreciation is not allowed to affect either the general price level, and therefore the real value of the money stock, or the price of our output and therefore our competitiveness. It is quite apparent that in fact we should expect at least some spillover into domestic prices and that this spillover will determine the extent to which the real effects of a monetary expansion are dampened. . . . The third limitation concerns the absence of any dynamics. This limitation is important not only in respect to the price adjustment that we just noted but also for the adjustment of trade flows. The existence of adjustment lags . . . implies the possibility that monetary policy in the short run may fail to be expansionary.

D. THE PORTFOLIO-BALANCE MODEL

The Mundell-Fleming model emphasizes the high substitutability between domestic and foreign assets. Capital mobility is perfect so that the slightest deviation of interest rates from the world level unleashes unbounded incipient capital flows. An alternative formulation emphasizes a more limited substitutability between domestic and foreign assets and introduces the level of the exchange rate as a variable that along with asset yields helps achieve balance between asset demands and asset supplies. The model concentrates on asset markets but can readily be extended to include the allocational effects of exchange rates in affecting the current account.

Consider now the basic model as shown in equations (11)-(13) and Figure 3. In equation (11) we show the condition of monetary equilibrium where W denotes nominal wealth and where $\phi(r,r^*)$ is the fraction of wealth people wish to hold in the form of domestic money:

$$(11) \qquad\qquad M = \phi(r,r^*)W \qquad \phi_r, \phi_{r^*} < 0$$

Equilibrium in the market for domestic assets requires that the existing supply, X, equal the demand:

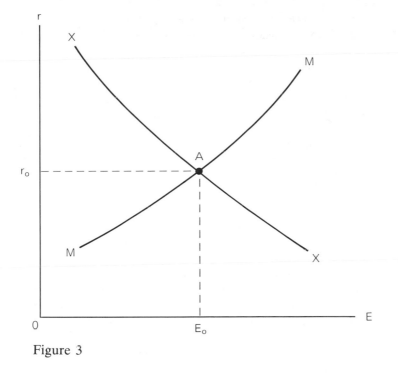

Figure 3

(12) $\qquad X = \psi(r, r^*)W \qquad \psi_r > 0; \psi_{r^*} < 0$

where $\psi(r,r^*)$ is the desired ratio of domestic assets to wealth. The ratio is assumed to increase with the own rate of return and to decline with the return on foreign assets. Equations (11) and (12) together with the wealth constraint:

$$W = M + EF + X$$

imply an equilibrium condition in the market for net external assets:

(13) $\qquad EF = (1 - \Psi - \phi)W = \rho(r, r^*)W \; ; \; \rho_{r^*} > 0, \rho_r < 0$

where F denotes net holdings of foreign assets measured in terms of foreign exchange. Note that since net external assets can be negative, ρ can be negative. We assume that assets are substitutes so that asset demands respond positively to their own yield and negatively to yields on alternative assets.

In Figure 3 we show the money and domestic-asset market equilibrium schedules for given stocks of each of the assets. Along MM the domestic money market is in equilibrium. Higher interest rates reduce money demand so that equilibrium requires a depreciation and thus a rise in the domestic currency value of foreign assets and hence wealth. The exchange rate thus plays a balancing role by affecting the valuation of assets. Along XX the domestic asset market is in equilibrium. Higher interest rates raise the demand for domestic assets and thus require an appreciation to reduce wealth and asset demand thus restoring equilibrium.

We want to establish next the effect of changes in foreign interest rates, changes in domestic money or net external assets. In terms of Figure 3 an increase in the foreign interest rate creates an excess supply of domestic money and domestic securities thus shifting the MM schedule down and to the right and the XX schedule up and to the right. Without question the equilibrium exchange rate depreciates.

Consider next an increase in the domestic money stock. At the initial equilibrium there will be an excess supply of money and an excess demand for domestic (and foreign) securities. Accordingly the MM schedule will shift down and to the right while the XX schedule shifts down and to the left. It is readily established that the net effect is unambiguously a depreciation of the exchange rate.[3]

Finally we consider an increase in net external assets. Now both the money market and domestic security market schedules shift to the left. They will shift in the same proportion, as inspection of (11) and (12) together with the wealth constraint will reveal. Accordingly the equilibrium exchange rate appreciates in proportion to the increase in foreign assets.

The implications of the portfolio balance model are summarized in equation (14) which shows the reduced-form equation for the equilibrium exchange rate:[4]

(14) $E = E(r^*, M, X, F); \quad E_{r^*} > 0; \quad E_M > 0; \quad E_X \lessgtr 0; \quad E_F < 0$

Furthermore since (14) is homogeneous in domestic nominal money and securities we can rewrite the equation as:[5]

(14)' $$E = \gamma(r^*, X/M)\frac{M}{F}$$

In this form we emphasize that the equilibrium exchange rate depends on relative asset supplies. In particular an increase in domestic nominal assets—money and securities—relative to external assets will lead to an equiproportionate depreciation. This homogeneity property is, of course, desirable since it corresponds to an ongoing, neutral inflation process.

The portfolio balance model draws attention to the substitution possibility between domestic and foreign assets. Domestic and foreign securities are no longer perfect substitutes and accordingly their relative supplies determine, along with the nominal money stock, equilibrium interest rates and the exchange rate. A link with the current account is established by virtue of the fact that external assets are acquired over time through the current account surplus. Accordingly, as Kouri (1976, 1977) and others have emphasized, the current account determines the evolution of the exchange rate over time. In particular a current-account surplus which implies accumulation of net external assets leads to an appreciating exchange rate.

The model remains a partial-equilibruim representation in two important respects. First, we do not consider the interaction between financial markets, the exchange rate, goods markets, and the current account. Second, we do not allow for any expectational effects.

What makes this model potentially attractive for the analysis of exchange-rate questions is the direct relation between asset-market disturbances and movement in exchange rates. It extends the monetary model because we do not have to rely on shifts in money demand or supply as sole determinants of exchange-rate movements but rather can consider shifts between domestic and foreign assets, for example, as motivated by, say, expectations.

E. EXPECTATIONS AND EXCHANGE-RATE DYNAMICS

We have so far concentrated on models of the exchange rate that are largely static and that do not emphasize the role of expectations. We extend the analysis now to questions of dynamics and to the place of expectations. The role of expectations is central to exchange-rate determination, and therefore to policies under flexible exchange rates. The spot exchange rate is almost entirely dominated by the course the public expects it to take in the near future. These expectations, of course, are influenced by the structure of the economy and institutional features such as indexing or systematic policy responses. We will in this section first review a fairly general model of exchange-rate expectations and dynamics and then extend the analysis to discuss the idea of a virtuous and vicious circle.

Expectations. We return to the assumption of perfect capital mobility to establish a relationship between interest rates, current exchange rates and expected exchange rates. With perfect capital mobility asset holders would find themselves indifferent between holding domestic or foreign assets provided they carry the same yield, that is provided the interest differential matches the anticipated rate of depreciation:

$$(15) \qquad\qquad r - r^* \cong (\bar{E}/E - 1)$$

where $r - r^*$ is the interest differential, and where $(\bar{E}/E - 1)$ is the expected depreciation of the domestic currency which is defined as the percentage excess of the expected future spot rate, $\bar{E}$, over the current spot rate, E. We can rewrite (15) to yield an equation for the spot rate:

(15)
$$E = \frac{\overline{E}}{1 + r - r^*}$$

Equation (15)′ is central to a correct interpretation of exchange-rate movements. It argues that movements in the spot rate are due either to changes in interest differentials, given expectations, or to changes in expectations over the future course of exchange rates. Specifically, an increase in our interest rate will lead to an appreciation. The anticipation of depreciation, given interest rates, will lead to an immediate depreciation in the same proportion.

We close the model of exchange-rate determination with a theory of nominal interest rates and a theory of how exchange-rate expectations are formed. This is the point where our model ties in with the earlier theories. Thus we can appeal, for example, to the Keynesian model to argue that interest rates are determined by income, the terms of trade, and the real money stock. Suppose the foreign interest rate is given. The domestic interest rate, using the condition of money-market equilibrium as implicit in an LM schedule, will depend on income and real money:

(16)
$$r = r(M/P, Y)$$

The expected future or long-run equilibrium exchange rate, $\overline{E}$ can be written as a function of the terms of trade, σ, and long-run price levels, $\overline{P}/\overline{P}^*$

(17)
$$\overline{E} = \sigma(\quad)\frac{\overline{P}}{\overline{P}^*} = \sigma(\quad)\frac{\pi\overline{M}}{\pi^*\overline{M}^*}$$

which in turn are proportional to long-run money stocks, $\overline{M}$, $\overline{M}^*$ with the factors of proportionality, π and π^*, determined by exogenous real variables. Substituting (16) and (17) in (15)′ gives us a reduced-form equation for the equilibrium exchange rate:

(18)
$$E = \frac{\sigma(\quad)(\pi\overline{M}/\pi^*\overline{M}^*)}{1 + r(M/P, Y) - r^*} = E(\sigma, M/P, Y; \pi, \pi^*, \overline{M}, \overline{M}^*)$$

What are the implications of our model for exchange-rate determination and monetary policy? The analysis is helped by Figure 4. The schedule QQ shows the equilibrium exchange rate of (18) for given long-run money, terms of trade and price levels and a given foreign interest rate.

The QQ schedule is downward sloping since, given money, a higher price level, say a move to point A‴—raises the equilibrium interest rate at home and thus creates a differential in favor of the home country. To offset the differential the spot rate must appreciate—E must decline—to the point where the anticipated rate of depreciation matches the interest differential.

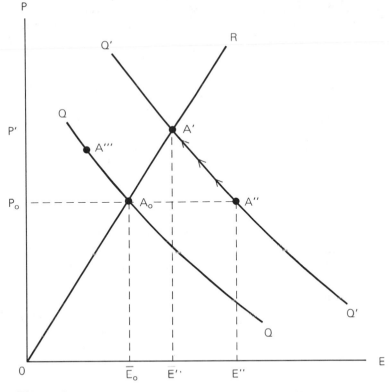

Figure 4

How will a permanent increase in the money stock work itself out in this framework? An increase in money in the long run, with all prices flexible will increase prices and exchange rates in the same proportion. This implies that the QQ schedule shifts out to Q'Q' and that in the final long-run equilibrium we will be at point A' with all real variables unchanged. In the short run, though, an increase in nominal money is an increase in the real money stock. Prices are unlikely to jump and therefore a lower rate of interest is required for the public to hold the higher real money stock. With a decline in interest rates there will be an incipient capital outflow until the exchange rate has depreciated enough to create the anticipation of appreciation exactly at the rate of the interest differential. This is true at point A" where the exchange rate has depreciated beyond its new long-run level. This *overshooting* of exchange rates is an essential counterpart of permanent monetary changes under conditions of short-run price stickiness and perfect capital mobility.

By how much will exchange rates overshoot? That depends on the nature of the price adjustment process. If prices rise very rapidly because interest response of money demand is low and that of goods demand is high or because demand is highly responsive to relative prices—then the overshooting will tend to be small. Conversely, if the adjustment process of prices is slow, then the overshooting is large.

The adjustment, following the impact effect of an increase in money, is shown in Figure 4 by the movement along $Q'Q'$. The exchange rate has depreciated thus making domestic goods more competitive. Interest rates at home have declined thereby raising demand. Both factors work to put upward pressure on our price level. Prices will rise, real money declines and interest rates rise back up until the new long-run equilibrium at A' is reached.

Virtuous and Vicious Cycles. The framework we have laid out here helps understand a controversy that has developed about the working of a flexible-rate system. It has been argued that flexible rates make inflation stabilization more difficult in soft-currency countries and easier in hard-currency countries. The reason is that monetary policy, through the rapid reaction of exchange rates and through the overshooting, exerts rapid inflationary pressure in expanding countries and inflation-dampening in relatively tight countries. Monetary policy becomes quite possibly ineffective if one recognizes that the inflationary pressure of depreciation is quite soon translated into domestic price increases. These price increases limit the gain in competitiveness from a depreciation. In these circumstances monetary policy is primarily inflationary; it has very little, if any, effect on real aggregate demand. All that would happen is that renewed attempts at stimulating aggregate demand would translate into increasing inflation rather than more employment.

What institutional factors would check or enhance such an ostensibly unstable process? It has been argued with force that the virtuous and vicious cycle is entirely a matter of monetary determination. Unless monetary policy validates the depreciation it will ultimately undo itself. There can be little disagreement with this conclusion, except that it is fundamentally irrelevant as an observation about policy. The relevant policy setting is one where widespread indexation, for example, will immediately translate depreciation into wage and price inflation with the consequence of growing unemployment if the central bank fails to accommodate through further monetary expansion. The central bank may in practice have very little power to stop this inflationary process and the right starting point is incomes policy not monetary policy. At the same time it is, of course, true that the prospect of an effective stabilization program will immediately receive the side benefit of an appreciation and a consequent bonus in terms of inflation reduction.

F. SUMMARY

We have now reviewed a wide spectrum of exchange-rate theories. There is little purpose in endorsing one particular formulation since each of these models seeks to capture a special effect and thus is more or less suitable for a particular instance of policy analysis. Some models view the place of the exchange rate mainly in its short-term effects on competitiveness and its long-term role in keeping prices in line internationally. Monetary and portfolio models assign importance to exchange-rate movements through valuation effects, exchange-rate movements change the real value of the money stock or the relative supplies of domestic and foreign assets.

If a choice has to be made between models, then I do see a difference between Quantity Theory-oriented models that leave for the exchange rate the purely passive role of keeping the current stock of real balances just right and expectations-oriented asset-market models in which the current level of the exchange rate is set primarily by references to its anticipated path. In this latter perspective changes in current rates bring about an adjustment dynamics the details of which depend on the differential speeds of adjustment in goods and money markets and where the adjustments that are taking place are quite possibily directed toward events that have not yet matcrialized but are already anticipated.

Monetarist models, of course, also recognize the importance of expectations. In those models, however, the spot rate is influenced by the effect of anticipated depreciation on real money demand. The anticipation of depreciation would reduce real money demand thus raising the price level and therefore, via PPP, lead to a depreciation of the exchange rate. The extent of the depreciation depends on the interest responsiveness of money demand. By contrast in the present model the anticipation of depreciation leads directly, as of given prices and interest rates, to an equiproportionate depreciation of the spot rate.

From the perspective of monetary policy these two strands of modeling differ of course quite radically. The Quantity Theory model assumes quite literally that prices are fully, instantaneously flexible. It thus cannot have any use for monetary policy, except perhaps to stabilize the price level in the face of money-demand fluctuations. All other models, of course, share a macroeconomic—as opposed to monetarist—persuasion where monetary policy works, more or less, because the central bank can move the real money stock. In this perspective exchange rates become a vehicle for monetary policy. One of the chief channels of monetary policy is the direct effect of money on interest rates and on the exchange rate and thereby on relative prices and aggregate demand. The empirical problem is of course whether this link makes price adjustment more rapid, or to put it differently, whether flexible rates make the Phillips curve steeper....

Notes

1. For extensive reviews see Officer (1976), Frenkel and Johnson (1978) and the collection of essays in the May 1978 issue of the *Journal of International Economics*.
2. The condition of goods market equilibrium is: $Y = A(r,Y) + C(EP^*/P, Y, Y^*)$ where $A(\ )$ denotes aggregate spending by domestic residents and C is the trade balance. We solve the equation for the exchange rate to obtain (9).
3. Using equations (11) and (12) along with the definition of wealth we have:

$$dE/dM = \left(\frac{1}{F}\right) \frac{\Psi_r(1 - \phi) + \Psi\phi_r}{\phi\Psi_r - \Psi\phi_r} = \frac{1}{F} \frac{\Psi_r\rho + \Psi(\Psi_r + \phi_r)}{\phi\Psi_r - \Psi\phi_r} > 0$$

which is positive on our assumption of substitution.
4. The effect of an increase in domestic securities on the equilibrium exchange rate is ambiguous.
5. To derive (14)′ we note that taking the ratio of (11) and (12) and solving for the equilibrium interest rate we have: $r = h(r^*, X/M)$. From (13) and the wealth definition we obtain:

$$E = \frac{\rho}{1 - \rho} (M/F + X/F) = (M/F) \frac{\rho}{1 - \rho} (1 + X/M)$$

Substituting the equilibrium interest rate $r = h(\ )$ yields (14)′, where $\gamma(r^*x, X/M) \equiv$

$$\frac{\rho(r^*, h(r^*, X/M))}{1 - \rho(r^*, h(r^*, X/M))} (1 + X/M).$$

References

Black, S. (1977) *Flexible Exchange Rates and National Economic Policy*. Yale University Press.

Fleming, J. M. (1962) "Domestic Financial Policies under Fixed and Flexible Rates." *IMF Staff Papers*, November.

Frenkel, J. and Johnson, H. G. (1978) *The Economics of Flexible Exchange Rates*, Addison-Wesley.

Isard, P. (1978) *Exchange Rate Determination: A Survey of Popular Views and Recent Models*. Princeton Studies in International Finance, No. 42.

Kohlhagen, S. M. (1978) "The Behavior of Foreign Exchange Markets—A Critical Survey of the Empirical Literature." New York University, Series in Finance and Economics.

Mundell, R. A. (1967) *International Economics*, MacMillan.

Officer, L. (1976) "Purchasing Power Parity Theory of Exchange Rates: A Review Article." *IMF Staff Papers*.

Schadler, S. (1977) "Sources of Exchange Rate Variability: Theory and Empirical Evidence." *IMF Staff Papers*, July.

Whitman, M. (1975) "Global Monetarism." *Brookings Papers*, 3.

Willett, T. (1978) *Floating Exchange Rates and International Monetary Reform*. American Enterprise Institute.

VI

Structural Change in International Financial Relations

Part VI is a potpourri encompassing international monetary reform, the European Monetary System (EMS), OPEC's influence on past and future international financial structure, and external-currency banking. The readings come in pairs. The substitution account (Group of Thirty) is one of several important proposals for international monetary reform (the subject of Thomas D. Willett's opening essay).[1] The second pair presents views of different enthusiasm and perspective (Jacques van Ypersele de Strihou versus Robert Triffin on the EMS). Still others combine retrospective and prospective emphasis (Robert M. Dunn, Jr. and Morgan Guaranty Trust on OPEC), and macroeconomic/microeconomic flavor (John R. Karlik and Gunter Dufey and Ian H. Giddy on external-currency banking). After separate introductions to each of these articles, we will mention briefly some common themes and overlapping threads.

Intervention Rules and Intervention Assets

Thomas Willett's opening contribution is a comparative critique of five recent approaches to international monetary reform. "International monetary reform" describes proposals for regularizing or harmonizing government oversight of international monetary transactions, usually under the overall supervision of the International Monetary Fund (IMF). As such, its justification depends very much on finding *some* reason why governments should have anything at all to do with the foreign exchange market. Underlying the discussion of international monetary reform, therefore, is an assumed resolution of the debate between fixed and floating exchange rates (Artus and Young, Wanniski in Part V) that makes clean floating in some measure undesirable or infeasible. (Clean floating will be infeasible if governments cannot resist the temptation to conduct economic war on each other, via what Willett calls "aggressive intervention," a form of beggar-your-neighbor policy).

The most important of any government's international monetary instruments is official intervention in the foreign exchange market, and Willett's paper discusses five proposed rules for such intervention. Since Willett supposes such previous knowledge of these rules, they are summarized below:

1. Reserve-indicator rules prescribe that maximum allowable intervention be some function of current and historical reserve stocks, reserve flows, and other conditioning variables (that might sometimes prohibit any intervention).
2. Target-zone rules prescribe recommended or required intervention that is some function of the divergence between current exchange rates and exogenously chosen exchange-rate targets. (The Bretton Woods system is an example.)
3. Reference-rate rules prescribe that maximum allowable intervention be some function of the divergence between current exchange rates and exogenously chosen exchange-rate targets, and of other conditioning variables (that might sometimes prohibit any intervention).
4. Leaning-against-the-wind rules prescribe recommended, required, or maximum allowable intervention that is some function of the divergence between current and historical exchange rates.
5. Judgmental assessment, or the case-history approach, suggests that the IMF use any or all of the rules outlined above as the circumstances of time and place warrant.

These rules differ in several dimensions. Some are permissive/prohibitive (full autonomy within allowable limits); others are directive. Among the directive varieties are presumptive rules (recommendations) and imperatives (requirements). Some focus on exchange rates, others on reserves. Some use historical values as the norm; others use policy-determined targets.

The issues that such rules raise are difficult (and Willett's discussion is at points quite subtle). Many of these issues relate to national discretion. Will governments "agree to be forced" (as they were under the Bretton Wood system), or can they only be encouraged? If they can only be encouraged, then encouraged to do what?—to take precisely specified action, or simply to consult with each other (note Willett's mention of "consultation points")?[2] Other important issues relate to market efficiency (see Part V). If the foreign exchange market is efficient, then it is not clear just what the grounds are for *any* intervention. If it is inefficient in certain carefully defined ways, then some rules seem to make more sense than others. Finally, if private agents discover the more rigid rules (rules 1 through 4) and factor them into their decisions as a piece of endogenous government behavior, then their actions can shrink or neutralize any systematic benefits from the rules (see

Part V.) This last problem, plus the suspicion that governments themselves have been the most frequent cause of inefficiency in the foreign exchange market, tilt Willett's preferences towards the ill-defined, but flexible proposal 5.

The substitution account is one aspect of international monetary reform that concerns intervention assets rather than intervention itself. There are strong indications that the dollar may lose its 35-year-old preeminent status as the world's official reserve currency. The rise of "parallel" reserve currencies, most importantly the German mark, the reasons behind it, and the problems encountered in a multiple-reserve-currency system are documented in the Group of Thirty's discussion of the substitution account. Its chief purpose is to formalize and insure a process by which governments diversify their official reserves without periodically "dumping" their huge "overhang" of official-reserve dollars whenever confidence slips.[3] The more fundamental aim is to avoid potentially wild fluctuations in exchange rates that can be brought on by such dumping, and thus to avoid their adverse consequences for trade, investment, growth, and resource allocation.

The U.S. supports some sort of substitution account, because these consequences would be particularly troublesome for it. They would make the dollar's reserve-currency status a U.S. burden in the same way as sterling's was for Britain in the early 1970s. Other nations support a substitution account, too. Some feel "locked into" their dollar reserves. Others feel that it is time for the U.S. and the dollar to play a more symmetric international role. The IMF supports the substitution account too. It would enhance the position of Special Drawing Rights (SDR's) as a reserve asset,[4] even though the envisioned "SDR denominated claims" would be scrupulously differentiated from SDRs themselves. The IMF/internationalist vision is for SDR-type assets eventually to replace all national currencies in official reserves, and for globally negotiated reserve creation to replace nationally-dictated deficit financing in the U.S. (or Germany, or anywhere else).[5]

With all this agreement, it may seem strange that the first serious outline of a substitution account was unceremoniously shelved in the spring of 1980. An underlying irony in these events was that governments themselves turned out to be suspicious of whether other governments or the IMF could create economically viable official reserves—reserves that were as attractive as those available to all in national markets. The SDR, for example, had a singularly uninspiring portfolio performance in the late 1970s.[6] This poor performance, coupled with gradually increasing German willingness to see marks held more widely as official reserves, made nationally-controlled substitution into marks tempting as an alternative to internationally-controlled substitution into SDR claims. When no agreement could be reached on the mechanism to guarantee global purchasing power of the dollar assets held by the substitution account, and thereby ultimately to assure its fiscal integrity, the whole proposal was tabled. The U.S. was unwilling to accept the bulk of guarantee/liquidation responsibility, perhaps because of the belief that it had already done its share over the years by bearing the "burden" of reserve-currency responsibility.[7] Developing countries in the IMF were just as unwilling to back the substitution account with IMF gold, because the gains from its alternative uses (IMF gold sales and restitution) accrue largely to them.

The European Monetary System

Some of the same misgivings that prompted portfolio diversification away from dollars have also encouraged the regionally-based return to pegged exchange rates that is the European Monetary System (EMS). Triffin describes European misgivings about the dollar at some length. He also reveals an important common motivation for the EMS: As mark assets are increasingly sought out for reserve purposes, the mark's link to weaker European currencies will dampen any tendency toward secular appreciation and overvaluation (which the Germans seem to fear primarily because of the export dependence of their real sector). The mark's link will also spread the exchange-rate effects of recurrent bouts of mark speculation throughout the EMS.

The EMS has also come about because European economists, politicians, and civil servants seem much more convinced of the virtues of stabilizing exchange rates than do their American counterparts. Von Ypersele de Strihou in his paper has set forth a cogent summary of the "European view" on this venerable theme. He stresses not only the familiar side effects of floating exchange rates (for example, overshooting) but introduces some that are less familiar in the U.S. For example, he claims that variable exchange rates are like unpredictable adjustable customs barriers; if we agree (in our trade courses) that the customs barriers would be detrimental to trade, then we should agree that the exchange rates are also. He also argues that under certain kinds of incomes policies and real-wage rigidity, both depreciation and appreciation discourage output: Floating exchange rates would thus cause smaller growth in output and employment than fixed. Finally, he stresses the policy discipline that the EMS might provide. A skeptical reader might ask, however, whether signing an agreement really enforces discipline. Will countries necessarily "have to give a high priority to internal policy measures rather than rely on exchange-rate changes"? Will they "compel themselves to aim at greater convergence"? If so, why didn't they do so before the agreement? And won't Germany feel less pressure for "discipline" under the EMS?

The EMS can be seen indeed as a test of the readiness of major countries to return to pegged exchange rates. It can also be seen as a first step toward a currency union (with a full-fledged common currency succeeding the European Currency Unit [ECU]) that might rival the U.S. in economic prosperity, hegemony, and reserve-currency responsibility. Finally, the EMS can be seen perhaps as a threat to the IMF. Its structures and obligations (parities, consultations, reserve depositions and loans, and the like) are remarkably similar. Spokespersons for the EMS and the IMF deny any such competition between them, but the potential is clearly present.

Oil Prices and International Finance

Oil pricing and investment policy of OPEC have greatly complicated the problems of international and regional monetary reform. Dunn's paper is an especially clear catalog of the reasons why. Employing a practical version of the "monetary/asset approach" discussed in Part V, and keeping careful track of the different kinds of pressures on the current account and the capital account, Dunn demonstrates how pegged exchange rates and managed floating provide no conventional means of payments adjustment to an OPEC oil tax. The reasons all relate to the absence of linkage between payments imbalance and domestic economic variables such as the money stock in OPEC countries. Cleanly floating exchange rates would not have necessarily been any better, although they might have brought "adjustment," because the adjustment would have come at the cost of a much higher and more burdensome relative price of oil than now exists. As Dunn remarks, ". . . the classical adjustment process is not always to be preferred over a continuing disequilibrium."

Dunn's paper is full of provocative challenges. Perhaps the relative price of OPEC oil *isn't* artificially high at present. Perhaps we should stop considering current-account deficits to be a sign of economic weakness and see them instead as a mark of national attractiveness to foreign investors. Perhaps the 1970s saw European and Japanese governments engage in the kind of aggressive foreign-exchange-market intervention that some of Willett's rules would outlaw.

And these are not issues only for economic historians, as the Morgan Guaranty Trust paper reveals. The OPEC nations raised oil prices again in 1979 by a dollar amount that far exceeded their increase in 1973. Thus Dunn's observations are more timely than he may have intended. The difficulties stemming from this new price hike are qualitatively the same but have different weights. Developing countries seem destined to experience considerably more severe burdens and payments adjustments this time than the last. Morgan Guaranty counsels developed countries to be even more prepared to welcome OPEC investments and, consequently, to bear larger current-account deficits. Morgan Guaranty then suggests they "recycle" OPEC investments to developing countries, thereby avoiding massive default and the potential collapse of some multinational commercial banks. But Morgan Guaranty gives no advice on how developed countries should sell larger current-account deficits to a protection-minded public who are facing national unemployment levels unprecedented in their lifetime and who are sharing in the global economic slump. These matters are certain to be among the most vexing of the coming five years.

External-Currency Banking

"External-currency" or "offshore" banking has grown tumultuously during the 1970s, due in part to the recycling of OPEC oil revenues and more importantly to OPEC's desire to hold wealth in highly liquid assets that are less accessible than conventional assets to monitoring, regulation, and seizure by hostile governments. Another source of growth during this period has been official-reserve diversification. Virtually all mark-denominated reserves are Euromark bank deposits. Many smaller countries have diversified their official reserves away from "U.S." dollars and toward Eurodollars, since as Dufey and Giddy reveal, this enables them to minimize the political-jurisdiction risk of their portfolio.

Karlik outlines other reasons for the growth of external-currency banking in answering his question 2. His questions 4 through 10 reveal the sweeping implications that this phenomenon has for international financial structure.

That external-currency banking is neither as unfamiliar nor as sinister as sometimes it appears is an important message found in the contribution by Dufey and Giddy. External-currency banking is nothing more than transnational financial intermediation, and Dufey and Giddy insist that it is distinguishable in only six important ways from other financial intermediation. Among the implications of these distinctions are that external-currency banking promotes both efficiency and equity (defined with reference to market-generated income distribution): It circumvents distortions introduced by bank regulation, and it undermines the preferred status attainable by some borrowers and lenders in cloistered national capital markets.

Dufey and Giddy also emphasize the way in which external-currency banking links the foreign exchange market to integrated national credit markets—through interest arbitrage and speculative capital movements. They point out that external-currency banking bridges national capital markets (markets for means of deferred payment) just as the foreign exchange market bridges national cash-balance "markets" (markets for means of current payment).[8]

Common Themes and Overlapping Threads

The readings in Part VI are less self-contained than they may at first appear, organization of the introduction notwithstanding. We will mention a few illustrations of this point; the reader will find it a useful study technique to look for more.

1. The EMS is an implementation of Willett's "target-zone" proposal.
2. Controversy over whether international monetary reform should lay down directives, presumptions, or invitations to negotiate is precisely what separates the U.S. from other countries on insuring the substitution account.
3. Because the ECU is even today something of a competitor to the dollar, it is already a potential "mechanism for substitution accounts" (Triffin).
4. International monetary reform may increasingly have to be oriented toward adjustment to oil prices, say through a new IMF Oil Facility, and the substitution account as initially proposed might aggravate the OPEC-related recycling problem (Morgan Guaranty Trust).

Notes

1. Other illustrations include the significant Second Amendment of the IMF's Articles of Agreement, and its gold sales. Trust Fund, and Special-Drawing-Right (SDR) innovations. We found them to be adequately treated elsewhere and readily available.
2. The EMS features commitments that span most options for governments—some actions are required, some recommended, and some result in consultations only. See the appendix to the van Ypersele de Strihou paper.
3. The substitution account is thus aimed at solving what many textbooks refer to as the "confidence problem."
4. The Second Amendment of the IMF's Articles of Agreement mandated an increased role for SDRs in international monetary affairs, without spelling out exactly how this change was to be accomplished.
5. To make universal substitution of SDR-type assets for national moneys feasible, SDR claims would have to become privately held, used by commercial banks, and traded in forward markets, as the Group of Thirty makes clear.
6. Its "real yield" from January 1975 through August 1979 has been estimated to be negative—approximately a 1 percent loss each year—and inferior to short-term investments in *all* major national capital markets, even the U.S. See Morgan Guaranty Trust Company, "Reserve Diversification and the IMF Substitution Account," *World Financial Markets* (September 1979), pp. 5–14. "Real yields" are adjusted for capital gains and losses due to inflation and exchange-rate changes.
7. Being a reserve-currency country also means benefits, alluded to indirectly by Triffin's insistence in his EMS paper that the U.S. "abused" its reserve-currency privilege.
8. Their observations are consistent with the asset approach to exchange rates and payments discussed in Part V.

27

Alternative Approaches to International Surveillance of Exchange-Rate Policies

Thomas D. Willett

I. INTRODUCTION

How can we best attempt to ensure that national governments do not abuse the freedom generated by floating-exchange rates by engaging in beggar-thy-neighbor policies to overdepreciate their exchange rates or unduly retard the operation of the international adjustment process by maintaining an overvalued exchange rate? The major purpose of this paper is to develop a basis for choosing among the major alternative approaches which have been proposed for the international surveillance of national exchange-rate policies. The following section attempts to characterize the basic logic of the alternative approaches and isolate the major causes of differences of views among the advocates of alternative approaches. Emphasis is placed on political as well as technical economic considerations. . . . The final section emphasizes the importance of strengthening the role of the I.M.F. in the international surveillance process if the judgmental approach is to be effective.

The major alternative approaches which have been suggested for the international surveillance of national exchange-rate practices under managed floating can be functionally classified under five categories:

1) reserve indicators
2) target zones
3) reference rates
4) leaning against the wind
5) judgmental assessment or the case-history approach

Proposals for allocating current-account positions will be discussed as a variant of the target-zone approach.

From Thomas D. Willett, "Alternative Approaches to International Surveillance of Exchange-Rate Policies," in *Managed Exchange-Rate Flexibility* by Jacques R. Artus et al. (Boston: Federal Reserve Bank of Boston, 1978). Reprinted by permission. Some footnotes omitted. Thomas D. Willett is Horton Professor of Economics, Claremont Graduate School and Claremont Men's College. The author is indebted to the participants in the economic workshop at Claremont Graduate School, and particularly Richard J. Sweeney, for helpful comments on an earlier draft of this paper.

As a first approximation we can consider the major objective of all of these proposals to be to limit the emergence and persistence of disequilibrium or incorrect exchange rates. All of the proposals are concerned with the possibilities of government policies creating such disequilibrium. Some are also concerned with possible deficiencies in private market behavior, for example, due to poorly behaved private speculation or externalities, which would require government intervention to establish correct exchange rates. The supporters of the various proposals have different views about the relative seriousness of these two types of causes of incorrect exchange rates, about methods of attempting to detect or estimate disequilibrium and correct exchange rates, and about the political and management problems involved in attempting to implement the alternative proposals.

The *reserve-indicator* approach takes reserve movements as the best indicator of government-induced disequilibrium in the foreign-exchange market and seeks to set limits on the amount of such intervention. A reserve-indicator approach to international surveillance of the adjustment process was advocated by the United States in the early stages of the post-floating negotiations on international monetary reform. It has a history going back at least to Keynes and was recommended by Mikesell and Goldstein in their recent analysis of rules for a floating-rate regime.[1]

The *target-zone* and *reference-rate* approaches seek to establish internationally agreed levels or zones for appropriate exchange rates. The target-zone approach focuses on requiring intervention to keep market rates from moving outside of the zone and thus is closely akin to the old Bretton Woods adjustable peg system. A version of the target-zone approach was advocated in the 1974 I.M.F. Guidelines for Floating (which have been repealed by the 1977 set of Principles for Exchange Rate Policies) and enjoys a great deal of support in Europe.[2] The reference-rate approach turns the Bretton Woods procedures on their head and prescribes when intervention is prohibited rather than when it is required. Leading advocates of the reference-rate approach include Ethier and Bloomfield, Fred Hirsch, and John Williamson.[3]

The *leaning-against-the-wind* approach essentially prohibits aggressive official intervention, that is, selling domestic currency when its value is falling in the exchange markets or buying domestic currency when its value is rising. The proposition that official intervention only be allowed to lean against the wind can be included as an element of reserve indicator or judgmental approaches, and is a generally accepted common-law principle. Its major violations occur when countries have intervened in dollars to meet obligations under the European snake arrangements or to counter movements in trade-weighted exchange-rate indices. Thus there have been many instances in which other countries have sold dollars even though the dollar was falling against their currency or have bought dollars even though it was rising. While such practices are inconvenient from the standpoint of the United States and have probably contributed somewhat to the variability of the dollar, cases of more broadly based aggressive intervention have been quite rare.

Perhaps the most notable alleged case concerned the plunge of the pound below $2.00 in 1976, but it is somewhat unclear whether the beginning of this decline was deliberately engineered or was a mistake based on operating procedures which called for intervention in dollars based on movements in the Bank of England's trade-weighted index. In any event, such aggressive intervention lasted at most for one day. During most of the subsequent drop of the pound against the dollar, the Bank of England was buying pounds to slow the fall. For the purpose of this paper, I will assume that the principle that countries should not usually intervene aggressively is generally accepted.[4] The discussion of this category below will concentrate only on whether it is sufficient to obviate the need for other procedures. Recent discussion of the leaning against-the-wind approach has been presented by Cooper (who refers to it as the "smoothing and braking strategy" as contrasted with the "tracking strategy" of the target-zone and reference-rate proposals), Grubel, Tosini, and Wonnacott.[5]

The *judgmental* or *case-history* approach was stongly advocated by the United States in the later stages of the reform negotiations and was adopted in essence in the 1977 I.M.F. Principles for the Guidance of Members' Exchange Rate Policies. Advocates of various varieties of the judgmental approach have included Artus and Crockett, Cooper, Roosa, Whitman, and Willett.[6]

The first best argument for a judgmental approach is based on the view that desirable balance-of-payments and exchange-rate behavior is too complex to be adequately captured by a set of exchange-rate or reserve indicators and that acceptable norms must be built up over time based on the cumulative treatment of concrete situations. The second best argument for the judgmental approach is that it represents the best fallback available when sovereign national governments are not prepared to agree on a more highly structured approach to international surveillance.

There are, of course, many variants under each of these categories, and sometimes variants under different categories merge into one another. Thus, for example, efforts to ensure that leaning-against-the-wind intervention policies are applied symmetrically on the up and down sides are likely to merge into a reserve-indicator approach. Similarly, some of the European proposals for target zones represent something of a halfway house between the pure target-zone and reference-rate approaches. For example, C. J. Oort has proposed a system of consultation points.[7] If exchange rates move outside of these points, multilateral consultations to discuss intervention are called for, while intervention on the wrong side of the consultation points would be prohibited. Target-zone proposals with asymmetrical intervention requirements have also been put forward, reflecting a greater concern with "excessive" depreciation than with excessive appreciation.[8]

In the following section I shall attempt to lay out the rationales for the various approaches in more detail. As will be discussed, advocates of the various approaches tend to differ greatly in their judgments about such issues as the behavior of exchange markets, the ability of governments to determine "correct" or equilibrium exchange rates and secure international agreement on them, and the social costs of exchange-rate variability and government exchange-rate manipulation.

One important point which should be kept in mind is that the best guidelines for international surveillance may differ from the best strategies for national intervention policies. A good set of international procedures should not rule out desirable national intervention strategies, but the purpose of international procedures is to place limits on the ability of national governments or the private market to produce anti-social outcomes which harm the international community. Thus, for instance, while reserve changes are probably a better indicator for national exchange-rate policies than are reserve levels, it may be more appropriate to use reserve levels to set bounds on the range of permissible national behavior. Likewise, . . . I do not believe that the available evidence indicates that foreign-exchange markets have operated in a manner that would make systematic leaning against the wind an optimal national intervention strategy, but I believe that barring exceptional circumstances, only intervention which leans against the wind should be internationally approved.

I should also note that this paper does not explicitly deal with issues of monetary and macroeconomic policy coordination. Where underlying conditions are highly variable, equilibrium exchange rates will display great variability and this can impose serious economic costs. Where private speculation is working reasonably well, attempts to substantially limit exchange-rate variations through exchange-market intervention are dealing with the symptoms rather than the basic cause of the problem. I believe that having a strong system of international surveillance of exchange-rate policies is important. But the creation and maintenance of relatively stable national macroeconomic policies and conditions are even more important for promoting international monetary stability. It is quite appropriate that a session at this conference be devoted to discussion of surveillance of exchange-rate policies, but we should be careful not to mislead ourselves into believing that effective surveillance of exchange-rate policies is a sufficient condition for the restoration of international monetary stability.

The officials of the International Monetary Fund have been well aware of this point, and perhaps the major focus of their attention recently has been on trying to induce more stable and better coordinated macroeconomic policies. Indeed a major aspect of the agreements among the major industrial countries at Rambouillet which cleared the way for international monetary reform was the emphasis on the need for more stable underlying economic policies if one hoped to obtain exchange-rate stability. However, there is still sufficient controversy about various aspects of proposals for narrowly defined exchange-rate policies to deter me from attempting in this paper to tackle the problems of international surveillance of macroeconomic policies as well.

I should also stress that although the International Monetary Fund has adopted one of the proposed alternatives for surveillance, I believe that it is quite appropriate that the alternative possibilities still be reviewed. It is certainly within the normal domain of policy research to focus on evaluating past decisions, as well as future possibilities. Adoption of the new I.M.F. guidelines has certainly not quelled advocacy of the alternative approaches. Obtaining a better understanding of the rationales for the alternative approaches is also quite important for understanding different points of view about national exchange-rate policies. Furthermore, as will be argued below, even when some of these proposals are rejected in their pure form, they still may have important, although less formal, potential roles to play in the implementation of the I.M.F.'s judgmental approach. And little appears to have been decided so far about how the new I.M.F. guidelines will be implemented.

II. THE LOGIC OF THE VARIOUS APPROACHES

The Reference-Rate and Target-Zone Approaches

Advocates of the target-zone and reference-rate approaches tend to assume that 1) "correct" or equilibrium exchange rates can be calculated relatively accurately, but that speculation in the foreign-exchange market is not sufficiently well behaved to keep market rates "close enough" to these "correct" rates, 2) that because correct rates can be calculated relatively accurately it will not be excessively difficult to achieve agreement among national governments as to what these rates or zones are and 3) that these figures can be renegotiated relatively promptly when changes in underlying conditions warrant.

In both of these approaches the idea is that officials can systematically do a better job of determining exchange rates than the market can, that official announcements of exchange-rate objectives will help to stabilize private speculative behavior. The advocates of the two approaches differ in their views of the costs of exchange-rate variability, however, as the reference rate supporters focus only on prohibiting beggar-thy-neighbor official intervention while the target-zone approach seeks to limit both national beggar-thy-neighbor policies and excessive exchange-rate fluctuations.[9]

On purely logical grounds the target-zone advocates appear to make a stronger case than do supporters of the reference-rate approach. If, indeed, officials can calculate and secure international agreement on correct exchange rates within relatively narrow bands, why should it not be as important to avoid incorrect exchange rates resulting from market forces as it is for those resulting from government manipulation?

It seems likely that reference-rate advocates may tend to be somewhat less confident than target-zone advocates of the ability to reach internationally negotiated agreements on exchange-rate norms that tend to be systematically better than market rates. Such a belief could justify a looser target-zone or consultation points approach which does not require mandatory intervention in opposition to strong market sentiments.[10] Reference-rate advocates could also believe that while the private market and government intervention may both lead to wrong exchange rates at times, there is a stronger tendency for incorrect rates to persist as a result of national policies than of market behavior. Such a tendency would be sufficient to establish a rationale for greater international concern with limiting national governmental behavior than with limiting market behavior.

In the first several years after the oil shock, a great deal of attention was focused on the allocation of the resulting oil deficits and a number of proposals were put forward to assign current-account targets to each country in order to avoid a beggar-thy-neighbor scramble for surplus positions which were not collectively feasible.[11] Functionally, comprehensive current-account allocation proposals may be considered a variant of the target-zone approach in which calculations of the exchange-rate norms are based on estimates of what is required to achieve the current-account norms. Proponents of the current-account allocations approach assume either that other policies can be adjusted to remove differences between the exchange rates which would yield overall payments balance and the current-account target or that, in the case of conflicts, achieving the current-account target is more important. Comprehensive versions of the current-account allocation entail the same types of problems of implementation as the more general target-zone approach (although most of the discussions have focused on the need to avoid a scramble for current-account surplus and how current-account targets should be allocated, with little explicit attention to the problem of achieving such targets once they had been accepted). Advocates of the judgmental approach would also argue that it will often be important to give considerable attention to current-account positions as well as overall payments but would tend to argue that this cannot usefully be done in a simple mechanical manner.

Leaning Against the Wind

Critics of the reference-rate and target-zone approaches tend to challenge the validity of all three of the propositions listed at the beginning of the previous subsection. Advocates of a leaning-against-the-wind approach are dubious of the ability to set internationally agreed accurate sets of exchange-rate norms. but usually assume that free markets will tend to display excessive volatility because of badly behaved private speculation and/or externalities resulting from exchange-rate fluctuations. Since they tend to be skeptical of the desirability of freely floating rates, advocates of leaning against the wind tend to support this approach both as a norm for national behavior and of international surveillance and would tend to be tolerant of fairly large reserve changes in support of efforts to reduce the magnitude of exchange-rate fluctuations.

The adoption of the proposal to allow only leaning-against-the-wind intervention as a complete solution to international surveillance implies a primary concern with avoiding aggressive beggar-thy-neighbor policies. However, while the avoidance of such aggressive actions is certainly to be desired, this has not really been a major problem since the 1930s. It is quite understandable that with the 1930s fresh in their memory, the architects of the Bretton Woods monetary system considered the avoidance of such aggressive beggar-thy-neighbor policies as a major rationale for adopting the adjustable-peg exchange-rate system. However, in my view, the much more serious problem of national government policies creating disequilibrium under both the adjustable-peg and managed floating has been not by overt exchange-rate changes, but rather through government policies which maintained exchange rates or allowed them to adjust only slowly in circumstances in which equilibrium exchange rates were changing by substantial amounts, in other words, through excessive leaning against the wind rather than aggressive policies.[12]

Reserve Indicators

To attempt to limit this problem, some type of provisions for symmetry between the extent of leaning in an upward and downward direction would need to be introduced into leaning-against-the-wind proposals for international surveillance. The most obvious method is to adopt bounds on the amount of net cumulative intervention in either direction. In her recent analysis of leaning against the wind, Paula Tosini accepts the proposition that intervention should be symmetrical over the long run but argues against quantitative limitation on cumulative reserve changes. She argues that such limitations would encourage the use of alternative methods of influencing the exchange rate and would increase exchange-rate volatility.

The existence of substitutes for intervention such as official borrowing from private markets, monetary policy, capital controls, and official guidance of private-capital flows clearly indicates that quantitative limits on reserve changes are not sufficient to eliminate the possibility of beggar-thy-neighbor policies, but it does not establish a case against the use of quantitative limits on cumulative reserve movements in conjunction with supplementary guidelines concerning the use of intervention substitutes. To argue against quantitative indicators on this score would require additional arguments such as that intervention substitute policies are so easy to adopt and would be so quantitatively important that it wouldn't be worth the trouble to attempt to negotiate reserve indicators or that agreement on quantitative reserve indicators would inappropriately deflect international attention away from the use of intervention-substitute policies.

The second type of argument cuts more directly against the basic case for reserve indicators. Tosini's assumption is that private speculation does not work well so that limitations on official intervention will reduce the ability of governments to counteract the excessive volatility of the private market. As I have argued elsewhere, the basic logic of the reserve-indicator approach rests on the opposite assumption that private speculation usually works fairly well.[13]

In the case of well-behaved private speculation and no intervention substitute policies, reserve changes or cumulative intervention would measure the extent to which national governments have caused exchange rates to diverge from their equilibrium levels.[14] Quantitative limitations would then be set on the basis of how much discretion would be given to national authorities to use exchange-market policies to achieve domestic objectives such as reducing inflation, stimulating employment, or correcting for externalities caused by exchange-rate movements.

Presumably these limitations would be set more stringently, the less important externalities from equilibrium exchange-rate movements were judged to be, and the more willing countries were to accept limitations on their own scope for discretionary action in return for similar limitations on the actions of others. Similar considerations would influence the width of exchange-rate bands under the target-zone and reference-rate approaches. In such a world, the width of reserve bands or permissible cumulative reserve changes would be determined purely by the trade-offs involved between the costs and benefits of international policy coordination in the exchange-rate area.

When the possibility of clearly recognizable poorly behaved private speculation is introduced, this would suggest a widening of the limitations on reserve changes in order for governments to combat disequilibrium movements in exchange rates, or the establishment of an international intervention authority with a mandate to intervene only to offset destabilizing speculation or make up for an insufficiency of stabilizing speculation. As the latter alternative seems unlikely to be a serious candidate for adoption over the foreseeable future, let us concentrate on the case in which the limitations on the extent of possible cumulative net national interventions are widened as views about the magnitude of private speculative deficiencies increase. As a set of statistical rules cannot distinguish between intervention in response to imperfections in private market behavior and interventions to achieve national objectives, countries can be given .greater scope to reduce excessive market volatility only at the risk of giving them more potential scope to engage in exchange-rate manipulation as well.

Thus the adoption of a reserve-indicator approach may make a lot of sense if private exchange markets work fairly well. If they work very poorly, reserve limitations sufficiently tight to set strong constraints on exchange-rate manipulations also would be likely to result in excessive exchange-rate volatility, while limitations broad enough to allow the elimination of excess volatility caused by poorly behaved private speculation might provide little effective check on the scope of exchange-rate manipulation by national governments. It is thus not surprising that Mikesell and Goldstein, who believe that the exchange markets work fairly well, recommend a relatively tight reserve indicator system, while Tosini, who assumes that the exchange markets work poorly, is highly critical of Mikesell and Goldstein's recommendation.

Two other types of economic objections to reserve indicators should also be briefly discussed. One is the argument that a reserve-indicator system might encourage disruptive private speculation. When reserves were close to their permissible limit, the market would know that future exchange-rate changes would be much more likely to be in one direction than the other and this tendency would be exaggerated in the face of rules that required some proportion of interventions to be reversed within a given time period. In reply it can be argued, however, that the prospect of such developments would place a healthy discipline on national governments to refrain from intervening so much that they get themselves out on such a limb. Obviously such an argument is much more persuasive to those who believe private markets work fairly well and are concerned primarily about excessive government intervention, than to those who believe that the private market works poorly and a considerable amount of official intervention is desirable. It should also be noted that the perverse speculative incentives which might be generated by a poorly working reserve-indicator system are unlikely to be as bad as the one-way speculative option which developed under the adjustable-peg system and which critics believe would be likely to reemerge if a target-zone approach were adopted.

The second additional objection concerns the feasibility of determining reasonable mechanics and quantitative values for the reserve-indicator approach. How should stock and flow considerations be combined? How tight should the quantitative limitations be and how should this vary for stock and flow indicators? How should base levels and rates of growth of reserve norms be selected? Such questions are the analogs for the reserve-indicator approach to the problem of deciding upon exchange-rate norms under the target-zone and reference-rate approaches.

While at first glance, it would seem that the technical difficulties involved in implementing the exchange-rate norm approaches are a good deal less than for the reserve indicator approach, it is not clear that this is really so. For example, would norms be set for each set of bilateral exchange rates or would it be sufficient to use some type of composite exchange-rate index for each country? And if it is granted that it may be appropriate at times for reserve deficient countries to recoup reserves (for example, the United Kingdom during 1976 and 1977) or for some reserve countries, such as Germany and Japan, to reduce their reserve holding (for example, the sales of some of their recently accumulated dollar holding at the beginning of the floating-rate period in 1973), then reserve considerations must be taken into account in the calculation of equilibrium exchange rates. This implies that, in fact, the determination of correct exchange rates may not be less difficult conceptually than the determination of optimal reserve levels and flows.

Furthermore, optimal reserve positions may not tend to change as rapidly as equilibrium exchange rates. Thus once adopted, the need for frequent revisions might well be less of a problem with the reserve-indicator approach than with the exchange-rate norm approaches. It also seems likely that where mistakes are made in calculating norms or norms are not adjusted promptly in the face of changing circumstances, incorrect reserve norms will cause less severe problems than incorrect exchange-rate norms, especially where the norms are used to require as well as prohibit intervention.

While the above considerations make me skeptical of arguments that problems of implementation are substantially less for the exchange-rate norm than for the reserve indicator approach, I find the technical difficulties involved in implementing either approach to be quite impressive. Recognition that such norms do not necessarily have to be optimal to be helpful reduces these difficulties, but not in my view to a manageable level.

The Judgmental Approach

This belief that the issues surrounding appropriate norms for exchange-rate behavior are too complex to be adequately captured in calculations of the exchange rate or reserve norms is the major basis for first best arguments for the judgmental or case-history approach. Advocates of this approach tend to be doubtful that government experts can forecast correct exchange rates sufficiently accurately to make such estimates a sound basis for internationally agreed intervention guidelines. As noted above, the accuracy requirements necessary to make a target-zone approach of mandatory intervention work well are greater than for the reference-rate approach. Conceptually, as the magnitude of expected official forecast errors increased, the appropriate response would be to widen the target zone or consultation points, just as one would increase the width of reserve indicators in response to increases in the magnitude of poorly behaved speculation. In both cases, however, one reaches a point in which the reserve or exchange-rate bands are so wide that at best they become almost meaningless and at worst they may become counterproductive by diverting attention from more important aspects of surveillance.

Advocates of the judgmental approach do not necessarily believe that it is inappropriate for national governments or international organizations to attempt to estimate appropriate exchange-rate zones and perhaps even to make these estimates public. They tend to be doubtful, however, that the market frequently behaves so obviously poorly that one could reach international agreement in advance on meaningful limits to possibly appropriate exchange rates.

Apart from the technical difficulties in estimating correct exchange rates, proponents of the judgmental approach also tend to emphasize the difficulties in reaching international agreement among governments on such estimates, and once having reached agreement, being able to revise such norms sufficiently quickly when unanticipated developments lead to changes in estimates in equilibrium levels or rates of change of exchange rates. The greater the variability in the underlying economic and financial environment, the greater this problem becomes.

If there were some simple set of calculations which gave good estimates of equilibrium exchange rates, these problems of political implementation might not be very serious. For example, if some standardized set of Purchasing Power Parity (PPP) indices gave good approximations of medium-term equilibrium exchange rates, then political negotiations would need only to focus on choosing the formula to be used. Calculations of exchange-rate norms could be automatically updated as new price data became available. Indeed, it is probably not coincidental that many of the advocates of the target-zone approach appear to believe that various types of PPP calculations can provide a reasonable normative guide to appropriate exchange rates.

In such circumstances, there would probably be some initial hard political bargaining over just what formula to use, as many countries attempted to secure an agreement which they believed was more likely to see their currency a little undervalued than a little overvalued. . . . Various PPP calculations can give an extremely wide range of values. Still there is a fairly high probability that such political negotiations could be reasonably successfully concluded. Unfortunately however, . . . there are serious questions whether PPP calculations can give a good guide to appropriate exchange rates. Even holding the degree of accuracy of forecasting constant, the more complicated are the procedures for forecasting, the greater is the extent to which the outcome of international negotiations over exchange-rate norms would be likely to reflect political bargaining strength rather than economic analysis. And as the ability to forecast accurately declines, the political component in negotiations would rise still further.

Perhaps even more significant, the less simple and accurate is the technical economic analysis, the more difficult it would be to renegotiate a new set of norms when underlying fundamentals change. In such circumstances a target-zone approach could easily take on the type of status quo bias which led to the breakdown of the Bretton Woods adjustable peg exchange-rate procedures. Critics argue that it is difficult enough to determine what equilibrium exchange rates are at any one point in time, much less to estimate the equilibrium pattern of exchange rates which will hold over a substantial period into the future. But if the latter cannot be done or some automatic formula for updating norms cannot be adopted, then the international community might well be in almost continuous negotiation over exchange-rate norms.

Negotiating Costs and Problems of Implementation

Advocates of the judgmental approach would argue that international cooperation and the time of top-level policy makers are very scarce and valuable resources. Where the technical issues are complicated, the use of a less formal judgmental approach allows a much more economical use of these scarce resources, concentrating them on the international economic issues which seem of greatest overall importance. It is a frequent, but unfortunate, characteristic of many proposals for international monetary reform to treat the supply of high-level attention and international cooperative behavior as if it were a free good.[15]

In general, advocates of the judgmental approach tend to give greater weight to questions of the allocation of policy-making resources and the willingness of countries to compromise than do advocates of the exchange-rate or reserve norm approaches. Under the ideal circumstances for the application of these objective norm approaches, these questions largely disappear. But as conditions begin to deviate from these ideals, then questions of international decision-making costs become increasingly important. This in turn increases the difficulties with the objective norm approaches more rapidly than on the basis of technical economic considerations alone.

It is also important to recognize that concerns with the maintenance of traditional areas of national sovereignty and appearances to their electorates (who are not international economic experts) will often keep national governments from engaging in as much international cooperative behavior as many international economic experts would judge to be desirable. While continuing to press the case for greater degrees of cooperative behavior over the long run, this leaves technical experts with the short-run problem of seeking second or n-th best solutions which utilize the currently available supply of cooperative behavior as effectively as possible.

An ideal system of surveillance would have a clear-cut set of rules and a well-specified schedule of penalties for violations of these rules. This explains much of the attractiveness of the exchange-rate and reserve norm approaches. They contain objective rules and lend themselves easily to graduated sets of penalties for violations of these rules. But even apart from the difficulties of finding objective rules which would be describable in practice, it may not be possible to get national governments to agree to give up traditional sovereignty in the interests of similarly constraining the range of behavior of other countries. In my judgment this had at least as much to do with the failure to agree on a set of reserve indicators during the earlier phase of the monetary reforms negotiations as did technical economic problems with the indicator proposals.

Precision and Sovereignty

As I argued in my earlier analysis of international surveillance issues,[16] it appears that at present many countries are willing to behave more cooperatively in actual practice than they are willing to accept explicit formal constraints on their behavior. It seems quite likely that adoption of an informal judgmental approach to international surveillance would make it more difficult to secure agreement to grant substantial explicit sanctioning authority to a surveillance body. On such issues, countries often tend to engage in worst-case analysis, making them very hesitant to give great power to international authorities. And the incentives against granting such power are greater, the more scope there is for discretion in the application of such power.

Thus I believe it should be granted by advocates of the judgmental approach that under such procedures the International Monetary Fund is unlikely to be given many additional powers to sanction explicitly the behavior of countries deemed to be engaging in beggar-thy-neighbor policies. (At Bretton Woods, the Fund was given the power to expel a country from membership and to authorize discriminatory trade measures against any country whose currency has been judged to be scarce, but these sanctions proved to be much too blunt to be useful in practice as methods of penalizing moderate beggar-thy-neighbor behavior.)

If my previous assessment of the willingness of countries to behave cooperatively is correct, however, then it seems likely that even without formal sanction, the informal judgmental approach may be the way to achieve the greatest amount of cooperative behavior under present circumstances. In practice, the moral suasion generated by international surveillance under the judgmental approach may be a much more potent method of inducing countries to refrain from or modify beggar-thy-neighbor policies than the more legalistically appealing blueprints for explicit rules and sanctions.

Again, political and economic considerations interact. The case for the judgmental approach becomes stronger, the less well simple explicit rules would conform to ideal surveillance norms and the stronger are political biases against the acceptance of formal constraints and penalties.

Even if it were believed that the greatest amount of effective cooperative behavior in the short run would be induced by the judgmental approach without formal sanctions, there are possible grounds for opposing this approach, however. The hope of the advocates of the informal judgmental approach is that this will not only maximize the effectiveness of surveillance in the short run, but also will be an effective forum for continuing to strengthen cooperative tendencies over time. It is also possible, however, that the judgmental approach could serve as a cover to hide fundamental disagreements and weaknesses in the surveillance process. This could breed a false sense of complacency and achieve the appearance of greater international harmony in the short run at the expense of the development of more serious difficulties over the longer term. While I am personally somewhat more on the optimistic side on this question, the history of international surveillance efforts over the postwar period contains enough examples of national and international officials giving primary concern to the public appearances rather than the substance of surveillance policies that the more pessimistic possibilities cannot be prudently overlooked.[17] . . .

CONCLUDING COMMENTS: STRENGTHENING I.M.F. SURVEILLANCE

In this paper I have attempted to lay out a framework for evaluating the major alternative approaches to the international surveillance of exchange-rate policies and indicate briefly why I believe that the judgmental approach adopted in the new I.M.F. principles for surveillance represents the best strategy given our current knowledge about the major economic and political factors involved.[18] It is important to stress, however, that merely adopting the judgmental approach does not resolve the various technical complexities discussed above, nor does it ensure informal political cooperation.

If there is to be effective international surveillance of exchange-rate policies, the I.M.F. must play an important role in attempting to analyze the many complexities of distinguishing between appropriate and inappropriate exchange-rate policies on a case-by-case basis. It must become a forum for international discussions of complaints about national exchange-rate policies and a leader in the exertion of moral suasion to secure the abandonment of policies which are judged to be seriously antisocial.

So far there is discouragingly little public evidence that the I.M.F. is beginning to play a substantially expanded role in the international surveillance process. It is hard for an outsider to judge accurately whether much progress is being made, for sometimes the most effective exertion of moral suasion is that which is kept the quietest. (Publicity may at times stiffen the backs of offenders and make it more difficult on domestic political grounds to appear to give in to foreign pressures.) I wish that there were more substantial external signs of progress, however. There are many unsettled issues concerning both economic analysis and political and administrative feasiblity which assure that we shall not quickly solve all of the questions concerning optimum surveillance, and it could discredit the whole process if the I.M.F. tried to push too quickly to enforce standards for which there is not reasonably widespread international acceptance, but if the I.M.F. does not move relatively swiftly to establish itself as a major forum for the discussion of the economic and political issues involved, it may miss an important opportunity for strengthening the international surveillance of exchange-rate policies and the adjustment process.

An important early step in this process should be the establishment of an extensive monitoring system which contains the latest available information on exchange-rate movements, official intervention, and reserve changes, and the many other types of policies which may influence exchange rates such as official borrowing from the international financial markets, controls, and other measures which may influence private capital flows, etc.[19]

One of the most important issues in the implementation of surveillance will be the respective roles of the Managing Director and senior staff, the Executive Directors, and the successor to the Interim Committee within the I.M.F. framework and the interrelationships between these and the surveillance activities which take place through other organizations such as the OECD and the BIS and bilateral and the less structured multilateral forums such as the recent series of Economic Summits. Again this is an area where an initial detailed blueprint would not be sensible. These relationships will have to evolve gradually over time. But it is important that the progress be begun with all deliberate speed. In this regard, I would favor that the management of the Fund be allowed substantial independence in exerting moral suasion concerning countries' exchange-rate policies.

It is clear that any formal reports or sanctions concerning the surveillance process should be the result of collective decisions of the representatives of national governments, but I believe that it would be useful to treat the Fund (i.e., its senior management) as an independent actor to a large extent in the early stages of surveillance investigations. Thus, for example, I think it might be well worthwhile for the Fund staff to begin to more formally estimate and update on a timely basis sets of reference rates or zones for a number of countries. To economize on scarce negotiating resources and to allow prompt adjustments, no attempt should be made to secure formal political agreement on the set of rates or their revisions. When any sizable amount of intervention contrary to the reference rate estimates takes place, however, discussions including both political and technical level representatives should be initiated on the reasonableness of the Fund staff's rate calculations and analysis of the national authorities in question. This will allow higher level attention to focus on the issues which appear to be most important.

Likewise, I believe it would be useful to begin to develop a presumption that national authorities should be called upon to justify cumulative net exchange market intervention which exceeds some order of magnitude and that the intensity of such discussions should increase as the size of the cumulative net intervention increases. Over time such discussions may lead to the development of widely accepted rules of thumb. In such ways I believe that elements of the reference rate and reserve indicator approaches could play an important role in the implementation of the judgmental approach.

There are a thousand and one more important questions concerning the implementation of I.M.F. surveillance. For example, should estimates of reference rates be made public and should this vary with the stage of surveillance? And should I.M.F. surveillance focus only on discouraging government actions which are impeding the efficient operation of the adjustment process or should it also to some extent attempt to encourage official intervention to offset the effects of poorly behaved private speculation? But this paper is already overly long. Adoption of the judgmental approach is just the beginning, not the end, of the search for the most effective operational principles and mechanisms for the international surveillance of exchange-rate policies.

Notes

1. Raymond F. Mikesell and Henry N. Goldstein, *Rules for a Floating Rate Regime* (Princeton Essays in International Finance, No. 109, April 1975). For discussions and references to the literature on reserve indicator proposals, see Thomas D. Willett, *Floating Exchange-Rates and International Monetary Reform* (Washington: American Enterprise Institute, 1977), ch. 4, and John Williamson, *The Failure of World Monetary Reform, 1971–1974* (New York: New York University Press, 1977) ch. 5.
2. See, for example, Samuel I. Katz (ed.), *U.S.-European Monetary Relations* (Washington: American Enterprise Institute, forthcoming).
3. See Wilfred Ethier and Arthur I. Bloomfield, *Managing the Managed Float* (Princeton Essays in International Finance, No. 112, Oct. 1975) and "The Reference Rate Proposal and Recent Experience," Banca Nazionale del Lavoro *Quarterly Review* (forthcoming); Fred Hirsch, "International Guidelines and Principles for National Financial and Exchange Rate Policies: Commentary," in Jacob S. Dreyer, Gottfried Haberler, and Thomas D. Willett (eds), *Exchange-Rate Flexibility* (Washington: American Enterprise Institute, 1978); and "I.M.F. Surveillance Over Exchange Rates: Comment," in Robert A. Mundell and Jacques J. Polak (eds), *The New International Monetary System* (New York: Columbia University Press, 1977); and John Williamson, "The Future Exchange Rate Regime," Banca Nazionale del Lavoro *Quarterly Review*, June 1975, and *The Failure of World Monetary Reform*, ch. 9.

4. "Aggressive" intervention might be desirable when a country needed to recoup severe losses. A more controversial rationale for desiring to intervene aggressively is the so-called "bear squeeze" in which a central bank attempts to punish speculators who have been "too pessimistic" about the outlook for the currency.

5. See Richard N. Cooper, "I.M.F. Surveillance Over Exchange Rates," and Herbert G. Grubel, "How Important is Control Over International Reserves," both in Mundell and Polak (eds.), *The New International Monetary System;* Paula A. Tosini, *Leaning Against the Wind: A Standard for Managed Floating* (Princeton Essays in International Finance, No. 126, December 1977) and Paul Wonnacott, *The Floating Canadian Dollar* (Washington: American Enterprise Institute, 1972).

6. See Jacques R. Artus and Andrew D. Crockett, *Floating Exchange Rates and the Need for Surveillance* (Princeton Essays in International Finance, No. 127, May 1978); comments by Richard Cooper and Robert Roosa in E. M. Bernstein, *et. al., Reflections on Jamaica* (Princeton Essays in International Finance, No. 115, April 1976); and Sam Y. Cross, "The Role of the I.M.F. under the Amended Articles of Agreement," and commentaries by Marina Whitman and Thomas D. Willett in Dreyer, Haberler and Willett (eds.), *Exchange Rate Flexibility*.

7. See, for example, Oort's presentation in Katz (ed.). *U.S.-European Monetary Relations*.

8. An example is the recent OPTICA Report, Commission of the European Communities, *Inflation and Exchange Rates: Evidence and Policy Guidelines for the European Community* (Brussels, 1977). For extensive discussion of the OPTICA proposal see Katz (ed.), *U.S.-European Monetary Relations*, and Giorgio Basevi and Paul De Grauwe, "Vicious and Virtuous Circles," *European Economic Review,* 1977, pp. 277–301.

9. Thus, as Ethier and Bloomfield stress ("The Reference Rate Proposal and Recent Experience,") it is not correct to group reference-rate proposals with target-zone proposals together as being on the pegged as opposed to flexible end of the spectrum of guidelines for floating. The pure reference-rate approach is much further toward the free-floating end of the spectrum than proposals that would impose a presumptive obligation for official intervention to lean against the wind.

10. There is a considerable range of opinion among reference-rate advocates about whether fairly heavy official management is desirable because of deficiencies in the behavior of private speculation. Both Fred Hirsch and John Williamson have argued that a fair amount of official intervention is needed, while Ethier and Bloomfield appear to have been less concerned about the behavior of private speculation. Thus the characterization of the reference-rate advocates as believing that governments can determine correct exchange rates better than the market would apply more directly to Hirsch and Williamson than to Ethier and Bloomfield.

11. See, for example, Andrew D. Crockett and Duncan Ripley, "Sharing the Oil Deficit," *I.M.F. Staff Papers,* July 1975; Robert Solomon, "The Allocation of 'Oil Deficits'," *Brookings Papers on Economic Activity,* No. 1 (1975); Thomas D. Willett, *The Oil Transfer Problem and International Economic Stability,* (Princeton Essays in International Finance, No. 113, December 1975); and John Williamson, "The International Financial System," in Edward R. Fried and Charles L. Schultze (eds.), *Higher Oil Prices and the World Economy* (Washington: Brookings Institution, 1975).

12. Some advocates of leaning against the wind argue that an essential part of this approach is that exchange rates must be allowed to move in the face of strong market pressures (although not by a market clearing amount). Such a provision would reduce the problem of cumulatively mounting disequilibrium which resulted from the excessive rigidity of the adjustable peg system.

I should also note that following the tradition of most discussions of the leaning-against the wind approach, I have assumed that monetary policy is set independently of exchange-market intervention, i.e., that reserve flows under managed floating are fully sterilized. As Richard Sweeney has pointed out to me, an alternative type of defense of leaning-against-the-wind policies would be as a guide to monetary policy. This would, of course, imply that reserve flows should not be sterilized, at least not fully. This is an intriguing idea which deserves more consideration. Along somewhat similar lines, see Ronald I. McKinnon. *A New Tripartite Monetary Agreement* (Princeton Essays in International Finance, No. 106, Oct. 1974).

13. Willett, *Floating Exchange Rates*, ch. 4, and "The Emerging Exchange Rate System," in Katz (ed.), *U.S.-European Monetary Relations.*
14. Because of nonmarket transactions such as interest earnings on official foreign currency holdings and some types of military payments, figures for reserve changes and net official intervention over the same period will not necessarily coincide. The appropriate standard would be to have such nonmarket transactions put into the market. For example, the interest earnings on foreign official dollar holdings should be sold in the foreign-exchange market to acquire the foreign countries' currency. Otherwise foreign official dollar holdings would grow even in the absence of any exchange-market intervention.
15. The importance of international decision-making costs is one of the major points of emphasis in a study being prepared by Robert Tollison and myself on *The Challenge of Economic Interdependence: A Public Choice Perspective.*
16. Willett, *Floating Exchange Rates*, ch. 4.
17. See, for example, the excellent chapter on multilateral surveillance in Susan Strange, *International Monetary Relations* (London: Oxford University Press, 1976). Strange concludes with respect to I.M.F. surveillance over the United Kingdom that ". . . the weight to be attached to particular instruments of Fund surveillance, and even the effectiveness of the surveillance itself, must remain to some extent a matter for subjective judgment . . . All that may be said with some confidence is that both parties were a great deal more concerned with appearances than with realities." (p. 146)
18. These principles were adopted by a decision of the Executive Board of the I.M.F. on April 29, 1977. They appear in *Annual Report of the Executive Directors for the Fiscal Year Ended April 30, 1977* (Washington: International Monetary Fund), appendix II and are reprinted in Artus and Crockett, *Floating Exchange Rates and the Need for Surveillance*, and Willett, *Floating Exchange Rates.*
19. Obtaining needed data is not a trivial problem. Most countries have been much more reluctant than the United States to make public data on their intervention activities even with a considerable lag and even on the strictest confidential basis and most major central banks have been hesitant to make available to the Fund the kind of information on exchange-market developments and official intervention which they exchange among themselves on a daily basis. Since the major function of the Fund would be surveillance over the broad course of policies, access to such information on a current daily basis would not be necessary, but it is important that the Fund be given access to more intervention information on a regular basis than it currently receives (or at least than it received when I left the U.S. Government in August 1977).

28

Reserve Assets and a Substitution Account: Towards a Less Unstable International Monetary System

Reserve Assets Study Group of the Group of Thirty[1]

STATEMENT BY DR. H. JOHANNES WITTEVEEN CHAIRMAN OF THE GROUP OF THIRTY

In a growing world economy, where economic and financial strength is more and more widely shared, the monetary system, based almost exclusively on one currency, the dollar, must naturally come under increasing strains. These strains, which will be aggravated by the continuing large payments surplus of OPEC countries now in prospect, have recently shown themselves in a tendency of many central banks around the world to "diversify" the composition of their reserves. A so-called "multi-currency reserve system" is developing.

Differing views may be held about the response (if any) that the international community should make to these developments. I and my colleagues in the Group of Thirty are of the opinion that if the process were left entirely to the interplay of market forces and the uncoordinated policies of individual central banks, the road ahead would indeed be a bumpy one for the world economy. A multiple currency reserve system is inherently unstable. Shifts in currency preferences of central banks would be an additional destabilizing element in foreign exchange markets. They would thus tend to increase fluctuations in exchange rates. Given the risks that these fluctuations would entail for trade, investment and employment, we believe that a cooperative approach to the problem is urgently required.

That is why we have chosen the subject "Reserve Assets and a Substitution Account" for the first of the policy statements which we plan to issue from time to time. The report that follows outlines some suggestions on how the world's financial community might respond to the challenge. In the first place, it gives strong support to the proposal, on which important official discussions are being held, for the establishment of a Substitition Accout in the International Monetary Fund. In addition, it suggests the development—as a complement to the Substitution Account

From the Reserve Assets Study Group, "Towards a Less Unstable International Monetary System" (New York: Group of Thirty, 1980). Reprinted by permission.

—of forms of cooperation between central banks which would guide their policies to a less destabilizing pattern.

None of these suggestions will solve all the problems of the monetary system. There is no panacea. But they would help. They would at least take away some additional elements of instability and would move monetary arrangements in the direction of the aims which the international community has set for itself in the amended Articles of Agreement of the I.M.F.

The report has been drafted by the Reserve Assets Study Group of the Group of Thirty, and discussed by the full Group; these discussions were in turn taken into account in the final report. Nevertheless, many members of the Group of Thirty hold official positions and cannot for obvious reasons be held responsible for all the views expressed in the report. Members of the Group of Thirty participate in its meetings in a personal capacity and our reports and policy recommendations should not in any respect be taken to represent the views of institutions with which members are associated.

TOWARDS A LESS UNSTABLE INTERNATIONAL MONETARY SYSTEM

It is clear, in the opinion of the Study Group, that there is a serious reserve asset problem in today's international monetary arrangements. In particular, it is unlikely that the dollar can continue indefinitely to provide some 80 percent of the world's foreign exchange reserves. It may be felt that it is inappropriate for any national currency to play this central role and that efforts should be made over the longer term to establish the primacy of an international reserve asset; or it may be felt that there is a disequilibrium in the existing pattern of reserve holdings which can only be satisfied over time with the growth of other national currencies as reserve assets; or, even if neither of these long-run aims is subscribed to, it may be felt that the present situation leads to avoidable instability in foreign exchange markets.

This report sets out the conclusions of the Study Group of the Group of Thirty which has been considering these questions over the past few months. Members both of the Study Group and of the Group of Thirty participate in their meetings in a personal capacity and the present report should not be construed as reflecting the views of the institutions with which members are associated.

The report is divided into the following sections:

(a) The trend towards diversification of currency reserves;
(b) An SDR Substitution Account;
(c) The role of the private sector;
(d) Possible supplementary or alternative arrangements;
(e) Conclusion.

The Trend Towards Diversification

Aggregate estimates suggest that since 1970 central banks have moved out of sterling and into Deutschemarks and other non-dollar currencies but that there has been no net diversification out of the dollar, since the proportion of dollar holdings in total currency reserves has remained remarkably stable, at around 80 percent. However, the country composition of reserves shows that a number of groups of countries have reduced the proportion of dollars in their reserves, with some showing reductions in the absolute levels of their dollar holdings. If the five "reserve currency" countries (defined to include France, Germany, Japan, Switzerland and the United Kingdom) are excluded, the dollar proportion of the foreign exchange reserves of the remaining 76 countries covered in estimates prepared for the Group fell from 71.7 percent at December, 1970 to 67.0 percent at September, 1978. The increase in the dollar proportion of the "reserve currency" countries (from 91.3 percent to 93.3 percent over the same period) probably stemmed less from deliberate attempts to increase the total, or change the composition, of their reserves, than from active intervention in foreign exchange markets designed to affect their exchange rates. The dollar proportion of the reserves of several developing countries has fallen sharply. In addition, there is evidence that diversification by certain groups of countries assumed significant proportions towards the latter part of the period. Finally, official or quasi-official institutions other than central banks in some countries may have diversified on a larger scale than is suggested by the figures, which are based on holdings of central banks.

The weakness of the U.S. balance of payments has been one important factor in this trend towards diversification. Anticipations of a fall in the value of the dollar naturally create an incentive to diversify into other currencies, as do expectations of continued volatility in exchange rate movements. However, it is unlikely that an improvement in the U.S. balance of payments, as has occurred over the past year, can be expected to bring about a complete and sustained reversal of the process. Many factors other than the state of the U.S. current account or the outlook for the dollar are likely to influence portfolio decisions by central bankers. These include not only the changing composition of world trade but also the increasing sophistication of the foreign exchange management of many central banks, particularly in the developing world; the desire to purchase foreign currency assets matching the expected pattern of foreign currency expenditures on large-scale projects, again particularly in the developing world; the comparable desire to purchase assets to match interest and principal payments on international borrowing, such as borrowing in the Eurobond or Eurocredit markets, denominated in non-dollar currencies; and the disappearance of the remaining inhibitions against using the Eurocurrency markets as means of diversifying into the currencies of those countries which do not wish to encourage the reserve-currency role of their national currencies.

Exchange rates may be influenced as much by anticipated as by actual diversification. While it may be questioned how far, if at all, the existing proportion of dollar holdings represents in aggregate "involuntary" accumulations, there can be little doubt that some large dollar holders have felt "locked in" in the sense that they believed dollar sales would adversely affect the values of their portfolios, i.e. their dollar holdings are believed to be too large for risk diversification. The desire for reserve diversification by some "reserve currency" central banks, which have in total increased the dollar proportion of their reserves, may also be significantly greater than the figures suggest, for reasons noted above.

The actual or potentially destabilizing effects of currency diversification are increased if, as is probable, central banks attempt (or are believed in the markets to desire) to change their portfolio mix at the margin at times of pressure on the dollar. In particular, such attempts, or market expectations of such attempts, may precipitate much larger private sales of the principal reserve currency, as was experienced at times during sterling's decline as a reserve currency. Expectations of both official and private sales may in turn trigger violent exchange-rate movements affecting the whole structure of the world's currency and trading arrangements.

The Study Group concluded that the pressures making for a greater degree of currency diversification by official and private holders were likely to persist; and that a system which relied on one national currency for the bulk of its currency reserves was likely, for that reason as well as others, to continue to experience large-scale, unpredictable and often destabilizing capital flows. At the same time, the internationalization of the banking systems of many countries, and in particular the gradual opening-up of the financial markets of some potential reserve-currency centers, would not only facilitate the emergence of currencies other than the dollar as reserve currencies but also in our view further increase the potentiality, unless accompanying measures were taken (see below), of such unpredictable large-scale capital flows. These flows would, however, be even less subject to control if holdings of non-dollar currencies continue to be diverted, as hitherto, largely to the Eurocurrency markets.

Although it is widely accepted that there is some unfulfilled desire on the part of official holders throughout the world to diversify somewhat out of dollars and into other currencies, a consensus has not yet developed as to the most appropriate means of meeting this demand. What is clear is that both existing and potential reserve centers are reluctant to promote the development of a multicurrency reserve system (MRS). This is understandable. First, both *a priori* analysis and the evidence from situations where bimetallism has prevailed in the past indicate the potential instability of any system based on more than one reserve asset. Secondly, the postwar years have highlighted the difficulties that can beset a mature reserve currency center if its performance is considered unsatisfactory. Thirdly, the exposure of a reserve center to large and sometimes sudden changes in the volume of externally-held short-term claims upon it can greatly complicate the operation of its domestic monetary policy. Fourthly, a decision to establish and operate new reserve currencies would be likely, unless very carefully handled, to have destabilizing effects on existing reserve currency centers and on major exchange rate relationships.

In the light of such considerations, and especially the intrinsic difficulty of managing a multi-currency system, the Group concluded that a major effort should be made to reach international agreement on a Substitution Account issuing claims denominated in SDRs.[2] The need to establish a Substitution Account is lent added urgency by the prospect that OPEC countries are likely to run a substantial aggregate current account surplus for a number of years. At the same time, recognizing that the trends towards currency diversification noted above are likely to continue over the next few years, the Group also considered possible ways in which the official international community might handle such pressures so as to minimize any disturbance or disruption they might cause while an SDR Substitution Account was being established and developed.

An SDR Substitution Account

A Substitution Account should serve the objectives both of promoting the use of the SDR as a reserve asset and of offering an alternative to the further diversification of currency reserves. A successful Substitution Account would therefore contribute to exchange rate stability, while in the long term it would also facilitate an orderly reduction in the reserve currency role of the dollar. An additional objective has occasionally been mentioned in this context—that of preventing renewed accumulations of dollars in national reserves. According to this view, agreement on the creation of a Substitution Account should be accompanied by an agreement to restrict further official accumulations of dollars. This would constitute, however, a large step towards what is referred to as "mandatory asset settlement" and would be impractical at the present time. It is, of course, possible that in the long run the international community may show itself prepared to make the important moves to an SDR-standard and a wider role for the SDR in official intervention in the foreign exchange market. The latter possibility points, in turn, even at this stage towards the desirability of promoting the use of the SDR and of SDR-denominated claims in the private market. However, the Group regards the role of an SDR Substitution Account at the present time as being essentially complementary to the range of existing reserve assets and to other steps that should be taken to improve the functioning of the system.

The basic framework of a Substitution Account might be as follows: participants would deposit foreign exchange (initially dollars) in an

Account administered by the IMF, in return for SDR-denominated claims or "certificates"; the managers of the Account would invest the funds in securities or other assets denominated in dollars; the Account would pay interest on the SDR claims and various arrangements would be made to ensure the full usability of the claims as reserve assets. There are, however, numerous questions and problems that have to be resolved in setting up an Account and we return to some of these below.

There are certain general principles and considerations that in the view of the Group should be followed for the scheme to make a worthwhile contribution:

(i) Participation should be voluntary.

(ii) Wide participation is essential.

(iii) The size of the Account should be significant in relation to existing foreign exhange holdings in the form of dollars. These totalled some SDR 150 billion as of June, 1979, but a sizable proportion is unlikely to be subject to diversification pressure; thus an account that amounted after a time to some SDR 50 billion would make an important contribution.

(iv) The scheme should be market-oriented, providing incentives for private-sector institutions to hold, and develop markets in, SDR-denominated claims.

(v) For all these reasons, the claims or certificates to be issued by the Account should be sufficiently attractive.
(It should be noted that substitution, which would not change the stock of reserves, should not be regarded as an alternative to the creation of SDRs by allocation).

The most important determinants of the attractiveness of the proposed SDR claim on the Substitution Account will be its yield and liquidity characteristics:

(i) Interest on the claims should be paid at a rate closely related to a weighted average of short-term rates prevailing in the major financial markets. It should be adjusted regularly, for example every three months. This aspect of our proposal is discussed further in the following section.

(ii) Interest could be paid either in dollars or in the form of additional SDR claims; one advantage of the latter method would be that the size of the Account would grow naturally over time.

(iii) Claims should be freely transferable between official participants, by mutual agreement.

(iv) Claims should also be freely transferable between official and private holders. This would enhance the liquidity of these claims, encourage their use by the private sector, and open the way to the eventual private use of SDRs proper (which cannot be held privately at present). However, private holders of dollars should not be permitted, at least initially, to deposit them with the Account, as this would unduly complicate its administration.

(v) We hope that over time a main way in which countries could obtain liquidity for their claims would be through the market; and if, as is suggested in (i) above, interest were paid at a market-related rate, the claims could be traded in a secondary market at or close to par. Initially, however, there would be a need for some official mechanism on which participants could rely, for selling their SDR claims in exchange for currencies, in case of balance-of-payments need; i.e. use of acceptance/designation rules such as those employed to transfer SDRs proper and, beyond this, if necessary, encashment of the claims at par at the Account (i.e. participants would receive the dollar equivalent of the face-value of the SDR claim, at the $-SDR rate prevailing on the day of the transaction). The United States, though not a depositor, could also have an acceptance obligation; this would further enhance the liquidity of the scheme. We would hope that the need for, and the role of, this kind of mechanism would rapidly decline as the private market in SDR claims developed.

(vi) The SDR claim should be of indefinite maturity because substitution should be regarded as permanent.

It is the opinion of the Group that an Account issuing a claim having these characteristics would attract wide participation. Central banks would then gradually become accustomed to holding and using the SDR claim as the internationally respectable reserve asset.

To bring the Account into being, a reasonably large number of IMF member countries would agree to participate for a sufficiently large aggregate amount. Participation by developing countries with appreciable reserves as well as by industrial countries is essential. Subsequently, additional deposits could be made on specific dates both by original and new participants. The dollars deposited would be valued in SDRs on the basis of the $-SDR rate on the day of deposit.

As has been found in market attempts to develop a composite currency unit, such as the SDR, the fundamental problem is that of reaching a combination of interest yield and exchange risk that renders instruments denominated in such units acceptable both to borrowers and to lenders. In the context of the Substitution Account proposal, this problem presents itself in two forms:

First, what arrangements can be made to ensure that the income of the Account will be large enough to cover its interest payments to participants? Second, in the event of liquidation, how would the Account's obligations be settled?

(i) *Interest payments and receipts:*

As already noted, the SDR claim should bear interest at a rate closely related to market rates in the major financial centers. The rate should be as high as is required to avoid the SDR claim being traded at a significant discount in secondary markets. The precise relationship of the SDR interest rate to other interest rates can only be discovered by experimentation and will certainly change over time, as the markets in these claims develop. We believe the managers of the Account should have discretion to vary the relationship of the rate to market rates from time to time, as they gain experience with private trading in the claim with the objective of avoiding a discount in the market.

How may the Account finance these interest payments? This raises the issues of the investment of the Account's assets and of possible ways of making good an emerging deficiency on interest account if necessary. On the first question, the Account could earn interest on its investments, which would naturally be in dollars, at the U.S. long-term bond rate, and, as long-term rates have on average been higher than short-term rates in the past, it might be expected that this would be sufficient to cover interest payments on its SDR obligations. However, since the interest rate on the SDR claim would be adjusted every three months or so, and short term rates may from time to time rise above long-term rates, we believe that the managers of the Account should be given a considerable degree of discretion in the conduct of their investment policy. For instance, a case could be made for allowing the managers some discretion to invest also in short-term claims, such as certificates of deposit issued by major banks. Funds might even be placed in the Euromarkets, if there were evidence that funds were being withdrawn on a large scale from the markets as a result of the establishment of the Substitution Account. The difficulty that might otherwise be created for borrowers is this market might be met in this way. This discretion for the managers of the Account would ensure that the interest earnings of the Account were related as closely as possible to its payments on its SDR obligations. At the same time, there would need to be firm safeguards to assure the United States and other countries that such investment would not cause additional complications for the conduct of their financial policies.

However, these approaches would not guarantee that the Account's interest earnings were sufficient in any given year to finance interest payments on SDR claims, given the possibility of changing interest-rate and exchange-rate relationships. Here one possibility would be to cover any deficiency which could not be met out of previously accumulated interest earnings by using some of the dollars in the Account (which transfers this problem to that discussed under (ii) below, as would also be the case if interest were to be credited in the form of additional SDR claims). Another possibility would be for the United States to agree to make a non-interest bearing loan to the Account in any year in which there was such a deficiency, with any surplus being invested in a non-interest bearing deposit in the United States. Yet another possibility, discussed further below, is to use some of the Fund's gold stock to back the Account.

(ii) *Liquidation provisions*:

We do not envisage liquidation of the Account; but some arrangements are necessary if only because the Articles of Agreement of the Fund provide for the liquidation of the SDR Department and indeed of the Fund itself. In this regard one possibility would be a simple risk-sharing arrangement. In the event that the dollar holdings of the Account were insufficient to redeem the dollar value of the SDR claims of participants, half of the additional dollars required might be supplied by the United States, and the other half by participants in proportion to their original participation; an inverse arrangement would be made in the event of a surplus. An alternative that has been proposed is that the Fund might make an allocation of SDRs proper, which would be turned into the Account.

One proposed solution to both aspects of the problem discussed above would be for some of the Fund's gold holdings (worth between $60 billion and $80 billion at the gold price of January, 1980) to be used as backing for the Account. The Account would then take on more of the character of a bank, with command over resources that could be regarded as the equivalent of capital funds, as well as interest earning assets and interest-bearing liabilities. This would have the advantage of making the solvency of the "SDR Bank" dependent on its own assets rather than relying exclusively on the guarantee of the United States and other participants. If, at the same time the managers were able to invest a portion of the dollars with considerable flexibility and were also able to vary the relationship of the interest offered on the SDR claim to market rates, the problem of establishing the attractiveness of the claim to potential diversifiers without asking too large a contribution towards any residual deficit from the

United States and other participants could be well on the way to being solved. The United States would of course still be called upon to make a commitment to the scheme and would certainly be a guarantor of the Account.

By thus consolidating a portion of the large short-term liabilities of the United States and placing them in firmer hands the scheme would facilitate in the longer term a gradual reduction in the dollar's reserve currency role. From the point of view of the United States the principal advantage of this would be to alleviate the vulnerability of the dollar and thus the pressure that would otherwise develop for that country to take, in the form of current-account adjustment, all the burden of adjustment to shifts in currency preferences. If the United States were forced to deflate its economy to prevent sales of the dollar by central banks from causing an undue depreciation of the dollar, the growth of U.S. GNP would fall further below its potential growth rate and unemployment would rise further. If on the other hand the U.S. government allowed the depreciation to take its course, inflation would worsen. Both courses would result in unnecessary damage to the U.S. economy. That is why the U.S. government should be prepared to make some contribution to the financial viability of the scheme (though again, we would stress that the United States might well not be called upon in practice to make any higher payments under the scheme than market pressures might otherwise require it to offer, as the recent sharp rise in U.S. interest rates testifies).

In general, participating monetary authorities should not base their decisions on how much of their dollar reserves to deposit in the Account on a narrow view of their self interest, or purely on a search for maximum profits. It should be realized that a cooperative effort is needed, particularly in view of the massive accumulation of reserves by the OPEC countries expected in the coming years. In its evaluation of costs and benefits each country should give proper weight to the desirability, in the common interest, of improving the monetary system and creating greater stability in the exchange markets. We believe that a scheme such as we are suggesting would promote these objectives.

The Role of the Private Sector

The private sector should in time play a major role in promoting the objectives of the scheme. Although the usefulness of the Substitution Account would not depend upon the development of a private market in the SDR claim, it would be greatly improved by such a market. A well-developed market would certainly enhance the liquidity of the scheme, and, more broadly, help to establish the SDR as the internationally respectable reserve asset. It would also lay the foundation for the development in the longer run of an intervention mechanism in SDRs.

It is thus desirable that a secondary market, in which SDR claims are actively traded and valued, be developed as soon as possible. This would assure holders that they can exchange the claims for dollars or any other currency without suffering a significant loss of value, as an alternative to the other courses of action open to them. . . . In this way encashment at the Account, and the use of designation mechanisms that would oblige creditor countries to accept large additional amounts of claims—making participation less attractive for them—would be avoided as far as possible, and the mechanisms themselves gradually phased out.

In order for a secondary market to be established, several conditions have to be satisfied:

(i) The rights of holders of SDR claims other than official depositors should be protected, in the event of the liquidation of the scheme. There should be specific provision ensuring that such holders would have a clear claim on the Fund to receive dollars equivalent to the full face value of their SDR claims (at then current exchange rates); and for the official participants to bear all the loss, if any, from the operation of the Account.

(ii) An efficient clearing mechanism should be established. This could be provided either by the IMF itself or by a commercial bank or group of banks.

(iii) It is important that the yield of the SDR claim be set in a manner that would ensure a good reception by the markets.

It may be impossible, however, to prevent the new SDR claim going to a discount in the secondary market if its yield were to be set in the same way as that of the existing SDR, even if it offered what is referred to as the "full combined rate," which is a weighted average of recent short-term interest rates in the United States, Germany, the United Kingdom, France and Japan. This is because banks and dealers trading the claims would generally base their carrying (or financing) cost on Eurocurrency rates, which are generally higher than domestic interest for comparable terms.

To avoid the emergence of a discount, which could in turn discourage participation in the scheme, we believe that the IMF might consider setting the rate by reference to the average of the Eurocurrency rates of the major currencies. As suggested above, a period of experimentation might be unavoidable, and the managers should be given discretion to alter the formulation on which the rate is based from time to time. We would hope, however, that as the markets developed the yield on the SDR claim would settle into a relationship with that of SDR bank deposits that reflected the official character of the SDR claim. There are various ways in which central banks, in the requirements they place on their commercial banks, might strengthen the official character of the claim.

Another interrelated aspect of the private use of SDRs is the readiness of banks and other commercial institutions to take deposits and make loans denominated in SDRs. At present, the supply of outstanding SDR-denominated deposits and bonds in the international markets is small. Publicly-issued SDR-denominated bonds in the Eurobond market have been modest in total at $250,000,000 and there have been only six issues of such bonds in the last four years.

Although no exact estimate is available on the size of the deposit market, the fact that only about 20 banks are active takers of deposits suggests that total deposits are at most a few hundred million dollars. These SDR-denominated deposits are quite different and distinct in form from that envisaged for use in a future Substitution Account mechanism. They are deposits with a commercial bank in a "composite of currencies" which happens to consist of the same currencies and percentage mix as the SDR. Interest rates quoted for these SDR-denominated deposits are based on rates at which the commercial bank can deploy the individual currencies for the same maturity. These will most likely be the "Euromarket" rates for the major currencies; where there is no Euromarket and domestic invest-ment is prohibited to foreigners the calculated interest rate used for the currency will be zero.

In the past, it has been argued that banks have not been willing to take SDR-denominated deposits because there is no forward market in SDRs. As a result, banks would face an open exchange risk because the currency actually deposited and the corresponding asset acquired by the bank would be dollars or another traded currency. However, this point may sometimes be exaggerated. Banks can invest and find forward cover in most of the traded currencies represented in the SDR and, if demand in-creased, an active market in SDR forwards might be created. The Study Group believes there might be a case for an official institution, such as possibly the Bank for International Settlements, to encourage this de-velopment by making a forward market in SDRs.

The critical requirement for the development of a bank deposit market in SDRs, in our opinion, is a source of large-scale investors. If the proposed Substitution Account were launched on a substantial scale, and central banks began using the SDR claims and trading them on secondary markets, commercial banks' awareness of this activity, and participation in it, might encourage them to offer SDR-denominated deposits on a wider scale both to central banks and to private-sector investors.

Once banks accepted SDR-denominated deposits on a substantial scale they could be expected to begin to offer borrowers the option of denominating loans in SDRs and so match their currency book. Syndicated loans denominated in SDRs could become a feature of the banking market. Official institutions, such as the World Bank, might equally be encouraged to issue medium or long-term securities denominated in SDRs.

We recognize that the development of a market in SDR claims and of the use of SDRs as a unit of denomination for private sector financial transactions will be a gradual process. The official scheme should be designed to encourage this process. We consider that a scheme such as we propose would provide incentives to private-sector institutions to develop such markets.

Possible Supplementary or Alternative Arrangements

While the Study Group emphasizes the necessity to reach agreement on the establishment of a Substitution Account, it also recognizes that the trends toward reserve diversification noted above are likely to continue over the next few years. The Group has accordingly considered possible ways in which the official international community might handle such pressures so as to minimize any disturbance or disruption they might cause while an SDR Substitution Account was being established and developed.

One point that may be made at the outset is that the present confusion in the provision of a reserve base for the system arguably itself contributes unnecessarily to the uncertainty felt by private and official holders and thus to the potential for erratic capital flows. To the extent that the developments that are taking place already—such as the gradual emergence of the Deutschemark and, on a smaller scale, the Swiss franc and the yen as reserve currencies—could be made more explicit and transparent, it could be argued that at least this source of uncertainty may be alleviated.

Further, because of the unwillingness of potential reserve centers to allow other central banks to hold significant amounts of their currency in domestic form, such holdings as have developed have predominantly been in external form—most notably in Euro Deutschemarks. (It is estimated that, subtracting the proceeds of the Carter notes issued in December, 1978 from total DM reserves, the proportion of remaining DM reserves held in the Euromarket at end-1978 was approximately 66 percent.) It could be argued that this situation has involved many of the disadvantages of running a reserve currency without using some of the possibilities for controlling its development. In these circumstances, other central banks will tend not to feel any great responsibility for the overall and long-run effects of the developments of which their individual decisions are a part—especially if their individual holdings are fairly small.

Recently, the central banks concerned have all begun to accept to some extent the different roles thrust upon them. This is important because it would facilitate more explicit discussion of the needs, or at least preferences, of the world's central banks. Such discussion might help to engender a much greater sharing of the responsibility for the stability of the system and hence slower and more predictable shifts in portfolio preference. Evidence of broad agreement on portfolio patterns among central banks should also help to reduce the volatility of private markets.

Such discussion and negotiation would be bound to be difficult and protracted. Compromises would be required between the preferences of potential or actual reserve centres among each other and with nonreserve centres as to the volume of reserve assets and the conditions under which they would be supplied in each currency. The Group recognizes, moreover, that quite apart from the formidable technical and negotiating problems that would be involved, significant developments in this direction could have implications for the wider and more fundamental questions of exchange rate and intervention policies and the global volume of reserves. Nevertheless, the Group believes that, for two main reasons, the possibility of more explicit arrangements for reserve currency holdings should be further explored. First, as has already been stressed, potentially disruptive pressures for diversification could still erupt at any time; and secondly, there would be genuine potential benefits for all parties if some forms of agreement, however rough and ready, could be reached on the way in which reserve-holding patterns might develop.

For example, potential reserve diversifiers might give formal or informal undertakings only to diversify their reserves in line with prearranged guidelines—such as an agreement on their part to acquire no further holdings in Eurocurrencies—in return for a degree of access to the money and capital markets of the new reserve centres. Such arrangements would offer developing countries, in particular, a limited freedom which they do not possess in many cases at present, whilst also offering to the reserve currency centers a somewhat greater degree of control over capital movements into and out of their currencies. Further, current exchange rate instability is at least partly caused by the inadequacy of the volume of borrowing in the capital markets of potential reserve currency centres in relation to potential capital inflows.

Whether such a framework for the discussion of reserve holdings contributed to exchange rate stability might depend to some extent on the methods used for achieving any further degree of diversification. Two broad approaches may be distinguished in principle:

    (i) the balance of payments channel.
    (ii) the foreign currency substitution channel.

The balance of payments channel. New reserve currencies might develop as the result of policies followed by the potential reserve centers whereby their customary surpluses on current account were substantially more than offset by deliberately stimulated long-term capital outflows. One implication of such developments that might be unwelcome is that, if the U.S. balance of payments remained unchanged, the total of world reserves would be thereby increased. There may in any case be a preference among the potential reserve centers to maintain in the future smaller current account surpluses, with occasional moves into deficit, rather than foster large net capital outflows: and there may also be practical difficulties in the relative lack of development of their domestic capital markets. On the other hand, should it prove very difficult permanently to reduce the current-account surpluses that these countries have generally experienced, it can be argued that fostering large net capital outflows would be a helpful contribution to the international adjustment process and to exchange rate stability.

An alternative or complementary approach to the balance of payments channel is the *foreign currency substitution channel*. Problems posed by the relative lack of development of surplus countries' capital markets might also, to some extent, be avoided by this approach which allows for diversification outside the markets. For example, the strong currency countries could issue obligations in their own currencies in exchange for dollar claims on the United States. The advantages would be that they could thereby arguably sterilize the domestic monetary effects of foreign currency inflows before they actually occurred; that such techniques would be independent of the state of the countries' domestic financial markets; and that if the claims were in the form of long-term placements with central banks they could be less volatile than short-term capital inflows. This approach might be considered analogous to a swap, with one leg of it in longer-term assets. However, strong currency countries would under this proposal have to accept further accumulations of dollar reserves and presumably the resultant exchange risk, unless bilateral arrangements are agreed between participating countries to share the exchange risk or the strong currency countries deposited newly-acquired dollar reserves in the Substitution Account.

Techniques of financial diplomacy which might influence the currency preferences of official holders at the margin are inappropriate when dealing with a very large and diverse group of private holders. Private holders will continue to respond to the actual and perceived underlying economic conditions. However, the experience of recent years suggests that private holders are often influenced by fears or beliefs that official holders are diversifying. To the extent that the fears could be calmed by the knowledge of the existence of inter-central bank agreements there might be an improved degree of stability in the currency distribution of private holdings.

CONCLUSION

The Study Group considers that there is an urgent need to reach agreement on a Substitution Account meeting the needs of all participants, attracting widespread support and with strong links to the private sector. The scheme would not solve all the problems of the international monetary system: it is not designed to do so. But it would mark an important step forward in the evolution of the system. Failure to reach such an agreement would risk adding to the volatility of exchange rates and the instability of current international monetary arrangements. At the same time, granted the likely strength of the trend towards the diversification of currency reserves, and the time it will take to put a Substitution Account into place, it is desirable that more explicit discussion should develop among the central banks concerned as to the ways in which the legitimate preferences of all parties may be met.

Notes

1. H. Johannes Witteveen, Peter B. Kenen, Christopher McMahon, I. G. Patel, Wolfgang Rieke, Robert V. Roosa, Robert Solomon, and Gengo Suzuki.
2. SDRs (Special Drawing Rights) are reserve assets issued by the International Monetary Fund. Their value in terms of the U.S. dollar is determined as the sum of the dollar values, based on market exchange rates, of specified quantities of 16 currencies.

29

Operating Principles and Procedures of the European Monetary System

Jacques van Ypersele de Strihou

Before analyzing the operating principles and procedures of the European Monetary System, I believe that it is useful to describe some of the motivations behind this effort. I will then discuss the basic principles of the EMS and its conditions for success. Finally, I will try to answer some of the criticisms of the EMS.

MOTIVATIONS

A principal economic motivation for the creation of the EMS has been dissatisfaction with floating exchange rates during the past few years and the conviction that this monetary situation was having adverse effects on economic integration in Europe and, in general, on growth and employment in the European Community (EC). Expressed in a positive way, the objective of the EMS is to contribute to a lasting improvement of the present economic growth and employment situation of the Community and to its economic integration through greater exchange rate flexibility. This objective will be met only if the system is conceived in such a way that it will be durable and credible and contains neither a deflationary nor an inflationary bias.

Before explaining how the EMS should contribute to growth and employment, let me first talk about greater exchange rate stability. The EMS can help in two ways:

—in a short-term sense, through ironing out excessive fluctuations;
—in the longer term, through fostering greater convergence of the Community economies.

First, the European system, with its intervention rules and credit mechanism, should be able to effectively fight the phenomenon of "overshooting." By this I mean movements of the exchange rate in excess of what would be warranted by differences in inflation rates between countries.

Overshooting has often occurred in the past. It can be initiated by strictly national causes. It can also be initiated—and it often has been—by movements of third currencies, particularly the dollar. When people move out of the dollar because of a lack of confidence in that currency, they do not move equally into all the European currencies. They often move specifically to one EC currency, the deutsche mark. This pushes the D-mark up and it widens the relationships between the D-mark and the French franc or the pound sterling. So one can say that sharp fluctuations of the dollar have also contributed to excessive swings, or overshooting, in European currencies.

Expressing the same idea in the economist's jargon, one can say exchange rates between major currencies have frequently been determined by portfolio adjustments. Such changes have often overshot the purchasing power parity level between these currencies themselves and also between the major currencies and others that are less used as instruments for investments in financial assets. These excessive movements are usually accommodated ex post by price movements, especially in the more open economies, and this tends to exacerbate inflation differentials. The new European exchange rate system, with its provisions for intervention and the available resources to carry out this intervention, should help prevent overshooting.

Second, there is a more fundamental way in which the EMS should contribute to greater exchange rate stability. Participation in this system assumes that in the adjustment process countries will have to give a high priority to internal policy measures rather than rely on exchange rate changes. Otherwise the effectiveness of the system itself would be jeopardized. Participating countries therefore have to realize that, by adhering to this scheme, they compel themselves to aim at greater convergence, through domestic measures, of the fundamentals of their economies. This factor is sometimes called the disciplinary element in the system. But the term should not be misinterpreted. It should not be taken to mean that adjustment is wholly a matter of restrictive policies by deficit countries. Rather the clear intention is that adjustment should take place in a symmetrical way through actions by surplus as well as by deficit countries.

How will greater exchange rate stability contribute to higher growth and employment? There are several ways.

In the first place, it should allow a higher level of both foreign and domestic demand to develop. Monetary instability in Europe has had a deflationary impact in both surplus and deficit countries. In countries with strong currencies, excessive appreciation has contributed to deflationary pressures by reducing profits in export industries and by reducing prospects for sales. This was one of the causes of the downward revisions of growth in Germany in 1977 and 1978.

On the other hand, in countries whose currencies have depreciated too much in relation to stronger currencies, downward overshooting has led to inflationary pressures through increased import prices and wage indexation. These inflationary implications have acted as a brake on economic revival. Governments have been afraid to allow their economies to grow faster lest the expansion increase the pressures on balance of payments and cause further currency depreciation and more inflation.

Thus greater monetary stability should have a positive impact on economic revival by making measures to stimulate higher levels of demand more feasible. This should have important multiplier effects, in view of the openness of EC economies and the high proportion of intra-Community trade in total trade. Trade with other EC partners represents 69 percent of total Belgian trade, between 45 and 50 percent of the trade of France, Germany, Denmark, and Italy, and 38 percent of British trade.

Greater monetary stability would also encourage business confidence and investment. In talks with European business executives, one often hears complaints that they are unable to give their companies a full European dimension because of the ever-present exchange risks and uncertainty about inflation rates. It has been difficult to forecast correctly the cost in national currency of inputs from abroad or the revenue in national currency from exports. These uncertainties contribute to the fact that businesses are not harvesting the potential benefits of a market as large as Europe. Furthermore, they reinforce protectionist pressures and paralyze investment.

In fact, one can safely say that exchange rate fluctuations have in part replaced the old customs barriers in their negative effects on growth and on the development both of a large European market and of enterprises with such a dimension. The dismantling of customs barriers and the progress toward integration contributed to the fast growth in Europe in the 1960s, but the instability of exchange rates between European currencies in the 1970s has been a brake on integration and on growth.

In short, I argue that monetary instability in Europe has had the deflationary bias that some people have wrongly attributed to the EMS design. I will come back to this point later.

OPERATING PRINCIPLES AND REQUIREMENTS FOR SUCCESSFUL FUNCTIONING OF THE EMS

Having analyzed the economic motivation for the creation of the EMS, the main elements of which are described in the appendix to this paper, I will now discuss the operating principles of the EMS and the conditions for its successful functioning. I stress three factors:

—the convergence of underlying economic conditions in the EMS countries;
—flexibility in the operation of the system;
—greater stability between EMS currencies and other currencies.

Convergence of the Community Economies

To be successful, the EMS, first of all, will have to be accompanied by policies designed to achieve a greater convergence of the economies of member states. The EMS cannot be durable and effective unless it is backed by complementary policies. As there are still important divergences in the situations of member states, great effort on the part of all countries and in all areas of policy will be needed if the system is to last.

Unless central rate changes are going to be very frequent, which would in itself limit the usefulness of the EMS, countries must, as noted, in principle give a higher priority to adjustment through internal policy measures than to changes in exchange rates.

Among these efforts, coordination of monetary policies deserves a special role. This is meant to assure a compatibility of the internal monetary objectives of member states with exchange rate objectives and with larger economic objectives. In this framework I believe that attention should be focused more on the coordination of domestic components of money creation, that is, on domestic credit expansion, than on one or more measures of the money stock. It would facilitate the monitoring of the EMS if members would broadly follow the principle of nonsterilization, through open market operations or other means, of exchange-market interventions. This would mean that countries losing reserves would allow tighter money and higher interest rates to reflect the liquidity effects of these losses, as has been the practice of the smaller countries in the "snake." A country facing a temporary accumulation of reserves will also have to remain calm and not try to offset quickly and completely the liquidity effect of sudden inflows of reserves.

Another approach to convergence is through coordination of global demand management policies. The concerted economic action decided upon in Bremen in July 1978, which modulated the extent of expansion of countries according to both balance-of-payments and inflationary problems, was an important approach to convergence. In the Bremen framework the strongest economy (Germany) took expansionary measures. This helped other countries to make necessary adjustments and makes it more probable that the right sort of adjustment and convergence policies will be followed under the EMS. This is one factor that is favorable to the initial functioning of the EMS.

Other elements of domestic policy also have an important role to play. In fact, the immediate issues affecting convergence these days are in the area of incomes policy, particularly in Ireland, Denmark, and Italy, where important wage negotiations are being discussed. The outcome of these negotiations will certainly affect the degree to which convergence can be achieved.

Let me also make a short comment here on the role of the divergence indicator,* which is the main novelty in the exchange rate system and which is described more fully in the appendix. When we proposed it, our purpose quite clearly was not only to find a compromise between the two views about what to use as a trigger for mandatory intervention—the parity grid* or the European currency unit (ECU)*—but also to find an objective indicator as a trigger for policy coordination. This the snake did not have, for it did not indicate who should take measures. Thus the divergence indicator should become one element of a more equilibrated adjustment process and should help induce convergence. It will be very important that all countries make this new element function effectively, as it could be a means of fostering real convergence. Its role is to signal early in the game where divergences are appearing and to induce countries to take corrective actions.

A second condition (in addition to monetary coordination) for successful operation is flexibility in the system. While the EMS by itself should help to reduce differences in inflation rates among countries, it should not prevent remaining significant differences from being reflected in exchange rates. It is necessary to avoid the rigidity of the Bretton Woods system and to "de-dramatize" exchange rate adjustments. Experience in the snake during the last three years has been positive on that score. A number of adjustments have been made, with exchange markets remaining calm. Several of these adjustments involved a general realignment. This

---

*[The terms *divergence indicator, parity grid,* and *ECU* are explained in the appendix to this paper.—Eds.]

was, for instance, the case in the October 1976 snake realignment, which gave new life to the snake when many outside observers were forecasting its imminent death. In a sense, the realignment two years later was also a very successful one. It was a kind of preemptive strike, which anticipated market tensions as the January 1 deadline for the EMS approached. This operation permitted the system to start in a quiet way, first unofficially in January, then officially in March.

If changes in exchange rates can be kept small, it will be an important element in deterring speculation. Often one hears that speculation cannot but gain from a system of stable and adjustable exchange rates. That is not right. To the extent that changes in central rates are smaller than twice the width of the margin of fluctuation it is not at all sure that speculation will gain. If before the change of the central rate a currency is at the floor rate, and after the change is at the ceiling, speculation will not have gained, provided the change in the central rate is smaller than twice the margin.

Experience with the snake has shown that central rates may be adjusted by as much as 4 percent without having much effect on market rates if a depreciating currency manages to shift position with the past strongest currency inside the regular EMS band.

Some commentators on the EMS have criticized it on the ground that it does not provide clear criteria for adjustments of central rates. I disagree. If you set specific criteria for what is to be allowed, you will activate market forces that push you to make those changes. As soon as a country moves toward the indicator, speculation will be triggered. There are many cases in which you might justifiably want to resist a move, even if a sophisticated indicator tells you otherwise. I have often mentioned the case of Belgium in this respect. If Belgium had slavishly followed indicators, it would have been led to adjust in a more significant way vis-à-vis the D-mark in the last few years. Its policy of staying close to the D-mark has allowed it, on the contrary, to rapidly decrease its inflation differential with Germany, from 7 percent in 1975 to less than 0.5 percent in the spring of 1979.

This, of course, is not to say that Belgium does not accept the role of an objective indicator, as is evidenced by its initiative in proposing the divergence indicator. However, this latter indicator can set off different kinds of action, among which I would especially emphasize domestic policy actions. It is true that adjustment in rates is one of the possible actions to be taken, but it is by no means the only one.

Let me now move to a third factor for success of the EMS. A stable relation between the dollar and European currencies is not an absolute condition of success but would greatly contribute to it. Obviously this is an element that is to a large extent outside the direct control of Europeans.

Erratic movements of the dollar have often contributed to the phenomenon of overshooting between European currencies. From this point of view, the smooth start of the EMS has been helped by the relative stability of the dollar. This reflects largely the new and effective concern of the U.S. authorities about the dollar, which has been manifested in monetary and budgetary policies since November 1, 1978. Continuation of such policies by the United States will be helpful to the EMS.

I wonder whether in the future we should not try to formalize somewhat the effort on both sides of the ocean to achieve greater stability. I wonder also whether it would not be feasible to devise a more comprehensive kind of divergence indicator, which would induce a divergent country or regional grouping to take action. Such a divergence indicator could be based on the IMF's special drawing rights. If the dollar, the ECU, or the Japanese yen diverged by a certain percentage against the SDR, this would trigger consultations in which possible action by the divergent country or group of countries would be considered.

OBJECTIONS

Many criticisms of the EMS have been heard in the Community as well as outside it. I will deal with some of them, realizing fully, however, that the best answers will not come from reasoning in the abstract but rather from the behavior of the new system.

The first and most important objection is that the economic situation in Europe is too divergent to allow a system of stable exchange rates among the European currencies. Those who raise this objection point out that the inflation rates of the nine members of the European Community vary at present between some 3 percent in Germany and 13 percent in Italy. This objection should be examined seriously.

Although comparisons of consumer price indexes are not, in my view, the best criterion for measuring existing inflation differentials, I think the answer to this objection is threefold.

First, it must be recognized that the exchange rate mechanism, if it is the only instrument of coordination, is of limited use. It seems essential that a system intended to stabilize exchange rates must go hand in hand with effective coordination of economic policies, in particular of internal monetary and budgetary policies, but also of incomes policies. It is not so much a question of imposing this convergence from outside. I believe countries have come to realize better in the last few years that it was in their own interests to take domestic measures toward convergence and that floating rates did not in fact grant independence to domestic policy. In other words, one can rightly say that those who adhere to the exchange rate system should be ready to adjust their internal monetary and economic policies accordingly.

Second, agreement on this point, however, does not imply that introduction of the system must wait for a complete disappearance of differences in inflation rates. Action should be taken to reduce them, but they need not be eliminated before the system can become operative. This EMS has sufficient flexibility to allow remaining real disparities to be reflected in exchange rates. In the snake mechanism, it will be noted, divergences have been reflected in changes in exchange rates, changes that have been carried out efficiently during the past few years.

Finally, the EMS includes an element of supplementary flexibility for the member states that did not participate in the snake in 1978. These countries may opt for wider margins (6 percent) around central rates, as Italy has done.

Another objection, partly linked with the first one, says that the system will necessarily be deflationary and will adversely affect employment and economic activity in the Community. The reasoning leading to this conclusion is as follows: those countries with higher inflation rates will be forced to adopt more restrictive monetary, budgetary, and incomes policies, which are detrimental to growth, in order to meet EMS exchange rate objectives.

I cannot agree with this objection, based as it is on what economists call "the Phillips curve," or on an assumption that there is a positive correlation between growth and increases in the price level. This comes down to saying that more inflation is necessary to growth. It is not a proven case. On the contrary, in many cases countries with a low inflation rate but greater confidence have had good rates of growth. The British in recent years have been compelled to recognize the error of this reasoning. Only after the introduction of anti-inflationary monetary, budgetary, and incomes policies did the performance of the British economy improve.

I do not intend to say that there may not be transitional problems for the poorer EC countries in the EMS. Demand management policies may be more difficult to apply in these countries. It is to meet this kind of difficulty that the issue of resource transfers to the poorer countries—Ireland and Italy in particular—has been raised.

The fear that the EMS will have a deflationary bias is also based on the proposition that the D-mark will pull up the other Community currencies above their purchasing power parity and that this will necessarily have deflationary effects through decreased competitiveness. This is an objection that cannot be met in the abstract. It would only be valid if one assumed that the country with a strong currency would refuse to take internal measures to prevent an excessive increase in the value of its currency and would also refuse to have its currency revalued in relation to other currencies. One answer is that the ECU divergence indicator is designed to induce countries whose currency is diverging to take the domestic measures necessary to prevent persistence of the divergence. Furthermore, experience with the snake has already shown that needed changes of the central rates can be carried out efficiently and flexibly.

A third objection is the opposite of the second: that the EMS will have an inflationary bias. Simplified, the reasoning is as follows: differences between inflation rates will continue, and speculation will take place on a large scale. Germany then will be obliged to grant important credits in order to support the weaker currencies. These credits in turn will raise the German money supply and lead to inflationary pressures in that country.

Here again, an answer cannot be given in the abstract. The objection assumes that inflation differentials will remain high and that adequate changes in central rates will be resisted. Let me repeat that a major factor in the efficient functioning of the system will have to be greater effective coordination of economic policies so as to reduce differences in inflation rates. Let me also repeat that, while the EMS itself ought to contribute to reducing divergences in economic performance, it should not prevent remaining real disparities from being reflected in exchange rates. The experience with the snake in the last few years shows that the normal adjustments have not been resisted. There have been periods of heavy intervention to fight speculation, of course, but most of these movements have been reversed within a short time.

CONCLUSION

An important initiative has been taken in Europe toward greater exchange rate stability. To function successfully, the EMS will have to foster convergence of the economic situations of member countries and be operated in a flexible way.

This initiative should also be seen as an element that can bring greater worldwide monetary stability. In this context the continuance of the recent American efforts to increase the stability of the dollar is an important consideration.

APPENDIX: CONTENTS OF THE EMS AGREEMENT

The EMS agreement contains three parts: an exchange rate system; the creation of a European currency, the ECU; and the first steps toward a European Monetary Fund.

The Exchange Rate System

Central Rates and Intervention Rules. Each currency has a central rate related to the ECU. These central rates have been used to establish a grid of bilateral exchange rates around which fluctuation margins of ±2.25 percent are established. EC countries whose currencies did not belong to the snake in December 1978 could opt for wider margins of up to ±6 percent at the outset of the EMS. Italy has availed itself of this opportunity. This wider margin should be gradually reduced as soon as economic conditions permit.

A member state that does not participate in the exchange rate mechanism at the outset—this is the case for the United Kingdom—may participate at a later stage.

Adjustments of central rates will be subject to a common procedure through mutual agreement of all countries participating in the exchange rate mechanism and the Commission of the European Community. When the intervention points defined by the fluctuation margins are reached, intervention in participating currencies is compulsory.

Intervention is also allowed before the margins are reached. In principle, such intervention will also be made in participating currencies, but intervention in third currencies is not excluded. The EMS agreement provides also for "coordination of exchange rate policies vis-à-vis third countries and, as far as possible, a concertation with the money authorities of these countries."

Indicator of Divergence. One of the new elements of the EMS that makes it different from the snake, which involves only the parity grid system, is the indicator of divergence. It is a kind of warning system and will signal whether a currency is experiencing a movement differing from the average. The indicator is based on the spread observed between the variable value of the ECU and the ECU numéraire. It flashes when a currency crosses its "threshold of divergence." The formula chosen to calculate this threshold is: 75% × (2.25% or 6%) × (1 less the weight of the currency in the ECU basket). This means that the threshold is set at 75 percent of the maximum spread of divergence allowed for each currency.

The divergence indicator also is calculated so as to eliminate the influence of the weight of each currency on the probability of reaching the threshold. If this had not been done, currencies that have a large weight in the ECU would reach the divergence indicator later than other currencies since they affect the ECU more than the currencies with smaller weights.

Before measuring the effective divergence compared to the threshold, the effective divergence must be adjusted to eliminate the effect of movements of some currencies—the lira and the pound sterling—in excess of 2.25 percent. Indeed, the lira has a margin of 6 percent and the pound sterling is subject to no margin. This is done so that, for instance, a wide movement of the pound would not by itself lead a currency across its divergence threshold.

When a currency crosses its threshold of divergence, the presumption is that the authorities concerned will correct the situation by adequate measures, such as the following:

—Diversified intervention. This means intervention in various currencies rather than in only the currency that is furthest away from the currency of the intervening country. Diversified interventions allow a better spread of the burden of intervention among currencies of the EMS.

—Measures of domestic monetary policy. This includes, among others, measures affecting the interest rate that have a direct effect on the flow of capital. In the snake system interest rate movements were an important instrument to alleviate tension.

—Changes in central rates. While the EMS itself ought to contribute to reducing divergences in economic performance, it should not prevent remaining real disparities from being reflected in exchange rates.

—Other measures of economic policy. These could include, for instance, changes in budgetary policy or incomes policy.

In case such measures, because of special circumstances, are not taken, the reasons for this shall be given to the other authorities, especially in the "concertation between Central Banks." Consultation will, if necessary, then take place in the appropriate Community bodies, including the Council of Ministers.

After six months, these provisions shall be reviewed in the light of experience.

To summarize this first part, the present EMS differs from the snake, especially in the following ways: (1) membership has been increased by the inclusion of the French franc, the lira, and the Irish pound; (2) one currency has a larger margin, 6 percent, than the standard 2.25 percent; and (3) the system is not only based on a parity grid but also has a new element, the divergence indicator.

The ECU and Its Functions

A European currency unit is at the center of the EMS. The value and the composition of the ECU are identical with the definition of the European unit of account.

The relative weights of the currencies in the ECU were as follows in early March 1979:

Deutsche mark	33.02	Belgian franc	9.23
French franc	19.89	Danish krone	3.10
Pound sterling	13.25	Irish pound	1.11
Dutch guilder	10.56	Luxembourg franc	0.35
Italian lira	9.58		

The ECU will be used (1) as the denominator (numéraire) for the exchange rate mechanism; (2) as the basis for the divergence indicator; (3)

as the denominator for operations in both the intervention and the credit mechanisms; (4) as a means of settlement between monetary authorities of the EC.

The weights of currencies in the ECU will be reexamined and if necessary revised within six months of the entry into force of the system and thereafter every five years or, on request, if the weight of any currency has changed by 25 percent. Revisions have to be mutually accepted; they will, by themselves, not modify the external value of the ECU on the day of the change. They will be made in line with underlying economic criteria.

To serve as a means of settlement, an initial supply of ECUs will be provided by the European Monetary Cooperation Fund (EMCF) against the deposit of 20 percent of gold and 20 percent of dollar reserves currently held by central banks. This operation will take the form of specified, revolving swap arrangements. The deposits will be valued in the following ways:

—for gold, whichever of these two prices is lower: the average of the price, converted into ECUs, noted each day at the two fixings in London during the previous six months, or the average of the two fixings noted the day before the last one of the period (so as to avoid a price above the current market value):

—for the dollar, the market rate two days before the date of the deposit.

Every three months, when they renew the swap agreements, central banks will make the adjustments necessary to maintain deposits with the EMCF corresponding to at least 20 percent of their reserves. This will be done to the extent that their reserves in gold and dollars have changed. The amounts of ECUs issued will also be adjusted according to changes in the market price of gold or in the exchange rate of the dollar.

A member state not participating in the exchange rate mechanism (the United Kingdom) may participate in this initial operation on the basis described.

The European Monetary Fund and Present Credit Mechanisms

The agreement of December 1978 stated:

We remain firmly resolved to consolidate, not later than two years after the start of the scheme, into a final system the provisions and procedures thus created. This system will entail the creation of the European Monetary Fund as announced in the conclusions of the European Council meeting at Bremen on 6/7 July, 1978, as well as the full utilization of the ECU as a reserve asset and a means of settlement. It will be based on adequate legislation at the Community as well as the national level.

In the meantime, existing financing and credit mechanisms will continue, adjusted in the following ways. The very short-term financing facility of an unlimited amount will be continued. Settlements will be made forty-five days after the end of the month of intervention with the possibility of prolongation for another three months for amounts limited to the size of debtor quotas in the short-term monetary support. Under the snake system, settlements had to be made thirty days after the end of the month of intervention. Debtor quotas in the short-term monetary support (which serve as ceiling for the three-month extension privilege) have been multiplied by about 2.5.

The credit mechanisms will be extended to an amount of 25 billion ECUs of effectively available credit. This is about 2.5 times the previous amount. Its distribution will be: for short-term monetary support, 14 billion ECUs; for medium-term financial assistance, 11 billion ECUs.

The substantial increase in the amounts of credit available and the lengthened duration of some credit mechanisms are important elements for strengthening the credibility of the system; they guarantee that, in the case of need, large means can be made available to countries to fight speculative movements. . . .

30

The American Response to the European Monetary System

Robert Triffin

A sensible response to the EMS requires, first of all, a determined attempt to "listen" before responding. I am very much concerned about American insularity, about our tendency to feel that we have the answers and that our only problem is to transmit our know-how to others who are less knowledgeable, less wise, less courageous, and less unselfish than we are.

Before summarizing my suggestions for an American response to the EMS, therefore, I shall, first, discuss the European motivations for taking such a step, in spite of the tremendous odds to be overcome, particularly the difficulties of reconciling national views and interests, of shaking the traditional inertia of bureaucracies, and of accepting the political— including the electoral—risks entailed in this bold attempt to reshape the future. And second, I shall outline a few crucial features of the EMS Agreement that seem to have escaped the attention of most official and academic observers in this country.[1]

MOTIVATIONS

Why did the European Community belatedly agree to adopt a monetary system of its own rather than continue to rely on the Bretton Woods system—on a de facto or de jure U.S. dollar standard?

Note that it would have had to do so anyway, at some stage, as a first step toward the full economic and monetary union repeatedly promised over the past ten years by its heads of state and government. But why now? I shall skip the purely political motivations that contributed for so long to blocking an agreement and that have now, at long last, made it possible. Being an economist rather than a politician, I shall limit myself to a review of some of the economic arguments that explain this switch from a U.S. dollar standard to an EMS standard.

The Bretton Woods system enshrined the dollar as a "parallel currency" for Europe as well as for the rest of the world; that is, as a currency of denomination for most transnational contracts, a currency of settlement, of market intervention, and of reserve accumulation by central banks, a currency in which private firms and individuals accumulated most of their international working balances, and finally the currency against which national exchange rates were measured, stabilized, and "readjusted" by all countries other than the United States. This system worked with remarkable success until the end of the 1950s, gave evident and growing signs of its ultimate lack of viability in the 1960s, and finally broke down in the early 1970s.[2]

The EMS agreement reflects European dissatisfaction not with the Bretton Woods system itself, but with the actual functioning of the inconvertible paper-dollar standard that took its place eight years ago and with the generalized, nationally managed, floating rate system that has been used to palliate some of the defects of this paper-dollar standard in the past six years. Speaking of Europe only—ignoring the views of the members of OPEC, of the other less developed and developed countries, and of the communist countries—I shall mention [five] major reasons for this dissatisfaction and for the Community's attempt to establish a different system.

The first is the inflationary flooding of the international monetary system by an unrestrained dollar creation. I shall mention only two broad developments as evidence of what we all know. The foreign exchange reserves (overwhelmingly dollars) of European central banks have grown tenfold since 1969 (from less than $13 billion to more than $133 billion at the end of 1978), increasing over these nine years by nine times as much as in all previous years and centuries since Adam and Eve. The inflationary implications of such a reserve explosion are obvious, since it entailed for the European central banks a $120 billion increase in their "high-powered money" issues, multiplied further by commercial banks under the traditional system of fractional reserve requirements, legal or customary. The parallel explosion in the foreign loans of the European commercial banks must also be noted. Those recorded by the Bank for International Settlements (BIS) amounted to nearly $500 billion in mid-1978; $92 billion of this was in domestic currencies and $400 billion in foreign "Eurocurrencies," of which $276 billion was in Eurodollars.

A second reason for the Europeans' growing dissatisfaction was the huge losses entailed by their accumulation of depreciating dollars. In real purchasing power, the dollar has declined by more than half over the past ten years (by more than 50 percent if measured by the rise of wholesale prices, and by about 60 percent if measured by the rise in the unit value of exports).

More relevant as a measure—considering conceivable alternatives to dollar accumulation of liquid reserves and working balances—is the depreciation of the dollar in relation to other currencies. The so-called effective exchange rate of the dollar vis-à-vis twenty major currencies (as measured by the International Monetary Fund and published monthly in *International Financial Statistics*) had declined in December 1978 by 24 percent since May 1970. While highly relevant in other respects, this measure is totally irrelevant as a guidepost for reluctant dollar holders, since a moderate decline was heavily influenced by the rise of the dollar relative to the Canadian dollar, the pound sterling, the Mexican peso, and so forth.

The practical alternatives for holders of U.S. dollars are not these weak currencies but the stronger currencies, particularly the Japanese yen, the German mark, and the Swiss franc, which had risen in the same period by 83 percent, 95 percent, and 161 percent, respectively, in relation to the dollar, entailing a dollar depreciation of 45 percent, 49 percent, and 61 percent vis-à-vis these currencies. These huge fluctuations were undoubtedly due in large part to capital movements by Americans as well as by foreigners. They may be "blamed" on "speculators," but in a free enterprise economy the private sectors are expected to be guided by the profit motive, and daily floating rates are expected to induce corporation treasurers and others to switch promptly from depreciating to appreciating currencies. The task of stabilizing the dollar, or at least avoiding unnecessary, excessive fluctuations, devolves not on them but on the public authorities.

As far as central banks are concerned, the use of the dollar as the main component of international reserve accumulation entailed enormous

bookkeeping losses. Those reported by the Bundesbank, for example, to-
taled 43 billion deutsche marks in an eight-year period (1971–78). At the
December 31, 1978, dollar-mark exchange rate (1.828 marks per dollar)
this would translate into a $23.6 billion loss, more than three times the
total international reserves of Germany at the end of 1969.

Third, even if full confidence in the dollar were restored tomorrow,
the desire for a different system less utterly dependent on it would still be
explainable so long as responsible policymakers did not base their decisions
on the unrealistic assumption that Americans—any more than they—could
be relied on to have permanent wisdom, courage, and luck in "keeping
their house in order" indefinitely. . . .

Fourth, widespread doubts about the future exchange rates of the
dollar are based not only on speculative forecasts of the current account
balance, but also on the danger of capital switches from the dollar "overhang" accumulated as a result of past deficits into other currencies or assets
abroad. . . .

Last but not least, the Europeans are deeply concerned about the
impact that a further depreciation of an already vastly undervalued, overcompetitive dollar rate would have on their own economic activity and
employment in the sectors competing abroad and at home with U.S exports. . . .

FEATURES OF THE EMS INSUFFICIENTLY
UNDERSTOOD IN THE UNITED STATES

I leave it to others to review the main features of the new EMS and
of its prospective evolution in the forthcoming months and years. All I wish
to do is dispel a few widespread misunderstandings still entertained in this
country by many economists, in official and particularly in academic circles.

Even those most in favor of European monetary and political
union remain basically skeptical about its success, and indifferent or even
downright opposed to it. This is to be expected, of course, from those who
are enthusiastic about free markets and floating exchange rates. I shall not
enter again this unending debate.

I can agree, on the other hand, with those who hold that commitments to exchange rate stability would be premature, harmful, and bound
to fail as long as member countries have not succeeded in reducing the wide
divergences still prevailing in their national rates of inflation (although
these are in part the result, as well as the cause, of divergent fluctuations in
exchange rates). This view is widely shared by the promoters of the EMS
and indeed has inspired some features, noted below, designed to accelerate
rather than prevent the exchange rate readjustments still expected to be
inevitable in the early years of the system. Full monetary union and ir-
revocable exchange rate stability remain distant hopes, not thought to be

achievable at this stage. The initial phase of the EMS centers—like the most successful monetary agreement ever concluded, the European Payments Union—on immediately feasible goals and acceptable commitments, rather than on blueprints for the distant future. Even the most chauvinistic opponents of full-fledged monetary union can agree on it insofar as it aims to promote the use of the ECU as an alternative to widely used foreign currencies and Eurocurrencies, including Eurodollars, in international payments.

Let me merely mention seven crucial features of the system that are highly attractive to its promoters.

In the first place, the system restores for the participating currencies a common denominator—or numéraire—sadly lacking in the revised IMF Articles of Agreement. In the absence of such an agreed-upon common denominator the dollar was the only common denominator used by the exchange market, and until recently tended to be the point of reference used by the authorities in calculating exchange rates and their readjustments. Perfectly logical under the Bretton Woods system, this procedure became absurd after the dollar became inconvertible and other currencies were left to fluctuate widely relative to each other and to the dollar. More and more countries thus began to calculate "effective" exchange rates in relation to national "baskets" of the currencies to the countries most important in their external transactions.

The U.S. dollar is not a major component of such baskets for any country of the Community. . . . The United States absorbs an average of less than 6 percent of the Community countries' exports, this percentage ranging in 1976 from a low of less than 3 percent for the Netherlands to a high of 9.6 percent for the United Kingdom. Intra-Community exports account, on the average, for 52 percent of the exports of participating countries, with a range of 36 percent to 77 percent for individual countries. The addition of services, such as tourism, transportation, and insurance, to merchandise exports would probably raise these percentages substantially as far as current account transactions are concerned.

Moreover, most other countries of Western Europe—to say nothing of Eastern Europe, Africa, and the Middle East—are likely to associate themselves de facto or even de jure with the EMS. Adding to the intra-Community trade only the Community's exports to other European OECD countries brings the average share of exports covered by the EMS arrangements to 67 percent—twelve times the Community's exports to the United States—ranging from a low of 51 percent for the United Kingdom's exports to a high of 92 percent for the exports of the Belgium-Luxembourg Economic Union.

All in all, the member countries of the Community and others closely associated with it in their external transactions are likely to account for three-fourths or even more of the Community's current transactions on trade account. The adoption of the ECU as a common denominator for exchange rate quotations, stabilization, and readjustments therefore appears to be a highly reasonable objective.

Second, the adoption of a "divergence indicator," which places on the country with the divergent currency the presumptive burden for the readjustment of domestic policies or exchange rates, or both, should help accelerate desirable readjustments. In contrast to the IMF Articles of Agreement as well as to the "snake" agreement, consultations on such readjustments are no longer left exclusively to the initiative of the country in question. The process can be triggered as well by partner countries complaining of the impact of an undervalued or overvalued exchange rate on their own economies. This is an unprecedented breakthrough in international monetary arrangements.

Third, Article 107 of the Rome Treaty requires that "each Member State handle its policy regarding exchange rates as a problem of common interest." The adoption of the ECU as common denominator gives, for the first time, an operational significance to this provision. I refer you to the March 1979 *Bundesbank Bulletin* for a full explanation of this matter, and quote only the following sentences from the relevant passage (page 13):

> It follows from the choice of the ECU as the fixed numéraire for the central rates of participating countries that a change in the ECU central rate of one currency necessarily leads to changes in the ECU central rates of other currencies. . . . Any change in a central rate in the EMS is therefore carried out in the context of a realignment of all ECU central rates, and it is consequently subject to the agreement of all the participants in the system.

Fourth, and particularly important to the United States, will be the replacement—in principle, at least—of the dollar by Community currencies in market interventions and by the ECU in the settlement of mutual credits. Americans have often justifiably complained of the dominant use of the dollar for both of these purposes, as strong—even though unintended—upward or downward pressure could be exerted on the market rates of the dollar, irrespective of any development in the underlying balance of payments of the United States, whenever Community countries' surpluses or deficits switched from eager to reluctant dollar holders, or vice versa. For instance, the dollar's strength in the exchange markets in 1977 was largely due to the accumulation by the United Kingdom and Italy of $17.5 billion of foreign exchange in 1977 (more than doubling Italy's depleted foreign exchange reserves and septupling those of the United Kingdom). Its precipitous decline in 1978 got much of its impetus because the United Kingdom had to sell dollars to finance its deficit, adding to the dollars that more reluctant dollar holders, such as Germany, Switzerland, and Japan, had to add to their already bloated holdings in order to slow the excessive appreciation of their currencies on the market. . . .

The substitution of the ECU for the dollar in such settlements might, of course, reduce the United States' deficit-financing facilities. Unpleasant as this would be in the short run, it might nevertheless be deemed beneficial in the longer run because it would restore a balance-of-payments and monetary discipline whose excessive relaxation has undoubtedly contributed for a long time to policies leading to a disastrous overvaluation of the dollar abroad and an inflationary weakening of its purchasing power at home.

One of the German motivations for the EMS is the hope that it may direct to other European currencies and to the ECU itself some of the speculative flows from weaker currencies into the deutsche mark. Germany, like Switzerland, complains bitterly about the excessive appreciation of its currency caused by the "refuge currency" status forced upon it by speculators. The first months of functioning of the EMS have indeed been encouraging in this respect (though in part for extraneous reasons, upon which I cannot dwell here). Weak currencies, such as the lira, the Irish pound, and the Danish krone have moved up well beyond their central rates while the D-mark has hovered around, mostly below, its central rate. The spreading of the previous "refuge currency" role of the strong currencies would, of course, be helpful to the dollar also by reducing its excessive bilateral depreciation relative to these currencies, often taken by speculators as a signal to unload more dollars on the market.

Fifth, the ECU is too often described by uninformed writers as a mere unit of account. The previous paragraphs—and the EMS Agreement—have already emphasized its roles as numéraire and as a means of payment and reserve accumulation by central banks. Its official use is spreading daily to many other Community transactions. It is also likely to be used in the near future as an alternative to Eurodollars, Euromarks, and so forth, in the flotation of bond obligations by the Community, the European Investment Bank, and even by national and local authorities. Equally important is the prospect that commercial banks may offer their customers ECU-demonimated loans and deposits as an alternative to the Eurocurrency denominations prevalent today. Actual and prospective developments in this respect were summarized in my December 1978 *Foreign Affairs* article and need not be rehashed here.

For a sixth point—and for brevity's sake—I merely refer to the same article for a discussion of the transition to full monetary union and the merger of national currencies, when and if EMS succeeds in attaining its ultimate objective of stability in intra-Community exchange rates.

Finally, let me mention that a full-fledged commitment to monetary union would require more than even a prolonged de facto stabilization of exchange rates. It would require a transfer of jurisdiction from national authorities—and their advisers—to Community institutions. The proposed European Monetary Fund would pave the way for such an evolution, modestly initiated already by the transfer to the European Monetary Cooperation Fund (EMCF) against ECU balances of 20 percent of each country's gold and dollar reserves. This percentage could be increased in time to encompass, not a pooling, as it is often improperly described, but joint management by their holders of international reserves now entrusted largely to the management of the U.S. monetary authorities and commercial banks.

SUGGESTIONS FOR THE U.S. RESPONSE

I now come to my personal suggestions for an American response to the EMS. First, I should say that I strongly favor a positive and constructive response, in a spirit of cooperation rather than one of skepticism, indifference, fear, or latent opposition.

The EMS should be viewed as an unprecedented opportunity to help the United States and the world resolve the awesome dollar problem, which is the legacy of the ill-advised and ill-fated dollar exchange standard of yesteryear. It might also, in a longer perspective, guide us toward a renewed, imperatively required effort to shape a worldwide monetary system worthy of its name and fair and acceptable to all concerned, including the less developed and the communist countries.

Europeans share with Americans a deep desire to restore the dollar as a currency worthy of the richest and most powerful country in the world. As stressed in the first part of this paper, a further weakening of the dollar exchange rates to even more undervalued, overcompetitive levels than is already the case would be as unacceptable to them as to us. It could hardly fail to trigger protectionist restrictions abroad against what would be called "exchange-rate dumping," followed by panicky moves here toward similar restrictions and even toward exchange controls that would be particularly disastrous for a world reserve center and a parallel currency.

The first requirement will be the correction of the huge and growing deficits of recent years, and indeed the restoration of healthy surpluses in the U.S. balance of payments on current account. This, in turn, will require an even more determined fight to reduce oil consumption and imports and a rate of domestic inflation that is double or triple that of Germany, Japan, Belgium, the Netherlands, or Austria, to say nothing of Switzerland. The clear affirmation of these prior policy objectives by the Congress and the administration, and their early implementation by concrete restraints on fiscal overspending, excessive money creation, price and wage increases, oil consumption and imports, and so on, should help restore confidence in the dollar and reverse bearish speculation against it by Americans and by foreigners. The measures announced and put into operation since last November have already shown substantial results.

Still, a total and lasting correction of external deficits cannot be expected overnight. Corrective policies—including past readjustments of exchange rates—produce their effects slowly. Avoiding an excessive depreciation of the dollar will still require considerable financing of foreign deficits for some time to come.

The United States can draw for this purpose on its own international reserves, which were estimated at $21 billion at the end of January 1979 but which would actually approximate $75 billion if gold holdings were revalued at the current market price of gold. This latter estimate is, of course, excessive, since gold prices would collapse in the event of massive sales. It is relevant, however, as one of the many reassurances to prospective creditors about the United States' solvency.

Far more important is the willingness, amply demonstrated already, of foreign countries to participate in a joint defense of agreed-upon dollar rates. This would include the adjustments, upward as well as downward, that might be deemed appropriate—or unavoidable—before any stabilization of the dollar in relation to the other major currencies could be realistically envisaged, even as a presumptive goal rather than as a legally binding commitment. The radical policy changes announced on November 1, 1978, are essential in this respect.

The U.S. government has agreed to intervene heavily in the exchange market rather than leave such interventions nearly exclusively to others. It has agreed to reduce the inflationary impact of borrowing abroad by borrowing in the financial market rather than nearly exclusively from central banks. The United States is now ready to denominate foreign borrowing in the creditors' currencies as well as in dollars in order to make them more attractive and acceptable to prospective lenders deterred by the risk of exchange losses on a depreciating dollar. It is now willing to explore with its IMF partners the opening of so-called substitution accounts in SDRs as a way to mop up some of the dollar overhang accumulated in the past.[3]

The EMS opens up new opportunities in all of these respects.

The adoption of the ECU as a parallel currency may soon enable the United States to denominate some official foreign borrowings in ECUs. Financially, this would expose the United States to smaller risks of exchange losses than alternative denominations in national currencies such as the mark or the Swiss franc. Politically, it would be a concrete and spectacular demonstration of the will to support the new European Monetary System. And it would be far more acceptable than borrowing in any national currency other than the dollar, borrowing that would open the way to charges that the dollar was becoming a satellite of, say, the mark.

A reinforced EMCF—and later a European Monetary Fund—should facilitate joint interventions and management of European exchange rates vis-à-vis the dollar. It should also provide an additional mechanism for substitution accounts. Reluctant dollar holders could exchange them for ECUs if they wished, as well as for SDRs. . . .

I shall comment only briefly on suggestions relating to the insertion of the EMS and the EMS-U.S. agreements into the broader framework of world monetary reform. I hope I am not entirely alone in feeling that floating rates and the second amendment to the IMF Articles of Agreement should not relegate to the trash can all the previous proposals for IMF reform, which were worked out during ten years of continuous, intensive negotiations. . . . I consider that a successful functioning of the EMS and of the links to be established between it and the dollar area may provide invaluable guidelines for the reforms that will be negotiable and feasible on a global scale. A decentralized IMF system should leave to regional organizations such as the EMS wide responsibilities and initiatives for the handling of problems between their members, and reserve for the IMF only the problems that cannot be dealt with as, or more, efficiently on a regional scale. This should elicit from like-minded countries that are interdependent and sufficiently aware of this interdependence closer cooperation—even integration—than is feasible in a broader framework between more heterogeneous groups of countries. It should also make it possible to reintegrate into the international monetary community the countries—especially the communist countries—to which a needlessly centralized Bretton Woods system anchored to the national currency of a single superpower was obviously unacceptable. . . .

Notes

1. For a fuller discussion of the EMS, see John Williamson, Alexandre Lamfalussy, Niels Thygesen, and others, *EMS: The Emerging European Monetary System* (Ires, Louvain la Neuve, April 1979).
2. I apologize for mentioning my early warnings of this impending breakdown, particularly in my testimony to the Joint Economic Committee of Congress in October 1959. The official collapse of the system began with the so-called two-tier gold price hurriedly adopted in March 1968, and was consummated by the "temporary" suspension of dollar convertibility in August 1971 and the generalization of floating exchange rates in March 1973. See the article by John Williamson in *EMS*.
3. Agreement on this technique, however, is likely to require a parallel agreement of some sort on the complementary proposal of the IMF executive directors and the Committee of Twenty on "asset settlements."

31

Exchange Rates, Payments Adjustment, and OPEC: Why Oil Deficits Persist

Robert M. Dunn, Jr.

INTRODUCTION

The balance-of-payments experience of the United States and other major oil importers in the period since 1973 produces an embarrassing paradox for many supporters of flexible or floating exchange rates. For decades it was argued that balance-of-payments disequilibria were solely the result of misguided decisions to maintain fixed parities and that, if the world would only adopt a system of floating exchange rates, payments problems would disappear. In 1973 most of the industrial countries abandoned parities and floated their currencies, not because of a general acceptance of academic arguments for floating rates, but because the Smithsonian Agreement collapsed and it was impossible even to guess what equilibrium parities might be under the circumstances existing at that time. Although flexible exchange rates were adopted by default rather than intent, the arguments to the effect that payments problems should then disappear remained relevant.

Seldom have the expectations of economic theory been more disappointed. The sharp increase in the price of oil in January 1974 produced a massive shift in the international payments pattern. As can be seen in Table 1, the OPEC countries moved into a large and sustained surplus, most of which was concentrated in a minority of the member countries. The oil-importing countries as a group necessarily had a parallel payments deficit. This payments pattern has continued for five years. Although the size of the OPEC surplus declined in 1978, it is now expected to be much larger in 1979 and 1980. A flexible-exchange-rate system of sorts was maintained by most of the industrial countries throughout this period, but it has remained strangely ineffective or even irrelevant to the adjustment of this payments disequilibrium.

The purpose of this essay is to analyze three related questions raised by this unhappy experience: (1) Why hasn't the payments disequilib-

From Robert M. Dunn, Jr., *Exchange Rates, Payments Adjustment, and OPEC: Why Oil Deficits Persist*, Essays in International Finance No. 137, December 1979. Copyright © 1980. Reprinted by permission of the International Finance Section of Princeton University and Robert M. Dunn, Jr., Professor of Economics at The George Washington University. Some footnotes omitted.

TABLE 1

OPEC Current-Account Balances by Country, 1973–80 (*in billions of U.S. dollars*)

	1973	1974	1975	1976	1977	1978	1979[a]	1980[a]
Algeria	−0.9	1.0	−1.7	−0.9	−2.8	−3.4	−1.4	−1.6
Ecuador	0	0.1	−0.2	0	−0.3	−0.3	−0.2	−0.3
Gabon	0	0.1	0.1	0	−0.1	0.1	0.4	0.4
Indonesia	−0.4	0.7	−1.1	−0.9	0	−1.3	0.5	0.3
Iran	1.1	12.7	4.7	4.7	5.1	−1.4	2.8	5.8
Iraq	0.5	3.0	2.8	3.8	5.0	4.5	10.0	7.4
Kuwait	1.5	8.1	5.9	7.0	5.4	5.8	12.2	11.5
Libya	−0.6	2.2	−0.2	2.3	2.1	1.5	5.5	5.7
Nigeria	0.3	5.0	0	0.3	−0.9	−3.4	0.5	−1.6
Qatar	0.1	1.6	1.0	1.0	0.4	0.9	1.9	2.2
Saudi Arabia	3.1	26.4	13.9	13.8	16.7	2.8	8.9	4.8
United Arab Emirates	0.3	5.6	3.2	3.9	4.1	3.5	6.0	7.2
Venezuela	−0.1	5.8	2.3	1.0	−2.1	−4.1	−2.1	−1.8
Total[b]	4.9	72.3	30.7	35.4	33.0	5.3	45.0[a]	40.0[a]

Note: These accounts are on an accrual rather than a cash-payments basis, meaning that exports of oil are counted when the oil is shipped rather than when final payment is made. The 1974 total would be about $12 billion less on a cash-payments basis, but the numbers for the other years would be only slightly affected.

[a]Preliminary U.S. Treasury projections, which assume no further increases in the price of oil beyond July 1979 levels. Informal estimates currently available in Washington suggest that the OPEC surplus will be about $60 billion during 1979, and that the 1980 total could be anywhere from $80 billion to $100 billion. The increases are expected to accrue primarily to Saudi Arabia, Iraq, Kuwait, and perhaps Iran.

[b]Totals may not add owing to rounding.

Sources: Estimates by U.S. Dept. of the Treasury and Chase Manhattan Bank.

rium caused by OPEC price increases been much affected either by the flexible-exchange-rate system adopted by the industrial countries or by other traditional adjustment mechanisms? (2) How would the adjustment process have worked if the necessary changes had been made in the payments system to produce exchange rates that forced payments positions into equilibrium, as the standard theory of floating rates suggests? Although it would have been possible to make the changes necessary to produce this conclusion, it turns out that the results would not have been pleasant or even acceptable. And (3) what has been the effect of floating exchange rates on the distribution of the oil deficit among the importing countries? Although the size of the total OPEC surplus, and hence the total deficit of oil importers, was unaffected by exchange-rate changes under the current float, the distribution of that deficit among oil importers is in large part determined by the workings of the managed, or "dirty," float that now prevails for most of the countries in the Organization for Economic Cooperation and Development (OECD).

THE IRRELEVANCE OF CONVENTIONAL ADJUSTMENT MECHANISMS TO THE OPEC SURPLUS

The massive payments disequilibrium that followed the 1974 increase in the price of oil has remained largely immune from the effects of exchange-rate changes or other traditional adjustment mechanisms because of an unusual arrangement that virtually isolates the domestic economies of the surplus oil-exporting countries from changes in oil revenues and from the resulting shifts in the balance of payments. Like most other exporters of primary products, the OPEC countries receive their export revenue in foreign exchange (dollars). Unlike most others, however, they do not have to provide parallel local-currency payments to domestic residents. The demand for OPEC exports is not matched by a demand for OPEC currencies by either foreigners or OPEC residents. Therefore, an increase in export receipts puts no upward pressure on the exchange rates for OPEC currencies and thus no downward pressure on the exchange rates for the OECD currencies as a group relative to the OPEC currencies. The maintenance of flexible exchange rates by a number of OECD countries produces no force for the adjustment of OPEC current-account surpluses.

One might still expect the classical fixed-exchange mechanism to operate; monetary expansion and rapid increases in disposable income in OPEC surplus countries would produce adjustment through inflation and the resulting increase in imports. But the governments of the OPEC countries are the oil producers and the recipients of the resulting revenues. Accordingly, increases in export proceeds do not result in automatic increases in either money supplies or domestic incomes. There are no pressures inside the OPEC economies that would rapidly expand private expenditures on domestic or imported goods when oil revenues increase sharply.

Although individuals in the OPEC countries receive no additional income when oil revenues increase, the governments of these countries do receive this income and might be expected to behave like individuals. Additional government revenue from exports increases both [government-owned] "cash balances," which in a monetarist framework will lead to increased expenditures on imports and to foreign investments, and government "incomes," which in a Keynesian framework will lead directly to increased expenditures on both domestic and imported goods. Although payments equilibrium is not reestablished through increases in privately held cash balances or private incomes, a similar result might occur through the responses of governments to these same forces.

These mechanisms have, in fact, operated in OPEC countries whose oil revenues are small relative to their populations and their development or military goals. As can be seen in Table 1, Indonesia, Nigeria, Venezuela, and similar countries have not run persistent surpluses; government expenditures on imports have been adjusted quickly to use all or most of the extra revenues provided by increases in the price of oil. These mechanisms have not operated, however, in Iraq, Kuwait, Saudi Arabia, and the United Arab Emirates, whose oil revenues and surpluses have largely dominated OPEC. (Iran was the only other OPEC member to run large and consistent surpluses from 1974 to 1977, but that situation changed dramatically in 1978. Libya has had modest surpluses since 1975, and these are expected to increase sharply in 1979 and 1980.)

The current-account surpluses have been concentrated largely in countries with very large oil revenues, small populations, and development or military goals that are modest relative to the revenues. Iraq and Saudi Arabia each have populations of just over ten million and massive incomes from oil. Because major investment projects were bunched up, resulting in inefficiencies from carrying them all on at once, and because the price of oil fell relative to the price of imports, Saudi Arabia spent almost all of its oil revenues during 1978. The recent increases in the price of oil and the likelihood that the Saudi government will respond to fundamentalist Islamic pressures by reducing the rate at which the country is modernized mean that Saudi Arabia is now returning to the previous pattern of large current-account surpluses. Tiny countries such as Kuwait and the United Arab Emirates probably cannot spend their receipts on sensible development programs. The governments of the major surplus countries cannot be expected to respond to increases in either cash balances or incomes in ways ascribed to individuals by theories of balance-of-payments adjustments. Libya would superficially appear to have the oil revenue and population characteristics of these four surplus countries, but it has apparently managed to spend almost all of its revenues on military equipment and "foreign aid." Treasury predictions of large Libyan surpluses in 1979 and 1980 are apparently based on the expectation that Colonel Qaddafi's financial support of radical efforts in the Middle East and elsewhere will not increase as rapidly as the price of oil.

As can be seen in Table 2, monetary expansion has been rapid in all of the OPEC countries in recent years. It was particularly rapid in Saudi Arabia and the United Arab Emirates, although a sharp deceleration occurred in the latter country from 1976 to 1978. Rates of growth of the money supply were considerably less extreme in the other major surplus countries, Kuwait and Iraq. The apparent lack of any relationship between rates of monetary expansion and the size of continuing current-account surpluses in the OPEC countries results in large part from the differing

TABLE 2

Percentage Annual Growth in Domestic Money Supply in OPEC
Countries, 1973–78

	1973	1974	1975	1976	1977	1978	1973–78 Average
Algeria	28.3	9.1	30.4	29.6	21.3	26.3	24.2
Ecuador	34.9	50.8	10.8	31.1	23.1	11.6	27.1
Gabon	24.1	66.9	54.7	76.4	−8.0	−6.2	34.7
Indonesia	41.6	40.4	37.3	23.7	25.3	24.0	32.1
Iran	29.9	37.1	20.2	45.9	23.1	n.a.	31.2[a]
Iraq	24.2	43.0	35.3	20.6	n.a.	n.a.	30.8[b]
Kuwait	21.1	14.0	48.0	35.9	24.6	29.5	28.9
Libya	24.5	46.7	15.1	31.2	26.8	n.a.	28.9[a]
Nigeria	24.0	51.1	85.5	44.6	38.1	1.7	40.8
Qatar	19.4	35.8	78.6	57.0	32.7	10.5	39.0
Saudi Arabia	39.9	41.4	89.6	71.2	58.3	28.1	54.8
United Arab Emirates	n.a.	57.3	69.5	81.5	10.4	10.8	45.9[c]
Venezuela	19.7	43.6	50.3	14.7	24.1	15.7	28.0

[a]Average for 1973–77.

[b]Average for 1973–76.

[c]Average for 1974–78.

Source: International Financial Statistics (October 1979, line 34 for each country).

roles of oil revenues in different economies. In countries such as Venezuela
and Ecuador, oil revenues are not large enough to dominate the economy
and relatively modest accelerations of growth in the money supply are
sufficient to produce adjustment when oil revenues increase. In countries
such as Kuwait or the United Arab Emirates, however, the oil industry *is*
the economy. This means that recent increases in oil revenues have been
so large relative to the economy and the money supply that even a rapid
acceleration of monetary growth will not produce current-account adjustment.

Although forces inside the OPEC surplus countries have not produced adequate adjustment, monetary and income changes in the oilconsuming countries might be expected to encourage a movement toward
current-account equilibrium on their side of the payments disequilibrium.
As noted earlier, the OPEC practice of accepting payment in dollars and of
maintaining surplus funds in dollars and other OECD currencies has meant
that there has been no exchange-rate pressure on the OECD currencies as
a group that would cause adjustment. To the extent that the OPEC governments hold their surplus funds in assets that are not liabilities of the

OECD central banks, there is also no automatic downward pressure on the money supplies of the OECD countries. If U.S. dollars are transferred from oil companies to OPEC governments, which hold them in commercial banks in New York or London, there is no decline in the reserve base of the U.S. commercial banking system. If the OPEC governments purchase U.S. Treasury securities in the open market, these funds move to the seller of the securities and are still in the commercial banking system. Only if the OPEC governments hold deposits in, or buy securities from, the Federal Reserve System would the U.S. money supply fall automatically. That decline, moreover, would probably be quickly sterilized. When the OPEC countries hold Eurodollar deposits or other U.S. dollar assets purchased from private parties, however, there is no decline in commercial bank reserves to sterilize.

Real incomes decline in the oil-importing countries because of worsened terms of trade, and this might be expected to be a modest force for current-account adjustment. The decline in real incomes in the oil-importing countries reduces other purchases, producing recessions and a reduction in current-account deficits. The recessions experienced by many OECD countries after the 1974 oil price increases were examples of this process, and they did produce a decline in the OPEC surplus from the 1974 peak of $72 billion. The combination of strong recoveries in the OECD countries and further oil price increases is producing a return to massive OPEC surpluses in 1979 and 1980, but the further worsening of the terms of trade of the oil-importing countries may soon produce another set of recessions and a temporary reduction in the OPEC current-accounts surplus.

The balance-of-payments adjustment processes that economists describe for regimes of either flexible or fixed exchange rates are based on direct linkages between shifts in the balance of payments and the domestic economy. The linkages are automatic in the sense that they do not require changes in government policy to produce adjustment. If the government remains passive, payments disequilibria either cause exchange-rate changes, which affect relative prices within one or both economies, or they affect the domestic money supplies and incomes in both the deficit and surplus countries. Under either exchange-rate regime, the balance of payments is linked to one or more aspects of the domestic economies of both surplus and deficit countries, and these linkages produce some degree of payments adjustment. The circumstances under which the OPEC countries sell oil eliminate all of these linkages in the OPEC countries and almost all of them in the oil-importing industrialized countries. The result is the current situation, in which there are no major automatic forces for adjustment of either the OPEC surplus or the deficit of the oil-importing countries as a group.

BALANCE-OF-PAYMENTS ACCOUNTING FOR OPEC

The fact that the same economic agents (the governments of the OPEC countries) who receive virtually all the oil revenue also determine what imports will be purchased and how the remaining surplus will be invested abroad makes the normal definition of a balance-of-payments surplus arbitrary or meaningless for these countries. The distinction between the capital-account and foreign-exchange-reserve items, on which the official settlements definition of payments disequilibrium is based, assumes that the economic agents who make investment decisions, which are recorded in the capital account, are different from those who undertake residual or accommodating transactions, which appear as foreign-exchange reserve flows. Since this assumption obviously does not hold for the dominant OPEC surplus countries, it is not at all clear how their balance-of-payments surpluses can be measured.

Saudi Arabia, for example, ran an accumulated current-account surplus of just over $54 billion from 1974 through 1976, but it accumulated only about $23 billion in foreign-exchange reserves during the same period. Since the government or its agents made almost all of the other $31 billion in foreign investments, the distinction between foreign-exchange reserves and the remainder of Saudi Arabia's foreign assets seems almost meaningless. It is at least clearly misleading to suggest that Saudi Arabia had a payments surplus of only $23 billion during this period.

Under these circumstances, it might be more reasonable to use the current account as the measure of payments disequilibrium, which would suggest a surplus of $54 billion for Saudi Arabia in 1974–76. One objection to this measure is that foreign-exchange reserves are supposed to be highly liquid, so that it is not reasonable to view Saudi investments in long- and medium-term assets as constituting reserves. The use of the "basic" balance-of-payments format, where the balance of payments is measured as the sum of the current and long-term capital accounts, avoids this problem by placing such nonliquid investments above the line as autonomous items, while short-term investments of all types are placed below the line with official foreign-exchange reserves. Since the vast majority of Saudi investments have reportedly been in short-term forms, the difference between the current-account and the "basic" balance-of-payments results would be quite small. In contrast, Kuwait has apparently made sizable long-term investments, so the difference between the two accounts there would be considerably larger.

The use of the "basic" format still leaves the question of whether Saudi and Kuwaiti medium- and long-term investments are really autonomous. Do these countries really "want" to invest abroad, or are they doing so only because huge current-account surpluses make it necessary to put the resulting surplus funds somewhere? The credibility of the latter explanation argues that these investments are accommodating, and consequently that the current account is the best measure of Kuwait's and Saudi Arabia's payments positions. The $54 billion figure appears to be a far better estimate of the Saudi payments surplus in 1974–76 than the $23 billion figure suggested by the official-settlements accounts or whatever figure the basic-payments format would indicate. Kuwait had a current-account surplus of $21 billion in 1974–76, while official foreign-exchange reserves increased by only about $1.5 billion. The $21 billion figure also appears to be the more reasonable estimate of Kuwait's surplus.

The current OPEC experience is not the only occasion on which revenues from a dominant export have been isolated from the domestic economy to block normal forces for payments adjustment. Other developing countries have responded to sudden and sharp increases in the price of a dominant export by applying heavy export taxes to prevent or at least greatly reduce an increase in domestic disposable income. They have also taken payment for these exports in foreign exchange to avoid pressure on their exchange rates or domestic money supplies. Colombia adopted this response to the increases in coffee prices that followed the partial destruction of the Brazilian crop by frost in 1975, and the operations of the government marketing boards for cocoa in Ghana and Nigeria have produced the same effects when cocoa prices have increased sharply. In these and similar instances, however, the payments surpluses were both small and temporary. The OPEC situation appears to be a unique combination of the absence of historic forces for payments adjustment and a huge and apparently far from transitory surplus.

THE APPLICATION OF CONVENTIONAL ADJUSTMENT MECHANISMS TO THE OPEC SURPLUS

The conclusion that the resistance of the massive OPEC surplus to standard adjustment forces results from the isolation of the internal economies of the OPEC countries from their international sectors might suggest that the solution to the current payments disequilibrium is to end this isolation and allow the traditional forces to produce adjustment. But how would such forces operate in the current context, and would the application of the classical remedies for payments deficits really be acceptable to the oil-importing countries? It appears that the adjustment mechanism would be so harsh in this case that a continuation of a difficult and disruptive disequilibrium is probably preferable.

If, for example, the OPEC countries had set prices and received oil payment in their local currencies, a decision to adopt floating exchange rates would have produced a sharp appreciation for a number of OPEC currencies and parallel increases in the U.S. dollar price of oil. If at the outset Saudi Arabia had set a riyal price of oil equivalent to $8 per barrel and then allowed the riyal to float, a Saudi decision not to make investments abroad during recent years would have necessitated a large appreciation of the riyal to clear the exchange market. There is no way of knowing what the dollar price of oil would have been if Saudi Arabia and its neighbors had adopted this approach, but the combination of the highly inelastic demand for oil in the consuming countries and demand for imports in Saudi Arabia and its neighbors suggests a very high price. The OPEC countries that are not in large current-account surplus have been producing oil at close to full capacity during recent years; their terms of trade would have improved with such a price increase, but they would have produced very little additional oil. The burden of adjustment would have been on reductions in world consumption of OPEC oil and increases in oil output and imports in the major surplus countries. The small populations of these countries suggest a very limited ability to absorb more imports, particularly since the governments rather than individuals receive the extra income from oil sales. If the governments of Iraq, Kuwait, Saudi Arabia, and the United Arab Emirates had decided not to make foreign investments but instead to allow the U.S. dollar price of oil to increase through an appreciation of their currencies sufficient to produce current-account equilibrium, the result would have been increases in the price of oil far in excess of those experienced by the importing countries between 1974 and 1978.

A similar result would have occurred in the unlikely event that the OPEC countries had adopted local-currency pricing of oil and fixed exchange rates before allowing their domestic money supplies to adjust to the payments surplus. If both the OPEC countries and oil importers had refrained from sterilizing the monetary effects of the payments disequilibria, the result would have been rapid inflation in the OPEC countries, which would have caused a rapid increase in imports. A parallel deflation in the oil-importing countries would have produced a recession (or worse) and an eventual decline in wages and prices.

If the OPEC countries did not increase the local-currency price of oil as other domestic prices rose, the only additional effect on the terms of trade would have been the decline in the prices of exports in the oil-importing countries. Equilibrium would have been established primarily through the effects of rapid inflation in the OPEC countries and a severe downturn in the oil-importing countries.

If the OPEC countries wanted oil revenues to remain a constant proportion of government receipts or wanted to recapture increases in wage rates and other oil-industry costs, the price of oil would have had to increase as domestic inflation accelerated. In such a case, the terms of trade of the oil-importing countries would have deteriorated far more rapidly and the adjustment process would have been even more painful.

Current-account adjustment would still have been achieved through the effects of deep recessions in the oil-importing countries and inflation in the OPEC economies, but the change in the terms of trade caused by the further increases in oil prices would have made the process even less pleasant for the oil-importing countries. Flows of capital from OPEC to the rest of the world would have continued until the adjustment process was completed. The OPEC countries would have accumulated foreign-exchange reserves, which are financial claims on the rest of the world, until their inflation and deflation in the oil-importing countries produced current-account equilibrium. These capital flows would not have been autonomous or voluntary but would instead have been necessitated by OPEC's decision to maintain fixed exchange rates for their currencies.

These scenarios have been developed not because they are likely but rather to suggest that the classical adjustment process is not always to be preferred over a continuing disequilibrium. Professors and central bankers in the industrialized countries frequently lecture officials of developing countries about the desirability of forcing rapid payments adjustment rather than depending on continued use of the Euromarkets, the International Monetary Fund, or other credit sources. Devaluations and domestic austerity are prescribed and accompanied by admonitions about "biting the bullet." Although these policies may in fact be necessary in some developing countries, the imposition of the same "bullet biting" adjustment mechanisms on the industrialized countries in general and the United States in particular during the last five years would have been more than painful: It would have produced a recession far worse than that of 1974–75.

Fortunately, the OPEC surplus countries are apparently willing to continue accumulating financial claims on the OECD countries, so this unpleasant process is unnecessary. The industrialized countries are not in the situation faced by many developing countries, because they appear to have a limitless source of credit.[1] As long as the Saudis and their neighbors are willing to lend, the OECD countries can finance continuing current-account deficits and the disruptive adjustment process described above will be unnecessary. But if ever the surplus countries decide that oil in the ground is a more attractive investment than financial claims on the industrialized countries, the result will be unpleasant. If the OPEC countries decide to stop making additional foreign investments (including increases in foreign-exchange reserves), they will have to force their current accounts into equilibrium, which implies the results described earlier. The industrialized countries would be well advised to see to it that the OPEC surplus countries continue to find it attractive to accumulate financial claims on the rest of the world. Whatever fears may have been raised by the prospect of OPEC surplus countries becoming major creditors or equity investors in the OECD countries, the alternative is worse. The United States and its allies may not like going into debt to finance oil purchases, but they ought to be pleased that it is possible to do so—that the OPEC surplus countries are willing to lend rather than force current-account adjustment.

The unpleasant and even destructive aspects of forced current-account adjustment result from the extremely low price elasticity of demand for oil in the importing countries in the short to medium term. If close or even partial substitutes for imported oil existed, the resulting increase in the price elasticity of demand for OPEC oil would make the movement to current-account equilibrium by the OPEC countries much less painful to the oil-importing countries. A far more modest increase in the relative price of oil would be sufficient to reduce oil consumption by enough to produce current-account balance. This fact is one more reason to hasten the development of substitutes for imported oil. The oil-importing countries had better develop large alternative energy sources and a far more successful conservation effort before the surplus OPEC countries decide to stop accumulating financial claims on the rest of the world. Unfortunately, it remains quite possible that the United States will develop alternatives to massive oil imports only when compelled to do so, perhaps through an OPEC decision to stop lending. Necessity would become the mother of invention, but it would certainly be a harsh parent.

It is often argued in the oil-consuming countries that the current OPEC price is purely the result of the exercise of monopoly power, and that this price is in no way fair or efficient. Despite OPEC's obvious market power, it is not clear that prices during the period since 1974 have been unreasonable. Oil consumption has not fallen, and known or proven reserves have risen so slowly that they are now a lower mutliple of annual consumption than in 1973. (According to the American Petroleum Institute statistics, proven world reserves of oil rose by 2.4 per cent between the end of 1973 and the beginning of 1979, and world oil consumption rose by 13.7 per cent during the same period; the ratio of proven reserves to annual consumption fell from 30.7 to 27.8.) The OPEC countries have produced at close to full capacity for much of this period, and serious shortages are widely predicted for the mid-1980s even if all of the OPEC countries are producing as much as possible.[2] Oil prices have only now reached levels at which some oil substitutes may become economically feasible.[3] If the world's oil industry has been operating at close to optimum capacity, and if shortages are widely expected in the mid-1980s because proven reserves are not rising as fast as consumption, it becomes difficult to argue that the price of oil has been "too high." It may have been higher than oil consumers wished, but it has not been high enough to compel the United States and other countries to reduce consumption of imported oil, to bring oil substitutes into the market, or to significantly reduce the rate at which the world is depleting a finite and irreplaceable resource.

FLEXIBLE EXCHANGE RATES AND THE DISTRIBUTION OF CURRENT-ACCOUNT DEFICITS AMONG THE OECD COUNTRIES

Although the post-1973 regime of flexible exchange rates will not lead to adjustment of the OPEC current-account surplus under current payments arrangements, this exchange-rate system does have major effects on the distribution of the resulting current-account deficits among oil-importing OECD countries.

Under a system of flexible exchange rates, the determination of the current account is based to a considerable degree on the fact that it must be a mirror image of the capital account, including foreign-exchange reserve flows if the float is "dirty" or managed. Exogenous shifts in net capital flows cause exchange-rate changes to which the current account must ultimately adjust. In the short run, both the current and capital accounts are likely to respond to exchange-rate movements caused by shifts in OPEC investment patterns, but the longer the new pattern of capital flows continues, the more important the current account becomes to the adjustment process. The appreciation of a currency resulting from such OPEC shifts can be expected to generate some capital outflows among speculators who conclude that the new exchange rate is higher than the long-term equilibrium. It will probably cause additional capital outflows by portfolio managers who want to maintain their previous ratio of assets in various currencies, since the appreciation has increased the value of assets in that currency relative to the rest of the portfolio. Finally, if stabilizing private capital flows do not develop quickly, or if private capital flows are destabilizing because of a speculative run on a currency, the change in the exchange rate may become large enough to encourage official capital flows as central banks use foreign-exchange reserves to stabilize the exchange market. These capital-account adjustments, however, are of a stock-adjustment type and so are unlikely to continue indefinitely. Once stabilizing speculative positions have been taken and portfolios returned to desired currency ratios, private capital flows are likely to decline sharply. Central-bank intervention may continue for longer, but it is also unlikely to continue indefinitely if the goal is to produce a stable exchange market rather than a return to fixed exchange rates.

Since the long-term price elasticities of demand for traded goods and services are typically much higher than short-term elasticities, the response of the current account to the exchange rate can be expected to increase as time passes. Shocks to the exchange market, caused by shifting flows of OPEC funds or other factors, produce payments adjustment through both the current and capital accounts as the exchange rate moves. Stabilizing capital flows are likely to be of greater importance in the short run, but current-account adjustment becomes more significant with the passage of time, as capital flows with stock-adjustment aspects decline and larger long-term elasticities of demand for traded goods and services become effective. OPEC decisions about the currencies in which their surplus funds are invested can then be viewed as affecting exchange rates, which in turn produce long-term current-account adjustments. Countries that attract large inflows of OPEC (and other) capital will have correspondingly large current-account deficits, and *vice versa*.

This long-term process can most easily be seen through an oversimplified example. Assume a three-country world consisting of Saudi Arabia, Japan, and the United States, in which Saudi Arabia sets oil prices and receives payments in U.S. dollars. Further assume that the United States and Japan maintain a clean float and there are no capital flows between these two countries. If Saudi Arabia has an annual current-account surplus of $20 billion, the distribution of the resulting deficit between Japan and the United States will depend solely on Saudi investment decisions. If they invest all $20 billion in U.S. dollar assets, the resulting exchange rate between the yen and the dollar will produce a $20 billion U.S. current-account deficit irrespective of how much oil the United States or Japan imports. A Saudi decision to switch $10 billion per year into yen assets will produce an appreciation of the yen sufficient to give Japan a $10 billion current-account deficit. Since all payments are made in dollars, the exchange rate for the riyal has no effect on this process: Saudi decisions as to the mix of currencies in which their surplus funds will be invested determine the yen/dollar exchange rate and hence the division of the current-account deficit between Japan and the United States.

If capital flows between Japan and the United States are allowed in our example and a clean float is still assumed, the distribution of the current account deficits becomes a function first of the original Saudi investment decisions as described above, and then of further flows of funds (often called secondary recycling) between New York and Tokyo. The current account of each country remains the mirror image of its capital account, but now the capital account is determined both by Saudi investment decisions and similar decisions in New York and Tokyo. If, for example, the Saudis invest all $20 billion in dollar assets but $10 billion in capital then flows from the United States to Japan, the resulting yen/dollar exchange rate will produce a $10 billion current-account deficit for each of the two oil-importing countries. Relative interest rates, speculative expectations, and a number of other factors determine first where the Saudis put their surplus funds and then how much is passed through to investments in the other country. The current accounts of the oil-importing countries ultimately adjust to shifts in net capital flows through the exchange rate, and countries with continuing capital-account surpluses will have parallel current-account deficits.

Viewed in this light, a sizable current-account deficit is no longer a sign of economic weakness but rather the result of a country's attractiveness to foreign investors. Countries that offer both high yields and safe investment climates will have exchange rates that overvalue their currencies in terms of purchasing power parity and the resulting current-account deficits. The strength of their currencies will protect their terms of trade and allow levels of investment well in excess of domestic saving. Oil-importing countries that fail to attract net capital inflows will be compelled to pay for their oil with real resources. Their currencies will depreciate by enough to force the current accounts into long-run equilibrium at the probable cost of worsening terms of trade. In a regime of clean floating exchange rates, a current-account deficit is no longer the result solely of inflation or other economic failures but is instead largely the result of economic strengths that attract net capital inflows.

OPEC INVESTMENT PATTERNS: 1974–78

Partial data on OPEC investment patterns can be found in Table 3. The totals do not match Table 1 because not all OPEC investments are reported and some are reported late. These figures do suggest, however, where the surplus OPEC countries have been putting most of their excess funds.

The most obvious conclusion to be drawn from this table is that OPEC investment patterns have changed sharply during the 1974–78 period. The British attracted large amounts of money in 1974, a significant proportion of which went into sterling assets. After 1974, however, the flow of funds into the United Kingdom dropped sharply and almost no new funds went into sterling assets. Virtually all the OPEC funds flowing to Britain were put into foreign-currency (Eurocurrency) deposits, which did nothing to support the sterling exchange rate. As Table 4 shows, the British current account declined sharply in 1974, when the OPEC countries put a sizable volume of funds into sterling assets, and then recovered during the next four years, when OPEC inflows declined.

While a number of factors—including relative rates of inflation and growth in Britain and its trading partners—may have contributed to this pattern of current-account changes, it is at least consistent with the earlier suggestions that OPEC investment decisions affect the current-account positions of oil-importing countries through movements of the exchange rate. Downward pressure on sterling during 1975 and 1976 could be viewed as a partial result of the decline in OPEC capital inflows and as a partial cause of the improvement in the U.K. current account. The strengthening of sterling in 1977, however, was clearly based on factors other than investment decisions by OPEC countries.

The relationship between OPEC investment decisions and the behavior of the current account is somewhat less clear for the United States

TABLE 3

Estimated Deployment of Oil Exporters' Surpluses, 1974–78[a] (*in billions of U.S. dollars*)

	1974	1975	1976	1977	1978
United Kingdom	21.0	4.3	4.5	4.1	−1.7
British Government stocks	0.9	0.4	0.2	—	−0.3
Treasury bills	2.7	−0.9	−1.2	−0.2	0.2
Sterling deposits	1.7	0.2	−1.4	0.3	0.3
Other sterling investments[b]	0.7	0.3	0.5	0.4	0.1
British Government foreign-currency bonds	0	0	0	0.2	0
Foreign-currency deposits	13.8	4.1	5.6	3.4	−2.0
Other foreign-currency borrowing	1.2	0.2	0.8	0	0
United States	11.0	10.0	12.0	9.2	1.3
Treasury bonds and notes ⎫	6.0	2.0	4.2	4.3	−1.6
Treasury bills ⎭		0.5	−1.0	−0.8	−0.9
Bank deposits	4.0	0.6	1.6	0.4	0.7
Other[b]	1.0	6.9	7.2	5.3	3.1
Other countries	20.6	17.4	18.7	19.9	12.2
Bank deposits	9.0	5.0	6.5	7.5	3.6
Special bilateral facilities and other investments[b,c]	11.6	12.4	12.2	12.4	8.6
International organizations	3.6	17.4	2.0	0.3	0.1
Total	56.2	35.7	37.2	33.5	11.9

[a]Excludes liabilities arising from net borrowing and inward direct investment and also, on the assets side, changes in credit given for oil exports.

[b]Includes holdings of equities, property, etc.

[c]Includes loans to less developed countries.

Sources. Bank of England Quarterly (September 1975) and *IMF Survey* (Apr. 4, 1977, and July 23, 1979).

TABLE 4

U.S. and U.K. Current-Account Balances (*in billions of U.S. dollars*)

	1973	1974	1975	1976	1977	1978
United Kingdom	−2.6	−8.6	−4.1	−2.0	0.5	1.0
United States	+6.9	+1.8	+18.4	+4.3	−15.3	−16.0

Source: Economic Outlook, OECD (July 1979, pp. 70 and 150).

than for Britain. The United States attracted a relatively stable flow of OPEC funds from 1974 through 1977 (Table 3), but the U.S. current account recovered sharply in 1975 and deteriorated in 1976 (Table 4), in large part as a result of the 1974–75 recession and the subsequent recovery. Because the U.S. dollar remains the dominant reserve currency and is also used heavily in a range of international transactions, a variety of official and private capital flows could easily have overwhelmed the effects of OPEC investment decisions. The U.S. current account remains a mirror image of all capital flows, but those flows include large shifts of funds by official monetary agencies of countries that still maintain fixed parities or manage their floating exchange rates.

The role of official reserve flows is particularly important in understanding the apparent lack of any relationship between OPEC investment decisions and the U.S. current account in 1978. OPEC investments in the United States declined sharply in 1978, at a time when other investors had doubts about the future of the dollar. The result was an acceleration of the downward pressure on the dollar that had begun in late 1977. Since the current account does not respond quickly to the exchange rate and since the U.S. economy was in the middle of a strong cyclical recovery, the U.S. current account did not recover in 1978. Official support for the dollar became necessary to stabilize exchange markets in 1978. The 1977–78 depreciation of the dollar, along with the possible effects of the end of a strong cyclical recovery, does appear to be causing a sharp recovery of the U.S. current account during 1979. OPEC and other investment decisions are apparently affecting the U.S. current account through the exchange rate with a lag of about a year.

There are two other points worth noting in Table 3. First, the proportion of OPEC investments going to countries other than the United States and Britain has increased steadily since 1974. Only one-third of such funds went to other countries in 1974, but this figure rose in the following years until it was over 100 per cent in 1978, when net withdrawal of funds from the United Kingdom occurred. Second, OPEC investments in international organizations such as the IBRD have been negligible since 1975. After modest investments in 1974 and much larger commitments in 1975, OPEC flows into the international organizations almost ceased in 1976 through 1978. Third-world complaints that the United States and its OECD allies are making insufficient commitments to the soft-loan window of the World Bank and to other concessionary lending facilities in the international financial institutions might be referred to Riyadh, Kuwait, and Abu Dhabi.

MANAGED FLOATS AND MERCANTILISM

The earlier conclusion that a current-account deficit could be viewed as the desirable result of a country's ability to attract OPEC and other capital inflows implicitly assumed that fiscal and monetary policies could be depended upon to offset the deflationary effects of currency appreciations fully and promptly, and that adjustment problems in individual traded-goods industries could be ignored. But there have been unfortunate and even disillusioning experiences with fiscal and monetary "fine tuning," and very real sectoral problems have resulted from the impacts of sizable appreciations on traded-goods industries. Thus current-account deficits cannot be viewed as favorably as the previous discussion suggests, despite the fact that they result from an attractive investment climate. Such problems have led governments to attempt to manipulate net capital flows, and hence the current account, under the existing regime of floating exchange rates.

The introduction of a managed or "dirty," float complicates the previous arguments and conclusions. Now the capital flows that affect the current account include flows of foreign-exchange reserves resulting from manipulative intervention by central banks. Returning to the previous and oversimplified three-country example, if Saudi and other private investment decisions produce a net capital flow into Japan of $15 billion, then Japan should have a current-account deficit of that size. If, however, the Bank of Japan decides to protect local traded-goods industries by absorbing $10 billion through exchange-market intervention, the resulting change in the yen/dollar exchange rate will shift $10 billion of the presumed current-account deficit to the United States. A U.S. decision to add $10 billion worth of yen to U.S. foreign-exchange reserves through similar intervention would produce the original exchange rate and shift the $10 billion current-account deficit back to Japan. Equal and offsetting central-bank intervention in Tokyo and New York produces the clean-float results.

The division of the $20 billion current-account deficit between the United States and Japan is now determined by *all* capital flows. The U.S. current account is simply the net capital account, including both private and official monetary flows, with the sign reversed. Under this exchange-rate regime, old-fashioned mercantilism can be practiced in a new way— through the manipulation of official capital flows and hence the exchange rate rather than through tariffs and quotas. The goals are the same, but the techniques are more subtle. Countries like Japan that want to protect and expand their traded-goods industries undertake exchange-market "stabilization" programs in which sizable and frequent additions are made to their foreign-exchange reserves. If this is too obvious, official guidance or "moral suasion" can be used to encourage domestic financial institutions to move large amounts of capital out of the country, which produces the same result. The currencies of such countries are systematically undervalued, and traded-goods industries are protected by such intervention.

Evidence of managed floating exchange rates can be found in Table 5. All the countries in this table were supposedly maintaining floating exchange rates (either individually or as part of a bloc) after 1973, but they all experienced sizable increases in their holdings of foreign-exchange reserves. From the end of 1973 through 1977, the Japanese "stabilized" their exchange market in a way that added about $11 billion to their

TABLE 5

Foreign-Exchange Reserves Excluding Gold, End of Period, 1972–78
(*in billions of U.S. dollars*)

	1972	1973	1974	1975	1976	1977	1978
France	6.2	4.3	4.5	8.5	5.6	5.9	9.3
Germany	19.3	28.2	27.4	26.2	30.0	34.7	48.5
Italy	3.0	3.0	3.4	1.4	3.3	8.1	11.1
Japan	17.6	11.4	12.6	12.0	15.7	22.3	32.4
Netherlands	2.7	4.3	4.6	4.9	5.2	5.7	5.1
Switzerland	4.4	5.0	5.4	7.0	9.6	10.3	17.8
United Kingdom	4.8	5.6	6.0	4.6	3.4	20.1	16.0

Source: International Financial Statistics (Oct. 1979).

foreign-exchange reserves. (1978 is excluded from this discussion because it included a major official support program for the dollar; reserve additions by many countries during that year were not purely voluntary but were instead a response to U.S. requests for aid in stabilizing exchange markets.) The Swiss doubled their reserves over the same period. After experiencing some decline in reserves during the first years of the float, the British responded to strong upward pressure on sterling by making huge reserve additions during 1977. The increases in Dutch, German, and French reserves might be viewed as the result of their participation in the European "snake" except for the fact that the participants as a group had large increases in reserves and no single member experienced a significant decline. Although the snake was supposed to float relative to the dollar, the float appears to have been managed in a manner that held the European currencies down relative to the dollar and other nonparticipating currencies. The sizable accumulation of reserves by the countries in the European snake indicates that, if the float had been clean, the group of participating currencies would have appreciated further against the dollar, improving the competitive position of U.S. firms exporting to Europe and having the opposite effect on European firms selling in the United States.

Table 5 includes every major U.S industrial competitor except Canada. (Canada had relatively stable reserves from 1972 through mid-1976 and hence could be viewed as operating a relatively clean float. The results of the late 1976 election in Quebec produced strong downward pressure on the Canadian dollar, and Bank of Canada support efforts caused exchange reserve losses of about $1.4 billion in 1977 and 1978.) The large increases in the reserves of these countries during the 1973–77 period suggest that their exchange-market interventions put U.S. exports and import-competing firms at some disadvantage. The impact may not have been large, but it created understandable frustration on the part of

U.S. firms and labor unions. The Japanese have been the principal target of the resulting criticism because of their dominant role in many U.S. import markets and the size of their reserve increases, but Table 5 indicates that the problem was widespread. One goal of the new IMF exchange-market surveillance system is apparently to discourage this new form of mercantilism. It is important that this system succeed. . . .

Notes

1. The payments problems of most oil-importing developing countries have been made more difficult by their inability to arrange large direct loans from the surplus OPEC countries. As the price of oil has risen rapidly, these countries have avoided the rigors of current-account adjustment only to the extent that they have been able to borrow from official international institutions such as the World Bank and the IMF, or from private financial institutions. A large part of this financing has been provided by private commercial banks in New York, London, and other financial centers. These banks raise money from the surplus OPEC countries, usually through Eurocurrency deposits, and relend to deficit developing countries. This process has now gone on for long enough and has involved such large amounts of money that questions are being raised about the prudence of its continuation. The debts of the non-oil developing countries have grown rapidly, and it is widely felt that many commercial banks are fully extended (or overextended) in a number of such countries. The recent oil price changes are expected to increase the current-account deficits of the developing countries to almost $60 billion in 1980, which will raise further questions about their credit-worthiness. If it is imprudent for the major commercial banks to lend large amounts of new money to these countries, it will become very important that the surplus OPEC countries either provide considerably more funds to the official intermediaries for lending to the non-oil developing countries or do much more direct lending to these countries.
2. See Walter Levy, "The Years That the Locust Has Eaten: Oil Policy and OPEC Development Prospects," *Foreign Affairs* (Winter 1978/79) for predictions supporting this view. There have been press reports recently that CIA studies also predict serious shortages of oil in the mid- and late 1980s.
3. See *The Economist* (Oct. 6, 1979, p. 124) for data on the costs of various oil substitutes from an engineering study by the Bechtel Corporation.

32

The Response to Higher Oil Prices: Adjustment and Financing

Morgan Guaranty Trust Company of New York

The effective price of crude oil—the weighted average of both official and spot prices—is now almost $30 per barrel and probably will average somewhat above that level for 1980 as a whole. Oil prices are currently almost 130% higher than at the end of 1978, or about twice as high in real terms. Relative to 1974, when oil prices already had quadrupled from the 1973 level, the rise has been nearly 170% and 50% in real terms (see [Figure 1]).

Last fall, when oil was still in the $20-$24 per barrel range, optimism predominated about the ability of the world economy to adjust to the higher oil prices and about the scope for financing the payments imbalances of the oil importing countries through the markets. Now that oil prices have risen much more than expected, sentiment has shifted.

These higher prices have compelled substantial upward revisions in projections of the OPEC current account surplus for 1980. Late last year, most official forecasts (e.g., those of the OECD and the Bank of England) called for an OPEC surplus after transfers of between $70–$75 billion in 1980 and projected a considerable shrinkage during the course of this year. In contrast, most projections now anticipate a 1980 surplus substantially above $100 billion. Last month, former U.S. Treasury Under Secretary Solomon forecast a surplus of as much as $120 billion.

As in 1974 the emergence of another major international payments imblance has sparked a debate about the adjustment process of the world economy to the higher oil prices and the need for special official financing to supplement the recycling of funds from surplus to deficit nations through the markets. . . .

THE ECONOMIC RESPONSE OF THE INDUSTRIAL COUNTRIES

Adjustment and financing will hinge more than ever on the response of the major industrial countries to the higher oil prices. Much of the adjustment by these countries to the 1973–74 oil shock occurred by

Reprinted with permission from "The Response to Higher Oil Prices: Adjustment and Financing," in the March 1980 issue of *World Financial Markets*, published by Morgan Guaranty Trust Company of New York. Some tables omitted.

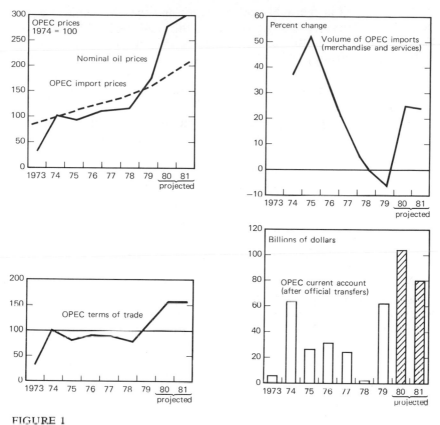

FIGURE 1
Trends in the OPEC Current Account

1975, when their combined current account deficit fell below $5 billion from more than $30 billion in the previous year. . . . This rapid adjustment was partly a consequence of the 1974–75 recession, which contributed to a 7% reduction in OECD import volume, including a 12% decline in net oil import volume. . . . The United States experienced a particularly severe recession and total import volume dropped by about 15%, resulting in the record $18 billion U.S. current account surplus in 1975. In addition, the industrial countries benefited from the large absorptive capacity of OPEC, whose import volume from the industrial countries doubled in this two-year period.

The 1974–75 recession, while it facilitated adjustment by the major industrial nations, exacerbated the problem for the non-OPEC LDCs. The latter's combined current account deficit after official transfers widened to $31 billion in 1975 from $5 billion in 1973—much more than the $9 billion increase in their net oil imports. It was not until 1976, when growth resumed in the industrial countries and the U.S. current account began to deteriorate, that the deficit of the non-OPEC LDCs began to shrink. The volume of industrial countries' imports from the non-OPEC LDCs surged 20% in 1976 compared with a 7% decline in 1975. There was also a 5% improvement in the terms of trade of these developing countries in 1976, partly reversing the 20% deterioration between 1973 and 1975.

Responding not only to developments in both the industrial and developing countries but also to OPEC's own spending boom, the OPEC current account surplus after transfers was reduced to the $30–$35 billion range in 1975–76 from a surplus of $64 billion in 1974. This narrowing of global payments imbalances strengthened the confidence of the credit markets in smoothly financing the balance-of-payments adjustment of the oil importing countries. Indeed, largely because of this smooth financing, the non-OPEC LDCs were able to maintain economic growth at close to 6% in 1974–76.

In subsequent years, the terms of trade of OPEC declined even further, while imports of OPEC continued to expand. Despite a pickup in oil consumption in the industrial countries, demand for OPEC oil remained relatively flat, mainly on account of rising oil output from non-OPEC sources, such as the North Sea, Mexico, and Alaska. By 1978, the OPEC current account surplus had virtually disappeared, while the current account deficit of the non-OPEC LDCs was trimmed to $25 billion.

There are a number of striking similarities between the present situation and the first oil shock. Once again, nearly all of the industrial nations are experiencing an acceleration of inflation, especially the United States where the rate of increase in consumer and producer prices has reached 18% per annum in recent months. Virtually all of these countries are responding, as in 1973–74, by tightening their monetary policies. . . .

One principal contrast to the 1974–75 experience is that the slowing of economic activity in the industrial countries is likely to be somewhat less severe this time. One reason is that economic activity among the major industrial countries is currently less synchronized than it was before the last recession. At that time most of the industrial economies simultaneously reached the end of an economic boom. . . . Real GNP growth for the major industrial countries as a group is likely to average between 1% and 2% this year and next, in contrast with zero average growth in 1974–75.

Another significant contrast is that non-OPEC LDCs are unlikely to hold up their growth rates as they did in the mid-1970s. A number of these countries have already taken steps that will reduce economic growth in the interests of curbing their inflation and containing their current account deficits. Real GDP growth of the major borrowing countries among the non-OPEC LDC group is likely to average only 3%–3½% this year and next, in contrast to nearly 6% in 1974–75.

NEAR-TERM OUTLOOK FOR PAYMENTS IMBALANCES

The slowing of economic growth in industrial countries and the near doubling of oil prices in real terms during the past fifteen months, as well as the mild winter, should lead to a decline in non-Communist world oil consumption outside OPEC of . . . about 1.5% in 1980 relative to 1979. Continued sluggish economic growth next year could keep oil consumption from rising. This, together with the very high oil stocks and the growth in non-OPEC oil production (mainly Mexico and the North Sea) . . . , may reduce world demand for OPEC oil. It could permit some OPEC members to cut their production gradually without upsetting oil markets. . . . Therefore, barring unexpected oil supply interruptions, oil prices could rise rather slowly during the next eighteen months or so and, in view of the high rates of world inflation, could even decline by a few percentage points in real terms.

The containment of the growth of OPEC oil revenues that this outlook implies is likely to be accompanied by a recovery in the growth of OPEC imports of goods and services from the sharp slowing of 1978–79. The virtual disappearance of the OPEC surplus in 1978 and the cutback in Iranian expenditures that accompanied the revolution kept the volume of OPEC imports of goods and services relatively flat in 1978 and led to a decline of some 7% last year [see Figure 1]. These expenditures are beginning to pick up as a result of the large rise in oil revenues that OPEC members are now experiencing. Merchandise exports of twelve major industrial countries to OPEC were up by almost 10% in nominal terms in the fourth quarter of 1979 from the year before, compared with an average decline of 6% in the preceding three quarters. . . .

THE IMPACT ON THE MAJOR BORROWING COUNTRIES

. . . The aggregate deficit of the non-OPEC LDCs is likely to rise further from an estimated $43 billion in 1979 and $58 billion in 1980 to more than $70 billion in 1981. . . .

The potential financing problems raised by higher oil prices and the resultant payments imbalances can not be fully gauged by looking only at the aggregate position of non-OPEC LDCs. . . . Indeed, a mere dozen non-oil LDCs, which include the major borrowers from the international banks, are expected to account for half of the projected current account deficit of the non-oil LDC group this year and next.

. . . External payments problems, particularly in 1981, will not be confined to the non-oil LDCs. The smaller non-oil industrial countries, outside the Group of Ten, are projected to experience a sizable deterioration in their aggregate current account deficit next year. . . .

TABLE 1

Banks' Claims on Selected Groups of Borrowing Countries[a]
(end-September 1979)

	In billions of dollars	% of total
Non-oil LDCs	103.4	30.2
12 major borrowers[b]	80.1	23.4
Other	23.3	6.8
Smaller non-oil industrial countries	107.6	31.5
11 major borrowers[c]	75.5	22.1
Other	32.1	9.4
Oil exporters outside the Middle East and North Africa	76.2	22.2
9 major borrowers[d]	66.8	19.5
Other	9.4	2.7
Eastern Europe	54.7	16.0
Total	342.0	100.0

[a]Based on claims reported by banks to the BIS

[b]Argentina, Bolivia, Brazil, Chile, Colombia, India, Ivory Coast, Korea, Philippines, Taiwan, Thailand, and Turkey

[c]Australia, Denmark, Finland, Greece, Ireland, New Zealand, Portugal, South Africa, Spain, Sweden, and Yugoslavia

[d]Ecuador, Indonesia, Malaysia, Mexico, Nigeria, Norway, Peru, Trinidad and Tobago, and Venezuela

Table 1 shows banks' claims on these two categories, together with their claims on a group of oil exporting countries outside North Africa and the Middle East. At the end of September 1979, claims on the major borrowers within these three groups accounted for two thirds of the banks' total foreign claims on all countries other than major industrial countries and offshore money centers. During 1974–79 the external indebtedness of these major borrowers roughly tripled. About two thirds of the increase was in borrowing from commercial banks. By the end of last year, commercial banks held more than half the total external debt of these thirty-two countries, and in some instances close to three quarters.

. . . Substantial increases in the . . . financing requirements of these groups of countries are [projected for 1980–1985. For details, see original article.—Eds.] . . .

THE OUTLOOK FOR BANK LENDING

While the implied average annual rates of increase in bank credit exposure to two out of the three groups of countries would be similar to those registered in the past four years, the banks may not be able to sustain this pace of credit expansion. There has already been a marked slackening in the pace of new Euro-currency credits arranged for developing countries. . . .

The rapid expansion of banks' international lending has contributed to a growth in their total assets that has exceeded the growth in many banks' capital, thereby contributing to a deterioration in their capital/asset ratios. Moreover, the rate of growth of banks' international lending, including their lending to these three groups of countries, has exceeded the growth of most banks' total assets, thereby resulting in an increase in the element of country risk in bank portfolios. Continued growth in banks' international credit exposure at rates similar to the recent past would tend to further accentuate these trends, a development which may be unacceptable to both bank managements and supervisory officials.

The increase in portfolio concentration in the past, of course, has applied to banks' total international loans in relation to banks' total assets and not just to banks' loans to the three groups of borrowers. In fact, in the past four years the rate of growth of bank's claims on these particular groups of borrowers has not been out of line with the rate of expansion of banks' total international lending.

Problems arising from concentration of country risk could be alleviated somewhat, but would not be removed, by improved lending margins and resulting increases in the growth of banks' earnings. Rapid growth of international lending could take place without erosion of bank capital/asset ratios in the context of slack domestic loan demand. This, however, would increase country credit risk concentration.

Two other issues will heavily influence the attitudes of banks toward international lending, including refinancing of maturing obligations. The first is the contribution of official international lending institutions and OPEC members to the recycling process, particularly in 1981–82 when the OPEC surplus still will be very large and the financing needs of the borrowing countries will be particularly heavy. The second issue is whether the major industrial countries and the principal borrowing nations pursue policies adequate to achieve satisfactory payments adjustment.

THE NEED FOR INCREASED OFFICIAL LENDING

Both the International Monetary Fund and the World Bank could play a somewhat more significant balance-of-payments financing role than in the past. While the Fund has some liquidity, additional resources would have to be marshalled for it to assist in recycling in an important way. . . .

The World Bank is currently considering a number of quickly disbursable "structural-adjustment" program loans, as distinct from project loans, which require as long as six or seven years to disburse. . . .

There is also need for increased bilateral assistance. . . . It is to be expected that the bulk of official development assistance will continue to be channeled to the poorest developing countries, and only to a very limited extent to the major borrowing countries.

Among official lending sources, the Fund probably is the only institution that can fairly quickly provide additional, large-scale balance-of-payments assistance to the major borrowing countries through direct borrowings from the surplus countries. After the first oil price shock such borrowing took the form of two IMF Oil Facilities, totaling $8 billion. These facilities have now expired and drawings from them are being repaid. In view of the similarity of the current situation with that of the mid-1970s, it would be desirable for OPEC surplus countries to funnel significant amounts either through the Fund's Special Financing Facility or through a new oil facility.

THE NEED FOR BALANCED ADJUSTMENT

Even with some expansion of official lending, the bulk of the financing of the deficits will still have to be done by the credit markets. For the markets to continue to play their important role, there will have to be (as in the mid-1970s) the prospect of adequate adjustment to the new international payments imbalance. Therefore, a policy strategy has to emerge that will assure a significant narrowing of this imbalance. The desired strategy would consist of three elements: continued willingness of OPEC members to expand the spending of their oil revenues, stronger energy policies in oil importing countries to permit their economic growth to resume without adding to the demand for OPEC oil, and readiness on the part of the major industrial countries to run large current account deficits and thus share the burden of the OPEC surplus.

Despite the current pessimism, the OPEC surplus could be reduced substantially beyond 1981. True, the exceptionally high import growth rates of the mid-1970s are not likely to be repeated, if only because OPEC is now starting from a much higher level of expenditure than the last time: more than $150 billion in goods and services imports last year versus only $30 billion in 1973. The reassessment of development plans that has recently been taking place in most OPEC countries and the realization of the adverse social and inflationary effects of too rapid development are also likely to contain the growth rate of spending. Nevertheless, pressures to spend their rising oil revenues are likely to continue, given the projects already underway, the need to spread the wealth, and the wish of most of them to diversity their economies and develop viable non-oil sectors for the period when the oil runs out. Thus, an *average* rate of growth in OPEC import volume on the order of 8%–10% per annum would seem plausible. Such a growth rate would go a long way toward reducing the present OPEC imbalance, but it will not be sufficient if oil prices keep rising rapidly in real terms.

A significant decline in the OPEC surplus, even in a stable political environment, will also require energy adjustments on the part of the industrial countries. The economic recovery of 1976 brought about an increase in industrial countries' oil consumption and imports, and it was only because of the steady rise in non-OPEC production that demand for OPEC oil remained fairly flat and oil prices continued to decline in real terms. This time, similar increases in oil supplies can no longer be assumed. The annual additions to non-OPEC supply are likely to be progressively smaller during 1981–85, while the willingness of OPEC members to meet incremental demand for their oil is even less now than it was during the 1970s. Statements on future production policies and growing oil consumption in OPEC countries suggest that OPEC oil exports may not again exceed the peak of 1979.

In the future macroeconomic policies of industrial countries will have to be tied more consciously with energy policies to contain demand for oil imports. The challenge is to achieve a structural change in the relationship of economic growth to oil import demand. Since the development of new oil or alternative energy sources can make little contribution in the next five years, whatever their longer-run benefit, it becomes increasingly clear that conservation provides the only feasible near-term relief. While all industrial as well as developing countries can make progress in this area, the major source of future improvement should be the United States, where, with the exception of the industrial sector, relatively little has been done until recently.

Conservation by government regulation can be helpful, but it places a severe burden on administrative competence. Conservation on the scale needed requires strong economic incentives, and realistic energy pricing policies in oil-importing countries should be the main means of fostering such conservation.

Industrial countries have been far from steadfast or consistent in recent years in this respect. . . . There are difficulties in raising energy taxes, or even in achieving full pass-through of world oil prices to the consumer. A major obstacle to an aggressive increase in final consumer energy prices is the apparent conflict with anti-inflation policy. In most countries higher consumer or industrial oil prices are eventually reflected in cost-of-living indices and, through various linkages, in wages and benefits. A balanced approach to achieving higher *relative* prices to energy users should therefore trade off higher taxes on oil for reductions in other *indirect* taxes, notably consumer sales taxes and taxes on business in general, to neutralize the effect on the cost-of-living indices.

Since the United States has no federal value-added or general sales tax, a well-designed trade-off for higher gasoline taxes requires the cooperation of state authorities. These political difficulties notwithstanding, failure of government initiative in this direction could have serious consequences. . . . If conservation cannot be effected by choice, whether through regulation or taxation, the alternative is likely to be curtailment of oil demand through successive OPEC oil price explosions, sluggish economic growth, and even worse inflation.

Reducing the OPEC surplus over the next few years by itself is not sufficient to ensure the confidence of the credit markets. Progress is also needed to secure a balanced distribution of the corresponding deficit among the oil importing countries, avoiding the mistakes of the post-1973 period. This time, the major borrowing countries, especially the non-oil LDCs, cannot escape some lowering of their growth rates, even assuming continued progress in economizing imports.

Moreover, the industrial countries must recognize the dangers of competitive restriction of domestic activity, whose major effect is to shuffle payments deficits from one oil-importing country to another. While large OPEC surpluses persist, the current-account deficit strain on oil-importing countries should be assumed by the world's strongest economies such as the United States, Germany, Japan, France, and Switzerland. It is no longer realistic to expect the United States to shoulder a disproportionate share of the deficit counterpart to the OPEC surplus. That situation was viable for a time in 1977, but its persistence contributed significantly to the 1978 dollar crisis. Exchange markets would be even less tolerant this time of such a maldistribution of current account balances.

Complicating the prospects for sustainable and balanced adjustment of industrial-country payments positions is the placement of the OPEC financial surplus. The priority today should be to channel this more evenly into Germany, Japan, and other oil importing countries to better assure the financing of appropriate current account deficits. Official action should not encourage disproportionate investment of the OPEC surplus in the United States. Unhappily, this is exactly what a successful IMF Substitution Account would do. It is envisaged that the account's assets would be held in U.S. government obligations, but this would merely aggravate the burden on U.S. intermediaries to onlend funds to deficit countries. In the context of present concerns for the smooth working of the adjustment process, the IMF substitution scheme is misdirected.

A more encouraging approach is now evident in the evolving attitudes of the new reserve countries—such as Germany, Japan, and Switzerland—toward the reserve currency function that market developments have thrust upon them. Negativism on the part of the central banks and governments has receded. Some first steps have been taken in recent weeks to strengthen their currencies' reserve function through offerings of official securities and acceptance by the central banks of deposits from OPEC and other official investors. These instruments provide a flexible tool for stabilizing exchange markets and provide suitable opportunities for diversification of OPEC portfolios, also demonstrating in practical terms that the world's multiple-currency reserve system is more manageable than some academic and official analyses have implied.

SUMMING UP

The payments imbalances facing the major countries in the next several years pose a challenge to the capacity of international markets to deliver the necessary new financing. The preponderant role of commercial banks in the recycling effort entails continued rapid growth in their international portfolios. Because adjustment to the second oil shock begins with international indebtedness already high by traditional standards, the financing of the new imbalances—and the refinancing of existing obligations as they mature—implies considerable risk to the world's financial system.

To lessen this risk, more balanced and speedy balance-of-payments adjustment should occur this time than was the case following the 1973 oil shock. This will undoubtedly require some short-term sacrifice of economic growth objectives, in both industrial and developing countries, for the sake of curbing inflation and making a determined start on measures of structural adjustment. Without such adjustment there is little hope of maintaining financial market confidence.

Tangible contributions are required of all the principal actors: from the developing countries, the recognition that sustainable growth in the early 1980s may be less than desired and should be of a less import-intensive character than hitherto, especially in energy use; from the OPEC countries, a greater willingness to accept portfolio risk, vigorous but carefully considered development programs, and a sense of international responsibility in setting oil production targets; from the industrial countries, a strong commitment to energy conservation and the avoidance of short-sighted shuffling of current account deficits among themselves or at the expense of the developing countries; from the international agencies, a greater flexibility in lending procedures and purposes; from the commercial banks and the supervisory authorities, a reasoned approach to questions of country risk.

First readings of the international response to last year's oil shock are modestly encouraging. A number of developing countries have moved swiftly to contain current account deficits within bounds that can be reasonably financed. OPEC import spending appears to be on the rise again. The industrial countries, particularly the United States, show clearer awareness of the energy problem and are beginning to take more practical conservation measures. Monetary policies have shifted to a more forceful anti-inflationary stance. Germany and other major countries are adopting a more responsible role in sharing the OECD current account deficit, which should limit exchange market tensions and improve financial market confidence. . . .

It cannot be emphasized too strongly that the road to an orderly world adjustment to the recent oil shock lies primarily through sound policies on the part of the industrial countries. . . . Neglect of energy conservation and any return of complacency in industrial countries risks another OPEC price explosion and accelerating inflation in the years ahead. The time is ripe to set the world on a better course. Understandably the election schedule over the coming year in several of the major countries tempts policy makers to procrastinate. This, the world cannot afford.

33

Some Questions and Brief Answers About the Eurodollar Market

John R. Karlik

The Eurodollar market is perhaps well understood only by the practitioners, employed by banks and other financial institutions, who deal in it as their chosen way of making a living. Academic economists disagree about how the market functions and what is its real economic impact. To the uninitiated, the Eurodollar market seems to be a financial black box into which goes American money and from which comes credit for foreigners. Persons attempting to understand this phenomenon frequently pose a set of fundamental and important questions about what the market is and how it operates. Since these questions arise repeatedly, it seems appropriate to attempt to provide some brief answers for interested Members of Congress and other readers. The questions discussed are the following:

1. What is a Eurodollar deposit?
2. How did the Eurodollar market originate, what factors have been responsible for its growth, and what is its current size?
3. How does the Eurodollar market operate?
4. Does the Eurodollar market create money?

From John R. Karlik, *Some Questions and Brief Answers About the Eurodollar Market*, a Staff Study prepared for the use of the Joint Economic Committee, Congress of the United States (Washington, D.C.: U.S. Government Printing Office, February 7, 1977). Some tables omitted. John R. Karlik is a Senior Economist of the Joint Economic Committee, U.S. Congress

5. What is the impact of the Eurodollar market on the U.S. balance of payments?
6. What is the impact of the Eurodollar market on the foreign exchange value of the dollar?
7. Is the Eurodollar market an engine of inflation?
8. Is a cumulative credit collapse likely?
9. Does the operation of the Eurodollar market undermine the implementation of monetary policy in the United States?
10. Can the Eurodollar market be regulated? Is regulation desirable?

1. WHAT IS A EURODOLLAR DEPOSIT?

A Eurodollar deposit is a dollar deposit in a bank outside the United States. The depositors may be, for example, foreign manufacturers who have exported goods to the United States and obtained payment in dollars. Or they may be American residents who have withdrawn funds from their own accounts in the United States and placed them in a foreign bank, generally but not always to obtain a higher interest return than is available in the United States on savings account deposits, the purchase of certificates of deposit, Treasury bills, commercial paper, or the like.

Except for an insignificant amount, dollar deposits in foreign banks are not demand deposit liabilities of those banks. They are deposits for a specified time period and bearing a stated yield. The period of deposit may be for as short a time as overnight. But Eurodollars are typically not an immediate payments medium; one cannot generally write a check against a Eurodollar account. To be used to make payments a Eurodollar account must usually first be converted into a deposit with a bank located in the United States; it must become a normal dollar demand deposit. Investing in a Eurodollar account is therefore more like placing funds in a savings account or buying a certificate of deposit than like opening a checking account.

Occasionally reference is made to foreign currency deposits with European banks in currencies other than dollars. Such Eurocurrency deposits are placed with banks outside the nation issuing the currency. For example, an account in a German bank denominated in Swiss francs is a Eurocurrency deposit.

2. HOW DID THE EURODOLLAR MARKET ORIGINATE, WHAT FACTORS HAVE BEEN RESPONSIBLE FOR ITS GROWTH, AND WHAT IS ITS CURRENT SIZE?

The amount of credits extended through banks operating in the expanded Eurocurrency market, which now includes not only dollars but also sterling, German marks, Swiss francs, and other currencies and which encompasses Canada, Japan, Hong Kong, Singapore, and the Caribbean, as well as Europe, has grown from about $7 billion in 1963 to approximately $250 billion at the end of 1975. A deposit denominated in other than the domestic currency in a bank anywhere in the world is now loosely referred to as a Eurocurrency deposit.

The motivation underlying the inception of the Eurodollar market was the desire to avoid regulation, either regulations already in effect or additional restrictions that depositors feared might be imposed.

Among the first depositors of dollars in European banks were the Russians. Soviet enterprises were earning dollars both by selling gold and by exporting to the United States and to other countries. They feared that accounts opened in U.S. banks might be attached by Americans who had claims against the Soviet Government. The preferred alternative, therefore, was to place their dollar earnings in European banks. The 1958 abolition of most exchange controls in Europe permitted the growth of the Eurodollar market to accelerate. By the mid-1960's this market was a recognized force in European credit markets.

During the credit crunch of 1968 and 1969, U.S. commercial banks relied on the Eurodollar market to escape the effects of the interest rate ceiling imposed by the Federal Reserve under Regulation Q. The larger American banks directed their foreign branches to bid for dollars by offering yields above the level permitted in the United States. The head offices then borrowed heavily from their overseas branches. A portion of the new deposits attracted by overseas branches during this period apparently represented funds transferred out of the United States by Americans. Additional deposits were also attracted from foreigners, including foreign central banks. In October 1969 the Federal Reserve imposed a stiff reserve requirement on head office borrowings from abroad. The incentive for American banks to obtain funds overseas was further reduced in June 1973 when large denomination certificates of deposit were exempted from Regulation Q limitations on maximum interest yields.

Obviously a credit market does not grow to the present size of the Eurocurrency market purely on the basis of avoiding government regulations and reserve requirements. Indeed, the tacit approval and even the assistance of governments in the main Eurocurrency centers is required. Some central banks—both European and others—have deposited a portion of their dollar reserves in European commercial banks rather than investing in, say, U.S. Treasury bills. Banks in London and other financial centers have found accepting deposits in dollars and other foreign currencies and extending loans in these currencies to be profitable because no reserves are required against such deposit liabilities and because this business could be added to their normal functions at modest cost. The extra expense is small because these banks were already engaged in a large volume of international transactions and had well-established relationships with customers in a variety of countries. Most Eurocurrency transactions are for large amounts and can be handled at wholesale rates. European banks can for all these reasons offer somewhat higher deposit yields and lower loan charges than American banks and still make an acceptable profit. Depositors and borrowers appreciate this configuration, for obvious reasons.

The Eurocurrency markets, the largest of which is the Eurodollar market, have also had an important positive impact on economic activity in the countries where they have evolved. These markets constitute a highly efficient system for allocating credit among lenders and borrowers. They have facilitated higher levels of domestic and international commerce than would have been likely in their absence. The removal in 1958 of most European restrictions on the conversion of foreign exchange and the rapid growth of international trade in the 1960s, a large proportion of which was financed in dollars, created a need for dollar loan and deposit services in Europe during normal working hours. Banks understandably strove to satisfy this demand and finance additional commerce. The resulting gain in output and employment is the chief real economic benefit produced by the banks and other institutions that have jointly constructed the Eurocurrency financial network.

3. HOW DOES THE EURODOLLAR MARKET OPERATE?

The Eurodollar and other Eurocurrency markets are largely interbank markets. When a European bank accepts a dollar deposit, it naturally attempts to lend the funds at a higher interest rate than the yield it is paying to the depositor. In some cases the borrower will be the ultimate user of the funds, such as a European importer purchasing merchandise in the United States. In many instances, however, an individual or corporate borrower will not be immediately on tap as an acceptable investment opportunity for the bank. In this event, the bank will place the dollars, most likely for a short period, with another bank that is seeking funds. Similarly, if a worthy ultimate borrower appears when a European bank does not have surplus dollars to invest, it may temporarily borrow in the interbank market in preference to rejecting the customer.

Because of the volume of interbank transactions and the consequent double counting of available dollar credits that can easily result, estimates of the size of the Eurodollar market must be used cautiously. The chief source of data on Eurocurrency markets is the Bank for International Settlements (BIS) located in Basle, Switzerland. The BIS is the one surviving institutional remnant of the League of Nations. Eight European central banks, those of Belgium, France, Germany, Italy, The Netherlands, Sweden, Switzerland, and the United Kingdom, are the majority stockholders. In publishing Eurocurrency market data, the BIS attempts to eliminate double counting among the eight member countries of available Eurocurrency credit. The totals cited above have been deflated in an effort to eliminate the effects of redepositing within the eight BIS-reporting countries. However, since substantial Eurocurrency markets have now been established in Canada, the Caribbean, Japan, Hong Kong, Singapore, and the Middle East, the totals may still be inflated.

Of the approximately $250 billion of Eurocurrency credits granted during 1975, $205 billion were extended by banks in the eight BIS-reporting countries.[1] The bulk of these Eurocurrency loans in the eight countries were to banks; only $61 billion were to nonbank residents and foreigners. The great difference between total credits extended and the portion granted to nonbank users illustrates the extent to which the Eurocurrencey market is in fact an interbank market.

4. DOES THE EURODOLLAR MARKET CREATE MONEY?

Eurodollar deposits, as noted above, are not money in a strictly defined sense; they are time rather than demand deposits and cannot be drawn upon to make payments. However, if the definition of money is expanded from cash and demand deposits to include time deposits (i.e., from M_1 to M_2), should Eurodollar and other Eurocurrency accounts be included in this expanded measure of liquidity? Yes. Furthermore, if one adopts this expanded definition of the money supply, creation of a Eurodollar deposit will lead under certain circumstances to an equivalent increase in the global stock of liquidity. How does this consequence come about?

Suppose an American individual or corporation has a quantity of funds invested in a certificate of deposit or time deposit with a New York bank and decides to invest these funds in the Eurodollar market instead.[2] The certificate of deposit or time deposit must first be transformed into a demand deposit.[3] The individual or corporate treasurer then writes a check on his demand deposit in the New York bank and makes it payable to a European bank. At that point, the European bank has a demand deposit claim on a New York bank, and the individual or corporation has a time deposit with a European rather than an American bank.

The outcome of this series of transactions is that M_2 in the United States is unchanged but is increased in Europe by the amount of the Eurodollar deposit. The broadly defined global money supply has increased by this amount, since deposits by foreigners, including banks, are considered part of the U.S. money supply. But at this stage, the supply of credit to nonbanks has not changed.

If the European bank initially accepting the deposit relends it to another European bank, use of credit by the nonbanking sector is still not increased. This statement remains valid regardless of how many times the funds are redeposited among banks. Only when the funds are finally loaned to an ultimate nonbank user is the total quantity of credit available to support economic activity increased.

If the user is either a foreigner making payments to Americans or an American other than a bank, the story ends with the conclusion that the total amount of liquidity available globally is expanded by the amount of the Eurodollar deposit. If the user is an American bank, there is no increase in the total volume of credit available to the nonbanking sector of any other economy.

As another possibility, if the user is a foreigner who converts the dollars into his own currency, and if his central bank buys the dollars and redeposits them in a European commercial bank, another round of dollar credit expansion may occur. Similarly, if the foreign user pays the dollars to another foreigner and the recipient—depending on the yields available in New York and Europe—redeposits the dollars in a foreign bank, a second real economic transaction may then be financed.

Thus, an initial dollar deposit in a European bank can lead to a variety of outcomes. The amount of additional liquidity provided to nonbanks may be zero, equivalent to the deposit, or some multiple of the deposit.

This uncertainty about who may be the borrower of dollars from a European commercial bank and how these funds will be employed raises the question of the size of the "Eurocurrency multiplier." In other words, if a dollar sum is deposited in a European bank, will a multiple credit expansion occur? If so, what is the average amount of the multiple? Most importantly, what is the ultimate economic significance of the initial transfer?

Economists studying the Eurodollar market generally fall into either of two groups in responding to these questions. One group views the Eurodollar market as the product of a fractional reserve banking system that creates dollar credits. The reserves of Eurobanks, according to this conception, are checking account deposits in commercial banks located in the United States. Since Eurobanks are not required to hold minimal reserves as a fixed proportion of their dollar liabilities, one might expect that, by comparison with the ratio of reserves held in the United States against time deposits, Eurobanks would maintain a lower fraction of reserves. Most attempts to measure the ratio of "reserves" that Eurobanks hold voluntarily to liabilities indeed show a low proportion. The change in total Eurodollar balances implied by an initial change in "reserves"—if the fractional reserve banking analogy is accepted—is therefore quite high.

The other school of economists views the Eurobanks as financial intermediaries that do not create money but shunt available credit from lenders with excess liquidity to borrowers short of funds. These analysts emphasize the "leakages" to which Eurobanks are exposed. There is little reason, they say, to expect that the dollars a borrower has obtained from a European bank and subsequently paid to a third party will necessarily be put back into the Eurodollar market. Therefore, each Eurobank must, according to this view, maintain a more-or-less balanced term structure of dollar claims and liabilities. Furthermore, they maintain, Eurobanks may prefer to safeguard their ability to meet withdrawals by arranging standby lines of credit with U.S. banks, rather than by maintaining checking account balances, which earn no interest. Thus, according to this second school of thought, the low apparent reserve ratios of Eurobanks do not necessarily indicate that the market is a powerful machine for generating additional liquidity.

An indication of the extent to which the Eurodollar market creates money is the size of loans to nonbank borrowers as compared with all loans. At the end of 1975, banks in the eight countries reporting to the BIS indicated that out of dollar loans totaling $190 billion, only $41 billion were to nonbank borrowers. Of loans denominated in other currencies totaling the equivalent of $68 billion, $20 billion were to nonbanks. These totals do not include the activities of the Eurocurrency markets located in the Caribbean and the Far East, but they do encompass the bulk of Eurocurrency credit creation.

5. WHAT IS THE IMPACT OF THE EURODOLLAR MARKET ON THE U.S. BALANCE OF PAYMENTS?

It is sometimes maintained that growth of the Eurodollar market is dependent upon net capital outflows from the United States or upon U.S. payments deficits. In the example discussed above, an American resident transferred a sum of dollars from an account with a New York bank to an account with a European bank. This action produces a capital outflow from the United States. But as is also evident in the above example, the full story extends far beyond the initial transaction. Particularly if the European bank receiving the funds is the branch of an American institution, the head office may borrow the dollars back from its branch. In this case, a subsequent capital inflow offsets the initial outflow, and there is no net transfer of funds internationally.

On the other hand, if the foreign bank receiving the dollars sells them to the central bank in exchange for the domestic currency, U.S. liabilities to foreign official institutions increase, and a U.S. official settlements deficit will be expanded (or a surplus diminished) by the amount of the transaction. If the foreign central bank then invests the dollars in U.S. Treasury bills, the impact on the U.S. official settlements balance is not further changed. Thus, while an initial transfer of dollars out of the United States arising from a trade, services or capital transaction, or the purchase of dollars in the exchange market with foreign currency is a requisite for the establishment or enlargement of a Eurodollar balance, the ultimate consequences of this action on the U.S. balance of payments are by no means clear. . . .

Financial markets in New York and Europe are competitors. The rate of growth of the Eurodollar market has been determined, more than anything else, by the relative attractiveness of investing short-term either in New York or in Europe and by the relative availability and cost of funds in the two areas. The particularly rapid growth of the Eurodollar market in 1968 and 1969 resulted from a credit crunch in the United States and Regulation Q ceilings on the interest rates that American banks could offer. The reaction of American banks to this combination of factors was to bid for deposits through their European branches. Although the widespread adoption of floating exchange rates brought about a sharp decrease in the U.S. payments deficit during 1973, this development did not inhibit the market's growth. In 1974, when the market expanded by one-third, the chief motivating factors were apparently the desires of oil producing countries to invest their expanded earnings in highly liquid bank deposits and the needs of both industrial and developing countries to finance high-cost oil imports. The same factors remained important in 1975.

To conclude, a transfer of dollars from the United States and into a European or other foreign bank cannot be presumed to produce a U.S. payments deficit of even approximately the same magnitude. The growth of the Eurodollar market is not linked with U.S. payments deficits in any readily identifiable way.

6. WHAT IS THE IMPACT OF THE EURODOLLAR MARKET ON THE FOREIGN EXCHANGE VALUE OF THE DOLLAR?

The foreign exchange value of the dollar tends to fall when Americans need to make increased payments to foreigners or when individuals desire to hold additional assets valued in other currencies. Conversely, the external value of the dollar tends to rise when foreigners' payments to Americans increase or when individuals desire to hold more dollar assets. The Eurodollar market has established convenient mechanisms for the temporary investment of excess dollar balances. It also offers another source of dollar loans for periods ranging from overnight to several years. In general, the market has made the dollar more useful and desirable relative to other currencies. Therefore, its net effect has probably been to increase the value of the dollar somewhat in comparison with other currencies.

From time to time, however, transactions have occurred in the Eurodollar market that have had a depressing impact on the external value of the dollar. Speculators believing that a particular foreign currency was likely to increase in value have occasionally drawn on Eurodollar credit lines and sold borrowed dollars to buy another currency. They hoped to realize profits by repaying the dollar loans after the expected upward revaluation of other currency.

If the anticipated exchange rate change indeed occurred, repaying the loan with interest consumed most but not all of the dollars obtained from converting the foreign currency balance at its new higher value. A margin constituting the profit remained. If the expected exchange rate change did not occur, speculators losses were limited to the cost of interest on the loan and the cost of two currency conversions. The shift in 1973 from fixed to flexible exchange rates eliminated many of the opportunities for speculative gain that had previously existed. The large international transfers of liquid capital that had resulted from this incentive have also largely disappeared.

Because the Eurodollar market has grown to constitute a major international financial market, the transfer of a dollar balance out of the United States can no longer be presumed to have an impact on the exchange value of the dollar. An international capital flow will produce exchange rate repercussions only if there is an exchange market transaction. But because of the Eurodollar market, dollars can be transferred out of the United States and easily be invested abroad as dollars; they need not be converted into any other currency. Similarly, dollars moved into the United States need not have been acquired through a previous sale of foreign currencies. The growth of the Eurodollar market in the last decade has considerably enhanced the usefulness of the dollar as an international transaction or vehicle currency and has therefore probably increased foreigners' desired dollar holdings. The foreign exchange value of the dollar is most likely a bit higher than it would have been in the absence of a Eurodollar market.

7. IS THE EURODOLLAR MARKET AN ENGINE OF INFLATION?

Would inflation rates experienced during recent years have been substantially lower if there had been no Eurodollar market? Of course, some inflation would have occurred anyway as a result of (a) increased prices for oil, food, and raw materials, as a consequence of (b) generally overstimulative monetary and fiscal policies in 1973 and 1974, and as an aftereffect of (c) dollar purchases by foreign central banks during the last throes of the fixed exchange rate system in 1971 and 1972. Central bank dollar purchases had the effect of increasing commercial bank reserves and money supplies in some countries.

If all these other factors are taken into consideration, has there been an additional increment of inflation that can be attributed to the operation of the Eurodollar and other Eurocurrency markets? (When considering the impact of these financial markets on prices and total economic activity, focusing on only the dollar component would omit an important segment). An answer to this question can be inferred from the data presented in Table 1. The first column in this table gives the level of M_2 in the eight European countries reporting to the Bank for International Settlements at the end of each calendar year from 1970 through 1975. It is appropriate to use M_2, the domestic money supply in these countries defined to include not only currency and demand deposits but also time deposits and certificates of deposit, as a basis for comparison because Eurocurrency deposits are also made for a specified time period. The second column gives for the same years the amount of Eurocurrency claims against nonbank residents of the eight BIS-reporting countries. . . .

If the Eurocurrency market is an engine of inflation, it must create money in excessive amounts in addition to the volume of credit created by domestic banking systems. But examination of the data presented in Table 1 shows that in most recent years the Eurocurrency market has usually contributed only marginally, and at most modestly, to the supply of credit available in Europe.

In 1971, M_2 grew in the eight BIS-reporting countries by nearly $80 billion, and in 1972 by a slightly greater amount. Yet in 1972 Eurocurrency claims against nonbank residents of the eight countries grew merely $1 billion, and on December 31, 1972, the total amount of these claims was

TABLE 1

Data Provided by Banks in the 8 BIS-Reporting Countries (In billions of dollars)

	M_2	Eurocurrency claims against nonbank residents
Level at the end of:		
1970	348.7	(¹)
1971	428.1	7.6
1972	511.2	8.6
1973	640.3	14.0
1974	773.5	23.7
1975	831.8	24.0
Change during:		
1971	79.4	(¹)
1972	83.1	1.0
1973	129.1	5.4
1974	133.2	9.7
1975	58.3	.3

¹Not available.

Sources: "International Financial Statistics" and the "Forty-Sixth Annual Report of the Bank for International Settlements."

only $8.6 billion, as contrasted with an M_2 of over $500 billion. M_2 expanded during the next 3 years by $129 billion, by $133 billion, and by $58 billion respectively. In comparison, from 1973 through 1975 Eurocurrency claims against residents expanded by $5 billion, by $10 billion, and by less than $1 billion respectively. In 1974 the Eurocurrency market made its largest percentage contribution to the supply of credit in Europe; that year the expansion of Eurocurrency claims against nonbank residents was the equivalent of 7.3 percent of the growth of M_2. . . . Therefore, even if one were to accept the thesis that excessive monetary expansion were an important cause of inflation, Eurocurrency markets hardly appear to be a major source of that expansion.

When appraising the inflationary impact of Eurocurrency markets, one should keep two additional considerations in mind.

First, not all credit generated by the Eurocurrency market is necessarily additional credit. In at least some years, central banks in Europe would probably have induced commercial banks to create more liquidity than they actually did had the Eurocurrency market never come into being.

Second, on the other side of the ledger, the Eurocurrency market should be recognized as having helped combat recession during periods when demands for credit were unusually strong. Such a period was 1974, the year following the quadrupling of oil prices.

The Eurocurrency market provided a vital service in accepting large deposits from oil producing countries and lending the funds to hard pressed oil importing nations. Developing countries contending with increased energy and food costs and, subsequently, with a drop in earnings for their own commodity exports, have been especially aided by credits obtained in the Eurodollar market. Although the problems of these nations are by no means solved and may become more serious, their transitional pains following the abrupt international price changes of recent years would have been far more severe without the financial cushion provided through the Eurocurrency market.

No authoritative summary measure can be offered of the inflationary costs versus the real benefits of credit creation in the Eurocurrency market. Part of the reason that costs and benefits cannot be simply set off against one another is that they have been experienced by different individuals in widely separated countries and with vastly divergent incomes. But in the record of the Eurocurrency market over the past five years, there is scant evidence to support an assertion that it has served as an engine of inflation.

Indeed, if there is a monetary engine of inflation in Europe, it is more likely to be discovered in the operation of domestic banking systems than in the Eurocurrency markets. From 1971 through 1974, M_2 in the eight BIS-reporting countries grew each year by nearly 20 percent or more.

8. IS A CUMULATIVE CREDIT COLLAPSE LIKELY?

The Eurodollar market, as explained above, operates efficiently because the banks and other financial institutions participating in it can invest or obtain funds easily via the market for periods of from one day to over a year. Interbank transactions constitute the bulk of the volume in the market, although it is the initial depositors and final borrowers who experience its real economic consequences. Because this market, like the foreign exchange market, operates on verbal commitments backed by mutual trust, and because fluid interbank operations are essential to efficient operation, the Eurodollar market would appear to be particularly vulnerable to the failure of even a modest-sized institution.

During the 6 or 9 months following the quadrupling of oil prices in the fall of 1973, many observers feared that the Eurodollar market would not be able to invest profitably the volume of liquid assets that would most likely be deposited by oil producing countries. The worriers went on to speculate that even if the institutions in the market somehow managed to accept and disburse the funds, an economic collapse in a European country or a major default by a developing nation that had borrowed heavily would provoke a financial crisis that gathered strength like an avalanche.

These worst fears have not been borne out for at least two reasons. First, when banks operating in the Eurodollar market began to run out of profitable opportunities for short-term investment of deposits subject to quick withdrawal, they lowered their deposit rates and announced their reluctance to accept additional large deposits. Second, as a consequence of both self-discipline and chiding by various central banks—notably the Bank of England—Eurodollar banks have tightened their lending requirements. At present there seems to be no imminent danger of a crisis, but numerous substantial loans to developing country borrowers remain to be repaid or refinanced.

Officials have taken two steps to help bolster the stability of the Eurodollar market and to curb excessive credit creation and the risk of a crisis.

First, the central banks of the major industrial countries agreed in the Spring of 1971 to limit the extent to which additions to their own dollar reserves are redeposited in the market. If redepositing became standard procedure, the increase in the money supplies of the nations encompassing the market could theoretically be limitless. Therefore, controlling the extent of redepositing is a step toward governing the credit-creating impact of the market.

Second, the central banks of the major industrial countries agreed in 1974 that in the event of a crisis, each will stand behind its own banks and the overseas branches of domestic banks to keep the crisis from spreading.

The precise terms of this mutual acceptance of responsibilities have not been spelled out, but the principle seems clear. For example, Federal Reserve Board member Henry C. Wallich said in testimony before the Senate Permanent Investigations Sub-committee in October 1974:

> The Federal Reserve is prepared, as a lender of last resort, to advance sufficient funds, suitably collateralized, to assure the continued operation of any solvent and soundly managed member bank which may be experiencing temporary liquidity difficulties associated with the abrupt withdrawal of petrodollar—or any other—deposits.

This commitment to back "any solvent and soundly managed member bank" extends to overseas branches as well.

Central bankers of the major industrial nations meeting in Basle, Switzerland, issued the following statement on September 9, 1974:

> The Governors also had an exchange of views on the problem of the lender of last resort in the Euromarkets. They recognized that it would not be practical to lay down in advance detailed rules and procedures for the provision of temporary liquidity. But they were satisfied that means are available for that purpose and will be used if and when necessary.

9. DOES THE OPERATION OF THE EURODOLLAR MARKET UNDERMINE THE IMPLEMENTATION OF MONETARY POLICY IN THE UNITED STATES?

In considering the impact of the Eurodollar market on the implementation of monetary policy in the United States, one must distinguish between recent developments in international financial institutions that merely make life more complicated for Federal Reserve authorities and other changes that could prevent or counteract the working of monetary policy in the United States. Some observers might conclude that the Eurodollar market has made life only a little more complex for American money managers, while others, at the opposite end of the spectrum, would argue that the existence of the Eurodollar market as an alternative source of credit can at critical times totally vitiate the intent of Federal Reserve policy. . . .

The record of policy actions by U.S. monetary authorities is an important indication of whether they perceive that international capital flows frustrate the implementation of domestic monetary policy. Such flows are certainly a complicating factor. But the progressive [1970s] reduction of reserve requirements [on the borrowings of domestic offices of U.S. banks from their foreign branches and from foreign banks] and the elimination of constraints on capital outflows suggests that in the minds of the authorities, the benefits of open money and exchange markets outweigh the disadvantages of the resulting complications. In any event, if serious problems did arise at some time, nothing prevents the authorities from introducing controls over international capital flows and exchange transactions.

10. CAN THE EURODOLLAR MARKET BE REGULATED?
IS REGULATION DESIRABLE?

Numerous individuals have from time to time urged that the Eurodollar market be regulated to limit credit creation or to reduce the risk of a credit collapse. Regulation can be discussed from two perspectives—feasibility and desirability. While somewhat greater regulation might be desirable, to date the inflationary consequences of excess credit creation have not been sufficiently demonstrable and the risk of an avalanching credit collapse has not been sufficiently evident to prompt monetary authorities to achieve the high degree of cooperation that would be necessary to regulate the Eurodollar market effectively. Even the eight central bank members of the Bank for International Settlements have not been able to agree on mechanisms for controlling the growth of the Eurodollar market or on standards of credit worthiness to be applied to lenders. At the present time, therefore, only the most modest degree of regulation seems possible.

Another factor severely limits the feasibility of any efforts that might be undertaken to regulate the Eurodollar market. In recent years the market has spread rapidly from its origins in the City of London and the financial centers of continental Europe to the Caribbean, the Mideast, Singapore, Hong Kong, and Tokyo. If burdensome regulations were imposed in the existing centers of Eurocurrency activity, most of the market's functions might well be transferred to some other area, particularly to a bastion of free enterprise. In the event of such a relocation, the profits and the jobs derived from the market's activities would move also. Reluctance to forgo these benefits, particularly in London, have deterred authorities from imposing as comprehensive regulations as they otherwise might have.

Should the evident difficulty of regulating the Eurodollar market be a source of concern? How much concern, since the possibility of a serious crisis can never be entirely excluded? Following the 1973 increase in oil prices, the Eurodollar market has gone through at least two distinct periods of stress. First, there was the danger—discussed above—that Eurocurrency banks would not be able to accommodate the huge volume of deposits from oil producing countries and lend these funds out at profitable rates of return. The banks did accept a major increase in deposit liabilities. But they eventually lowered their interest rates to discourage further acquisitions of massive short-term deposits and gradually tightened their lending criteria. Second, a few banks—most notably Franklin National and Herstatt—speculating in the foreign exchange market, not in the Eurocurrency markets, suffered severe losses. These events brought into question the quality of bank management and their ability to control the exposure of their institutions. For a subsequent period all new deposits were placed only with the largest and most respected institutions, and some funds were withdrawn from smaller banks. The announcement of central banks' commitment to stand behind their own national banks and these banks' overseas branches helped reassure depositors.

A third time of stress is presently foreseen. Developing countries have borrowed heavily in the Eurodollar market to finance oil imports and to compensate for the loss of earnings resulting from the subsequent drop in export prices for many of their commodities. Some of these nations are approaching the limits of their borrowing and loan servicing capabilities. How well Eurocurrency banks would be able to withstand defaults on outstanding loans to some developing countries or the rescheduling under duress of loan repayments is the subject of present concerns.

The real economic adjustments to the increased prices of oil, bauxite, and perhaps other commodities will continue. Some industrial and developing countries will be able to continue borrowing in the Eurocurrency markets to help lengthen the period during which real adjustment will occur and so mitigate the pain of that transition. In others, the bite has begun to take hold, and the need to curtail some incomes and transfer resources is imperative. However, the adjustments need not and will not occur everywhere simultaneously. Exporters in industrial countries are benefiting from growing sales to oil producing nations. Some of these industrial exporting countries will have excess funds to deposit in U.S. and Euro banks. Oil producers will also continue to make deposits. Banks operating in the Eurocurrency markets will most likely be able to adjust to strains of future demands as flexibly and as successfully as they have in the recent past.

All participating financial institutions recognize that the maintenance of stability in the Eurocurrency markets is in their own best interest. The issue is whether competitive instincts among institutions can be sufficiently curbed through self-discipline to preserve the soundness of the entire structure.

CONCLUSION

The Eurodollar market, like virtually all modern economic institutions, is a mixed blessing. It has produced important benefits in terms of helping to expand international trade, to stimulate economic growth, and most recently to distribute the excess earnings of oil producers among consumers needing credit to finance their imports. On the other hand, it may have raised rates of inflation somewhat. It has generated substantial business for the countries in which it is located—most of all for banks in the City of London. The financial institutions and individuals operating in the market can and will elude extensive regulation, if attempted. Unwillingness to forgo profits generated by the market and inability among central banks to agree on appropriate operating guidelines and on joint monetary policies have enabled the Eurodollar market to continue enjoying virtually no formal regulation. At the same time, the banks operating in the market know that the maintenance of stability is in their own best interest. Given the record of what is now a tested and mature market, there is reason to hope that—under the surveillance of concerned officials—the sometimes uneasy balance in the Eurocurrency markets is maintained so that lenders and borrowers can continue to enjoy its benefits.

BIBLIOGRAPHY

The literature on the Eurodollar market is extensive and difficult. Much of the difficulty results from conceptual muddiness and confusion about how the market operates. The following is a selected list, with brief comments, of readings that may be useful to individuals desiring to pursue further the issues raised in the preceding discussion.

Books

Stem, Carl H., Makin, John H., and Logue, Dennis E., editors. *Eurocurrencies and the International Monetary System.* Washington, D.C.: American Enterprise Institute for Public Policy Research, 1976.
  Contains selections by Thomas D. Willett on the inflationary impact of Eurocurrency growth (pp. 214–221), by Carl H. Stem on Eurocurrency credit expansion and regulation (pp. 283–332), and by John H. Makin on the "multiplier" versus the "new-view" analysis of how the Eurocurrency market operates.

Articles

Bell, Goeffrey L. "Credit Creation Through Eurodollars?" *The Banker*, vol. 114 (August 1964), pp. 494–502.
  A good discussion of whether the Eurodollar market creates money or merely redistributes existing liquidity.
Crockett, Andrew D. "The Eurocurrency Market: An Attempt to Clarify Some Basic Issues." *International Monetary Fund Staff Papers*, vol. 23, no. 2 (July 1976), pp. 375–386.
  Argues that the fractional reserve banking model is inappropriate for analysis of the Eurocurrency market.
Friedman, Milton. "The Eurodollar Market: Some First Principles." *Federal Reserve Bank of St. Louis Review*, vol. 53, no. 7 (July 1971), pp. 16–24.
  Basic presentation of the viewpoint that the Eurodollar market creates money in a way similar to a fractional reserve banking system.
de Grauwe, Paul. "The Development of the Eurocurrency Market." *Finance and Development*, vol. 12, no. 3 (September 1975), pp. 14–16.
  Historical review for readers unfamiliar with the Eurocurrency market.
Hewson, John and Sakakibara, Eisuke. "The Eurodollar Deposit Multiplier: A Portfolio Approach." *International Monetary Fund Staff Papers*, vol. 21, no. 2 (July 1974), pp. 307–328.
———. "The Eurodollar Deposit Multiplier: A Note." *International Monetary Fund Staff Papers*, vol. 22, no. 2 (July 1975), pp. 565–568.
  Contains estimates of the Eurodollar multiplier based on a portfolio rather than a fractional reserve model.

Klopstock, Fred H. "The International Money Market: Structure, Scope and Instruments." *Journal of Finance,* vol. 20, no. 2 (May 1965), pp. 182–208.

    A comprehensive discussion of international money markets, including how the Eurodollar market links national money markets.

———. "Money Creation in the Eurodollar Market—A Note on Professor Friedman's Views." *Federal Reserve Bank of New York Monthly Review,* vol. 52, no. 1 (January 1970), pp. 12–15.

    Disputes the Friedman view that the Eurodollar market is a source of multiple credit creation.

Lutz, F. A. "The Eurocurrency System." *Banca Nazionale del Lavoro Quarterly Review,* vol. 27, no. 110 (September 1974), pp. 183–200.

    Discussion of alternative conceptions of how Eurocurrency markets work and of whether they redistribute available credit or create money.

Mayer, Helmut, W. "Multiplier Effects and Credit Creation in the Eurodollar Market." *Banca Nazionale del Lavoro Quarterly Review,* vol. 24, no. 98 (September 1971), pp. 233–262.

    Argues that the credit creation mechanism of a self-contained commercial banking system cannot be applied to credit creation in the Eurodollar market.

———. "Some Analytical Aspects of the Intermediation of Oil Surpluses by the Eurocurrency Market." *Banca Nazionale del Lavoro Quarterly Review,* vol. 27, n. 110 (September 1974), pp. 201–226.

    Discusses the capability of the Eurocurrency market to help finance the payments deficit resulting from the increase in oil prices.

McClam, Warren D. "Credit Substitution and the Eurocurrency Market." *Banca Nazionale del Lavoro Quarterly Review,* vol. 25, no. 103 (December 1972), pp. 323–363.

    This discussion argues that in the absence of the Eurocurrency market, national central banks would have had to expand domestic money supplies more.

Meulendyke, Ann-Marie. *Causes and Consequences of the Eurodollar Expansion.* Research Paper No. 7503. Federal Reserve Bank of New York, March 1975.

    Analyzes the Eurodollar market as a fractional reserve banking system a la Friedman and measures the money creating potential of the market.

Sakakibara, Eisuke. "The Eurocurrency Market in Perspective." *Finance and Development,* vol. 12, no. 3 (September 1975), pp. 11–13, 41.

    Basic explanation of the Eurocurrency market not as a fractional reserve banking system, but as a mechanism for redistributing available credit.

Sweeney, Richard J. and Willett, Thomas D. "Eurodollars, Petrodollars, and World Liquidity and Inflation." *Journal of Monetary Economics,* forthcoming.

    Good evaluation of the extent to which money creation in the Eurocurrency market contributed to inflation.

Willms, Manfred. "Money Creation in the Eurocurrency Market." Unpublished paper DM/75/112, International Monetary Fund Research Department, December 17, 1975.

    Compares and evaluates the operation of the Eurocurrency market as a fractional reserve banking system using different definitions of reserves.

Notes

1. The data cited here are from the "*Forty-Sixth Annual Report of the Bank for International Settlements*." published June 14, 1976.
2. Since most Eurocurrency transactions are interbank transactions, the series of events recounted in the following paragraphs is not intended to be typical. A more typical Eurocurrency transaction might be between two commercial banks, or among a central bank and several commercial banks. Such alternative transactions would have effects on the supply of available credit in various countries different from the sequence discussed in the text. The example presented in

the text illustrates in a simple way the diverse impacts on the global availability of credit that may result from the transfer of a dollar balance from a U.S. bank to a European bank. Variations on this theme would include, for example, a decision by a foreign exporter to place his dollar earnings in a bank in London rather than in New York, or a decision by the central bank of, say, a Latin American country to deposit dollars in Frankfurt rather than buy U.S. Treasury bills.

3. This action will increase the total amount of reserves the U.S. banking system is required to hold, since demand deposits carry a higher reserve requirement than time deposits. But suppose the Federal Reserve through open market operations increases the total stock of reserves by the incremental amount required to permit this marginal increase in the U.S. money supply (narrowly defined).

34

The International Money Market: Perspective and Prognosis

Gunter Dufey and Ian H. Giddy

I. WHAT'S SO SPECIAL ABOUT THE EUROCURRENCY MARKETS?

There are few important aspects about the international money market that cannot be explained with reference to the following ideas:

1. The external (Eurocurrency) and internal (domestic) money markets are merely competing segments of the larger markets for the assets and liabilities of financial intermediaries.

2. Financial institutions in the external market are largely free of both informal constraints (such as pressures to allocate credit to certain borrowers) and formal regulations (such as reserve requirements). Eurobanks can therefore operate on narrower margins than can domestic banks.

3. On the other hand, from the point of view of the depositor or borrower, deposits in and loans from Eurobanks are generally riskier, because transactions with Eurobanks are subject to restrictions on funds transfers and for credit extension by *two*

political jurisdictions, whereas domestic transactions are subject to the political risk of only one government. Hence Eurobanks—as a rule—offer more attractive deposit and loan rates than do domestic banks.
4. While entry to virtually all national banking systems is restricted, in effect if not *de jure*, there is no limit to participation by any financial institution in external financial intermediation.
5. The close links between the domestic and external credit markets in a particular currency may be partially broken when capital controls restrict transfers of funds into and out of the country of that currency.
6. The links between segments of the Eurocurrency markets denominated in different currencies are governed by exchange-rate expectations. Arbitrage within the Eurocurrency market occurs through the foreign exchange markets, whereby the interest differentials equal the respective forward exchange premium or discount.

The Eurocurrency markets do differ from domestic markets in ways other than those summarized above. In most cases, however, these differences can be explained as the result of one or another of the basic features noted or can be dismissed as not being fundamental features of the external markets per se. *In all other respects, therefore, there is nothing special about the Eurocurrency markets.*

Indeed, most aspects of the external market can be explained by means of an analogy with a particular segment of the domestic banking market. There are many aspects of the international money market that we have, by intent or omission, neglected to discuss. But we have attempted to provide the reader with the tools with which to dissect virtually any problem relating to the market. The basic rule is this: if the problem cannot be interpreted by analogy with a segment of the domestic market, it must be the result of one of the six distinguishing characteristics we have listed. We have found this to be a remarkably powerful principle.

II. DOMESTIC AND EXTERNAL CREDIT MARKETS AND THE INTERNATIONAL FINANCIAL SYSTEM

The fact that the international money markets involve few concepts that are not already familiar to students of money or banking does not reduce their central role in the modern international financial system. The Euromarkets serve as the bridge between the financial markets of countries and currencies. They enable, for the first time, the *currency of denomination* of an asset to be separated from the *country of jurisdiction*. Stated differently, they enable borrowers and lenders to systematically separate the *currency risk* from the *political risk* of an asset or liability.

It is therefore instructive to examine precisely how the domestic and external markets for credit and the foreign exchange markets fit into the international financial system in general. Table 1 provides a schematic summary of the issues arising from the existence of international payments, capital flows, and financial markets. Let us explore some of these questions.

In a fundamental sense the financial system performs two functions: (1) the collection of savings and the allocation of resources into real investments, and (2) the facilitation of payment for transactions. Efficient performance of both functions requires financial assets and money balances, serving as convenient stores of value and means of payments, respectively. Internationally, there exists a need for the same services. Differences in the intertemporal preferences of economic transactors in different countries can be efficiently evened out through the international exchange of financial assets (international capital flows). And the working balances that financial institutions hold in other countries make possible an efficient transfer of funds to settle various kinds of international transactions. However, virtually all money balances are of a strictly national character, reinforced by national monopolies on issuance of currency and buttressed by legal tender laws. If trade and payments were effected only on a bilateral basis, using only the currency of the transactors, every international company or bank would be forced to hold money balances in all countries where payments might have to be made. Hence the use of a common vehicle currency considerably improves the efficiency of the

TABLE 1

Role of the External Markets in the International Financial System

Phenomenon	Function
Existence of financial assets	Satisfies intertemporal preferences
Existence of money balances	Minimizes uncertainty and cost associated with future payments
Use of a vehicle currency	Reduces the costs and uncertainties involved in international payments
Currency denomination of financial assets and liabilities	Guards the international purchasing power and stability of portfolios
Extent of financial intermediation	Reconciles different risk and maturity preferences of borrowers and lenders
Determination of external versus internal intermediation	Reflects relative cost and risk perceptions
Market for spot and forward foreign exchange	Reconciles currency preferences and expectations
Arbitrage between domestic and external markets and among Eurocurrency markets	Assures equality of effective interest rates in the absence of controls

system for international payments because it permits transactors to economize on the number and amount of foreign money balances held. The choice of a national currency as a vehicle currency depends largely on three factors: (1) the relative number of "natural transactions" favoring large countries; (2) the availability of an efficient money market that permits transactors to adjust their liquidity positions at a low incremental cost; and (3) a strong expectation that the authorities will not restrict nonresidents in their use of working balances (technically this is known as the *maintenance of nonresident convertibility*).

Although the existence of money balances in a certain foreign currency will also promote the denomination of financial assets in that currency, because transactions cost (conversion costs) will be minimized, in a world of uncertainty of exchange rates and international consumption, it is considerations of portfolio diversification that determine the currency denomination of financial assets and liabilities.

Such assets and liabilities are issued either directly by (ultimate) investors as a means of obtaining funds for productive assets, or by financial intermediaries who interject themselves between savers and investors, performing a risk and maturity transformation. The extent of financial intermediation relative to the total savings-investment process depends largely on the ability of such institutions to better reconcile different risk and maturity preferences of borrowers and lenders than would be possible through organized securities markets. Given the institutional barriers involved in international capital flows, it is not surprising that financial intermediaries play a dominant role in the international flow of credit.

International capital flows, however, do not explain the existence and growth of extensive external ("Euro-") financial intermediation sectors; these phenomena are explained by different cost structures and risk perceptions relative to domestic financial intermediation. However, because of the special operating conditions, external financial intermediaries play an important role in the collection of savings and the allocation of credit, both internationally and in respect to the national financial market, of which they represent the external sector.

It is the special operating characteristics of the Eurocurrency markets that make them the integrating mechanism of what are basically different, and to a certain extent independent, functions: the international transmission of credit and payments. To the extent that payments are made in the future, markets for foreign means of payments and international credit markets are linked through arbitrage: the foreign exchange market, where currency preferences and expectations are reconciled, determines the relationship among various segments of the external markets, which, in turn, tie together national financial systems. How close these links are depends largely on the extent of governmental controls on international payments and credit transactions.

III. HOW DO THE EUROMARKETS AFFECT ECONOMIC GROWTH AND THE DISTRIBUTION OF INCOME?

. . . The development of large, competitive financial markets facilitates the transfer of resources from ultimate savers to ultimate investors at low cost, and so promotes economic growth. As broad, competitive, and liquid financial markets, the Eurocurrency markets contribute to the efficient transfer and allocation of resources to their most productive use. The Eurobanks enlarge the financial sector of those countries whose currencies are used to denominate the assets and liabilities of external financial intermediaries. As a result of their diversity of geographical location and national origin, these Eurobanks may have a less domestically oriented bias in seeking out borrowers and depositors. Thus there is a strong presumption that they may contribute more to the efficient *international* allocation of credit than would the growth of an equal volume of intermediation in purely domestic markets.

But is there anything about the fundamental nature of the Eurocurrency system which suggests that its effect on economic growth and its distribution might differ from that of domestic markets? The answer is "yes," and the basis for that answer is grounded in two facts: (1) Eurobanks are not subject to pressures and legal constraints on investment behavior, and (2) they allow both international investors and borrowers to separate their choice of political risk from the choice of currency in which the asset or liability is to be denominated.

How do these features affect the growth and distribution of output? Consider first the effect on the distribution of credit, and therefore of income, in a purely domestic context. Domestic banks are almost universally expected to allocate a portion of their loan and bond portfolios to "socially preferred" borrowers who are less able to compete for funds in the open credit market. In addition, domestic banks are required to hold non-interest-bearing reserves, which are obligations of the government (in effect, a free loan to the public). Each of these constraints means that banks earn less on their portfolios, given the level of risk, than they would otherwise choose to do. Each constraint, therefore, implies (1) a transfer of income to preferred borrowers (including the government itself) from the bank's shareholders and depositors, and (2) a suboptimal allocation of credit, in the sense that the bank is prevented from allocating funds to their most profitable and productive uses.[1] By conducting their business in the external rather than the domestic market, banks escape such constraints, with the result that there is a redistribution of credit away from privileged borrowers and in favor of more productive borrowers and therefore in favor of economic growth.

Similar reasoning applies to the international as opposed to domestic allocation of credit through the external markets. Since the class of privileged borrowers (whose credit needs are perforce favored by domestic banks) seldom extends to foreign borrowers, the latter are, when credit-worthy and productive, favored by the effective removal of political constraints on bank portfolios. The redistribution and growth-promoting effect of the Euromarkets occurs on an international as well as on a domestic scale.

It would be a mistake to infer from this argument that the growth of Eurocurrency banking is necessarily accompanied by a capital flow from countries with an external market to those without one. Although this may occur—developing countries, for example, now have freer access to dollar credit than might otherwise have been the case—the flow of loans to such countries may well be offset by a flow of deposits from the same countries to the Euromarkets. And such flows are even more likely now that savers are able to invest in dollar assets, for example, without necessarily placing their funds in the United States.

This brings us to our second point. International capital flows tend to increase total (world) welfare by equalizing the marginal efficiency of capital, differences in preferences for present as opposed to future consumption, and differences in preferences for liquidity. It may be argued . . . that the Eurocurrency markets increase the international mobility of capital and hence enhance economic welfare and growth. The reason lies partly in the institutional mechanism (it is easier to switch currencies in a single institution, place and time zone), but also in the separation of currency risk from political risk. An individual may respond to an attractive yield differential by switching his deposit or loan from one currency to another without altering the nature of the jurisdiction in which his deposit or loan is booked; the same would not be true in the absence of the Euromarket.

IV. BANK REGULATION AND THE EUROCURRENCY MARKET

If it is true that the external market enables banks to circumvent the government's efforts to allocate credit by way of the private financial system, what can we conclude about the need for, and nature of, a response on the part of the regulatory authorities? For although the Euromarkets may redistribute credit in such a way as to promote economic growth, one cannot be sure that such a redistribution actually is in the social interest of any particular country. A redistribution that increases total output does not necessarily increase total welfare. All one can say is that if a government is to tax some citizens to improve the income of others, the tax should not be levied in such a way as to discourage efficient use of resources.

The simple answer, then, to the dilemma posed by unregulated external markets is for the government to impose a *direct* tax and provide a *direct* subsidy to favored sectors or institutions. In this way the transfer of income would be effected without additional distortions in financial markets occurring. Instead, however, the usual method is to increase the burden of credit allocation on those institutions that remain subject to domestic regulatory influences, thus distorting domestic financial markets even further. But there is a limit to the extent to which authorities, such as the U.S. government, can increase the burden of indirect credit allocation on domestic institutions without forcing *them* into the external market. This limit may be stated in terms of the *law of maximum distortion: for a given level of restrictions on international capital flows, there is a limit on the extent to which a government can distort domestic financial markets.*

The reasoning behind this statement is quite simple. A government can force financial markets and institutions to allocate credit in a suboptimal fashion to a certain degree, even if an external market exists and capital inflows and outflows are relatively unrestricted. If the manipulation of banks' portfolios or market decisions is carried too far, however, depositors and other investors will find themselves receiving returns insufficiently high for the level of risk involved. Therefore, either the financial markets and institutions themselves will shift to the external market (taking borrowers and depositors with them), or they will lose intermediation business to the external markets. Taking the United States as an example, let us assume that there is a given volume of credit intermediated in dollars. Part of the dollar credit system is external: the Eurodollar market. The more the U.S. authorities impose restraints and regulations on the rates that domestic banks can pay for deposits or obtain on assets, the greater the proportion of credit that will be intermediated externally. And the more dollar credit intermediation occurs outside the U.S. authorities' jurisdiction, the more difficult it will be to allocate credit domestically. The only recourse for the U.S. government is to accept the limits to market distortion, or to impose restrictions on investing or borrowing abroad—that is, to raise the level of capital controls. And a policy of financial isolationism has its own costs, which we need not discuss here.

What can we conclude? Since . . . there is little that the U.S. government or even the major industrial countries' governments in concert can do about controlling the Eurodollar market directly, domestic financial institutions will continue to bear a disproportionate burden of regulation. Reserve requirements and other nonmarket constraints on banks' asset or liability decisions can be regarded as an indirect tax.[2] The existence of external markets means that this tax falls more heavily on domestic banks, their owners and depositors, than would be the case in the absence of external markets. This is not necessarily "unfair," because many domestic banks benefit from protected markets that result solely from regulation-related barriers to entry. But it does suggest that such a tax might be more equitably and efficiently collected by some means other than the distortion of credit markets.

Indeed, some observers have suggested that the only way for the U.S. authorities to regain controls over financial markets is to allow domestic institutions to be sufficiently competitive to attract credit intermediation business back to the United States. This could be done, for example, by (1) removing reserve requirements on bank time deposits, (2) by paying a competitive interest rate on the required reserves, and (3) by eliminating most of the explicit and informal constraints on portfolio choices that banks face. Under this scheme, both domestic banks and Eurobanks could, for a fee, buy deposit insurance such as that offered by a deposit insurance institution such as the FDIC in the United States, and be subject to examination. But these higher costs would mean that depositors who favored such banks would have to accept a slightly lower interest rate.

V. THE CONDITIONS FOR EXISTENCE OF EXTERNAL CREDIT MARKETS

The Eurocurrency market is a creature of regulation and as such depends largely for its existence on the nature and degree of banking regulations and capital controls. Of course, it is not regulation per se that matters, only regulation that imposes a greater cost than it provides benefits. The banking authorities of many countries provide supervision and examination of domestic banks that is regarded as a useful service by the consumers of banking services. And the test of such effects of regulation is when both borrowers and depositors are willing to accept less favorable interest rates in return for the assurance that the bank's books are subject to regular review by competent and objective authorities. The most successful of the Eurobanks, then, tend to be those that are subject to such review.

But domestic banking regulation that imposes a cost without any associated benefits provides an incentive for the banking public to avoid this cost, and it does so by means of the external money market. We conclude that, other things being equal,

$$\begin{pmatrix} \text{Size of external credit} \\ \text{market relative to total} \\ \text{credit market in that} \\ \text{currency} \end{pmatrix} = \begin{matrix} \text{a} \\ \text{function} \\ \text{of} \end{matrix} \begin{pmatrix} \text{Costs of} \\ \text{domestic} \\ \text{banking} \\ \text{regulation} \end{pmatrix} - \begin{pmatrix} \text{Benefits from} \\ \text{domestic} \\ \text{banking} \\ \text{regulation} \end{pmatrix}$$

It follows that if domestic banking regulation were to disappear, there would be little incentive for the Eurocurrency markets to exist. Yet we need not go so far. Even in the presence of banking regulation, most of the external market would shift back to the domestic market if banking regulation were such that it did not distort financial decisions.[3]

This raises a related question: If the size and existence of external markets are largely a function of the burden of domestic regulation, why is it that external credit markets have not developed in the many currencies whose countries distort banks' decisions to a much greater degree than does the United States? Why is there not a large Eurocurrency market in Brazilian cruzeiros, Indian rupees, or even Japanese yen? The answer lies in the mechanism of the market. Every transfer of funds into, out of, or between Eurobanks is made by means of a transfer in domestic banks; hence the ability to undertake such transfers is an absolute prerequisite for the existence of a Euromarket in a particular currency. To the extent that financial transactions between domestic residents and nonresidents are restricted, it becomes more difficult to establish and maintain an active external credit market. Thus it is a mistake to suppose that the Eurodollar market grew during the 1960s because of the U.S. capital controls; more accurately, it grew in spite of them. At no time, however, did the United States restrict *nonresident convertibility*—that is, foreigners were always free to increase or decrease their balances in U.S. domestic banks. The same is not true of Japan even now, hence the virtual nonexistence of a market in Euroyen.[4]

There is another reason for the absence of external credit markets in most of the world's currencies. This reason is that paradoxically, one can obtain Euroloans or Eurodeposits in any particular currency without there actually being a Euromarket in that currency. How can this be? The answer lies in the fact that an asset or liability in, say, dollars, can be effectively converted into any other currency by buying or selling that currency in the forward market. . . . Assume, for example, that a Mexican resident wishes to hold a Europeso deposit in London but discovers that no Europeso market exists and that even if it did, it would be narrow, illiquid, and inefficient. What he can do, instead, is sell his pesos for dollars in the spot foreign exchange market, deposit the dollars in a Eurobank, and simultaneously buy Mexican pesos forward. He will now effectively own a peso-denominated asset earning an interest rate that equals the Eurodollar rate plus the forward discount on the Mexican peso.[5]

Taken to its logical extreme, this argument implies that when an external market in one currency (such as the U.S. dollar) exists, there is no need for parallel deposit markets in any other currency, since Eurodollars can be "swapped" into any given currency as long as a forward market exists for that currency. Alternatively, since transactions in external deposit markets are perfect substitutes for forward foreign exchange transactions, the depth and liquidity of the market for forward foreign exchange is greatly enhanced by the existence of the Euromarkets.

VI. SOME UNRESOLVED ISSUES

As long as the Euromarkets continue to exist in their present form, we will be able to employ the framework laid out in Section I to reinterpret any issues that arise. But the answers to specific questions in particular instances frequently depend on purely empirical issues. Indeed, it is our belief that differences in various researchers' interpretations of the market would be largely resolved if they could reach agreement on certain empirical characteristics of the external markets and their linkages with domestic credit markets. And such knowledge would certainly improve policymakers' understanding of how to respond to the Eurocurrency phenomenon.

What are these questions? The first concerns simply the size of various segments of the Eurocurrency market and related aggregates. What, for example, is the effective size of the external market in each currency, after taking into account the conversion from one currency into another through forward hedging? What fraction of the total *comparable* credit market in each currency does the external market form? And how does the inclusion of the external market alter various domestic monetary aggregates?

The next set of questions concerns the size of interest elasticities, or the responsiveness of capital flows between the domestic and external markets, and between various external markets, to a given change in interest rates in one market. And what is the impact on interest rates of a given shift in deposits? Related questions are: How much credit business shifts from the domestic to the external market (or vice versa) in response to a given change in domestic regulations, such as reserve requirements? How sensitive are Eurocurrency depositors to a given change in the political risk associated with a particular offshore market location? In what way, if at all, are lending practices of banks affected by the geographical location of deposits?

Next, how much exactly is the distribution of credit and economic growth affected by a given shift of deposits out of or into the external credit market? What is the additional cost to domestic banks of being obliged to bear the burden of "taxes" in one form or another imposed by the regulatory authorities?

Finally, there remain several empirical issues relating to the quantitative effect of various attempts to control the Eurocurrency markets and their implications for the cost and efficacy of conducting domestic banking and monetary policies. To what extent, for example, would the imposition of small reserve requirements on one particular segment of Eurobanks cause business to shift to other segments or geographical locations? And what is the impact of a given proportion of credit being intermediated externally on the domestic credit multiplier—its size and variability, the lags involved, and the difficulty of gauging the final impact on total credit of a given reserve change?

These are the kinds of issues that we do not propose to resolve here but which will provide grist for the mill of anyone who believes that no interesting questions remain concerning the international money market.

Notes

1. Of course, domestic banking regulations often protect banks from competition, too; so the final effect of being subject to domestic regulations on a particular bank's profitability cannot be stated unequivocally.
2. This tax is akin to a sales tax rather than a tax on income or profits.
3. Even in the absence of costly regulations, however, some credit business would continue to be intermediated externally as a result of *fear* of the later imposition of restrictions on domestic banks.
4. In Japan, yen balances in Japanese banks can be held only if they result from authorized transactions; these become "free yen." And the short-term capital transactions that are required for Eurocurrency borrowing and lending do not fall into that category.
5. Note, however, that this example or any similar transaction presupposes some degree of freedom for capital transfers into and out of the country in question.

Index